ALLEN COUNTY PUBLIC LIBRARY
3 1833 00387 05
Y0-BFY-277
STO
WITHDRA
ANNEX

9Feb'4
7May'4
6Jun'4
14Jul'49
DEC 8
16Mar'5
30 Mar'
14Apr'5
27Jun'51
YAR31

THE BEST PLAYS OF 1945-46

EDITED BY

BURNS MANTLE

The Best Plays of 1899-1909
(*With Garrison P. Sherwood*)
The Best Plays of 1909-19
(*With Garrison P. Sherwood*)
The Best Plays of 1919-20
The Best Plays of 1920-21
The Best Plays of 1921-22
The Best Plays of 1922-23
The Best Plays of 1923-24
The Best Plays of 1924-25
The Best Plays of 1925-26
The Best Plays of 1926-27
The Best Plays of 1927-28
The Best Plays of 1928-29
The Best Plays of 1929-30
The Best Plays of 1930-31
The Best Plays of 1931-32
The Best Plays of 1932-33
The Best Plays of 1933-34
The Best Plays of 1934-35
The Best Plays of 1935-36
The Best Plays of 1936-37
The Best Plays of 1937-38
The Best Plays of 1938-39
The Best Plays of 1939-40
The Best Plays of 1940-41
The Best Plays of 1941-42
The Best Plays of 1942-43
The Best Plays of 1943-44
The Best Plays of 1944-45
The Best Plays of 1945-46
Contemporary American Playwrights (1938)

Photo by Vandamm Studio.

"STATE OF THE UNION"

Grant—Now stop that nonsense and make up that bed again . . . You wouldn't get any sleep there on the floor, and I wouldn't get any sleep there (points to bed) worrying about you.

Mary—Good-night, Mr. President!

(*Ralph Bellamy, Ruth Hussey*)

THE BEST PLAYS OF 1945-46

AND THE
YEAR BOOK OF THE DRAMA
IN AMERICA

EDITED BY
BURNS MANTLE

With Illustrations

822.08
M319
1945-46
V.27

DODD, MEAD AND COMPANY
NEW YORK - - - 1946

"State of the Union," copyright, 1945, by Howard Lindsay and Russel Crouse
Copyright and published, 1946, by Random House, Inc., New York
"Home of the Brave," copyright, 1945, by Arthur Laurents
Copyright and published, 1946, by Random House, Inc., New York
"Deep Are the Roots," copyright, 1945, by Arnaud d'Usseau and James Gow
Copyright and published, 1946, by Charles Scribner's Sons, New York
"The Magnificent Yankee," copyright, 1945, by Emmet Lavery
Copyright and published, 1946, by Samuel French, Inc., New York
"Antigone," copyright, 1945, by Lewis Galantiere
Copyright and published, 1946, by Random House, Inc., New York
"O Mistress Mine," copyright, 1945, by Terence Rattigan
Revised and published version, copyright, 1946, by Terence Rattigan
"Born Yesterday," copyright, 1946, by Garson Kanin and Ruth Gordon
Copyright and published, 1946, by Viking Press, Inc., New York
"Dream Girl," copyright, 1945, 1946, by Elmer Rice
Copyright and published, 1946, by Coward-McCann, Inc., New York
"The Rugged Path," copyright, 1946, by Robert Emmet Sherwood
Copyright and published, 1946, by Charles Scribner's Sons, New York
"Lute Song," copyright, 1945, under title of "Pi-Pa-Ki," by
Will Irwin and Sidney Howard
Revised and published version, copyright, 1946, under title of "Lute Song,"
by Will Irwin and Leopoldine Howard

COPYRIGHT, 1946,
BY DODD, MEAD AND COMPANY, INC.

CAUTION: Professionals and amateurs are hereby warned that the above-mentioned plays, being fully protected under the copyright laws of the United States of America, the British Empire, including the Dominion of Canada, and all other countries of the Copyright Union, are subject to a royalty. All rights, including professional, amateur, motion picture, recitation, public reading, radio broadcasting, and the rights of translation into foreign languages, are strictly reserved. In their present form these plays are dedicated to the reading public only. All inquiries regarding them should be addressed to their publishers or authors.

PRINTED IN THE UNITED STATES OF AMERICA

610767

INTRODUCTION

THE theatre (meaning the American theatre and more particularly the American theatre as reflected in the play productions brought to Broadway, New York) behaved quite normally as a refugee from the Second World War. It took time out for emotional readjustments.

Having continued excitingly through its third and last wartime season, which was the season of 1944-45, it greeted its first Victory season of 1945-46 with jumpy nerves and but little confidence in any of its divisions, save that of the box office.

There was still plenty of money for spending purposes and there were still long queues of eager ticket buyers for even the quasi-successes. But there was not much in the way of superior drama to be bought—not enough to satisfy either the theatre's older and more discriminating supporters or to thrill its newer and less demanding discoverers.

Six of the ten plays chosen as most creditably representing the season's list reflect the war in one way or another. And yet only two of the six are out-and-out war plays—Sherwood's "The Rugged Path" and Laurents' "Home of the Brave." Neither of these was what Broadway would accept as a hit. "The Rugged Path," the experts insisted, held on for ten weeks largely because of the popularity of Spencer Tracy, who came East from Hollywood to play the hero. "Home of the Brave," many of the same experts reported, was not given a fair chance, although its producers did keep it playing for eight weeks.

It is this editor's considered opinion that a sort of war-play weariness had crept into the minds of playgoers. This handicapped the chances of both plays, as it also condemned a number of other war plays, notably a well-written and well-played drama of the Cassino siege, "A Sound of Hunting," written by Harry Brown, which was withdrawn after 23 performances.

Robert Sherwood's "The Rugged Path" was an honest crusader's protest against influences that were permitted to warp, if not to bias, the judgment of certain newspaper owners and editorial writers, to the embarrassment of the government's war effort. Woven into this theme was a GI Joe's search for an answer to his own mystified query: "What the heck is it all about? And what does it, or should it, mean to me?"

FEB 7 1947

Arthur Laurents' "Home of the Brave" was, I think, the best of the season's personal-adventure type of war play. It was given both purpose and stature by the author's use of an experiment conducted by Army psychiatrists in their effort to cure a case of nerve-shock resulting in the paralysis of a soldier's legs. Incidentally Mr. Laurents preached a healthy sermon against a bigoted racial intolerance.

The Lindsay-Crouse "State of the Union" rightfully earned the Pulitzer award that goes annually to the best play of American authorship produced in New York. This is a timely, significant and keenly observant study of American politics and politicians of the recent past, the foaming present and a reasonably predictable future.

Arnaud d'Usseau and James Gow's "Deep Are the Roots," having to do seriously with the Negro problem as it is pretty certain to rear a troubled post-war head in the Southern states, was the first and the most effective of several dramas inspired by a similar theme. Others included Lillian and Esther Smith's "Strange Fruit" and Robert Ardrey's "Jeb." Each of these attracted adherents who were quick to protest the superiority of one or the other. "Deep Are the Roots," however, proved more to the liking of the general playgoing public. It boasted a sincerity in writing and in performance that cut definitely through a certain overlay of theatricalism, and ran out the season.

Emmet Lavery's "The Magnificent Yankee" did full sentimental justice and honor to the home life of the late Justice Oliver Wendell Holmes and Fanny Dixwell Holmes, his wife. There was mild objection offered in some quarters that the play did not go far enough in presenting the great dissenter as an early political progressive, but a majority vote of playgoers favored both the play and the quite exceptional performance of Louis Calhern as Judge Holmes.

"Antigone" was brought home from Paris by Katharine Cornell, and served her well for a short season, to which she added a revival of "Candida." The "Antigone" of Sophocles, modernized by Jean Anouilh as "Antigone and the Tyrant," and produced directly under the Hitler nose during the Nazi occupation of France, was interesting: First as a nobly defiant and subtle gesture on the part of the captive race; second, as a novelty in dramatic form in the English adaptation by Lewis Galantiere.

With the acknowledged help of several outstanding characterizations and performances, the comedies stood up very well. Alfred Lunt and Lynn Fontanne found a comedy to their liking while they were in England helping to keep the bombed and the brave cheerful. This was "O Mistress Mine," Terence Rattigan's happy, and inferentially meaningful, account of a young radical's serious attempt to save his mother from too intimate contact with a capitalistic world—amusingly represented by a capitalist in the flesh. The Lunts were frank to confess that playing "O Mistress Mine" represented a deliberate effort on their part to help as many thousands as they could reach to escape for two hours from war-weighted miseries and memories.

Elmer Rice's "Dream Girl" was also a cheerfully escapist entertainment. Having to do with the daydreams of a young, charming and imaginative heroine, and being played by the young and charming Betty Field, it added definitely to the season's playgoing satisfactions. When health considerations took Miss Field out of the cast, Haila Stoddard carried on most successfully, thereby disproving the charge that Mr. Rice's comedy was no more than a personality triumph for Miss Field.

Garson Kanin's "Born Yesterday" came swaggering into town in midseason. It might have proved another of those typically American satirical swings at pompousness plus ignorance so frequently aimed at the producers of motion pictures. Mr. Kanin cleverly evaded this classification by making his hero a pompous and ignorant junkman instead. Then, by sending the junkman to Washington on a power-grafting mission, he added, by implication at least, a serious note of warning to a thoughtless citizenry.

"Lute Song," an adaptation of a two-thousand-year-old Chinese classic, written some years ago by the late Sidney Howard and Will Irwin, brought a picturesque novelty and unusual scenic beauty to the season. Robert Edmond Jones decorated "Lute Song" with a strikingly handsome background. This setting unquestionably helped to make the play, but it also seemed, suggestively at least, to smother slightly the fairly delicate text. There were two publics for "Lute Song." One raved of the beauty of setting and text, and the other swore by the generously attractive Mary Martin, the star, who in other years had won attention by singing the Broadway confessional, "My Heart Belongs to Daddy."

And so we have come to the completion of the twenty-seventh volume of the "Best Plays" series, dating from the issue covering the season of 1919-20. Adding the two Mantle-Sherwood volumes which came later, "The Best Plays of 1899-1909" and "The Best Plays of 1909-19," we have twenty-nine volumes in all, and a pretty complete record of the drama in America from the turn of the century to the present time. A grand total of 290 representative "best" plays, practically all of which have been endorsed and supported by American playgoers, and 239 of which were written by American playwrights.

Again, as happened last year, when your editor retired from active play reviewing to become what is known locally as the dramatic critic emeritus of the New York *Daily News,* John Chapman has helped to keep an eye on the Broadway proceedings. Mr. Chapman also contributed the digests of "Home of the Brave" and "Born Yesterday" to the current volume.

Let these added words carry the editor's grateful appreciation to loyal readers and supporters of the Best Plays series.

B. M.

Forest Hills, L. I., 1946

CONTENTS

ILLUSTRATIONS

THE BEST PLAYS OF 1945-46

THE BEST PLAYS OF 1945-46

THE SEASON IN NEW YORK

WE could, with reason, write the hand of destiny into this report of our first Victory theatre season following close upon the successful conclusion of World War II. It has served to bring the chief English-speaking allies much closer together in the entertainment field. In place of the more familiar cartoon of weather-beaten, war-scarred, and perspiring hands indulging an emotional hands-across-the-sea clasp, we could have two super-transport airplanes passing each other in mid-air (and also mid-ocean), loaded with American and British theatre talent. A caption would explain, not too obviously, that they were on their way to the exchange of morale-stimulating visits with troops at the front and beleaguered citizens at home.

We did do an unusual amount of theatre talent sharing during the year, capped at season's end by the importation of London's fine Old Vic Theatre troupe by Theatre Incorporated. Not only did the Old Vic actors play six highly successful weeks of repertory—the most satisfying six weeks of the season, probably—but one of its chief players, Laurence Olivier, was generously voted by New York critics to have proved himself the best actor of the season.

It was all very nice and friendly, and interesting as well. We, on our part, had loaned the British our favorite acting couple, Alfred Lunt and Lynn Fontanne, practically for the duration. We had taken (and held) Maurice Evans, who joined our military forces and quickened Shakespeare's Hamlet nearer to the GI's heart's desire. We had cheered the magnificent courage of those English cousins who had so bravely faced the London, Plymouth and Coventry blitzes, and they had cheered as admiringly our complete success in outfitting and implementing an arsenal of democracy without which the war could not have been won.

This Victory season also embraced other features of which we trust future theatre historians will take note. For one, the formation and development of that same altruistically minded, nonprofit organization, Theatre Incorporated, which, in addition to the importation of the Old Vic troupe, revived Bernard Shaw's "Pygmalion" with English Gertrude Lawrence and Canadian Raymond Massey starred, and Sir Cedric Hardwicke directing.

This new producing company is quite the most promising organization of its kind that has put in an appearance since the Theatre Guild took over the Garrick Theatre, and an Otto Kahn loan, to make American playgoers more familiar with the better samples of continental drama. I quote from its first prospectus:

"Theatre Incorporated is a non-profit, tax-exempt corporation, committed to a sustained program of great plays of the past and outstanding plays of the present. Its income is devoted to the continuation of such a program on a permanent basis; to the encouragement of young playwrights, directors and actors through a subsidiary experimental theatre; to the utilization of the stage as an educational force, and to the ultimate development of a true people's theatre."

A second repertory organization also coming to life this year is one called the American Repertory Theatre. Margaret Webster, Eva Le Gallienne, Cheryl Crawford and others have banded together for a November production of Shakespeare's "Henry VIII," to be followed by revivals of Barrie's "What Every Woman Knows," and Ibsen's "John Gabriel Borkman." A considerable company, to include Miss Le Gallienne, Victor Jory and Walter Hampden as a leading trio, has been signed. There will be nothing non-profit about this one, but it is promised that its standards and ideals will be scrupulously maintained on a high level.

While nearly every theatre season stages some sort of battle royal between playwrights and drama critics, or producers and critics, or actors and critics, this 1945-46 season offered one that topped most recent explosions. It was set off by the production of a new Maxwell Anderson drama, "Truckline Café." Partly because they found in the play many marks at which to shoot, and partly because they had a feeling that on the Anderson record they had a fair right to expect better things of this particular dramatist, the critics were fairly brutal in their attack.

Mr. Anderson, his sense of justice and fair play outraged, his pride grievously hurt, bought advertising space in which to reply to the more violent of his critics.

"The public is far better qualified to judge plays than the men who write reviews for our dailies," protested the playwright, in bold-face type. "It is an insult to our theatre that there should be so many incompetents and irresponsibles among them. There are still a few critics who know their job and respect it, but of late years all plays are passed on largely by a sort of Jukes family of journalism who bring to the theatre nothing but their own hopelessness, recklessness and despair."

By going to their library records, the critics discovered that the Jukes "was a name given to a family of New York state that had an unusual record of crime and pauperism," a large majority of whose members were "of low physical and moral standard." One by one the critics either replied in kind or refused to be drawn into so undignified a controversy.

Mr. Anderson's public statement was followed by a like protest from the Playwrights' Company, co-producers of "Truckline Café," and by Elia Kazan and Harold Clurman, their associates. Week-end columns flared with sizzling comments and letters to the editor. It was a good two weeks before charges and countercharges were dropped and the play withdrawn.

There were only three Summer shows this season, and we could easily have done without one of them. "Oh, Brother," a plotty little something by Jacques Deval, started in June and played for 23 performances to nobody's gain. "Marinka," which was the Mayerling tragedy involving the Crown Prince and his mistress who mysteriously disappeared from a mountain hideaway in Hungary (with music added), did very well. The critics of the press, however, did not care much for it. Starting in July it ran through to December, with Joan Roberts and Harry Stockwell, one of the more successful "Oklahoma!" pairs, playing and singing the leading roles.

"The Wind Is Ninety," a war fantasy written by Ralph Nelson, a service man, came as near to being a popular success as a play can and still fail to make the grade. This was the story of a lieutenant of the air force who was shot down over Germany. Hoping to cushion the shock his family would suffer when they received the news officially, the hero goes home quickly from the spirit world, accompanied by the shade of the Unknown Soldier. The lieutenant finds he cannot get his message through to the family, but he is able in the end to make his widow understand that whenever the wind is 90—which means from the east—he will always be with her in spirit.

The season had the usual official opening in September—first with a musical comedy called "Mr. Strauss Goes to Boston," then with a drama, "A Boy Who Lived Twice"; then with a comedy entitled "Devils Galore" and finally with another comedy, "Make Yourself at Home." They were all washed up and out of the way before the end of the month.

Then there were three that started the same week, which was the last week in September, that helped to revive playgoers' hopes—a comedy by Edmund Goulding of Hollywood called "The Ryan Girl"; a romantic comedy of which Tennessee Williams was co-author with Donald Windham entitled "You Touched Me," and the first outstanding hit of the season, "Deep Are the Roots," from the studios of Arnaud d'Usseau and James Gow, happy co-authors of the 1942-43 season's hit, "Tomorrow the World."

"The Ryan Girl," with June Havoc playing the heroine, her second serious dramatic role, counting "Sadie Thompson" her first, tried desperately to interest audiences. The story was of a former "Follies" girl who gave her illegitimate son up for adoption and then shot his father to save the boy's name. It couldn't quite get past its fifth week. "You Touched Me," helped greatly by the performance of Edmund Gwenn, the star, and helped a little by the fact that Mr. Williams' first success, "The Glass Menagerie," was still a smash hit at the Playhouse, held on for 109 performances.

"Deep Are the Roots" was the first of the newer war plays to deal with the problem faced by colored heroes of World War II when they try again to take up life in their home communities on the same level they had laid it down when they were drafted. It proved an overnight hit of such proportions that it was still a favorite late in the summer of 1946. It was the first play selected for this record of the theatre year.

About this time we had two ambitious musical productions, "Carib Song" and "Polonaise." The first was a vehicle in which it was hoped Katherine Dunham, a favorite colored dancer, together with her troupe, could ride through half the season at least. Thirty-six performances and the demand for seats was more than satisfied. "Polonaise," also leaning heavily on the accepted popularity of its stars, Marta Eggerth and Jan Kiepura, who had done well with a "Merry Widow" revival the year before, succeeded in achieving 113 performances, despite a not-too-enthusiastic press reception.

Eva Le Gallienne was paired with Victor Jory, the popular screen actor, in a new Thomas Job adaptation of Emile Zola's old-time "Therese Raquin." With the superior support of Dame May Whitty, they managed to carry "Therese" through 96 performances, but were not very happy doing it.

The first of the major revivals, with which the season was generously sprinkled, was that of "The Red Mill." This old-time Victor Herbert-Henry Blossom success, which Dave Montgomery and Fred Stone played for three seasons, starting in 1906, again captured large audiences with its superior Herbert score and a Blossom book rewritten to make room for Dorothy Stone and Charles Collins, the dancing duo. Paula Stone, Dorothy's sister, joined Hunt Stromberg and Edwin Lester in promoting the revival. They brought it to Broadway, following a successful season on the Pacific Coast, with Eddie Foy, Jr., the star comedian of the cast.

Irwin Shaw, in the service and bitter over the Darlan incident in Africa, dramatized in "The Assassin" the wiping out of the Admiral (Marcel Vesperry in the play), but had no success with it. Oscar Serlin, who hasn't been any too successful in picking plays on which to venture his "Life with Father" profits, failed again with a Theodore Reeves number called "Beggars Are Coming to Town." He brought Paul Kelly back from the coast to help Luther Adler play the leads, a pair of gangsters caught in a double-cross. Even their good performances could not save the drama.

Everybody was greatly disappointed when Fay Bainter, a favorite in the old "Arms and the Girl," "East Is West" days, tried a Broadway return with Mary Chase's "The Next Half Hour." Miss Bainter gave excellent support to Mrs. Chase's drama, which was based on the superstitions of the Irish (a little something she had dug up following the sensational success of her "Harvey"), but the folks wouldn't buy the play.

Another pair of "the-war-as-we-saw-it" dramas, written by service men, suffered from the growing apathy of playgoers for reminders of the too recent conflict. One was Harry Kleiner's "Skydrift," relating the adventure of an excited crew of paratroopers flying a mission in the South Pacific theatre. Following an air attack they awake to the discovery that they are all dead in a shattered plane. After some debate they decide to bail out and visit their nearest of kin on earth before resigning themselves to their heavenly future. They have the usual difficulty getting a message across to their folks. They (the casualties) try to tell the folks that they will be quite all right in spiritland if their kin will only quit grieving for them.

The second was a more effective drama by Harry Brown called "A Sound of Hunting." In this Mr. Brown followed the adventure of a squad of American GI's on patrol in the bombed and crumbling city of Cassino, Italy. Just as the squad is about to be relieved for a rest period they discover that one of their number has been cut off by a German machine gunner. They refuse to go back until their pal is rescued, even though none of them has much use for him. Pvt. Dino Collucci finally manages to sneak up on the machine gunner and liquidate him, but he finds the trapped Yank dead. "A Sound of Hunting," well treated by the critics, gave up after 23 performances. "Skydrift" lasted only 11.

Broadway was happily cheered about this time by the arrival of the first smash hit of the season. This was Howard Lindsay and Russel Crouse's "State of the Union," with Ralph Bellamy and Ruth Hussey playing the leads, splendidly supported by Minor Watson and Kay Johnson. This story of a search for a liberal, but not too liberal, candidate for President, to head the Republican ticket in 1948, immediately went into the sold-out class. For months there were nothing but capacity audiences, a reason for which may be found in the digest of the comedy to be found in this volume.

"The Day Before Spring" proved to be one of the more intelligent of musical comedies. Alan Jay Lerner wrote the story and Frederick Loewe the music to fit it—the story being about the tenth reunion of a university class. Two members of the group recall having tried to elope during their senior year, when they were balked by a motor car accident. At the reunion they decide to try a repeat performance, and fail again when the heroine's husband catches up with them.

The customarily sure John Van Druten failed with "The Mermaids Singing," though it did get 52 performances. And Lillian Smith and her sister, Esther, failed with their dramatization of Lillian's sensationally successful novel, "Strange Fruit." Many playgoers, casual and professional, attributed this failure to the more effective theatrical quality of "Deep Are the Roots," which had become firmly established as an accepted favorite before "Strange Fruit" came in.

Maj. Maurice Evans, home from the wars in the Pacific, offered his GI version of "Hamlet" in mid-December. He played it successfully through to April. The tragedy was lightly trimmed, as previously recorded, the elimination of the grave diggers' scene and Ophelia's funeral representing the principal cutting.

Elmer Rice, having fallen into the pleasant habit of writing plays for his actress-wife, Betty Field, decided to arrest the tendency. The result was a fantastic comedy called "Dream Girl." The star part was promptly offered to a number of screen celebrities as a vehicle which might conceivably carry them back to Broadway, but they could not see it. As a result Miss Field had to play "Dream Girl" after all, which she did with great success until late Spring, when Haila Stoddard took over so Betty could have a rest.

S. N. Behrman wrote a comedy about the daughter of a New York politician and a ruthless American industrialist. Apparently the Playwrights' Company, of which Mr. Behrman was one of the founders, did not agree with him as to the promise of the script. He thereupon took it over to the Theatre Guild. The Guild produced it, with Dennis King playing the industrialist and June Havoc the daughter. This would be Miss Havoc's third dramatic role. The performances were good, but the play wasn't—not in the estimation of both its critics and the playgoing crowd. It lasted through the Guild's subscription list and was withdrawn.

One of the last of George Bernard Shaw's more popular comedies was "Pygmalion," produced in 1914. Sir Herbert Beerbohm Tree played it in London, with Mrs. Patrick Campbell as his leading lady. In the Fall of the same year the play was imported by the late George C. Tyler and played in New York by Mrs. Campbell and Philip Merivale. In 1926 the Theatre Guild staged a revival, with Lynn Fontanne as the heroine and Reginald Mason as the phonetics professor who wins a bet that he can so transform a flower girl of the London streets that in six months' time she will be accepted as a lady at a Buckingham Palace garden party. "Pygmalion" was this season chosen as the introductory bill for the newly formed Theatre Incorporated producing unit. Gertrude Lawrence was co-starred with Raymond Massey and the revival proved so successful and so popular that it ran out the season.

Another popular revival was that of the Jerome Kern-Oscar Hammerstein-Edna Ferber "Show Boat," which started making American theatre history back in 1927. Mr. Hammerstein has always held this most satisfying of all American musical comedies in particularly high esteem. It played a definite part in establishing him as one of the country's leading librettists. Having capitalized further on the career that "Show Boat" started, and having acquired the necessary funds to do what he most wanted to do, Mr. Hammerstein decided that he would make his own revival of his own favorite old-time hit. The result was such another hit that the new "Show Boat" practically outshone its original production, and likewise that of a revival Florenz Ziegfeld made in 1932.

Bobby Clark, the irrepressible, had long had his eye on Molière's "Le Bourgeoise Gentilhomme" as a proper framework for a bridge between old-time and modern burlesque. For months he devoted all his spare time to writing an adaptation of the comedy, which Michael Todd was eagerly awaiting to produce. "The Would-Be Gentleman" was the title chosen, and while the Clark version did not live up to all its comedian-author's hopes, it did bring him a series of as handsome personal endorsements from the critical fraternity as any funmaker ever received. The comedy held on for ten weeks, thanks to Bobby's personal following, and then went back into the familiar collection of classical discards.

The Theatre Guild, now lousy with assets, as the saying has been going since "Oklahoma!" provided this worthy institution with new life, decided that it could not suffer much, if any, from a revival of Shakespearean dramas. The Guild hit upon the seldom played "The Winter's Tale" as the proper medium for its first experiment. On tour the reviews were favorable and business good. In New York "The Winter's Tale" got 39 performances and a conservative critical endorsement. Encouraged by its first step, the Guild immediately put "The Merry Wives of Windsor" into rehearsal. Charles Coburn, newly come into a widely scattered fan popularity radiating from Hollywood, was selected as the star. A preliminary Spring tour gave promise of an expanding success the season of 1946-47.

Two popular acting couples, Alfred Lunt and Lynn Fontanne, Louis Calhern and Dorothy Gish, found plays to their liking, and both plays have been made a part of this record. The Lunts brought back from England with them a light comedy written by Terence Rattigan and called, over there, "Love in Idleness." For America the title was changed to "O Mistress Mine" but the play remained otherwise unaltered. It was, explained the Lunts, their contribution to a happier world, after five years of war. They had not the slightest trouble selling their play for as long as they were willing to play it. The Theatre Guild and John C. Wilson made the production.

Mr. Calhern and Miss Gish played Mr. and Mrs. Oliver Wendell Holmes in Emmet Lavery's sentimental biographical tribute to the home life of the jurist and his devoted mate. This was titled "The Magnificent Yankee." Theirs, too, was a quick and popular success, and Arthur Hopkins was its sponsor.

Comedies were doing well in mid-season. Garson Kanin's "Born Yesterday" caused quite a furore, as a result of which it, too, finds a place in our favored ten selections to represent the season. The players in this instance were practical unknowns to the Broadway theatre, a lad from the radio field, Paul Douglas, playing an amusingly vulgar hero, and a new character ingénue,

Judy Holliday, scoring a big personal success as a dumb but triumphant heroine.

Walter Huston, also tiring of the silences and limitations of the screen drama, came East with a little something called "The Apple of His Eye." This turned out to be the simple romance of a simple farmer. Because Walter played the farmer a good deal better than he really deserved to be played, and because there was a supporting bankroll of sufficiently generous proportions to stand out against the critics' thumbs-down first-night verdict, "The Apple of His Eye" stayed with us for 118 performances. Kenyon Nicholson and Charles Robinson were the authors.

Mary Martin, having won her first success as the lovely loyalist whose heart belonged to daddy, and then moved on with a slightly raucous fantasy, "One Touch of Venus," decided the 1945-46 season was a good time to change her pace. With this in mind she agreed to play a Chinese fantasy called "Lute Song." Backed by an unusually effective display of scenic beauty, designed by Robert Edmond Jones, "Lute Song," which the late Sidney Howard and Will Irwin wrote some years ago, attracted and satisfied a good many playgoers. Starting in February it ran the season out. Daddy's girl was very happy.

As is more fully related in later pages, Katharine Cornell came upon Jean Anouilh's "Antigone" in Paris, when she was playing "The Barretts of Wimpole Street" for America's GI's on the continent. She brought the play home and gave it a handsome production. When she sensed that "Antigone" was nearing the end of a normal Broadway demand for modernized Greek tragedy, Miss Cornell revived Shaw's "Candida" to please the other half of her following. She played "Antigone" and "Candida" alternately to fill out her season.

Robert Ardrey, who has not been too lucky as a Broadway peddler of plots, though one of the most promising, wrote the third of the season's plays devoted to the Negro war hero's problems, a drama called "Jeb." As was the case with "Strange Fruit," "Jeb" was declared by a minority to be the best of the dramas written on that now familiar theme, but it went down just the same, being withdrawn by Herman Shumlin after 9 performances.

Ray Bolger, the dancer, saved an otherwise uneven revue called "Three to Make Ready" from early extinction. Rowland Stebbins, producer of "The Green Pastures," came back to Broadway briefly with something fairly odorous called "Flamingo Road." The Theatre Guild, still riding the crest of success, decided to restage a revi~ed version of Molnar's "He Who Gets Slapped."

Dennis King played the role of "Funny," who turned out to be the "He" of the original production, and a little lady named Susan Douglas, who came from Czechoslovakia and trained in radio, was the youthful heroine. These roles were played in 1922 by Richard Bennett and Margalo Gillmore. As happened twenty-four years ago, those who understood the drama did not go, and those who did go did not understand the drama.

Oscar Karlweis, one of the more successful, because one of the more talented of refugee comedians, made his first hit in the operatic "Rosalinda." He built upon that in "Jacobowsky and the Colonel." But he did not do so well his next time out, which was as the lightly bemused hero of a comedy called "I Like It Here." This time he was Willie Kringle, an amiable Austrian whose impulses were perfect and his wit keen, even if his dialect was a little uncertain and his conclusions a bit fantastic. Answering an advertised call for help, Willie lands as a house man in the family of a college professor and helps the daughter of the house outwit her parents and marry the lad of her choice. Starting in March, "I Like It Here" was through in early May.

"The Song of Bernadette," which had been successful as a novel by Franz Werfel and as a motion picture by a couple of other fellows, did not live up to the expectations of its adapters when Jean and Walter Kerr rewrote the Werfel story for the stage. Mr. Kerr first staged his adaptation for the Catholic University in Washington, D. C., where it was well received.

Two of the late season musicals were successful beyond the average. One was "St. Louis Woman," telling a racy story of an attractive colored trollop who reserved her charms for winners. Leaving a wealthy saloonkeeper for a winning jockey, she quit the jockey as soon as he began riding losers. A second winning streak, however, sent her back to the arms of her diminutive rider. An all-colored cast, headed by the Nicholas Brothers, Ruby Hill, Pearl Bailey and Rex Ingram, carried "St. Louis Woman" well into the Summer. Arna Bontemps and Countee Cullen wrote the book, Harold Arlen the score.

A second and even greater hit was earned by a GI revue, "Call Me Mister," written by Harold Rome, Arnold Auerbach and Arnold B. Horwitt, all ex-service men. It was played by a troupe made up of service men, with a sprinkling of Wacs and Waves. Not a single condemnatory press review barred the way of this one, which gave promise at its April 18th premiere of going on through the Summer and probably the season to follow as well.

An interesting near success was Don Appell's sensible treatment of the racial intolerance theme in "This, Too, Shall Pass." In this one Mac Sorrell had saved the life of his friend, Buddy Alexander, in World War II. Buddy's sister, striking up a correspondence with Mac, comes to love him, and when the boys come home from the war they are engaged. Then Mrs. Alexander discovers that Mac is a Jew, and also that deep down she still resents Jews. Mother does what she can to break off the match. She has practically succeeded when God takes a hand and there is a sentimental recovery of sorts.

The repertory season of the Old Vic Company from London began, as heretofore noted, on May 6 and continued through June. The two weeks of San Carlo Opera that Fortune Gallo delights in presenting at the Rockefeller's Center Theatre each Spring was again happily successful, but without added novelty in the repertory. It started with "Aïda" and ended with "Faust."

The last of the Negro problem plays was one called "On Whitman Avenue," written by Maxine Wood. A liberal-minded daughter takes advantage of her parents' absence to rent an apartment in their home to a Negro and his wife. The return of the family precipitates a row that extends to the community and results finally in the eviction of the Negroes.

Determined to prove that their judgment and playwrighting skill were still as dependable as they were in the days of their "The Front Page" and "Twentieth Century," Ben Hecht and Charles MacArthur wrote a drama called "Swan Song" based on a story by Ramon Romero and Harriet Hinsdale. It was produced as "Crescendo" on tour and later revised and brought to Broadway. A majority of the play reviewers did not care for it, but audience response was excellent. At the end of the season it had played for three weeks and was still going—not strong, but going. The story was of a frustrated pianist and his determination to clear his path of threatening rivals. The chief of these, a young girl of twelve, was played by the brilliant Jacqueline Horner of Hollywood.

The favored and favorite Ethel Merman, after having taken time out to start a family, came galloping back at the end of the season as the heroine of a musical comedy fashioned by Dorothy and Herbert Fields from the life of Annie Oakley, sharpshooter. The musical score, which the late Jerome Kern had planned to write before his last illness, was taken over by Irving Berlin and, as anticipated, turned out to be a major attraction. "Annie Get Your Gun" was the title.

The season's closing attraction was an extravaganza, conceived, written and staged by no less a theatre personage than Orson Welles. Taking Jules Verne's novel, "Around the World in Eighty Days" as a base, Mr. Welles built up a loose but lively entertainment featuring everything from two or three Cole Porter songs to a full-stage circus, with tumblers, wire walkers and a magic show doing some violence to a crateful of ducks, geese, rabbits and Mr. Welles. The critics didn't like it, but neither did Mr. Welles like the critics' comments. Honors were easy and the fight was going merrily on as the season passed out. "Wellesapoppin" they called it.

There were, according to a statistician's figures, eighty new plays, which was some fifteen less than there were last season. There were also ten holdover successes from the previous season. The sturdy "Life with Father" added to its score, which stood at 2,755 performances the first of June. This leaves it 427 performances to make up if its producers insist on breaking the "Tobacco Road" record of 3,182. "Oklahoma!" is trailing with 1,372 performances and a stout heart.

Some of the motion picture millionaires are again threatening to keep their money in their Hollywood vaults rather than risk it on Broadway legitimate productions, as they have done in considerable number the last several seasons. Broadway will not miss the millions until after its angels have sold all their war bonds. By that time the cinema hoarders will doubtless have changed their minds again.

THE SEASON IN CHICAGO

By Claudia Cassidy
Drama Editor of the *Chicago Tribune*

TO say that Chicago will not soon forget the season of 1945-46 is not to encourage the theatre to take too deep a bow. It was a busy season and often a bright one, but it was memorable for calamitous confusions not a single producer tried to write off as acts of God. This was the season Katharine Cornell opened "Antigone" in street clothes on an improvised stage because the truck attempting to thwart the railroad strike was washed up in a Pennsylvania flood. This was the season our theatres generated their own electricity during the dimout, the season the Metropolitan Opera kept its Civic Opera House engagement, which had piled up $100,000 in advance sales, only because some ingenious soul thought of piping in electricity from the Diesel-operated cargo boat, the *Mainsheet Eye*.

But there were compensations, even in calamity. "Antigone" made its point despite polka dot boleros and checked sports coats, the gayer customers found darkened playhouses rather a lark, and everything was fine at the opera, pictorially speaking, except the night the *Mainsheet Eye* blew a fuse at "La Gioconda" and the afternoon it so bashed the riverside plaza of the building occupied by the *Daily News* and the Chicago *Sun* that thereafter the *Metropolitan's* press agent prefaced all calls to those newspapers with "Pardon my boat."

Although we had fewer shows—42 productions this season to 46 last season—they ran longer, a total of 329 playgoing weeks between the end of May, 1945, and the beginning of June, 1946, and according to *Variety's* trusty statisticians they took in more nearly $6,000,000 than last season's $5,500,000. Something in the neighborhood of $5,800,000 seems a fair estimate.

Some of this—more than $1,000,000 of it, to be specific—was due to our acquisition of what to many Chicagoans was a brand-new theatre, the Shubert. Longer memories knew it once was famed as the Majestic, but it had been dark a dozen years when the Shuberts decided they could use its 2,000 capacity and proceeded to restore its rose and gold gaiety, dust off its bronze and crystal and make it their musical flagship. They booked Olsen and Johnson, which looked rather like inviting the wreckers before the departing builders had turned the corner, but it worked like magic. "Laffing Room Only" ran 30 weeks to the musical championship and piled up a neat $1,114,800.

This not only rescued an expensive show from the blight of a none-too-happy past, but caused Olsen and Johnson to grow nostalgic. They prowled through Chicago *Tribune* files until they came across a Sunday paper of 1920 vintage showing when "Two Likeable Lads Loaded with Laughs" made their downtown bow in that same Majestic. That was quite a Sunday page. Percy Hammond was writing on it, and among the people here for him to write about were Ethel Barrymore, Richard Bennett, Leo Dietrichstein, Arthur Byron, Frank McGlynn, Nance O'Neil, John Charles Thomas, Donald Brian, Wallace Eddinger, Margaret Lawrence—this list could go on for a paragraph. On the Majestic bill in slightly smaller type than the almost infinitesimal "Two Likeable Lads" was Jack Benny. Bert Lahr could be discovered with a microscope at the Star and Garter, but Sophie Tucker was more buxom at the Palace. Altogether, Olsen and Johnson were so enchanted they sent hams to all the drama critics, the subtlest comic gesture of their sojourn.

While they were piling up grosses at the Shubert, "Anna Lucasta" captured the nonmusical record with 36 weeks at the Civic, where even at small capacity it had taken in some $580,000 before turning the corner into the new season with Janice Kingslow, a Chicago girl, replacing Hilda Simms in the title role. "Anna Lucasta" is not only a good show, but an example of how a producer took a chance and made it pay. John Wildberg sent Chicago the New York company last Fall and gave New York a substitute. There has been much visiting back and forth, but the standard has been kept high, partly because Harry Wagstaff Gribble, the director, has spent so much time here, some of it planning his piebald production of "Romeo and Juliet."

However, despite the encroaching champions, the Selwyn, Harris and Erlanger Theatres held their edge as the town's favorite playhouses. The Selwyn was busy 50 of the 52 weeks, 32 of them with "The Voice of the Turtle," which rounded out its 68-week run and went to the West Coast where its leading actors, K. T. Stevens and Hugh Marlowe, lived up to the title by getting married. The Selwyn also had Ethel Barrymore for 10 weeks in a revival of "The Joyous Season," the special Chicago company of "Deep Are the Roots" for seven weeks, and Ruth Chatterton's ill-fated "Second Best Bed" for one week.

Thirty-five of the Harris' 48 weeks went to the holdover "Dear Ruth," which ran 41 weeks in all. Kay Francis kept the trivial "Windy Hill" going for 12 weeks, and Katharine Cornell played one of the two repertory weeks combining "Candida" and "Antigone." Sir Cedric Hardwicke left for England after the first week, and George Mathews became Mr. Burgess.

The Erlanger's 47 weeks began with nine featuring a fresh and charming return of "Life with Father," with Carl Benton Reid and Betty Linley, who stayed over from the previous seasons to make it 10 weeks in all. Billy Rose sent his crackling "Carmen Jones" for 19 weeks, Willie Howard came for 6 in a mournful revival of "The Passing Show." "The Late George Apley" clung to its stalwarts, Leo G. Carroll, Percy Waram, Janet Beecher and Margaret Dale, for 12 distinguished weeks, one of them blacked out by the coal strike. The current visitor, the Theatre Guild's rather dusty "The Merry Wives of Windsor," with Charles Coburn "in person" as Falstaff, has two of three weeks to its credit.

The Blackstone's 40 weeks began with a week's holdover of "Jacobowsky and the Colonel," then went on with 12 weeks of the returning "Good Night Ladies," 3 of the Theatre Guild's "The Winter's Tale," 1 of "The Ryan Girl," another of Guy Kibbee's "A Joy Forever," 4 of "The Hasty Heart," 12 of the brilliant folk play, "Dark of the Moon," and 6, so far, of our company of "State of the Union," with James Rennie topping the cast with his powerful portrait of a political boss.

New as it is and late in entering the joust, the Shubert ran fifth with 37 weeks, 30 of them devoted to Olsen and Johnsoniana, 6, to date, of Michael Todd's vastly popular "Up in Central Park," which had more than $250,000 to its credit at season's end. "Anna Lucasta's" 36 weeks put the Civic next in line, with the Studebaker following, its 33 weeks divided between 3 for "The Tempest," 4 for Tallulah Bankhead's "Foolish Notion," 4 each for returns of "Blossom Time" and "The Student Prince," and 10 for "St. Lazare's Pharmacy," the Eddie Dowling show with Miriam Hopkins and the French-Canadian Fridolin, given superb setting by Jo Mielziner. Jan Kiepura's "Polonaise" came next for 6 weeks, and "The Day Before Spring" had 2 before it gave up in the face of the dimout.

The Great Northern's 30 weeks began with Elisabeth Bergner's mercurial brilliance in the tawdry "The Two Mrs. Carrolls," and went on with 2 weeks of "The Overtons," 3 of Milton Berle's "Spring in Brazil"—he told an audience from the stage one night, "Look out, we outnumber you"—3 of a poor version of "Suds in Your Eye," 3 of a dull probing at the Negro problem, "A Young American," 4 of the engaging "On the Town," 1 of a dismal gibe at book publishers, "Between Covers," and another 3, so far, for "Windy City," a musical with imagination and more possibilities than it had been able to exploit.

Not counting several Yiddish shows, the Civic Opera House, busy most of its time with concert, ballet and opera, devoted 8 weeks to theatre, 1 to a holdover "Countess Maritza," 4 to Edwin Lester's "The Desert Song," notable in that it proved the house had won the amplification battle, and 3 to a curious adventure called "Second Guesser," which attempted to sell peanuts, popcorn, hot dogs and Al Schacht in a play about the Dodgers.

THE SEASON IN SAN FRANCISCO

BY FRED JOHNSON

Drama Editor of the San Francisco *Call-Bulletin*

THE war was over and San Francisco theatre-goers were wondering what peace would mean in their amusement life. They were certain of one thing—that more normal times would see an end of the boomtown period which had meant more in profit at the box office than in quality of entertainment.

The war years, which had crowded this throbbing embarkation point with hordes of transient diversion-seekers in uniform, also had brought in a succession of mediocre stage offerings which would have had much less chance of passing muster in ordinary times. But with eager crowds at the wickets, more concerned with the earthier and spicier conceits of the theatre than with matters of uplift, there was opportunity, even invitation, for attractions of rank shoddiness, enabled to draw full houses at such top prices as once were rewarded with entertainment of the highest caliber.

Came peacetime, "the party was over," as showmen put it, here and in other large centers as well. But in San Francisco the change was even more fortunate for the show patron who had been denied for the duration such Broadway hits as "Oklahoma!", "Dear Ruth," "Harvey" and "Foolish Notion."

Arrival of these and other top-grade entertainments highlighted the late season, which was further marked by the exceptionally long runs of all these except the last-named, although the Tallulah Bankhead play had its month's profitable stay. It also launched the Theatre Guild-American Theatre Society's subscription series in San Francisco, a project that met with fervent response, due to "Oklahoma!" 's second date in the schedule. The musical, with its well-favored Chicago company, played to record turn-away patronage for twelve and a half weeks.

Third attraction in the series, arriving at season's end, was "The Merry Wives of Windsor," starring Charles Coburn as Falstaff and featuring Jessie Royce Landis, Gino Malo, Whitford Kane and Romney Brent. Coburn, in jubilant spirit over the town's mirthful reception, gave over part of his opening night curtain chat to a plea for support of the Guild's repertory theatre plan. Romney Brent's direction and Stewart Chaney's settings were factors in the splendid production.

The theatrical season of 1944-45 had ended, as had others in late years, midway in the San Francisco and Los Angeles Civic Light Opera festival, with "The Red Mill" and "The Desert Song" as first of the offerings. These were followed in midsummer by "Rose Marie" and Billy Rose's "Carmen Jones," which played to capacity.

This year an even more brilliant series was promised with a lavish revival of Jerome Kern's "Roberta," with special orchestrations and dance arrangements by Edward Ward and new choral embroidery by Dudley Chambers. San Francisco had its first view of the explosive comedy star, Luba Malina, of whose performances in "Mexican Hayride" and "Marinka" the word had been advanced. Film comedian Sterling Holloway's expert direction was widely commended.

"The Vagabond King" was a second revival offering of like opulence, well performed by Barytone John Tyers, Dorothy Sarnoff, Marguerite Piazza, Eduardo Ciannelli and Comedian Billy House. Scheduled for early July was the Associations' most pretentious production since "Song of Norway," under the title of "Fortune Teller," but combining Victor Herbert music of that operetta with that of his "Serenade," with a new book by Henry Myers. Helena Bliss, on leave from "Song of Norway," was to head the cast. "Bloomer Girl," with the New York production and company, was scheduled to close the season in July-August.

"Song Without Words," a new operetta based on the romance and music of Tschaikowsky, was a futile attempt by another producing organization to follow up the success of "Norway" as a combination of melody and biography. Margit Bokor, the late prima donna of "Waltz King," was starred as the French opera singer involved in romance with the composer, with John Maxwell Hayes in the latter role. Frederick Jackson's book and Tschaikowsky's music as adapted by Franz Steininger were insufficient as a foundation for success of the piece.

Still under the musical heading were repeat visits by the Shuberts' "Blossom Time" and "Student Prince" troupers, playing to fair business. Paul Small made one more venture into the vaudeville field, with the usual San Francisco premiere. Dropping the "Time" handle of his previous exhibits, he presented "Merry-Go-Round," with Jay C. Flippen and Jack Pearl as comedians and Everett Marshall as principal singer. It was the least successful of his variety series that began with "Show Time" a few seasons before.

The year's phenomena was a shoddily staged and acted version of Mary Lasswell's novel, "Suds in Your Eye," which played two engagements to near-capacity profits under the banner of Louis Macloon. Originally produced at Pasadena Playhouse, it bore the directorial stamp of Gilmor Brown, previously associated with offerings of more integrity. After appearing in various coast towns, the comedy, adapted by Jack Kirkland, won similar patronage in midwestern centers until it reached Chicago. Critical consensus was to the effect that Kirkland had overlooked several worth-while elements of good theatre in Miss Lasswell's work in favor of added characters and extraneous horseplay.

Another fiasco was the premiering of a new comedy titled "Adam Ate the Apple," by Herbert Rudley and Fanya Lawrence, and staged by Melville Burke. Ernest Truex and Sylvia Field were the main principals, concerned as man and wife with a visit in their household of the latter's old flame. The injection of labored sexiness served only to worsen an amateurish script and the mixture was shelved after brief runs here and on tour.

Three revivals met with indifferent success. One was "The Bad Man," starring Leo Carrillo; another, "Rain," with Gladys George, and the third, Victor Herbert's "The Only Girl." Alonzo Price's revised book and lyrics and his own direction of the latter comedy with music failed in offsetting its vintage flavor—or winning patrons.

A touring company of "Ten Little Indians" played more than a month's engagement to virtual capacity and an even more profitable run was accorded "Rebecca," teaming Bramwell Fletcher and Diana Barrymore.

Not until the year was nearing its close did the theatre begin to pick up with the arrival of "Dear Ruth" and a road company headed by Philip Ober and Marjorie Gateson, to be rewarded by a 9 weeks' engagement. A run of equal length was chalked up by "Harvey," with Joe E. Brown in the Frank Fay role, moderating his accustomed comedy style to the demands of his crowning stage characterization.

"The Voice of the Turtle" followed in the same theatre, headed by K. T. Stevens, Hugh Marlowe and Vivian Vance, playing to virtual capacity for 13 weeks, or a few nights longer than "Oklahoma!" From San Francisco the tour was continued, with a change of cast.

With the Curran and Geary Theatres solidly booked as the city's regular legitimate houses, Elisabeth Bergner was disadvantaged by bringing "The Two Mrs. Carrolls" into the Tivoli, a former stage theatre given over to motion pictures. Its location and acoustics were detriments she deplored. The three weeks' engagement might have been of greater length under more favorable auspices.

With the season's end, Basil Rathbone and Eugenie Leontovich appeared at the Curran for a limited ten days in "Obsession," a new adaptation of Louis Verneuil's two-character French drama which had been played here seventeen years ago by John Halliday and Fay Bainter under the title of "Jealousy." Under the aegis of Homer Curran, of "Song of Norway" identification, Russell Lewis and Howard Young, the new version was well received, due in part to its added values in dramatic quality and sophistication under Reginald Denham's direction and with setting by Stewart Chaney.

The season's collegiate event on the stage was University of California Theatre's presentation in Hearst Greek Theatre on the Berkeley campus of the Oresteian Trilogy of Aeschylus, "Agamemnon," "Choephori" and "Eumenides." The university's music and drama departments gave the combined dramas a spectacular and impressive staging.

In San Francisco the Theatre Arts Colony was virtually alone in the little theatre field, climaxing its year with an outstanding revival of "Winterset," acted by a cast of near-professional caliber.

THE SEASON IN SOUTHERN CALIFORNIA

By Edwin Schallert
Drama Editor of the *Los Angeles Times*

REDISCOVERY of a stage-minded public was the most important single facet of the season of 1945-46 in Southern California. Two productions, "Harvey" and "Oklahoma!", served to evidence its broad-dimensional existence. Reactions to the New York Theatre Guild's whole footlight program, as expressed through its allied American Theatre Society, even more strongly disclosed a large latent interest in what might be described as potentially worth-while theatrical events. Even the very weak "Foolish Notion," starring Tallulah Bankhead, and written by Philip Barry, seemed to evoke enthusiastic response. This was the opening Guild attraction, and that organization, after the premiere of "Oklahoma!" which followed later on, was encouraged to contemplate a more expansive invasion during 1946-47.

Taken by and large, the theatre had its most promising outlook in many years toward the end of June, 1946. Summer shows were establishing themselves, notable being the Gryphon Productions project at Laguna Beach. "Angel Street" with John Emery and Peggy Converse inaugurated this enterprise just at the close of the regular season, and the Gryphon included "Dark Victory," "Goodbye Again," "Room Service," "Blind Alley," a new play called "George," "Beautiful People," "Twentieth Century" and "Amphitryon 38" in the ambitious prospectus of its offerings—though naturally the actual appraisal of these will have to be made at a later time.

Prime figures in the undertaking were Walter Rathbun, formerly with Summer groups in the East, Richard Irving, and John Merdyth Lucas. Three ex-servicemen, they were connected with entertainment for the armed forces during the war. They enlisted an amazing attention for their plan in Hollywood itself, among guest stars tentatively named being Claire Trevor, Keenan Wynn, Constance Moore, the noted British actor, Rex Harrison, Sally Eilers and others, while the advisory committee comprised such personalities as Bette Davis, Edgar Bergen, Van Johnson, Dorothy Lamour, Charles Bickford, Joan Crawford, Otto Preminger, Norman Krasna, Jerry Wald, Hal B. Wallis, Michael Curtiz,

Charles Beahan, Louella Parsons and others.

Other heralded prospects in Summer theatre were a production of "Hamlet," with a cast from the films, in the Pilgrimage Play Theatre, which was rebuilt during the Summer with the consequent abandonment of the Life of the Christ drama for 1946. Mike Todd announced his intention of sponsoring the Shakespearean venture, and also secured the Hollywood Bowl for the Fall presentation of one of his musical shows.

Summer light opera was planned for the Greek Theatre in Griffith Park, which had been quiescent throughout the war, with Irene Manning, Kenny Baker, Allan Jones mentioned among the stars, and the opening bill, "Two Hearts in Three-Quarter Time."

June, in fact, was seeing plans expanding in every direction, and if even half of them attained materialization it would have suggested a festival spirit that was not only all-prevailing, but that had never previously been rivaled in the Los Angeles show-giving area.

Actors' Laboratory, for instance, was a late June entrant with its "Awake and Sing" by Clifford Odets, which starred John Garfield, with J. Edward Bromberg, who earlier gained renewed fame in "Volpone"; Morris Carnovsky, Sam Levene, Phoebe Brand and others in the cast. That organization not only had its primitive set-up, where it has given a number of interesting presentations, but also the Las Palmas Theatre in Hollywood, which was formerly the Playtime. At this establishment, where "Awake and Sing" was staged, "The Twig Is Bent" by N. Richard Nash and "The Inspector General" by Gogol were slated for Summer and early Fall rendition, respectively. Actors Lab made one of its finest records during the season with "A Bell for Adano," in which Kent Smith played the Major Joppolo role. This was their most noteworthy effort, apart from the "Volpone" revival.

Whatever the scope of the reawakening, which mostly took place during the early part of 1946, it still left no space for even the slightly mediocre. The shows and the enterprises that score with Southern California audiences still require big-league qualities. It must be a circus to succeed in the Los Angeles territory. Other conflicting interests too quickly intrude for aught but the most dazzling entertainment to thrive. The races, the seaside, the movies, and just plain automobile travel furnish a constant and relentless competition.

The long build-up for "Oklahoma!" explains its popular enticement. Nobody who had heard about it wanted to miss the production. Even those who felt, as some did, that the show itself was overrated, or that the company, out of Chicago, was not everything they anticipated, could not summon a strong enough word-of-mouth campaign to overcome the great advance pulling power that "Oklahoma!" had gained. It is difficult to believe that anybody could be allergic to this event, but some people were. But no single voice, or even small chorus of voices raised against it could ever have shunted the long lines away from the box-office, or stopped the terrific procession of mail orders for tickets. "Oklahoma!" sold before it arrived; it sold double after its arrival.

Even if the presentation was less brilliant than Broadway, it was still great entertainment. For the record, James Alexander, Mary Hatcher, Dorothea MacFarland, Walter Donahue, Richard H. Gordon and Mary Marlo were in the aggregation that appeared. Local interest attached to the fact that Alexander at one time sang at Florentine Gardens, while Miss Hatcher was a contractee of Paramount studios on loan for the big stage musical, and Miss MacFarland had come originally from Glendale, near Los Angeles. There was probably never a more lively back-stage party held after any production than that which celebrated the advent of "Oklahoma!" in Los Angeles. The film professional world gave this troupe a gala greeting.

"Harvey" was almost equally festive socially, and heretofore cinema premieres have had an "exclusive" on that sort of thing. But Joe E. Brown was the star, and that seemed to mean a lot in the community. Moreover Brown proved the fine restraints of which he was capable in his acting. His performance avoided completely the suggestion of his usual comedy routines, and his speech about Harvey, which is a climaxing event of the play, was genuinely moving. Brock Pemberton did splendidly by the western public in bringing Marion Lorne to the stage in the sister role. She is one of the finest mature actresses to have been viewed on the Pacific Coast in a long while.

While "Oklahoma!" had a 12 weeks' staging with promise for a return engagement, "Harvey" played a busy 6 weeks, and was also hovering on the repeat list. The welcome was also good for "The Two Mrs. Carrolls" with Elisabeth Bergner, and "Voice of the Turtle" among visiting plays. K. T. Stevens, Hugh Marlowe and Geraldine Jones composed the three-people cast for "Turtle." Marlowe made the most efficient impression, though the sum total of Miss Stevens' performance was good. Miss Bergner in "The Two Mrs. Carrolls" drew big houses, and was keenly enjoyed.

Apart from this one definite line of development so strongly marked, there was much of the usual "snafu" aspect to the theatre in Los Angeles and vicinity. It should be called the annual hodge-podge, through which any appraiser has to thread his way to discover a few slight diamonds, which are often very likely to be in the rough. Any mixed metaphor will, perhaps, fit the pattern as displayed.

The Pasadena Playhouse premiere of "Yes Is for a Very Young Man" by Gertrude Stein was inordinately dull. One went expecting at least some of that fantastic alleged originality of the author as a fillip, but aside from a few early sorties in that direction, the play seemed shortly to settle down to a kind of pseudo-conventionality, and very little vitality was discernible either in plot or characters, while most of the situations even with the French wartime background carried little or no impact. The play can be written off as amateurish.

"The Avon Flows" was almost equally unbearable before it was through. George Jean Nathan's idea for putting "false faces" on regular Shakespearean characters by changing Romeo into Othello and then into Petruchio, and Juliet into Desdemona and then Katharine the Shrew may have seemed a novel experiment to its author, but it was only mildly diverting for a certain proportion of the audience to which "The Avon Flows" played. The whole contraption seemed to sag terribly in the second half, and juggling the Bard's plays doesn't exactly appear to be Mr. Nathan's forte, regardless of whether he gave years of time to the experiment. One says this, too, regrettably of a critic who has made himself very successfully heard in that field for a number of years.

Of more moment in the premiere line was the mystery melodrama, "I Give You My Husband," by Al York, first presented on a non-professional basis at the Jewel Box Theatre, and a late season production at the Belasco under the title "All Women Are—!" There was much thought of transporting this eventually to New York, and the tryouts therefore were to be regarded as a preliminary. It is an intriguing and novel thriller.

Pasadena Playhouse gave the world premieres of "Men Coming Home" by Denison Clift, and "The Happy Family" by James Rennie, drawn from Dickens sources, as well as the first American performance of "Angels Amongst Us" by Frantisek Langer. Both "Men Coming Home" and "Angels Amongst Us" received commendation. "Chicken Every Sunday" and "While the Sun Shines" were offered for the first time on the Coast by this organization.

In addition to the Actors Laboratory, a further effort was made to draw the professional group from pictures to the stage at the Phoenix Theatre in Westwood, site of the University of California at Los Angeles, where the Campus Theatre holds forth.

At the Phoenix, "Candida," with Freddie Bartholomew and Anne Revere, and "Bad Angel," with Reginald Owen and Hugo Haas, were proffered. "Bad Angel" lacked in solid values as a new play.

Such varying affairs as "Trio" and "Suds in Your Eye," as well as the fifth revival of "Tobacco Road," which, this time, starred John Barton, were prominent among downtown Los Angeles events of Coast origin. "Trio" was the most provocative.

Guy Bates Post tried out "Good Morning, My Son," but it was a hopeless excursion in sentimentality. "Over 21" was well given late in the season, but collided with the street car strike which forced its premature closing. "School for Brides" was another short-lived and less meritorious effort.

Not even street car strikes can interfere with the serene progress of "The Drunkard," "The Blackouts" with Ken Murray, or the Turnabout with Elsa Lanchester, Lotte Goslar, Forman Brown, the Yale Puppeteers and the others. Murray in his vaudeville revue, which is about the only continuous and continuing show of this kind in the country, departed his comedy tradition by acting in the dramatic "The Valiant" for a time. What's more, audiences seemed to like this departure from the normal entertainment.

"Dear Ruth" managed to pay a visit during the year with Philip Ober, Marjorie Gateson, Randee Sanford, Russell Hoyt and Peggy Romano in the cast. Also those never-failing musicals, "The Student Prince" and "Blossom Time." This was in the early and rather arid part of the theatrical year. "The Red Mill" also preluded its transference to New York with a short engagement at the Biltmore under the Paula Stone-Hunt Stromberg, Jr., management, after it had been played during the regular Los Angeles Civil Light Opera season. "The Only Girl" was another of the early musical shows, but the production was not to be compared with "The Red Mill." Also "Song Without Words," hopefully trying to find "The Song of Norway" trail, was produced, but missed the right landmarks. It essayed to "immortalize" Tschaikowsky, and had merit in the staging.

"Rain," with Gladys George, paid a brief visit, while Diana Barrymore and Bramwell Fletcher starred in "Rebecca." Featuring Eva Gabor, "Candle-Light" was well acted at the new Masque Theatre. The outdoor spectacle "Ramona," which ceased during the war, resumed at Hemet, California.

There is scant need to chronicle such things as "Motel Wives," "Nellie Was a Lady," "Two in a Bed," "A Honey in the Hay" and "Maid of the Ozarks," which grow up like weeds in the Los Angeles vicinity. Madge Bellamy contributed some betterment to "Holiday Lady," which was hardly any more worthy of note fundamentally than the others, and Betty Rowland was seen in "Anybody's Girl."

Revues such as "Insanities of 1945," with Shaw and Lee and Harry Savoy, and "Merry Go Round," presented by Paul Small, with Jack Pearl, Jay C. Flippen, Everett Marshall and Corrinna Mura, had something to recommend them.

The Civic Light Opera was due to cross the million-mark as one of the West Coast's biggest show projects. That figure represents the combined receipts derived in Los Angeles and San Francisco. Impresario Edwin Lester sponsored a production of "The Vagabond King," with John Tyers and Dorothy Sarnoff, and "Roberta," with Luba Malina in the sensational class as a star. He also brought out "Bloomer Girl" from New York. But his most original undertaking, "The Fortune Teller," blending that Victor Herbert work with the composer's "The Serenade," belongs to the 1946-47 season, as it wasn't produced until July. Lester was weighing the New York possibilities of this last-named operetta especially.

Earl Carroll's "Sketchbook" came onto the scene about the end of 1945, and even more importantly this veteran revue producer was planning a huge new theatre. His success has been phenomenal.

Pasadena's eleventh annual Midsummer Drama Festival from June to August, 1945, dealt with Living American Playwrights, while Clyde Fitch was heralded for 1946.

Callboard Theatre, the Geller Workshop, the Bliss-Hayden, Rainbow, Village, New Hampshire and other smaller establishments all seem to have a hold for one reason or another, and the Callboard appears verging on the professional status. Little theatres will always have a field, as long as there are film talent scouts in Southern California.

STATE OF THE UNION

A Comedy in Three Acts

By Howard Lindsay and Russel Crouse

THERE was a story floating around Broadway shortly after the production of "State of the Union" that no less prominent a theatre person than Helen Hayes had suggested the play to its fortunate authors, Howard Lindsay and Russel Crouse. A true story only in part, later evidence revealed. The authors of "Life with Father" had had a comedy in mind for Miss Hayes, and there had been conferences. Then Miss Hayes decided that what she needed more than a new play was a year's rest from constant devotion to the theatre. So she went back to her Nyack estate and the playwrights returned to their search for a proper subject.

It had been agreed that there might reasonably be a good comedy with a touch of political significance, stemming inferentially from the colorful adventures of the late Wendell Willkie. His nomination and campaign for the Presidency in 1940 had furnished excitement, suspense and conflict enough for a dozen plays. But the conviction that their play should not in any sense be a Willkie play was definitely fixed in the minds of both authors.

To combine politics and romance in the same comedy is a good trick if you can do it. Such a comedy is pretty sure to appeal to both men and women. But few playwrights have been able to turn that trick. So the Messrs. Lindsay and Crouse elected to have a try at it. If it should please critics and playgoers to read hints of the Willkie adventures into the story, that would be their privilege, though completely unauthorized.

As it turned out, "State of the Union" became a very human domestic comedy with serious dramatic overtones—a comedy in which the dramatists' basic impulses were swayed by both their love of laughter and their love of country. The comedy is a tribute to the Lindsay-Crouse playwriting skill, and to the keenness of their observation of American character.

It had been a dull theatre season in New York up to November 14, 1945, when "State of the Union" was produced at the

"State of the Union," copyright 1945 *by Howard Lindsay and Russel Crouse. Published by Random House, Inc., New York.*

Hudson Theatre. Only one other play had stirred anything like a majority enthusiasm in critical ranks. That was the controversial d'Usseau-Gow "Deep Are the Roots." Playgoers who had been paying extravagant prices for disappointing drama were heartily disgusted. Little wonder that this happy comedy ran through the season.

Being ushered into the studio of James Conover's home in Washington, D. C., at the opening of "State of the Union," we find three other guests have arrived ahead of us. They are Kathryn Thorndyke, known to her intimates as Kay; "Spike" McManus and Grant Matthews. Mrs. Thorndyke is "a handsome woman in her late thirties . . . the kind you would find talking to men more often than women." McManus "has been for years a Washington political reporter, pudgy and genial, and with a rough charm. He knows how to make friends and influence people." Grant Matthews is "a distinguished-looking man in his middle forties, a successful business man, but also much more than that."

At the moment the host, Conover, is seated at a desk, engaged in a conversation over the phone. He is "a quiet-spoken man of about 60, of good appearance; not quite the type an audience would expect to be a politician."

The three guests are obviously waiting, though not impatiently, for their host to finish telephoning. This he does shortly and with this final and forceful statement to whomever is listening:

"Has this occurred to you? The reason you and the Senator are fighting over this one appointment is because we lost the last election and the one before that and the one before that! We have to win the next one! The Senator feels that appointment will strengthen the party in his district. So there's no argument."

With that curt dismissal Conover hangs up the receiver and comes back into the circle. It soon appears that Mrs. Thorndyke is the publisher of several newspapers in the Middle West; that "Spike" is probably the best informed political reporter in Washington, whom she is ready to loan to Conover for a coming presidential campaign, and that Grant Matthews is a hugely successful industrialist whom Conover is seriously considering as a possible candidate to head the Republican party ticket in 1948.

"If we can get a strong candidate in '48 we've got better than a fighting chance," Kay Thorndyke submits. "Jim, my newspapers are city papers, but small cities, with a rural circulation too. They make a pretty good sounding board. Here's what comes back to me: The party's best chance in '48 is to put up a candidate who's never been identified with politics."

"Look what happened in '40," adds Spike. "If the election had been held a month after Philadelphia, Willkie would have won."

KAY—Yes, and why? Because the people had the idea Willkie was somebody you politicians didn't want.

SPIKE (*to* CONOVER)—You wouldn't mind if that impression got around about the candidate in '48, would you?

CONOVER—Not if the candidate was somebody I *did* want.

SPIKE—That's what I mean.

CONOVER—Well, it seems to me at this point we ought to hear from Mr. Matthews. (*They all look at* GRANT.)

GRANT—Let me make this clear—I don't want to be President of the United States. (*They smile at his vehemence.*)

CONOVER—That decision may not be in your hands.

GRANT—Mr. Conover, I can understand Mrs. Thorndyke telling me I should be President. But you—you must be talking about somebody else.

CONOVER—You're a national figure—and you have been ever since the war started.

SPIKE—Is Henry Kaiser a national figure? For every ship he's built you've built a hundred planes.

KAY—Grant, everybody in the country knows you and everybody respects you.

GRANT—Oh, they know I make good airplanes and I've made a hell of a lot of them.

SPIKE—They know more than that. When you fought the aluminum combine! When you slugged it out with the War Production Board until they broke those bottlenecks! The time you talked back to that Senate Investigating Committee. Three times you crowded the war off the front page!

CONOVER—Mrs. Thorndyke and I aren't the only Republicans who've been thinking about you. Those speeches you've been making—especially that last one in Cleveland.

GRANT—When I made that speech in Cleveland I was trying to put both parties on the spot. I wasn't speaking as a Republican. I was speaking as a citizen. I'm worried about what's happening in this country. We're splitting apart. Business, labor, farmers, cattlemen, lumbermen—they're all trying to get the biggest bite of the apple. We talk about the war being over—well, we've got a war on here at home now—a civil war—an economic war.

That's what I said in Cleveland. That's why I was surprised you asked me down here.

Conover—Why were you surprised?

Grant—Because you politicians are trying to make capital out of this situation—you appeal to each one of these pressure groups just to get their votes. But let me tell you something. I don't think that's good politics. A lot of people wrote me after that speech in Cleveland. (*With a grin.*) Of course I will admit that the business men liked best what I said about labor, and the unions said I was absolutely right about big business, and the farmers were pretty pleased with what I said about everybody but the farmers. But they all knew what I was talking about. They know we've all got to work in harness, if we're going to take our place in this world. And if we don't there won't be any world. We may be kidding ourselves that our party is going to win in '48—that the people here will want a change the way they did in England—but if our party does win, whoever is President has to have guts enough to pull us together and keep us together. I'm for that man, Mr. Conover—I don't care who he is.

There is another phone call for Conover. This one he decides he had better take in another room—seeing that Spike McManus is there. Spike understands. He will hold the line and hang up as soon as Conover gets the other phone. But Conover is too smart for that.

"Mrs. Thorndyke, do you mind?" he asks, handing Kay the phone. "Spike has a little Drew Pearson blood."

Grant Matthews has been pacing the floor. Now, with Conover gone, he announces that not only is he feeling mighty uncomfortable, but that as soon as Conover comes back he is going to ask him to drop the whole business. He and Kay have had a lot of fun dreaming about this situation, Grant admits, but it doesn't follow that they should ask Conover to take their dreams seriously. The Republican party can't be *that* desperate for a candidate—

"Don't think he isn't serious about you," Spike warns Grant, with his finger between the pages of "Who's Who"; "there's a book mark in this at your page. . . . Are you 47 years old? You don't look it. . . . You know this even impresses me—Twelve boards of directors! Say, there's a lot of swell angles about you!—For instance, Honorary President of the Society for the Preservation of Wild Life. How can we use that in the campaign?"

"Spike, I don't think the wild life vote is very important."

"No, I mean from a publicity angle. Say, for instance, a picture in *Life*. (*He points to* GRANT.) You and a grateful duck."

Conover is back from telephoning and frankly in need of a drink. That, argues Spike, would indicate that he (Conover) has been talking with Senator Taft. Which reminds Kay: Does Conover think that Taft can be serious about becoming a candidate himself?

"Well," Jim dodges, "you can always figure that Senator Taft is serious."

It is Grant's opinion that, whatever happens, Truman is not going to be easy to beat. "He's made a damn good impression," declares Grant. "He's made some strong appointments."

"He's also made some weak ones," says Kay.

"Those are the ones that interest me—the weak ones," inserts Conover. "Between now and the campaign the administration can run into some ugly trouble."

"Well, all we can do is hope." Spike is passing the drinks.

The talk on Grant's chances as a candidate becomes general. Kay is of the opinion that they are excellent. No employer in the country has a better labor record. And business is bound to go along with him. Kay is sure Grant would command the votes of both Sewell Avery and Philip Murray, even though he would refuse to promise either of them a thing—

"You'd have to promise them something," Spike insists. "Still, Dewey outpromised Roosevelt and it didn't get him anywhere."

At this point Spike decides to take a one-man Gallup poll: What does Jim Conover think of the Matthews chances? Jim can't say just yet. After Grant makes his Washington speech he will have a better line on the feeling in the Capital. Incidentally, is Mrs. Matthews coming to hear her husband speak?

No, she isn't. "She takes bringing up the children more seriously than she does my speeches," explains Grant. And, anyway, as he was saying to Mrs. Thorndyke, Grant thinks it would be a good thing to drop the whole idea.

"Jim, Tuesday Grant's starting a tour of his plants," says Kay, quickly. "Everywhere he's going he's been invited to speak."

"Minneapolis, Seattle, San Francisco, Los Angeles, Denver, Wichita, Detroit," adds Spike—

"If Grant made those speeches, at the end of the tour could you tell him whether he had a chance, or whether we should give up the whole idea?"

"That covers a lot of territory. Yes, I think if Mr. Matthews made those speeches I could be pretty definite."

"Grant, you've got to go along with us that far." Kay is very earnest. "You've got to make those speeches."

"Look—Kay, I'm going to be pretty busy on this trip. I've got problems in every one of those plants. I've got to do my damnedest to keep those men working. Besides, I wish I knew how much you had to do with those invitations for me to speak."

"Spike, you're going to make the trip with him." Kay is decisive. "You've been telling everyone for years how to run a political campaign. Now we'll find out whether you can run one. The bureau can get along without you for a couple of weeks. It will be a vacation for you."

"It will be a vacation for everyone in Washington," declares Jim Conover significantly. "Now we've reached that decision, there's a lot for all of us to talk about. On this tour, Mr. Matthews—"

Before they can get any farther there is another phone call for Conover. This time Kay, holding the phone, isn't quite so quick to set it down as she was before. After she has pressed the disconnector as a signal to Conover to go ahead, she carefully picks up the phone again and listens. What she has to report a moment later is a little startling. Conover has been talking with someone in New York who has been looking into Grant's record. They have picked up some gossip about Grant and Kay. And there has been talk, too, about Mrs. Matthews and some Major. Grant is more than a little disturbed by that report. What's the Major's name? Kay didn't get it. What did it sound like? They hear Conover coming and Spike is quick to cover—

"On the other hand, if what you say is true, Mr. Matthews," ad-libs Spike loudly as Conover comes into the room, "that makes the migratory flamingo a very interesting bird."

"What makes the flamingo an interesting bird, Spike?"

Spike is caught short, but not very—"Tell him what you just told us, Mr. Matthews."

"I don't think Mr. Conover's interested in the wild life of America."

"Staying up this late is a little more wild life than I'm used to. I think we'd better call it a night."

Conover's note of dismissal is something of a surprise, but they accept it gracefully. Spike promises to stop in at the White House, if they still have the lights on, and warn the Trumans to start packing. Which reminds Jim that if Grant will linger for a little they can finish their drinks and talk over a few things. Kay hasn't finished her drink either—but she is not asked to stay.

Kay has said her good nights and started for the door. At the door she turns back and goes straight to Grant.

"Mr. Conover, I want you to know how completely we trust you," she says, putting her arm around Grant and kissing him. "Good night, darling." She has started out again when Conover stops her—

"Mrs. Thorndyke. You might as well finish your drink here. That's what I was going to talk about."

Conover (*continuing*)—Naturally, Mr. Matthews, when your name first came up as a possible candidate, I made some inquiries. It seems there's been some talk about you and Mrs. Thorndyke.

610767

Grant—What kind of talk?

Conover—I think you know what I mean when I say talk.

Kay—We wouldn't pretend to deny there's basis for it, but it can't be very widespread.

Grant—Kay, let Mr. Conover tell us what he's heard.

Conover—That's about all. (Spike *strolls back into scene.*) There's been some gossip. That's nothing unusual, and as long as it's about a man who makes airplanes, even though you're very well known, I don't think it would spread a great deal, but the minute you become a public figure—

Kay—Do you think it might be used against Mr. Matthews?

Conover—Not openly. What it would come down to would be a whispering campaign.

Grant—Frankly, Mr. Conover, I don't give a damn for the kind of opinion that sort of thing would influence.

Conover—I haven't any respect for it, either; but I have to reckon with it. You see, Mr. Matthews, while Mrs. Thorndyke happens to be divorced, you're a married man.

Grant—Well, if you think that's a major—(*His mind sticks momentarily on the word "major."*)—a vital factor . . . Kay, that seems to settle it.

Kay—Wait a minute, Grant! Jim, there must be some way around this.

Conover—Yes, there's a very obvious one.

Grant—So? What is it?

Conover—I'd like to see your wife with you when you speak here Monday night, and I'd like to see her make this trip with you.

Grant (*laughing*)—That's not the solution. If Mary knew

that I even thought of myself as President of the United States—

KAY—Jim, we've got to think of something else. It's a little difficult for me to talk about Mrs. Matthews in this situation but —you've seen the kind of wife—the more important her husband becomes the more determined she is to make him feel unimportant.

GRANT—Now, wait a minute, Kay. Be fair to Mary. (*To* CONOVER.) I don't want you to get the wrong impression of my wife, Mr. Conover. She's no shrew. She's a damned bright woman.

KAY—Grant, you know Mary's always cutting you down.

GRANT—I can't deny that. Still, I suppose her criticism of me has been valuable sometimes. (*To* CONOVER.) But a man does reach a saturation point.

CONOVER—If you become a candidate you'll have to take a lot of criticism.

SPIKE—Yes, your wife might be good training for you. Toughen you up.

KAY (*to* CONOVER)—I think it's more important that Grant should have his self-confidence.

CONOVER (*sitting on edge of desk*)—The most important thing of all is to kill this gossip. We haven't got a chance unless we do. The American people like to think of a married candidate as happily married. They want to see him and his wife together. They like to see them make the campaign together. It's an American tradition. You'd have to face that sooner or later. I think the sooner you face it the better.

Grant isn't sure that Mrs. Matthews would campaign with them, even if he were to ask her. The quickest way to find out, Conover suggests, would be to call her up and ask her. To which Grant agrees.

Spike would like to relieve the situation and also reassure Grant and Kay. "There's been that gossip about every candidate except Herbert Hoover," he reminds them. "They didn't pull it on Hoover because nobody would have believed it."

While they are waiting for long distance, their talk turns again to the possibilities of Grant's candidacy and his own increasingly belligerent attitude respecting his freedom to say what he wants to. If, for instance, he were elected, what would Conover expect him to do by way of showing his gratitude?

"I can't ask for more than an open mind," asserts Conover. "Mrs. Thorndyke said you two came down here for my advice.

Well, politics is my business. If we do get into a campaign together I hope you'll be open-minded about any advice I might give you then."

"I'd welcome it—only I can't promise I'd always follow it."

"Now, Grant, don't turn down advice before you get it," suggests Kay.

"All right, give me some." Grant's nervous laugh is intended to be disarming.

Well, for one thing, Conover would advise cutting Minneapolis out of the speaking tour. That's Stassen territory and Grant's speech might start a backfire.

Also, Conover would suggest, in this preliminary tour Grant should keep his remarks pretty general. Grant isn't sure he can follow that line strictly. "The only reason I have for speaking at all," he says, "is because there are some things I feel deeply about." He would like it thoroughly understood that he is not going to pull any punches.

"Mr. Matthews," observes Conover, serenely settling himself in one of the easier chairs, "most candidates have to spend a lot of time explaining things they wish they hadn't said. You're not carrying that weight because you haven't said very much yet. Your danger at this point might be in raising minor issues that would come back to plague you later."

"Grant, this isn't the airplane business," adds Kay. "You're used to dealing with tangible things. I know what Mr. Conover's talking about because I have to go out after circulation. You'll have to go out after votes."

Grant thinks he understands the situation pretty well. He would like to have Conover look over the speech he is to make in Washington, and he expects to get a lot of advice from Spike on the tour of the plants.

Spike, to the contrary, promises to be modest with his advice. His job, as he sees it, will be to humanize Grant. "I've got a lot of things dreamed up," he admits. "Do you know what first sold Willkie to the country as a human being? His going on Information Please. He came over as a regular guy and he held his own, too."

"Just a minute," protests Grant; "I'm no Wendell Willkie—I'm willing to take on Harry Truman, but not John Kieran."

Long distance is on the wire. Mrs. Matthews has been located. "Hello, Mary. I'm in Washington," is Grant's greeting as he takes over the call. "How's Joyce? . . . Doctor been there today? . . . That's fine. If she's that well, Sonny won't catch it now. . . . Mary, I'm making another speech down here Monday night. . . . No, they asked me to! I'd like to have you come down and listen to it, if it wouldn't bore you too much. . . . As a matter of fact I won't be home for a few weeks. I'm making a tour of the plants. How'd you like to make the trip with me?—I wish you would. We haven't made the circuit together in a long time." . . . "But how about coming down here anyway? We'll be house guests at Jim Conover's . . . Conover—a friend of mine, but in spite of that you'll like him. . . . Get here tomorrow night. . . . It doesn't matter how late. I'll send a plane back for you. . . . Swell! . . . Bring enough clothes for the trip, anyway. We can talk it over when you get here. . . . Mary, you'll need a dinner dress here Monday night. It's a banquet. You'll get my speech for dessert. . . . What? . . . All right. . . . Of course you'll look a little funny, sitting there with earmuffs on. Good night."

"I'm not sure the Presidency's worth it," sighs Grant, as he hangs up.

"She's coming?"

"Yes, Heaven help me."

"Grant, you know what that means. If Mary's coming here I've got to go home tomorrow." Kay's tone is something less than cheerful.

"I confess that would ease the housing situation," admits Conover. "The National Committee seems to think I run a hotel."

"H-m-m! Well, for the next few weeks I'll be sitting alone in New York while you tour the country with your wife." Kay is still serious.

" 'Politics makes strange bedfellows,' " chirps Spike.

Kay gives him a look. Catching the look, Spike quickly picks up his hat and starts out.

The curtain falls.

The bedroom in the Conover house that has been assigned Grant and Mary Matthews is attractively furnished. There is a double bed, with bed stands and reading lamps at either side. There are several overstuffed armchairs. The entrance door is from the left and the door leading to a dressing room and bathroom at the right.

At the moment Grant is editing his speech, taking out a few things that might have confirmed Spike McManus' idea that occasionally he (Grant) was inclined to become a little fancy as a speechmaker.

Jim Conover stops in to report that he has sent a car to the airport to meet Mrs. Matthews. Grant doesn't think she will get in much before midnight. He would have gone to meet her, but she couldn't give him any idea when she might get in.

"Where are you putting Mary?" Grant would know.

"In here with you. If we're going to create the impression about you two that we want to, this would be a good start."

Grant is troubled. "I don't think she'd welcome the idea," he protests. "We rushed into this decision and it's been on my conscience ever since. Look, Jim, when Mary finds out what's up, she can still say no. But moving her in here with me tonight—"

"Well, Fosdick's room is about the only one. He's in there alone. But where can I put Fosdick? There's nothing left but the billiard table."

Spike has come for the speech and is well pleased with the changes Grant has made. Still— "This spot in here sounds a little like a speech," he admits, with a shade of doubt in his voice.

"Damn it! It *is* a speech!"

"That's what I meant," confesses Spike.

A moment later Norah has arrived with Mrs. Matthews' bags, which, Grant quickly explains, are to be put in another room. Before Norah can find out which other room, Mary, chaperoned by Conover, is there. "Mary is an attractive woman in her thirties, dressed in a smart traveling suit and hat."

Mary offers her lips to Grant in greeting and turns to meet his new friend, Mr. McManus. Her host she had met downstairs and thinks it fine of him to have them there. As for the other room she was to have, according to Norah, it is quite all right with Mary if she and Grant stay where they are. "We're really married," she reports with a smile.

"Mr. Conover just thought you'd be more comfortable with a room to yourself," Grant explains.

"I'll stay here," announces Mary. And Norah takes the bags into the dressing room. . . .

Conover has adroitly cleared the room. Grant and Spike have gone downstairs to meet a couple of politicians, one of them Governor Dunn. Conover and Mrs. Matthews are alone with their highballs. Their talk turns naturally to Grant and their mutual admiration for the man. Mary's admiration goes back some time. Conover's is of more recent growth, and is centered largely in the breadth and understanding of Grant's vision for his country's needs. This, Conover is convinced, places on Grant a certain responsibility to the country.

That's why he has been trying to persuade Grant to take an active part in the Government. That's why he has arranged this speechmaking tour, that the country can be made aware of Grant's potentialities as a possible candidate.

"Is he going to make speeches on the trip?" Mary asks anxiously.

"Yes, in several places."

"Oh, dear!" Mary is quite dismayed, but quickly catches herself. "Oh, I didn't mean that the way it sounded. Grant really can make a very good speech. But public appearances for me—I'm not good at that—I'm so uncomfortable. Would it be bad form if I just stayed quietly at the hotel and listened to him over the radio?"

"Yes, I'm afraid it would. It would defeat the whole purpose."

"Purpose? What purpose?"

"Mrs. Matthews, you must know how concerned your husband is about this country splitting apart—how deeply he feels that it must be held together."

Mary—Oh, yes. We've been talking about it for months. Grant's been trying to figure out what could be done.

Conover—I think you can help him do something about it.

Mary—Oh, not me. I just get angry! I can't read the newspapers any more! While the war was on we were a united country—we were fighting Germany and Japan. Now we're just fighting each other. No, I just get angry.

Conover—I'm glad you feel that strongly about it because it's important that wherever Grant goes now—wherever he makes these speeches—you're right there alongside of him.

Mary—Why should that be important?

Conover—Well, for a man who's going to be in the public eye—people like to know his wife—like to see what she looks like—like to see the two of them together.

Mary (*thoughtfully*)—Oh! I was a little puzzled by Grant's invitation to make this trip with him.

Conover—Oh! Grant wants you to go along. These public appearances—they're my idea. It's just an old politician's habit of cashing in on an opportunity.

Mary (*rising*)—It all fits in a little too neatly, Mr. Conover. I don't know whether you know—(*She stops and looks at him sharply.*)—or perhaps you do—that Grant and I haven't been very close for the last year or so.

Conover—Wouldn't you prefer to create a contrary impression?

Mary—Oh, then you do know! Let's be open about this. These public appearances that Grant and I are to make together—are they designed to kill off any talk about my husband and Mrs. Thorndyke?

Conover (*putting his drink on table*)—There's that kind of talk about every important man. But if there are any rumors about your husband, this would be a good chance to kill them.

Norah has come from the dressing room with a print dress she is planning to press for Mrs. Matthews. Quite suddenly Mary has changed her plans. Now she wants to get back to New York as soon as she can—Conover has followed her to the phone and is standing before her—

Conover—Mrs. Matthews, I think any man who has a chance to become President of the United States deserves that chance.

Mary (*staring at him in astonishment*)—President of the United States?

Conover—Yes. (*There is a short pause.*) Don't you think he'd make a good President?

Mary (*after consideration*)—Yes, I do.

Conover—Then you understand this goes beyond personal considerations. Let's not think of this in terms of you—and Grant—

Mary—And Mrs. Thorndyke.

Conover—And Mrs. Thorndyke. I'm sure you will go along with us. You're a good citizen.

Mary—Right now, Mr. Conover, I'm not feeling like a good citizen! I'm feeling like a woman!

Conover—All right, as a woman!

Mary—As a woman, no, I won't go along with you. . . . I resent being used!

In that case Conover thinks they should both consider the situation in terms of the country. Let the American people make the choice. No one knows what will come of the speech experiment, but after they have made this tour it will be possible for Conover to decide whether Grant should go ahead with his candidacy or forget it. Forget it? Mary doesn't think it likely Grant could ever do that—

"I'll bet he's running a pretty high fever right now," she says. "When he left the room I thought he walked as though he was trying to be two inches taller."

"Mrs. Matthews, you see your husband at pretty close range. Take my word for it, he's a big man."

"There's no argument about that, Mr. Conover. I know he's a big man and you know he's a big man. My bad days are when *he* knows he's a big man! You don't suppose there's any way of Grant being elected President and keeping it a secret from him, do you?"

It is when Conover takes a long distance call from one of his workers that Mary changes her mind. By the time he has tried to stir the loyal enthusiasm of a worker to arouse the Italians and the Poles in his district to a firm faith in the Republican party as a party that will most completely meet their hopes, she has decided to go along with Grant. Jim Conover is greatly pleased.

"That's our first big campaign contribution," says he, raising his glass. "To you, my dear, the most attractive plank in your husband's platform."

"That's a heck of a thing to call a woman," laughs Mary.

It is also the Conover idea that by the time the tour is finished Mary and Grant will find themselves much closer together—

"Even if that could happen, I don't think you'd want it to," counters Mary. "It might cost you the support of Mrs. Thorndyke's newspapers."

"Don't worry about that. They're Republican newspapers in Republican territory. They couldn't afford to risk their circulation. A chain of newspapers is a very valuable property."

"Mrs. Thorndyke must have thought so. In the divorce settlement Dick Thorndyke got the children and she got the newspapers. And if that sounds bitchy, I hoped it would. You may succeed in killing the rumors, but unfortunately you won't kill Mrs. Thorndyke."

Which reminds Conover of another rumor that may be killed on this trip—a rumor about Mrs. Matthews and a certain Major. Mary is enormously pleased to hear about that. That's the best news she has had in weeks. She hopes Grant has heard about the Major. It happens the Major's been in China for six months, but she wouldn't want Grant to know that! So far as Conover is concerned the whole thing is a military secret. . . .

Grant has come from his meeting with the Governor and other assorted politicians. He is a little depressed. The Governor, he reports, has almost talked himself to sleep. Conover decides that he had better take over the Governor. But before he goes he tells Grant that he has told Mary everything. . . .

The atmosphere is a bit tense after Conover leaves. This is the first visit Grant and Mary have had since she arrived. She is, she is quick to say, very proud of him. And however he may feel, she is prepared to take his presidential chances very seriously. It isn't only that he has the brains for the job, but more importantly, he has always tried to be honest. Even when he has had to cut corners in business he has at least had the decency to be unhappy about it.

Grant is scared. Not about the Presidency, but about what is happening to the country—it's breaking up again.

"What do you think you can do about it?" Mary asks.

Grant—I think somebody can appeal to what's best in people instead of what's worst.

Mary—And still be in politics?

Grant—That's my whole case, Mary. If I can make the people see the choice they've got to make—the choice between their own interests and the interests of the country as a whole —damn it, I think the American people are sound. I think they can be unselfish.

Mary—All of them?

Grant—Hell, we both know there are plenty of bastards in this world who'll always be out for themselves. But that's where I differ from Conover. I think they're in the minority.

Mary—I do, too. (*A pause.*) How much do you and Mr. Conover differ?

Grant—He's a politician. Politicians think you have to bribe people to vote for you, one way or another.

Mary—You mean groups like the Poles and the Italians?

Grant (*turning to* Mary)—Yes—and labor and the farmers and the rest of them. But I'm not going to play politics.

Mary—That will take a lot of courage.

Grant—No, it won't. I have faith in the American people.

Mary—So have I. (*A pause.*) The Presidency's a great temptation.

Grant—I don't even want the job. Whether I become President or not is completely unimportant. (*A longer pause.*)

Mary—Grant, when I first learned the purpose of this trip, I wasn't very happy about making it with you.

Grant—I can understand that.

Mary—But I am now.

GRANT (*looking at* MARY)—Mary, there are some things I should say—(*Pause, and he turns away.*)—but I can't.

MARY (*after a hopeful pause; taking up her hat and gloves from the bed*)—Well, I think I'll get out of these clothes.

Through the open door of the dressing room a Matthews family conversation is carried on. Mary thinks Grant should telephone Joyce next day, and Grant decides if he calls Joyce around dinner time he can talk with Sonny, too. The time is rapidly approaching when they will have to begin thinking about a boarding school for the children.

From the family their confidences swing back to the political situation that is developing. They are going first to Minneapolis, Grant says, in answer to Mary's query. But he is not going to speak in Minneapolis. That's Stassen territory, and Conover thought—

"Uh-huh. I suppose that's good politics," Mary suggests significantly. "Tell me some more about your differences with Conover."

"Now, wait a minute, Mary!" Grant is plainly irritated. "That was my decision! I'm making all the decisions. I've told Conover where I stand and he knows I'm going to tell the American people where I stand. The American people are facing problems today that will affect the future of the entire world. There's only one way to face them—with complete honesty—with utter frankness—"

His tone has become oratorical and his manner a little pompous. "Take it easy," Mary calls from the dressing room. "I'm going to vote for you!" And when she has finished dressing and he is still booming about his conviction that the one thing he can do for the people is to "change the whole complexion of political campaigns" she asks quietly: "Wouldn't you feel more comfortable if you took off that stuffed shirt?"

With a disgusted "Aw, hell—I don't want to be President!" Grant throws himself into an easy chair.

"Darling, when we were talking a little while ago, you said the same things and they sounded so right—I wish you could just talk to the people that way."

"That's the way I plan to talk to them." Grant is not entirely mollified.

"That's all I meant," sweetly concludes Mary.

Grant is in the dressing room when Norah comes with Mary's gown she has pressed. She would not have been late except that just as the iron was hot another guest arrived. They had put him on a cot in Mr. Conover's room. The situation gives Mary a guilty feeling, but Norah is reassuring—

"Don't you worry, Mrs. Matthews. A cot's good enough for most of them. They just come down here to get something out of Mr. Conover. Not the people we put in this room. This room is for special guests. We even had a Democrat in this bed one night."

"Oh, I wish you hadn't told me that."

"He wasn't a Roosevelt Democrat." Norah has finished the bed. "When you wake up in the morning just press that button and I'll have breakfast right up for you. And here is the light switch here."

"Thank you, Norah. Good night."

"Good night, ma'am. (*She starts out, then stops and turns.*) Oh, I was going to ask your husband but maybe you can tell me. Do you know Mrs. Thorndyke's address?"

"Mrs. Thorndyke?"

"She forgot her glasses when she left this morning. And I know what it is to be without glasses. I want to mail them back to her."

"Are you sure they're Mrs. Thorndyke's?"

"Yes, they're them Chinese kind. What women won't do! Won't they?"

"Yes—won't they? (MARY *puts her drink down and goes to the dressing room door.*) Grant, can you step out for a minute? Norah wants some information."

Grant is tying his dressing gown as he appears. "Hello, Norah. What can I do for you?" he asks cheerfully.

"Mrs. Thorndyke left her glasses. I wanted to know where to mail them back to her."

"Oh!" A quick glance at Mary, and then: "1276 Park Avenue. Shall I write it down for you?"

"No, I can remember it. 1276. 76—that's the year of the revolution. And twelve for the Twelve Commandments."

Another glance at Mary and Grant returns to the dressing room, closing the door after him. Mary stands for a moment in thought. Then she comes to a decision and promptly goes into action. It does not take long for her to strip two of the chairs of their cushions, which she lines up on the floor. This she follows by ripping top sheet and blanket off the bed and spreading them out on the improvised mattress. She finds an extra blanket for the bed, folding blanket and sheet double. She takes a pillow from the bed and makes up the bed on the floor, also by doubling sheet and blanket.

When Grant appears from the dressing room in pajamas and dressing gown his first glance takes in what she is up to. Mary continues to work, completely ignoring him.

"Mary, what do you think you're doing?" Grant demands. "Now, stop that nonsense and make up that bed again. . . . Damn it, I'm not going to let you do this! . . . You wouldn't get any sleep down there on the floor and I wouldn't get any sleep lying there (*He points to bed.*) worrying about you!"

Mary has crossed to the bed, turning out the lights as she lies down: "Good night, Mr. President!" she says.

The curtain falls.

ACT II

The living room of the suite in the Book-Cadillac Hotel in Detroit to which Mr. and Mrs. Grant Matthews have been assigned is furnished, not to make a mystery of it, "the way a living room in the Book-Cadillac would be furnished." The entrance is from the hall, and there are doors at either side of the room leading to bedrooms that go with the suite.

It is dark when a bellboy ushers Grant and Mary in, arm-in-arm. A second later he has put down their three bags and switched on the light, with a hearty "Well, we made it!"

Then it appears that the Matthewses have dodged a mob in the lobby by coming up in the servants' elevator. At the station, too, there had been a crowd. To Mary it has been quite exciting.

Spike McManus was supposed to meet them. While Grant is at the phone trying to locate Spike Mary tries to decide which of the bedrooms she will take. It doesn't really matter—only—

Grant has located Spike, and learned that Jim Conover is also expected any minute. That, decides Grant, is a good sign. "It looks as though Jim's afraid somebody might get his front seat on the bandwagon," he says. Mary isn't so sure. In any event, says she, Grant will be wise not to talk to Jim about what he is going to say in his Detroit speech.

Grant, going through a bunch of telegrams that have been waiting for him, is excited to find that they are mostly about his Wichita speech, and that they are terrific. "I've never had anything like this before!" he chortles.

"That's what I mean," warns Mary. "Spike tried to talk you out of making that speech. So, remember what I just said . . . Don't talk to Jim about your speech tonight."

They go through the telegrams together. Practically all are wildly enthusiastic.

"Grant—these are simply wonderful," Mary is saying. "You see, you didn't have to be afraid of shooting the works. That's the way they want to hear you talk."

"Just look at these, Mary—it shows how hungry the American people are for leadership."

"This one's nice, Grant. It speaks of your modesty and humility."

Grant has come on one wire that is less than favorable. It is from the Executive Secretary of Local 901— Into the waste basket it goes. Mary comes on another. "Look, darling—they want you to speak in Omaha next Monday."

"That's nothing. They want me in New Orleans on Thursday and Atlanta on Friday."

Mary thinks it would be fine to go to all these places. Grant points out how impossible would be the transportation problem. Not only that, but think of the work piling up on his desk—

"I don't know why you bother with business when this is so much fun," says Mary. They grin at each other.

"Do you know, this trip has done you a lot of good? You have no right to look that young at your age!" says Grant. Mary puts a warning finger to her lips, but that doesn't stop him. "On the field at Denver, just before we took off, I had the damnedest sensation. You were standing there in the moonlight with the wind from the propeller blowing your hair and dress—I knew we were in Denver, but you were the girl standing on the deck of the boat on our way to Victoria."

"Now I'll tell you something," answers Mary, after a reminiscent pause. "Remember when we stood on the balcony of the hotel in Victoria, and you were telling me what the world should be like? That same boy was standing on the platform last night at Wichita."

"I'm glad you said that, Mary. It was a wonderful satisfaction, that speech—just saying what I really believed."

"You see what that speech did!" She has picked up another wire. "Grant, who is Herbert Bayard Swope?"

But she will have to take the Swope matter up at another time. A smart knock on the door now heralds the approach of Spike. Spike is full of talk. He has been worried about them. The grounding of their plane had jammed up a lot of appointments he had made for Grant. The fact that Conover is coming out makes things look pretty hot. Also it makes him sore, seeing he will have to split his bed with the boss.

"You know what kind of a split a politician takes," moans Spike. But Mary has a solution for that one—

"That's silly," she says. "We have two bedrooms here and we don't need both of them. Grant, you're moving in with me. We're putting Jim in the other bedroom." Grant is deep in an editorial in an evening paper and doesn't hear. "Grant! Yoo-hoo! Mr. Candidate! Mr. President!"

"Huh?"

"That got him!" says Mary, with a gay little snap of her fingers. "I'm playing a little politics for you. I'm saving Jim from sleeping with Spike. He's moving into our extra bedroom."

"Fine! Be with you in a minute, Spike, let me finish this editorial."

Jim Conover has arrived. He is happy to find that politics agrees with both Grant and Mary, seeing they are looking fine. But he is not as excited as they are about the reaction to the Wichita speech. Nor is he too much impressed with Mary's report that it was the best speech Grant had ever made—

"It was the first time I felt sure that Grant would be elected," Mary tells Jim. "You never heard such applause!"

"Mary, if applause elected Presidents, William Jennings Bryan would have had three terms." You can't fool an old campaigner.

Spike is sure he can juggle Grant's appointments between the two bedrooms and keep the living room free. They can order their dinner sent up and Grant can dodge from one bedroom to the other, grabbing a bite of food between calls. Mary attends to the ordering. Having had one drink, she thinks they might have another, but none of the men will join her. So— Let the waiter bring her a Martini to the bedroom—

"That's the difference between Grant and me," she explains; "I'd rather be tight than be President."

Conover is getting a little nervous about Grant's speech. He would like to read it, if Grant doesn't care. Grant doesn't, but he only made a few scratchy notes. If Conover would like to, he can read some of Grant's fan mail! With that suggestion he disappears into his bedroom to dress. He has no sooner disappeared than Spike disgustedly throws the telegrams he has been reading on the desk and turns to Conover.

"You're a hell of a campaign manager!" growls Jim.

Spike—That's why I wired for you, Jim. He's gotten away from me.

CONOVER—It's a damn shame! The boys in the Northwest and all along the Coast—they were swinging right in behind him. Then he had to stick out his chin in Wichita.

SPIKE—How much damage has he done?

CONOVER—We may have lost labor. I must have had thirty calls after that speech. How did you let it happen.

SPIKE—I talked him out of that labor stuff in Denver—that is, I gave him something to use instead—local stuff—Rocky Mountain stuff.

CONOVER—Didn't you get a look at the speech for Wichita?

SPIKE—No, and I'll tell you why. She—(*He points to the bedroom.*)—knew he was planning to talk about labor in Denver and when he didn't she spent the rest of the night tossing harpoons into him. But the next day on the plane to Wichita they were clubby as hell—and I couldn't get any advance copy of the speech. You just sent the wrong dame with him!

CONOVER—I even talked him into taking her along.

SPIKE—When we get back to New York, Kay can straighten him out. She put this presidential bee in his bonnet. She never tears Grant down. She always builds him up. If you ask me, that's why he fell for her. But that doesn't help us tonight.

CONOVER—What are you afraid of tonight?

SPIKE—I don't know—(*Telephone rings.*)—but she's too damn happy. (*In phone.*) Hello. . . . (*Pause.*) Oh—give me the desk. (*To* CONOVER.) That's why I sent for you. We can't take a chance on his making another mistake here tonight. (*Into telephone.*) Hello. This is McManus. There are some people down there to see Mr. Matthews. And there are a lot more coming. Send them all up to the third floor, Parlor B, and tell them to wait for me there. (*He hangs up. To* CONOVER.) You've got to find out what he's talking about here.

CONOVER—That's what I was trying to do—and you saw how far I got.

SPIKE—Well, keep after him.

CONOVER—If you've got people coming to see him, what chance have I?

SPIKE—I wasn't sure you were going to get here. I figured I had to put some kind of pressure on him. I've got everybody —dairy farmers, automobile people, even the Labor boys, mad as they are.

CONOVER—Maybe they ought to be talking to Mrs. Matthews.

SPIKE—Look, Jim, this guy's vulnerable. He's got the bug.

CONOVER—That's what I was counting on. How bad has he got it?

SPIKE—He wants to be President, all right. So what I keep throwing at him is votes—get those votes—don't lose those votes. (SPIKE *has read two or three wires.*) Maybe that Wichita speech didn't do as much harm as we thought it did.

CONOVER—Oh, those are just from people.

SPIKE—They don't count, eh?

CONOVER—You don't see any signed "State Chairman," do you?

SPIKE—Don't kid yourself, this guy does something to people. I've been on a lot of campaigns. They don't shake hands with Grant just to say they've shaken hands with him. They're up there with a light in their eyes—they practically mob him. If he gets away from us, you may be heading a "Stop Matthews" movement.

CONOVER—Stopping him wouldn't be any trouble. He hasn't any organization. I don't want to stop him. I think we can elect him, if we can keep him in line.

A further threat that their dark horse may be taking the bit in teeth is discovered in a telegram confirming a speaking date for Grant under the auspices of the Foreign Policy Association in New York on the 23rd. He can't do that, Conover insists, and not admit that he is a candidate. "Well, I guess we've got to fence him in. Damn!" sighs Jim.

The waiter has brought the dinner and Mary's extra cocktail. The dinner, Mary announces, is to be served when ready in the living room. Spike can do as he likes with the two bedrooms and his expected delegations. Spike does. Grant has just sat down to his hamburger steak when Spike announces the arrival of a delegation of dairy farmers in Parlor B.

"My hamburger's waiting," protests Grant, with something like a smothered sob.

"Hamburgers don't vote!" snaps Spike. And as Grant is going out he adds: "The fellow with the mustache is the one to play for."

Mary and Conover continue with their dinner. It is, thinks Jim, a time for congratulations. Mary so far has certainly done a fine job. Mary, beaming at the compliment, would like to confess, in strictest secrecy, that she has enjoyed every minute of the tour—

"Even the speeches?" asks Conover.

"That's been the best part of it. I don't mean just listening to Grant. I mean listening to the people—feeling the way they respond. Of course they laugh and yell when he talks about the troubles he's had getting things through in Washington . . ."

"Yes, I've heard those laughs. He does it very cleverly. That's what they like to hear."

"Jim, over the radio you only hear the audience when it's making noise. What you don't hear is the silence—when Grant has them do that they're not thinking of themselves—when he has them thinking of the country—that's when it takes your breath away."

"I'm glad to hear Grant can do that. I know how effective it can be in a speaker."

"Jim, I'm not talking about Grant. When they rush up after the speeches—I wish you could see their faces . . . You know, I'd forgotten how good it was to be with people—I used to see a lot of them when Grant first started and had small plants—when we moved to New York I got too far away from them—they're so eager to do whatever is the best thing to do—and they're so quick—they're so intelligent. (*She laughs.*) They've thrown a couple of questions at Grant that had him stopped cold. He just had to admit he didn't know enough to answer them. And they liked him for it."

"That's smart. Shows he uses his head."

Mary is sitting back in her chair, regarding Conover quizzically. "Jim, you fascinate me. You have such a complete lack of faith in sincerity—and you're so sincere about it. (CONOVER *gives her an understanding smile.*) And what puzzles me is that I dislike so thoroughly the way your mind works—and yet I'm so very fond of you."

"It is puzzling, isn't it, because I feel the same way toward you."

Grant is back from the dairy conference and is just about to take a bite out of his steak when Spike bursts in. The A.F. of L. is waiting in Parlor A.

"Look, Spike, give me a chance to eat."

"Nope. This is a crisis. I have to know you're holding the A.F. of L. in there while I sneak the C.I.O. into the other bedroom."

"Put them both in the same room, I'll talk to them both at the same time."

"Little Boy Blue, haven't you heard? They ain't keeping steady company any more. Besides, these aren't big shots—just small fry—officers of the locals."

"They're both labor groups. They both want the same things.

That's what I've been talking about all this time—getting people to work together—now let's put it into action."

"Now, boss—"

"I'm serious about this, Spike. Tell those men in there you're bringing in the C.I.O., and then I'll come in and talk to them!"

It is Conover's opinion that Grant may be just looking for trouble, but Grant is positive he knows best. He has both labor organizations working in his plants, and he has never had any trouble talking to them. Bill Green and Phil Murray will sit down together if they're properly approached—

"Jim, if I can ever make people like these in the next room see something bigger than their job as head of their own locals and the little power they get from that—"

That brings them to the Wichita speech. That's what brought Conover to Detroit. He didn't like it. Yes, he had read the telegrams. And it is entirely possible that Grant had picked up a few auditorium votes. But— He had "chilled off most of the Labor leaders in the country."

Grant can't understand. Hadn't he said that business would have to give Labor a voice in management? Hadn't he said Labor should have to have a larger share of the profits? He had, admits Jim. But it was the stand Grant took on strikes that had been the trouble maker—

"No, Jim, not on strikes," protests Grant. "I mentioned only one kind of strike. I asked Labor to give the people of this country the answer to this question: 'Is there any moral justification for the jurisdictional strike?' Can you answer that question? Can the Labor leaders you talked to answer that question?"

"Of course they can't. That's what makes them so sore. Too bad you didn't talk about the other kind of strikes."

"All right, it's true—some unions are abusing their right to strike at this time. They're sacrificing the country for their own special interest. What do you propose to do? Take their right to strike away from them? Freedom of the press is being abused. Do you want to take that right away from the publishers?"

"Well—Labor's pretty sore about what you said about opening their books, too."

"Not all of them are. Some of the biggest and best unions in the country have opened their books."

"Jim, the audience was full of union men—I don't mean union leaders, I mean union members, and they cheered Grant. I had a feeling they would like to get a look at those books themselves."

"Some of that money goes into campaign contributions," admits Conover, sulkily.

Spike is back from the Labor groups. They refuse to meet together. "They're even mad they're in the same hotel together," reports Spike.

That makes Grant pretty mad, too. Now he *will* speak to them. And he goes to do just that.

"Jim, Grant's got something," insists Mary, when she and Conover are alone. "Don't take it away from him. When he's just cockeyed drunk with sincerity people can't resist him."

That statement would, to Jim, seem to indicate that it includes Mary, too. But Mary is quick to assure him it doesn't. "Our personal relations are strictly political," she says. The highly personal looks Jim may have seen Grant toss in Mary's direction didn't mean a thing. If he were a married man he would understand that—

"When a man and woman have been married for a long time," says Mary, "even their closest friends can't always tell whether they're still in love with each other. They themselves wonder about it sometimes."

"Well, then the trip's accomplished something—if you're at the point of wondering."

"No, there are things that happen that make you sure—little things that don't really mean anything except that you know how much they mean. For instance, Grant found out once the girls at school used to call me Maizie. He knew I hated it. So sometimes he used to call me Maizie—just to tease me— But you don't tease people that way unless you love each other. Well, Maizie doesn't live here any more. And another thing—Grant always hated to hear me swear—whenever I let go with something—he used to smack me on the behind—hard. I've done a lot of swearing on this trip—"

"And no smacks?"

"It's a small request—but I'd give anything for a good smack on the behind."

"I wish there were something I could do about that, but—"

Presently Spike appears from one bedroom and Grant from the other. Everything is set for the merger. While Conover turns his back, Grant leads three stony-faced Labor leaders from one bedroom to the other. Not to miss a chance, Mary springs up from her chair and comes down to meet them as they pass—Mr. Vincent, Mr. Solly and Mr. Mack. As Grant, with a wink, closes the door after the laborites, Spike puts his fingers in his ears to cushion any shock that may result. When no explosion occurs he relaxes with a grin—

"You know," says he, "Grant might be able to unite the United Nations."

Conover is still harping on the speech Grant is to deliver in Detroit. As soon as they are alone again, he would find out more from Mary. Because it is the last speech of the tour, says she, it is a sort of summary. Is it controversial? Jim would know. "Isn't a Presidential campaign supposed to be controversial?" asks Mary.

Detroit is a dangerous city politically, Conover warns. "They've had a lot of trouble here—strikes—race riots—and for some reason or other it seems to be the headquarters of some of the lunatic fringe."

"You mean subversive groups—"

"Mary, subversive is a very dangerous word—(*Apprehensively.*) —Grant's not using that word in his speech tonight, is he?"

"I think Grant's saving anything like that—and the international situation—for his speech in New York."

Grant is back from the Labor front. Again he eagerly attacks the hamburger. As for the Labor situation everything is great.

"As a matter of fact," he reports, "The Congress of Industrial Organizations has just extended an invitation to the American Federation of Labor to have a glass of beer."

"Under whose jurisdiction?"

"The Arcade Bar and Grill!"

And then Spike appears to announce one more group. These are representatives of Grant's own—the Detroit tycoon set. Somebody he really wants to see for a change! Spike must be slipping!

Mary takes advantage of this interlude to thank Conover for having told Grant about the gossip involving her and a Major. At least somebody must have told—Grant has recently been so very rude to all army Majors—

"And it's so unfair to those poor Majors," adds Mary. "My Major's been a Colonel for months."

Sam Parrish, an exuberant old friend, has come with the Detroit delegation. Barging in from Parlor A he is delighted to see Mary, and almost as keen about discovering that old son-of-a-gun, Jim Conover. Well, well!

"Jim, do you know you're psychic?" demands Sam. "I'm due in Washington on the 18th—I had it all planned to come and see you with the idea of selling you Grant Matthews for President, and, dammit, you beat me to it. Frankly, I was going to bribe you—with the biggest campaign contribution you ever saw."

"That's a date, Sam!" Conover has grabbed Sam's hand and is pumping it vigorously. "Lunch in Washington on the 18th and bring Cash!"

"Mary," Sam calls, "you go right home and start packing. You're moving into the White House. Give me another kiss! I've never been so happy about anything in my life. Wait until I tell Hilda!"

"Sam, you're not telling anybody, including Hilda."

Sam's coming has set Mary thinking. How will he be taking Grant's speech? The last time they met, Sam and Grant had had a knock-down dragout fight about reconversion and full employment. But Sam isn't worried—

"You know Grant," he says. "Likes to talk like a radical. But, hell, anybody that's made as much money as Grant has is a sound American."

Sam has read Grant's Wichita speech, and approves it—or at least two-thirds of it. The other third Sam is ready to take if he has to. "I suppose you've got to say those things . . . but look out people don't get the idea you're too far to the left. Talk to you about it later."

"You're talking about reconversion and full employment tonight." Conover's tone and attitude are accusing.

"Touching on them, among other things," admits Grant.

CONOVER—What angle are you taking?

GRANT—We talked about it in Washington. You know how I stand.

CONOVER—In Washington you were pretty specific. You're not being that specific here tonight?

GRANT—You're damn right I am!

CONOVER—What are you going to say?

GRANT—I'm going to tell them they did a great job in war production—and they did! But I'm going to remind them there wasn't any risk in that— The Government paid them for it. They had their engineering brains and plenty of manpower to do the work.

CONOVER—All right. Why don't you let it go at that?

GRANT—Oh, no! I've got to tell them that now they're up against the test. Now they're on their own. They talk about how they want to save the private enterprise system. All right, now they've got a chance to do it!

CONOVER (*agreeably*)—Yes?

GRANT—They're not going to save it by lowering production so they can raise prices. And they're not going to save it by closing down plants to cut down competition. They're not going to save it if they don't work with unions instead of against them. And those babies who are stirring up war veterans to fight Labor—I'm going to take their hide off!

CONOVER—Grant, you can't do that!

GRANT—Jim, you know reconversion goes deeper than re-tooling our plants. We need a moral reconversion. Take Full Employment. I don't mean the Bill—I mean the principle of it. What's behind most of the opposition to Full Employment—behind opposing the whole idea of the Government supplying work. To give private enterprise the chance to supply the employment? Nuts! It's to keep prices up on everything but Labor. Let Labor starve for a while! Jim, there isn't going to be a free enterprise system if it means that men are free to starve!

CONOVER—Grant, you can't say those things now, and you can't say them here. This town is one of my best sources for silent money.

GRANT—You'll have to take your chances on the silent money, Jim.

MARY—What is silent money?

CONOVER (*to* GRANT)—I warn you, Grant, you can't get out on this limb before the nomination.

MARY—People ought to know where he stands before they nominate him.

CONOVER (*angrily*)—The people have damn little to say about the nomination. You two have lived in this country all your lives. Haven't you got that through your heads yet? You're not nominated by the people—you're nominated by the politicians! Why? Because the voters are too damned lazy to vote in the primaries! Well, politicians are not lazy! Remember what happened to Willkie in Wisconsin!

GRANT—They've got to know what I think, Jim! I told you that from the start. I've got to be on record.

CONOVER—All right—but not here—not tonight! Later. When you're out in Nebraska or Oklahoma.

Spike is in to announce the last visitors of the day—"And are they fruity!" They call themselves the Americans Incorruptible, and, as Mary suggests, with that name they are not likely to be *for* anything, but *against* something. However, Spike insists,

Grant should remember that they've got votes. "The Head Incorruptible is the fat dame with the big cowcatcher."

Ten minutes later Grant has met the Americans Incorruptible —and lost them.

"Who were they? What did they want?" Mary asks.

"They don't want America to be too harsh on poor little Germany and Japan." Grant's tone is heavy with sarcasm. "We shouldn't have gotten into it in the first place."

"Oh, that crowd! Against war—but we may have to fight the Russians!"

GRANT—Exactly! I wound up making a campaign speech for Stalin. Where's Jim?

MARY—He'll be back in a minute. He had a telephone call. Grant, what is silent money?

GRANT—Oh, it's a way they get around the Hatch Act.

MARY—What's the Hatch Act?

GRANT—It's a law they passed a few years ago about campaign funds. Only individuals can give money and nobody more than $5,000, and you have to account for how it's spent. It's a very pretty law—and we feel very moral that it's on the books—but it just doesn't work.

MARY—There must have been some reason for passing it.

GRANT—Yes, there was! It had gotten to be a bad situation. But you know how we do things in this country, sometimes. When human nature gets to behaving like human nature, they pass a law repealing human nature. But the Hatch Act is too tough. So men who can afford it, walk in and put silent money down on the barrelhead—cash, that can't be traced. It's been done by both parties before the law was passed and since. I've told you before, Mary, there's damn little difference between Democrats and Republicans.

MARY—But if silent money's illegal, I don't think you should take it!

GRANT—Oh, I wouldn't take it. That would be Jim's business.

MARY—But, Grant—

GRANT (*stopping her*)—Now, Mary, we both drank during Prohibition, didn't we? Put it down to political education, the way the PAC does. (*Seeing she is still troubled.*) I can't be too righteous about taking silent money. I've given it.

MARY—If you take money, you have to pay it back some way.

GRANT (*indignant*)—Mary! You know damn well I'm not for sale!

Mary—You've arranged it very neatly in your mind, Grant. All they have to do is to buy Conover. I warned you the Presidency was a great temptation.

Grant (*after a tight-lipped pause*)—You certainly have a gift for making it tough for me. You didn't used to be that way.

Mary (*distressed with herself*)—I know. I hear myself saying those things. I suppose it's a gift I picked up in exchange for some illusions.

Grant (*with sober reasoning*)—Mary, people change. We've both changed. Life does that to you. We would have been happier if we could have stayed the two kids who went on a honeymoon to Victoria. I'm just as unhappy as you are that we didn't.

Mary is worried about Conover's having got a line on what Grant's speech is to be about. But, Grant assures her, Conover's knowing will not alter the speech. He is going to speak his mind on reconversion. He has been frank with Labor, now he intends to be equally frank with Business.

Mary, standing beside Grant's chair, is smoothing his hair. "Grant," she says quietly, "you know you don't have to be President."

"Oh, I don't even expect to be," he answers. "But I know this much—I could do a lot of good."

It is nearing time for them to start for the banquet. Conover would still like to know a little more about the speech, but Grant is sure there isn't time. Anyway, Spike has just reported the arrival of a surprise delegation. He will have to see them.

And now there is a favor Conover would like to ask of Mary. When she has the Parrishes to dinner on the 17th, will she invite him, too? Mary would love to. And, continues Jim, will she include four or five other fellows?

"If Grant's speaking on the twenty-third on International Policy," Jim explains, "it may be important for him to see these people first."

Again Mary is agreeable. She and Grant have been away from home so long they must have saved up a few extra red points—

"And there's one other I'd like to talk to you about," Conover goes on. "You remember the reason I wanted you to make this trip in the first place?"

"Yes, I remember well enough."

"Mary, I've been looking into how that talk got started. Mrs.

Thorndyke used to be a frequent guest at your house. Then about a year ago she was crossed off your list, but Grant went on seeing her."

"Yes."

"Let's kill off those rumors once and for all. I want Mrs. Thorndyke to be there on the 17th."

"No, Jim. Not in my house. And of all nights not on the 17th. It happens to be our wedding anniversary."

"Look, Mary, I'm doing my damnedest to go along with Grant, even though he doesn't always go along with me. I need Mrs. Thorndyke there for more reasons than one. Let me win this, will you?"

"Sorry, Jim, that's more than I can take."

There is a knock at the door. A bellboy has found a radio for them, despite an unusual demand. "Everybody wanted a radio tonight," reports the boy. Grant, coming from the bedroom, smiles proudly. "Special broadcast from Hollywood—Bob Hope and Jack Benny," explains the boy.

Spike has rushed Grant and Mary to a waiting elevator.

Conover, straightening up the room, stops to open a bedroom door and call: "We may as well sit in here and be comfortable." As Mrs. Thorndyke appears he adds—"I have a radio. Do I dare listen?"

"I think so. Of course I had less than five minutes with him."

"Yes, and Mary's had five weeks!"

"I think he was glad to see me. I told you in Washington I could handle him."

"Well, we'll find out."

"I made it pretty strong. I said the Democrats would never take a chance like that. But that brought up a question that's on his mind, Jim, and you'd better have an answer for him."

"An answer to what?"

"Is there any real difference between the Democratic Party and the Republican Party?"

"All the difference in the world. (*He turns on the radio.*) They're in—and we're out!"

The curtain falls.

ACT III

The living room of the Matthews duplex apartment in New York is large and handsomely furnished. The entrance from the hall is through an archway, and there is an alcove with a built-in bar this side of the door to the dining room at the opposite side of the room. A practical fireplace in the right wall is faced by a large ottoman, with a sofa nearby. An oil painting of Mary and the children decorates the center wall.

At the moment Spike McManus is going over a list of expected Matthews dinner guests with Swenson, the Matthews butler. As Spike indicates individual drinking habits Swenson makes notes.

Judge Alexander, for example, is tagged as a straight bourbon and plain water man, though he has been known to take a cocktail on occasion. Mrs. Alexander is just naturally wedded to Sazarac cocktails, and if Swenson doesn't know how to make a Sazarac he had better start learning. Let him take an old-fashioned glass, put a lump of sugar in it soaked in Pernod. (SPIKE *has brought the Pernod to make sure.*) Then a jigger of bourbon, a twist of lemon peel on top, and a good stir. "Don't sample that one, Swenson; it'll light up your vest buttons," cautions Spike. It will be all right for Mrs. Alexander to get tight, but Spike would like Swenson to do what he can to keep the others sober.

Senator Lauterback prefers Martinis before and a steady diet of Scotch and soda after dinner. Manhattans for Mr. Parrish and then rye. A very dry Martini for Mrs. Thorndyke before dinner, Swenson remembers. Haig and Haig Scotch and soda for Jim Conover.

"And remember, Swenson, except for Mrs. Alexander, nobody gets too much to drink—and that goes for Mr. and Mrs. Matthews, too. . . . If there's one thing I don't want around here tonight it's too much frankness." There's a Mr. Hardy on the list. "Those Labor boys are smart cookies," answers Spike when Swenson asks about the Hardy preferences. "He doesn't drink anything."

Grant is home. He calls Mary from upstairs to help Spike with the table seating plan. Mary is looking very lovely in an evening dress as she comes downstairs. It will be all right, Mary agrees, to put Senator Lauterback at her right, Mrs. Draper at Grant's right, and Sam Parrish at Grant's left—

"Don't you want Sam up near you?" asks Grant. "It will give you someone to talk to."

"Well," answers Mary, "I thought that after what you *didn't* say about reconversion in Detroit, you and Sam might want to hold hands under the table."

"Mary, we've been over that often enough. I *did* talk about reconversion in Detroit."

"I wouldn't say *about* it, Grant. I'd say *around* it. You did come right out and mention the word once."

"Mary, I've heard all I want to hear about Detroit," announces Grant, with angry finality.

"Here is a good couple to pair off," speaks up Spike, as a rescuer of the situation. Hardy and Mrs. Alexander. He never opens his mouth and she never closes hers . . . How about Mrs. Thorndyke up here?" He is pointing to a location.

"How about Mrs. Thorndyke down there," promptly answers Mary, and that settles that. It is easy to place Judge Alexander and Conover, and the seating plan is set.

Grant would thank Mary for helping him with the dinner, even if it isn't going to be much fun for her, but she is quick to assure him that she is glad to do it, and that she hopes it will be everything he wants it to be—

"Just to show you how serious I am about it, I'm not even going to have a cocktail," she adds.

Grant is on his way upstairs to dress when he notices a box in the hall. "This is for tonight," he says, handing it to Mary.

There is an eager expression in Mary's eyes as she unwraps the box. "I didn't think he even remembered it," she mutters. "This is our wedding anniversary," she explains to Spike, as she takes off the last wrapping and reveals a box of cigars. "My error!" she admits. . . .

There is one thing Mary would like to know. Why had Grant changed his speech in Detroit? Spike thinks it probably was because Jim Conover had warned him against endangering the campaign contributions from that territory.

"No, Spike, it wasn't for money. So if you do know, you won't tell me. You're not on my team. And I've often wondered why. You know, Spike, you've got a very wide streak of decency."

"Yes, if I don't watch it, it gets in my way. (*Seriously.*) Mary, I'll pull every trick I know to get Grant in the White House, but once he's there and I'm back on the newspaper, I'll be on the same team with you; and if Grant isn't in there pitching for the people, I'll burn his pants off!"

"I'll light the matches for you."

Judge and Lulubelle Alexander arrive. They are from the Deep South. He is tall and lean. She is short and heavy. Mary is glad they could come. Especially Mrs. Alexander. The women are going to be outnumbered by the men. To Lulubelle that doesn't mean a thing. Being a Democrat she is used to being outnumbered at all Republican dinners. "But you can speak freely," she assures them. "You Republicans can't say anything about the Administration mean enough for us Democrats down South."

When Swenson serves cocktails, and Lulubelle discovers her Sazarac, she is delighted. The Judge, however, is worried for fear Lulubelle's reputation may be getting a little too far north.

"Do you get up North often?" Mary asks.

"Being a Republican down South," explains Lulubelle, "the Judge only gets important every four years—around Convention time. Jim Conover getting him way up here this early must mean they're pretty serious about running your husband for President, which I hope they don't."

"Really?"

"Yes, you seem like such a nice woman. Politics is too good an excuse for a man to neglect his wife."

"Well, if you're neglected tonight—you and I will be neglected together."

The guests are arriving in groups now. Jim Conover and Mrs. Draper; Bill Hardy and Senator Lauterback. Introductions and greetings are general. Hardy is beginning to feel conspicuous. He's the only one so far wearing a dinner jacket—

"Isn't that what you're after, Bill?" asks Conover. "Put evening clothes on Labor and let the rest of us go without?"

Bill's answer, if any, is smothered. When Kay Thorndyke arrives she stands for a moment in the archway. As Mary catches her eye and advances to greet her Kay comes forward.

"Hello, Mary. You're looking very pretty tonight," she says, her hand outstretched in greeting. But Mary has turned and taken a Martini from Swenson's tray.

"You're just in time for a cocktail," she says, sweetly.

A moment later, introductions over, Mrs. Draper has turned to Mrs. Thorndyke. "Kay, after you left, Jim and I went into the situation in Chicago. (*Turns to* CONOVER.) Jim, tell her what you said."

"Oh, Grace, let's take time out of politics for a little drinking. (*To* MARY.) You're in for a bad evening, Mary."

"Oh, no! Politics is new to me, but I'm very interested."

"You've got the 'very' in the wrong place, Mary," Conover corrects, his tone amiable but sardonic. "Interested but very new."

"Mr. Conover means that I have not lost my amateur standing." Mary is smiling to the others.

"You're learning—I hope!"

"That's a dangerous hope, Jim. You politicians have stayed professionals because the voters have remained amateurs."

Sam Parrish has burst in, alive with excuses and high spirits. He kisses Mary and then kisses Mrs. Thorndyke twice—once for Hilda.

"Senator! You'll be glad to hear I'm starting a back-to-the-farm movement," says the jovial Parrish in greeting Senator Lauterback. "Just closed down two plants."

"And have you met Mrs. Thorndyke?" Mary is asking as she continues the introductions.

"Oh, yes, we know each other," Kay is quick to answer. "Nice seeing you, Mr. Parrish."

"Where did you get to that night?" demands Sam. "I looked all over the banquet hall for you."

There is an embarrassed pause before Kay answers. "I didn't go to the banquet."

"Sam, how's Hilda?" Conover tries but fails to rescue Kay.

"She's fine now," says Sam, and promptly turns back to Kay. "I thought that was why you were in Detroit—to hear Grant's speech."

"Were you in Detroit when we were there, Kay?"

"Yes, you must have seen her, Mary. She was on her way to your suite. I'd just left you, remember?"

"I didn't see Mrs. Thorndyke in Detroit." Mary turns to Kay. "Oh, you must have dropped in to talk to Grant about reconversion."

"What Grant said about reconversion in his speech that night was all right. You couldn't argue with it."

"Well, I think you can thank Mrs. Thorndyke for that."

"Sam, did you get that finance report I sent you?" This time Conover succeeds in breaking up the group.

"Well, Jim, you hoped I'd learn," says Mary, as she moves away. "I'm learning!"

Judge Alexander, drawn into service by Lulubelle, has been devoting a large part of his evening mixing Sazaracs for his wife. Now, coming from the bar, he has two drinks on the server. He hopes to save a little time. But Mary has decided that she also will try a Sazarac. Jim Conover would warn her that Sazaracs are pretty powerful. All right. Let the Judge make her a second one, too.

"I thought you weren't drinking anything tonight," protests Jim.

"I have just been reconverted," says Mary.

Grant Matthews comes down the stairs and is rapturously greeted. Especially by Sam Parrish. "Grant! All I've got to decide tonight is whether we're going to run you for a third term."

Grant shortly gets around to Lulubelle and Mary. "Handsome, isn't he?" observes Lulubelle, acknowledging Mary's introduction. "He's the first good reason I've ever seen for voting Republican. I warned your wife I was a Democrat."

"Some of my best friends are Democrats."

"Well, you know us Southerners. We vote Democratic at home, but we've got an awfully good Republican record in Congress."

Mary and Lulubelle have settled to their drinking. Two more Sazaracs is what Lulubelle would have the Judge mix so she won't have to interrupt him when he gets started talking. That one drink is for Mary is a surprise to Grant. He thought—

Now politics has raised its troubled head. Kay Thorndyke has brought Grant and Mrs. Draper together. "Grant," Kay is saying, "Mrs. Draper is very interested in what you plan to say at the Foreign Policy Association Thursday night."

GRANT (*to* MRS. DRAPER)—Yes, Thursday's the night I settle world affairs.

KAY—Grace is the Party's expert on the foreign vote.

MRS. DRAPER—I think the election in '46 is going to turn on it, and in '48, too.

KAY (*to* GRANT)—Take the Italians, for instance. Everybody knows we've made a mess of things in Italy.

MRS. DRAPER—The Italians over here are all unhappy about it, and they're going to be even unhappier when the final peace terms are drawn up.

KAY—Truman has to take responsibility for the peace terms. So it's not going to be hard to appeal to the Italian vote.

GRANT—I think we have to wait and find out what the peace terms are.

KAY—We don't have to wait. We just have to demand justice for Italy.

MARY (*who has been listening*)—If you favor Italy, won't that lose you the Abyssinian vote?

MRS. DRAPER (*turning to* MARY)—Mrs. Matthews, there isn't any Abyssinian vote.

MARY (*taking a drink*)—Good! We don't have to worry about justice for the Abyssinians.

KAY (*to* GRANT)—Grace thinks that in this election the Polish vote is the most important.

MRS. DRAPER (*to* GRANT)—Indeed I do! Now in your speech Thursday night you should come out for the reopening of the whole Polish question—boundaries, government, reparations—

KAY—Any strong stand, Grant, would clinch the Polish vote.

MARY—I thought the Poles voted in Poland.

KAY (*to* MARY)—We're talking about Polish-Americans.

MARY—Oh, can you be both?

SAM (*looking up from his papers*)—Mary, you're a sweet girl and I love you, but this is practical politics, and you're way out over your head.

MARY (*to the group around* GRANT)—If they're Americans I should think you'd ask them to vote as Americans, not as Poles!

GRANT (*too heartily*)—Mary, I think we could all use some more hors d'œuvres.

KAY—Take Pennsylvania for instance . . .

MARY—Is this what's called power politics?

SENATOR—Mrs. Matthews, power politics is what they play in Europe.

MARY—It seems to me we're beginning to play it here. Let's disunite the United Nations and keep Pennsylvania safe for the Republicans.

The talk is becoming a little mixed. Mary has started on her third Sazarac with Lulubelle's sympathetic encouragement. Senator Lauterback has got around to issuing a warning word to Grant—

"Mr. Matthews, in your speech Thursday I know you have to tie up world peace with tariff reductions and we realize industry has to make some sacrifices along that line—"

"Oh, Industry has to make the sacrifices!" protestingly calls Sam Parrish from his table.

"But," the Senator goes on, "I think you'll have to reassure the American farmer that he won't be forced to compete with Russian wheat and Danish butter and Argentine beef."

Grant is sure there is a direct connection between world trade and world peace. But, Kay would remind him, the farmer has a special case. And twenty million votes, puts in Senator Lauterback.

"Senator," Grant is saying, "I want you to talk to me very, very frankly and very fully, and give me all the information you can—but please don't expect me to make any decisions here tonight."

"That's the way Grant works," Mary informs them, resting her drink on the table. "He likes to listen to people before he makes any decish—before he decides anything."

Sam Parrish is getting worried. It was his impression that they were "going to talk turkey" at this dinner. Nor is he completely reassured by Jim Conover's promise that there will be a caucus later—

"You know what we're worried about. Are we going to be in for a lot of government competition, or is this country going to be put back in the hands of private enterprise?"

"Oh, Grant believes in private enterprise," puts in Mary, staring at Kay. "Doesn't he, Kay?"

Swenson has come from the dining room. He is trying to catch Mary's uncertain eye.

"Dinner is served, ma'am!"

"Dinner! Good! Take your cocktails with you if you haven't finished."

As the guests move toward the dining room, chattering volubly, Grant tries to edge in a word with Mary, but doesn't quite make it.

"Grant, Mary's tight!" explodes Kay, in cold anger as Mary disappears. "Is there any way you can talk to her?—do something with her?"

Before she can explain further Mary is back. She sees Grant and Kay. Kay passes her and goes into the dining room.

"Mary, I'm depending on you to help me tonight," Grant warns.

"I'm afraid I interrupted you and Kay before she had a chance to tell you what you think." She is reaching for her drink.

"Leave that drink here, and get some food into you as soon as you can!"

"Well, seems to me you're getting a little 'belligerel.' "

"Mary, I'm on a spot here tonight. We both are. We have to be ready to do some quick thinking."

"Don't worry about me," says Mary, starting for the dining room. "I'm a very thick quinker."

The curtain falls.

The Matthews dinner is over. Most of the guests have returned to the living room. Mary and Lulubelle are again sitting together. Lulubelle is working on a bourbon highball. Mary has finished her own coffee and, with Lulubelle's permission, she annexes a second cup. She takes her third and fourth cups when Swenson appears with the silver coffee pot.

"I can't remember anything that happened before the salad," Mary admits.

"You missed the best part. You certainly were whamming away at them. You picked them off one by one—like settin' birds. I haven't enjoyed myself so much since Huey Long died."

MARY (*taking another gulp of coffee*)—Can you remember any of the things I said?

LULUBELLE (*thinking*)—Now let me see—what was it you said to the Senator? I kept wishing I had a pencil so I could write 'em down. It may come back to me later. That was the time Sam Parrish had the choking spell. You remember that, don't you?

MARY (*disconsolately*)—No. (*Another gulp of coffee.*)

LULUBELLE—Oh, he had to leave the table. Then when he came back you started on *him*.

MARY—Oh, dear! (*She puts her empty cup down and takes up* LULUBELLE's *full one.*)

LULUBELLE—It was something personal that I couldn't rightly follow. Your husband got it. That's when he knocked over his wine. My!—and that looked like an expensive dress Mrs. Thorndyke is wearing. (MARY *comes out of coffee cup with broad smile and turns to* LULUBELLE.) I don't think she likes you, honey. She was the only one that tried to get back at you, but you took care of her.

MARY—What were they talking about?

LULUBELLE—It was kinda hard to keep track of it, because every time you said something they changed the subject. (MARY *suffers.*) After we've gone, you better make up to your husband. I don't think he thought that talk about the thermometer was very funny.

MARY—Thermometer? What thermometer?

LULUBELLE—Oh, you just kept bedeviling him to take his temperature.

MARY—Why?

LULUBELLE—Well, you said he was getting another one of his attacks of gallopin' self-importance. (MARY *winces.*) I remember that one! I'm saving that up to use on Jeff!

MARY—I certainly picked a good day for this. (*Turns to* LULUBELLE.) It's our wedding anniversary.

LULUBELLE (*thoughtfully*)—Well, honey, this is one anniversary you'll both always remember.

Spike McManus has arrived in time to get in on the table discussions as to party policy. He is a little disturbed to hear of

Mary's verbal indiscretions, but there apparently is nothing that can be done. "And don't ask for a copy of my speech," advises Mary. "No matter what they tell you, I've been misquoted."

The others have gone back to the dining room when Jim Conover finds Mary alone. His attitude might be defined as paternal, but unsympathetic. Mary is ready to agree that she has behaved badly as a hostess. She is not so sure she would not be proud of much of what she has said—if she could remember what it was—

"You did let go of some beauts," admits Conover, amused in spite of himself.

"Well, I think they're all stupid, selfish people."

CONOVER—I'd like to tell you how stupid I think you are. Mary, I think it's time *you* were a little selfish, *and* a little intelligent. There's such a thing as enlightened self-interest you know. Why should you be stupid just because Kay's being stupid?

MARY—Jim, that's one thing even I can't say about Kay—she's not stupid.

CONOVER—Isn't she? She's in there now doing her damnedest to get Grant into the White House. And the White House is the one place where she can't be with him. She can't follow him there, Mary. Have you ever thought of that?

MARY—No, I hadn't.

CONOVER—Well, isn't it a little unintelligent of you to do anything to stop Grant from getting there? If he doesn't become President, I'm not sure what's going to happen between you and him. But if he is elected—then you'll be the First Lady—in more ways than one.

MARY—That doesn't necessarily follow.

CONOVER—I think it does—and I'll tell you why. I know how you feel toward Grant. You've never bothered to conceal it from me.

MARY (*looking down*)—Okay. So I love him.

CONOVER—Mary, when I saw you and Grant in Detroit—before he spoke that night—there were two people in love. Maybe Grant hadn't said so—maybe Grant hadn't shown it in those little ways you were looking for—but if you had had another month alone together, you know what would have happened.

MARY—I think you're wrong, Jim.

CONOVER—No, my dear, what he feels toward you goes pretty deep—and I'll tell you how he gives himself away. It's in his respect for your opinion—for what you think.

MARY—Don't kid me, Jim. We both know what happened to Grant's speech on reconversion.

CONOVER—Well, here's something you don't know—how unhappy Grant is about that. He's good and sore at himself and I know in my bones that some day what he thinks about reconversion—and Big Business—and what you think—is going to pop right out in the middle of a speech. I'm only praying that it doesn't happen before the nomination, and you'd better add a prayer, too.

MARY—But I want him to say it.

CONOVER—No, Mary, not before the nomination. That's playing Kay's game.

SPIKE (*from arch*)—Jim, can you come back in here? They're just breaking up.

CONOVER (*as* SPIKE *goes back*)—I'll be there in a minute. Mary, use your head. You can keep Grant from being President, but if you do, you're going to lose him. Will you do something for me before I go tonight?

MARY—What?

CONOVER—I'd like to hear you say something to Grant that would let him know that if he does come our way a little bit, you wouldn't make life miserable for him. (MARY *is silent.*) You're not the only one to be considered, Mary. Think of your children. That's a pretty good heritage—to be able to say, "My father was President of the United States."

MARY—Thanks, Jim. You're better than black coffee. You'd better get back in there.

CONOVER—Oh, I'll hear it all later.

MARY—Oh, yes, Grant and Spike are going over to your hotel with you.

CONOVER—No, Mary, we're going over to Mrs. Thorndyke's.

Now the party is breaking up with the usual exchange of thanks and congratulations. "You don't mind my falling in love with your husband, do you?" Mrs. Draper is asking Mary.

"I don't see how you could help it," answers the loyal wife of a political possibility.

Mrs. Draper turns to Grant. "I hope you and Jim get together on everything," she hopes.

"Whoever the candidate is, you're going to be very valuable to him. I realize that," says Grant.

"Well, if there's one group I do know how to swing, it's the foreigners. I don't pretend to be an intellectual, but since our so-called great minds have gotten us into the United Nations, we can't overlook the political advantage it gives us. Remember, there are lots of voters who are afraid of Russia!—and you'd be surprised how many people hate the British!"

"I don't think we can capitalize on that, Mrs. Draper. We can't build world peace on world hate. We have a certain leadership in the United Nations. We have to be very jealous of it."

"Yes, but, Grant," speaks up Kay Thorndyke, "if we're to win, remember each nationality in America will be thinking of their home country. We can use that. Am I right, Jim?"

"In Jersey City, Mayor Hague promised the Italians we'd rebuild Italy."

"Exactly!"

"We've got to promise them that, and more too."

"It's bound to be part of the campaign. I don't see how we can very well avoid it. (*He has been eyeing* MARY *and now speaks to her.*) Do you, Mary?"

"Well, some of the Democrats are being pretty open about it."

Mrs. Draper has grown restless. "I do have to run," she insists finally. "Good-by, Mr. Matthews. You'll find I'm right about all this! Good night, Mrs. Matthews. It was a wonderful dinner—and such good talk! Of course my friends accuse me of thinking God is a Republican. But I'm fair-minded. I thank him every night for Senator Bilbo."

Soon the others have followed her. The Alexanders have had a wonderful time. Lulubelle can't begin to tell Grant how wonderful Mary is. It's nice, too, to be able to congratulate him on this, his wedding anniversary!

Sam Parrish is also on his way. He and Jim Conover will make the same train back to Washington. That will give them a chance to talk everything over.

"Grant, you're in a spot now where you can't indulge any more of that radical talk," is Sam's parting shot. "My God, look at the effect it has had on Mary!" He has found a leather picture case in his pocket. In it is a picture of his son, Bobby, who has made a whale of a record in Japan—sixteen Jap planes. Bobby wants to get right into the business when he comes back. And Sam wants to make it the soundest business in the whole country before he leaves it to Bobby.

There is a little more politics before Kay and Conover get away. Of course there will have to be compromises, Kay is sure of that. And Jim agrees. "We can't get through life without conceding some things, can we, Mary?" Conover asks. His arm is around Mary's shoulder. He doesn't wait for an answer.

"I don't think the Senator is going to be half as tough as Mrs. Draper," ventures Spike. "I started kidding her. I said it was too bad we couldn't dig up Hitler. There might be some votes in it. (*He chuckles.*) She didn't know whether I was on the level or not. And from her answer, I don't know whether she was on the level or not."

GRANT (*getting into his coat*)—If you ask me, I don't think she was kidding. (*To* CONOVER.) I can't go whole hog with her, Jim.

CONOVER—Of course she goes overboard—but you can't dismiss the fact those issues are coming up, and we've got to find some way of making a play for the foreign vote.

KAY—We know that every nation is going to feel the peace terms have done them an injustice. We can make a perfectly honest appeal for justice, and if that gets us some votes—I don't think we should quibble.

GRANT—What are you thinking of first, the votes or the justice?

CONOVER—Grant, we can't help ourselves. The Democrats are going to play that side of the street—they're doing it already. Mary agrees with us on that. We can find some way to take a stand for justice and still appeal to the foreign vote—and with a clear conscience. Don't you think so, Mary?

MARY—No. I don't. I tried to get out of the room before I got sick but you wouldn't let me! I've sat here listening to you make plans for Grant to trade away the peace of the world to get a few votes!—Now that we're in the United Nations let's use it! —use it to get Italian votes and Polish votes—let's use it to get the votes of those who hate the Russians and those who hate the British! How long is it going to be before you ask us to forgive Germany to get the German vote?

CONOVER (*warningly*)—Mary!—

MARY—You heard Mrs. Draper and how much did it mean to you? "She's a little overboard"—"You can't quite go whole hog with her." And you heard Kay, too, cheering her on! None of you had the guts to tell them they are starting another war and to slap them down for it!

KAY—Now, Grant. Really!

CONOVER—Mary, do you know what you're doing?

MARY—Yes, Jim, I know what I'm doing! Look at Sam—he

wants to leave a fortune to Bobby. What kind of a world is he going to leave to Bobby? The kind he wants isn't good enough for my children. Don't you know what's happened in the world? Are you willing to trust the people you brought here tonight with atomic power?

CONOVER (*harshly*)—We may not be as bright as you are, Mary, but the people here tonight were pretty representative.

MARY—Representative of what? Nobody represented the American people! They don't even represent the Republican party. You represent what's dead in the Republican party . . . and what's dead in the Democratic party!

KAY—For heaven's sake, Mary, have a little faith in Grant.

MARY—What have *you* got faith in? The people? You're afraid to let them know what Grant really thinks. Don't you believe in Democracy?

KAY (*sharply*)—Why do you suppose we were here tonight? What do you think we were doing? All we were planning was the next election.

MARY—Yes, I know. Everybody here tonight was thinking of the next election. Well, it's time somebody began thinking of the next generation.

Mary has covered her face with her hands. She is sobbing as she runs upstairs.

For a moment they are all too stunned to speak. Then Kay suggests that what they need most is a drink. Let them go over to her house and get it. Grant isn't ready. Slowly he unbuttons his coat and takes it off. A worried look from Kay and Conover would stop him—

"Grant, I've got to talk to these people, and that means you've got to talk to me," pleads Jim.

"I'm talking to a lot of people in my speech Thursday night," answers Grant. "You'll be one of them. I promised myself when I went into this that I'd appeal to the best in the American people. The only advice I've ever had from any of you was to appeal to their worst. And that's what both parties are starting to do today. Let's end rationing! Who cares if Europe starves? Let's lift the price ceilings—suppose it does bring inflation. Let's lower the taxes and all get rich."

"I see. You're the only honest man in politics."

"No, Jim! We have some damn good men! There are some wonderful men in the Senate and in the House, too—Democrats and Republicans. But dammit, Jim, there are not enough of them to shape the party policies. So, to get votes, both parties are out to buy the American public. I can't do that, Jim. So I'm afraid I can't be of any use to you."

Neither Conover nor Kay is willing to accept that decision as final. Let Grant sleep on it first. They will see him tomorrow. But Grant stands firm.

"Well, Grant, you're wrong," Conover is saying, a little sadly. "In this country we play politics—and to play politics you have to play ball."

"I'm sorry, Jim. I've become very fond of you."

"Oh, don't send flowers. It's not my funeral!"

They have gone. For a moment a heavy silence prevails. Then Spike takes over: "Mr. Matthews, will you marry me?"

That sets Grant laughing. "Be careful, Spike, I'm in the mood for it! I've never felt so relieved in my life. Thank God that's settled. I hope they're all listening in Thursday night! I'm going to burn their ears off. Any candidate for any office who threatens world peace for the sake of a few votes—there's the international criminal for you, Spike. I'll take care of them Thursday night—and from now on!"

"You know Jim may have to take you on your own terms."

"No, Spike, it's all over but the shouting—but, oh, boy, am I going to shout!"

Presently Mary comes down the stairs. She is surprised to find them there. "Where's Jim?" she asks.

"I think he's cabling General MacArthur," ventures Spike.

Grant is pacing the room collecting his thoughts. He has taken off his jacket and is rolling up his sleeves—

"We've got to run business on a different basis. . . ."

"What's happened?" asks Mary anxiously.

"Quiet, please, we're on the air!" Spike cautions.

GRANT—Sam and his type are dead. They want to go back to something they've had before. We've got to move on to something we've *never* had before. And I'm going to tell off the Senator, too. . . . (*Crosses to* MARY.) It's time somebody spoke up for the farmers. The American farmer is not the unpatriotic, selfish, grasping bastard the farm-bloc makes him out to be. Thank God I can speak my mind now— (*He looks at* SPIKE.) I don't have to worry about being a candidate!

SPIKE—Now you're on the beam. Talk as though you're not a candidate and I think they'll have to make you one.

GRANT—Forget it, Spike. (*He shakes hands with* SPIKE.)

It's been great working with you. But it's all over. I'll be seeing you. This isn't good-by.

SPIKE—You're damn right it isn't good-by. I'll be around first thing Friday morning. See you later, Mary.

GRANT—No, Spike, it's cold. But I'm in a great spot for my speech Thursday night. I haven't any commitments.

SPIKE—You've got one.

GRANT—What?

SPIKE—You promised not to make me Postmaster General. But I'll tell you what I'm doing, Grant—I'm releasing you from that. I'll be Postmaster General. (SPIKE *leaves.*)

MARY—But, Grant, what happened?

GRANT—Mary, I'm not running for President. But that doesn't mean I'm out of politics. Nobody can afford to be out of politics. I'm going to be yelling from the sidelines; you've got to be yelling; everybody's got to be yelling. I'm going to be in there asking questions, and I'm going to see that the people get the answers.

MARY—There are a lot of questions to ask, Grant. You're going to be a busy man.

GRANT—You're damned right I'll be busy. Say, I didn't do a real job in any one of my plants. Let's make the trip all over again.

MARY—But, Grant, you need a rest first. We both do.

GRANT—All right, what do you say we go back to Victoria?

MARY—Victoria?

GRANT—Say—do you know something? (*He shakes his finger at* MARY.) You forgot this is our wedding anniversary!

MARY (*pretending surprise*)—I did? Oh, damn it all to hell!

GRANT (*smacking* MARY *on the behind*)—Cut that out, Maizie! (*The realization comes to* MARY *that he has smacked her and called her Maizie. Her face lights up.*) Darling, you're right about the future. We've got something great to work for! (*He reaches* MARY *and enfolds her in his arms.*)

THE CURTAIN FALLS

HOME OF THE BRAVE

A Drama in Three Acts

BY ARTHUR LAURENTS

(Digest by John Chapman)

WHEN the New York Drama Critics' Circle met to vote upon best plays of the season, two war dramas received enthusiastic if minor support. They were "A Sound of Hunting," by Harry Brown, and "Home of the Brave," by Arthur Laurents. Before the war Mr. Brown was a poet; during the war he was a GI writer, and in "A Sound of Hunting" he wrote a play about an incident in the battle for Cassino, in which a group of men were pinned down by enemy fire in the wreckage of an Italian house. Mr. Brown's play was praised for the naturalness of its soldier dialogue and for realistic performances by a company headed by Sam Levene.

Mr. Laurents' "Home of the Brave" was a battle drama, too, with much of its action incident to jungle warfare; but it also had something of a postwar angle in that it dealt with psychoneuroses resulting from warfare and the methods of curing them.

The theatre is usually on the losing end of a "raid." If the films want a writer or an actor, they usually take him from the stage—and in recent years the radio has followed the same practice. However, the stage has begun to do a little raiding of its own. It has found some promising dramatists in Hollywood, and an occasional screen-bred actor like Ruth Hussey of "State of the Union." Radio can be credited with the early development of Arthur Laurents, and his four years of service in the Army were largely devoted to the writing of broadcast programs and dramas like "Assignment Home" and "The Man Behind the Gun." His first play won the outspoken support of three or four of the New York reviewers and such adjectives as "promising" from the remainder; and because of "Home of the Brave" he was given a grant of $1,000 by the American Academy of Arts and Letters.

According to army psychiatrists, the fear of death is, obviously, the greatest mental strain and the most common cause of a break-

"Home of the Brave," copyright 1945 by Arthur Laurents. Published by Random House, Inc., New York.

down; but next comes the guilt complex. Survival, when some of a man's companions have been killed, carries with it a sense of guilt. It is the business of the army medicos to try to find out what has caused a mental or physical breakdown, and this is the problem faced by Capt. Harold Bitterger when they wheel into his hospital room Pvt. Peter Coen, who has lost his memory and the ability to walk.

Capt. Bitterger's room at a Pacific base is also his office. Tropical foliage and bright sunlight can be seen through the rear window—a lush contrast with the office itself, with its battered desk, a couple of chairs and an army cot. Bitterger is trying to learn all he can about Pvt. Coen's case before he sees the lad himself. As the scene begins he is talking with two men who know something of its case history. One is Maj. Dennis E. Robinson, Jr., a cigarette ad with a blond crew-cut who is self-conscious about his rank—for he is only 26—and who tries to hide his youth with a stalwart military manner. The other is Corp. T. J. Everitt, a thin, sallow, paunchy man of 35 who resents the Army, the war and practically everything—for he lost a good civilian income.

Maj. Robinson has given the Doctor a written report on the facts of Coen's case. Complete as they seem to be, they appear to be of no great help to Bitterger. "They're not quite enough," he says. The Corporal, searching his memory for more facts, volunteers, "I just happened to remember. There was something else. There was a fight the last day we were on the island."

The Major, worried about the young man who has been in his command, pleads with the Doctor, "Coney's going to be all right, isn't he?" Bitterger doesn't know—maybe yes, perhaps no. "I'm a psychiatrist, Major, not a clairvoyant. The boy suffered a traumatic shock. Now he has paralysis. Amnesia. Physical manifestations."

"How are you treating him, Captain?"

"Narcosynthesis. You administer a drug that acts as a release for the patient. Usually, he will relive the experiences immediately preceding shock if the doctor leads him."

Corp. Everitt, known in his outfit as T. J., goes to a ward and wheels in Private Coen, a young, frightened, melancholy lad dressed in the dark red "zoot suit" of the hospital. The Major gives him a friendly greeting, but Coen regards him blankly. He recognizes the officer's rank and says "sir," but does not remember him as an individual—nor, when they ask him, does he remember Mingo or Finch.

The Doctor is ready to begin treatment. Coney, as he is nicknamed, is lifted to the cot and the Major and T. J. leave the room. Gently, Bitterger tells the frightened lad that he is a doctor. "I'm going to make you well, Coney. I'm going to fix you up so you'll remember everything and be able to walk again."

Into Coney's arm he injects a solution of amytal. "Start counting backwards from 100," he orders, and Coney begins—"one hundred, 99, 98, 97 . . ." His speech gets thicker and slower and he stops between 81 and 80. The drug has now taken full effect, and now the Doctor's work begins.

"Who do you work for, Coney?"

"Maj. Robinson." The reply comes without hesitation, and Bitterger continues his questioning. Coney thinks the Major is all right, but not as smart as Mingo. Mingo's a sharp boy, but sensitive—sensitive about his wife. His wife's sharp, too; she writes poetry, and Mingo recited one of her poems once.

"Why shouldn't he recite it to you? You're his buddy."

"Oh, no, I'm not his buddy. He doesn't have a buddy."

"Who's your buddy, Coney? Finch? Finch is your buddy, isn't he?"

Coney is oddly uncomfortable at this mention of Finch and the Doctor senses that he is on a promising lead. He pursues it. Coney admits he likes Finch and that Finch likes him—and then almost hysterically denies it. Under obvious emotional stress, Coney wavers between expressing violent hatred of Finch and a gentle friendship for him—a dumb Arizona hayseed and a sweet kid. "He doesn't seem like the others—only I wonder if he is."

"What others?"

"The ones who make the cracks."

Suddenly Coney, brooding about the hateful T. J. Everitt and his cracks, springs to a sitting position and, frightened, demands where Finch is. "Finch?" he calls. "Finch?"

The Doctor throws his arm around the paralyzed boy. "Hi, Coney," he says in a GI greeting, and to Coney it is Finch who is talking. "Where the hell have you been? The Major wants us in his office," Coney chides affectionately.

Under the influence of the amytal, Pvt. Coen has begun to relive an experience. The hospital room fades out, and in its place appears an office in a Quonset hut somewhere in the Pacific. Again the sun is burning down through tropic trees as Coen and his buddy, Pvt. Wally Finch, enter. Wally is a likeable, simple and gentle soldier, even younger than Coen. There is no one else in the office and the boys speculate on why they were sent for

—cleaning up, or a health inspection, or what? Maybe it's a furlough.

The greatest of all soldier dreams was a furlough—a furlough home. Seeing the family. Seeing the girl. Eating wonderful food. Ice cream. Milk. Meeting the old gang. Coney and Finch, day-dreaming, think of how they'll go to Finch's mother's ranch in Arizona, and how they'll look for a spot where they can start the bar they plan to run after the war—only Finch has written his mother that it's going to be a restaurant.

"Does your mother know who I am?" asks Coney.

"Of course." Finch has written all about his Pacific buddy, and his mother even has ideas about mating Coney and Finch's sister. "I mean," says Coney, "does she know my name?"

This pleasant day-dreaming is interrupted by the arrival in the hut of T/Sgt. Carl Mingo, a red-haired man of 27 whose bearing indicates spiritual and physical strength. Sgt. Mingo doesn't know why they've been summoned to the Major's office, but he doubts that it's a furlough. A rest camp, maybe—and they need it. But, on the other hand, moving out to "where the little men make with the big bullets."

In the faded coveralls like those which the others are wearing appears "T. J." He doesn't know what the summons is for, either, but is in a temper about it. "I heard a rumor," taunts Finch, "that they were going to give you a commission, T. J." But Everitt can't be kidded out of his temper, nor out of his violent disregard for the Major.

Speculation and soldier banter come to an end when Maj. Robinson comes from the inner office of the hut. "At ease, men." He invites them to sit and have a smoke, because they are in for a session. The Major talks cheerfully, hearteningly, like a college coach, and is sorry that furloughs aren't the subject. There's a job to do now, but afterward, maybe, they'll get the furloughs. Right now, the subject is "top secret," and anyone talking will be court-martialed.

"You four men," he begins, "are the best engineers in the outfit. We need A-1 engineers for the job."

The job is an island—never mind where—which is next on the invasion program. Taking it will shorten the war—but there are 15,000 Japs on it. "To take it and hold it," explains the Major, "we'll need airstrips. . . . Well, I'm flying to that island tonight."

"With fifteen thousand Japs on it, sir?" asks Finch.

Exactly. And the Major needs four men to go with him, to draw maps and survey for the proposed airstrips. Natives will pick them up offshore in canoes, and the whole job can be done in four days, when they'll take to the canoes again and a plane will pick them up.

"This is purely voluntary, fellows. . . . Talk it over. . . . I'm sorry, but I can't give you more than ten minutes—but it came up damn fast and—well, you men know the Army."

They know it, all right. "Oh, my aching back!" . . . "That vaseline about volunteering." . . . "With a nice little bribe of furloughs." . . . "Keep your eyes open, your mouth shut and never volunteer." . . . "The dirtiest trick you can play on a man in war is to make him think." But, when the Major returns in ten minutes and asks "Yes or no?" Coney says, "Yes, sir."

Again, hot muggy sunlight pours through tropic trees, but now there is no hospital room, no office in a Quonset hut; for this is a Pacific island with 15,000 Japs on it—the Japs on the other side of it, facing the American enemy, and here on the side facing Japan are Coney and Finch. They are on the edge of a clearing, and Finch, propped against a pile of equipment, is completing a map on a sketch pad while Coney cleans a rifle.

The screaming of jungle birds has got on Coney's nerves. "They make you jumpy, Finch?"

"Coyotes are worse. . . . They're kind of scarey—if you wake up and hear them in the middle of the night."

"I remember waking up in the middle of the night and hearing something. I was ten years old."

"What'd you hear?"

"A human coyote." Coney gets up from his rifle-cleaning. "I've got the jumps."

"We'll be out of here tonight. Why don't you relax. It's a fine day," soothes Finch, and he leads Coney into time-passing conversation about girls; and the bar they're going to have; and Mingo; and Mingo's poetry-writing wife, and the spiteful T. J. Shortly T. J. emerges through the bushes. "The Major wants the clinometer."

FINCH—You know where it is.

T. J.—Why don't you get the lead out of your can and do something for once?

CONEY—You finish your map.

FINCH—It is finished, Coney.

CONEY—Well, let T. J. Rockefeller do something besides blowing that tin horn.

T. J.—Look who's talking.

FINCH—Yeah, look! He stood guard two nights out of three while you snored your fat face off. The Major told me to take it easy today and you know it.

T. J.—The little kike lover.

FINCH—You always get around to that, don't you?

T. J.—Every time I see your friend's face.

CONEY—You son-of-a-bitch.

T. J.—Watch your language or I'll ram it down your throat, Jew boy.

Finch, thoroughly aroused, takes a swing at T. J. and a rough scuffle is under way when Mingo comes through the brush and orders them to break it up.

"Why don't you jerks save it for the Japs?"

Coldly he orders T. J. to take the clinometer to the Major, and T. J. gets the instrument from the pile of gear and goes into the jungle. Finch keeps muttering, "That bastard," and Mingo soothingly agrees. "Hell, the guy's 35, 36. He can't adjust himself to the Army, so he winds up hating everything and resenting everybody. . . . But you ought to try to understand him."

Coney, still seething, snaps, "YOU try to understand him. I haven't got time. I'm too busy trying to understand all this crap about Jews." And to Finch he explains:

"I told you I heard something in the middle of the night once. Some drunken bum across the hall from my aunt's yelling, 'Throw out the dirty sheenies!' . . . That was us. But I just turned over and went back to sleep. I was used to it by then. What the hell! I was 10. That's old for a Jew. When I was 6, my first week in school, I stayed out for the Jewish New Year. The next day a bunch of kids got around me and said, 'Were you in school yesterday?' I smiled and said, 'No.' They wiped the smile off my face. They beat the hell out of me. I had to get beat up a couple more times before I learned that if you're a Jew you stink."

Coney continues in this vein for a moment or so more, until Finch cuts in: "Maybe I'm an Arizona hayseed, like you say. But I never met any Jewish boys till I got in the Army. I didn't even realize out loud that YOU were, until somebody said something. . . . And I took a poke at him, too. . . . O.K., I'm a jerk, but to me—you like a guy or you don't. That's all there is to it."

Coney's mood softens to one of affection for Finch, but amiable banter is cut short by a shot from the jungle. Finch, Coney and Mingo freeze, then start for cover just as the Major and T. J.

run into the clearing. A Jap sniper has taken a shot at them. "Grab the gear and let's beat it fast," orders the Major.

Finch, T. J. and the Major begin picking up equipment, while Coney and Mingo hold their rifles at the ready. The last piece of equipment to be picked up is a walkie-talkie, which Mingo goes to get. There is another shot, and Mingo drops his rifle and grabs his right arm. Coney fires twice, and there is the sound of a body crashing through the trees. "Got the bastard," whispers Coney. The Major crawls to Mingo, makes a tourniquet on his arm with a handkerchief.

"We'll make for that clearing near the beach," he orders. "You got the maps?" he asks.

"Yes, sir," says Finch.

The Major, T. J. and Mingo set out, and Coney urges, "Let's go, Finch." But Finch, wandering around the clearing, can't find the map case. "This is a helluva time!" snarls Coney. "Listen, we'll lose them."

"We gotta have those maps."

"The maps won't do us any good if we get picked off!"

"That's the only thing we came here for."

"You'll get us both killed, you dumb Arizona bastard!"

Finch, overwrought, turns upon his buddy. "I'm not asking you to stay, you lousy yellow—" he catches himself, with an effort, and continues, "—jerk."

Coney stands for a moment, staring at his friend, then makes for the bushes, just as Finch locates the map case.

Another shot from the jungle and Finch clutches his belly and falls. Coney scrambles back to him.

"I didn't mean—" Finch begins.

"Never mind. Are you hit?"

"Take the maps."

Coney tries to carry his friend, but Finch pushes him down. "I'll follow," he whispers. "Go on, quick!" Coney disappears in the brush and Finch, badly hit, begins a painful crawl in the same direction. As he, too, vanishes, the bushes behind him begin to rustle. The Japs are at hand. In the distance Coney can be heard calling, "Finch! Finch! Finch!"

The curtain falls.

ACT II

The Doctor and Coney are again in the hospital room. Following another amytal injection, Coney is counting backward. The numbers fade away and the young soldier says, "I shouldn't have left him. I should have stayed with him." The Doctor argues that the maps were the main job and if Coney had remained with Finch they would have been lost. But Coney keeps muttering, remorsefully.

Suddenly the Doctor pretends he is Finch. "Coney, take the maps and get out of here. . . . Go on!" Slowly Coney raises himself from the cot as though to get out of bed. "Go on!" The soldier makes a great effort, then sinks back. "I can't." He realizes for a moment that he is in the hospital and that it is the Doctor, not Finch, talking.

The Doctor tries another tack. He asks Coney what he thought of when he heard the shot and saw that Finch was hit. Coney is vague. "I—I got a bad feeling." The Doctor pursues this lead. Coney didn't want to leave his buddy, but Finch told him to. The Doctor assures him he was right in going—assures him over and over again. The logic of the argument is plain to Coney, but he still has "that bad feeling." He can't remember when he first got the bad feeling, or whether it was worse after he found he couldn't walk; he can't even remember when he discovered he couldn't walk. "When? When? When?"

The questions continue. As Coney makes a great effort to remember, the scene changes to another clearing on the Pacific island.

This clearing is smaller than the one where Finch was shot. Leading from it is a faint path to the beach, where, that night, buried canoes will be dug up and a rendezvous kept with the pickup plane. Coney is peering anxiously through the trees. T. J., sitting near, is drinking from his canteen. Mingo, reclining against some equipment, is having his arm ministered to by the Major.

"We ought to be able to hear him coming," insists Coney, but T. J. argues that if they could hear him the Japs could, too, and Finch isn't that dumb. Mingo's arm looks pretty bad, and the Major thinks it has two slugs in it. "Ready to be lopped off," adds Mingo.

There is an air of distress, not helped any by the screaming of jungle birds, as the men try to ease each other's anxiety about Finch and Mingo's fatalistic opinion about his arm.

"The plane will be here in about an hour, Mingo," the Major comforts. "You can be in the hospital tomorrow."

This adds to Coney's anxiety. Suppose Finch hasn't arrived when the plane comes—what then? They'll worry about this when the times comes, says the Major.

"I wonder," muses Mingo, "how a one-armed linotyper would make out."

Mingo and T. J. have begun an argument, when a distant scream is heard. A bird? No. . . . Again a scream—and this time it is recognizable as Finch calling "Coney!"

Coney starts for the sound, but the Major grabs him. "They're sticking him just to make him yell like that. Just to make us come after him."

As the screams continue the struggling Coney breaks loose and again makes for the jungle. He is brought up short by Mingo, who snaps, "Coney, stop trying to be a goddam hero!"

Mingo takes his turn explaining it is a Jap trick, and if Coney goes after him they'll kill him and Finch, too. Mingo talks fast—about Coney's home; about the bar he's going to have—anything to distract the frantic young soldier as the sounds of torture keep on. He even turns to poetry—a poem he says his wife wrote. As Finch's cries grow weaker, Mingo recites:

"We are only two and yet our howling
Can encircle the world's end.
Frightened, you are my only friend.
And frightened we are, every one.
Someone must take a stand—
Coward, take my coward's hand."

To break the tension the Major orders T. J. to reconnoiter the spot where the canoes are buried, although it's still daylight and they can't be dug up yet. T. J. obeys hesitantly.

"I guess the big executive is a little afraid," observes Mingo.

"I guess he doesn't like to take orders from me."

"He doesn't like much of anything, Major."

"Does he—Mingo, does he make cracks about Jews?"

T. J. does, indeed, and to Coney, who is a Jew. "Funny," observes the Major, "I never think of him as a Jew."

"Yeah, it is funny. I never think of you as a gentile."

The Major feels that he is in an awkward spot. Suddenly he opens his heart to Mingo. He's young for his rank—only 26—but he's got to have the respect of his men. The only way to get it is to know his job and run it. He feels that an officer should always be an officer. Mingo gently observes that "us guys" also want respect—"and an officer is a guy, isn't he?"

This little talk does the Major good, and, treating Mingo as a "guy," he asks him about going home. The wounded man isn't enthusiastic. The Major ventures that he's just worried about going back to his wife with a—well, a bum wing, and Mingo retorts bitterly that she wouldn't care. "She sounds like a fine girl . . . from that poem."

Mingo starts to say "What po—" and then remembers. "Oh, sure, she's a great little writer, and pretty, too. . . . She writes good letters, too. I remember the first one, the first one she wrote me in the Army. 'My darling darling, I will never again use the word love—except to say I love you.' "

"Oh, that's very nice," bitterly continues Mingo. "Almost as nice as her last letter. I can remember that one, too. I got that about a week ago. That began, 'My darling, this is the hardest letter I've ever had to write. But it's only fair to be honest with you and tell you that—' "

He is too choked up to go on. The old "GI" letter.

There is a rustle in the bushes. The Major grabs his rifle and Coney sits up with his own gun ready. But it's just T. J., coming in from the wrong direction because he lost the trail. The light is fading. The Major thinks it's time to get going. First dig up the canoes, then come back for the gear. Coney volunteers to remain with the equipment. The others go down the path. Coney, in the quickly gathering dusk, smokes silently, then freezes at a sound.

Catlike, he leaps to the edge of the clearing and calls, softly, "Finch? Finch?" Then he sinks to the ground and covers his face with his hand. He doesn't hear the bushes move. Nor does he sees a body slowly dragging itself toward him. A hand gestures, as though the man were trying to talk and can't.

With a final great effort Finch drags himself further into the clearing. He sees Coney, tries again to call, and at last manages a shrill scream. His clothes are slashed and bloody and his face is battered. Coney, overcome, puts an arm around his groaning buddy—

CONEY—Finch! Oh, Christ, Finch! Finch! . . . Oh, I'm glad! I'm so glad, Finch! You all right? You're going to be all right now, Finch. You're going to be all right now— (FINCH *cannot hold the water* CONEY *has given him and spews it up.*) Easy, fellow. Easy, Finch. (FINCH *begins to retch.*) Oh, that's charming. That's really charming. You go right ahead. That's fine and charming, Finch.

FINCH (*just getting the word out*)—Delightful.

CONEY—Oh, you bastard! You damn son-of-a-bitch bastard! I might've known they couldn't finish you off, you damn Arizona

Photo by George Karger, Pix, Inc.

"HOME OF THE BRAVE"

Doctor—Peter, I want you to listen hard to what I am going to tell you. . . . Every soldier in this world who sees a buddy get shot has that one moment when he feels glad. . . . Because deep underneath he thinks: "I'm glad it wasn't me! I'm glad *I'm* still alive."

(*Joseph Pevney, Eduard Franz*)

bastard! Let me see what they— (*He touches* FINCH, *trying to see his wounds.* FINCH *gasps in pain.*) I'm sorry. I'm sorry, kid, but I—what? What, Finch? I can't hear you. What? (*He bends down.*) Oh, for Chrissake! Sure the lousy maps are all right. We've got to get you fixed up. . . . You can goldbrick out the rest of the war in the hospital, you lucky bastard! (*As* CONEY *keeps talking* FINCH'S *head rolls and flops to one side.*) Finch? Finch? Aw, Finch, please don't be dead! (FINCH'S *body rolls back, stomach down.* CONEY *looks at it for a long moment and then, suddenly, with a violent, decisive, brutal gesture, shoves the body so it rolls over on its back. He stares at the horror for a few seconds. Then, swiftly, he lifts the head into his lap with one hand, cradles the torso with his other arm and bends across it.*) Oh, no, Finch! Oh, no, Finch! Oh, no, no, no! (*From some distance Jap voices begin to be heard.*)

FIRST JAP—Hey, Yank! Come out and fight!

SECOND JAP—Hey, Yank! Come out and fight!

CONEY—Finch, they're after you again! But I won't leave you this time. I promise I won't, Finch.

THIRD JAP—Come and fight, Yank!

CONEY—I won't leave you, Finch. I promise, I promise, I promise! (*He takes his bayonet out and starts to scoop up the ground furiously. The Japs continue yelling.*) Don't worry, Finch. I told you I wouldn't let them get you. I promised, didn't I? Didn't I? And I won't. Because I'm not a yellow bastard. I'm not afraid. I won't leave you, Finch. (*The Jap yelling is coming closer. The* MAJOR *and* MINGO *come into the clearing.*)

MAJOR—Coney!

MINGO—He's got Finch!

MAJOR—Get the map case. . . . Coney, come on. We've got to—oh, God! He's dead!

FIRST JAP—Fight, you yellow bastard!

CONEY—They won't get him, though, Major. They want to, but they won't. I'm going to bury him!

MAJOR—Bury—listen, Coney—we— Coney, you can't bury him. We've got to get out of here.

MINGO (*coming over with map case*)—Got them, Major.

MAJOR—Coney—

MINGO—What's the matter with him?

MAJOR—Finch is dead and he's trying to bury him.

MINGO—Oh, God! Coney, get up.

CONEY—I can't leave Finch.

MINGO—We'll take him. Come on. Get up.

CONEY—I can't leave Finch.

MINGO—Get up, Coney.

CONEY—Finch—

MAJOR—We'll take him.

MINGO—Come on, Coney.

CONEY (*tries to get up*)—I *can't!*

MAJOR—What do you mean you can't?

CONEY—I can't move, Major. I can't move!

MINGO—Holy God! Try.

CONEY—I am—but I can't.

MINGO—Now stop that. You've got to get out of here.

CONEY—I can't, Mingo. I can't walk. I can't move.

MINGO—Were you shot? Were you hit?

CONEY—No.

MAJOR—Then why can't you walk?

CONEY (*building to hysteria*)—I don't know!

MINGO—What's the matter with you?

CONEY—I don't know! I don't know! I don't know!

(*The screaming laughter of the Japs is getting louder and louder as the lights dim.*)

The curtain falls.

For a third time in the base hospital room Coney has had an injection. The Doctor, with the tenacity of a detective, is still looking for a clew to what set Coney's mind and body awry.

The lad thinks he remembers how he got off the island—that Mingo picked him up and carried him to the canoes. And he remembers everything that happened on the island—

"Then why can't you walk?" Coney still doesn't know.

"Do you remember waking up in the hospital? Do you remember waking up with that bad feeling?"

"Yes."

"When did you first get that bad feeling?" He doesn't know. Was it right after Finch was shot? No.

"What did you think of when Finch was shot?"

"I don't know."

"You said you remember everything that happened. And you do." The Doctor is hammering home now. "You remember how you felt when Finch was shot, don't you, Coney? Don't you?"

Coney sits bolt upright. "Yes." In flat tones he relates: "When we were looking for the map case he said—he started to say, 'You lousy yellow Jew bastard.' He only said 'You lousy yellow jerk,' but he started to say 'You lousy yellow Jew bastard.' So I knew. I knew."

"You knew what?"

"I knew he'd lied when—when he said he didn't care. When he said people were people to him. I knew he lied. I knew he hated me because I was a Jew, so I was glad when he was shot."

This, the Doctor is certain, is the key to the trouble. He goes doggedly on. Coney ran through the jungle, he points out, and walked around the clearing. If anything happened to his legs it must have happened afterward when Finch crawled back. What was it? Think back!

Coney covers his face. The Doctor, moving across the room away from him, calls in a cracked voice, "Coney!"

"Oh, Finch, Finch! Is that you, Finch?" Coney cradles an imaginary head in his lap and rocks back and forth. Then he stops short, bends down as though to listen to Finch's heart, then makes the same decisive, brutal gesture as before, when he shoved the body so that it rolled over.

The Doctor now calls, "Hey, Yank! Come out and fight!" Coney begins a frantic pantomime of digging. The Doctor grabs Coney's arm and says, curtly, "What are you trying to bury him in? This isn't earth. This is a bed. . . . You're in a hospital, Coney, and I'm your doctor. . . . And you remember now that nothing happened to your legs at all, did it?"

"No, sir."

Continuing to drive the logic of his argument home, the Doctor urges his patient to get up and walk, but Coney can't. Then the Doctor harshly commands, "Coney, get up and walk! You lousy, yellow Jew bastard, get up and walk!"

Shaking with rage, Coney grips the edge of his bed, swings his feet over, starts to walk toward the doctor with his hands outstretched as though he intends to kill him. First one foot, then the other—and then, beginning to weep violently, he sinks to the floor.

"All right, son," says the Doctor, gently. "All right, son."

The curtain falls.

ACT III

It is two weeks later. In the hospital room Coney is typing at the Doctor's desk. T. J. and the Major enter, give him warm greetings, tell him he looks great, kid him a bit about his easy job. He's not exactly a patient any more, but he and the Doctor talk once a day. The Major informs Coney that their island has been invaded and that their little mapping outfit has got commendations a yard long.

When the Doctor comes he jokingly, but firmly, orders the visitors out.

"Nice boy, the Major," he observes. Coney agrees.

"And how'd you get on with T. J.?"

"All right—no. Not really all right. He makes me think of things and I want to jump at him."

The Doctor observes that it's a good, healthy reaction. Coney tries to keep on typing but the medical captain stops him and resumes questioning. Something still is bothering Coney, quite obviously. That feeling—that bad feeling—that sort of guilty feeling.

"When did you feel it first, Peter? Right after Finch was shot, wasn't it?" It was.

Coney explains he thought he felt guilty because he left Finch, but everybody has persuaded him he had to leave his buddy to get the maps back. He is convinced in his mind that this is right—but he still has that guilty feeling. He didn't mean it, that first session in the hospital, he explains, when he said he hated Finch. But he was glad when his buddy got shot, because he thought Finch was going to call him a lousy yellow Jew bastard.

"Peter," urges the Doctor, "I want you to listen hard to what I'm going to tell you. . . . Every soldier in this WORLD who sees a buddy get shot has that one moment when he feels glad. . . . Because deep underneath he thinks, 'I'm glad it wasn't me! I'm glad I'M still alive!' "

Coney can't grasp it, but the Doctor repeats what he has said. "You've been thinking you had some special kind of guilt. But you've got to realize something. You're the same as anybody else."

"I'm a Jew."

This sensitivity, explains the Doctor, has been like a disease and Coney must cure himself of it. Cure himself and help cure others. "Don't you understand?"

"Yes, sure," agrees Coney. He understands perfectly in his head, but in his heart he just can't. The Doctor wishes he had more time to help the boy—but now he breaks the news. Hospital space is needed, and Coney is being moved back home.

"I don't want to leave you, Doc! I'm scared!"

"You won't be if you work. If you think every minute about what I told you. . . . Come on, Pete. Work!"

Coney works. "Every guy who sees his buddy get shot feels

like I did. . . . So what I felt when Finch got shot had nothing to do with being a Jew. Because I'm no different. . . . Oh, Doc, help me. . . . Get it through my dumb head. Get it through me —here" . . . and he indicates his heart.

It is another morning in the office and there is an air of activity. T. J. is packing crates. Records and papers are piled around. Mingo, in dress uniform, is sitting in a chair.

"And if you think I'm going to shed any tears over leaving this hole you're crazy," says T. J.

"You and me both," agrees Mingo.

"Yeah, but we're moving on to another base. You're going home."

It is now noticeable that Mingo's sleeve is empty—his arm has been amputated. He's waiting for a jeep to take him to the airfield. T. J. has heard that Coney is flying back, too. Is Coney all right? Are they sending him back in Mingo's care? That makes Mingo mad.

"O.K. I was just asking. You know as well as I do that cases like Coney get discharged from the hospital and then one little thing happens—and off they go again."

"Look," says Mingo grimly. "You leave that guy alone! Do you hear?"

"Leave him alone! Why in hell don't you guys lay off of me for a while?" T. J. is sorry for himself. Everybody picks on him—picks on anybody who made a halfway decent living as a civilian. . . .

Coney, carrying a barracks bag and also wearing dress uniform, joins the group. "He looks better now, but his stance, his walk, his voice show that he is still a little unsure."

The greetings are friendly. How is Coney feeling? Fine. And Mingo? "A little underweight," reports Mingo, tapping his empty sleeve.

They have talked much about going home. Now it feels kinda funny to be leaving. But they'll snap out of it. "Oh! What the hell!" demands Mingo. "We're going back to the land of mattresses and steaks medium rare!"

T. J. is back. T. J. is sore. Coney and Mingo are going home. He and the rest will have to stay on and clean up the mess single-handed!

The Major is in to wish the boys luck. His attitude is different. He's going to miss Mingo and Coney a lot. Feeling the way he does, it is plain the Major is a little embarrassed.

"I wish I knew how to say it," he almost stutters. "The three of us have been together for such a long time that it's—well—like saying good-by to your family."

T. J. is in again and still ugly. Mingo is struggling awkwardly to light a cigarette. Coney starts to help, but draws back—sensing that Mingo had rather get along alone. Not T. J. With a flourish he strikes a match and proffers it.

"It's more fun this way," says Mingo.

"Okay. Does it bother you, the arm, I mean?"

MINGO—No. It makes me light as a bird.

T. J.—I didn't mean that. I meant does it hurt?

MINGO—Some.

CONEY—What they put us in O.D.'s for?

T. J. (*still to* MINGO)—They'll give you a new one back in the States, kid.

MINGO—I know.

T. J.—You ought to be able to work them for a good pension, too.

MINGO—Sure.

CONEY (*quietly*)—Shut up!

T. J.—What's eating you?

CONEY—Shut up.

T. J.—Why, Mingo's not kidding himself about—

CONEY—Shut up.

T. J.—Take it easy, Coney, or—

CONEY—Or what?

MINGO—Coney . . .

CONEY—No. (*To* T. J.) Or what?

T. J.—Are you trying to start something?

CONEY—I'm trying to tell you to use your head, if you got one.

T. J.—If *I* got one? Look, friend, it takes more than a few days in the jungle to send me off my trolley. It's only your kind that's so goddam sensitive.

CONEY—What do you mean, my kind?

T. J.—What do you think I mean? (*There is a second's wait. Then* CONEY'S *fist lashes out and hits* T. J. *squarely on the jaw, sending him to the floor.* CONEY *stands with fists clenched, trembling.*)

T. J. (*getting up*)—It's a good thing you just got out of the booby hatch or I'd—

MINGO—You've got to get those crates out, don't you?

T. J.—Look, Mingo— (*He carries a crate out.* CONEY'S *trembling gets worse.*)

MINGO—Nice going, kiddo. . . . Coney! Coney, what's the matter?

CONEY (*numbly; starting to lose control*)—I'm just like anyone else.

MINGO—Take it easy, kid. Sit down.

CONEY—I'm just like anyone else.

MINGO—Sure, sure. Sit down.

CONEY (*getting wilder*)—That's what the Doc said, Mingo.

MINGO—And he's right. Ease up, Coney. . . .

CONEY (*jumping up in a wild outburst*)—Yes! Who're you kidding? It's not right. I'm not the same!

MINGO—Kid, you gotta get hold of yourself.

CONEY—You know I'm not!

MINGO—Kid, stop it. Listen to me.

CONEY—I'm tired of listening! I'm sick of being kidded! I got eyes! I got ears! I know! . . . You heard T. J.!

MINGO—And I saw you give him what he deserved.

CONEY—What's the use? He'll just say it again. You can't shut him up. . . . You can't shut any of them up, ever!

MINGO—All right! So he makes cracks about you. Forget it!

CONEY—Let's see you forget it.

MINGO—What the hell do you think I'm trying to do? . . . He makes cracks about me, too. Don't you think I know it?

CONEY (*the idea has struck him*)—But those cracks—it's not the same, Mingo.

MINGO—To him, it's the same. To that son-of-a-bitch and all of the son-of-a-bitches like him, it's the same; we're easy targets for him to take potshots at.

CONEY—But we're not—

MINGO—No, we're not the same! I really *am* something special. There's nothing in this sleeve but air, kiddo.

CONEY—But everybody around here knows you . . .

MINGO—Around here I'm in khaki, so they call me a hero. But back in the States, put me in a blue suit and I'm a stinking cripple!

CONEY—No. Not you, Mingo!

MINGO—Why not me?

CONEY—Because you're—you're . . .

MINGO—What? Too tough? O.K. That's what I keep trying to tell myself: Mingo, you're too tough to eat your lousy heart out about this. O.K., you lost a wing, but you're not gonna let it go down the drain for nothing.

CONEY—You couldn't.

MINGO—You should've seen me in the hospital. When I woke up and found it was off. All I could think of was the close shaves I'd had; all the times I'd stood right next to guys, seen 'em get shot and felt glad I was alive. But when I woke up—

CONEY—Wait a minute!

MINGO—I wasn't so sure.

CONEY—Wait a minute! Mingo, wait! Say that again!

MINGO—Huh?

CONEY—Say it again.

MINGO—About waking up in the hospital and . . .

CONEY—No, no. About standing next to guys when they were shot.

MINGO—Oh. Well, it was pretty rugged to see.

CONEY—But how you felt, Mingo, how you felt.

MINGO—Well, I felt sorry for them, of course.

CONEY—No, that isn't it. . . . When you saw them, Mingo, when you saw them get shot, you just said you felt—you felt—

MINGO—Oh. I felt glad I was still alive.

CONEY—Glad it wasn't you.

MINGO—Sure. Glad it wasn't me.

CONEY—Who told you to say that?

MINGO—Who *told* me? . . . Nobody told me, kiddo. I saw it. I felt it. Hell, how did you feel when you saw Finch get it?

CONEY (*almost growing*)—Just like you, Mingo. Just like you! Just like you!

MINGO—Hey, what's got into you?

CONEY—I was crazy . . . yelling I was different. I *am* different. Hell, you're different! Everybody's different. But so what? It's O.K. because underneath we're—hell, we're all guys! We're all, oh, Christ, I can't say it, but am I making any sense?

MINGO—You're making a helluva lot of beautiful sense!

CONEY—And like what you said about your arm; not letting it go down the drain for nothing. Well, I'll be damned if I'm gonna let me go for nothing.

MINGO—Now we're riding, kiddo. Hey!

CONEY—What?

MINGO—Maybe this is cockeyed.

CONEY—What?

MINGO—That bar you were going to have.

CONEY—Bar?

MINGO—With Finch. . . . You want a partner?

CONEY—A—

MINGO (*timidly*)—A one-armed bartender would be kind of a novelty, Pete. (*A great smile breaks over* CONEY'S *face. He tries to talk, to say what he feels. But all that can come out is*—)

CONEY—Ah, Judas, Mingo! (*A jeep horn sounds offstage.*)

MINGO—Hey, that sounds like our chauffeur. Soldier, the carriage waits without! (*They go to their barracks bags, but* MINGO *has to struggle to lift his with his left hand.*) You'll have to keep an eye on me, you know. This arm's gonna—dammit!

CONEY—Hey, coward!

MINGO—What?

CONEY (*lifting bag up on* MINGO'S *back*)—Take my coward's hand.

MINGO—Pete, my boy, you've got a charming memory.

CONEY (*happily*)—Oh, delightful!

(*The two start out proudly.*)

THE CURTAIN FALLS

DEEP ARE THE ROOTS

A Drama in Three Acts

BY ARNAUD D'USSEAU AND JAMES GOW

THE authors of "Deep Are the Roots" had come to New York from their accepted field of labor, the cinema farms of Hollywood, following the success of their hit drama, "Tomorrow the World." For the first time in their respective careers they were in a financial position to do about what they wanted to do. And then the Army got them. They were assigned to the Signal Corps Photographic Center in Long Island City, and were thereafter kept pretty busy helping to win the war. They counted themselves fortunate in being with the same outfit, and their playwriting ardor was in no way dimmed in service. Tremendously stimulated by their previous season's success with the study of a youthful Nazi loose in a democratic world, they began talking about another play.

It takes a long time to write a play, working only nights and Sundays, and they were eager to hit upon a theme that would still be of timely and vital interest after the war. Having in their first play forced a Nazi youth successfully through his fight with a reconditioning period in his life, they finally decided to see what they could do with the reactions and adventures of a Negro war hero returned to his home town in the deep South. "Deep Are the Roots" developed as the result of their debates.

It took the Messrs. d'Usseau and Gow eighteen months to complete the script. It was turned over to Leah Salisbury, one of the more active of the Broadway play agents, and duly submitted to several Broadway producers. Several were interested but timid. Timid, first, about submitting still another war play to a playgoing public that had been pretty well fed up with them, and second, about stirring up further controversy having to do with both the Negro problem and "the white problem," as Lillian Smith, who wrote the best-selling "Strange Fruit," calls it.

Finally the script came to the attention of George Heller, also

"Deep Are the Roots," copyright 1945 *by Arnaud d'Usseau and James Gow. Published by Charles Scribner's Sons, New York.*

an eager young man of the theatre. The only thing Mr. Heller was timid about was his own ability as a business man. So he called in a second courageous theatre adventurer, Kermit Bloomgarden. Together they decided to see "Deep Are the Roots" through to a production.

The drama, tried first in Philadelphia with definitely encouraging results, reached Broadway September 26, 1945. It proved the first real hit of the new season, and continued prosperously the season through. In November a dramatization of Miss Smith's "Strange Fruit" was produced on Broadway. It was, some reviewers and playgoers insisted, the better play of the two. But it had little or no effect on the forward sweep of "Deep Are the Roots." "Strange Fruit" was withdrawn after fifty-two performances. This may reasonably be attributed to the fact that the d'Usseau-Gow drama was much the more dramatically effective of the two, and much more enthusiastically received by the critical fraternity.

In the play, Senator Ellsworth Langdon's home is on the outskirts of a small town in the Deep South. Mid-morning of a day in early Spring, 1945, it has been thrown open to such breezes as were blowing through the garden just beyond the terrace onto which three high French windows open. The fabrics of the comfortably furnished living room are worn, but the furniture is old and very handsome. "Treasures and mementoes belonging to the past are at various strategic points; an ormolu clock; silhouettes of distant cousins; two painted oil lamps brought from Paris long ago, and now converted to electricity. The appointments and atmosphere of the room suggest family, wealth and tradition."

Honey, "a thin, not unattractive Negro girl of twenty," has just brought in the morning paper, which she puts on the table. Spying a low bowl of magnolias, Honey is moved to try one blossom in her hair. She is enjoying the effect of her reflection in a mirror when she is interrupted by Bella Charles. "Bella is a Negro woman of fifty who has been in the Langdon home for twenty-four years and thus occupies a favored position; of this she is fully conscious and conducts herself with dignity."

"Gal, you sure are a tonic to yourself!" observes Bella, as Honey, hand on hip, strikes a pose "winning and flirtatious."

"All I'm doing is fixing to meet Brett," announces Honey, defensively.

"Well, suppose you fix to get upstairs and take care of those unmade beds," suggests Bella, sharply. "Listen, you! My son will have more to think about than a frisky, no-good gal three weeks out of a cotton patch!"

Senator Langdon comes briskly into the room looking for his paper. The Senator "is almost seventy, white-haired and with a strong face that has been rutted by age and illness. A man of wealth, in his time he has been a powerful political figure; and now, like all men who have once been active, he detests the penalties of old age. He walks with a cane and his eyesight is failing. He wears a black silk waist-coat, a fat gold chain suspended from one pocket to the other."

"Well, you're anxious to see that boy of yours, aren't you?" the Senator asks, as Bella hands him the paper. "He was always a good boy. . . . Is Jackson driving you down in the car?"

"Yes, sir."

Bella has started to go when Genevra Langdon comes quickly down the stairs. "Genevra is a pretty girl of twenty-two, slim and dark. She is introspective and at moments impulsive. This is one of her impulsive moments." Genevra has decided to go with Bella to the station to meet Brett. When both Bella and the Senator question that suggestion, she quickly overrides the objection with a touch of defiance.

"Stuff and stuff! Don't you think I'm proud of Brett, too?" . . .

"I know Bella will excuse me if I have to remind you that one does not go to the station to meet a colored man," observes her father.

"Are you worried about what people will say? The great Senator Langdon."

"I said you're not to go." The Senator is firm.

"I'm sorry, Father, but I'm going. If people are shocked, it's just too bad. It'll give them something to talk about over their 'cokes.' Come on, Bella."

"It's all right, Bella. Go on. Don't be late."

"We'll be careful, Senator. When we're at the station, I won't let her get out of the car."

Bella and Genevra have left when Alice Langdon joins her father. "Alice is thirty-two and attractive. She has enormous self-confidence and good humor." Alice, too, is momentarily stunned by the news that her younger sister has gone to the station to meet a colored man, but she quickly absorbs the shock. Nor is she greatly impressed when her father accuses her of spreading the contagion of "fine ideas" that Genevra has caught. Alice is much more deeply irritated by the inopportune arrival of her cousin, Roy Maxwell. "Maxwell is forty-five, pink-faced, with a professional desire to be pleasant."

Cousin Roy is quick to note that he is not too welcome to either of the Langdons, but he accepts their attitude as quite normal. Besides, he has come to do a good deed. Knowing their interest in Brett Charles, whom they were instrumental in sending to Fisk University, Roy is pleased to report that the Rev. Richardson, pastor of the Negro Church, had asked his support in getting Brett appointed principal of the Negro School, a support he was perfectly willing to give. In fact, at a meeting of the school board the previous night Brett had been given the appointment. "After all, a thing like this is beneficial to the equilibrium of the community," concludes Maxwell.

"But, unfortunately, Brett can't take the job," calmly interposes Alice.

"I don't understand."

ALICE—Why, I couldn't let Brett spend his life teaching school in that grubby little shack.

MAXWELL (*hastily*)—Oh, I know he's outstanding for a Negro.

ALICE—He's outstanding.

MAXWELL (*bridling*)—Cousin Alice, are you trying to say that teaching school isn't a good enough job for this colored boy? What on earth do you expect him to do?

ALICE—He's going to the University of Chicago and work for his doctor's degree.

LANGDON—What?

ALICE—He's going to be a bio-chemist.

LANGDON (*rising with difficulty*)—Great suffering Jehoshaphats! This time you've really done it! Give me a drink.

ALICE—Father, you know you're not supposed to—

LANGDON—Damn it! Give me a drink!

ALICE—Roy, there's some whisky in the cabinet. Sit down, Father.

LANGDON—Just because he can read and write, making a doctor of philosophy out of a nigger! Why wasn't I told before of this monstrous stupidity?

ALICE—Simply because I wanted to put off as long as possible this demonstration you've just given us.

MAXWELL (*handing* LANGDON *a drink*)—Here you are, Senator.

LANGDON—Thank you. (*He drinks. After a moment, when he is more calm.*) Why should I get excited? He's your property. Go on—do what you want with him. The Federal Government's given him a good start. They've made him a first lieutenant. By an Act of Congress he becomes a gentleman. Has it occurred to you that your boy Brett may have changed?

ALICE—I should hope he's changed. He's been away from us for three years.

LANGDON—So he has. Over in Europe killing white people. With legal sanction, he's been driving his bayonet through white flesh. Day after day he's seen white bodies blown apart, white faces shattered. What do you suppose that has done to his black soul? (*There is silence for a moment.*)

MAXWELL (*nervously*)—Well, let's not lift the lid of Pandora's box before we have to. (*Then, more resolutely.*) Alice, there's nobody in this town who supports your advanced ideas more than I do. But why should we deliberately send away one of our educated Negroes? What if *all* our darkies got the notion to go North? *Then* where would we be?

At that moment Howard Merrick walks into the picture, coming from the terrace. "Howard is forty. A large man, handsome in an unconventional fashion, his manner is pleasantly urbane."

Cousin Roy is glad to meet Howard Merrick. He knows him already as a Northerner who is visiting the Langdons; knows, too, that he is a successful novelist. But Cousin Roy is frank to say that he considers Mr. Merrick's last novel as a libel on the whole South—

"You've got a character in there," recalls Maxwell, "a Southern girl who goes North—the way you portray her—why, it's a calculated slur on Southern womanhood."

"Shall I have him horsewhipped, Cousin Roy? Or perhaps you'd prefer a duel. Shall we ask him to name a friend?" Senator Langdon's irritation is mounting.

"Senator, at times your levity tends to be most unpleasant," protests Maxwell.

"I'm a very wealthy man and I learned a long time ago that gives me the privilege of being unpleasant to my relatives. Why should you get your feathers ruffled over this impolite novel? Even Southern authors insult the South these days. It's their most profitable line. They cultivate two favorite myths. Either we're swaggering around with a rose and a sword, or we're rotting in shiftlessness. Both are lies, but what difference does it make?"

Cousin Roy has turned again to Howard. What he would like to know is why, feeling about Southern women as he does, why did Howard ever come South? It wasn't, explains Merrick, his idea. It was Alice who dared him to come. This statement Alice is happy to confirm.

Alice and Howard, it appears, had met in New York at a literary tea. A literary tea, Howard explains, is "an affair at which everybody has to get quite drunk in order to tell an author they like his book."

Alice, not drinking, had told Howard that she did not like his novel. This led to his inviting her to dinner, which naturally led to an argument about the South, and this to Alice's invitation to Howard to go home with her.

LANGDON (*chuckling to* HOWARD)—You've been here two weeks. Have you changed your opinion of the South? Or are you still helping Grant take Richmond?

HOWARD—I think your daughter Alice is the loveliest woman I've ever known.

ALICE—He's nice, isn't he? (*To* HOWARD.) Now answer the gentleman's question, Howard. Have you changed your opinion of the South?

HOWARD (*with a private smile*)—I would say so, wouldn't you?

ALICE (*to* MAXWELL *and* LANGDON)—Last night this skeptical visitor from the North—this arch critic of the South, who makes fun of our clichés—surrendered completely. And you know what finally got him? Our oldest cliché of all. Moonlight and magnolias.

HOWARD (*to* MAXWELL, *pleasantly*)—Do you think that will satisfy your Aunt Carrie and Cousin Ferdinand?

MAXWELL—Well—I will grant that you are a man with an open mind. You see, it's just that we down here are proud of our South. We believe in it. . . . Of course we have problems—I don't have to tell you what some of them are—but we are learning to handle them, and I must say, quite successfully.

LANGDON—Cousin Roy is running for Congress next year. We're getting his morning work-out.

MAXWELL—The Senator likes his little joke. But I *am* going to run for Congress. Because I am deeply concerned. Now you take this problem of our colored people— They aren't what they used to be—with all these war factories springing up in the most unlikely places—of course it's good for business—but after all, you know it's practically impossible any more to get decent servants. Aunt Carrie has had four cooks in the last month. She rebukes them and they up and quit. (*Back to* HOWARD.) And the war has given us a very special cross to bear. So many of our white young men have been drafted. For example, in our county here, for the first time there is an actual majority of blacks. You can see the implications of that, can't you?

HOWARD (*kindly*)—Indeed I can.

Cousin Roy is leaving. As Alice goes to the door with him Senator Langdon turns to Howard—

"Drivelin' idiot!" he says, with a head toss in the departing Maxwell's direction. "Yes, we have problems—but they'll never be solved by Cousin Roy—nor by my daughter Alice. We need strength and we're not strong any more. I see you're giving me one of those skeptical Yankee looks. You're thinking this old fossil is a Southern Aristocrat, or perhaps a Bourbon. Well, I am. History seems to be against me. But until the day I die, I'll fight for the rights and privileges of the superior person."

Alice is back, and is so noticeably solicitous as to the Senator's comfort that she excites his suspicion. She has tried to signal Howard that this is obviously the time for him to speak, but with no success. Suddenly she is summoned—

"Alice, come out from behind my back."

"Yes, Father."

"You contemplate marrying this young man?"

"That's the general idea, Father."

"I knew it. It was in your eyes this morning—it was in the way you walked . . . Merrick, come here. (HOWARD *obeys.*) I don't know you. I don't know who your father is, nor your mother. For all I know you may come from a long line of horse-thieves. But that sort of thing doesn't seem to matter any more. Are you marryin' my daughter for her money?"

"Oh, I have no prejudice against money."

"Those books you write—do you get paid for them?"

"When a character in one of my novels says 'No,' that one word is worth two dollars," reports Howard.

There are other things the Senator would know. What are Howard's politics? He is a Democrat. That's good. Has he ever been married before? Yes, he has. To a surprised Alice, Howard is quick to explain—

"It's a long time ago. I'd almost forgotten. I was twenty-two and she was younger. After a while she got tired of my prose and ran off with a very bad poet."

"You sound awfully callous about it," observes Alice.

"You would be, too," Howard assures her, "if you read any of his poems."

There are a few other things the Senator would know—Will Howard be taking Alice to live in the North? No. They'll probably live six months in New York, six months in the South. Has Howard ever been in jail?—

"Father," interrupts Alice, "you've played Grand Inquisitor long enough. Say something nice to Howard. Tell him what a lucky man he is to get me."

"Yes, I think he is," Senator Langdon admits, judiciously. He is looking at Alice as he adds: "Well, it's the *end* of the Langdons. The name will stay for a few years in the history books, and then slowly disappear as they're revised. It's the end of this house, too. Langdons have lived here for a hundred and three years. (*He takes a large gold watch and chain from the pocket of his waistcoat.*) Here, I want you to have this. It's a Jurgensen stem-winder. You've never seen one, have you? Well, it belonged to my father, the gentleman in that portrait. (*Indicates portrait above the fireplace.*) The gold chain you see there is the same you have in your hand. The chain and the watch were given my father by his uncle, Alexander Stevens, vice-president of the Confederate States. If you open the back, you will see an inscription: 'Honor Above All.' To you, of course, such phrases are mere rhetoric, but to us—in the old days—a word like *honor* really meant something. Don't judge us too harshly, young Yankee. Don't judge us by our Cousin Roys, or by those moss-ridden shell-backs who sit in Congress these days. They're only chattering shadows of a once noble tradition. There was once a South that had virtue and valor. When you look at this watch, perhaps you will be able to think of us kindly."

"Thank you, Senator, but I'm not sure I should accept it." Howard is visibly impressed.

"Take it. Take it. I have no son, so I give it to you."

"Dear Father." Alice has risen to kiss the Senator on the cheek.

"My treasure, did I rise to the occasion properly?"

"Darling, it's the greatest speech you've made in years, and it's a crime it won't be in the Congressional Record."

Now there is some commotion at the front door. A moment later Genevra has burst into the room in a pleasant state of emotional excitement. "Brett's here," she all but shouts. "He's here! He's home! I told him to come in the front door. Here he is. Doesn't he look wonderful? Lieutenant Brett Charles!"

Brett and Bella stand hesitantly in the hallway. "Brett is a good-looking Negro of twenty-six. He is in uniform. His manner is polite, poised; he seems mature for his years." Alice is the first to rise to the situation.

"Welcome home, Lieutenant. Brett, we are all glad to see you."

"Thank you, Miss Alice." He turns to the Senator. "Good day, Senator."

"Well, boy, how was it?"

"In one sentence, sir?" Brett is laughing.

"He doesn't seem wounded at all," announces Genevra, excitedly. "And he says his leg is practically as good as new!"

Bella has stepped in from the hallway, and is still thirstily drinking in the sight of her son. "Six battles and seventeen pieces of shrapnel in his leg and he was still whole!" she announces proudly. "The good Lord never let him out of His sight."

"That's right, Mama. And together the Lord and I dug some mighty fine foxholes."

Howard Merrick is introduced. As he shakes hands with the Lieutenant the Senator is quick to explain that Mr. Merrick is from the North. Howard is impressed by Brett's four decorations. He's wearing them, the Lieutenant explains, for Mama—

"Some of the boys on the train started kidding me. They said with that much salad I should have French dressing."

"Now don't start being modest, Brett," protests Alice. "Those medals are not only for your mother. They're for all of us. We're terribly proud of you."

Alice insists that the Lieutenant shall sit down, which he does a little diffidently. She finds him thinner—and older; older than three years would normally have added to his age. She thanks and praises him for his letters and is greatly appreciative, too, of the kindnesses the English family he had met in London extended to him.

"The packages were magnificent, Miss Alice," reports Brett. "They made a big hit with my men. Of course, some of my men couldn't understand how come I had a white friend who would send things like that."

Genevra would have Brett tell just how terrible his experiences in Italy were, but Alice and the Senator are not sympathetic listeners.

"Brett . . . How did you feel when you killed a man," asks the Senator.

There is a moment's silence. "Sir," answers the Lieutenant, "the only feeling I had when I killed a man was that I had saved my own life . . . which I had. The only men I killed were men who were out to kill me."

"Lieutenant, may I ask a question?" asks Howard. "Did you like being in the Army?"

"That's a tough one to answer, sir."

"Go on, boy! Don't be afraid to speak up. They didn't treat you any too well, did they?" The Senator is curiously eager.

"It's very difficult to be a Negro in the Army," answers Brett, carefully; "even a Negro officer. And yet in the Army I was able to see things—do things. The Army gave me privileges I never had before."

Genevra doesn't think conversations should be allowed to grow so serious, when there's a celebration going on. Doesn't anyone realize that Brett is a hero? A hero who was met at the station by a delegation?

It seems the delegation was mostly composed of the Rev. Richardson and a Dr. Wayne, who had taken care of Bella when she was sick. Brett's friends, however, are planning to give him a big luncheon in the churchyard, and Bella had grabbed him away until twelve o'clock.

"Brett, son, I reckon you'll have to make a speech after they've ate their belly full. You better get in mind what you're going to say to them."

"I'd sure enough like to hear that speech," announces Genevra, with enthusiasm. Then she turns to her father: "Do you realize he's the first Distinguished Service Cross we have in this town?"

"Of course I realize it. Stop prattling." The Senator has had about as much as he can stand.

Bella and Alice have gone to show Brett how they have fixed up his room, with new curtains and all.

As the Senator starts toward the terrace he has a word of caution for Howard—

"Mr. Merrick, in this house, to use a modern phrase which I detest, 'anything goes.' We do as we please. But in the South, one doesn't usually shake hands with a Negro. As long as you're going to be with us, I mention it as a useful point of etiquette."

"Old fogey!" Genevra has waited until her father disappears. "I 'specially noticed you shook hands with Brett, and I liked you for it."

"Your father sometimes is charmingly naive. Apparently he really thinks I didn't know that one doesn't shake hands with Negroes—in the South. Or maybe he doesn't realize that I shake hands with whom I like."

"And you like Brett?"

"He's a ray of hope. With a person like Brett, it's possible to *connect.*"

"You're talking just like a writer," Genevra warns him. "I love it, but what does it mean?"

"Just this. I don't like it when I walk down the street and a Negro steps timorously into the gutter to let me pass. I'm uncomfortable when a Negro snatches off his hat and gives the white man the obsequious smile. I'd like to be able to say: 'Look, I don't want these deferences, these symbols of servility. It's not my fault I'm a white man.' (*He shrugs.*) But down here there's no way of communicating—connecting! You're caught in the tradition. If I'm to stay here it helps to know that there are people like Brett. That's what I mean."

GENEVRA—It all seems so strange and serious now, seeing him in that uniform. When we were children—well, Brett and I always played together.

HOWARD—Was that allowed?

GENEVRA—Father considered none of the white children around here good enough to play with me. So—Brett was my best friend.

HOWARD—I was under the impression that Alice was his best friend.

GENEVRA (*with a quick look*)—Is that what Alice told you? . . . It's true that every day she gave him his lessons, but then she was practically grown up. She's ten years older than I am.

HOWARD—How old are you?

GENEVRA—I'm— Say, do you think I'm going to betray my sister? If Alice has told you she's barely old enough to vote, I'll swear it's the truth and I'm not a day over thirteen . . . Do you want to hear more about Brett? He taught me to catch fish—perch—bass—eels. I'll bet you can't catch an eel. And he taught me not to be afraid of snakes. I could still kill a copperhead if I had to. Come to think of it, the only useful things I ever learned were from Brett.

HOWARD—Why were you the only one who went down to the station to meet Brett?

GENEVRA—Because I felt like it, I guess . . . We used to play theatre, too. I was in one of the rooms over the stable. I was going to be a great tragic actress—oh, much greater than Bernhardt. Suddenly, one day we discovered *Shakespeare.* I was about twelve and Brett was fourteen. When it came to playing Desdemona, I had a wonderful idea. Here was a really good part for Brett—he could play Othello! It worked marvelously. We were so pleased we gave ourselves a long run—four days. Until, one afternoon, just as Brett was very realistically choking me, who should walk in but Alice. She was furious!

HOWARD—Why?

GENEVRA—Can't you guess? Alice hustled me off to the house, sat me down and gave me the facts of Southern life. I cried and shrieked, but Alice was very firm. It was all right when I was a little girl to like Brett. But now I was growing up—I was twelve years old—and I would have to stop liking Brett; that's what Alice said. How can you suddenly not like somebody who's been your best friend? . . . But after that, Brett and I never played together again.

HOWARD (*from the heart*)—Nevvy, you're going to make an adorable sister-in-law.

Genevra was hardly expecting that. The news that Howard has decided to "take out the papers" and marry Alice is enough to knock a young sister practically speechless, but she recovers happily. Howard is certainly taking an awful chance, but that's up to him. Alice is a wonderful girl, Genevra admits, but she is awfully darn sure of herself. "Alice likes to make up the rules," reports Genevra. "And there always comes a time— Well, if you don't play her way, you just don't play. . . . But you know something? I think maybe *you* can handle her. . . ."

The others have gone when Brett comes to the living room looking for Miss Alice. Honey, the maid, in to straighten up the room, thinks this a perfect time to better her acquaintance with the returned hero. Honey always has admired men with broad shoulders. But Brett isn't interested. He is planning to spend his first night at home getting himself a little rest. He is in no mood to "pay Honey some mind," as she suggests—"Honey, you're a nice girl; now act that way," advises Brett. "Be a little more proud of yourself."

"You mean act uppity like you, and play Uncle Tom for the white folks?"

Brett has grabbed Honey by the wrist. "Listen, you! I'm no Uncle Tom! Don't you ever say so again!"

"Brett, honey, you're hurting me," wails Honey. "But I like it." She is pressing herself close to him.

Honey's campaign might have continued if Bella had not arrived to break it up. Honey is smartly ordered out of the room, and Bella turns to her son. She earnestly hopes that he is not going to raise trouble—

BELLA—You're a good boy. But you act different. Them white folks couldn't see it . . . What'd they do to you, Brett, boy? Why you act so careful? You're like a pan of water waitin' to boil.

BRETT (*after a moment*)—You heard Miss Alice talk about that English family. Well, that English family treated me fine. . . . But in that same English town three of my men got beat up by white American soldiers. You know why? They dared to go dancing with English girls.

BELLA—You shouldn't of let your men go dancing with English girls.

BRETT (*rising*)—I'd have got beat up myself, except that I was an officer.

BELLA (*startled*)—You danced with a white girl?

BRETT—The English like us, Mama. We don't criticize their food or their little cottages, because over here most of us haven't had very much ourselves. And on Sunday we're happy to go to church and sing in the choir, and afterwards tell the minister what a fine sermon he preached. Somebody invites us home for dinner, and we're not afraid to show how we appreciate it. They like us, and so they ask us to dance with them. They don't seem to mind that our skins are dark . . . Things are changing, Mama.

BELLA—Careful, son.

BRETT—I tell you things are changing. You saw how the Senator looked when Mr. Merrick shook hands with me . . . Well, one of my best friends in the Army was a white officer. In a hotel in Naples we slept in the same bed together. How would the Senator like to know that?

BELLA (*alarmed*)—Hush that talk. When you think like that, the earth has split wide open, and you're standin' on the edge looking down.

BRETT—Maybe down, maybe up. Maybe way high up.

BELLA—Turn back, son. If you believe in the Good Lord, turn back.

BRETT (*shaking his head*)—Too late now.

BELLA—God likes us humble.

BRETT—No! No more humbleness.

BELLA (*frightened*)—Sh—!

BRETT (*more quietly*)—We've seen a little bit of fairness,

Mama. And we'll make it so white and black can live together, fairness all around.

Genevra has come down the stairs. She is carrying a rag doll by its ankle. It is an old rag doll, with a stitched-up face, but those were Brett's stitches and she thought he'd be interested in remembering. Brett remembers all right. "Her name was Sarah Ann and you snagged her on the iron fence out front," Brett recalls.

Sarah Ann reminds Genevra of a lot of things, but Brett is not eager to talk of them, even after Bella has left. His strained politeness, his "Miss Nevvy," and all, irritate Genevra—

"Stop being like that," she snaps impatiently. "Don't you realize that things are different now? I'm grown up. So are you."

"Yes, Miss Nevvy."

"Do you have to call me 'Miss Nevvy'—when we're alone like this?" Brett does not answer. "All right, Brett, you win. You don't think any white person can be your friend, except maybe Alice. My mistake."

She has started to go and is almost to the hall when she hears him say: " 'Soft you; a word or two before you go.' " She has turned and come toward him with a smile of pleasure as he continues:

" 'When you shall these unlucky deeds relate,
Speak of me as I am; nothing extenuate,
Nor set down aught in malice; then must you speak
Of one that loved not wisely but too well . . .' "

It takes a moment for Genevra to recall the answer. When she does she falls into Brett's mood and answers him in kind—

" 'Upon my knees, what doth your speech import?
I understand a fury in your words,
But not the words.' "

" 'Why, what art thou?' "

" 'Your wife, my lord; your true and loyal wife.' "

They are laughing now, and remembering other experiences, including the time Nevvy played Lady Macbeth and put such childish force into the "Out, damned spot!" speech. Nevvy was engaged to be married then. But she never married. "Hank (her fiancé) went to the dogs magnificently," she reports, with a smile. "For a boy who was going to inherit a soft-drink fortune he was sure fond of hard liquor."

That reminds Genevra of something else—of the time when she and Brett were told that they could never play together again. How did he feel then?

"Well, I didn't like it much when Mama switched me," Brett remembers. And shortly adds: "She said it was for my own protection. She said, 'You got to live in a white man's world.' And she switched me."

Genevra resents the unfairness of that switching. "Brett, what makes it so that people have to do such mean things? Even people like Bella—and Alice—sometimes. People down here—people everywhere, I guess—talk about the brotherhood of man, but when it comes right down to it, they don't act like brothers at all. (*Frowning.*) Am I saying anything, or am I just being high-flown and elegant? . . . But anyway, you and I don't have to act like strangers. Of course, we can't go swimming together as if we were still kids, but at least we don't have to blush and be embarrassed.—Isn't that right?"

"Yes, Miss Nevvy."

"That's just what I'm talking about." Genevra is plainly impatient.

"I'm sorry, Miss Nevvy."

"Yes, of course. I'm a Southern lady and you're a— But why? Why can't we talk without this damn formality? Why? I won't believe it's right! I won't!"

"Careful, Nevvy."

"Well, is it right?"

"No." Brett's answer is slow, but definite.

"Well, then—"

Alice has come down the stairs to tell Brett of her wonderful news. She has arranged a scholarship for him at the University of Chicago. Now he will be able to work for his doctor's degree. The application is all ready for him to sign. Both the Senator and Howard Merrick are in from the terrace to witness the ceremony. But Brett can't sign. He quite frankly doesn't want a scholarship anywhere. He just wants to stay in the South and be the principal of the Negro school—

"Sounds innocent enough; but I can see through you," snaps a surprised Senator Langdon. "Get hold of our colored folk around here and make them dissatisfied—put ideas in their heads—stir up trouble!"

"No, sir; no trouble. But I will put ideas in their heads, I hope."

LANGDON (*to* ALICE)—What did I tell you? Gone off to war and comes back with a lot of foreign theories. Send me my lunch on a tray. I'm going to bed! If he told you the truth, you'd probably find out that over there he slept with white women. (*He storms out.*)

ALICE—Brett, this was very embarrassing for all of us. I apologize for my father.

BRETT—I had to speak out, Miss Alice.

ALICE—Of course. You and I can always be honest to each other . . . Mr. Maxwell was here this morning, and I told him under no circumstances would you become principal.

BRETT—You see, I wrote Rev. Richardson.

ALICE—Yes, I understand now. But, Brett? What is the best way to help the colored people? Isn't it to become an exceptional person—somebody we can all point to with pride?

BRETT—That's one way, Miss Alice.

ALICE—You used to think it was the only way.

BRETT—But here in the South is where the most work has to be done.

HOWARD—Lieutenant, I can't understand why in God's name any Negro would stay here— Why they don't *all* just pick up and go North.

BRETT—This is my home! And people love their homes, even when things are tough. My Grandma Celia lives in a shack with a dirt floor. She can't read or write, and she's suffered a great deal. But this is her country too, and she loves it.

ALICE—But you can't help your Grandma Celia by being—

BRETT—Coming back here on the train after three years I kept looking at things so hard my eyes began to hurt. The first cotton field, I almost cried. Sometimes I even forgot I was riding on a Jim Crow car.

ALICE—That's just it. You won't have to suffer Jim Crow cars. You can go North. You can be so great, so famous, that you can—Brett, I can't let you be an obscure little schoolmaster in a Negro community.

BRETT—That's what I want to do.

ALICE—But why, Brett? *Why?*

BRETT—You know what my main job in the Army was? It was to make my men believe they were fighting for a better world for themselves—as well as for you, Miss Alice . . . A lot of my men thought I was clean crazy. Some of them even hated me. They called me a white man's nigger. They called me a Communist . . . It's true that some of the Negroes aren't very good soldiers. How can they be? They're illiterate, a lot of them . . . But with my men, I was lucky. When it came right down to it, they all turned out to be good fighters. Because I was able to persuade them that this was their big chance to prove themselves. . . .

ALICE—Yes, of course, Brett, I know, I know. But you're no longer in the Army. . . .

BRETT—All through this war we've been living on promises—we've had to fight on faith. Now the promises have to be made good, even if we have to begin at the beginning. Even if we have to teach the alphabet.

ALICE—And it will be the alphabet—and two times two—things that anyone can teach. Brett, you're a talented man. You owe it to yourself and—well, I'll be quite selfish about it—you owe it to me, too.

BRETT—I owe you a great deal, Miss Alice. But I have to pay that debt in my own fashion. I'm staying in the South, Miss Alice. If I can't have the school—then I'll pick cotton if I have to. And I'll teach at night.

Genevra is the only one who agrees with Brett. She thinks it is time people were allowed to do what they want to do, instead of always doing what people tell them to do.

Finally Alice goes to the phone and calls Cousin Roy Maxwell to tell him that Brett will take the job of school principal. His salary from the state will be five hundred dollars a year, but the Langdons will probably do something about that. About the best thing anyone can do right now, Brett suggests, will be to help them get a new schoolhouse. . . .

Bella has arrived, nervously pulling on a pair of gloves for her trip to the luncheon with Brett. They are gloves she hasn't worn since the family left Washington. She is very happy to hear of the school offer. Now she knows her son has come home to stay.

"The Lord's treated me good this day," Bella exclaims, happily. "My son's come home safe, and we'll make him *stay* home safe. You and I, Miss Alice—we'll take good care of him."

"Have a good time at the luncheon—both of you. Brett, tell

them about the new schoolhouse. Make it good. And whatever you promise we'll try to get it."

After the others have left, and Bella and Brett are starting out, Bella spies the rag doll. Now, she decides, she can throw the trashy thing away. Always before there would be Miss Nevvy's protest—"No, no, I got to show it to Brett—"

Brett takes Sarah Ann from his mother. "She saved it for me. Maybe I want to keep it," he says.

"Boy, what you saying?"

"I didn't say anything."

"Why you look like that? What you thinking?"

"A man can't help what he thinks."

"No! No! Don't you dare! Don't you ever dare think about things like that! You listen to me. And don't ever forget it! Black's black and white's white. . . ."

Bella has hurled the doll into the waste basket. Brett watches her without a word. She makes a desperate effort to calm her emotions. "Come on, son," she mumbles. "Now we'll go to the churchyard."

Brett takes a step toward the waste basket, then turns and follows her out.

The curtain falls.

ACT II

On a hot afternoon, a week later, Senator Langdon is expressing another of his moods. He resents the fact that although he is perspiring freely, his feet are like ice. He resents having to take the capsule and water that Bella has brought for him. Nor does he think much of Cousin Roy's belated wedding present for Alice. In fact, the whole wedding arrangement is not as the Senator would have had it—

" 'I promise to love, honor and obey'—and life goes on exactly as before," he laments; "except that he will probably move into her bedroom. No splendor any more. The vivid colors have all gone. . . ."

When the Senator and his Sophia were married they had a private car, filled with flowers, and three musicians to play Miss Sophia's favorite melodies all the way to New Orleans.

"That's the way things should be done," agrees Bella.

Genevra has come through the front hall. Her greeting for her father, to his distress, is both short and curt. When the Senator has gone back to the garden Genevra would ring for Honey and dismiss Bella. But Bella has something for Miss

Nevvy. It is a lipstick she had found. It is Bella's advice that Miss Genevra had better be less careless with her things. They get themselves in strange places.

A moment later Howard Merrick has appeared with a copy of the local newspaper, *The Sentinel.* Howard depends on *The Sentinel* for all the town news and gossip, but frequently the editorials ("medieval propaganda," he calls them) both puzzle and alarm him. This issue has one headed "Our Negro Veterans"—

"I can't quite make out their point of view," admits Howard, handing the paper to Genevra to read. "They seem to want to be fair, but every sentence is a threat. 'We love our Negro veterans and they, of course, love us. But just because they've had the privilege of wearing a uniform, they need not think we will dine and wine them as if they were liberated Italian peasants and French radicals. This is America, our prejudices are sacred, and we're proud of them.' "

"Idiots! That's just the sort of drivel they always write," says Genevra.

"Is it drivel? Perhaps. It's a perfect reflex action to the speech of Brett's. Maybe they're worried too, because the Negro children traipse after Brett on the street as if he were the Pied Piper. I'll bet your father doesn't think it's drivel. Where is he?"

"Out in the garden. You know, Howard, it's going to be a terrific strain on Father, having to give you his blessing tomorrow."

"Oh, I don't know. I think he considers me repulsive but awfully likeable."

"I'm sure he's already sorry he gave you that watch of Grandpa's."

"So am I. I mislaid the damn thing and I can't find it."

Brett has come in answer to Genevra's summons. To him she is glad to report that she has been able to get him a lower berth, round trip, for his trip to the Atlanta Conference. Everybody had thought the ticket was for her. Has he asked Miss Alice's permission to go?

Brett doesn't like that word permission. He's sure Alice would want him to go. But he is plainly nervous about the ticket—

"Are you afraid they won't let you on the Pullman or something?" asks Genevra.

"Oh, no, there won't be any trouble. I'm still in uniform."

Still there is something wrong. Genevra can see that. "We

had so much fun last night," she reminds him. "Now you're getting moody and sentimental again. That's silly."

"I'm sorry, Miss Nevvy."

GENEVRA—Oh, my God, you *are* worried. Whenever that "Miss Nevvy" starts coming out— Look, Brett, I know we did something very daring and shocking, but it was hot as hinges, and it was a beautiful night, so we went for a walk down by the river. Now, that's terrible, isn't it? (*Suddenly.*) You don't really think it was wrong, do you?

BRETT—No.

GENEVRA—Well, all right then. I was even going to ask you if we could go again tonight. Maybe take some sandwiches and go out in the old rowboat.

BRETT (*sharply*)—NO! No, Nevvy! No!

GENEVRA (*startled*)—Why, Brett—!

BRETT—You mustn't do this! You don't know what you're doing!

GENEVRA (*after a moment*)—That car that passed us last night. You're afraid they saw us.

BRETT (*grimly*)—They saw us. I hope they didn't recognize us.

GENEVRA—We can be more careful—much more careful. The car was going too fast. They couldn't have seen us . . . (*Impatiently.*) It just doesn't make sense, does it? When we were children we played together right out on the front lawn.

BRETT (*with great deliberation*)—Nevvy, you've got to forget that I ever called you anything but Miss Nevvy . . . No, we can't even be friends. And this time don't ask me why.

GENEVRA—All right. Why?

BRETT—No! No! It can't be evaded by being impudent or daring. I'll try to tell you. Yesterday afternoon in the post-office, when I asked to buy stamps, old man John Weylin threatened me. I forgot to say, "Mr. Weylin, please, sir" . . . In Italy I was an American officer. Here I'm a nigger. I had forgotten some of the things that means . . .

GENEVRA (*bewildered*)—But why do I have to care about old Mr. Weylin, or Italy, or anything else? I don't know what you're talking about.

BRETT—Don't you? Couldn't it possibly enter your head? No, it couldn't. (*Bitterly.*) Damn it, Nevvy! Use your eyes! Use your heart!

GENEVRA (*after a moment, softly, gently*)—Oh, no, Brett.

Brett (*wretchedly*)—Now maybe you'll stop piping on about rowboats and sandwiches!

Genevra—I didn't think—I didn't realize—

Brett—I've done just what they all expect us to do. I've come back and laid my eyes on a white woman.

Genevra—Brett, I'm quite helpless. There's nothing I can say, is there?

Brett—Now maybe you'll know how to treat me.

Genevra—Well, I don't know . . . You talk as if you expected me to be horrified or revolted. As if suddenly you were a stranger—somebody to be feared . . . Well, I don't think I'm horrified. Maybe I should be, according—according to everybody. But I'm not. That doesn't help much, does it?

Brett—You're being kind to me.

Genevra—Please believe me, Brett. I'm not being kind. I never thought about such a thing before, but you're the nicest person who's ever said to me, "I love you."

Brett—I didn't say it. But I will. God help me, I'll say it, and then I'll never say it again, not even to myself . . . Nevvy, I've loved you for as long as I can remember. I'll go on loving you for quite a while.

Genevra (*rising*)—Brett . . . I'm not sorry you said it. I'll always remember. (*After a moment.*) Look, Brett— There is one little thing I can do. I'll go away. When you come back from Atlanta, I'll be gone.

Alice comes down the stairs. She is wearing her wedding dress and is seeking the approval of Howard. The groom should not, she knows, have a peek at the gown until the wedding, but here it is. Howard thinks it is beautiful, even without orange blossoms. He greatly approves the model, too.

Alice would also have her sister's approval. "Nevvy, you've got to say something. You've got to tell me you like it or I'll be broken-hearted."

"It's beautiful, Alice. You look more beautiful than I've ever seen you. You're terribly happy, aren't you?"

"Happy? I'm delirious. And you'll be just as happy one day. And you probably won't have to wait as long as I did. Somebody will come along and fall in love with you, and then—"

"Please. Please don't say that," pleads Genevra, tremulously.

"What's the matter, dear?"

"Just don't say that! Just don't say that!" With a stifled sob Genevra turns and runs up the stairs.

"I know people are supposed to cry at weddings, but Nevvy is starting a day ahead of time. (*Suddenly to* BRETT.) There's nothing really wrong with her, is there?"

"It's nothing, Miss Alice. It's just that— Well, Miss Nevvy was telling me how lonesome she's going to be without you."

Brett would change the subject, but Miss Alice is not ready to listen until she tells him the good news about the colored school house. It is, Mr. Maxwell has assured her, "practically in the bag." Brett is glad to hear that. Even if building priorities hold them up, he says, they can have blueprints and maybe a corner-stone-laying ceremony. But there is also something else. It is a conference in Atlanta—

"Black and white folk meeting together," pictures Brett. "Discussing everything. Better school houses; more of them. Abolishing the poll-tax. Jobs for soldiers coming home. Miss Alice, I think I'd like to go to that conference!"

"Naturally I believe in all those things, Brett," slowly answers Alice. "You know that. But I can't believe in the *people* who go to a conference like that. A lot of them are Communists."

"I'm not a Communist. You know that."

"Of course not. But what would the people in this town think? And I mean especially the colored people. Why not face it? Half of them would distrust you if you went off to a black and white get together like that."

In the garden Senator Langdon ("mighty achey today," Bella reports) is calling for Alice. As Howard is partly responsible for having shown the Senator the *Sentinel* editorial, Alice insists he shall go with her to help pacify the old gentleman. As they go, Alice turns to Brett. She knows he is terribly disappointed about the Atlanta Conference, but she is still sure that her judgment is best.

As soon as they are alone Bella would know what all the talk is about. Brett tells her. Alice doesn't want him to go to Atlanta, but he's going just the same. This time he is willing to disobey even Miss Alice.

"All right! You go to Atlanta! You go anywhere! You go *North!* And don't come back!" storms Bella.

"Mama!"

BELLA—Don't you come back! You get out of this town! (*With great bitterness.*) You talk about helping your people! Then doing something like this. I raised you to be a God-fearing man, free from sin! First chance you get, you transgress God's holy law!

BRETT—Mama, listen to me! I haven't done anything wrong!

BELLA—Where were you last night? Where were you? . . . Can't think of any fine words for that, can you? . . . I found her lipstick in your coat pocket . . . You were out with a white girl . . . Answer me. You were out with a white girl.

BRETT—All right. What if I was? (BELLA *suddenly slaps* BRETT *across the face, hard.* BRETT *stands motionless.*)

BELLA—You want to hang from a tree by your neck? (*There's a long silence. When* BELLA *again speaks, it's almost apologetically.*) Boy, I warned you. The day you came back, I warned you.

BRETT (*quietly*)—Nothing happened, Mama. It didn't even start to happen. And now it's over. It's over and done with.

BELLA—No. If you're in this house, if you're in this town, it ain't over. Don't you think I know what hot blood and foolishness are? . . . You went out with a white girl, and that's written on the book of what is and what ain't. It's there for somebody to ferret out. And when that happens— (*With a sob.*) Better you died in one of them foxholes.

Overcome by her emotion, Bella runs from the room. Brett, a little bewildered, sinks into the chair nearest him. It's the Senator's chair and the Senator has just come in from the garden, still angry. Not only would he order Brett out of the chair, but he also would have him go and take off his uniform. The Government may permit him to wear it for thirty days, but the Senator won't. Alice is quick to countermand the order as soon as the Senator leaves them.

Howard is responsible for this flare-up, says Alice. He never should have shown the Senator that stupid editorial. But Howard has a defense. The cause of the Senator's anger stems from his insistence that the editorial wasn't strong enough. Much too tolerant. Howard loves the Senator, but he can't help baiting him now and then because he (Howard) is curious about the old gentleman's reactions. "Your father is a wonderful relic," he tells Alice, and immediately regrets the speech. "Darling, I'm sorry. Maybe it's just the heat," he says. "Or maybe it's the South."

"What?" Alice's resentment is immediate and flaring.

"Oh, I don't know." Howard would be conciliatory. "On top the flower is quite beautiful, full of grace and very delicate. But

Photo by Alfredo Valente.

"DEEP ARE THE ROOTS"

Brett—This afternoon neither you nor I were thinking of getting married. It never entered our heads. If it wasn't right then—it's still not right. No, Nevvy, no! We would have to cut ourselves off. We'd be on an island. We could never live in the world as it is.

(*Barbara Bel Geddes, Gordon Heath*)

underneath are the roots, and occasionally you glimpse them, twisted and crossed as if choking each other."

Alice is still unhappy, but Howard convinces her with a kiss that he has not the slightest desire to recant—not with all those wedding presents in the East Room. It is just as well, he agrees, that they could not put the horse that Cousin Ferdinand has given them in the East Room, too. Howard had visited the horse in the stables and frankly he (the horse) had scared hell out of him.

Senator Langdon, joining them, is still perturbed about his inability to rest properly. When he discovers that Howard is not wearing the gift watch he is still more perturbed. But when Howard is forced to admit that he has evidently mislaid the timepiece the Senator is unexpectedly quite understanding. After all, it was only a trivial keepsake.

"But things like that just don't get lost!" insists Alice . . .

Cousin Roy Maxwell has come to confirm his congratulations. So long as Howard has won Alice, it must be because he deserves her. But Cousin Roy also has come to speak about a threatening crisis of which Brett is the center. The Senator might as well hear this too. It's all over town.

"It's not the first thing that has occurred since he's come back," warns Cousin Roy. "It's an unhappy chain of events—starting right with that speech he made. Telling our good-hearted darkies that segregation is *morally wrong* and that it won't always exist. Why, I'm told—"

"I've heard all those stories before, Roy," protests Alice, good-humoredly. "And I know Brett does not act like your Reverend Richardson, who's always bowing and scraping. But I can't see that he's done any harm."

But Alice doesn't know what happened yesterday afternoon. Brett had walked right up to the front door of the Public Library, proud as Punch. Any number of people had seen him. More than that, Cousin Roy reports, Brett had also walked right up to the desk and threatened Miss Chatham, the librarian—

"They say he demanded to have a book," continues Cousin Roy. "Poor Miss Chatham was terrified. But with admirable self-control she asked him if he had a note from you or the Senator. Miss Chatham was sure there was a gun bulging in his pocket—"

Such a charge, Alice insists, is simply ridiculous. Brett has no gun—

"Anyway," Cousin Roy continues, "they say he had this Luger

in his pocket. They say he wouldn't have gotten the book otherwise. Miss Chatham was trembling so she could hardly walk to the shelves. She couldn't say the library didn't have the book, because he followed right behind her. She had to give it to him. They say she felt her life was at stake."

Still Alice is not convinced. Miss Chatham, as everybody knows, "is a silly neurotic woman"—

"It's true she's poor, but she comes from one of our best families," snaps Roy. "And it's not absurd. They say people will be afraid to use the library."

Now Howard Merrick is impelled to take a hand. Who is this mythological "they" Roy talks about? "You introduce every statement with 'they say.' I want to know who is 'they.'"

"Well, everybody," ventures Maxwell, a little feebly.

In that case, Howard declares, everybody is a liar. Including Cousin Roy—

"Senator, do you permit this in your house?" Cousin Roy is bristling.

"Mr. Merrick is not always aware of our Southern amenities," answers Senator Langdon, wearily. "Like the many carpet-baggers who've preceded him, he's fond of moralizing."

HOWARD—Senator Langdon, I was at the library myself yesterday afternoon. (*To* ALICE.) Your library is the only place I can find the *New York Times*. I was there when Brett came in. I saw exactly what happened.

ALICE—But why didn't you tell me immediately?

HOWARD—There was no reason to tell you, because nothing happened; absolutely nothing. Surely you don't believe this concoction Roy's been telling?

ALICE (*slowly*)—Did Brett enter through the front door?

HOWARD—Yes, he did. But he was extremely polite to Miss Chatham. He very courteously asked her for a copy of the new biography of Justice Holmes. Miss Chatham may have been annoyed, but I certainly couldn't see that she was agitated.

ALICE—Did he follow her to the shelves?

HOWARD—He *accompanied* her to the shelves, which was thoughtful of him, because Miss Chatham would not have been able to reach the book without the ladder.

ALICE—Was there anyone else in the library at the time?

HOWARD—As I recall, there was only one other person—an elderly woman. (*Suddenly.*) Of course! That's how the whole thing started. The moment Brett left, this woman went over to

Miss Chatham's desk, they put their heads together and began whispering, and now the whole town's in an uproar and Miss Chatham decides to have a nervous collapse!

To Alice, Brett admits his visit to the library; admits that he did go through the front door. There is no written law or regulation against that. Brett made sure of that before he tried it.

But why can't Brett do as he has always done before—ever since he was twelve—come to her for a note to Miss Chatham whenever he wants a book?

"But I'm not a child, Miss Alice. I'm principal of a public school."

"Perhaps you're right," sighs Alice. "I don't know. I don't really give a damn about the library, or Miss Chatham, or what anybody thinks. I do know, however, it's dangerous for you and embarrassing for me. Brett, whether you're right or wrong, the next time you want a book at the library, just as a favor to me . . . will you ask for a note?"

But Brett doesn't promise.

Now Senator Langdon takes a hand. He asks Brett to send Honey to him. While they are waiting, Genevra comes down the stairs. Her eyes meet Brett's as he passes her. Immediately she feels the strain of the situation and demands to know the cause. No one is prepared to tell her, but she soon learns.

It is Senator Langdon's conviction that Howard did not lose the watch he had been given. It was stolen! And the Senator believes that Brett took it.

Genevra is quick to resent such a charge. She resents her father's even saying such a thing. But there is no stopping the Senator. His cross-questioning of Honey is quiet but pointed. When she was cleaning Mr. Merrick's room yesterday, did she see a watch and chain? No, and she didn't take anything neither. Was there anyone else in Mr. Merrick's room? Well, Honey hesitantly admits, Brett was there, fixing an old window sash.

That's all the Senator wants to know.

Dismissing Honey, the Senator is ready to shout his conviction of Brett's guilt. Against Genevra's hysterical protest, against Alice's declared belief in Brett's innocence, he stands firm. He has an instinct about such things that they could not have.

Again, over their excited protests, the Senator announces his intention of searching Brett's room. When they would lay restraining hands on his arm he orders them away. "This is the most disgraceful thing that has ever happened in this house!" declares Alice, as she follows her father from the room.

"Damn fools! Alice too!" Genevra is explosive. "She lets him get away with it!"

"What's the matter with him? What happened to him?" Even Howard is bewildered.

GENEVRA—Have you ever seen a lynching?

HOWARD—No.

GENEVRA—I did—once. I was thirteen years old. Nobody knows I saw it, not even Alice. It was across the river where I'd go to be alone, in the woods. There were shouts, scattered and wild. Then I could see them coming, and I hid. But I watched through the bushes. I could see everything. He was all beaten and bloody, and they had ripped off all his clothes. They shoved a boy up the tree with a rope. There was a woman with a child in her arms. She was laughing. And she laughed harder when the body went up in the air. The body did a terrible dance, like a doll on a string. Someone threw an empty whiskey bottle. And the men all cursed as if they were angry he was dead and they couldn't hang him again. I can forget, maybe, that poor black body; but I can never forget the faces on those people.

HOWARD—I'd like to know about those faces. What were they like?

GENEVRA (*shaking her head*)—I can't describe them, but sometimes in faces I know, I see just a little of that same look. That look of—well, sort of ecstatic perversion. There will be men sitting on the porch of the Country Club, and they'll talk about what a problem the "niggers are getting to be," and there'll be a little bit of that look on their faces. I remember I went with a boy once. Henry Westcott. Very rich and rotten. He talked that way too, and there was just a little bit of that same expression. When he'd say that the "niggers have to be kept in their place," he'd get that look of self-righteous lust. I was supposed to marry him, but I didn't.

HOWARD—Why did you want to talk about this, Nevvy?

GENEVRA—I don't know. I honestly don't know, Howard. But my father had that look on his face . . . When he searches Brett's room it's a tiny little lynching. It's an act of cruelty and he's enjoying it.

HOWARD—But why did you want to talk about this?

GENEVRA—But he can't really believe that Brett took the watch . . . or maybe he does. If you hate somebody enough . . . then you can believe anything about him, can't you? But my father doesn't realize how strong Brett is. He can't crush him. No matter what he does . . . he can't crush him.

HOWARD (*quietly*)—You love Brett.

GENEVRA—What?

HOWARD—I said, you love him.

GENEVRA—Really, Howard, you don't know what you're saying!

HOWARD—You've identified yourself with Brett because you hated the cruel white faces. And because as a child Brett was the first object of your natural affection. You love him.

GENEVRA—Howard, you're making me very angry. And you're completely cock-eyed. Really you are. You don't know how dangerous it is, just to talk like that. Don't you realize what happens to a woman in the South who's accused of a thing like that? Why, she's hated worse than the Negro! (*Desperately.*) I'm really very angry!

HOWARD (*gently*)—Okay, I'm wrong. I'm completely wrong.

GENEVRA—This time I think I really need that drink.

HOWARD—I take it all back. Every word of it. (HOWARD *goes to the liquor cabinet, pours a drink, and brings it to her.*)

GENEVRA—You see how angry you've made me? My hand's shaking. (*She sips the drink.*) And yet . . . why should I be so offended? Is it because— Well, what I mean is this: If I *did* feel that way about Brett, I honestly don't think I'd be ashamed of it. I'd try to be honest about it—to myself, I mean . . . He's a wonderful person, Howard. He's strong and he's gentle—why, you have no idea.

The Senator and Alice are back. The Senator is still storming. Is Alice going to call the Sheriff or not? If she doesn't, he will. But he had rather she would do it. He leaves it that way.

In Brett's room the Senator and Alice had found evidence that Brett has not been completely honest about the Atlanta trip. He had already got his ticket. There was good cause for suspicion in that. Why he had been so careless as to leave the ticket on his bureau, and why he had bought a round trip ticket, she can't quite understand. But Brett had promised her he would not go to the conference—

"I'm sorry, darling, but I didn't hear him agree to anything," interposes Howard. "You told him he couldn't go. There's rather a difference."

"Why, Howard?"

"I'm only trying to keep the record straight."

"Well, perhaps it's a matter of interpretation, but why didn't he tell me he already had a ticket? And how on earth did he get a *Pullman* ticket? What's he trying to do?"

"Darling, the answer to that is so simple, I suppose you can't see it. He's trying to buck Jim Crow. And, by God, I hope he succeeds."

"But this is no way to 'buck' anything. He must have done something wrong to get this ticket."

"Why?"

"They certainly didn't sell it to him."

"I bought it." Genevra faces them calmly.

"You what?"

"I bought the ticket. Brett gave me the money and I went down to the station and bought the ticket."

"Why did you do that?"

"Because he asked me to."

They can get no more satisfaction from Genevra than that. She has always resented Alice treating Brett as though he were her exclusive property. Ever since they were children, she has resented that. Now, when Alice would send for Brett, she pleads earnestly that Brett be saved from that embarrassment.

Bella has brought a note to Alice. It is unsigned and there is no return address. And it reads, when Alice has the voice to read it—

"Alice Langdon, you nigger lover. Everybody's been putting up with you because you've got a lot of money. But look out! Last night you were seen with your big nigger boy Brett Charles coming out of the woods. Look out!"

Alice's face is white with horror. This must be the work of someone insane, some stupid maniac— She must call Cousin Roy at once! Both Genevra and Howard beg her not to. Howard would have her forget she ever received such a note. Genevra pleads with her not to call Cousin Roy. "Please, Alice! For Brett! He's already had so much trouble!" She has followed Alice to the phone. "Whoever the person is, there's nothing he can do! He has no proof and nobody would believe him!"

Slowly suspicion is born in Alice's mind. "Genevra—where were you last night?" she demands. Genevra would evade the answer. She was out. She had gone to the movies. She had seen a picture with Fredric March in it. But she can't remember the picture—

ALICE—You were out with Brett.

GENEVRA—Yes, I was.

ALICE—You've been out with him before.

GENEVRA—No.

ALICE—But last night somebody saw you.

GENEVRA—Yes. It was unfortunate.

ALICE (*with deep bitterness*)—Unfortunate! . . . How did it happen? He forced you to go with him, isn't that right?

GENEVRA—No, he didn't force me. I asked him to go. We went walking down by the river.

ALICE—At night. All alone. Walking!

GENEVRA (*calmly*)—Yes.

ALICE—You don't think anybody will believe that? You don't think I can believe it?

GENEVRA—Why not?

ALICE—You're trying to protect him.

GENEVRA—Of course I am.

ALICE—*Why?* Why should you defend him?

GENEVRA—Because I like him.

ALICE (*in a whisper*)—Nevvy! Nevvy! You couldn't have wanted him to touch you?

GENEVRA—That's what you're bound to believe, isn't it?

ALICE—My God, you must have tried to stop him.

GENEVRA—Pretty soon you'll be saying something even worse. Rape. . . .

ALICE—Nevvy! Tell me that you tried to stop him!

GENEVRA—I didn't try to stop him, because he didn't try to touch me.

ALICE—You're lying.

GENEVRA—No, I'm telling the truth.

ALICE—Then why didn't you tell me before? Why did you try to hide it?

GENEVRA—Yes, that was stupid. Because there was nothing to hide.

ALICE—Then why are you frightened? Are you ashamed?

GENEVRA—I'm *not* ashamed! And I *am* telling the truth! And I may as well tell the *whole* truth. (*Slowly, painfully.*) I realize now, if he had—if he had put his arms around me—I wouldn't have—well, I don't think I would have minded at all.

I think maybe I would have been glad.

ALICE—My sister. My own sister.

GENEVRA (*very simply*)—Yes, maybe I *do* love him.

ALICE—Stop it! Don't use that word!

GENEVRA—I can't help it. Maybe I do love him. And it's no use covering your face or closing your ears. If it's the truth, you've got to hear it. Why shouldn't I say it? I love him.

ALICE—I wish you were dead.

GENEVRA—Yes, that would solve everything, wouldn't it? Except that I don't want to be dead . . . I'm going away.

ALICE—How could I have been so unaware.

GENEVRA—You're not listening to me. I'm telling you that I'm going away. I know that it's completely impossible, and so does Brett.

ALICE—The very first day he came home— You went to the station—

GENEVRA—All right, don't listen to me—don't believe me. But I don't think you'll call Cousin Roy or anybody else. You can't do anything to Brett without exposing me, too. And you'd never do that. You'll have to face the fact that it happened and then you'll have to forget about it.

Alice has sunk into a chair. Genevra, starting upstairs, stops to say she's sorry, but Alice draws away from her. Even Howard's sympathy after Genevra has gone, Alice finds callous and cold. Her own sister! How could such a thing have happened? Even though Nevvy is terribly young! Even though her mother died when she was a baby! How could this terrible thing have happened? Brett must have used some horrible persuasion! He must have bewitched her! That's what happened! Nevvy was bewitched!

"And he did it deliberately!" she concludes, sweeping aside Howard's effort to force her back to a sane reasoning. "He's done *everything* deliberately. The library, the conference at Atlanta, everything. And now we know he's stopped at nothing. He'd do anything."

Alice has stopped pacing the floor and gone directly to the telephone. Again Howard would restrain her, but she will not listen. Sheriff Serkin is called and told that there has been a theft in the Langdon house. Yes, the thief is known. He is Brett Charles and he is still there.

No longer will Alice tolerate Howard's contention that Brett did not steal the watch. Howard does not understand these things. Howard is, as he admits, a Northerner. Brett has "gone bad"—

"Oh, I know," says Howard. "Something like a thoroughbred horse who breaks a leg. You feel quite unhappy about it, but you have to shoot him. But Brett's not a horse. He's an intelligent man. You've got an investment there. Twenty years of patience and kindness—to say nothing of your liberal convictions. Shouldn't you hesitate a moment before you—shoot him? . . . Alice! Alice, darling! You're an intelligent woman. You've always used your head. You've got to use it *now*. Let's not lose our powers of reason. Let's not luxuriate our emotions by riding off on a witch hunt."

"Father was right. He saw what had happened to Brett."

"And now, I suppose, you'll agree with every wild declaration of your father's."

"My father may be old, but in his time he was considered by many to be a great man. And nobody ever questioned his sincerity."

"As you say, 'in his time.' But are you living in his time, or in your own time? . . . Whatever your father may once have been, today he's the dying South. He's decay; he's age; he's everything that's corrupt and evil. At first I thought your father was harmless, but I can see now that he wields a terrible power. The moment he thought he could frame Brett, he was off and away. He forgot he was ill, and that soon he would be dead. And now his greatest triumph: he's captured *you*—completely!"

Alice is in tears. She loves Howard very much, but she is greatly troubled. What would he do, were he in her place? If Genevra were his sister? What would he do?

Howard is honest in saying that he doesn't exactly know. But he would at least try to behave rationally—

"I'd try to realize this is no case for crime and punishment. I'd try to act with compassion, rather than with vengeance . . . And if I'd made the mistake of calling the Sheriff, then, when he came I'd send him away."

That would be doing nothing at all, in Alice's estimation. Howard, she feels, still doesn't understand. Certainly not when he contends that it is very likely none of his business, nor Alice's business, either.

"Of course it's my business," she hurls at him. "It's every white man's business. How do you think we live down here? How do you think we keep our sanity? When a thing like this happens, we stamp it out . . . And you babble on about compassion. You're a sentimental fool!"

"Because I don't want to join your private lynching!"

"Lynching!"

"Yes. If you need a support, go down and get those hooligans who sit on the curbstone outside the courthouse! They'll help you! They'll even *hang* Brett for you! Maybe you'd like *that!*"

"I don't want to talk to you any more. Please go away." She has turned away, trembling. Howard goes to her and takes her by the arms, speaking with considerable force—

"Alice—Alice, darling, there's just one chance for us; just one! When the Sheriff gets here, send him away! Don't let him have Brett! I can't stand up to be married tomorrow while that man's in jail! Send the Sheriff away! We'll try to help Nevvy. Maybe we can help Brett too. Let's for God's sake make a civilized effort."

"I have to do what I know is right."

"Well, Miss Alice, it's been an interesting four weeks' visit in the romantic South."

As Howard goes out, Senator Langdon comes in. The Senator is glad to hear that the lady who was "acting as a champion for her black friend," and the "Lovely zealot who believed the Negro could do no wrong" has come to her senses and that the Sheriff is coming for Brett Charles. With Alice in tears, confessing she will not be married the next day, he is gently sympathetic, but not displeased. Now they can go back to living as they have always lived, since those days in the long past when she used to sit in the Senate gallery and listen to her father make a speech. "You thought I was the greatest man in the world," he remembers, proudly.

The Senator is helping himself to a liberal drink when Honey comes quickly through the door. She has one hand in her apron pocket and she has something to tell the Senator. Strangely enough the stolen watch has reappeared. Honey had found it—

The Senator doesn't have to be told where. She found it in "that nigger boy's room." That's where she found it. And to make sure she is telling him the truth, the Senator takes a violent hold of Honey's arm. He is twisting the arm when she confesses that he is right.

"Honey, you're a good girl," the Senator admits. And to help her realize what it means to be good he gives her a ten-dollar bill to buy a dress. She would go then, but the Senator has one more thing for her to do. He insists that she shall stay and face Brett and tell the truth. But Honey is in tears, protesting that she is afraid of Brett. He might kill her for telling the watch story. He might. Anyway, he didn't steal the watch, really. She had found it in the basement. It just fell down the clothes chute somehow—

"The black boy made you steal it," the Senator reminds her. "Then you got scared."

"Nobody stole it. I found it."

"Damn niggers," the Senator explodes. "You never know what to believe . . . But the black boy's going to jail for this—that I know! He's a bad nigger."

"Senator, *I* ain't a bad nigger! Honest I ain't."

"Listen, I don't care about you," the Senator tells her, grabbing her wrist again. "But you're going to keep your black mouth shut, do you hear? Open that silly mouth of yours just once, and you'll find yourself in jail, right alongside the black boy!"

"Please let me go! I ain't never opening my mouth again. Not for nothing or nobody, no, sir!"

"Damn right you're not! That jail down there is just waiting for you. Now go answer that door."

Sheriff Serkin and two deputies are at the door. All three are armed. "Sheriff Serkin is a broad-shouldered, gross-featured man with a gun buckled cruelly around his enormous stomach."

Senator Langdon explains about the watch being taken, and the railroad ticket they had found in Brett's room.

"That's the nigger's been struttin' around in a uniform, eh? I ain't surprised. He's a bad nigger," recalls the deputy, Izay.

"Been expecting something from him," agrees the Sheriff. "Been shooting off his mouth to the other blacks. Well, where is he?"

"I've sent for him," reports the Senator. "He doesn't even know we suspect him, so you can take him by surprise. He'll be coming in this door presently."

Alice has come in. She hears her father tell Sheriff Serkin that Brett is to get fair treatment. His daughter will swear out the warrant. But, the Sheriff assures them, there is no hurry about that.

"We got some niggers down in that jail been waitin' for two months for warrants," adds Izay, "but we feed 'em good and it keeps 'em shut out of mischief."

When Brett comes into the hallway the Sheriff and his deputies deploy themselves professionally about the room.

"All right, boy. You're coming with me," announces Sheriff

Serkin, advancing toward his prey, and taking a pair of handcuffs from his pocket. "Stick out your hands! Stick 'em out, nigger!"

Senator Langdon has stepped forward and faced the confused Brett. "I'm sorry about this, boy. We trusted you . . . Admit that you stole the watch. If you'll admit it, we'll withdraw the charges . . . (*Pause.*) Well, Sheriff, I guess it's no use."

Brett turns appealingly to Alice. "Miss Alice! Miss Alice, do you think I stole a watch? . . . Are you going to let them—Miss Alice—!"

The Sheriff and his men start to close in on Brett. He turns quickly toward the hallway. That way is blocked by Izay. Brett starts in another direction and is tripped by the second deputy. As Brett falls the deputies fall upon him. The Sheriff yanks out his gun and brings the butt down on Brett's head. Alice is protesting in anguished cries of "No! No! No!" Howard Merrick appears on the stairs as the blow is repeated a second and a third time.

"Bastard! Are you trying to kill him?" shouts Howard, grabbing the Sheriff's arms.

The Sheriff steps back, breathing heavily. He ignores Howard. "Pick him up, boys!" he calls to his men.

The deputies have carried the unconscious Brett out. The Sheriff follows. Senator Langdon goes to his room. Alice's face is anguished at what she has seen.

"Well? Are you satisfied?" demands Howard. He is leaving the room as the curtain falls.

ACT III

It is nine o'clock that evening. The lights are on in the Langdon living room. The French doors onto the terrace are still open. Senator Langdon is at the sideboard pouring himself a drink and trying a little desperately to feel at peace with the world.

Presently Alice brings in a tray of food. Alice is pale and perceptibly troubled, but she is trying "to conceal her state of mind by being matter-of-fact and efficient."

The Senator would have Alice join him in a drink, but she declines. Nor is she visibly responsive when he proposes a toast to her:

"To my daughter, Alice, beautiful and wise, who will learn as she grows older that as a lady it is more pleasant to enjoy her own privileges than to demand rights for others."

Alice calls her father's attention to the food. He had better eat his eggs before they get cold. She has no urge to talk with him, even when he turns the conversation to her future without Howard—

"There will be times when you'll regret losing this Yankee," admits the Senator. "He's a bright customer . . . When is he leaving?"

"I don't know," Alice answers, sharply. "Will you want anything else?"

There is nothing else the Senator craves, unless it be that his daughter be less gloomy. His discovery that the Langdon household is practically in rebellion—that Lolly, the cook, deserted just an hour before dinner; that Honey also is missing, and that Bella has not been seen for hours—is irritating, but that situation will right itself in due course.

"Bella's a rare woman," muses the Senator. "She represents some of the best qualities of our heritage—loyalty and true kindness. There are not many left like her. She's devoted to me."

"But why did they have to hit him?" demands Alice, suddenly and passionately. "They hit him after he was on the floor. Why did they do that?"

"I abhor violence. I do not excuse it. But Negroes are violent creatures. With the slightest opportunity, they would do violence to us. That they are sometimes the *victim* of violence is perhaps inevitable."

"But they might have killed him!"

Cousin Roy Maxwell has called. He is considerably excited. He has just left the Mayor, who is also deeply concerned about the "hornets' nest" that has been stirred up. No fewer than twelve disturbed citizens have called Cousin Roy.

"Bosh!" explodes Senator Langdon.

"But a war veteran! They'll call him a hero—he has that Distinguished Service Cross!"

"The man is a thief!"

MAXWELL—Then why is he being held incommunicado, with no charge against him? How do you think it will look in those Northern scandal sheets? I'm told he was beaten up while wearing his uniform. There are a lot of folks who don't like that. And you know something? I'm one of them.

LANGDON—You weren't talking that way this afternoon.

MAXWELL (*bewildered*)—This afternoon?

LANGDON—Then you were thrashing about like an angry porpoise because he'd got a book from the library.

MAXWELL (*hotly*)—Yes, indeed. But I wasn't suggesting that he be arrested and knocked unconscious. (*Shaking his head.*) Cousin Alice, I don't understand you. You've always had an exemplary understanding of our civic problems.

ALICE—What are you suggesting I should do, Cousin Roy?

MAXWELL—I seriously believe you should call Judge Sweetwell and ask him to have Brett set free—immediately. (LANGDON *bursts into bitter laughter.*) With all due respect, Senator—I do not think the situation calls for laughter.

LANGDON—Cheap, tawdry, picayune politician. Constantly wetting your diapers.

MAXWELL—It's all very well for you to talk, Senator—

LANGDON—Talk, hell! I did something! I caught the rascal red-handed and got rid of him!

MAXWELL—Senator, you live in this house in comfortable isolation. You don't really belong to this community as I do. You don't realize the winds that are blowing—(*To* ALICE, *earnestly.*) Surely you know what I mean, Cousin Alice. There'll be a lot of Negro soldiers coming back. We have to bear that in mind.

ALICE—Some of them will be bad; they will have been corrupted.

MAXWELL—I see. Apparently you agree with the Senator. The Senator says I'm scared. Frankly, I *am*. We make them hate us and they're bound to want revenge . . . We haven't had any trouble here in a long time. Our record's been very good, even excellent. (*Taking a deep breath.*) Cousin Alice, this is a difficult moment for me. I'm going to oppose you on this.

ALICE—Very well, Cousin Roy.

MAXWELL—I'm going to ask Judge Sweetwell to have that boy released! I think the Judge will see the wisdom of this somewhat better than you seem to. (*Glances at his watch.*) It's nine-thirty. I'm going to urge them to get him out of that jail right away and put him on the north bound train tonight. He'll be gone. He'll never come back, and nobody can make an issue of it. Let it be over and forgotten.

LANGDON—So you want to run for Congress. I'll show you whether I live in isolation. Without my help, you couldn't be elected dog catcher.

MAXWELL—After today, I certainly don't think I could be elected *with* your help. Good evening.

Cousin Roy has gone. Bella has quietly appeared in the hallway and is staring at Alice and her father "with impassive hatred."

Bella has just come from the jail. They would not let her see her son. She has come to bring them her key. She wants nothing more to do with that house nor with either of them. "Right here I got the wrath of God," Bella announces, touching her breast.

The Senator, with soft tones and an ingenuous smile, would placate the angry Bella. How can she think of leaving them? Who is to take care of him?

"Yes. I've took care of you." Bella has walked toward the Senator. "For a long, long time I've took care of you. Giving you medicine, coming when you call, tending your mess, most of the time you acting like an ornery child. Yes, I been nice to you. I been nice to you when my back was tired and my soul was sick."

"Bella—"

"Bella do this; Bella do that! And I done it, every time, because I figured this man was the path the Lord appointed me to follow. But when you put my son in prison, path or no path, I step off. It's my son I hold to. Not you, old man. If you think I'd forswear my son to stay with you, then you got the evil of a serpent and the dumbness of an ox!"

Bella turns and leaves them. For a long minute the silence is oppressive. Then the Senator would try to find some justification for what has happened. He realizes that there is still a gulf between the races that can never be spanned. "It seems for a long time that a woman like Bella has crossed that gulf to join us," he says, "but at the first crisis she fails us."

There is no sympathy in Alice's tone. She wonders if Brett really did take the watch. The Senator is startled. If Alice didn't believe Brett guilty, why did she call the Sheriff? Why?

"He did steal the watch, didn't he?" Alice insistently demands an answer. Getting none, she answers herself. "He did steal it! And if we have to, we can prove it. He did! He did!"

Genevra and Howard appear in the hall. They, too, have been to the jail. The Sheriff would not let them see Brett. No bail has been set.

"Brother, there is one thing I hate more than a nigger, and that's a Northerner," the Sheriff had said to Howard when he suggested that Brett be taken before a Magistrate. "Now get out of here before I punch your nose!"

They had tried to get a lawyer. Three of them were very courteous and even greatly disturbed, but not one of them would take the case. So Howard had wired New York for legal help.

"You're awfully clever, Alice," Genevra is saying. "You

couldn't admit publicly what his horrible crime was; so you had him arrested for something else. Something he couldn't possibly have done."

"Brett is being freed. They're putting him on a north bound train tonight. (*Glances at the clock.*) They must be taking him to the station right now— And that's the end of it."

"That's dandy. If you can't prove your case, or don't care to, get rid of the accused. Send him North. Get him out of town . . ."

Slowly Genevra reaches a decision. She must see Brett. If she can't get to the train in time, as Howard insists she can't, she will follow Brett. She will find him, even if it takes years. She will trace him through his best friends in the North.

But, warns Howard, Genevra is not considering consequences. She has no idea of the suffering she would undergo, even after she found Brett.

"Would you marry him?" he suddenly demands.

"If that's what he wants—yes!" calmly answer Genevra. And to his somewhat horrified "Why?" she answers—

"You think I'm going to say 'because I love him.' But it's a lot more than that. He's lost everything; we've taken it all from him—his faith in us and his friendship. We're all guilty."

"You want to atone for all the sins of the white race. By yourself—alone?—"

"I want to go to him. I want to say to him, 'I'm sorry. I'm sorry for all these wrongs that have been done. I reject these people and all their cruelties. I'm with *you* . . .' Do you understand, Howard? (*Very quietly.*) Anyway, I don't want to stay in this house another day . . . I can catch the midnight express at Junction City. Will you drive me over? I'll have time to pack and get ready."

Genevra has hurried upstairs to pack. Howard is still looking after her wonderingly when Honey appears in the doorway. She is nervous and distraught and obviously afraid to come in. Honey is looking for the Senator. She's just got to see him, even if he has gone to bed. It is Howard's suggestion that she had better wait until morning—

"But I got to give him back his mean old ten dollars," wails Honey. "Judas money, that's what it is . . . Judas money. When I heard what they were saying down in colored town, why I like to died of shame. (*Passionately.*) I didn't want to be no Judas. He took my arm and made me say it."

Soon the whole truth is out. Senator Langdon had given Honey the money because she had found the watch—

"I brung it right to him. Then the first thing I knew the Sheriff come and took Brett away. (*Thrusts the money toward him.*) Here, you take it. You give it to Mister Senator. Me, I'm leaving. I never want to see that old man again. I'm going back to my ma, she'll have me . . . Please, Mr. Merrick, take this dirty old money and let me go free."

"All right, Honey. I'll give it to him."

"Thank you, Mr. Merrick. (*She backs away from him.*) I ain't a bad girl, Mr. Merrick. I guess it's like everyone says: I just ain't bright."

Howard is looking after Honey, and slowly putting the bill in his pocket, when his eye is caught by a portrait of Gen. Langdon above the fireplace. He salutes the picture with the bill. "I may be mistaken, sir, but I think you're blushing," he says sardonically, as he goes up the stairs.

For a moment the room is empty. Then Brett appears at the French windows. His head is crudely bandaged, his uniform is soiled. He hesitates a moment and then comes into the room. He is near the hallway when he hears someone coming and hides behind draperies at a window.

Alice has come to turn off the lights. As she reaches the last light there is the sound of a distant train whistle, very faint and far away. She frowns.

"No, Miss Alice, I'm not on that train," says Brett, softly. She is staring at him, speechlessly as he continues: "Yes, they put me on the train—took me right to my seat. They told me if I ever showed my ugly face in this town again, they'd hang me. But they made a mistake. They left before the train pulled out."

"What do you want?"

"What's the matter, Miss Alice? Can't we talk? Are you no longer my friend?"

"Why did you come back here?"

"You seem to be frightened. Why? You don't need to be afraid of me. I have a question to ask you. There's something I must know. Could you really make yourself believe I'm a thief? Tell me, I've got to find out. No matter what I did, couldn't you let me talk? . . . defend myself? Couldn't you give me a hearing?"

"Get out of here."

"Why did you do it? Why? Why?"

"Get out of here."

"That's all I have to know . . . Human beings are allowed to defend themselves—to explain—to use words. But not a 'nigger.' Human beings are permitted to have feelings. But not a 'nigger.' In your mind I'm still a slave."

"Brett, you've gone mad!"

"Damn you, Alice Langdon, I would have died before I would have brought harm or suffering to Nevvy! Damn you, I would have cut off this arm, rather than touch her!"

Alice has turned around and grabbed the telephone. She is calling frantically for the operator when Brett snatches the phone from her. So that is her answer? To call the Sheriff and get him hanged? Very well. If it is to be his life against hers—they had taught him about that—

"When I know somebody is my enemy, I can kill her," he says.

Alice slaps the black face soundly. Brett grabs her by the arms and is holding her motionless when his anger fades.

"No . . . No! I don't have to kill you!" he says. "You're not worth killing! Go on living! And shake with fear every time you see a black face!"

He is still holding Alice when Bella, carrying a suitcase, comes into the room. With a scream she throws herself between Alice and Brett. Desperately she tears Brett's hands from Alice's arms. Alice falls weakly against the table and Bella turns excitedly on her son. "Go to my room!" she orders. "Stay there! Don't come out!"

Brett is looking down upon the fainting Alice. "Look at her! White scum!" he sneers, contemptuously.

"Go to my room, you hear!" Bella repeats. And he goes.

With the glass of water Bella gives her, Alice quickly revives. She will be all right now. Bella may go—

BELLA—What did you expect? An eye for an eye, a tooth for a tooth? That's in the Bible too . . . I'm sorry for you; yes, I am, young white lady in your big house. You walk a high, proud path.

ALICE—Please, Bella.

BELLA—No humbleness, no loving kindness . . . All right, live like that. Grow old like that. Always being the one to pass judgment, until your heart is like a rock and you've nothing left but your almighty righteousness.

ALICE—Bella—Bella, you don't know what he did.

BELLA—What he did—and what Nevvy did. Or what they did not do—

ALICE (*helplessly*)—But, Bella, it was wrong.

BELLA—Yes. But did God appoint you to cast the first stone?

ALICE—But if it was wrong—? You know it was. You know we can't let such things happen.

BELLA—Who can't let it happen? It happens. You fine and mighty white folk let it happen every day.

ALICE—What?

BELLA—At least *them* two are pure in heart . . . But this land sees real evil. Sees it all the time. Ask any black woman, young and ripe. She'll tell you about those lily-white gentlemen.

ALICE—But it's not the same.

BELLA—Isn't it? Is my woman's body less sacred than yours? No, we ain't good enough to claim a place among the chosen people. But we're good enough to share a white man's bed. And when we do, God punishes us as he sees fit—but nobody calls the sheriff.

ALICE—Why, Bella—

BELLA—Well, maybe you'll learn. We all got to accept the misery we make for ourselves, and there's plenty of it without making misery for other folks too.

Howard has come down the stairs in time to hear this last speech. He heartily sympathizes with Bella. Isn't Alice going to face the fact that in her heart she knows Brett did not take the watch? Or is she going on supporting the lie her father has invented?

When she does not answer, Howard summons Senator Langdon from his room and gives little heed to the Senator's angry response. Howard has a message for the Senator from Honey. She wants to give him back his ten dollars. Howard would also like to know where the Senator has hidden the watch. If the Senator persists in denying that he has the watch it will be necessary for Howard to search his room, and even his pockets—

"Yes, yes. I think you would," sneers the Senator. "Your vulgarity does not surprise me! . . . Very well, here! . . . Here it is . . . Take it if you like!" He has taken the watch from his pocket. . . . Do you think I'm sorry? I'm not. I'd have let him rot in jail. If I could have done it, I'd have him hanged."

"And *you*, Alice. Would *you* have let him rot in jail?"

"In such a conflict any means are justified."

"Is that true, Alice?"

"The watch is nothing; the threat to our security is everything." The Senator has answered for Alice.

"Yes, your father is right," Howard goes on. "The watch is

nothing. If it hadn't been the watch, you would have found something else, and you would have justified it. What you've done to Brett is bad enough. What you're doing to yourself is even worse . . . Think about it, Alice. It's tough, I know. The prejudice is rooted deep . . . so deep it will take every ounce of your strength to root it out and look at it squarely. But think about it, Alice, for God's sake, think about it."

With Alice's assurance that Brett has nothing to fear, Bella agrees to send her son to them. The Senator is appalled—

"Heed my words, Daughter," he warns Alice. "Make your choice before it's too late. They'll return from Europe—this black horde—reeking with rebellion and ready to turn their guns on us, their masters. . . . I warn you, the wind is rising . . . the storm is gathering. . . ."

"Yes!" mutters Alice, intensely, "the storm has already broken. It's a very personal little storm, and there is nothing you can do about it—nothing in the world . . ."

"What do you mean?"

"It's your own daughter."

"What?"

"Yes, Nevvy. Nevvy and Brett."

"No! No! You're lying!" The Senator's voice has sunk to a low whisper. His shoulders shrink as he turns slowly toward his room. "No, you wouldn't lie about that!" he mutters. "Nobody lies about that. Great God Almighty! Great God Almighty!" He has gone to his room and closed the door.

Alice, having appealed vainly to Howard for sustaining support, meets Brett a little self-consciously—

"I'm not sure that anything I can say will mean very much now," she begins, carefully, almost painfully. "I'm not even sure I can say it properly."

"Say your piece, Miss Alice."

"There's a difference between us: Your skin is dark and my skin is white. In the world we live in today, everything conspires to make that a very great difference indeed. It's wrong, it's base, but there it is. I tried to call you my equal, I was very nice to you, but I realize now that always in my heart I felt you were *different*. (Brett *turns away.*) No, that's wrong. I'll try to tell it honestly. In my heart I felt you were inferior. I hid this feeling with noble deeds; I pretended to be fair and judicious. I was even able to impress myself with my own great good will. (*Pause.*) Well, with one blow you destroyed my lovely self-satisfaction. Whatever understanding I had, I lost in a moment.

I just couldn't stop to think that you were intelligent and truthful. Like any red-necked planter, I leaped to conclusions. I invoked the white man's law. . . . I don't want to be that kind of person, Brett. I don't want hatred on my conscience. I want to be free too. Free from fear and free from guilt."

What is she to do? Brett can think of but one thing. Let him go away. Let his life be his own. What else would they expect of him? That he should ask for a check for ten thousand dollars? Or a written apology announcing that he is not a thief? No. He can do without further favors.

Nor will he stay there, and risk hanging, just to give Alice a chance to show him that her faith in him is again established. That would mean little. They are, says Brett, and will go on being, on opposite sides of a high wall.

True, when he came back from Europe Brett was ready to scale that wall, or knock it down. But now he knows he was a fool—

"My men were right," says Brett. "My boys in Italy. They knew when it comes right down to it, it's white against black—the black underneath. They weren't deceived by having an expensive education and a generous white friend. They had the satisfaction of hating—hating all white people."

And that's the way it will have to be, concludes Brett. White hating black; black hating white. Even if Alice doesn't want to hate all black people, she can learn, as he has. Yes, Brett insists, he has come to hate Miss Alice, and all whites. Even the family in England, that entertained him; and the Italian peasants with whom he sat at table and shared a bottle of wine. They are ignorant, but they will learn. There are plenty of white Americans teaching them.

"Brett . . . What about Nevvy?" Howard sharply demands. "Nevvy is white. Do you hate Nevvy, too? Go on, tell me! Tell me that you hate Nevvy! As long as there's one white person in the world whom you trust, you can't call us all unjust and vile. There's a—"

"Shut up!" Brett is shouting now.

"You admit there is one white person who is good. Then you can't declare war, because there may be others. If Nevvy—"

"Damn you, shut up!" Brett is furious.

"Please, Brett," Alice pleads earnestly. "It's more than you and I and Nevvy. If decent people—whatever the color of their skin—can't live and work together, then there's no security in the world. There is no peace."

For a moment Brett does not reply. Then he answers, solemnly: "Then there is no peace!"

Genevra is coming down the stairs carrying her suitcase. With a hearty cry of surprise at finding Brett there she goes quickly to him. Eagerly she would know what they had done to him? Isn't it funny that he would be right there all the time she was planning to go to him, wherever he was? Now they can go together. They will go North, and she will take care of him. "We'll manage somehow!" Genevra says confidently.

"No. No!" It is a tortured Brett who speaks. "You don't know what you're saying."

GENEVRA—But I know exactly. I'm saying: Will you marry me? (BRETT *stares at her, stunned.*) Yes, Brett. Will you marry me?

BRETT—You would do what I would never ask you to do? You would be my wife?

GENEVRA—Yes. . . . Yes, Alice, I'm going to marry him. There's nothing much you can say, is there? You had your say and it wasn't a very nice one. I can see you're frightened. You're terrified. You needn't be.

ALICE (*pale and rigid*)—I can't help it. I can't feel any other way. (*She touches* GENEVRA.) Nevvy, dearest.

GENEVRA—Yes, Alice.

ALICE—This is a mistake. A tragic mistake. For every practical reason in the world. (*She breaks off.*) It's for you and Brett to decide. Yes, and whatever you decide, I shall try with all my strength to be your friend.

GENEVRA (*turning to* BRETT *who has sunk into a chair and has put his head into his trembling hands*)—Brett, what is it? Brett, look at me. Please, Brett.

BRETT (*slowly looking at her*)—This afternoon—neither you nor I were thinking of getting married. It never even entered our heads. If it wasn't right then—it's still not right. (*Shaking his head.*) No, Nevvy. No. We would have to cut ourselves off. We'd become an island. We could never live in the world as it is.

GENEVRA—All right, then, we can make our own world.

BRETT—An island of perfection and happiness, but all in a dream. Until one day you'd awaken, and discover that no man and woman can create a world apart. There are no islands. There is no escape.

GENEVRA—But don't you need me, Brett?

BRETT (*taking her hand*)—I've loved you all my life, but I didn't come back from Europe to marry you. You want the world to be different—it's not a very nice world, and you want it to be different—and so do I—but marriage is not the way.

GENEVRA—Is there a way? Is there any way at all?

BRETT (*after a moment*)—I don't know. I don't know any more.

GENEVRA—What will you do, Brett?

BRETT—I don't know that either.

GENEVRA (*after a moment*)—Well . . . whatever happens, I guess I could never stay here. After all, we knew it was impossible. We knew it first, didn't we? . . . Anyway, maybe I ought to be happy, getting out of this little old town. Maybe I ought to learn to do something, or get a job, like other girls. My goodness, I don't have to go through life doing nothing . . . Good-by, Brett. I'm glad that you have loved me. I'll always be glad. (*Turns to* HOWARD.) Howard, I'm ready. If you don't mind driving me over—

HOWARD—Of course.

GENEVRA (*going to* ALICE)—Well, Alice—

ALICE (*with an embrace*)—I shan't say good-by. When we meet again, we—

GENEVRA (*urgently*)—It'll be all right then, won't it? We can look forward to it, can't we?

ALICE (*nodding*)—Yes, Nevvy. I hope that one day you will be happy. (*They separate.* GENEVRA *turns to look at* BRETT, *hesitates, then goes out.*)

HOWARD (*as* GENEVRA *and* ALICE *separate*)—Well, I'll drive you over . . . Alice, I'd like to continue my visit in the South.

ALICE (*smiling*)—Drive carefully, Howard. Hurry back, but please drive carefully.

HOWARD—Okay then.

As Howard and Genevra disappear, Alice turns back to Brett. "Well?" she says. "Maybe that wall is not quite so high."

Brett does not answer. He has picked up the Senator's watch and calmly snapped open the case. "'Honor above all!'" he reads. After a moment he hands the watch back to Alice.

"Say it, Brett," she invites him. "Say it, if it makes you feel better."

"It doesn't," he admits.

The Senator has come from his room, wearing his hat. He

stops suddenly at sight of Brett and then turns to Alice, carefully ignoring Brett—

"Do I intrude?" the Senator asks. "You think I'm defeated—I'm not. For a brief few hours, I had high hopes for you, my daughter. But you're lost—lost. Fortunately, there are others who see the danger, there are men in this very village, armed and awaiting the day. Not Cousin Roy and his colleagues, but others, they are ready to fight and kill. They have their arsenals—they have their guns. I have already given them money. I'll give them more money. I go to join my allies."

"Father."

"You wish to reconsider?" he asks, hopefully.

"No."

"Then why did you address me."

"You forgot your watch." She hands it to him and he continues to the hall.

"Alice—" Brett has come to her, extending his hand.

"Yes, Brett?"

"We're on the same side."

"Yes, Brett, yes . . . yes." They are clasping hands.

THE CURTAIN FALLS

THE MAGNIFICENT YANKEE

A Biographical Drama in Three Acts

By Emmet Lavery

JUST before the production of "The Magnificent Yankee" in New York Arthur Hopkins, the producer, had a talk with the cast. They were not to be nervous over this particular opening night, he advised them, a little paternally, in keeping with a Hopkins characteristic. "After all, this isn't like opening an ordinary play," he said. "You are bringing something of your own country to the theatre. It's like bringing a gift—a beautiful present—which is rare."

The advice was quoted following the play's success in a New York *Evening Post* interview with Dorothy Gish, who played the role of Fanny Dixwell Holmes, the honored jurist's most loyal and helpful wife. The longer the play ran the more significant did the Hopkins tribute become.

"The Magnificent Yankee" is frankly not a great play, judged by strict dramaturgic rules. Nor even a great play, judged as theatrical entertainment. It is an honestly written and confessedly sentimental biographical drama. It does scant justice to the greatness of its subject as one of the truly great dissenting liberals who contributed to the history of the United States Supreme Court. But it does tie together episodes from the domestic life of the beloved Justice and Mrs. Holmes that are moving and rewarding sidelights in the career of a truly magnificent Yankee.

Emmet Lavery, the author, makes particular mention in a foreword to the published play of his great indebtedness to "John Palfrey, Esq., of Boston; to Attorney General Francis Biddle and to Mr. Justice Felix Frankfurter of the United States Supreme Court."

Mr. Palfrey was Justice Holmes' friend and legal aid; Mr. Biddle was one of the twenty-seven or twenty-eight young men picked from the Harvard Law School to serve, one year each, as Holmes secretaries. Justice Frankfurter was, with Justice Louis

"The Magnificent Yankee," copyright 1945 *by Emmet Lavery. Published by Samuel French, Inc., New York.*

Brandeis, among his closest and most respected associates on the bench.

Justice Frankfurter summed up most reasonably for the three principal contributors in his defense of their willingness to help with the work. "I go on the theory that Holmes belongs to the Nation," he told Mr. Lavery, "and anyone who wants to know more about him should be encouraged. As to the propriety of bringing Justice Holmes and his wife to the stage, I should say the only impropriety would be if it were not a good play." Both professional critics and a liberal section of the play-going public concurred in that decision. "The Magnificent Yankee," produced January 22, 1946, ran out the season.

However, it was generally conceded that the individual characterization of Justice Holmes by Louis Calhern, and the notably sympathetic support he received from Dorothy Gish as Mrs. Holmes, was greatly responsible for the play's popular success. It seemed to this observer at the time as though Mr. Calhern had been in training for this particular success most of the years of his professional life. It was for him a magnificent opportunity to play this magnificent Yankee, and he rose to it magnificently.

It was in December, 1902, that Judge Oliver Wendell Holmes, Jr., and his wife, Fanny Dixwell Holmes, journeyed from Boston to Washington to take up a new life. The Judge had just been lifted out of his position as Chief Justice of the Supreme Court of Massachusetts and elevated to one of the nine seats on the bench of the Supreme Court of the United States, succeeding Justice Gray.

Justice Holmes was 61 years old that year, and Fanny Holmes was willing, if inquiry were persistent, to confess to a like age. Both had been assured many times that they did not look it. There had been considerable discussion as to where they were going to live in Washington, and Mrs. Holmes had finally selected a house in I Street. Most of the Holmes furniture had been moved in before Fanny thought of bothering the Justice with so trivial a matter as a confirmation of her choice.

We meet the Holmeses in "The Magnificent Yankee" the afternoon that Justice Holmes has his first glimpse of the library of the house in I Street. Preceded by the broker, who is hoping to have the sale confirmed, the Justice, "a tall figure of a man, bundled comfortably in a big winter overcoat," is having a good look around.

The bookshelves are bare, the furniture covered with canvas

sheets against the muss painters have been making. "Despite the touches of white in his hair and mustache, there is a youthful, elastic quality to his step. . . . He is impressed with the place, but with true Yankee caution is not prepared to say so too soon."

The Judge likes the view from the window, which he throws open that he may the better sniff the air. It is, he allows, very good air—especially for December—

"Tell me, can you really smell Spring out here—when it is Spring, I mean?" he asks.

"Well, I suppose so, sir . . . I mean . . . well, no one's ever asked that before, sir."

"You see, that's the trouble with you real estate fellers. No imagination. You have your feet on the ground when it ought to be your nose."

As to his liking or not liking the house, much will depend, the Judge insists, on what his wife thinks. It is difficult to tell about a woman and a house.

"Pardon me, but would it be impertinent to ask what your line of work is?" queries the broker.

"It certainly would, but I'll tell you just the same. You might say that I was a missionary sort of—a missionary from Boston," explains the Judge with a chuckle.

It is at that moment that Fanny Dixwell Holmes steps through the door. "She is not a pretty woman in the accepted sense of the word: but at 61 she has an inner fire and radiance which match and at times surpass that of her illustrious husband." The Washington adventure for Fanny, no less than for the Judge, is a new lease on life.

She has caught the Judge's "missionary" line, and does not approve. "Wendell, you ought to be ashamed of yourself. A missionary indeed! Pay no attention to him, Mr. Dixon!"

"But if he isn't a missionary—"

"It would be a lot closer to the truth to say he was a traveling salesman—with a consuming passion for naughty French novels."

"Not necessarily French, my dear," corrects the Judge, with a wink for the broker.

Even before the question of the house can be settled they have a visitor. He is Henry Adams. Living close by, Adams has come over hoping to be among the first to welcome them to Washington. Adams is 58. "He speaks with the voice of destiny—and a very tired and weary voice it is."

At this particular time, Adams is greatly upset about the state of the country and quite sure that Justice Holmes is greatly needed in Washington.

"I'm worried—terribly worried," Henry confesses, after Mrs. Holmes and the broker Dixon have gone to continue an inspection of the premises. "It's—it's that man in the White House."

"Theodore Roosevelt?" questions Holmes, dryly. "I thought you were old friends."

ADAMS—We still are. I was one of the first to congratulate him when he named you to the Court.

HOLMES—Then what's the trouble?

ADAMS (*moodily*)—He's doing too many things . . . and saying too many things. Do you know what he said only the other day? That no nation could be great that was ruled by clerks, women and lawyers. Why, the man is beginning to attack the very law itself!

HOLMES (*chuckling*)—Adams—did you ever hear of a strong President who *didn't* think all lawyers were a damned pest?

ADAMS (*hardly hearing him*)—Maybe, but I don't like the tone of the country, Holmes. Cabot Lodge says the Spanish War has made us a nation. But I think it has only made us like the old nations—selfish, grasping, imperialistic.

HOLMES—Oh, I don't know . . . I look around me and I see more hope and enthusiasm in the young men than in our day. At least they are building their America on hopes—not on regrets.

ADAMS—But it's all so crude . . .

HOLMES (*reflectively*)—Crude? Maybe . . . but it's real . . . it's alive . . . and it isn't always selfish. Why, every day I meet boys capable of denying the material order of things—still capable, by God, of doing the spontaneous, uneconomic thing!

ADAMS—Yes, but the President is trying to do too many things too fast. Every day he's stirring up the people about something new . . . and where is it all going to end?

HOLMES—Cheer up, Adams. I think the country is young enough and strong enough to survive almost anything . . . including Theodore Roosevelt.

ADAMS—Well, I hope so—I certainly hope so. But I wish he'd remember that this isn't the millennium. This is only the year 1902—and he might leave a few things for someone else to do.

HOLMES (*with a grin*)—I'll tell him that the next time I see him.

ADAMS—Watch out, Holmes—or he'll swallow you up just as he has everyone else in Washington.

HOLMES—I'll take my chances on that.

ADAMS (*extending hand*)—Well, good-by for a while—and the best of good fortune to you.

HOLMES—Thank you—

ADAMS (*at door*)—I wish I knew what it is that always makes you so infernally unworried about everything.

HOLMES—Listen, Adams—when I was mustered out of the Civil War—almost forty years ago—people told me the country was going to the dogs. When I went on the Bench in Massachusetts, twenty years ago, they told me the same thing. Well, we may not be out of the trenches yet, Adams, but we're a long way from the dogs!

ADAMS—Maybe—but I hear them barking.

Henry Adams is no more than out of the house before the Judge gives way to a verbal explosion aimed directly at his departing visitor. What's the matter with Adams, anyway? "Forty-one years ago he was telling me the same things at Harvard—and he hasn't changed a goddamned bit."

What's Adams got to grouse about, anyway, the Judge would like to know. Certainly the country has done all right by the Adamses—his grandfather President and his great-grandfather!

"If Henry isn't equal to the strain of being an Adams, it only means *he's* going to the dogs—not the country."

Fanny, who admits that she, too, can take just so much of the Adamses, is still a little worried about Wendell's swearing. Quickly she brings the talk back to the house. Mr. Dixon is waiting for a verdict. Does Wendell like the house?

Of course Wendell likes it—but what has he had to say about it? Who was it found the house? Who told the postman that they had decided to take it? Who had had the furniture moved in? And all without consulting him—

"You might have let me have the fun of thinking I was the commanding officer around here—just once," concludes the Judge, with mock severity.

But Fanny knows that mood, and is very happy. Nor is she at all concerned with his apprehension as to the future. She knows that he will have his chance at greatness in Washington.

"But, Fanny, a man might fool himself at 61 and not know it. Not a chance of us having arrived in Washington just a bit too late, is there?"

"You know there isn't." She has gone to him and is holding his arm tightly. "Here you'll have a chance to work things out on a scale you never had in Massachusetts."

"Yes, you're right, Fanny." He has caught something of her spirit now. "This is the promised land and I'm as excited as if I were a boy seeing it all for the first time—"

But of course it isn't the first time. There was the time he and his soldiers had fought for this town of Washington, and won; the time he had to tell his Commander-in-Chief, Mr. Lincoln, to "get the hell down" when he popped up on the ramparts at Fort Stevens—

"We'll win this fight, too, only we won't win it in a day or a year," he says, a little sadly. "I saw that just now talking with Henry Adams. Right now, Fanny, you and I stand alone. We're a couple of generals without an army. Our folks fighting the Indians, before there was a union, my great-grandfather a Judge in Boston when the British entered Old South Church in 1776. And now—well, we're down at the bottom of the barrel."

Fanny, hurrying to his side, would stop him if she could, but he insists on going on. The truth is, he points out, there is no one left to carry on for the Holmeses as there is for the Adamses. And why, he wonders.

"I don't know, Wendell . . . maybe it's just that the Lord wanted a few more Adamses than Holmeses—" There is a tone in Fanny's voice that brings the Judge quickly out of his reverie. He has gone to her as he adds: "I was just daydreaming, that's all . . . I've nothing to complain of . . . I've had a full life and a merry one . . . and I've had the most wonderful wife an undeserving Yankee could ever hope for."

"Yes. We could almost make an epitaph of it, couldn't we? 'Here lies Fanny Dixwell, wonderful wife of Oliver Wendell Holmes, Jr.' "

"Fanny, please—"

"But you know and I know that a Yankee wife is only a good wife . . . when she's a good mother too."

"There, Fanny," he says, comfortingly, "you're the strong one and always have been. You have the joy of living in you and you've shared it with me. It wasn't your fault that we couldn't have passed some of it along. That . . . that . . . Oh, damn Adams! We'll carry on somehow."

There is a discreet tap at the door, followed by the appearance of a rather frail, blond young man. He stammers through a self-introduction, nervously and with a marked deference that at first amuses, then lightly irritates the Judge. Copeland is the name—Law School, 1902; Law Review—Notes editor—

"Hmmm. Well, Mr. Copeland, my needs don't really require a law editor," the Judge informs him. "What I really need is someone who can handle writs of certiorari, balance a check book—and listen to my talk. Think you can do that?"

"I think so, sir." Young Mr. Copeland is quite confident.

"You understand, the job is good only for a year. Professor Gray has suggested that it might be a good idea to take a different man from the Law School each year. Bound to be hell on me, of course, but it ought to be fine for the Law School."

"Yes, sir. It's wonderful."

So far as Holmes is concerned, Mr. Copeland can cut down on his "sirs," but let him understand that he doesn't have to say "yes" unless he means yes. And why does he think he would like to be the Holmes secretary—

"Well, I've been studying you and trying to understand your ideas," says Copeland. "Of course, I don't hold with everything you say about the law, sir—"

"Well—that's a promising beginning anyway. Go on—"

"But you're on the right track, sir—whether the rest of the country knows it or not. The law isn't just the dead hand of precedent—it's a living thing and it has to grow with the time in which it lives—it has to. It—"

The boy has become suddenly diffident. He would recover balance with an apology. The Judge understands. He is quite pleased, in fact, with the unleashed eloquence of the young man. He will find that his employer's needs are few, but his rules are fixed—

"The Government will pay you $2,000 a year but there are certain conditions. Do you have a girl you're in love with?"

"Oh, no, sir! No—indeed, sir." He speaks a little too fervently to suit the Judge.

"Well, there's no harm in having one. Nice thing, girls. But just make sure you don't marry while you're in my employ. Understand?"

"Very good, sir."

"Hmmm. I don't know how good it is, but it's the way I prefer to work. Well, there you are, Copeland—not a bad arrangement any way you look at it. If you're a credit to me and I'm a credit to you, we'll both have something to brag about. If we disappoint each other, no harm is done. You see, my boy, I intend to have all the pleasures of parenthood without any of the responsibility. If there is anything there, perhaps I can enrich it and you will go away not altogether ungrateful. Perhaps—"

Suddenly, as though the words "boy" and "parenthood" were re-echoing in his ear, the Judge breaks off abruptly. He dismisses Copeland and is whistling and strutting about the room as Fanny looks in—

"Wendell Holmes—whatever do you think you're doing?" she demands.

"Quiet, woman. I've just discovered that I'm going to have lots of children—lots of 'em—and they're going to be *all* boys!"

The curtain falls.

By March, 1903, the Holmes library has undergone a pleasant change. Now "it has a lived-in look and a clean sweep of line that is inevitably New England, even in Washington."

There is a new secretary, another modestly attractive young man named Mason. At the moment he is going through the day's Washington newspapers comparing reports of Justice Holmes' decision in the Northern Securities case with copy he has on the table. Mary, the Holmes housekeeper, brings in the New York papers and Mason is quick to grab these for further comparison.

Now Fanny Holmes joins him. "There's considerable change in Fanny. Washington has been kind to her and she has literally had a second blooming. . . . Her style of clothes has changed, too, and the afternoon dress she is wearing has, like Fanny herself, a discreet but definite sparkle."

The newspaper comments, Mason tells her, are quite flattering, all things considered. But the President seems to be quite angry. Why? Probably because, although in his favor, the vote was very close—five to four. And the President had evidently rather counted on the Judge—

"The fact that the Judge's dissenting opinion gets almost as much space as the majority won't make the President any happier," opines Mason.

And now Fanny has come upon something that causes her to explode excitedly. "Just listen to this: 'When asked to comment on the unexpected dissent of Mr. Justice Holmes, one of his own appointees to the Court, President Roosevelt replied with a bark: I could carve a man with more backbone out of a banana!'" She has put the paper down and is looking grimly at Mason. "Well, merciful Heaven, what does the President want—a judge or a banana?"

"If you don't mind my saying so, ma'am, I think the President would be content with a banana."

"Well, just wait till I see Mr. Roosevelt!"

Photo by Lucas-Pritchard Studio.

"THE MAGNIFICENT YANKEE"

Judge Holmes—I wonder if that will sound the same in another fifty years? . . . Ah, the trouble is few books are worth reading twenty-five years after they have been written.

(*Dorothy Gish, Louis Calhern*)

Mary has reported the presence of several reporters waiting below. One of them has penetrated even to the kitchen. Quite a gentleman he is, too!

"If you could have heard the way he said: '*I* am the Boston *Transcript!*' . . . Like you might say: '*I* am the Archangel Gabriel!' " says Mary.

Fanny is plainly impressed. "Well, of all things—the *Transcript!* That's different, Mary. Show him up—show him up right away!" And as Secretary Mason shows signs of concern she explains that, though she knows the Judge never gives interviews, she hasn't seen an Archangel around in a long time—especially a Boston one!

Fanny has time to run through the Judge's mail before the *Transcript* man arrives. One letter intrigues her intensely. She sniffs it suspiciously. Mason can take the rest of the mail but she will leave this one on the Judge's desk, seeing it is marked "Personal."

Leave it she does, though that isn't easy. She is still sniffing, and holding the rather flossy envelope up to the light when a knock heralds the arrival of the *Transcript's* Mr. Palmer. He easily answers Mary's description. "There is a deliberate condescension about the man that is almost regal."

Mr. Palmer is quite surprised to find Mrs. Holmes so young a woman. He had been given to understand that she was very much older—

"That must have been the Judge's first wife," suggests Fanny, sweetly.

"First wife? But I had always understood that Justice Holmes had married only once."

"Ah, it only goes to show—you never can tell about people from Boston, can you, Mr. Palmer?"

"My apologies, Mrs. Holmes," apologizes Palmer, stiffly. "I assure you—"

"Oh, it's quite all right, Mr. Palmer. It is quite the nicest compliment I have had in a long time."

Mr. Palmer grows increasingly fidgety. He would like to leave and come back, but he does manage to get out one question: "Mrs. Holmes, I was only wondering . . . Does Mr. Justice Holmes know that President Roosevelt has said he will throw him out of the White House if he ever sets foot there again?"

"Why, Mr. Palmer! Mr. Palmer!" Fanny is honestly aghast.

Mason has burst through the door to warn them that the Judge is coming up the walk and there is a good bit of scurrying to get

Palmer of the *Transcript* down the back way and back into the kitchen.

"But, Mrs. Holmes!" He is protesting as Fanny edges him toward the door.

"Now—now, Mr. Palmer. Just say that we love Washington—and that we adore Mr. Roosevelt at all times."

"Adore him, Mrs. Holmes?"

"Yes. We adore everything about him—except his taste in bananas. Good-by, Mr. Palmer." . . .

There is a problem confronting Mr. Mason: What time will Judge and Mrs. Holmes be wanting a cab to carry them to the White House for dinner. Fanny had forgotten all about that engagement. She would get out of it now, if she could. But, as Mason reminds her, one doesn't decline invitations to the White House.

That problem is soon settled by the Judge himself. He has come bursting in filled with enthusiasm for the Spring, and with a fresh crocus blossom in his buttonhole.

He has met the enemy below stairs and silenced them with Mary's sugar buns. He kisses Fanny with a dashing air, reports the noisy enthusiasm of the birds for the Spring, and settles the dinner question with a sweeping affirmation. Going? Of course they're going. "Company is bound to be a bore, but the food is always good."

What if the President carries out his threat to throw him out? "Well, my dear, in that event, I shall simply say to myself: 'Holmes, what would a man from the Boston *Transcript* do in a situation like this?'—and then be sure to do the opposite."

But he would like to have an explanation of what Fanny means by telling people that she is the second Mrs. Holmes? What does she think people back in Boston will think of that?

"Do you care what the people in Boston think?" she demands, after explaining that the *Transcript* man had simply jumped to conclusions. "Back there you were merely the good-looking son of the famous Autocrat of the Breakfast Table. To them you were just some sort of literary ornament on the Bench, more brilliant than sound. To them—"

Fanny has suddenly remembered the perfumed note and given it to the Judge.

"It came for you in the afternoon mail," she reports, with a knowing look in her eye. "It was marked personal—so I thought you might like to open it yourself."

She starts out, but such is her interest she must stop at the door and watch the Judge as he reads the note. Nor is he conscious of her being there until he has read the letter through twice and she speaks to him—

"Well, Wendell—who is she?" He does not look up. "Is she pretty?"

"Yes—she's pretty. Very pretty." Then he realizes that he is talking to Fanny, and not to himself. "Eh, what? What's that? Oh, it's nothing—nothing at all! . . . For just a moment I was back at Antietam . . . on the road to Hagerstown with a bullet in my neck . . . and no one to care for me until the Kennedys took me in . . . and a girl named Ellen Jones nursed me back to health . . . I never saw her again but she's in town now and . . ."

"Well, let's have her out to dinner by all means."

"Yes, that would be very nice but . . . she wants to know if I'll have dinner with her at the Shoreham some night."

"The Shoreham?"

"That's where she's stopping. Of course it's all a little silly. I don't want to go at all but—"

"Don't be absurd, Wendell. Of course you want to go!"

"You don't think I should though—do you?"

"My dear, what possible difference could it make to me? It's only that—"

"Only what?"

"Some people do change, you know . . . in forty-two years . . . even if you don't."

"Oh, not Ellen Jones. She was the prettiest thing that ever came out of Philadelphia. (*Then catching himself.*) I mean—well, it can't be forty-two years, Fanny. It can't be. Why, it was only yesterday. I can still hear the pound of cannon in the hills. . . . I can still smell the powder burning. I can—"

"Can you still smell the perfume she used? Or has she changed the brand by now perhaps?"

Fanny's tone has brought the Judge to with a start, but there's a rather pleasant gleam in his eye. "Fanny—you're not jealous—not at this late date?"

"What do you mean by 'this late date'? Was there a time when it would have been quite in order for me to be jealous of Miss Jones?"

"Now, Fanny—"

"I always knew that half the girls in Boston had lost their hearts to you . . . but I had never given a thought to Philadelphia."

"I'll have you know, Mrs. Holmes, that in a democracy a man can still look at a pretty woman without violating either his marriage vows or the Constitution of the United States."

"Don't you talk about the Constitution to me, Mr. Holmes. Save that for Mr. Roosevelt. If you want to spend an evening mooning over the dear old days with an elderly hussy from Philadelphia—"

"But she's not a hussy. She's a nice girl—at least she was when I knew her."

"—why, you go right ahead. I have no objections. Only don't bring the Constitution into it. Take her some nice flowers—buy her a good wine and a wonderful dinner. But leave the Constitution home. You won't need it!"

She would flounce out of the room, but Mary stops her to report that a Mr. Owen Wister is calling. He has asked to see Mrs.—not Mr.—Holmes. The Judge is not disturbed by that. Let Wister be shown up—and right away.

Wister is 44. *The Virginian* is two years behind him. He is what the Judge would call a swell, but he is also pretty much what the Judge might have liked in a son. He has "dash, fire, character and a nice sense of humor."

The enthused greetings over, Wister announces that he is there as an unofficial ambassador from President Roosevelt—

"As far as I can gather," says Wister, "the President would like to refuse the Judge admission to the White House at any and all times— But, as regards Mrs. Holmes—I am permitted to express the hope—oh, most unofficially, you understand—that at dinner this evening Mrs. Holmes will do the President the great honor of sitting on his right."

HOLMES (*flabbergasted*)—Well, I'll be damned.

FANNY (*rising quickly*)—Mr. Roosevelt is most kind, Mr. Ambassador. But it will not be possible for Mrs. Holmes to accept.

WISTER—What?

FANNY—Because Mrs. Holmes isn't going to the White House dinner tonight.

HOLMES—Eh? What's that?

WISTER—But, my dear, decline an invitation from the White House. It just isn't done.

FANNY—Oh, isn't it? Well, we'll see about that.

HOLMES (*explosively*)—Damn it, Fanny—what's all this about anyway? Of course we're going. I don't give two straws for Teddy Roosevelt, but wild horses wouldn't keep me away from the White House tonight. I'm going to look him straight in the eye and if he blinks behind those glasses of his, I'll—

FANNY—Very well, Mr. Holmes. Look him in the eye if you want to—but you can look alone. (*Then more softly.*) Good heavens, Wendell. Where's your Yankee pride? Did you leave it behind you in Boston? Sit to the right of him, will I?—(*Turns to* WISTER.) You can tell the President for me, Mr. Ambassador, that he could carve a better dinner companion out of a banana! (FANNY *starts out—pauses at door with a nice smile for* WISTER.) But you can tell that nice Mr. Wister that the Holmeses would be deeply honored if he would stay for tea.

HOLMES (*softly, as* FANNY *goes out leaving an admiring* WISTER *and baffled* HOLMES *behind her*)—You know, my boy—I'm married to a wonderful woman. She has made life poetry for me—(*Then fingering perfumed letter and putting it away.*) but there are times when I can never be equal to her. Right now I'm not sure whether it's me or Mr. Roosevelt she is punishing.

WISTER—But what am I going to tell the President?

HOLMES (*with enjoyment*)—My boy, I haven't the least idea in the world.

Fanny having left them, the men settle to their visit. How does the Judge like Washington? Well, the New Willard isn't the Parker House, but the thing he misses most are those three-alarm fires he, Fanny and "Whiskers" used to run to—

"Of course Washington is full of Congressmen and Senators," admits the Judge, with a grin, "but every now and then you find a fellow whose mind begins to wriggle with the first sparks of thoughts."

Wister would know if there isn't some way that Judge Holmes and T. R. could bury the hatchet. T. R. would never admit a mistake, naturally, but he's a wonderful person, once you get to know him. What's the real trouble, anyway?

"Well, my boy—mostly it's just that we are two different men doing two different jobs," the Judge explains. "Our problems are different but, you see, my problems began to straighten out quite a lot when I woke up one fine day and decided that I was *not* God Almighty!"

"But, seriously, Judge—"

"I am serious. The magic moment is when you decide that there are other people in the universe, and that it isn't your high destiny to be the one and only boss of the Cosmos. But you take Theodore Roosevelt now—he hasn't discovered yet that he is *not* God Almighty. And that complicates matters for him."

Anyway, Wister would point out, the people all like Roosevelt. That, says the Judge, may be because T. R. "doesn't care a damn for the law." To settle the point they ask Mary, who has come to lay the tea things, what she thinks of Mr. Roosevelt—

"Well, sir—as Mr. Dooley says—I guess he is a great hand for getting things done," says Mary.

"There, you see?" beams Wister.

"Yes, he gets things done all right," admits the Judge. "Only trouble is he doesn't care how. Oh, I'll admit some of his aims are steps in the right direction. That "square" deal he's always talking about . . . some of it pretty good stuff. But he ought to remember once in a while that this is the United States of America . . . not the United States of Theodore Roosevelt."

"Come, Judge. He's not that swell-headed."

"Oh, no? I met a fellow the other day who read the proofs on the President's book about the Spanish War. Tells me they made T. R. cut out the line which read—"The bravest man I ever knew followed me up San Juan Hill—!"

It was entirely understandable that T. R. would hope Justice Holmes would see things his way in the Northern Securities case, insists Wister, seeing he (Holmes) was T. R.'s first appointee to the Court.

"Yes, because I happened to go labor's way in some cases back in Massachusetts, he thought I was a freebooter— His freebooter. (*Then challengingly.*) But he's all wrong. A good judge isn't anybody's judge. And most of all, he isn't something that a President carries around in his vest pocket."

"I'm sorry, Judge. You're either with T. R. or against him."

"That wasn't what it said in the statute the day I took my oath of office," answers the Judge, with something of a bark. But his tone softens as he adds: "Ah, look here, Whiskers—I know it was a hard case but hard cases can make bad law. If the President wants to crack down on the big railroad mergers, let him go ahead and crack. But damn it to hell, let him get something stronger than the Sherman Anti-Trust Act."

There is a trace of anger in the Wister tone as he suggests that the President has little time to waste. "Any stick to beat a dog is a good stick."

"Of course, that's what every strong man thinks when he begins to swing the big stick. Follow me, or get out of my way."

"Very well, sir. If that's the way you feel about it—" Wister has risen and is starting for the door. "I guess there isn't anything that anybody can do to bring you and the President together."

"Hold on, Whiskers—this isn't going to make any difference as between you and me, is it?"

"I don't know, sir. That all depends on you."

"Now, look here—"

But Wister has reached the door and briskly pulled it open. There stands Fanny in a beautiful new evening dress.

"Do you think Mr. Roosevelt will like this?" she asks, demurely.

In a moment both men are figuratively on their knees before her. What made her change her mind about the dinner? "That's hard to say," says she, blithely. "Maybe it was the dress— Or maybe it was poor Mr. Roosevelt. After all, men are so easily misunderstood—aren't they, darling?"

With a smile the Judge is willing to admit that she may be right. As for Wister, he would like very much to know what it is all about.

"Why, Mr. Ambassador, it's just life—that's what it is," says Fanny, sweetly. "Some of us suddenly acquire a great passion for dining with Mr. Roosevelt . . . others for dining with old flames from Philadelphia."

The clanging bell of a passing fire engine reaches them through the windows. Judge Holmes' excitement is keen. "I say, that sounds like a big one—three alarm. Come on, boy, let's go!"

The Wister excitement is also bubbling. The Judge and "Whiskers" start out together, but they can't lose Fanny—

"Oh, no, you don't. If you can still go racing to fires, so can I—"

"But what about your new dress?" asks Wister.

"And what about the man you're wearing it for tonight—that man in the White House?"

"What's the man in the White House compared to a fire—Come on!"

It's Fanny who leads them through the door.

The curtain falls.

ACT II

Eight years have made but little difference in the appearance of the Holmes library. There are new curtains. One or two sectional extensions have been added to the book shelves and there is a new print or two on the walls.

At the moment the Judge is sitting at the table playing solitaire. Fanny is reading to him—

"And when the wind in the tree-tops roared,
The soldier asked from the deep dark grave:
'Did the banner flutter then?'
'Not so, my hero,' the wind replied,
'The fight is done, but the banner won,
Thy comrades of old have borne it hence,
Have borne it in triumph hence.'"

Fanny stops reading. The Judge is intent upon his cards. "Wendell, you're not listening," Fanny complains. Wendell goes on silently with his cards until he completes his play.

"Not listening? It takes me back fifty years . . ." He takes up the poem from where Fanny had left it—

"Then he heareth the lovers laughing pass,
And the soldier asks once more:
'Are these not the voices of them that love,
That love—and remember me?'
'Not so, my hero, the lovers say,
We are those that remember not;
For the Spring has come and the earth has smiled,
And the dead must be forgot!'

Then the soldier spake from the deep dark grave,
'I am content.'"

The Judge has moved over to the windows. He is "restless with a reflective kind of uneasiness—"

"I wonder if that will sound the same in another fifty years . . . ?" he wonders. "Ah, the trouble is few books are worth reading twenty-five years after they have been written . . . the things that struck sparks for you as a boy have a way of fizzling out by the time you're—(*Then wryly.*)—you know, I begin to suspect that I must be quite an old man."

"Humph!" Fanny has taken up her embroidery. "You've been saying you were an old man ever since you were forty!"

The newest of the secretaries hasn't come back at eight-thirty as promised, and the Judge is worried and a little peeved. He has a speech to work on—a speech for a crowd of his old classmates who "are going to get together in June and paint the town red."

"What am I going to tell them, Fanny?" he asks, a little plaintively, when she chides him for not having let her know about this speech. "What can I tell them? Fifty years we've been out of Harvard now—and fifty years ought to add up to something, but do they—and if so, how much? I could put all I know about life on one small piece of white paper but on the other side I'd have to write 'not proved.' "

"It's right pretty talk," agrees Fanny, knowingly, "but it doesn't take me in a bit. When you're in a tight spot, I notice you always begin to twist the tail of the cosmos. . . . You're awfully scared somebody may find out about it some day. So you retire behind those beautiful white whiskers of yours and mutter, 'Ah, me; ah, me, what is life?' Why don't you come out in the open just once and let us all in on the secret?"

The secretary has arrived. He is very much like the others. A shade handsomer, perhaps. He is wearing a smart linen duster and holds in his hand a dashing motor cap with goggles attached. His name is Northrop and he is very, very sorry to be late. There was a break-down near Mt. Vernon—and—and—the fact is Mr. Northrop fears he will have to resign. He is going to get married.

"Married? That's preposterous!" This from the Judge with something of a bark. "Why, you promised you wouldn't. You—"

"I realize that, sir. But you know how these things are."

"I know nothing of the sort. Why, Northrop, this is amazing! This is unprecedented! This is—"

"Nonsense, Wendell. Secretaries are getting married every day," puts in Fanny.

"Not my secretaries!" snaps the Judge.

Then Fanny takes over and, offering her congratulations to the flustered and troubled Northrop, gets the story from him: He and his young lady had been engaged for a year. The car broke down. There was nothing to do but wait for the horses to come. And—well—anyway Northrop is the happiest of men—or would be, if it were not that he will be leaving the Judge.

Fanny fixes that, too. "I know, dear—a rule is a rule—but you only made up the rule for your secretaries. You can't possibly expect it to be binding on the girls they are in love with. . . ."

"All right, Northrop," agrees the Judge. "I know when I'm licked. Consider your resignation refused."

Given the evening off, an excessively grateful Northrop promises to get back to his bride as soon as he can, and to be sure that he will be on time in the morning. Fanny stands watching him off, smiling tenderly.

"Now, as for you, my good woman—" The Judge is eyeing Fanny sardonically.

"Did you notice his eyes, Wendell? Did you ever see anything so shining bright? No wonder folks say some people carry their hearts in their eyes. They do, you know—and sometimes it's just a little dazzling. You want to look closer and closer . . . and then suddenly you feel like a trespasser."

"Very pretty! But let's face the facts, woman. You tried to blackmail me just now!"

"I thought I got away with it rather well. Besides, milord, as I understand the law—it's only blackmail if there was anything black to back up the threat with. And surely there wasn't anything that wasn't pure white between you and Ellen Jones—except that she *was* a little fat when you finally caught up with her forty years later. Remember?"

"Well, maybe she was a little plump—but—"

"Oh, Wendell—Wendell—what difference does it make? This boy is almost like a son—just like all the others."

"That's neither here nor there. And if you ever say anything to any of them—I'll disown them—"

"Oh! He's so young . . . and it's so wonderful to be young."

Henry Adams is calling. What can be troubling Henry this time, the Judge wonders. "Each year it's something different. You can be sure it's President Taft now. Every administration brings new woes to Adams—and, God, how he enjoys it!"

But the Judge has no time for Henry just now. Let Mary tell him that Mrs. Holmes will be down in a few minutes. Meantime he and Fanny will return to his talk.

"What kind of an account am I to give of myself to my old classmates?" asks the Judge. "What can I say I've learned in all these years? Listen to me, Fanny, while I gather wool."

"Very well, but Mr. Adams is waiting."

"Mm-m-m! Adams—my mistake has been that I was trying to add up the years the way Adams would add them up. (*There is something electric and exciting about the* JUDGE *now.*) But life isn't doing a sum. It's painting a picture . . . and sometimes you have to have confidence that the canvas will fill out as you go along. . . . What difference does it make that I haven't reached all my objectives in my few years down here? No man ever can—we are lucky enough if we can give a sample of our best and if in our hearts we can feel it was well done. At least

I have helped them to see that the Constitution is a living thing . . . and a broad thing too . . . I've helped them see that the personal views of judges ought not to determine what is allowed and what is not allowed under the Constitution . . . that it takes a lot of live and let live to put a republic together and keep it going . . . and that we ought to give the individual states as much leeway as we can in social experiments for the common good. We must not be afraid to trust our people."

As Judge Holmes pauses Fanny looks up at him with a smile. He goes on: "Well, you were right, Fanny. I *am* a believer in spite of everything. I believe in my country. I believe in the people in it. I even at times believe in myself—and the universe I'm a part of, though I'm damned if I know yet just what it is that holds them both together from one day to the next. . . . Oh, I know—I don't have evidence to back all this up, but, Lord, life isn't a matter of how much evidence you have . . . because you never will have enough . . . It's a matter of how much faith you have . . . faith in a universe not measured by your fears. Ah, there's the trick, Fanny, the real trick. Not to measure things by our fears but by our faith."

FANNY—Now, Wendell, you *are* beginning to come out from behind those beautiful white whiskers.

HOLMES—Yes, I feel naked but warm somehow—warm. Why, that's the trouble with Henry Adams, he has no fire in his belly. And where there's no fire, there's no hope. There's no—

FANNY (*firmly*)—Now, Wendell—belly is not a nice word.

HOLMES (*explosively*)—Well, I'll be damned. Here I go pouring out my very soul to you and all you can say is "belly is not a nice word."

FANNY—Well, it isn't . . . to some people.

HOLMES—Very well. If the word belly will shock the delicate sensibilities of the old boys at Harvard, we won't use it. But belly was what I said and belly, by God, is what I mean . . . it's the thing you crawl on when the bullets get too thick overhead . . . it's the thing you march on, by Heaven, when everything else fails you. A belly, my good woman, is the place where a soldier's faith is born . . . a belly— (FANNY *gives way to laughter and can't stop.*) Well, what's so funny about that?

FANNY (*rising*)—I'm sorry, Wendell. I didn't mean to laugh. Really I didn't . . . but suddenly—I got to thinking about poor Mr. Adams . . . I'm sure he never even thought of the word belly in his whole life . . . and if he did . . . if he did just once . . . I'm sure he wouldn't have the stomach for it.

Fanny, convulsed with laughter, leaves the Judge—leaves him looking after her, "puzzled and a little frustrated."

The curtain falls.

It is June in Washington, the June of 1916. The five years last passed have made little change in Judge Holmes' appearance. He is a little older, but as erect as ever. He is working at his desk, going through the texts of some of his brother justices. Another of Harvard's bright young men is working with him.

It is too nice a day, the Judge observes, for them to stay bottled up with a lot of printer's ink. But before they get away—at least before the secretary can get away—another batch of papers has arrived from the Court.

"You know, the double damned fertility of my brethren will kill me yet," says Holmes. "Time was when a Judge could sneak away on a nice afternoon and commune with nature—or whatever his luck turned up. But now . . ."

Having left the new work with his secretary (the name is Hamilton), the Judge has gone to see how things are along the Potomac when his wife comes into the room. Fanny is 75 now, but still as "slim, striking and indomitable as ever."

Fanny is worried about their getting away for Beverly Farms. No, Mr. Hamilton has not made their reservations. There is no telling how soon the Senate will be ready to confirm the appointment of Louis Brandeis.

And now the Judge comes gaily back, followed by Owen Wister, whom he tells Fanny he found on the doorstep. Of course Owen will be staying to tea, but Holmes does wish Fanny would get over the tea habit. A good cup of tea may be even better than a good glass of wine—but everybody to his taste—

"Said Aristotle unto Plato:
'Do have another sweet potato?'
Said Plato unto Aristotle:
'No, thank you. I prefer the bottle.' "

That happens to be a Wister verse. "Will I never be able to live that down!" sighs the author.

Wister, just back from a trip to Europe, is surprised to find the Judge still working through the June heat. He is also a little concerned about the happenings of the day: Will we or will we not be able to keep out of Kaiser Wilhelm's fracas? Holmes doesn't believe we can—

"I had a commander-in-chief once who said a country couldn't endure half slave and half free. What's the difference between a country and a world?"

It may be, Wister observes, that Hughes will have a war left on his doorstep—if he can beat Wilson. Whether he will or not, the Judge hates to see Hughes resign from the bench—

"There's a man with a real sense of humor and a neat turn of mind," says Holmes.

There is also talk of Chief Justice White resigning. If he does, who will be the appointee most likely to succeed him? Supposing Wilson should name Mr. Taft?

"Whiskers, you ought to stick to stories about the great outdoors," advises the Judge, teasingly.

Wister is ready to admit that Taft would not be a bad choice, but he can't see any reason why, if White resigns, the President should not name a fellow named Holmes—

"Easy, Whiskers," cautions Holmes. "I'm getting to be an old man—well, seventy-five, anyway."

He is prowling about the room now, evidently bent on making it appear that he really isn't interested in any appointment—but he is.

"I'm only what we call a side Judge," Holmes is saying. "They never name a side judge to be Chief. It's much easier to designate someone who isn't already on the Court. (*Then breaking off abruptly.*) Besides, I'm fond of White . . . even if he was a Johnny Reb in his day . . . not bad fellows the Johnny Rebs . . . they had to be discouraged of course but they fought like gentlemen . . ."

The secretary is back. Henry Adams, he reminds Judge Holmes, is still downstairs, and insists on being seen. Wister would get out of the way, but the Judge will not let him off that easy. Let Adams be shown up there.

"If he bothers you too much, why do you keep on seeing him?" Wister wants to know.

"I don't know. The duffer is a fascinating kind of bird, though. He's like a hen that's always brooding and never hatching anything. Just stand by and maybe he won't stay very long."

It is the Louis Brandeis appointment that is troubling Adams at this time. Not that he has anything against Brandeis but if a fight against his confirmation should be prolonged, as threatened, it would be certain to divide the country as it has not been divided since the Civil War. Jew will be lined up against non-Jew and—

"Poppycock!" explodes Judge Holmes. "This isn't a Jewish issue at all."

"Of course it isn't. But people are beginning to think it is—and already it is being said that even the Court itself might not be too disappointed if—"

"Nonsense. A few of the brethren may not be keen for Brandeis, but it's his ideas they are afraid of—not his religion. And the same is true of the die-hards in the Senate. If Brandeis had never fought the utilities, if he had never taken the part of labor, if he hadn't been quite so successful at it, they would have called him a nice Jew—and accepted him. When you come right down to it, Adams, very few people are against the Jews because they *are* Jews. The real reason is always something else but they never admit it. The Jews have contributed a lot to this country and one of their prize contributions is Brandeis—and if I were Wilson I'd hang on until hell freezes over—and then I'd skate on top of it!"

A moment later, another of Fanny Holmes' conspiracies is uncovered—Louis Brandeis is calling. Fanny had asked him to stop by for tea. She knew that the Judge had made it a point never to see appointees while their nominations were still before the Senate, but she feels that this occasion is a little different. The Judge may not know it (as he doesn't), but the Administration is calling up the Brandeis appointment this afternoon, and evidently they have the votes to put it over.

"But if what you say is true, surely I would have heard of it?" protests Holmes.

"Darling," Fanny answers sweetly, "the justices of the Supreme Court are the last people in the world to hear anything about anything. And that's as it should be. You are sweet old darlings who live in a cloister . . . and try not to see too much of the wicked world outside. But senators and the wives of senators are something else again . . . especially the wives."

A few moments later Mary has shown in Mr. and Mrs. Brandeis, a pleasant, modest pair, who seem nervously conscious through the introductions. It is certainly a bit early for congratulations, Brandeis protests. But he is quite pleased with the compliments and the hopes of these friends. A little later a messenger from the Senate brings the happy tidings—the Brandeis appointment has been confirmed.

"There were only twenty-two votes against me," says the new Justice, with a happy smile.

With his arm around Judge Brandeis' shoulders, Judge Holmes beams his congratulations. "Welcome, brother—welcome to the Hall of—of—Disagreement." He turns to the others. "My friends, I give you Mr. Justice Brandeis—a Daniel come to Judgment!"

"Hear! Hear!" This from Henry Adams.

"Come along, Daniel," invites the Judge. "I know a better way than this to celebrate."

"I'm with you," laughs Wister, following after.

The curtain falls.

It is a Sunday evening in March, 1921. Just two days before Justice Holmes' eightieth birthday. Again the library shows only minor changes—further extensions to the bookcases and a new print or two.

The Judge, standing before a bull's-eye mirror, is trying to give his white tie a debonair angle and swearing at all inventors of bull's-eye mirrors.

Fanny Holmes, still charming at 80 as she was at 60, is able to fix the tie, and explain, a little slyly, to the Judge, that the reason he is all dressed up for this particular Sunday night dinner is because he is "80 years young."

"You're not fooling me, old man," she teases. "You love to step out in your best bib and tucker, and you know it."

"Woman—you are a dangerous—and beautiful creature."

"Humph! That's what you say to every pretty woman you meet."

"True . . . but I never mean it with the rest of 'em!"

"Thank you, my love . . . I've really begun to believe that, I think."

The newest of the secretaries, a presentable young man named Mapes, has stopped by to leave some papers. His evening dress is concealed by overcoat and white scarf, but it isn't easy for him to announce convincingly that he is on his way to a party with some of the boys.

Now Judge Brandeis has called. He knew that Justice Holmes was going out to dinner with his wife, but he also knew about the coming birthday. He had picked up an etching he thought perhaps the Judge might like. It's a Zorn and the Judge is a Zorn enthusiast. He thanks Brandeis very sincerely—

"Does one have to thank a friend for thinking of him?"

"You know what I mean," says Holmes, with a nice growl. "I used to think there was no one . . . except Pollock in England . . . or Canon Sheehan in Ireland . . . who really knew or cared what I was driving for. But it's been a little different with you in there beside me."

"It's been different for me, too. You know (*With some eagerness.*)—sometimes I begin to believe that our dissenting opinions may yet change the mind of the public—and the courts too."

There is a sharp contrast as between the rather nice detachment of a Holmes, and the crusading spirit of a Brandeis. "I wonder!" Holmes is saying. "We dissented pretty vigorously in *Hammer v. Dagenhart* and where did it get us? If a judge happens to like the idea of child labor, he can still go on making his personal prejudice the law of the land."

"But it won't always be that way, mark my words. Some day *our* dissent will be the law of the land. Smile, if you want to, Holmes—but the world is getting better. And the judges along with it."

"Really, Sir Launcelot? What about those free speech cases? The brethren went clear against us on most of them."

"I know—I know. But give time a chance, Holmes."

"I'd like to, my boy—I really would. But somehow I can't get that Abrams case out of my mind . . . think of it . . . twenty years in prison for men . . . who printed a few pamphlets and shouted, 'Workers of the World, Awake' . . . I suppose you'd like to tell me that our dissent there will be the law of the land some day too?"

"Why not? People *can* change, can't they? You've said so yourself. You've said that change is the law of life—and the life of the law. You've said—"

"All right, you old fire-eater, all right." Holmes has put both hands on Brandeis' shoulders. "I don't like being a dissenter any more than you do but if that's the way to make people think —let's keep on kicking—kicking like a pair of Army mules!"

Brandeis suddenly realizes that Holmes has been ragging him deliberately. "I see—you were just twisting the tail of the cosmos again, eh? Or was it the tail of a man named Brandeis?"

Brandeis has left. Presently Fanny tiptoes her way into the room, motioning for silence behind her. And now there is a faint hum of male voices down the hall—voices getting ready to burst forth with "Happy Birthday." The doors are thrown open and fifteen young men, dressed to the teeth in white ties and tails, file in. They are fifteen of the Holmes secretaries and they have brought their own champagne.

Proudly they file past the Judge, speaking their individual birthday compliments. Then they line up with their glasses for a toast. The Judge is plainly a little fussed.

"Fanny, you're to blame for this!" he mutters.

"Is that all you can say on an occasion like this?" Fanny demands, as everybody giggles.

The Holmes recovery is quick and he tells them of his eagerness to say something worth saying to them. When he was a boy his father had made it a practice to serve him a second helping of marmalade whenever he said anything bright at the breakfast table. He has never liked marmalade since then, but at the moment he would very much like to earn such a reward—

"You've been pretty good boys," he tells them. "Some of you have turned out to be pretty important pumpkins. I couldn't be prouder of you if you were my own sons—and yet you are in a way—sons-at-law, I guess you'd call it."

It is a bad pun and he knows it. He accepts the small ripple of laughter with a wry grin.

"Sorry. Even the Governor never inflicted a worse pun than that," he goes on. "Well, I wish I had something special to pass on to you boys at a time like this. But you know how I feel about hunches. Any one of yours is just as good as any one of mine. I will say this, though—I always had the idea that, when I got to be fourscore, I could wrap up my life in a scroll, tie a pink ribbon around it, put it away in a drawer, and go around doing the things I wanted to do. But I'm just beginning to see once more that the good fight is never over . . . there's always a new firing line just beyond . . . and that is as it should be . . . You boys remember, no man has the right to intellectual ambition until he has learned to set his course by a star he has never seen—to dig with a divining rod for springs he may never reach. (*Turns to* FANNY *with a teasing smile.*) And now, my dear, may a grateful but surprised host enquire how the devil we're going to cheer these boys, now that Mr. Volstead's moral tornado has become the law of the land?"

"The champagne is cooling downstairs and we've had it for years. It's perfectly all right, darling. All very legal."

"Then, gentlemen, we will toast the United States of America . . . and a new firing line."

"And the Supreme Court of the United States—and its next Chief Justice, Oliver Wendell Holmes," adds Mason, the current secretary.

"Hear! Hear!"

But the Judge can't go along with them in that. "Sorry to disappoint you, boys," he says. "White *is* retiring soon . . . The President wants a conservative—I think Taft will be the man . . . but it isn't anything for me . . . I'm too old for that kind of going's on . . . and besides I never did understand ambition for high office . . ."

There is a wonderful dinner waiting for them downstairs, Fanny announces, and a wonderful cake with eighty-one candles on it—including the one to grow on. The secretaries are filing out singing *"Guadeamus Igitur."*

"Wendell—it doesn't really matter, does it, about the Chief Justiceship?"

"No. Not really."

"Sure?"

"Of course. It's only for a moment—just for a moment—I had the strange idea that it might have mattered to some of the boys. I caught something in their eyes . . . as if they might have liked it . . . why, damn it, I felt just like a father who's let his sons down somehow . . . and they're not my sons . . . they're just a lot of fresh young rascals from Harvard . . . listen to them now . . . drinking my champagne and singing about how good it is to rejoice when you are young . . . that's all they know about it . . . the real trick is to rejoice when you're eighty . . . the real trick . . . Fanny, what the devil am I talking about anyway?"

"I'm sure I don't know Wendell—and if I did I wouldn't tell you."

Fanny touches her head lightly to his shoulder, grips his arm and they start toward the singing together.

The curtain falls.

ACT III

On a clear, crisp afternoon in January, 1929, we find Judge Holmes sitting at his desk in the Holmes library. With young Mr. Rogers (Harvard Law '28) he has been going over his work and finds that he is just about caught up. "At 88 the Judge is still a dominating and gallant figure, but now he has the look of a man who is fighting an enemy who cannot be defeated." Fanny Holmes has been in poor health for three years. Her devoted life partner is just beginning to face the parting of the ways.

Justice Brandeis has called. At 72 Brandeis is still vigorous and eager. He has come to inquire about Fanny. She's getting better all the time, the Judge tells him. "Just won't admit the possibility of a Yankee being an invalid."

As for himself, Holmes has not been too good, but perhaps he has just been spoiling for a good fight. The chances are good that they'll be getting that in the Rosika Schwimmer case. The decision is some time off, but so far as they know there will be only the two of them and, possibly, McReynolds on the dissenting side.

"By Heaven, I'd like to win one of these big fights just once . . . and this is a big fight," declares Holmes, with spirit. "This isn't just a matter of denying citizenship to a sincere woman pacifist. It's a matter of denying to ourselves just what that citizenship means . . . freedom of opinion doesn't mean merely freedom for the ideas we happen to like—it means just as much freedom for the ideas we happen to despise. For either this country of ours is a country where each man's right to his own point of view is respected and protected by every other man or—or—"

For a moment the Judge falters and seems unable to go on. "I'm sorry, Brandeis. My heart's with you, but I can't seem to make my mind behave. I'm worried . . . I'm worried about Fanny." A moment later he is trying to justify this human weakness. "—I wouldn't mind if it were I . . . I think for myself I could face the unknown without a quiver . . . but to stand by and watch it strike down the woman you've been married to for fifty-seven years . . . it breaks you up in little pieces."

"But none of us is eternal," says Brandeis.

"I know . . . I know . . . but people in love like to think they are. . . . Oh, it's a good joke on me in a way . . . all my life I've shouted that I didn't believe in heaven and I didn't believe in hell . . . felt pretty smart about it, too . . . I was so all-fired legal about it . . . 'not proved' I shouted at the universe and the universe shouted back 'not proved' . . . or so I thought . . . but now . . . maybe I wouldn't be so finicky about the proof if anybody thought he *could* prove it . . ."

"Damn it, I don't want things to wind up on me forever," he is saying a moment later. "Oh, I know I've bragged that life came out of nothing and would dissolve into nothing . . . but those are mere words . . . and I've always urged people to think things instead of words . . . well, I am thinking things now . . .

I wish to Heaven I had one of those souls Dante is always talking about. I wish—"

The door has opened and Fanny has come in quietly. "At 88 she is still an indomitable spirit—but there is an almost transparent air about her now."

For a little Fanny would joke with them, and chide the Judge for his too apparent concern for her. She is quite all right. When the Judge would go to get his guest a good cigar, Fanny suggests that he bring her one, too. With her husband gone, Fanny would make a slight confession to Brandeis. Not only is she worried about the Judge—(*He smokes too many cigars.*)—but—

"Sometimes lately I have the feeling . . . I haven't very much more time." She quickly passes by his assurances that she is looking wonderful. "I don't mind going when I have to . . . it's just that . . . he'll be so lonely without me . . . and women are so much better at waiting than men . . . especially when the men are not too sure just what it is they're waiting for . . ."

She would, if she could, pin Judge Brandeis down to a statement of his own belief about the hereafter—

"My dear, who can say for sure?" he answers her. "But I do believe this: Nothing good is ever lost. It renews itself constantly."

Holmes has come gaily back. He holds behind his back two cigars in one hand and a small nosegay of violets in the other. "Of course they're only hothouse stuff, ma'am . . ." he says as he gives the posies to Fanny, "but I understand they bespeak a loving heart."

"Silly—" Fanny raises his hand to her lips.

For a little they try desperately to appear natural. Judge Holmes is anxious that Fanny reassure him that it is all right for her to be up. For a moment it seems as though Fanny might break down and tell the Judge something of her doubt about the future. Then both find a way out by going back to the Rosika Schwimmer decision.

"What seems to be the trouble?" Fanny would know.

HOLMES—Oh, the real trouble is I don't agree with the dear lady's pacifist ideas at all.

FANNY—But whether you agree with them or not has nothing to do with whether she will make a good citizen, has it?

HOLMES—Of course not. That's exactly what the case is about. But the fact that I don't have much personal enthusiasm for the lady's slant on things is likely to make for a pretty flat opinion . . . when I come to defend her point of view.

FANNY (*now very interested*)—Just what's wrong with her point of view?

HOLMES (*in his old stride again*)—Now isn't that just like a woman? The trouble with Rosika Schwimmer is . . . she thinks like a woman. She thinks the destiny of mankind is to unite in peaceful leagues and alliances. She—

FANNY—Would that be so bad?

HOLMES (*rushing on*)—And as a consequence she will not promise to bear arms for her country in time of trouble. Well, considering the fact that Rosika Schwimmer is well past 50 now, I don't think the promise would mean much one way or the other.

FANNY—I suppose it's odd of me, Wendell, but everything you say about her sounds most attractive.

HOLMES—Now isn't that just like a woman? Look, Fanny—I know what war is. When you're at it, it's a messy and a dirty business . . . an organized bore. But out of it sometimes comes heroism . . . and a faith in heroism. For you can't fight for a thing without believing in it . . . Call it a soldier's faith if you like, but there it is. Now I'm not saying it's the only kind of faith there is, but—

FANNY (*with deep intensity*)—No, after all, there's the faith that takes the Sermon on the Mount as gospel truth.

HOLMES—Eh? What's that?

FANNY—And I suppose we have never held it against the Quakers that they seemed to take the Sermon on the Mount a little more seriously than some of us do . . . or can . . .

HOLMES (*with excitement*)—Fanny, my dear—that's it—I have it now—the twist I need to give it. Old girl, you're worth two of me any day. I don't know what I'd do without you, I—

FANNY—You've never tried.

Again an Adams has called. This time it is Charles Francis Adams, Secretary of the Navy. Fanny is anxious that Wendell should be nice to this Adams—"He's quite different from his uncle—and besides, you don't have to be jealous of the Adamses any more . . . you have twenty-seven boys all your own now, remember?"

"By Jove, that's right . . . why, by now they outnumber all the Adamses put together . . . and they'll be around a long time after . . . (HOLMES *was about to say "after you and I are gone" but he corrects himself quickly.*) . . . after the people who hound

Rosika Schwimmer are gone and forgotten. Oh, I forgot Adams. Cheer up, old girl, if a man has enough secretaries, a good cause is never lost . . . there's always somebody left to carry the battle to the enemy . . . another day."

He blows her a kiss as he leaves her. She is standing at the window looking out, "as one might who is taking a last look at many things."

"Another day!" she murmurs, softly. She has lifted the nosegay to her lips.

The curtain falls.

The Holmes library is still practically unchanged in March, 1933. Fanny's bird is gone and there is a small radio in the corner—an addition to the furnishings she probably would not have approved. It is a cold, clear day and there is a fire in the fireplace. Mary, grown a bit ancient on her own account, is dusting the room. When she gets to the radio she debates half a minute, and then turns it on. An announcer's voice comes in briskly—

"All up and down Pennsylvania Avenue the people are shouting themselves hoarse. The President and officials have left the balcony, and so, ladies and gentlemen, Franklin Delano Roosevelt has just become the thirty-second President of these United States. In a few moments the President's party will leave the Capitol for—"

The door opens, and in comes Owen Wister. "He is 75 now, but it is a trim 75." Wister is down from Philadelphia for the day. Sorry not to find Justice Holmes in. (MARY *thinks the* JUDGE *probably has gone out to Arlington Cemetery, a daily custom when the weather permits.*) How is the Judge—?

"Oh, he's wonderful, sir . . . wonderful," reports Mary. "But since Mrs. Holmes died—well—it's just—well, it's just as if someone had taken away the light from inside a lamp. But he never lets on, sir—he never lets on. Can I get you anything, Mr. Wister?"

"Nothing, Mary— Oh!—Just one thing more. I shouldn't be asking you this, but I wouldn't dare ask him. What does he do with himself now that he has resigned from the Court? Does time hang heavy on his hands or—"

"Oh, no, sir. He's quite busy and quite happy, sir . . . after a fashion. If you ask me, I don't think he needed to resign at all, sir. I'm sure no one wanted him to."

"You're right, Mary—no one did."

"But I suppose he was a little tired . . . I suppose anyone gets a little tired once they pass ninety . . . but, most of all, I think he wanted to stop while he was still as good as ever he was . . . and sometimes I think—(*Softly.*) Sometimes I think . . . he just wanted time to face . . . the end of things. Anybody else would rather things just caught up with them at the end . . . quite suddenly . . . without time for facing anything . . . but not the Judge. He has to look everything square in the eye . . . including the very devil himself!"

Presently from down the hall they can hear the voices of Justice Holmes and one of his secretaries (a visiting secretary this time, come back from the past).

The Judge doesn't see Wister at first, being busy with putting a German pessimist named Spengler in his place: "But what's he mean—'Decline of the West'? I tell you, boy, there's a lot of fire left in the West yet and, so far as I can see—the only thing that's declining in the West is Mr. Spengler."

Now he has caught sight of Wister and, with a glad shout of "Whiskers, my boy! Well, I'll be damned!" he has rushed over to greet him. Rushed, that is, in a relative sense. At 91 the Judge is still an impressive figure. "He carries himself with the alertness of the eternal soldier," despite the slight stoop to his shoulders. "His hair is snow white and his mustache too, but both are trimmed with the same precision that a young captain might have permitted himself."

The meeting of the old friends is friendly and most cordial. A casual mention of Fanny slows up the Judge's exuberance for a moment, and Wister suggests that perhaps he had rather be alone.

"That's just it, boy," answers Holmes. "I'm alone now . . . and somehow I can't quite get used to it."

"Perhaps you try too much . . ."

"No. A man has to keep on trying . . . no matter how alone he may be . . . no matter how little time he may have left . . . it's as I said on the radio . . . the day I was ninety . . . The riders in a race don't stop short when they reach the goal. There's a little finishing canter . . . just before the end . . . there's the time to hear the kind voice of friends and to say to one's self . . . 'the work is done' . . . but just as you say that, the answer comes . . . 'the race is over but the work is never done while the power to work remains' . . . and so the canter that brings you to a pause need not be the end. It cannot be while you still live. For to live is to function. To live—"

Mary has brought in the sherry and biscuits and is putting them on the table—

"You see what I mean, boy? To live is to function—to reach for a bottle of sherry when you can . . . and to leave your mind alone."

They are sitting at the Judge's desk, enjoying their sherry, and gradually becoming lightly reminiscent. Why did Whiskers come to Washington just now? Especially on a day like inauguration day? How could he stay away—with another Roosevelt being inaugurated? demands Wister.

"By the great horn spoon you're getting old, too," Holmes charges, with a sly twinkle in his eye. "Positively ancient, now I stop to look at you. Must be nearly all of 75, eh?"

"Just about . . ."

HOLMES—Infant!—Well, you know what I say every time I see a pretty girl—oh, to be 80 again!

WISTER—We've had some good times together . . . remember our first big argument about T. R.?

HOLMES (*softly*)—Will I ever forget it . . . that was the day Fanny set out to charm the President.

WISTER—But took time out for a three alarm fire along the way.

HOLMES—Well, Fanny did charm him . . . but I was never quite sure the old boy ever forgave me.

WISTER—Judge, you'll laugh at me for saying so—but I'm just as worried about this Roosevelt as you were about the other one.

HOLMES—Eh? You're joking.

WISTER—Never more serious in my life.

HOLMES—Oh, come now, Whiskers. For a second you sounded just like Henry Adams.

WISTER—I can't help how I sound. I'm worried. All kinds of things are in the wind now. (*Getting up and moving around.*) Do you know the newest—they say the President is going to declare a bank holiday before the day is over.

HOLMES (*casually*)—About time, isn't it? If that's the only way to save the banks.

WISTER—And after that?

HOLMES—I don't know. Maybe, if I were still on the Court, I wouldn't agree with Cousin Franklin any more than I did with Cousin Theodore. But I do know this—no one President ever wrecked this country yet and no one President ever will.

WISTER (*stiffly*)—I hope you're right—

HOLMES—Hold on, boy. This is 1932—not 1902. (*Getting up.*) And I, Heaven help me, am defending a Roosevelt while you're attacking one. Come on, Whiskers—where's your sense of humor?

WISTER (*still unyielding*)—Sorry, Judge. I guess I lost my sense of humor the day this new Roosevelt was elected to office.

Holmes is at the window. He looks back with a puzzled expression. He has lost the thread of the argument for the moment. He is, he explains, living a little behind a cloud these days. He hadn't caught all of what Whiskers was saying. But—Wister will be back for dinner. They will be having a bit of chicken and a dab of homemade ice cream—and maybe they can dig up a bottle of fizz! . . .

The newest of the secretaries is another presentable young man named Halloran. He comes now with letters he has written as he thinks the Judge would like to have them done. There is one, another of those darned requests that the Judge serve on a committee— But this one is a little different. It's a committee from a school in New York to help refugee scholars who have had to leave Germany on account of Hitler—

"Hitler? Eh—of course—of course. I remember now. That wild man is breaking all the rules . . . I might as well break one. Tell them I accept, my boy—and send them a check, too.— I don't understand what's going on in Germany," he adds, drowsily; "I don't understand it and I don't like it . . . lot of things I don't understand any more . . . lot of things you don't see so clearly . . . when you're living behind a cloud . . . when . . . (*Then more softly.*) . . . last night I drove out to Spottsylvania . . . to the Bloody Angle where we fought when I was twenty-one . . . I got out of the car and walked along the ridge just as night was coming in . . . and once more I heard the spat of bullets on the trees . . . I heard . . ."

He has drifted off now, and suddenly becomes aware of it. "Oh! I've been daydreaming again," he says, owlishly. "Oh, well, I suppose the strongest clock has got to unwind once in a while."

The Judge has settled into his chair, ready for a nap. Yes, he would like to have Halloran read to him—that should put him to sleep very easily. But before they start the reading, there are a couple of things he would like to speak about: His will is one. The original is with John Palfrey in Boston—

"I say, sir—are you feeling all right?" Halloran is a little worried.

"When you get to be my age, boy, you'll understand that death isn't the same to an old man . . . as it is to a young one . . . to die a little sooner now would be to miss the bits of pleasure . . . not the point of being . . . (*Opening one eye.*) . . . If you are wondering what I've done with all my ill-gotten gains, I'll be glad to tell you."

He dozes a little. Soon he is muttering drowsily, as though he were dictating a will—

". . . To my nephew, Edward J. Holmes, the portrait of my great-grandfather by Copley . . . to my servants gifts in cash . . . to the Library of Congress my library and works of art . . . to the Harvard Law School and Boston Museum $25,000 each . . . and all the rest to the United States of America."

"You do believe in the government, don't you?" says Halloran, softly.

"It isn't much, boy . . . a quarter million maybe . . . it would have gone to my wife if she had lived . . ."

Now he is ready to be read to—"the stuff about Roland and the Saracens again . . . you know . . . where they left him for dead, and fled before the horns of Charlemagne's returning host . . ."

Now the door has burst open and Mary, in a great state of excitement, rushes in. Something has happened! The Judge will have to do something about it right away—nap or no nap—

"Do you know who's downstairs this very minute? It's President Roosevelt—that's who it is—and he's driven over just to see you, sir!"

"What? Teddy Roosevelt in my house? What's he want now?"

"Oh, no, sir. It's not Theodore Roosevelt—it's Franklin Roosevelt. They're just taking the elevator down for him now!"

"Well—well! Show him in! Show him in!" The Judge is preening himself now; nervously starting to straighten his tie. Suddenly he seems years younger.

"I can't make it out—the President here—what can he possibly want with you, sir?" Halloran is completely stumped.

The Judge is beaming. "I don't know, my boy. I was born a Republican and he was born a Democrat. But he's my commander-in-chief, by God, and we'll receive him accordingly."

"But there's no precedent for a thing like this . . . the White House never does the calling . . . it's the other way around . . .

and besides, he's only been in office an hour . . ."

"Now, my boy—don't you worry about all this. This is the last canter . . . and I'm going to enjoy every moment of it. Now, let me see—you stand over there—and I'll stand over here. No, you'd better go out and meet him at the elevator—hurry—and I'll—"

"But, Mr. Justice, what will you say to the President? What *can* you say to him on a day like this?"

"Easy, son. When you bring my commander-in-chief in, I'll tell him what any good soldier could tell him on a day like this. I'll simply look him in the eye and say, 'Young feller, you're in the middle of a war . . . Fight like hell!"

Halloran goes quickly into the hall. The Judge moves over to face the door, drawing himself up to a soldier's salute, his tired back to the audience—

"For a flashing second he is nearly straight and erect, a soldier with a soldier's faith . . . first . . . last . . . always, awaiting his commander-in-chief—"

From the hall we hear the secretary's greeting:

"Mr. President, Mr. Justice Holmes is waiting."

THE CURTAIN FALLS

ANTIGONE

A Tragedy in One Act

By Jean Anouilh

(English Adaptation by Lewis Galantiere)

IT was while she was satisfying her own urge to help with keeping the American Army overseas as happy as could be hoped for that Katharine Cornell saw a production of "Antigone and the Tyrant" at the Theatre Antoine in Paris. She had been playing a lightly skeletonized version of "The Barretts of Wimpole Street" at various Army theatres, establishing a record of some 40 performances eventually. Incidentally she also had been confounding those GI directors of entertainment who had contended that the chief, if not the only, show soldier audiences were interested in was the old burlesque formula of "legs, lingerie and license," with the lingerie mostly eliminated. The boys had taken to "The Barretts" with enthusiasm, and had written home in great numbers that their morale had been immeasurably stimulated by seeing "something decent at last."

Miss Cornell had, as said, dropped into the Theatre Antoine for a bit of relaxation and immediately found herself intensely interested in the tragedy she was seeing. "Antigone," she decided, should most certainly be produced in America, preferably by Cornell & McClintic Productions, Inc.

Immediately thereafter she began investigating the matter of American dramatic rights. She contacted the author of "Antigone" and discovered that the American rights had already been disposed of—to Metro-Goldwyn Pictures. She suggested that her New York associates get in touch with Metro-Goldwyn and see if the dramatic rights could not be obtained. Metro-Goldwyn executives reported that they knew nothing about either Jean Anouilh or his play. Back again to Paris then, and the discovery that the American rights to the play had indeed been sold to a representative of the O W I and that Gilbert Miller was interested in the deal.

Finally, Mr. Miller, having decided to join Miss Cornell and

"Antigone," copyright 1945 *by Lewis Galantiere. Published by Random House, Inc., New York.*

Mr. McClintic in the production of the play, went back to Paris, saw the holder of the American rights and also the author, made certain down payments and the American production was started on its way. It reached Broadway February 18, 1946, in an English adaptation by Lewis Galantiere.

The first-night press reviews were favorable, largely because of Miss Cornell's participation in the play, but they were not too encouraging either. The critics' second thoughts the following Sabbath repeated the pattern.

"In Paris, during the Nazi occupation, 'Antigone' was something more than a theatrical experiment," wrote Howard Barnes in the New York *Tribune*. "Men of good will, muted to the verge of silence, discovered that a modernization of a Greek tragedy afforded them elliptical communication with their comrades. Sophocles became an honorary member of the French resistance movement. His stern account of a young girl defying a persuasive tyrant must have needled the Wehrmacht no end in its colloquial translation, but the Germans could do nothing about it." Miss Cornell's discovery of the play under these conditions, thought Mr. Barnes, could easily account for her enthusiasm.

"Anouilh's 'Antigone,' unlike Sophocles', is not moved by religious feelings," wrote Louis Kronenberger in the newspaper *PM*. "Far more than Sophocles', she is shown to be passionately and happily in love with Creon's son, and passionately, preternaturally in love with life; and beyond that she had never liked her brother and had not seen him for years. Saddled with the burial theme, Anouilh can only portray Antigone as a sort of fanatic about 'principle,' and he cannot make us believe she is even that. As an inspirational figure for an occupied Paris she undoubtedly had her value; as a human being she is quite unreal."

Speaking in justification of her own enthusiasm for the play, Miss Cornell told Harriet Johnson of the New York *Post:* "I like to talk about the character of Antigone because I love and admire her. We can't live by Antigones alone, but if we have no Antigone within us we are spiritually barren. She was remote and willful, but she was uncompromisingly true to the things she believed. The conflict between Antigone and Creon is the conflict between the spirit and the flesh."

A gray silk cyclorama encircles the room in the palace of King Creon in which the action of "Antigone" is centered.

There is a circle of three steps around the sides of the room and arched entrances at either side. A table in the center has matched chairs at either end, and next to the chair at the right is a small stool.

At curtain rise the characters who are to give the play are variously disposed and completely static. Mostly they are sitting or standing on the encircling steps. The curtain is no sooner up than Chorus, who has been standing idly at the back of the room, steps down and begins a recital of who the characters are and what they represent in the story about to be told. This, says he, indicating the heroine, is to be the story of Antigone—

"That dark-haired girl sitting by herself, staring straight ahead, seeing nothing, is Antigone. She is thinking. She is thinking that the instant I finish telling you who's who and what's what in this play, she will burst forth as the dark, tense, serious girl who is about to rise up and face the whole world alone—alone against the world and against Creon, her uncle, the king.

"Another thing that she is thinking is this: she is going to die. Antigone is young. She would much rather live than die. But there is no help for it. When you are on the side of the gods against the tyrant, of Man against the State, of purity against corruption—when, in short, your name is Antigone, there is only one part you can play; and she will have to play hers through to the end.

"Mind you, Antigone doesn't know all these things about herself. I know them because it is my business to know them. That's what a Greek Chorus is for. All that she knows is that Creon won't allow her dead brother to be buried; and that despite Creon, she must bury him. Antigone doesn't *think,* she acts, she doesn't *reason,* she feels. And from the moment the curtain went up, she began to feel that inhuman forces were whirling her out of this world, snatching her away from her sister Ismene—whom you see smiling at that young man; making *her* an instrument of the gods in a way she cannot fathom but that she will faithfully pursue. You have never seen inhuman forces at work? You will, tonight."

And so Chorus goes on, from Antigone to the golden Ismene, Antigone's beautiful sister; from Ismene to Hæmon, the king's son, to whom Antigone is engaged (though you might reasonably think he would have preferred Ismene as more his type). As a matter of fact Hæmon had flirted desperately with Ismene at a certain ball, but the gods intervened and Hæmon, suddenly leaving Ismene, had gone straight to Antigone and proposed marriage—

"It didn't seem to surprise Antigone in the least," reports Chorus. "She looked up at him out of those solemn eyes of hers, then smiled sort of sadly and said 'Yes.' That was all." . . .

"That gray-haired, powerfully built man sitting lost in thought with his little page boy at his side is Creon, the King," Chorus is now explaining. "His face is lined. He is tired. He practices the difficult art of a leader of men. . . . When he was younger, when Œdipus was King and Creon was no more than the king's brother-in-law, he was different. He loved music, bought rare manuscripts, was a kind of art patron. He used to while away whole afternoons in the antique shops of this city of Thebes. But Œdipus died. Œdipus' sons died. Creon's moment had come. He *took* over the kingdom."

Here Chorus slips into further confidences. Creon, for instance, has a tendency to fool himself. Creon thinks, if he could, he would step down and let who would be King. But he wouldn't, says Chorus. Creon loves being King. And he is quite sure he is the only one who knows what is best for the common people.

Also Creon has a wife, Eurydice, who is sitting over there on the stair, knitting. She will go on knitting all through the play. A good woman, but of no help to her husband. Next to Eurydice is the old Nurse who brought up Antigone and Ismene—

"That pale young man leaning against the wall—that is the Messenger," Chorus continues. "Later on he will come running in to announce that Hæmon is dead. He has a premonition of catastrophe. That is what he is brooding over. That is why he won't mingle with the others. As for those three pasty-faced card players—they are the guards, members of Creon's police force. They chew tobacco; one smells of garlic, another of beer; but they're not a bad lot. They have wives they are afraid of, kids who are afraid of them; they are bothered by the little day-to-day worries that beset us all. At the same time they are policemen: eternally innocent, no matter what crimes are committed; eternally indifferent. For nothing that happens can matter to them. They are quite prepared to arrest anybody at all, including Creon himself, should the order be given by a *new* leader."

Well, that's the lot of them, and now Chorus is ready for the play. One by one the actors have left the scene. Chorus lights a cigarette and moves closer to the proscenium. Œdipus, the father of Antigone and Ismene, he reminds his hearers, also had two sons, Eteocles and Polynices. When Œdipus died it was agreed his sons would reign over Thebes in alternate years, but at the end of the first year Eteocles, the elder of the boys, refused to give over the throne to Polynices. Civil war broke out, being finally won by Polynices and his foreign allies. Then the boys met in combat and killed each other. Their Uncle Creon became King, and a reign of terror ensued.

Now, in an effort to quell the uprising King Creon "has issued a solemn edict that Eteocles, on whose side he was, is to be buried with pomp and honors, and that the younger brother, Polynices, is to be left to rot. The vultures and the dogs are to bloat themselves on his carcass. And above all, any person who attempts to give him decent burial will himself be put to death.

It is, explains Chorus, against this blasphemy that Antigone rebels. "What is for Creon merely the climax of a political purge, is for her a hideous offense against God and Man. Since time began, men have recoiled with horror from the desecration of the dead. It is this spirit which prompts us today to suspend battle in order to bury our dead, to bury even the enemy dead."

And now the lights have dimmed and the play begins. The stage is bathed in a dark blue color. A clock is heard to strike four. Presently Antigone comes stealing into the house, carrying her sandals in her hand. Cautiously she starts to cross the room when her nurse appears and stops her. *Where* has Antigone been?

Antigone has no intention of telling. The morning has been beautiful. Nurse will have to get up earlier if she is to enjoy the mornings. With all the world breathless and waiting; with all the world colorless and the garden still asleep! That's all very pretty, but Nurse isn't interested—

"You will do well to wash your feet before you go back to bed, Miss," she advises coldly, kneeling before her mistress and taking one foot after the other to chafe warmth back into it.

Antigone has no intention of going back to bed. "Do you think that if I got up every morning like this, it would be just as thrilling *every* morning to be the first person out-of-doors?"

"*Morning* my grandmother!" snorts Nurse. "It was night. It still is. And now, my girl, you'll stop trying to squirm out of this and tell me what you were up to."

"That's true. It was still night. There wasn't a soul out-of-doors but me who thought it was morning."

"Oh, my little flibbety-gibbety! Just can't imagine what I'm talking about, can she? Go on with you! I know that game. I was a girl myself once; and just as pig-headed and hard to handle as you are." Nurse has put Antigone's sandals back and brushed off the hem of her skirt. "You went out to meet someone, didn't you?" she persists. "*Deny* it if you can."

"Yes. I went out to meet someone."

"You have a lover?"

Photo by Vandamm Studio.

"ANTIGONE"

Creon—I may be your uncle, but we are not a particularly affectionate family. . . . Are we?

(*Cedric Hardwicke, Katharine Cornell*)

"Yes, Nurse, I have a lover."

This is almost too much for Nurse. "Ah, that's *very* nice now, isn't it? Such goings-on! You, the daughter of a King, running out to meet lovers. And we work our fingers to the bone for you, we slave to bring you up like young ladies! You're all alike, all of you. Even you—who never used to stop to primp in front of a looking-glass, or smear your mouth with rouge, or dindle and dandle to make the boys ogle you, and you ogle back. . . . And now you see? Just like your sister after all. Only worse: a hypocrite! God save us! I took her when she wasn't that high. I promised her poor mother I'd make a lady of her. And look at her! But don't go thinking this is the end of this, my young 'un. *I'm* only your nurse and you can play deaf and dumb with me, I don't count. But your Uncle Creon will hear of this! *That,* I promise you."

"Yes, Creon will hear of this!" A weariness is creeping into Antigone's voice. She would dismiss Nurse if she could, but at the very suggestion her faithful guardian is bathed in tears. She must be calmed with loving protestations and the whole truth about the lover fabrication.

"Nanny, dear—don't cry." Antigone has put her arms about the old one's shoulders and she is caressing her tear-stained cheeks. "There, now, my sweet red apple. Do you remember how I used to rub your cheeks to make them shine? My dear, wrinkled red apple! I didn't do anything tonight that was worth sending tears down the little gullies of your face. I am pure, and I swear that I have no other lover than Hæmon. If you like, I'll swear that I shall never have any other lover than Hæmon. Save your tears, Nanny—save them, Nanny dear: you may still need them. When you cry like that, I become a little girl again; and I mustn't be a little girl to-day."

Ismene, too, is disturbed by her sister's early rising but she has a feeling that she knows what has inspired it. Ismene also has spent a sleepless night—thinking, thinking, thinking. And now she is a little terrified by her thoughts.

"Creon will have us put to death," prophesies Ismene, woefully.

"Of course he will. But we are *bound* to go out and bury our brother. That's the way it is. What do you think *we* can do to change it?"

ISMENE—I don't want to die.

ANTIGONE—I'd prefer not to die, myself.

ISMENE—Listen to me, Antigone. I thought about it all night.

I may be younger than you are, but I always think things over, and you don't.

ANTIGONE—Sometimes it is better *not* to think too much.

ISMENE—I don't agree with you! Oh, I know it's horrible. I *know* Polynices was cheated out of his rights. That he made war and that Creon took sides against him, and he was killed. And I pity Polynices just as much as you do. But all the same, I *sort* of see what Uncle Creon means.

ANTIGONE—I don't want to "sort of see" anything.

ISMENE—Uncle Creon is the *king* now. He *has* to set an example!

ANTIGONE (*turning to* ISMENE)—Example! Creon orders that our brother rot and putrefy, and be mangled by dogs and birds of prey. That's an offense against every decent human instinct; against every law of God and Man. And you talk about examples!

ISMENE—There you go, off on your own again—refusing to pay the slightest heed to anybody. At least you might try to understand!

ANTIGONE—I only understand that a man lies rotting, unburied. And that he is my brother, and that he must be buried.

It is not easy to allay Ismene's fright. She has, Antigone charges, thought it all out: "The howling mob; the torture; the fear of death! They've made up your mind for you. Is that it?"

"Yes."

"All right. They're as good excuses as any." And on Antigone's promise not to leave the palace, Ismene agrees to go back to bed.

Soon Nurse has come with coffee and toast to find her mistress deep again in a depression it is hard to conquer. Nurse would serve gladly as confessor and comforter if she could, but there are no confessions that Antigone can make, save that she feels that she is not quite strong enough to do what she has to do.

"Not strong enough for what, my kitten?"

"Nothing—just all this," answers Antigone. "Oh, it is so good that you are here. I can hold your calloused hand that is so prompt and strong to ward off evil. You are very powerful, Nanny."

"What is it you want me to do for you, my baby?"

"There isn't anything to do—except: put your hand like this—against my cheek . . . There! I'm not afraid any more."

Still, there is one small request Antigone would make of her old nurse: she must promise that she will never again scold Antigone's dog, Puff. And Nurse must promise to talk to Puff, just as she, Antigone, talks to her—if anything should happen—

"And if she got too unhappy; if she moaned and moaned, waiting for me with her nose under the door the way she does when I'm out all day; then the best thing, Nanny, might be to have her mercifully put to sleep."

It is all quite beyond Nurse. Surely something strange must have happened to her charge this morning. But she promises . . .

Hæmon has come. With a glad cry Antigone is in his arms and he, puzzled at her sudden burst of emotion and her plans for forgiveness, is tender in calming her fears and holding her close to him. The fact that she had come to his room, glamorously attractive with Ismene's cosmetics, is already forgiven.

"Don't laugh at me this morning, Hæmon," Antigone is pleading. "Be serious."

"I am serious."

"And hold me tight. *Tighter* than you have ever held me. I want all your strength to flow into me."

"*There!* With all my strength."

"That's good!" sighs a breathless Antigone. A moment later she asks, anxiously: "Hæmon, you loved me! You did love me that night, didn't you? You're sure of it!"

Eagerly she forces him to further confessions of his love; his love for her as a woman; as a woman wants to be loved; of his assurance the night he came to her at the dance that his love was hers and not by any chance Ismene's. Nor is she stopped when lightly he insists that she is a bit idiotic, and kisses her fondly—"Antigone, my darling, I love you!" he assures her, and kisses her again.

"And now I have two more things to tell you." Her tone has changed. "And when I have told them to you, you must go away instantly, without asking any questions. However strange they may seem to you. However much they may hurt you. Swear that you will!"

HÆMON—What are these things that you are going to tell me?

ANTIGONE—Swear first that you will go away without one word. Without so much as looking at me. (*She looks at him, wretchedness in her face.*) You hear me, Hæmon. Swear it, please. This is the last *mad* wish that you will ever have to grant me.

HÆMON (*after a pause*)—I swear it.

ANTIGONE—Thank you. Well, here it is. First, about last night, when I went to your house. You asked me a moment ago why I wore Ismene's dress and rouge. I did it because I was stupid. I wasn't sure you loved me as a woman; and I did it because I wanted you to want me.

HÆMON—Was that the reason? Oh, my poor . . .

ANTIGONE (*placing her hand on his face*)—No! Wait! That was the reason. And you laughed at me, and we quarreled, and my awful temper got the better of me, and I flung out of the house. The reason why I went to your house last night was that I wanted you to take me. As a matter of fact, I'll tell you why. I wanted to be your wife last night because I love you that way very—very strongly. And also because— Oh, my beloved—I'm going to cause you such a lot of pain. I wanted it also because—I shall never—never be able to marry you, *never!*

HÆMON (*moving a step toward her*)—Antigone . . . !

ANTIGONE—Hæmon! You took a solemn oath! You swore! Leave me, now! Tomorrow the whole thing will be clear to you. Even before tomorrow: this afternoon. (*He makes a slight gesture toward her.*) If you *please,* Hæmon, go now. It is the only thing left that you can do for me, if you still love me.

He stares at her for a moment, turns and leaves her. She is motionless for a moment and then, in a strange, gentle voice, she mutters:

"Well, it's over for Hæmon, Antigone." . . .

Ismene has come excitedly in search of Antigone. Ismene can't sleep. Ismene is terrified; afraid that even in the daylight her sister will still try to bury Polynices.

"Antigone, you know I love you; you know I want you to be happy," wails Ismene. "And you remember what he was like. He was our brother, of course. But he's dead; and he never loved us. He was a bad brother. He was like an enemy in this house. He never thought of you: why should you think of him? What if he does have to lie rotting in a field— . . . It's Creon's doing, not ours. . . . Don't try to change things. You can't bury Polynices. I won't let you!"

"You are too late, Ismene. When you first saw me this morning, I had just come in from burying him."

Before the startled Ismene can recover, Antigone has left the room. A moment later Ismene follows excitedly after her.

The lights are dimming. A clock is heard to strike a single note. There is a pause. When the lights are brought up, King Creon and his page boy are just entering the room.

A private of the guard left to watch over the body of Polynices has a report to make. At Creon's request he is brought in. He is a very frightened guard. Private Jonas, Second Battalion. A very good man, too, by his own account. A man of seventeen years' service, and never a black mark against him; a volunteer with two citations. He knows his business and he carries out orders. Let the King ask anyone—

"Stop chattering and tell me why you are here!" orders Creon. "If anything has gone wrong with that body I'll break all three of you!"

"Nobody can say we didn't keep our eye on that body," stammers Private Jonas. "We had the two o'clock watch: the tough one. You know how it is, Chief. It's nearly the end of the night. Your eyes are like lead. You've got a crick in the back of your neck. There's shadows, and the fog is beginning to roll in. A fine watch they gave us! And me, seventeen years in the service. But we was doing our duty, all right. On our feet, all of us. Anybody says we were sleeping is a liar. First place, it was too cold. Second place . . ."

"Ahh!" Creon's impatience is mounting.

"Yes, Chief. Well, I turned round and looked at the body. We wasn't only ten feet away from it, but that's how I am. I was keeping my eye on it. (*He shouts.*) Listen, Chief, I was the first man to see it! Me! They'll tell you. I was the one let out that yell!"

"What for? What was the matter?"

"Chief, the *body!* Somebody had been there and buried him. It wasn't much, you understand. With us three there, it couldn't have been. Just covered over with a little dirt, that's all. But enough to hide it from the buzzards."

"By God, I'll—!" He looks intently at the guard. "You are sure that it couldn't have been—a dog, scratching up the earth."

"Not a chance, Chief. That's kind of what we hoped it was. But the earth was scattered over the body just like the priests tell you you should do it. Whoever did that job knew what he was doing, all right."

No, there were no indications of who the culprit might have been. The guards have no suspicions. They had found a shovel—a kid's shovel, no bigger than that—all rusty and everything. Maybe a kid had done it—

The suggestion intrigues Creon. Polynices' friends might have thought of that. Or the envious princes. Or the temple priests.

"Always ready for a bit of fishing in troubled waters." A kid; a baby-faced killer; "creeping in the night with a toy shovel under his jacket."

"There is something, now, to soften the hearts and weaken the minds of the people! Very touching! Very useful to them, an innocent child. A martyr. A real white-faced baby of fourteen who will spit with contempt at the guards who kill him. A free gift to their cause: the precious, innocent blood of a child on my hands."

Creon has turned to the still frightened guard. "Listen, now! You will continue on duty. When the relief squad comes up, you will tell them to return to the barracks. You will uncover the body; keep a sharp watch, and if another attempt is made to give the corpse burial, you will make an arrest and bring the prisoner straight to me. And you will keep your mouths shut. Not one word of this to a human soul. You are all guilty of neglect of duty, and you will be punished; but if the rumor spreads through Thebes that the body received burial, you will be shot—all three of you."

"Chief, we never told nobody," excitedly protests Jonas. "I swear we didn't. Anyhow, I've been up here. Suppose my pals spilled it to the relief; I couldn't have been with them and here, too. That wouldn't be my fault, if they talked. Chief, I've got two kids. You're my witness, Chief, it couldn't have been me. I was here with you. I've got a witness. If anybody talked, it couldn't have been me! I was . . ."

"Clear out! If the story doesn't get round, you won't be shot."

Creon, still pondering the thought of a child as the guilty one, calls the page to him.

"Would you defy me with your little shovel?" he asks and answers himself. "Of course you would. You would do it, too. A *child!*"

They disappear back of the curtain.

The lighting suggests a bright afternoon. Chorus, coming again into the action of the play, strolls toward the front of the room. "And now the Spring is rolled up *tight!*" His tone is expectant. "It will uncoil of itself. That is what is so convenient in tragedy. The least little turn of the wrist will do the job. Anything will set it going."

Chorus has moved over to stand by the table. He is rather pleased with the convincing quality of his logic. ". . . Tragedy is clean, it is firm, it is flawless. It has nothing to do with melodrama—with wicked villains, persecuted maidens, avengers, gleams of hope and eleventh-hour repentances. Death, in a melodrama, is really horrible because it is never inevitable. The dear old father might so easily have been saved; the honest young man might so easily have brought in the police five minutes earlier. In a tragedy, nothing is in doubt and everyone's destiny is known. That makes for tranquillity. Tragedy is restful; and the reason is that *hope,* that foul, deceitful thing, has no part in it. There isn't any hope. You're trapped. The whole sky has fallen on you, and all you can do about it is to shout."

Chorus is moving toward an archway now, preparing to clear the way for the play to go on. ". . . In a melodrama you argue and struggle in the hope of escape. That is vulgar; it's practical. But in tragedy, where there is no temptation to try to escape, argument is gratuitous: it's kingly."

There is a sound of scuffling and muffled voices from the hall. Chorus looks in that direction. "The play is on," he says, in a changed tone. "Antigone has been caught. For the first time in her life Antigone is going to be able to be herself." With which he disappears.

The scuffling and voices outside increase. Presently the guards appear. Two of them have Antigone by the arms and are dragging her along. The third guard, holding her handcuffed hand, is giving orders—

"Come on, now, Miss. Give it a rest. The Chief will be here in a minute and you can tell him about it. All I know is my orders. I don't want to know what you were doing there. People always have excuses; but I can't afford to listen to them, see. Say, if we had to listen to all the people who want to tell us what's the matter with this country, we'd never get our work done."

"They are hurting me," Antigone pleads. "Tell them to take their dirty hands off me!"

"*Dirty* hands, eh? And what about stiffs, and dirt, and such like. You wasn't afraid to touch them, was you? 'Their dirty hands!' Take a look at your own hands!"

"Tell them to let me go. I shan't run away. My father was King Œdipus. I am Antigone."

"King Œdipus' little girl! What do you know about that! Listen, Miss, the night watch never picks up a lady, but they say, you better be careful; I'm sleeping with the Police commissioner."

The guards enjoy the humor of their mate. They have a grand time, too, listening to the story of Antigone's capture and the fierceness of her fight when she was taken; of her hysterical determination to finish the task she had set herself, that of burying the body they were guarding. Maybe they will get a bonus for their capture, and if they do, what a party they will throw! At the old woman's—behind Market Street.

Now Creon has appeared. He stands on the stair, astonished at the sight of Antigone handcuffed to a guard. Let them take the handcuffs off and explain at once what has happened.

The First Guard is eager to tell the story of his discovery of this woman by the body they were guarding by Creon's orders.

"What were you doing near your brother's body?" demands Creon of Antigone. "You knew what my orders were!"

"What was she doing? Chief, that's why we brought her in. She was digging up the dirt with her nails. She was trying to cover up the body all over again."

"Do you realize what you are saying?"

"Chief, ask these men here. . . ."

The story comes tumbling from his lips. He had gone back to the body; he and the other guards had uncovered the body and moved it to a small ridge where it would be out of the sun and catch the breeze and thus lessen the smell of it. And then, in the broad daylight, there was this woman "clawing away at the dirt with both hands— And when I grabbed her, she scratched and bit and yelled to leave her alone, she hadn't finished yet, the body wasn't all covered yet, and the like of that!"

"And was it *you* who covered the body the first time? In the night?" Creon asks.

"Yes, it was," Antigone admits defiantly. "With a toy shovel we used to take to the seashore when we were children. It was Polynices' own shovel: he had cut his name in the handle. That was why I left it with him. But these men took it away; so the next time, I had to do it with my hands."

The guards are dismissed. Creon turns again to Antigone. Had she told anybody of what she intended to do? No. Had she met anyone on the way, going or coming? No. Then she is to go straight to her room and go to bed, Creon orders. She will say that she has not been out since yesterday. Her nurse will tell the same story. He will dispose of the three guards.

"Uncle Creon, there's no reason to kill those three guards. You must know that I'll do it all over again tonight."

"Why did you try to bury your brother?"

"I owed it to him. Those who are not buried wander eternally and find no rest. Everybody knows that. I owed it to him to unlock the house of the dead in which my father and my mother are waiting to welcome him. Polynices has earned his rest."

"Polynices was a rebel and a traitor, and you know it."

"He was my brother."

Nor is it possible for a temporarily defeated Creon to get much farther than that with his determined niece. Nor possible for him to name an answering argument that Antigone would accept. That Creon will put her to death she is convinced.

"The pride of Œdipus!" mutters Creon. "Œdipus and his head-strong pride all over again. . . . You come of people for whom the human vestment is a kind of strait-jacket: it cracks at the seams: you spend your lives wriggling to get out of it. Nothing less than a cozy tea-party with death and destiny will quench your thirst. The happiest hour of your father's life came when he listened *greedily* to the story of how, unknown to himself, he had killed his own father and dishonored the bed of his own mother. Drop by drop, word by word, he drank in the dark story that the gods had destined him first to live and then to hear. How avidly men and women drink the brew of such a tale when their names are Œdipus—and Antigone! And it is so simple, afterwards, to do what your father did, to put out his eyes and take you, his daughter, begging on the highways."

But those days are over for Thebes, Creon assures Antigone. He is less ambitious than Œdipus was; he will be content to "introduce a little order into this absurd kingdom." Nor does he find the job of being a king at all romantic; it is just a trade a man has to work at every day. ". . . *Kings*, my girl, have other things to do than to surrender themselves to their private feelings."

He has risen and is walking about the room. He has stopped now and is leaning against the end of the table as he faces Antigone. "Hand *you* over to be killed!" he repeats. "I have other plans for you. You're going to marry Hæmon, and you're going to give him a sturdy boy. Let me assure you that Thebes needs that boy a good deal more than it needs your death. Now, you will go to your room and do as you have been told; and you won't say a word about this to anybody. Don't fret about the guards; I'll see that their mouths are shut. And don't annihilate me with those eyes. I know that you think I am a brute, and I'm sure you must consider me very prosaic. But the fact is, I have always been fond of you, stubborn though you always were. Don't forget that the first doll you ever had, came from me."

Antigone does not answer. Boldly she starts to leave the room. Where is she going? He knows very well where she is going, she answers. She is going again to bury her brother. Nor is she impressed with his threat that unless she listen to him and follow out his plan there will be no possible way for him to save her.

Neither does she admit that all the flummery attached to religious burial is ridiculous, as Creon insists. Or because there are priests who cheat the ritual that God is mocked. "No, Creon. There is God and there are His priests. They are not the same thing. You are not free to do with men as you wish—not even when they are dead."

"And you are going to *stop* me, are you?"

"Yes, I am going to stop you."

There is only one thing that he can do, Antigone repeats, again and again: He can have her put to death!

Creon's anger is mounting now, as Antigone continues to taunt him with his own weaknesses. He knows, he says, that she has cast him for the villain in her little play, and herself for the heroine. "If I were one of your preposterous little tyrants that Greece is full of, you would be lying in a ditch this minute with your tongue pulled out and your body drawn and quartered. But you can see *something* in my face that makes me hesitate to send for the guards and turn you over to them. Instead, I let you go on arguing; and you taunt me, you take the offensive. . . ."

". . . What are you driving at, you she-devil?"

Creon has grabbed Antigone's wrist and is twisting her arm. Her features are distorted with pain, and she is moaning audibly.

"I may be your uncle, but we're not a particularly affectionate family, are we? Eh?"

He gives the arm another twist. "What fun for you, eh? To be able to laugh in the face of a king who has all the power in the world . . ."

"Now you are squeezing my arm too tight," calmly reports Antigone. "It doesn't hurt any more."

Creon stares at his victim, and finally drops her arm. "I shall save you yet!" he mutters between clenched teeth. A second later he has recovered some of his poise and adds: "I am not going to let politics be the cause of your death. For it is a fact that this *whole* business is nothing but politics: the mournful shade of Polynices, the decomposing corpse, the sentimental weeping and the hysteria that you mistake for heroism, politics—nothing but politics. Look here. I may not be soft, but I'm fastidious. I like things clean, ship-shape, well scrubbed. Don't think that I am not just as offended as you are by the thought of that *meat*—rotting in the sun. In the evening, when the breeze comes in off the sea, you can smell it in the palace, and it nauseates me. But I refuse even to shut my window. It is vile; and I can tell you what I wouldn't tell anybody else: it's stupid, monstrously stupid. But the people of Thebes have got to have their noses rubbed into it a little longer. My God! If it was up to me, I should have had your brother buried long ago as a mere matter of public hygiene. But if the feather-headed rabble I govern are to understand what's what, that *stench* has got to fill the town for a month!"

"You are a loathsome man!"

"I agree. My trade forces me to be. We could argue whether I ought or ought not to follow my trade; but once I take on the job, I must do it properly."

Creon has found justification for his life, and the manner of his living it, in the memory that one morning he had awakened to find himself King of Thebes. He had not the courage to refuse the decree, and so he had gone on with the job. He was afraid to say no.

Now again he is afraid, Antigone charges. He knows that he is going to have to put her to death, and it frightens him. That is why he would save her if he could. He is frightened—

"Poor Creon!" she says pityingly, scornfully. "*My* nails are broken, *my* fingers are bleeding, *my* arms are covered with the welts left by the paws of your guards—but *I* am a Queen!"

"Then why not have pity on me, and live? Isn't your brother's corpse, rotting beneath my windows, payment enough for peace and order in Thebes?"

"No. You said *yes,* and made yourself king. *Now* you will never stop paying."

"But, God in heaven! Won't you *try* to understand me!" Creon pleads earnestly. "I'm trying hard enough to understand *you!* There *had* to be one man who said yes. Somebody *had* to agree to captain the ship. She had sprung a hundred leaks; she was loaded to the water-line with crime, ignorance and poverty. The wheel was swinging with the wind."

Creon had taken the wheel and righted the ship. It was no time to play with words like yes and no. Antigone should understand that much.

"I am not here to understand *these* things. I am here because I said no to you."

"It is easy to say no . . . To say yes you have to sweat and roll up your sleeves and plunge both hands into life up to the elbows. It is easy to say no, even if saying no means death. All you have to do is to sit still and wait. Wait to go on living; wait to be killed. That is the coward's part. *No* is one of your man-made words. Can you imagine a world in which trees say *no* to the sap? In which beasts say *no* to hunger or to propagation? Animals are good, simple, tough. They move in droves, nudging one another onwards, all traveling the same road. Some of them keel over; but the rest go on; and no matter how many may fall by the wayside, there are always those few left who go on bringing their young into the world, traveling the same road with the same obstinate will, unchanged from those who went before."

"*Animals!* Oh, what a king *you* could make, Creon, if only men were animals!"

Though his part is not a heroic one, Creon will play it through. But he is still impelled to make one more plea to Antigone. He wants to be sure that she knows what she is doing as well as he knows what he is doing. He would tell Antigone the story of her brothers—the true story of Eteocles and Polynices, which in Thebes he alone knows.

Does Antigone remember her brothers? They were older than she. They probably tormented her. Pulled her pigtails, broke her dolls, whispered secrets to each other just to put her in a rage.

"They were big and I was little," Antigone reminds him. And again: "They were boys and I was a girl."

There were times, Creon is sure, when Antigone, seeing her mother in tears, knew that her brothers were making her unhappy; times when her father would fly into a rage because of them; times when her brothers would come home "laughing noisily in the corridors—insolent, spineless, unruly, smelling of drink."

Antigone would only admit that she had seen them one night when Polynices, handsome in his evening clothes, his eyes shining, had given her a big paper flower that he had brought home.

"Poor little Antigone! With her night-club flower! Do you know what your brother was?"

"Whatever he was I know that you will say vile things about him," she answers.

CREON—A cheap, idiotic bounder, that is what he was. A cruel, vicious little voluptuary. A little beast with just wit enough to drive a car faster and throw more money away than any of his pals. I was with your father one day when Polynices, who had lost a lot of money gambling, asked him to settle the debt; and when your father refused, the boy raised his hand against him and called him a vile name.

ANTIGONE—That's a lie!

CREON—He struck your father in the face with his fist. (*He pauses for a moment.*) It was pitiful. Your father sat at his desk with his head in his hands. His nose was bleeding. He was weeping with anguish. And in a corner of your father's study, Polynices stood sneering and lighting a cigarette.

ANTIGONE—That's a lie.

CREON—When did you last see Polynices alive? When you were twelve years old. *That's* true, isn't it?

ANTIGONE—Yes, that's true.

CREON—Now you know why. Œdipus was too chicken-hearted to have the boy locked up. Polynices was allowed to go off and join the Argive army. And as soon as he reached Argos, the attempts upon your father's life began—upon the life of an old man who couldn't make up his mind to die, couldn't bear to be parted from his kingship. One after another, men slipped into Thebes from Argos for the purpose of assassinating him, and every killer that we caught, always ended by confessing *who* had put him up to it, *who* had paid him to try it. And it wasn't only Polynices. *That* is really what I am trying to tell you. I want you to know what went on in the back room, in the *smelly kitchen* of politics; I want you to know what took place in the wings of this drama in which you are burning to play a part. Yesterday, I gave Eteocles a State funeral, with pomp and honors. Today, Eteocles is a saint and a hero in the eyes of all Thebes. The whole city turned out to bury him. The schoolchildren emptied their piggy-banks to buy wreaths for him. Old men, orating in quavering, hypocritical voices, glorified the virtues of the great-hearted brother, the devoted son, the *loyal* prince. I made a speech myself; and every temple priest was present with an appropriate show of sorrow and solemnity in his *stupid* face. And military honors were accorded the dead hero. Well, what else could I have done? People had taken sides in the civil war. *Both* sides couldn't be wrong: that would be too much. I couldn't have made them swallow the truth. *Two* gangsters was more of a—*luxury* than I could afford. And yet—*this* is the whole point of my story. *Eteocles,* that virtuous brother, was just as rotten as Polynices. That great-hearted son had done *his* best, too, to procure the assassination of his father. That loyal prince had also offered to sell out Thebes to the highest bidder. Funny, isn't it? Polynices lies rotting in the sun while Eteocles is given a hero's funeral and will be housed in a marble vault. Yet I have absolute proof that everything that Polynices did, Eteocles had plotted to do. They were a pair of blackguards—both engaged in selling out each other; and they died like the cheap gangsters they were, over a division of the spoils. . . . But, as I told you a minute ago, I *had* to make a martyr of one of them. I sent out to the holocaust for their bodies: they were found clasped in one another's arms—for the first time in their lives, I imagine. Each had been spitted on the other's sword, and the Argive cavalry had trampled them down. They were—*mashed*—to a pulp, Antigone. I had the prettier of the two carcasses brought in, and gave it a State funeral; and I left the other to rot. I don't know which is which. And I assure you, I don't care.

Why does Creon tell her all this, Antigone would know. Because he would have her appreciate life, he says, and the joys of living—his way. It would have been wrong to let her die, the victim of that obscene story he has just told. Let her find Hæmon and get married quickly. Let her not throw life away. Whatever others may tell her about life she should promptly discredit—

"Believe me, the only poor consolation that we have in our old age is to discover that what I have just said to you is true. Life is perhaps, after all, nothing more than the happiness that you get out of it."

For a moment Antigone is lost in thought. "Happiness . . ." she murmurs to herself. "What kind of happiness do you foresee for me?" she asks quietly, turning to Creon. "Paint me the picture of your happy Antigone. What are the most unimportant little sins that I shall have to commit before I am allowed to sink my teeth into life and tear happiness from it? Tell me: to whom shall I have to lie? Upon whom shall I have to fawn? To whom must I sell myself? Whom do you want me to leave dying, while I turn away my eyes?"

"Antigone, be quiet!"

Antigone—Why do you ask me to be quiet when all I want is to know what I have to do to be happy. You tell me that life is so wonderful: I want to know what I have to do in order to be able to say that myself.

Creon—Do you love Hæmon?

Antigone—Yes, I love Hæmon. The Hæmon I love is hard and young, and difficult to satisfy, the way I am. But if what I love in Hæmon is to be worn away like a stone step by the tread of the thing you call life, the thing you call happiness; if Hæmon reaches the point where he stops growing pale with fear when I grow pale, if he stops thinking that I must have been killed in an accident when I am five minutes late, if he stops feeling alone on earth when I laugh and he doesn't know why—if he too has to *learn* to say *yes* to everything—why, no, then, *no!* (*She rises and crosses the room.*) I do *not* love Hæmon!

CREON—You don't know what you are talking about!

ANTIGONE (*turning to him*)—I *do* know what I am talking about! It is *you* who can't hear me! I am too far away from you now, talking to you from a kingdom you can't get into, with your preaching, and your politics, and your persuasive logic. I laugh at your smugness, Creon, thinking you could prove me wrong by telling me vile stories about my brothers or alter my purpose with your platitudes about happiness!

CREON—It is *your* happiness, too, Antigone!

ANTIGONE—I *spit* on your idea of happiness! I *spit* on your idea of life—that life that must go on, come what may. You are all like dogs, that lick everything they smell. *You* with your promise of a humdrum happiness—provided a person doesn't ask too much of life. If life must be a thing of fear, and lying and compromise; if life cannot be free and incorruptible—then Creon, I choose *death!*

CREON—Scream on, daughter of Œdipus, in your father's own voice!

ANTIGONE—*Yes!* In my father's own voice! We come of a tribe that asks questions; and we ask them remorselessly, to the bitter end. You have just told me the filthy reasons why *you* can't bury Polynices. Now tell me why *I* can't bury him!

CREON (*rising*)—Because it is my order.

ANTIGONE—The order of a coward king who desecrates the dead!

CREON (*grasping her by her arms*)—Be quiet! If you could see how *ugly* you are, shrieking those words!

ANTIGONE—Yes, I am ugly! Father was ugly, too. But Father became beautiful. And do you know when? At the very end. When *all* his questions had been answered. When he could no longer doubt that he *had* killed his own father; that he *had* gone to bed with his own mother. When he was absolutely certain that he had to die if the plague was to be lifted from his people. *Then* he was at peace; then he could smile, almost; *then* he became beautiful. . . . Whereas you! Look at yourself, Creon! That glint of fear and suspicion in the corner of your eyes—that crease in the corner of your power-loving mouth. Oh, you said the word a moment ago; the smelly kitchen of politics! That's where you were fathered and pupped—*in a filthy kitchen!*

It is no good for Creon to order Antigone to shut up; she will pay no attention to these orders from a "cook." Nor is she impressed when Ismene runs in and offers hysterically to go with her; to die with her. Oh, no! Ismene had her chance and refused it.

Now let Creon call his guards! Let him at last show a little courage! "It only hurts for a minute! Come on, cook!"

"Guard!" shouts an angered Creon. "Take her away!"

To the protests of a weeping Ismene are added those of Chorus, who has appeared suddenly upon the scene.

"You are out of your mind, Creon!" ventures Chorus. "What have you done?"

"She had to die."

"You must not let Antigone die. We shall carry the scar of her death for centuries."

"What do you want me to do for her? Condemn her to live?"

Now Hæmon has rushed into the room, crying out to his father that the guards are dragging Antigone away. This must not be. Creon must stop them. It is too late, Creon tells his son. The King may be master of Thebes *under* the law. Not above the law. Antigone must die. Hæmon must live; must resign himself to life without Antigone—

"Sooner or later there comes a day of sorrow in each man's life when he must cease to be a child and take up the burden of being a man. That day has come for you."

Hæmon is not impressed. He will not live without Antigone. Can this Creon be the father he has always known? Can this be "that massive god who used to pick me up in his arms and shelter me from shadows and monsters—was that you, Father? Was it of you I stood in awe? Was that man you? . . . You are not that man today. For if you were, you'd know that your enemies were abroad in every street. You'd know that the people revere those gods that you despise. You cannot put Antigone to death. She will not have been dead an hour before shame will sit on every Theban forehead and horror will fill every Theban heart. Already the people curse you because you do not bury Polynices. If you kill Antigone, they will *hate* you!"

"*Silence!* That edict stands!"

Hæmon, bewildered, stares at his father, then runs from the room. The lights are growing dim. The guards have brought

Antigone back. The people are crowding into the palace, they report.

"Creon, I don't want to hear them howl any more!" pleads Antigone. "You are going to kill me; let that be enough! I want to be alone until it is over!"

By Creon's order the palace is cleared. The first guard is left with Antigone. He lets her sit in a chair at the end of the table. Presently Antigone recognizes him as the one who had arrested her that morning. His is probably the last human face she will ever see. She would have him talk to her—talk of himself, and of his family. That pleases the guard. That appeals to his vanity. He is proud of being a guard; proud of his record; being a guard is really something. But now she has interrupted him—

"Listen . . . I'm going to die soon. . . . Do you think it hurts to die?"

"How would I know? Of course, if somebody sticks a saber in your guts and turns it round, it hurts."

"How are they going to put me to death?"

"Well, I'll tell you. I heard the proclamation, all right. There isn't much that gets away from me. It seems that they don't want to dirty up— Wait a minute. How did that go now? 'In order that our fair city shall not be pol-luted with her sinful blood, she shall be im-mured—immured.' That means they shove you in a cave and wall up the cave."

"Alive?"

"Yes . . ."

"O tomb! O bridal bed! Alone!"

"Yep! Outside the southeast gate of the town. In the Caves of Hades. In broad daylight. Some detail, eh, for them that's on the job? First they thought maybe it was a job for the army. Now it looks like it's going to be the guards. There's an outfit for you! Nothing the guards can't do. No wonder the army's jealous."

There is something Antigone would have the guard do for her. She would write a letter and have him give it to someone. The guard does not relish the assignment. It might be as much as his job's worth. No. Not even for the ring she offers him would he risk that. But—he has an idea—

"Listen, tell you what I'll do. You tell me what you want to say, and I'll write it down in my book. Then afterwards, I'll tear out the pages and give them to the party, see? If it's in my handwriting, it's all right."

Now the bargain is struck; the guard will keep Antigone's ring and deliver the letter she dictates. With one foot on the stool and his notebook on his knee he writes, a little laboriously, as Antigone dictates—

" 'My darling. I had to die, and perhaps you will not love me any more. . . . Perhaps you think it would be simple to accept life. . . . But it was not for myself. And now it's all—so dreadful here alone. I am afraid . . . And these shadows . . .' "

"Hey, take it easy!" protests the guard, as Antigone, gazing wildly about her, gives way to a momentary hysteria. "How fast do you think I can write?"

"Where are you?"

" '. . . dreadful here alone. I am afraid' . . ."

"No. Scratch that out. Nobody must know that. They have no right to know. It's as though they saw me naked and touched me, after I am dead. Scratch that out. Just write: 'Forgive me!' "

" 'Forgive me, my darling. You would all have been so happy if it hadn't been for Antigone. I love you.' "

The letter is finished. "Now, who's it to?" the guard asks.

There is a sudden sharp roll of drums. The second and third guards join the first. Antigone and the first guard rise—

"But I haven't finished yet," Antigone is saying.

"SHUT UP!" shouts the guard, pocketing his notebook. The drum roll rises in a sharp crescendo. It is heard again, as from a distance, striking a measured beat five times.

"It is over for Antigone!" announces Chorus. "And now it is Creon's turn."

The lights have dimmed, and then come up again. It is late afternoon. Suddenly a messenger lurches in, breathless and exhausted. It is seconds before he can cry out for the Queen. When Chorus would know what message he has for Her Majesty, the messenger recites a tale of horror, based on what had happened at Antigone's execution—

They had not finished heaving the last blocks of stone into place, reports the messenger, when they heard a sudden moaning from the tomb. It was not Antigone! It was Hæmon's voice! Recognizing the voice, Creon had howled like a man demented: "Take away the stones! Take away the stones!"

Thereupon the slaves, aided by Creon, attacked the blocks, working feverishly with bleeding hands, until an opening was made.

"Antigone had hanged herself by the cord of her robe, by the red and golden cord of her robe, twisted around her neck like a child's collar! Hæmon was on his knees, holding her in his arms and moaning, his face buried in her robe."

When the opening to the cave was enlarged, Creon had gone in, pleading with his son to rise to his feet. But Hæmon was deaf to his father's words. . . . Suddenly, in a burst of terrible anger, Hæmon had risen and grappled with Creon. Anguish was in Hæmon's face when suddenly he drew a knife and attacked Creon.

The King, avoiding the knife, stood trembling at the far corner of the tomb, his son staring wildly at him. There, without a word, Hæmon stabbed himself and lay down beside Antigone, "embracing her in a pool of blood."

Creon and his page come into the room as the messenger emotionally completes his tale. The King can add something—

"I have had them laid out side by side," he says. "They are together at last and at peace. Two lovers on the morrow of their bridal. Their work is done."

"But not *yours,* Creon!" Chorus has come from the upper step to face the King. "When the Queen was told of her son's death, she waited carefully until she had finished her row, then put down her knitting calmly—as she did everything. She went up to her room, her lavender-scented room, with its embroidered doilies and its pictures framed in plush; and there, Creon, she cut her throat. She is laid out now in one of those two old-fashioned twin beds, exactly where you went to her one night when she was still a maiden. Her smile is still the same, scarcely a shade more melancholy. And if it were not for that great red blot on the bed linen by her neck, one might think she was asleep.

CREON—She, too. They are all asleep. (*A pause. Then in a dull voice.*) It must be good to sleep.

CHORUS—Tomorrow they will sleep sweetly in the earth, Creon. And you will bury them. You who would not bury Polynices today will bury Eurydice and Hæmon tomorrow. And Antigone, too. The gods take a hand in every game, Creon. Even in politics.

CREON—The task is there to be done.

CHORUS—Why must dirty work be done? (*A pause.*) And now you are alone, Creon.

CREON—Yes, all alone. What time is it?

PAGE—Five o'clock, sir.

CREON—What have we on today at five o'clock?

PAGE—Cabinet meeting, sir.

CREON—Then we had better get along to it.

Chorus watches Creon and the page as they disappear. "And there we are," he announces, turning to the audience. "All those who were meant to die, have died: those who believed one thing, those who believed the contrary thing, and even those who believed nothing at all, yet were caught up in the web without knowing why. All dead: useless, rotting. Creon was the most rational, the most persuasive of tyrants. But like all tyrants, he refused to distinguish between the things that are Cæsar's and the things that are God's. Now and again—in the three thousand years since the first Antigone—other Antigones have arisen like a clarion call to remind men of this distinction. Their cause is always the same—a passionate belief that moral law exists, and a passionate regard for the sanctity of human personality. Well, Antigone is calm tonight. She has played her part."

The three guards have come back to resume their card game on the stairs.

"A great wave of unrest now settles down on Thebes," continues Chorus; "upon the empty palace, upon Creon, who can now begin to long for his own death. Only the guards are left, and none of this matters to them. It's no skin off their nose. They go on playing cards."

THE CURTAIN FALLS

O MISTRESS MINE

A Comedy in Three Acts

By Terence Rattigan

IT was in the first month of the glad new Victory year that Alfred Lunt and Lynn Fontanne returned to Broadway, after three war years in Europe. That return definitely made January one of the happiest theatre periods of the Winter.

The popular acting couple came back with a new play, a light and, some thought, quite trivial domestic comedy called "O Mistress Mine." It was written by Terence Rattigan, the English actor-playwright whose "Flare Path" and "While the Sun Shines" were pleasant but unsuccessful contributions to our war-time playgoing.

In London the Lunts had been playing Robert Emmet Sherwood's revised version of "There Shall Be No Night" (Best Plays, 1939-40) in which the background had been changed from that of an embattled Finland to that of an embattled Greece, without in the least weakening its basic human values.

Deciding amidst the bombing of London that their loyal play-supporting friends were really entitled to such relief as the so-called escapist drama gave them, the Lunts put aside "There Shall Be No Night" and took up the Rattigan comedy, then called "Love in Idleness." They played it first in the English provinces, brought it back to London for a run during the peak of the V-2 bombing, and then took it to all the GI camps on the continent to help with the Victory celebrations.

During the London run, as Howard Barnes of the New York *Tribune* wrote, "Victory in the European theatre of war was still a nebulous possibility. Most Londoners were walking around like somnambulists, dead tired, undernourished and waiting for the whine of the rocket explosive that smashed large districts of the city to pieces before it could be heard. There was a grim wake in progress which was curiously out of key with a frothy farce. . . .

"It was curious theatregoing in those days. One caught an opening curtain at 5 o'clock in the afternoon, and scrambled out

"O Mistress Mine," copyright, 1945, *by Terence Rattigan. Revised and published version, copyright,* 1946, *by Terence Rattigan.*

of the Lyric Theatre just as the blackout was descending. Tea was served in the theatre, of course, in imperturbable English fashion, and the queues lined up even when theatre patrons knew there was no more chance of getting home after the theatre than there was of buying a couple of oranges or an egg."

After their successful GI tour of the continent the Lunts came home in August, 1945, and went directly to their Wisconsin farm. In the Fall they resumed playing, and as reported, got to Broadway in January. Their welcome was a little noisy and generously hearty. Their reviewers were inclined to stress the fact that this favorite acting couple might easily be doing more serious things in the theatre, but— There were no empty seats in the Empire the rest of the season.

At curtain rise in the showing of "O Mistress Mine" we are ushered into the sitting room of a house in Westminster. It is a pleasant room in which "the furniture and decoration give an impression of tasteful opulence." There are large curtained windows at the back, and doors leading to various adjoining rooms, Sir John Fletcher's study being one of them. It is about 7 o'clock in the evening of a Summer day.

On a large and comfortable sofa in the center of the room Olivia Brown is stretched out, telephoning. The phone rests on her stomach and there is an engagement book in her lap. Olivia is a smart woman, in her thirties, and she is wearing an attractive negligee. The conclusion would be natural that she was both comfortable and happy.

She dials the phone, is shortly in conversation with a person named Dicky, who, she hopes, will put her through to the Chancellor. Dicky is reluctant to disturb the old boy, but finally does put him on. The Chancellor would be Sir Thomas, and Olivia is ever so anxious that he will be able to come to dinner on Thursday night. Sir Thomas doesn't think he can make it, which distresses Olivia—

"Oh, that is a shame," she protests, "I'm so disappointed. Celia Wentworth, the novelist, is simply aching to meet you; she's simply mad about your memoirs. She says she thinks you're wasting your talents as a politician. You ought to have been a writer. . . . Oh, that's sweet of you. Thank you so much. She would have been heartbroken. . . . Yes, eight-thirty. I'm very grateful. Good-by."

This engagement having been happily arranged, Olivia must now call Miss Wentworth and make sure of her coming on Thursday. The ballet? Surely she can cut the ballet. She certainly can cut the last ballet—at least—

"What is it?" asks Olivia. ". . . Oh, my dear, you don't want to see that again . . . all those great swans chasing that absurd young man. . . . I've got the Chancellor of the Exchequer coming and he's such an admirer of yours. . . . Yes, he absolutely worships your 'Resplendent Valley' . . . You will? Splendid. Yes, eight-thirty. You know the address, don't you? You'll find it in the book under Fletcher . . . John Fletcher . . . That's right. . . ."

She hangs up, but the phone is silent for no more than a short minute. It is someone calling Olivia—"Joan, darling" in fact—to tell her that Freddy is to have the post of Under Secretary of War. Yes, indeed—poor old Freddy—

"Oh, I *am* glad," gurgles Olivia. ". . . It just shows how right he's been to have sat there all those years looking stern and saying nothing. . . . Oh, no, darling, he wasn't thinking anything either. . . ."

It is during the talk with Joan that Polton ("a middle-aged, highly respectable-looking parlormaid") brings Olivia a telegram. Reading this, Olivia suddenly emits a shriek and all but drops the phone—

"Oh . . . Sorry, darling, it's the most wonderful news. It's a wire from Michael . . . my little son, he's arrived—in England" —and she quotes: 'Arrived safely. See you late tonight.' I knew he was on his way from Canada," Olivia explains, "but I didn't know he'd sailed— They never tell you a thing. . . . No, I haven't seen him for five years. I sent him over in '39. . . ."

Now there is considerable excitement and many things to think of. Olivia must explain to Polton that, strange though it may seem, Michael is not such a "little self" as Polton thinks. He was twelve when he went away and that would make him—er—well, quite old enough to look after himself. A cold lunch will have to be left out, against the possibility of Michael's being hungry when he arrives, and the little room next to Olivia's will have to be made up for him. It would have been much simpler if Michael had indicated at what station he would arrive, but—

Miss Dell, who is Sir John Fletcher's secretary, is in to remind Olivia that there are papers on Sir John's desk to be signed, and that he should not fail to call R.M.B.3. "His wife's solicitors want an answer by tomorrow," concludes Miss Dell.

"What about?" Olivia is alertly anxious.

"The Barton and Burgess affair."

"What's that?"

"Sir John will know."

"Come on, tell me."

"It's not at all important. You won't forget R.M.B.3, will you? It's vital he rings them as soon as he comes in." And Miss Dell leaves to collect a report Sir John is eager to have.

The situation seems well in hand. Polton will see that Sir John's bag is packed so he can stay at his club tonight. Cook has been told to have something left out for Michael—something a bit more substantial than the milk pudding Polton suggests.

"Well, Madam, if he's very late we don't want anything to sit too heavily on his little tummy, do we?"

"No, I suppose we don't—except that as I've told you, Polton, it really isn't such a little tummy as all that. It may even be quite a big tummy by now."

"Oh, no, Madam."

"Well, I don't know, Polton. Isn't it funny not to know what one's own son looks like? I think we'd better make it cold meat and salad."

"Very good, Madam, if you think so."

Sir John Fletcher, who arrives shortly, "is a man about 45, dressed in formal clothes." Olivia gives him an affectionate peck on the cheek and pours him a drink. She remembers, a little vaguely, that his secretary did leave a message for him. He is to call up his wife's solicitors, and he is to give them an answer tomorrow morning on the Barton and Burgess affair. And what is the Barton and Burgess affair?

"Barton and Burgess are my wife's bookmakers," explains Sir John. "She incurred a very large debt with them, mostly after we were separated. Her solicitors think I should pay. I don't. That is the Barton and Burgess affair. Any other messages?"

"No, I don't think so. Darling, I think you ought to pay that debt, don't you?"

"Frankly, no. She receives a very handsome settlement, and can well afford to pay her own racing debts. Are you sure there aren't any other messages?"

"Wait a minute now." Olivia is searching her mind. "There was a thing you had to ring up. Three letters and a figure. R something. Darling, don't you think if you paid that bill it would avoid a lot of unpleasantness?"

"That's not the way I see it. Do you think you can possibly remember what the other two letters and the figure are of the thing that I have to ring up?"

"Now, let me think. There was an R and a B, I think."

"R.B.Y.4?"

Well, it might be that. Or maybe it was R.M.B.3, as Sir John suggests. Or possibly B.R.F.*6*. At any rate it doesn't matter. They will probably call again, and Sir John expects to be sitting up working.

And that presents a problem. If Sir John expects to sit up he will have to do it at the Club. Why? Well, Michael's arrived! He'll be home in a few hours.

Michael! Olivia's son! Of course Sir John is very glad—even if he doesn't look it. He's very glad for Olivia's sake.

"Oh, darling, you'll find him most companionable," chirrups Olivia. "He's mad about politics. He's the head speaker for his little organization. Terribly amusing. You'll love him, you know."

Sir John is not so sure. Will Michael's arrival mean that he is to stay at his club so long as the boy is in the neighborhood? Oh, no. Only for the night. Olivia is sure of that. How old is Michael, really? He must be over sixteen, his mother thinks. Or maybe seventeen, seeing he has come back to join up. But even if he is, as Sir John figures from Olivia's facts, all of seventeen and eight months—that doesn't mean that he is really grown up.

"You know what Polton said, when I told her how old he was? She said she simply didn't believe it."

"I don't believe it, either. But as the papers say, we must face facts, and the facts are you have a grown-up son—or nearly a grown-up son, about to descend on you at any moment to face a situation which I gather you have not yet had the courage to tell him in any of your letters."

Olivia (*protestingly*)—Darling, it's not the kind of thing you can write about in a letter. The censor wouldn't have passed it—

John—There seems to be some confusion in your mind between the Department of War Censorship and the Archbishop of Canterbury. Anyway, whatever your excuse is, it is true, isn't it—you've told him nothing whatever about me?

Olivia—Oh, yes, I have told him something.

John—What?

Olivia—That I'd met you, and that you were very nice.

John—Thank you. When did you tell him that?

Olivia—Well—when I did meet you—about two years ago.

John—About three years ago. Anything since?

OLIVIA—Well, I occasionally told him I'd been to a theatre with you or something—or that I'd had dinner with you—or something.

JOHN—I see. In this case "or something" appears to cover quite a wide field.

OLIVIA—Darling—he's only a little boy. How could I tell him things he wouldn't understand.

JOHN—Olivia, darling, he is *not* a little boy—

OLIVIA—Yes, he is. Just because he's seventeen doesn't mean he's grown-up. I'll show you his letters—they're absolutely crammed with corking and top-hole and—white mice and sling-shots. He's just a little boy and he wouldn't understand.

JOHN—Well, then—what are you going to tell him?

OLIVIA—The truth, I suppose.

JOHN—But you've just said he's too occupied with white mice and sling-shots to understand the truth.

OLIVIA—Then I'll tell him as much of the truth as he can understand.

As to how much that will be, Olivia is not prepared to say. To Sir John the fact is plain that she is facing a crisis in her life that, left to deal with herself, she would probably make an awful mess. Therefore he thinks it would be an excellent idea if they were to have a little rehearsal and find out, if they can, exactly what it is Olivia intends to tell Michael—

"Well," begins Olivia, ". . . I'll say: 'One day I went to a cocktail party given by your Aunt Ethel who married the gas light and coke company, and lives in Park Lane, and there I met a man called John Fletcher whom I didn't know was *the* John Fletcher, in spite of his Canadian accent, because he seemed too amusing and young to be a Captain of Industry and a Cabinet Minister and all the rest of it, and who seemed to like me.' "

"You understate . . . However, go on."

" 'Well, I went to lunch with him a couple of times and then one night I had dinner with him—' "

"Or something."

"Shut up. 'And he told me he was in love with me.' "

"He said nothing of the kind. He was much too cautious for that."

"Well, in a sort of underhand roundabout politician's way he gave me to understand that he didn't find me altogether repulsive, but that he was unable to proceed any further in the matter because he already had a wife from whom he was separated and who anyway was a bit of a bitch—"

"Tell me, darling, what's that?"

" 'He already had a wife who didn't understand him, but whom he couldn't divorce until after the war, on account of Dr. Goebbels. So—"

"Wait a minute, wait a minute. You're skating over the crux of the whole thing. I think Michael would want you to expand this Goebbels theme—"

Well, in that case Olivia will tell Michael practically everything —that Sir John couldn't divorce his wife, although God knows she had given him every reason, because meantime he had been taken into the Government, and a scandal involving a British Cabinet Minister wouldn't do at all; that therefore Sir John had asked Olivia, oh, very *comme il faut,* if she would wait until after the war when he would be free to ask her to marry him, and that Olivia had replied that that would be quite silly—

"After all, we're neither of us getting any younger and the war might go on for years and years and years," Olivia had pointed out, to which Sir John regretfully agreed.

Whereupon Sir John had said he would resign from the Cabinet, and Olivia had said oh, no, he wouldn't, he being far too useful making tanks.

"You said you would exert every endeavor to find a way to suit everyone," concludes Olivia, cheerfully, "so I just packed my things and moved in that night. Since when not a ripple has stirred the calm surface of our domestic bliss. . . ."

Of course, if pressed, Olivia is willing to admit that she probably will not tell Michael anything like this. She will just explain that Sir John is a very old friend; that they are going to be married after the war, and that meantime he has made her a present of one of his houses.

"Don't you think it's rather odd my giving you a house and then coming and sleeping in it myself?"

"Not odd at all," insists Olivia. "You'll be here as my guest."

"Thank you."

"Not at all. Stay as long as you like."

Sir John is not happy. The more he considers the situation the more is he convinced that there is only one thing to do—Olivia must tell Michael nothing but the full, unvarnished truth. Anything less than that is likely to prove fatal.

"But surely the truth is not the kind of thing one should tell one's sixteen-year-old boy," protests Olivia.

"Madam, your son is nearly eighteen, and I think it better that he should hear the truth from his mother's lips than from one of his bar cronies."

"Oh, John, I feel quite embarrassed. I've never been embarrassed by the situation before, and now I find myself blushing whenever I think of it. I feel like a bad, bad woman."

"In the eyes of many people, that's just what you are."

"Oh, surely not in this day and age."

"In this day and age."

"In that case you must be a bad, bad man."

"A vile seducer."

And that makes Olivia laugh. Sir John a vile seducer! He couldn't seduce a fly! He may have been "the madcap of the Toronto Elks" as a young man, but never a seducer.

"Well, anyway, I seduced you," insists Sir John.

"Oh, no, you didn't. If there was any seducing to be done, I was the one that did it."

"Yes, I think that's true."

Sir John has taken off his shoes and Olivia has lifted his feet to the couch and made him comfortable. He would relax for a moment if she would promise to tell Michael the truth, the whole truth and nothing but the truth. This she promises to do. But can he trust her? Not an inch.

Olivia has turned the lights low and is sitting beside Sir John, listening to the trials of his day and comforting him sweetly. He had had a tiring day, he tells her. They had bullied him at question time. All about the new tank. At least ten of them were fairly screaming for his blood. That, to Olivia, just wasn't fair. She'll have the bulliers there and bully them. . . .

Sir John is drowsy now. . . . Let him sleep, Olivia suggests, while she writes a few letters. . . . He will, if she promises not to go too far away. . . . Why? . . . Because he adores her. . . .

For a moment all is peacefully quiet. In the distance Big Ben is chiming the three-quarter hour. And then Polton, in some agitation, bursts in, quickly followed by young Michael.

"Hullo, Mum!"

"Michael, darling!" Olivia is embracing her son with enthusiasm. "Your telegram said late tonight. I wasn't expecting you for hours!"

Sir John has sat up abruptly and is trying, awkwardly, to put on his shoes.

"I didn't see why I should wait all day for a train," explains Michael. "I got a lift from a pilot chap I know. He was taking an hansom down to Reading, and I came on from there."

Olivia's arms are around him again. "You don't look much older, but you're much thinner. Didn't they give you enough to eat over there?"

"Of course they did."

"Oh, it's wonderful to see you, Michael—"

Olivia puts on the lights and Michael becomes conscious of Sir John, who is still trying to get into his shoes. He has just succeeded in getting one shoe on as Michael turns toward him and waits to be introduced.

"Oh, I'm sorry." Olivia is not at all embarrassed. "This is Sir John Fletcher—my son Michael."

"How do you do?"

"How do you do, sir?"

"Poor man, his shoes were hurting him."

"Oh, really?"

"So I told him to take them off if they were hurting him."

"Yes, I see."

John's laugh is purely social. "Well, they've stopped hurting me now, so if you don't mind I'll put them on again."

"Oh, yes, do." She turns to Michael. "You remember I told you all about him in my letters. I want you to be particularly nice to him, Michael—because he's a very old friend of mine—that's to say, anyway, I want you to get on—"

"Oh, yes," agrees Michael, a little stiffly.

"Did you have a good trip?" Sir John would know.

"Yes, thank you, sir."

"Oh, don't call him sir, Michael. Call him—I know—call him Uncle John."

"Why?"

"Well—because it would—well—be nice."

"I agree with Michael," quickly speaks up Sir John. "I don't see why he should call me Uncle John when I'm not his Uncle John."

"Yes—but you're such a very old friend."

"Quite so, but that's hardly the point."

Michael is quite impressed with the house. Does Olivia get it furnished? She does, in a sort of way, his mother admits. And does the sofa become a bed? No. There are bedrooms upstairs. That's good, Michael allows. He can sleep there. He thought he might have to go out. But how much does she pay for all this? Can she afford it?

"Darling—don't let us talk about such things at the moment," Olivia quickly suggests, taking her son affectionately by the arm.

"Remember there's someone else in the room."

John is quite conscious that Olivia and Michael would like to be alone, but unfortunately he can't leave them until he has the papers that are being sent over from his office. Perhaps they wouldn't mind if he waits in the other room?

No, Olivia doesn't mind. But let him not forget that they are all having dinner together.

With Sir John out of the room, Michael is naturally a bit curious. His mother would do what she can do to acquaint him with the facts. "You know who he is, don't you?" she asks.

Yes, Michael knows. "He's the Minister for Tank Production."

"That's right, he's in the Cabinet."

"That doesn't make him any the less of an old poop."

"Michael!"

"You should *hear* what my organization in Canada says about him."

"But surely your organization in Canada speaks very highly of him."

"Oh, no, they don't. Not *my* friends, anyway. They say he is a menace to world industrial reorganization."

Neither does Michael's organization think much of Sir John's book, "A Defense of Private Enterprise," which Olivia hasn't got around to reading. It was the vote of Michael's friends that the book proved Sir John was nothing "but a rank, monopolistic reactionary."

But— Enough about Sir John. What about his mother? How has she been getting on? She doesn't look too awfully well. Sort of haggard, somehow. But that may just be because she is older—

"Poor old Mum. I bet you've had a pretty rotten time of it. Are you glad to have someone to take care of you at last?"

Olivia has found her handkerchief and is dabbing her eyes. "It's nothing. I'm sorry. It's just that you're not quite how I expected you somehow."

"I'm older, you know."

"Oh, darling, you don't look any older—"

"Oh, Mum, I must—"

"No, you don't." She has put her arms around him. "You still look my little Michael. How was Canada?"

Canada, reports Michael, was corking. And everybody was fine to him. When he told her his father had died, his landlady, old Mrs. Wilkinson, had actually cried. Is there anything more Olivia could tell him about his father?

"You know how ill he was before you went away—overwork, of course, and then because of the war there was even more work. I tried to get him to let up, but you know him, he wouldn't. I suppose I should have tried more—I don't know. . . ."

"Poor old Mum. I'm most terribly sorry."

"Thank you, darling."

Suddenly Michael is impressed with the gown his mother is wearing. He is willing to wager she didn't get that at Ponting's. No, as a matter of fact, she didn't. She got it at Molyneux's. Molyneux is—er—much nearer. And why hadn't she gone to any of the old shops? The telephone ringing helps end that inquiry. . . .

Michael and his mother are back now filling in the lapses. Why had Olivia left Baron's Court? Well, for one thing it was, as he knows, rather a gloomy flat. Then the blitz came and Olivia had taken a "basement bed-sit in—er—Swiss Cottage." Olivia by now is fanning herself with her engagement book. Had she ever let the old flat? No. No, she hadn't. It was still in the hands of the agents.

This brings up the subject of money. Michael can see that he will have to be looking around for something. And this reminds Olivia that she had already done something about that. Michael had written so often about wanting a job between now and the time that he would be called up that she had made inquiries. She had found something, too, something rather nice—about seven or eight pounds a week. Oh, gosh! To Michael that is a bit startling. *What* is it?

"Well, you're to go tomorrow morning and see a Mr. Symonds; he hasn't promised anything, but if you make a good impression he may give you something in the Ministry of Tank Production."

"Has *he* got anything to do with it?"

"Yes, he has, darling. He's gone to a great deal of trouble, and I want you to thank him very nicely."

"Gosh, seven or eight pounds; well, I suppose one can't afford to be too choosey, if the job's worth all that money. Still, I can't say I care for the thought of having him as my boss all the same."

It isn't very likely that Michael will be seeing too much of the Minister. And, anyway, Olivia does wish that he (Michael) would be forgetting all his tiresome prejudices and try to like Sir John just a little. It is terribly important for her that he does. Why? Well, John is such a very old friend— Besides—

Olivia has begun to walk about the room. Passing Michael she leans over to kiss him. There is, she admits, something she has to say to him—

"Yes, Mum, what is it?"

OLIVIA—Michael, do you think of me as being terribly old?

MICHAEL—Oh, no, Mum. Not old at all. Sort of middle-aged, really—

OLIVIA—Yes, I see. Well, now, you know how fond I was of your father, don't you?

MICHAEL—Yes, Mum, of course I know.

OLIVIA—Well, after all, that's really no reason why I should think of spending the rest of my life entirely alone—

MICHAEL—Of course you won't be alone. You're going to have me from now on.

OLIVIA—I know, dear, and I'm more grateful than I can say to have you with me. But, darling, you'll get married yourself one day, and then I shall have no one—

MICHAEL—Don't worry about that. We'll have you to live with us.

OLIVIA—Oh, I see.

MICHAEL—Besides, I don't think I'm going to get married.

OLIVIA—Why not?

MICHAEL—It's a bit frustrating, I think.

OLIVIA—Oh, is it?

MICHAEL—Yes. Go on, Mum. What were you going to tell me?

OLIVIA (*nervously*)—Oh, dear, Michael, what would you say if I told you that I was thinking of getting married again?

MICHAEL—What?

OLIVIA—What are you laughing at?

MICHAEL—Oh, Mum, oh, Mum! Poor old Mum!

OLIVIA—Why poor old Mum?

MICHAEL—I'm awfully sorry. Most rude of me—only—

OLIVIA—Only what?

MICHAEL—Nothing. Yes, of course, go ahead and get married. We'll just have to find the *right man* for you, that's all. Poor old Mum.

OLIVIA—Don't call me poor old Mum.

The papers for which Sir John has been waiting have arrived. Coming from his studio to get them he finds Michael smoking a cigarette, plainly to the distress of his mother. Would Michael also like a whisky and soda? Yes, Michael would. But Olivia

Photo by Vandamm Studio.

"O MISTRESS MINE"

Michael has recovered his book . . . What is he reading? A work called "Study and Diagnosis of Poisoning!" Why? Because it is a subject in which he is interested.

(*Alfred Lunt, Lynn Fontanne, Dick Van Patten*)

cannot permit that. If Michael has anything it will be a glass of sherry, which John pours for him.

Michael has wandered up to the window and is having a look at London. The minute his back is turned there is excited pantomime between John and Olivia—John trying to ask if she has told Michael all; Olivia shaking her head despairingly that she has not. John would then indicate that he is very, very angry. Michael turns around and nearly catches him at it.

"Well, I think I had better go and read this report," says John, picking up his papers.

Olivia is not to be trapped again. "No. You stay here and talk to Michael. I have to go and change for dinner."

"Oh, but surely—haven't you got a lot more to say to Michael —a *lot* more?"

"Yes, after dinner. He has something to say to you. He wants to thank you very nicely. I'm sure you two are going to get on quite corkingly." And she has gone.

Left to themselves, Michael and Sir John do a bit of polite verbal sparring. They are both interested in meeting each other. John hopes that Michael is going to like his new job—

"Anyway, you'll be getting a helluva lot of money for a boy of your age. Do you know how much I got when I first started?"

"No. How much?"

"About eight dollars a week. I started as an office boy."

"Really? According to my organization you inherited Fletcher-Pratt from your father—Black Fletcher—who fought the Canadian Trades Unions."

"Black Fletcher was not the name I knew my father by. However, it is quite true that my father, James Fletcher, was chairman of the Board of the Canadian branch at the time, but I had to work my way up like anyone else."

"Yes, but surely from slightly nearer the top than anyone else—"

"No—no nearer the top than anyone else. Tell me, are you terribly left wing?"

No, Michael doesn't think so. Not more than most people. He's just an anti-fascist. Maybe we are all anti-fascist, as Sir John suggests, but Michael has his doubts. Michael gets that idea from the treasurer of his organization, James P. Whitstable, who is convinced that "our real enemy is not so much the enemy, as some of *those* who pretend to be the enemy's enemy."

Young Mr. Whitstable, it appears, is well over nineteen. ". . . Fascism doesn't only wear a brown shirt. It can wear a black coat and a stiff white collar." That's another of the Whitstable sayings.

"If James P. Whitstable were only here, Michael, I might, who knows, be able to answer him," says John, covering his white collar with one hand. "But as a matter of fact I am a little out of practice at this sort of argument. You see, for the past three years I have been working on an average of fourteen hours a day trying to produce certain engines of war, designed to kill with maximum efficiency as many of my country's enemies as possible. So you see, Michael, I'm just a little tired."

Michael has heard of the new tank, too. He doesn't think much of it. According to the *Evening Standard* there is likely to be quite a stink about it. . . . A chap on the boat had said you could put your hand through the armor plate . . . Another said the turret was an absolute disgrace . . . Another that the only way you could get it up hill was to drive it up backward . . .

"Oh, it's the folly of the whole system," announces Michael. "Big business men running a public service. What happens? They cut each other's throats; they line their own pockets. And then people are surprised when after three years they get a tank that can't even go up hill in the ordinary way. . . . I see you have no answer," concludes Michael, as something suspiciously like a sob comes from Sir John; "I can't say I'm surprised."

Olivia has returned. She can see that Sir John has been terribly upset and insists that Michael apologize. A truce is declared for dinner, and Michael goes to get ready.

"Well, John? You didn't get on," surmises Olivia.

"I'm afraid we didn't get on."

"Politics?"

"Politics. He also accused me of nepotism, fraud, incompetence, Speculation and treachery."

"Did he really? Isn't he naughty?"

"At times, my darling, you have a positive genius for understatement."

Michael, they are now agreed, is certainly a problem. "He's too old to spank and too young to punch on the nose," declares Sir John. But Olivia thinks she has found the proper approach toward handling her son. She will wait until he is in bed and then, taking him a cup of nice hot Ovaltine, she will sit on the side of his bed and talk to him as though he were forty years old, a real man of the world. . . . And she will probably spill the Ovaltine and spoil everything, predicts Sir John.

Before they can decide on anything resembling a concrete plan their problem is again decidedly active. Michael has been talking with Polton, the parlormaid, and learned that not only does the house belong to Sir John, but everything in it is his as well. Is that true? Yes, that's true. And all those dresses in his mother's room—did she or did she not pay for them? She did not. Sir John paid for them and for "all those jewels and things on the dressing table?" Sir John paid for those, too—

"And the weighing machine in the bathroom?"

"Oh, no, Michael, I paid for that," insists Olivia, quickly.

"With your money, or the money he gave you?"

"Well—"

"With the money I gave her," answers Sir John.

"I don't need to hear any more. I understand the situation perfectly." Michael has gone quickly into the hall.

"No, darling, you don't understand," Olivia calls, as she follows after him; "and I beg you to reserve judgment until you've heard the whole story."

"I don't need to hear it," Michael's voice rumbles back; "you've been weak, he's been vile."

A compromise of sorts is agreed upon. They will all three go to dinner and during their meal John and Olivia will tell Michael the whole story, from beginning to end.

To that Michael agrees—on condition that he buys the dinner. And they'll not go to the Savoy; they'll go to the Tuck Inn—"in Puffin's Corner, off Belvedere Road, Baron's Court."

"We used to get a jolly good three-course meal there for one and fourpence," Michael promises. "Don't you remember? You used to take me there on Annie's night out. Besides, they'll know me there and we'll get service."

Now Sir John, having discovered that he has the wrong papers from the Ministry, and having ordered that the right ones be sent to the Savoy, must telephone the Ministry and change his order from the Savoy to Tuck's Inn.

It's pretty far to Tuck's Inn, Olivia fears. It won't be too far on the Underground, Michael assures her. Here again an aroused Sir John takes over. They'll go by bus—

"We'll queue up and get a number 24, to Trafalgar Square. Then we'll change and queue up for a number 96. At South Kensington we'll change and queue up for a number 49. That'll take us to the top of Belvedere Road. We can walk the rest."

"If we're going to walk I'd better change my shoes," says a dismayed Olivia.

"Yes, and, Olivia, you'd better take a mackintosh, it looks like rain," adds Sir John.

The curtain falls.

ACT II

It is early evening a few days later. In the Fletcher sitting room Olivia is busy with her accounts at her desk. Sir John is pacing the floor trying to dictate a speech to Miss Dell, who is sitting, notebook in hand, on the arm of the sofa.

Dictating, Sir John is finding, is a considerable chore, what with frequent interruptions by telephone, and not a few by Olivia. He is about ready to give up when Michael arrives, a little depressed by his long day at the office. They are working Michael a bit too hard, Olivia fears. Nine to seven is a long time for a boy of his age. Perhaps John will be able to do something about that—

"Olivia, my dear, roughly five thousand people work in my Ministry. I'm afraid I can't see my way to ordering the loss of some thirty thousand man hours per week in order that Michael may get home a little sooner." John is controlling himself with some difficulty.

Sir John resumes his dictation. Michael tiptoes his way to the desk, gets a book and tiptoes back to a chair. When he is finally settled Sir John goes on—

" 'Before I begin I would like to make it quite clear that I am no politician. It was as a business man that I was brought into this government, and it is as a business man, pure and simple, that I address you now.' " He has reached the fireplace and is standing before it. "Cut out 'pure and simple,' " he orders. " 'It is as a plain business man that I address you now—' " Michael nods, but Sir John pretends not to see him. " 'As many of you know, I am a Canadian by birth. All my life I have stood for a policy of closer industrial union and co-ordination within the Empire. Our left wing friends have dubbed this policy as reactionary and imperialistic. Very well, then. If it is reaction, if it is imperialism, then I am a reactionary, and I *am* an imperialist. Am I ashamed of being so? Far from it. Very far from it indeed. I glory in my unrepentance.' "

Michael, with no change of expression, is staring fixedly at Sir John. " 'So let our young intellectuals scoff and sneer, let them hurl their odium at my head. I still stand where yet I stood—' "

Both Olivia and Miss Dell suggest that this should be changed to "stand still" but Sir John will have none of that—

"I do not stand still. I still stand. 'Sticks and stones may break my bones, but words will never hurt me.' "

"Harm me," suggests Michael. "Hurt me," contends Miss Dell. "Injure me" is the way Olivia remembers having learned it—

" 'Hurt me. Words can never hurt me,' " prompts Miss Dell.

"Oh, yes, they can, Miss Dell. Oh, yes, they can," interpolates Sir John. He turns to the others, with controlled fury: "Now may I please have ten minutes of quiet? That's all I ask, and it's not very much, and I shall have finished my speech."

One more interruption and Sir John gives up. He dismisses Miss Dell. He'll do the whole thing over when he can get back into his studio next day.

Michael has recovered his book and is going upstairs. What is he reading? A work called "Study and Diagnosis of Poisonings." Why? It is a subject in which he is interested, he tells his mother, and he leaves them.

It is now plainly evident to Sir John what is happening to Michael. He is not still unhappy over his home situation, as Olivia fears. To the contrary, he is having the time of his life. Michael is playing Hamlet—

"Hamlet? What do you mean?" Olivia is puzzled.

JOHN—Haven't you noticed? You watch him.

OLIVIA—I have noticed an odd look about him at moments. Do you think that's what it is?

JOHN—Certainly. That's his "antic disposition." He does it at the office too, so Symonds tells me. He's always coming in giving the typists a demoniac glare. It scares them out of their wits. And then what about that black tie?

OLIVIA—Isn't there an office rule about that?

JOHN—Darling, he can wear any damn tie he likes. That's his "inky cloak."

OLIVIA—Oh, John. Then he must be upset about it.

JOHN—Nonsense. You told me yourself he never cared for his father. Besides, it's well over three years since he died. It's just sheer play-acting—for your benefit.

OLIVIA—Come to think of it, I believe his school did do Hamlet once.

JOHN (*triumphantly*)—There you are! And I bet he played the Prince.

Olivia—No, I don't think so. I think he played a lady-in-waiting.

John—Well, it doesn't matter. He knows the play anyway. You'd better watch out for a closet scene, Olivia. He'll be telling you to throw away the worser part of your heart and live the purer with the other half.

Olivia (*laughing*)—I'll smack his bottom for him, if he does. Oh, it really is rather sweet, isn't it?

John—It isn't so sweet if you remember how the play ends. That book! Don't you see?

Olivia—No, what?

John—Well, you remember how he tried to get me to admit I'd known his father?

Olivia—Yes, that's true. I had to deny it, too, you know. Then he suggested that Jack had probably been your doctor without my knowing it—as if I wouldn't have known it.

John—In default of a ghost he's trying to find out how I poisoned him.

Olivia—Oh, darling! Really!

John—Your son has a very lively imagination. He's having a lovely time. He's up to tricks. Still, at least he means to absolve you from complicity, in the crime— (*Chuckling.*) "Nor let thy soul contrive against thy mother aught." *I'm* the villain—the "bloody, bawdy villain! Remorseless, lecherous, treacherous, kindless, villain! Oh, vengeance!" Oh, God! I've scared myself, now.

It is while Michael is in his room that Olivia would check with Sir John on certain features of their situation about which she would be reassured. Why, she would like to know again, did John leave the first Mrs. Fletcher? There were, he repeats, several reasons—one being because the first Mrs. F. really preferred the embraces of a certain young Guard's officer to his own. How long was he in love with her? About ten days. How long was she in love with him? Never. She married him for his money.

"Has it ever occurred to you that I might be living with you for your money?" asks a lightly worried Olivia.

"That thought is never absent from my mind."

"Seriously. I mean it. Have you ever thought that?"

"I refuse to answer such a lunatic question seriously."

"It's not such a lunatic question really. Michael thinks I am."

"Michael thinks I poisoned his father. . . . Does it really matter what a crazy adolescent thinks of you?"

"He's my son.". . .

Michael has decided that he will not come down to dinner, if his mother doesn't mind. He'd rather be alone. But the following night, if they are free, he would like them to come see a show with him. That, Olivia insists, is a charming thought. They would love to come. What's the play?

"Well—it's a sort of thriller, I think," says Michael. "It's called 'Murder in the Family.'"

With that Sir John guffaws loudly and quickly leaves the room. Olivia is angry with Michael. There has been enough of this Hamlet nonsense and she demands that he stop it.

"In future I want you to behave less like a moonstruck little half-wit and more like a human being. Is that understood?"

"Yes, Mum."

"Good."

By the time she has reached the door Olivia has relented. She comes quickly back.

"Darling, I didn't mean to be unkind," explains Olivia, handing her son back the "ridiculous black tie" she has made him discard. ". . . You can dress in black silk tights if you want to, for all I care—only you'd better not—it might annoy John." She has forced a tight little smile from him before she leaves.

Michael's next move is to take up with Polton the matter of his mother's position in the house. He doesn't get much satisfaction there.

"Well, sir, I look at it like this. Mind you, I wouldn't have no truck, in the normal way with two people who carried on without being married. Living in sin, you might call it—begging your pardon, sir, if I'm taking a liberty—"

"No. After all, that's what it is—"

"Oh, no, sir, it's not. Not with Sir John and Mrs. Brown. It's different with them. They behave just like two people who've been lawfully married for years and years, and to see them together you wouldn't know they hadn't been, bless 'em."

"But don't you find that wrong?"

"Wrong? I wouldn't be staying in this house if I did, I can tell you that straight."

The doorbell has rung. With a quick glance out the window, Michael dismisses Polton. This is someone to see him. A moment later he has ushered into the room a considerably mystified young woman of 25, and very decorative. Yes, he is "the mysterious Mr. Brown" who has requested the interview, and she, it transpires, is Diana, the current Lady Fletcher. She has come in response to a summons from Michael, who has intimated over the phone that it is a matter of life or death and that she will learn something to her particular advantage. Now, after he has explained a little awkwardly how fortunate it is that everyone's out at the moment, making it unnecessary that he smuggle her into his bedroom, she is convinced that she had better be going—

"Oh, no. Please, Lady Fletcher. There's no danger. You'll regret it forever after if you do."

"Well, then, will you kindly say what you have to say to me."

"Yes. O.K. . . . Lady Fletcher, I hate to distress you unnecessarily, but I feel it my duty."

"Oh."

"Lady Fletcher, do you know whose house this is?"

"No—I don't think so—whose?"

"Your husband's."

"John's?" Diana has hurriedly risen. "Now I've got to go. I'm definitely not going to run into him, if I can avoid it."

"No, it's all right. He's at his office—he'll be there for hours. I do understand how you must feel about seeing him again, after the way he's treated you."

"What?"

It is in this house, Michael explains, that Sir John is living with —his mistress. Yes, the Olivia Brown about whom Lady Fletcher confesses having heard such a lot. And it is Michael's idea that Lady Fletcher should swallow her pride and confront Olivia. Confront her, and reason with her.

". . . I'm sure you could get her to see how wrong it all is," he says.

"How wrong all what is?"

"What she's doing, of course."

"Oh, do make sense. What *is* she doing—for Heaven's sake?"

"Living in sin with your husband."

Diana is laughing softly now. After all, there is something rather charming about Michael's wanting her to tell his mother to stop being a wicked woman. But she couldn't do that—

"I'm afraid I can't very well confront Mrs. Brown and reason with her, because, you see, it really isn't any business of mine."

"But of course it's your business. You don't seem to understand. After all, it's *your* husband who's her paramour."

Again Diana is laughing. "Paramour" is such a funny word to use in connection with John. . . .

Presently Olivia appears. Her meeting with Lady Fletcher is friendly and formal. Perhaps they both overdo the formalities a little. Michael is plainly annoyed. Olivia would have Lady Fletcher sit down, and have a drink, but Lady Fletcher doesn't think she will, if Mrs. Brown doesn't mind—

"It's no trouble, really," Olivia assures her guest. "I'm making one anyway. We're having a party tonight, it's such a strain on the rations but John does love to entertain his friends so of course I have to try to cope—"

"I know. Such a bore, isn't it, in wartime, trying to do anything in the way of entertaining? Still, if you'll forgive me, I think I really must begin to wend my way home. I have a few friends coming in to see me."

"Oh, well, in that case it would be wrong of me to keep you. Well, it's been so nice to have met you at last."

"It's been charming. Perhaps you'll drop in on me, one day."

"I'd love to—"

Olivia and Lady Fletcher are beaming at each other and advancing toward the door when Sir John suddenly appears. His surprise is well covered, and he listens interestedly to both Olivia's and Michael's explanations of how the meeting came about, followed by Diana's added declaration that she really must fly—

"Lady Fletcher has some friends waiting for her, John," says Olivia.

"Oh. Well, remember me to him, will you?"

"Yes, I will. How are you, John?"

"Very well, thank you, Diana. How are you?"

"Bearing up."

When Michael comes back from seeing Lady Fletcher out there are marked indications that Sir John is planning to have a pretty serious talk with the young man. Olivia is quick to save that situation by suggesting that John hasn't much time to get ready for dinner. With John out of the way she is herself prepared to take up this latest action of Michael's. She would like to know exactly what is in her son's mind. Is it true that he is playing some sort of game with her and John? That could be true, Michael admits. Otherwise what chance would he have fighting a man like John on even terms?

"Why do you feel you have to fight him?"

"Because I hate him."

Olivia—Oh, no, Michael, you don't hate him; you've just worked yourself up into thinking a lot of ridiculous things about him, but you don't hate him. Nobody could hate John.

MICHAEL—I hate him more than anything on earth. I hate him for what he's done to you.

OLIVIA—What do you mean?

MICHAEL (*passionately*)—Don't you know what he's done to you? He's changed you—so that you're no more like my mother than—than any of a hundred society women I could pick out for you any day of the week at the Dorchester. You're not *you* any more. That's why I hate him.

OLIVIA—Darling, that's a bad thing to say. Are you sure it's true?

MICHAEL—Don't you know it's true? *Think* back to Sandringham Crescent, when Dad was alive and there were just the three of us. You were happy then, weren't you?

OLIVIA—I wasn't unhappy, Michael.

MICHAEL—But you *were* in love with Dad, weren't you?

OLIVIA—Darling, it's a long, long time ago. It's hard to remember what one felt like at the beginning—

MICHAEL—You mean you didn't stay in love.

OLIVIA—No, darling, I'm afraid we didn't.

MICHAEL—Oh, Mum, but why?

OLIVIA—There isn't any why about these things, Michael. They happen, and that's all. Perhaps we married too young, or perhaps it was the difficult struggling life we led that made it so hard to stay in love.

MICHAEL—But surely Dad made an awful lot of money out of his practice, didn't he?

OLIVIA—Not an awful lot, Michael. And less and less as the years went on.

MICHAEL—You mean he wasn't a success.

OLIVIA—He was unlucky.

MICHAEL—But, Mum, I thought—that he—

OLIVIA—Of course you did, you were only a little boy. Thank God we managed to keep it from you. Don't think I ever resented his not being a success. I never asked for nor expected another sort of life with you and him. I suppose it was you who turned the scales— (*She kisses him.*) I would have been quite content to have lived the rest of my life as the wife of an unsuccessful doctor in Baron's Court.

There is still the question of Michael's future to be settled. He knows now his mother's defense. He knows what she is going to say—that when she first met Sir John Fletcher she fell in love for the first time in her life. Yes, she was going to say that, Olivia admits, because it is true.

"You're going to say that all this—grandeur—doesn't really mean anything to you, because you'd be just as happy with him in a slum as you are here."

"No, I wasn't going to say that," Olivia answers quietly. "All this grandeur—as you call it—is very important to me. I sometimes think I only began to live when I moved into this house. It's hard to separate that feeling from my love for John, and if in falling in love with John I've become a Dorchester society woman and therefore you no longer recognize me, I'm sorry, but there's nothing I can do about it."

Michael cannot agree with his mother's program—that he should go on living with her. After a little, she is sure, he really will grow fond of Sir John. Michael thinks the better thing for him to do is to go on his own; to find himself "digs." He wouldn't be going too far away. They will still see each other.

Olivia is resigned to this plan. After all, Michael is nearly eighteen. The next day they will go together in search of "digs." But she still is a little hopeful—

"Michael—you don't think you might grow to dislike him a little less?"

"I'm sorry, Mum, but I can't help what I feel."

"I see. Well, we're still friends, aren't we?"

He has gone to her quickly, now, and put his head in her lap.

"Don't go on with it, Mum. Please don't. Please. I can't bear it."

Sir John's voice in the hall brings Michael quickly to his feet. It is Sir John's idea that if Michael would be saved from a dull evening, Mr. Symonds at the Ministry would doubtless be glad to have his help. Michael, unimpressed, goes back to his room.

Absently Olivia is at the drink table mixing the cocktails. John, watching her, is puzzled and anxious. Presently she tells him. Michael has won. For her the decision had to be made—either Sir John or her son. And she has chosen Michael.

"Does it mean that you are going to leave me?" slowly asks Sir John.

"Yes."

"I don't know what to say, Olivia. If I told you that your love for me is the one good thing that ever happened to me and that if you left me it will be the hardest blow I've ever had to bear, would that make any difference?"

"It would be very nice to hear, darling, but it wouldn't make any difference—"

"If I resigned tomorrow, got my divorce, and asked you to marry me?"

"It would still be you or Michael—"

"I just can't see life ahead without you—I'm not threatening suicide or trying to get your sympathy, but it's a plain and simple fact that if you leave me, life will not be worth living—"

"Don't go on, darling. No matter how ever much I cry, it won't make any difference."

The guests are beginning to arrive—Miss Wentworth, Sir Thomas and Lady Markham.

"The Randalls have been delayed at the theatre, they'll be late," reports John, taking the call from the telephone.

"I hear they are rehearsing a new comedy," says Olivia. "I do think that in times like these it's far better to make people laugh than to make them cry. Darling, you haven't been for ages—" Olivia has gone into the hall to greet Sir Thomas and Lady Markham.

The curtain falls.

ACT III

Some months later Olivia and Michael are back in the sitting room of the Browns' flat in Baron's Court. It is at the top floor of a tall Victorian mansion and through a Gothic window at back a line of Gothic roofs can be seen across the street.

The radio is playing "I'll Be Seeing You." Michael, just home from the office, can't read his *Labour Monthly* comfortably to music and shuts it off.

Olivia, coming from the kitchen to greet Michael, is prepared to give him his food promptly, seeing that he has an early date. "It's a dried egg omelette again, I'm afraid," she apologizes. "All they had were dehydrated frankfurters."

Two things are interesting Michael at the moment—his date with Sylvia Hart to see a film at the Forum, and another article by Laski in the *Labour Monthly*. He isn't too happy about Sylvia, knowing that she is probably going with him only because Sparky Stevens has gone back from leave and Bill Evans is away. But he is enthused by the Laski article. It is on Inflation and the Standardization of Wages. No, Olivia isn't particularly interested. She has found a copy of the new *Tatler* and is much more concerned about a startling picture she has found in that. "Sir John Fletcher and his beautiful wife enjoying a joke at Ciro's." That's the caption Michael reads over her shoulder. It unquestionably is Sir John and Diana Fletcher.

"Well—why not?" demands Olivia. "They were still quite friends—I hope he has gone back to her. It would settle everything very nicely. . . . Go on with your dinner, darling, or you'll be late." She returns to the picture. "My God—she's still wearing that same idiotic hat she had on the day you brought her round."

"It was a jolly nice hat. You admired it yourself."

"I admired it because when a woman sticks a thing like that on her head you've got to say something or burst. Poor darling, what does she look like—a sort of agitated peahen."

Olivia isn't surprised that John doesn't make a better showing in the picture. He never did photograph well. Anyway, why should she care if he does go and make a fool of himself again?

"You still mind about it, don't you?" Michael asks.

"I've far too much on my hands trying to feed you and keeping this flat clean to worry about whether I'm happy or not. As a matter of fact, I've been perfectly happy these last three months."

"Gosh! Is that true?" demands Michael, wistfully.

"Of course it is. It's a clear conscience. I know my omelettes are uneatable and my gâteaux sit down, but at least I try and cope—which is more than some people do. Enjoying a joke at Ciro's! In a happy mood at the Dorchester! I wonder if that crowd realizes how ridiculous they all are. What does your paper say about them?"

"Oh, Laski says that in the New World everyone will have to work his passage or be pushed overboard."

"He's right."

"He says that crowd's absolutely finished, even though they don't know it yet."

"He's absolutely right. Pushed overboard—every one of them. I must read that article."

There is still a danger that he will be late for his date, Olivia reminds her son. Does he like Sylvia? A bit more than "like," Michael admits—

"Darling! Are you in love?"

"Sometimes I am and sometimes I'm not."

"Which are you at the moment?"

"I am."

"Oh, you poor little lamb." She has taken his face in her hands. "Is she in love with you?"

"Gosh, no! She's not in love with anyone. I'm only about fifth or sixth on her list. *I* can't *afford* to take her to the Savoy."

"I must say she really doesn't sound awfully nice. Why do you love her so much?"

"We men can't help our feelings."

Michael doesn't like leaving his mother alone, but she assures him she is quite content. Recently she has taken up a hobby. She is teaching herself to type on his typewriter.

" 'The time has come for all good men to—' I'm getting very good at it, you'd be surprised. Except that I can never find the 'y.' I love to hear the bell. How much does a typist earn, Michael?"

"Not much, I'm afraid, Mum."

"Oh, well, enough to keep me in my old age, I expect."

Michael has gone. Olivia goes briefly back to the picture in the *Tatler,* making a face in imitation of Diana Fletcher to indicate her contempt for that sort of thing. Into the kitchen she goes to put a few things in the cupboard and to decide to let the washing-up go. Now as she comes back, she is pretending in pantomime that she is a typist coming into her office. Mr. Jones she greets; and Mr. Peters. She hopes she isn't late! Then she goes directly to the desk "and with care and concentration begins to type, mostly with one finger, though at certain bolder moments, with two."

Her back is to the door. She does not see Sir John as he appears noiselessly in the doorway. "He is breathing heavily but soundlessly," and after resting a second to recover his breath he tiptoes up to Olivia and looks over her shoulder—

John—"Now is the time for all good men—"

Olivia—John!

John—"—to say that Diana Fletcher is a silly bitch!" Really, Olivia!

Olivia—John! Go away! Go away at once.

John—You ought to warn your visitors to bring their alpenstocks with them.

Olivia—How did you get in?

John—Through what I gathered was the front door.

Olivia—That little idiot left it unlocked again. Go away, John. I'll get Mr. Dangerfield to throw you out.

John—Who's Mr. Dangerfield?

Olivia—He lives in the flat below, and he's as strong as a bull.

John—Go and get him. I need exercise.

Olivia—Oh, John, please go. Please. You gave me your sacred solemn word of honor not to try and see me again.

JOHN—Yes, I did, didn't I?

OLIVIA—Well, then, aren't you ashamed of yourself?

JOHN—Yes, I am.

OLIVIA—Then why don't you go? Don't you see, every second you stay makes it worse.

JOHN—Yes, it does, doesn't it. Much worse.

OLIVIA—I warn you—Michael's in that room there—

JOHN—Oh, no, he isn't. It's not for nothing I've been sitting in my car at Puffin's Corner for the last half hour waiting for him to come out. It was rather exciting. Like a gangster film. My driver was most intrigued. I told her I was watching a hot-bed of international spies—

OLIVIA—Anyway, he's just gone around the corner for a packet of cigarettes. He'll be back in a minute.

JOHN—Oh, no, he won't. He's gone to the cinema with his girl friend—Miss Sylvia Hart—and he'll be away for hours.

OLIVIA—How do you know?

JOHN—You forgot he works in my Ministry.

OLIVIA—Really, John! You, the Minister, spying on a little boy to find out when his mother's going to be alone. That's pretty, I must say.

JOHN—I can only repeat, Olivia—I'm bitterly, bitterly ashamed of myself.

OLIVIA—Well, you don't look it.

JOHN—It would never do for a Cabinet Minister to look ashamed of himself. Oh, darling, I'm so glad to see you again. Have you—or is it my imagination—have you put on a little weight?

OLIVIA—Certainly not. As a matter of fact I've taken it off.

JOHN—Well, whatever you've done it certainly suits you.

When Sir John finds the flat charming he is not, he insists, patronizing the Browns, nor the late Dr. Brown's taste. He really finds it very pleasant. And he especially approves Olivia's gay apron. He had never seen her in an apron before. Nor has he come to taunt her.

". . . I want you to know, John, that this apron is an article of clothing that I am very proud to wear," announces Olivia, with dignity.

"But of course you are. I understand that perfectly."

"Oh, no, you don't. You don't understand at all—how could you, you and your crowd, understand what a wonderful feeling it gives me to know that I'm working my passage at last. As for your crowd, John, they're finished—absolutely finished. In the New World they're all going to be— What's the phrase?"

"Swept aside like so much chaff?"

"No, no . . . not swept . . ."

"Pushed overboard?"

"That's it, pushed overboard—they're all going to be pushed overboard. You should read what the *Labour Monthly* has to say about them."

Olivia cannot quite recall the name of the chap who wrote the *Labour Monthly* article, but John suspects it might be Professor Laski. A writer of forceful stuff, is Laski, he admits, and one with whom he finds himself in frequent agreement—but not in all things.

And now Olivia is through. Will John please go back to Westminster—and to his wife—who, she is sure, is waiting for him with open arms—

"What are you talking about?"

"You're not the only one who has ways and means of finding out things."

"You don't really think I've gone back to Diana, do you?"

"I don't care whether you have or you haven't, John. I've finished with you. Can't you understand that? I've finished with you for good and all."

"Do you mean that?"

"Of course I mean it. I've made my decision and I'm not going back on it, and I'd be grateful if in future you don't come slumming."

John doesn't seem to know exactly what to do. He searches for a cigarette. Olivia supplies this want, but insists he can only have one. When that is smoked he will have to go.

"You've gone awfully gray these last three months," ventures Olivia. Would that mean that he has been working terribly hard—or does it indicate too many late nights at Ciro's?

"Since you left me, Olivia, I've been out one night and one night only," protests John, seriously. "I took Diana to Ciro's to discuss a matter of business."

"Funny business."

"Serious business, the Barton and Burgess affair."

John doesn't say that he has made a settlement with Diana covering her suit, but he does admit that Diana has promised to give him a divorce, and Olivia puts the two together. And now he wants to know if Olivia will marry him? He has left the

Ministry. The new tank is in production and everything is fine. He practically has just come from 10 Downing Street. The nice things "he" had said about the tank are still very much in mind.

But still Olivia can't marry him, and again because of Michael. "It's still a question of you or him, and unfortunately he hates you."

"Well, I hate him."

"Don't say that."

"Well, it's true. Our lives have been split and blasted apart by a little moral gangster with an Œdipus Complex and a passion for self-dramatization."

Yes, it's true that John had trekked from Downing Street to Puffin's Corner to ask Olivia to marry him. "I had hoped against hope that three months of Baron's Court would have sickened you of this nonsense."

Olivia is still firm. She is happy doing what she is doing.

"Of course I was happy with you, John—gloriously happy, and you know it. But Michael was right about me, all the same. It was a silly, idle life to live. If I'd gone on like that, what sort of place would I have had in the New World?"

"Look, Olivia. I'll resign from Fletcher Pratt tomorrow, I'll give all my money to the *Labour Monthly,* I'll take a tenth floor flat in Bethnal Green—with no life, no sofa, no telephone—I'll conform in any way you like to this New World of yours and Michael's."

"It's no good, John. You don't want a New World."

"I want you, Olivia, and if I can get you I'll take a New World, an Old World, a Middle-Aged World, or any damn world at all. Don't I stand the faintest glimmer of a chance?"

"As long as Michael is with me, none at all."

John is going. There are several things he wants to do at Westminster before he leaves for Canada next day. The news of the Canadian trip is something of a shock to Olivia. She supposes that he will be settling down in Canada and getting married. Settle down he may, but he doesn't think he will marry again.

John has his hat and is at the door now. Olivia has followed and is calling advice to him in the hall. He should not work late at night, and he certainly should have his dinner. He doesn't see why.

Olivia has come back into the room. She is sitting on the sofa, softly crying when Sir John quietly reappears. He might consider dinner if she will have some with him. It will be their last dinner together, and he promises not to mention marriage—or Michael. He will confine himself to the new tank and what the Prime Minister said.

Olivia has gone to slip on a dress. John has turned on the radio. It is playing "Tiger Rag." A glance in the kitchen gives him an idea. He takes off his jacket, puts on an apron and starts to wash the dishes. He is still at it when Michael comes.

John's explanation is simple and direct. He had come to Baron's Court to ask Michael's mother to marry him. She had refused. That pleases Michael—and starts Sir John walking threateningly toward him—

"Yes. Well, your mother's refusal of me, Michael, at least has one compensation. It has relieved me of the bitter obligation of having to be polite to you. So from now on, young man, one more crack out of you will end in tears, and the tears, this time, will not be mine."

"So—you'd assault a chap in his own flat, would you?"

"No. I'd take the chap by the seat of his pants down six flights of stairs and assault him on the pavement in front of his own flat."

"You could get six months for that."

"You underestimate my feeling towards you, Michael. I could hang for it."

Michael would get out if he could, but John is too quick for him. Finally he decides to sit down and talk things over. He even produces a flask of gin from his pocket, and they have a drink. Michael had hoped to entertain a girl friend that evening and gin was the only thing she'd drink. Michael and his girl friend, it develops, had had a terrible row. When she saw that the picture at the Forum was "The Life of Maxim Gorky—Part VI," she had walked out on Michael. By now she is probably at the Savoy with Sparky Stevens.

Whether she is or not can be easily determined. Sir John will call his friend Mr. Gondolfo at the Savoy and see if Flight Lieutenant Sparky Stevens has a reservation for tonight. Sir John calls. As it happens, Lieutenant Stevens and a young lady are just coming in—a young lady "in a green dress with a red thingummy on the collar," which fits Michael's description of Sylvia Hart perfectly. Michael is visibly depressed—

"What's the answer to it—*that's* what I want to know," he wails.

"I'm not sure if there is one," admits Sir John, taking another sip of gin, and finding it just as bad as it was before. "I know from my own experience that if one is unlucky enough to fall in love with one of the Sylvia Harts of this world, there's nothing to do but sit back, take what comes, and pray for a quick release."

It is a little startling to them both to find their love experiences have closely paralleled each other. Michael has had his Sylvia and "Sparky" Stevens; John has had his Diana and his "Stinky" Buckridge. Still, it is difficult for Michael to believe that Sir John is really in love with Olivia. Sir John is certain the evidence is strongly in favor of that fact—

JOHN (*urgently*)—Michael—when you walk into a room and you find Sylvia in there, do you suddenly feel as though someone had hit you very hard, right here? (*He thumps his stomach.*)

MICHAEL—Well—yes—I do.

JOHN—Do you say the wrong things when you talk to her?

MICHAEL—Oh, yes, often.

JOHN—Do you find yourself stammering and blushing?

MICHAEL—Yes.

JOHN—And at night when you try to remember what she looks like, and then when you finally do, do you feel as if someone had hit you very hard here again, then there's a flutter of doves comes up like that—

MICHAEL—Gosh, yes! I do.

JOHN—Those are your symptoms, Michael. I'm more than twice your age. Double their intensity and you'll know what I feel for your mother.

MICHAEL—Oh, well, she couldn't feel anything like that about you.

JOHN—Why do you say that, Michael?

MICHAEL—I know it, that's all.

JOHN (*taking off apron*)—All right, Michael, we won't say any more. I'm sorry I raised the subject. As you said a moment ago, you've won and I've lost. Let it rest at that. But you will admit that your mother is a very beautiful and charming woman.

MICHAEL—Well, yes, I suppose so.

JOHN—Well—thanks to you, she's decided to work her passage through the New World. Very right, very proper. Only—tell me this—is there no better use to be made of beauty and charm—austerity age though this may be—than to consign them to a hermit's life in the kitchen? I'm only asking for information,

Michael. It's going to be your world—you and your generation are going to administer it.

MICHAEL (*hotly*)—And we're jolly well going to administer it too—without the help of any reactionary old fogies—

JOHN—All right, all right. Only remember this—ten years from now, when you're a successful commissar living in an enormous mansion in Park Lane with huge Adamses' ceilings, with Sylvia Hart as your paramour, drinking bottle after bottle of black market gin, I shall have a very good chuckle as I pass by selling my state-owned matches in the street.

That, to Michael, is "mere deviationism." And what is deviationism, Sir John would know. Well, as a matter of fact, it is just a word Michael uses in an argument when he can't think of anything else to say.

They are back now to the immediate problem concerned with Sylvia Hart and Sparky Stevens. What's to be done about that? Michael would jolly well like to appear suddenly at the Savoy and surprise them. He would, too, if he had the money.

Sir John can easily remedy that—and Michael can take all the time he may need to repay. But John also has a better idea. Suppose he calls Gondolfo of the Savoy and gets a table for Michael as near to the Sparky Stevens table as possible. Michael could sit there and glare.

Then Michael has a still better idea: Why shouldn't Sir John come along to dinner with him? Gosh! Wouldn't Sylvia have a fit if he (Michael) were to come walking into the Savoy with a Cabinet Minister! Sylvia's such a snob.

"I tell you what we can do," John agrees. "We'll have the head waiter walk in front of us, and just as we go past their table he can say in a very loud voice, 'Table for the Right Honorable Sir John Fletcher, Bart., and his friend, Mr. Michael Brown.'"

"That's a good idea."

"Then you might pretend to recognize Sylvia suddenly, give her a polite but frigid bow, and another to Sparky, and then we'll pass on to our table—with me still talking about the Prime Minister in a fairly loud voice."

However, a program as elaborate as this one should have a bit of rehearsing. Let them pretend they are in the Savoy, suggests Sir John. He will set the stage and direct the action. And he does.

Just as they get to the scene in which Sylvia is supposed to have fainted, Olivia appears.

"Oh, hullo, won't you join us?" calls John. His invitation is hearty and gay. "Let me give you the idea. This is the Savoy. That young lady you see being carried out unconscious is Miss Sylvia Hart—"

"John, John, don't you think it would be an even nicer idea if you were to put your feet up on this lovely sofa just for a few minutes."

"Don't worry, Mum."

"It's overwork, you know—"

"Sir John's all right," says Michael, "we're just going out to dinner together." He is off to brush up a bit.

With an effort, John is presently able to make sense for Olivia. Yes, he has been drinking—drinking gin, and with her son. And wouldn't she like to dance?

Whether she would or not, Olivia presently finds herself in John's arms. They are still dancing when Michael comes back. He glares at them for a moment. Then he turns off the radio and asks Sir John if it would be possible for them to get a table for three at the Savoy.

They are not going to the Savoy, they're going to Antoine's, Olivia corrects him. Convinced that it will have to be the Savoy, Olivia refuses at least to drive there in John's car. They'll walk. Or take a bus.

"Are you sure you know how to get there by bus?" asks John.

"Of course I do. We'll take a number 72—or is it a 73?"

"Or number 74?"

"No. You get to Notting Hill Gate, and then you change. Or does a number 72 go to Notting Hill Gate?"

"Perhaps it would if we asked it nicely."

"Well, wherever it does go to, you change and take a number—anyway, we'll get to the Savoy, somehow."

"Someday."

The dish washing is still to be done, but they can all do that later. Now they are ready to go. Michael has covered his mother's typewriter and put the light on the stairs. He kisses her gaily on his way out.

"Get my macintosh, John," calls Olivia. "It might rain."

John has taken the macintosh from the hall. As he puts it on Olivia he takes her in his arms—

"Oh, darling. I do love you so much." He takes the macintosh off and throws it on the sofa. "I don't think you'll need this. It's going to be a lovely evening."

"Come on, you two, for Heaven's sake, get cracking." An impatient Michael is calling from the hall.

"All right, in a minute. You must remember, Michael, your mother and I are getting on," answers Sir John.

He is kissing Olivia as—

THE CURTAIN FALLS

BORN YESTERDAY

A Comedy in Three Acts

BY GARSON KANIN

(Digest by John Chapman)

MAX GORDON'S production of Mr. Kanin's play in February, 1946, was a matter of good fortune all around, for "Born Yesterday" was a great success at the box office. But the ill fortune of one player resulted in extraordinary luck for another, and Mr. Kanin's chance casting of a third was another happy circumstance.

When Mr. Gordon and Mr. Kanin cast their play, the role of Billie was given to Jean Arthur, the screen star. During the tryout, however, Miss Arthur fell ill and had to be replaced. The actress chosen for the role was Judy Holliday (born Judy Tuvim, daughter of a newspaperman on the Yiddish language press of New York). Miss Holliday, as a member of a group of entertainers called the Revuers, had had considerable night club experience, but she first came to attention on the legitimate stage in the 1944-1945 season when she played a bit in a comedy titled "Kiss Them for Me." Her bit—that of a girl willing to give her all to make the U. S. Navy happy—was vividly played and won for her the annual Clarence Derwent award. Miss Holliday's performance as Billie in "Born Yesterday" established her as a comedienne of unusual skill.

The chance casting, according to the story told on Broadway, involves Paul Douglas, who plays Harry Brock. Mr. Kanin, who directed his own play, is reported to have been discussing casting with a friend. "I need somebody like Paul Douglas," he said. The friend suggested, quite simply, "Then why not get Paul Douglas?" With his performance Douglas, too, has become an actor of standing in the theatre. He had acted before, to be sure, and had been in some films; but he was more frequently occupied with sports announcing and other tasks on the radio.

As we move, in "Born Yesterday," to crowded, politically fever-

"Born Yesterday," copyright 1946 *by Garson Kanin and Ruth Gordon. Published in the Dominion of Canada by MacMillan Co. of Canada, Ltd. Published in the United States by Viking Press, Inc., New York.*

ish Washington, D. C., we come to the best hotel in the city and there, on the sixth and seventh floors, find a duplex apartment, Suite 67D. "It is a masterpiece of offensive good taste. Colorful and lush and rich." From its sitting room a broad and gaudy staircase curves upward to a suite of bedrooms, and in the rear wall is the door giving access to the hotel hallway. The door is open. The beginning is somewhat traditional, in that a maid is discovered straightening up and carrying flower vases, and in that a telephone rings; but this beginning breaks with tradition in that the maid pays no attention whatever to the bell ringing and pretty soon it stops.

A man can be seen passing down the hallway, looking in as he passes. In a moment he returns and stands in the doorway. He is in his middle 30s, handsome, bespectacled, carrying several books, magazines and newspapers. There is, the author believes, nothing wrong with him at all, except perhaps for a tendency to take things—and himself—too seriously. And well he might, for he is Paul Verrall, of the Washington staff of *The New Republic*.

Paul addresses Helen, the maid. He wants to know who is checking into the suite—a Harry Brock, by any chance? Paul is supposed to meet Brock. Helen doesn't know, but she looks at a card stuck among the hotel roses she has been arranging in a vase and reads the name—Brock. "Never heard of him," says Helen.

"You will, Helen," Paul assures her. "Big man. Ran a little junk yard into fifty million bucks, with no help from anyone or anything—except maybe World War II."

Helen is unimpressed. "Anybody checks into 67D I got no desire to meet. Believe me."

"Why not?"

"Listen, you know what they charge for this layout?"

"Two hundred and thirty-five a day." Paul, a reporter, has found that out already. "What about it?"

Helen, a chambermaid earning $18 a week, answers bitterly, "Listen, anybody's got two hundred and thirty-five dollars a day to spend on a hotel room there ought to be a law."

"I know some people who'd call you a Communist." To which Helen replies, darkly, "Tell them I'm thinking about it."

Paul, off on a serious tack now, begins talking about postwar Washington and Helen observes that the trouble with him is he thinks too much. Her advice on how a fellow his age should act is interrupted by a procession entering the suite. A bellhop carries a large leather box and several brief cases. Next comes Eddie Brock, who is Harry Brock's cousin—and servant.

Paul starts to leave, and so does the chambermaid, but at the door they stand aside for some more of the procession. Harry Brock stamps in, followed by an unctuous assistant hotel manager. Harry is a big bull of a man in his late 30s. Trailing him in is Billie Dawn, who is wearing one mink coat and carrying another. She is "breathtakingly beautiful and breathtakingly stupid."

The assistant manager goes into the routine of explaining the glories of the suite. Brock, trying to show he is not impressed, growls that it is all right. Paul steps into the picture by extending his hand and greeting the new guest with a "Hello, Mr. Brock." Brock ignores the hand and brusquely replies, "How are you?" Rebuffed, Paul leaves.

"Who the hell was that?" queries the big junk man, and Eddie, who has been busy taking liquor bottles out of the leather case and arranging them on a side table, says, "Search me!"

During Paul's attempt to greet the newcomer, the assistant manager has been showing Billie Dawn the upper quarters of the duplex, and he returns now to inform Brock that Mrs. Brock seems delighted with the bedchambers.

"It's not Mrs. Brock."

The assistant manager gulps.

"All right. Just don't get nosey. . . . There ain't no Mrs. Brock, except she's my mother. And she's dead."

With a snap of his fingers Brock orders Eddie to "take care of" the confused hotelman, and Eddie peels two $10 notes from a roll of bills. Brock cuts into the assistant manager's expressions of gratitude with, "All right, all right. Just listen. Anybody works in this room just tell 'em to do it good and do it quick and nobody'll get hurt. I'm a big tipper, tell 'em, and I don't like a lot of people around all the time and I don't like to wait for nothing. I ain't used to it."

Brock waves the fellow out and hollers up the stair for Billie, who appears boredly on the balcony. To Brock's "Not bad, huh?" she replies with an unenthusiastic "It's all right." She is not impressed with the rental of $235 a day. With a languid wave of her hips she returns to her bedroom.

The buzzer rings. Eddie opens the door and admits Ed Devery, who is slightly drunk—a permanent condition. Devery is a lawyer. He began a brilliant career as secretary to a Supreme Court justice—but with the years the brilliance faded and so did his standing in his profession. His only client now is Harry Brock—and a good one. Harry, who might find it difficult to get a reputable lawyer to serve him, pays Devery $100,000 a year, which is enough to buy Devery all the good whiskey he needs.

"You plastered again?" queries Brock.

DEVERY—Still.

BROCK—I told you I got a couple things can't wait.

DEVERY—Don't worry about me, Massa, I can see a loophole at twenty paces.

BROCK—How'd we make out?

DEVERY—It's going to be all right. May cost slightly more than we estimated, but there is no cause for alarm.

BROCK—How much more?

DEVERY—It's negligible.

BROCK—Why more?

DEVERY—Supply and demand, Harry. A crook is becoming a rare item in these parts. Therefore he comes high. Don't worry.

BROCK—What do you mean, don't worry? This kind of stuff ain't deductible, you know.

DEVERY—I'm not sure. Perhaps we should make a trial issue of it. (*Dictating.*) To the Collector of Internal Revenue: Herewith additional deduction for tax return now on file, one bribe, $80,000.

Brock's yowls about this increase from an originally estimated $50,000 are interrupted by the telephone. Eddie, who has answered, reports that it is some guy named Verrall for the lawyer. Devery takes the call.

To Brock's inquiry as to who that was the lawyer explains, "Paul Verrall. . . . He's a writer. *New Republic.* Wants an interview. Smart boy. He's just back from a long time in the service with lots of ideas and lots of energy."

Brock doesn't want to talk to no writers—he's got to get shaved. But Devery is insistent. "This is one of the few fellows in Washington to look out for. Thing to do is take him in. Then he doesn't go poking."

Brock yells for Eddie to get him a shave, a manicure and a shine. Devery has still more advice for his bull-necked client. Billie, for instance. She should wear something nice and plain for the Senator because the Senator might be bringing his wife—and, anyhow, why did Brock *have* to bring Billie? He has a chance to be one of the men running this country, but it is going to take judgment and intelligence.

Paul Verrall buzzes at the door and the lawyer makes the introduction. Brock is on the sofa, coatless and with his shoes off. Devery withdraws to join Billie upstairs and Brock yells for Eddie to provide some drinks. Brock explains about Eddie. "He's worked for me I don't know how many years. Also, he's my cousin. He knows me insides out."

"Maybe," ventures Paul, "I should be interviewing Eddie."

Brock wants to know about the interview—is it going to be a plug or a pan? "No angle. Just, well—just the facts."

Brock, remembering his lawyer's advice, decides he had better butter up Paul. He assumes a genial air, gives the writer a magnificently boxed cigar. "Five bucks apiece they cost me."

"Well, in that case," says Paul, pocketing the gift, "I'll give it to a Senator." Brock is disgusted. "Listen," he says, "you know what a Senator is to me? A guy who makes a hundred and fifty bucks a week." Paul pencils a note about this little joke on some copy paper, then plunges into the interview with a direct question:

"How much money have you got?"

"How should I know? What am I, an accountant?" counters the startled interviewee. Paul can prod out of him only that he has more than one million—plenty.

Brock—And listen, I made every nickel. Nobody ever give me nothing.

Paul (*sitting*)—Nice work.

Brock (*rising*)—I can tell already. You're gonna give me the business.

Paul—Wait a minute—

Brock—Go ahead! I like it.

Paul—You've got me wrong.

Brock—Go ahead. Work for me. I got more people workin' for me than knows it.

Paul (*after a pause*)—What do you think about—?

Brock (*violently*)—Go ahead! Pan me. Tell how I'm a mugg and a roughneck. You'll do me good.

Paul—Listen, Mr. Brock—

Brock—Lemme tell you about Cleveland. In 1937 there's a big dump there, see, and the city wants to get rid of it. High class scrap. So I go out there to look it over myself. There's a lot of other guys there, too. From Bethlehem even and like that. I didn't have a chance and I knew it. I figure I'm out of my class on the deal and I'm ready to pull out when all of a sudden the goddamnedest thing comes out there in one of the papers.

About me. A big write-up. It says my name and about how come the city is gonna do business with hoodlums. Mind you, I was out of my class. I didn't have the kind of buttons a guy needs for a deal like that. So the next day—again. This time they got a picture of me. Next thing you know, a guy calls me up. A guy from the Municipal Commission. He comes up to see me and he says they don't want no trouble. So I naturally string him along and I get busy on the phone and I raise some dough with a couple of boys from Dee-troit. Then comes the big pan. On the front page. Next day I close the deal and in a week, I'm carting.

PAUL—What's your point?

BROCK—My point is you can't do me no harm if you make me out to be a mugg. Maybe you'll help me. Everybody gets scared, and for me that's good. Everybody scares easy.

PAUL—Well, not everybody. (EDDIE *is ordered to provide more drinks, over* PAUL's *protest, and the interview continues.*) Where were you born?

BROCK—Jersey. Plainfield, New Jersey, 1907. I went to work when I was twelve years old and I been working ever since. I'll tell you my first job. A paper route. I bought a kid out with a swift kick in the keester.

PAUL (*writing*)—And you've been working ever since.

BROCK (*missing the point*)—Right. I'll tell you how I'm the top man in my racket. I been in it over twenty-five years. In the same racket.

PAUL—Steel.

BROCK—Junk. Not steel. *Junk.*

PAUL—Oh.

BROCK—Look, don't butter me up. I'm a junk man. I ain't ashamed to say it.

PAUL—All right.

BROCK—Lemme give you some advice, sonny boy. Never crap a crapper. I can sling it with the best of 'em.

PAUL—Twenty-five years, you say?

BROCK—I'll tell you. I'm a kid with a paper route. I've got this little wagon. So on my way home nights, I come through the alleys picking up stuff. I'm not the only one. All the kids are doing it. The only difference is, they keep it. Not me. I sell it. First thing you know, I'm making seven, eight bucks a week for that. Three bucks from papers. So I figure out right off which is the right racket. I'm just a kid, mind you, but I could see that. Pretty soon, the guy I'm sellin' to is handin' me anywheres from fifteen to twenty a week. So he offers me a job for ten. Dumb jerk. I'd be sellin' this guy his own stuff back half the time and he never knew.

PAUL—How do you mean?

BROCK (*relishing the memory*)—Well, in the night, see, I'm under the fence and I drag it out and load up. In the morning I bring it in the front way and collect.

PAUL—Twelve years old, you were?

BROCK—Something like that.

PAUL—So pretty soon you owned the whole yard.

BROCK—Damn right! This guy, the jerk? He works for me now. And you know who else works for me? The kid whose paper route I swiped. I figure I owe him. That's how I am.

The barber, manicurist and bootblack arrive and begin their ministrations while Paul continues with his interview. It is an unsuccessful one, for he can get no real information. Brock says flatly that it is none of Paul's —— —— business what he is doing in Washington. Paul thinks it *is* his business. Devery, coming down from the balcony, says, vaguely, that it's "just a little tax stuff."

Billie follows the lawyer down, makes for the liquor table, selects a bottle and starts back upstairs. Devery introduces Paul to her. Brock, noticing the bottle, orders Billie to put it back.

"We got somebody comin'. Somebody important. I don't want you stinkin'." Billie pleadingly inquires if she can't just have a little one.

"No," snaps her master. "Now put it back and go upstairs and change your clothes and don't give me no trouble. . . . Do what I'm tellin' you!"

Paul and Devery have turned away in embarrassment. Billie, humiliated, obeys. About halfway up she turns and regards Paul with strange interest and the faint beginnings of a smile. Even Devery is not thick-skinned enough to avoid feeling sorry for the girl. Addressing the barber, he inquires, "What'll you take to cut his throat?"

The effect of this question upon Brock is violent. He sits up so suddenly that the barber almost does cut his throat, and yells that there are some jokes he doesn't like. He strides over to Devery and pushes his face, hard. Paul keeps the lawyer from falling. Even though the shave and manicure are not quite finished, Brock orders his beauty team to beat it. Paul, too, wants to beat it and finally manages an exit after promising to stick around. He explains that he lives right down the hall.

Now Devery wants some work done. He takes some papers from his brief case and says he needs Billie's and Eddie's signatures on a few things. Brock yells for Billie to come down right away, which she does. She is wearing her most dignified dress. "That's all I do around here is sign," she complains.

"When is he comin'? This Senator guy," Brock asks the lawyer.

"Any time now."

"I better get fixed up, huh?" He goes upstairs and Devery and Billie get to work on the papers.

"I bet," she observes, "I've signed about a million of these."

That is what she gets, explains Devery, for being a multiple corporate officer. "You've come a long way from the chorus, all right."

"I wasn't only in the chorus. In 'Anything Goes' I spoke lines," says Billie, pridefully. "Five lines. I could of been a star, probably. If I'd of stuck to it."

"Why didn't you?"

"Harry didn't want me being in the show. He likes to get to bed early," sighs Billie.

She is troubled about Harry. He has changed. He used to be like more satisfied, but now he's always running around, always talking. "Now he's got me up half the night tellin' me what a big man he is. And how he's gonna be bigger. Run everything." Personally she doesn't care one way or the other.

Billie makes for the liquor again and Devery warns her to take it easy. She'd better drink later, after "they" have gone.

"What's the deal, anyway?" she inquires.

"No deal. Just important people, that's all."

"Who? This Senator guy?"

"And *Mrs.* Hedges."

"Harry told me this fellow works for him."

Devery admits that, in a way, the Senator fellow does, and it's very important that Billie be nice and use no rough language. "I won't open my mush," she promises.

The buzzer sounds and Eddie opens the door to Senator Norval Hedges and his wife. The Senator is a worried, thin man of 60; Mrs. Hedges looks uninteresting. Devery greets them and impressively introduces Billie Dawn, formerly of the stage. Eddie serves drinks around.

"How," inquires the Senator's wife of Billie, "do you like Washington, Mrs. Brock?"

Billie doesn't realize for an instant that she is being addressed. She catches Devery's warning glance and does not correct Mrs. Hedges' mistake. "I haven't seen it yet," she replies.

The Senator genially says they must show her around. "Too bad the Supreme Court isn't in session. You'd love that," offers Mrs. Hedges.

"What," asks Billie, "is it?"

Devery saves the moment by bursting into laughter. "Lots of people would like to know the answer to that one," says he. The Senator and his wife settle for Billie's remark as some kind of metropolitan humor.

When Brock enters they all rise—even Mrs. Hedges. Brock is almost violently cordial. He talks of his drive to Washington, and of stopping in Baltimore to look at one of his junk yards. Mrs. Hedges wants to know how many yards he has.

"Hell, I don't know," says Brock. He stops abruptly and makes blushing apology. *"Excuse me."* To the Senator he says, "I don't know why I like that little Baltimore outfit. I just always get kind of a feeling from it. You know what I mean?"

"Sentimental."

"That's it! I'm sentimental. Like you say."

"I think we're *all* a bit sentimental," says Mrs. Hedges, keeping the conversation going.

It seems to be Billie's turn to speak, and there is a pause. "Well," observes Billie, "it's a free country."

Mrs. Hedges wants to know if Mrs. Brock plays bridge. No, only gin—gin rummy.

Devery, getting down to business, asks the Senator how he is fixed for time tomorrow. The Hedges schedule is pretty tight, but would ten o'clock be all right?

"How's that for you, Harry?" asks Devery of Brock.

"In the morning?"

"Yes."

"Pretty early for me."

Billie, the cynic, puts in her oar. "I'll say." Brock throws her a dirty look. The date finally is made for eleven, and the Senator lamely observes that he can drop by the hotel at that time; it's "right on his way."

Billie, feeling that she should do something cordial, asks the shocked Mrs. Hedges, "You want to wash your hands or anything, honey?" Mrs. Hedges' "No, thank you" is almost inaudible. Billie, in an atmosphere of tense embarrassment, moves upstairs. The Senator addresses Brock softly. "I want to thank you, Mr. Brock. For everything."

Brock—Call me Harry, Senator, will you?

Hedges—I haven't written you about it, Harry. Not considered good form. But I want you to know that I'm grateful for all you've done. For your support.

Brock—Don't mention it. Just tit for tat. (*He stops, confused, then turns to* Mrs. Hedges.) Excuse *me!*

Mrs. Hedges (*at sea*)—Quite all right.

Brock—You see, Senator, what I think is—there's a certain kind of people ought to stick together.

Hedges—My feeling.

Brock—You know what I'm interested in. Scrap iron. I wanna buy it—I wanna move it—and I wanna sell it. And I don't want a lot of buttin' in with rules and regulations at no stage of the game.

Hedges—Obviously.

Brock—I ain't talkin' about peanuts, mind you. All this junk I been sellin' for the last fifteen years—well, it's junk again. And I can sell it again once I lay my hands on it. Do you know how much scrap iron is layin' around all over Europe? Where the war's been?

Hedges—No, I don't.

Brock—Well, I don't either. Nobody knows. Nobody ever *will* know. It's more than you can think of. Well, I want to pick it up and bring it back where it belongs. Where it came from. Where I can use it. Who does it belong to, anyway?

Mrs. Hedges—Why—isn't that interesting?

Hedges—I have a copy for you of the preliminary survey made by—

Brock—Boil it down and give it to me fast. I didn't come down here to have to do a lot of paper work. See, the way I work is like this. It's every man for himself—like dog eat dog. Like you gotta get the other guy before he gets you.

Hedges—Exactly.

Brock—What I got in mind is an operating combo—all over the world. There's enough in it for everybody—if they're *in*, that is. Up to now, I'm doin' fine. Everybody's lined up, everybody understands everybody. I want to get movin', see?—That's all. Only thing is, Ed here comes up with some new trouble every day. *This* law, *that* law, tariffs, taxes, State Department, *this* department, *that* department—

Photo by Vandamm Studio.

"BORN YESTERDAY"

Brock—How can anybody get so dumb?
Paul—We can't all know everything, Harry.
Billie (to Brock)—Who's Tom Paine, for instance.
Brock—What the hell do I care who he is?
Billie—*I* know!

(*Paul Douglas, Gary Merrill, Judy Halliday*)

DEVERY—I'm sure you understand, Norval, that in an operation of this kind—

BROCK—Listen, all that stuff is just a lot of hot air to me. There's a way to do anything. That's all I know. It's up to you guys to find out how.

DEVERY—Norval's been working along those lines.

HEDGES—Yes. The Hedges-Keller Amendment, for example, guarantees no interference with free enterprise—foreign or domestic. We're doing everything we can to get it through quickly.

BROCK—Well, see that you do, 'cause that's why I'm here, to see that I get what I paid for.

At last Hedges and his wife depart—he with a handful of Brock's gaudy cigars. Billie returns in time to say good-by. After the guests leave she would confide a personal opinion—

"Drips. . . . I said they're drips."

"Who the hell are you to say?" demands Brock, angrily.

Billie stretches out on the sofa. "I'm myself, that's who."

Brock orders her upstairs. "Not yet," she says.

"Get upstairs, I told you."

Billie goes quietly, attempting to retain her dignity by giving him a look of contempt. Devery busies himself with getting several documents signed by Eddie, while Brock fumes about his mistress. "Right now," he says, "I feel like giving her the brush."

This, says the lawyer, would be complicated—because, on paper, she owns more of Brock than Brock does.

"You better think something up. She's gonna louse me up all the way down the line. Goddamn dumb broad."

Devery suggests that she be sent home, but Brock says "No." His reason? He says, softly—and to Devery's great surprise—"I'm nuts about her."

Brock wonders if there isn't some way of smartening her up a little—some kinda school, maybe. Devery agrees to think about it—but in the meantime there's something Brock could be thinking about: namely, marriage.

Brock wants none of this. He was married once and he didn't like it. His eight or nine years with Billie has been a better arrangement. "This way, I give her something; I'm a hell of a fella. We get married, she's got it coming, she thinks."

Devery still urges marriage. Brock is moving up to bigger places and bigger people, and there are certain rules in this big league. Brock agrees to think it over and let the lawyer know—but in the meantime something must be done about Billie.

"Every time she opened her kisser tonight, something wrong come out."

Brock gets one of his rare ideas—the interview guy. He will hire Paul Verrall to educate Billie.

Devery doesn't think there's a chance, but Brock gets Paul on the phone and asks him to come right over. Paul does, and Brock plunges in. "How much," he asks, "do you make a week?"

Paul counters with a line from Brock's earlier interview: "How should I know? What am I, an accountant?"

"Listen, Paul," urges Brock. "Here's the layout. I got a friend. Nice kid. I think you probably seen her in here before. . . . Well, she's a good kid, see? Only to tell you the truth, a little on the stupid side. Not her fault, you understand. I got her out of the chorus. For the chorus she was smart enough, but I'm scared she's gonna be unhappy in this town. She's never been around with such kind of people, you know what I mean?"

Brock proposes that Paul take Billie in hand—show her the ropes, sort of. Paul refuses. "No, I don't think I could handle it."

"Means a lot to me," pursues Brock. "I'll give you two hundred bucks a week."

"All right," agrees Paul, "I'll do it." Billie is to become the Washington equivalent of the girl in Shaw's "Pygmalion."

Billie, summoned by a yell, appears on the landing. She is brushing her hair and wearing a negligee "that does all the proper things." To her objection that she's not dressed Brock replies that it's all right because Paul is a friend of the family. He and the lawyer go to another room, leaving the young people alone.

Paul explains Brock's proposition that he show Billie the ropes and answer any questions. Billie says she's got no questions—but, at that, she'd like to take in the Supreme Court. "What's he paying you?" she asks.

"Two hundred."

"You're a sucker. You could of got more. He's got plenty."

Paul, eyeing the seductive girl, says he'd have done it for nothing.

Billie has no illusions about what's happening. She knows Brock thinks she's stupid. "He's right. I'm stupid and I like it."

"You do?"

"Sure. I'm happy. I got everything I want. Two mink coats. Everything. If there's somethin' I want, I ask. And if he don't come across—I don't come across. If you know what I mean."

Billie's interest in the project, however, is developing. There is one thing she *would* like—to learn how to talk good. Paul suggests reading a few books, and says he'll correct her speech now and then.

Billie asks him to call her Billie, not Miss Dawn. "Billie," he says. "Sort of an odd name, isn't it?"

"What are you talking about? Half the kids I know are named it. Anyway, it's not my real name."

"What is?"

Billie has to think a moment. "My God! Emma."

PAUL—What's the matter?

BILLIE—Do I look to you like an Emma?

PAUL—No. You don't look like a Billie, either.

BILLIE—So what do I look like?

PAUL—To me?

BILLIE—Yuh, to you.

PAUL—You look like a little angel.

BILLIE (*after a pause*)—Lemme ask you. Are you one of these talkers, or would you be interested in a little action?

PAUL (*stunned*)—Huh?

BILLIE—I got a yen for you right off.

PAUL—Do you get many?

BILLIE—Now and then.

PAUL—What do you do about them?

BILLIE—Stick around and you'll find out.

PAUL—All right, I will.

BILLIE—And if you want a tip, I'll tell you. Sweet talk me. I like it. Like that angel line. (PAUL *looks upstairs with a frown.*) Don't worry about him. He don't see a thing. He's too dizzy from being a big man.

PAUL (*rising from the sofa and moving away*)—This is going to be a little different than I thought.

BILLIE—You mind?

PAUL—No.

BILLIE—It's only fair. We'll educate each other.

PAUL (*in a weak attempt to get on safer ground*)—Now, about these books. . . . I'll get them for you tomorrow. I'll look around my place, too. If there's anything interesting, I'll drop it by later.

BILLIE—All right.

PAUL—We can figure out time every day the day before.

BILLIE (*beckoning* PAUL *to her, taking his lapel and bringing his ear close*)—Or the night.

Brock and Devery come downstairs—Brock in a silk lounging jacket. Paul tells his new boss he thinks he and Billie are all set. Devery leaves, and Paul, too, says good night.

Brock takes a deck of cards from his pocket, shuffles them on the table, and he and Billie settle down to their nightly routine. She pours a couple of drinks and they begin to play, swiftly, professionally, with no sense of personal enjoyment. She picks up Paul's first three discards and quickly goes "gin"—lays down all the cards in her hand.

As the game proceeds it becomes obvious that Brock is no match for Billie at gin rummy. Their playing is intense and their conversation intermittent. Again Billie goes "gin," gets Paul's score and announces a Schneider. She has scored enough points to win without Brock having scored at all. She does some figuring on a pad—

"Fifty-five dollars. And sixty cents."

Brock throws down the cards and gets another drink. "All right, that's all!"

"Pay me now."

"What the hell's the matter? Don't you trust me?"

"What are you hollering for? You always make *me* pay." Billie, taunting him as a sore loser, makes him pay—including the sixty cents. Brock starts for the stairs and orders, "Come on up."

"In a minute."

"Now."

"In a minute, I told you."

This is the one moment of the day of which Billie is boss. Brock goes up quietly and shuts the door and Billie, singing a number from "Anything Goes" to herself, starts a game of solitaire—a game which is interrupted by the buzzer and the reappearance of Paul. He has brought some books and two morning newspapers.

"You could of saved yourself the trouble," offers Billie. "I don't read papers."

"Never?"

"Once in a while the back part."

"I think you should," advises Paul. "The front part. . . . It's interesting."

"Not to me."

"How do you know if you never read it?"

"Look, if you're going to turn out to be a pest, we could call the whole thing off right now."

Paul murmurs a "Sorry."

"I look at the papers sometimes," continues Billie. "I just never understand it. So what's the sense?"

"Tell you what you do," suggests Paul. "You look through these. Anything you don't understand you make a mark." He gives her a red editing pencil. "Then tomorrow, I'll explain whatever I can. All right?"

Billie is game—but doubtful about her eyesight, which isn't so hot. Paul suggests glasses.

"Glasses!" exclaims Billie.

"Why not?"

"Because it's terrible." She notices Paul's glasses now, but can't think of anything to say that will soften her remark. She moves closer to him. Paul puts his arms about her and kisses her —a long, expert kiss. As they come out of it Billie, having thought of a face-saving explanation, adds, "Of course, they're not so bad on men."

Paul leaves. Billie switches out the lights in the sitting room and starts up the stairs, slowly. She has resumed her song from the musical she had five lines in once.

> "Good authors, too, who once knew better words
> Now only use four-letter words
> Writing prose—tyah dah—"

She stops, looks back at the books and papers. These are her new key to something or other. She moves back into the other room, picks them up and, clutching them tightly, starts up again, singing— "Writing prose—tyah dah—"

She turns out the balcony light, sings the "tyah dah" at the door of Brock's room as though they were two notes of derision; then she goes into her own room and slams the door as we hear her last triumphant "Anything goes!"

The curtain falls.

ACT II

The scene is the same hotel suite, but now it looks lived in, for two months or so have passed. There is an added piece of furniture—a desk, piled with books, papers, magazines and clippings. On the walls are some framed reproductions of French and American moderns and one or two small originals. In another part of the room is a large terrestrial globe, and against a wall is a big phonograph with a stack of record albums on the floor beside it. It is early evening.

We discover Billie, in pajamas and wearing glasses, sitting on the sofa intently reading a newspaper. She makes a mark on it, and as she lifts it high to continue reading to the bottom we notice that the paper is covered with red pencil marks. For a momentary break in her concentration, Billie goes to the phonograph and puts on some records. As she returns to the sofa we hear the soothing music of Sibelius' violin concerto.

The door buzzer sounds and the ever-faithful Eddie comes through the sitting room to answer it. Paul has arrived for his daily visit with his pupil. Billie quickly takes off her glasses.

"Hello, smarty-pants," greets Paul. "How you coming?"

"Not so bad."

"Hm?" prompts Paul.

"*—ly*. Bad*ly*. Would you like some tea?"

And, indeed, Billie has not done so badly in two months or so. She has had Mrs. Hedges for tea and has discovered that Mrs. Hedges is pretty stupid, too. Pretending she had read "David Copperfield," for instance, when Billie knew she hadn't from the way they were talking.

From a coffee table Billie picks up a letter. "I got this letter today. From my father."

PAUL—New York?

BILLIE—Yes. I can't get over it.

PAUL—Why?

BILLIE—Well, it's the first time he ever wrote me in about eight years. We had a fight, sort of. He didn't want me to go with Harry.

PAUL—What does he do?

BILLIE—My father?

PAUL—Yes.

BILLIE—Gas Company. He used to read meters, but in this letter he says how he can't get around so good any more so they gave him a different job. Elevator man. (*A pause as she remembers back. The music is still playing.*) Goofy old guy. He used to take a little frying pan to work every morning, and a can of Sterno, and cook his own lunch. He said everybody should have a hot lunch. . . . I swear I don't know how he did it. There were four of us. Me and my three brothers and he had to do everything. My mother died. I never knew her. He used to feed us and give us a bath and buy our clothes. Everything. That's why all my life I used to think how some day I'd like to pay him back. Funny how it worked out. One night, I brought home a hundred dollars and I gave it to him. You know what he did? He threw it in the toilet and pulled the chain. I thought he was going to hit me, sure, but he didn't. In his whole life, he never hit me once.

PAUL (*carefully*)—How'd he happen to write to you? I mean, after all this time.

BILLIE—Because I wrote *him.*

PAUL—Oh.

BILLIE—He says he's thought about me every day. God. I haven't thought about him, I bet, once even, in five years. That's nothing against him. I haven't thought of anything.

PAUL—Be nice to see him, maybe.

BILLIE—I guess so—but he said I should write him again and I should have a hot lunch every day and I should let him know how I am but that he didn't want to see me if I was still living the life of a concubine. I looked it up. . . . He always used to say, "Don't ever do nothin' you wouldn't want printed on the front page of the New York *Times*." . . . Hey—I just realized. I've practically told you the whole story of my life by now practically.

PAUL—I've enjoyed it very much.

BILLIE—How about the story of *your* life?

PAUL—Oh, no. It's too long—and mostly untrue. What'd you do this morning?

It is a new Billie. She has been to the newsreel and to the National Gallery. She liked the Gallery—quiet and interesting and nice-smelling. She wants to go again and wishes Paul would go with her. "Boy, there's sure some things *there* that could use some explaining."

Also, Billie went to Brentano's and walked around and picked out some books she thought she'd like. Pretty soon she had a pile too big to carry. "So I stopped. And I thought, my God, it'll take me about a year to read this many. Then I looked around, and compared to all the books there, my little pile was nothing. So then I realized that even if I read my eyes out till the day I die I couldn't even make a little dent in that one store. Next thing you know I bust out crying."

Paul comforts her in her dejection, assures her that nobody reads everything—but, by the way, did she read his piece in *The*

New Republic? She has read it twice. As to what she thinks of it: "Well, I think it's the best thing I ever read. I didn't understand one word." She takes Paul's copy of the weekly to show him what she didn't understand, and as she puts on her glasses Paul laughs.

"What's so funny? That I'm blind practically?"

"Practically blind."

Billie is sorry she looks funny to him in glasses. "You don't," earnestly says Paul. "They make you look lovelier than ever."

As to the piece in *The New Republic,* even the title is a facer—"The Yellowing Democratic Manifesto." Paul explains "yellowing"—meaning like an ageing piece of paper. Surely she knows what "democratic" is—and surely Billie does. It means not Republican. So Paul has to explain the idea of a democracy. A manifesto is a set of rules and ideals on which the United States is based.

Billie now gets the idea of the title: Paul thinks the rules and ideals are turning yellow, and that's bad. Billie plunges into the body of Paul's article, reading, "Examination of contemporary society in terms of the Greek philosophy which defines the whole as a representation of its parts sends one immediately to a consideration of the individual as a citizen and the citizen as an individual."

Billie looked up every word, too, and still doesn't understand. Another little thing she didn't get is Robert G. Ingersoll's piece about Napoleon, where in the end he says he'd rather have been a happy farmer.

Paul quotes the Ingersoll passage: "—and I said I would rather have been a French peasant and worn wooden shoes. I would rather have lived in a hut with a vine growing over the door, and the grapes growing purple in the kisses of the Autumn sun. I would rather have been that poor peasant, with my loving wife by my side, knitting as the day died out of the sky—with my children upon my knees and their arms about me—I would rather have been that man and gone down to the tongueless silence of the dreamless dust, than to have been that imperial impersonation of force and murder known as Napoleon the Great."

There is a break in the seriousness of the moment when, on the phonograph, a Debussy number comes to a close and is followed by a wild Benny Goodman recording. Billie turns it off, resumes brooding. So who wouldn't rather be a happy peasant?

"So Harry wouldn't, for one," observes Paul. Under Billie's repeated questioning, Paul confesses he doesn't like Brock and thinks he is a menace; he never did anything for anyone except himself.

"Well," counters Billie, "I got two mink coats."

"That was a trade. You gave him something, too." Paul is off on a lecture about selfishness versus unselfishness, and how selfishness can even be organized as a government. "Then it's called Fascism."

Billie, however, is not entirely for brooding and lecturing. She still goes for Paul. "After that first night when I met you," she confesses, "I figured it was all going to work out dandy. Then, when you wouldn't step across the line—I figured maybe the way to you was through your head. . . . Anyway, it doesn't matter now—but I like you anyway. Too late for the rest."

Paul wants to know why.

"Why? Look, Paul, there's a certain time between a fellow and a girl when it either comes off or not and if it doesn't then, then it never does."

"Maybe," says the hopeful Paul, "we haven't got our time yet."

"I think we did. And you dropped the ball." Billie has gone through a rugged time for Paul, getting all mixed up in the head and wondering and worrying and *thinking*. "And," she concludes, "I don't know if it's good to find out so much so quick."

They talk more of books, and of Paul's belief that a world full of ignorant people is dangerous, of his belief in Pope's statement that the proper study of mankind is Man.

"I *been* studying different mankind lately," reports Billie. "The ones you told me. Jane Addams last week, and this week Tom Paine. And then all by myself I got to thinking about Harry. He works so hard to get what he wants, for instance, but he doesn't know what he wants."

"Money, more people to push around, money," opines Paul.

Speak of the devil—Harry enters, irritated because Ed Devery isn't here. Paul continues with Billie.

PAUL—What did you find out about Tom Paine?

BILLIE—Well, he was quite a fella.

PAUL—Where was he born? Do you remember?

BILLIE—London. Or England. Some place like that.

BROCK—What do you mean, London or England? It's the same thing.

BILLIE—It is?

BROCK—London is *in* England. It's a city, London. England is a whole country.

Billie—I forgot.

Brock (*to* Paul)—Honest to God, boy. You got some patience.

Paul—Take it easy.

Brock—How can anybody get so dumb?

Paul—We can't all know everything, Harry.

Billie (*to* Brock)—Who's Tom Paine, for instance?

Brock—What?

Billie—You heard me. Tom Paine.

Brock—What the hell do I care who he is?

Billie—*I* know.

Brock—So what? If I wanted to know who he is I'd know who he is. I just don't care. (*To* Paul.) Go ahead. Don't let me butt in.

Paul—Which of his books did you like best?

Billie—Well, I didn't read *by* him yet—only about him.

Paul—Oh.

Billie—But I made a list of—

Brock (*suddenly*)—Who's Rabbit Maranville?

Billie doesn't know, but Paul does, and Brock sneers that he must be some kind of genius. Paul is telling which Paine book to read first—"The Age of Reason"—when Brock comes up with another sample of erudition. "Who's Willie Hop?" Paul immediately answers, "National billiard champion. And I think it's pronounced Hoppe."

Brock won't give up. "What's a peninsula?" Billie knows this one, she thinks. "It's that new medicine!" Triumphantly Brock says a peninsula is a body of land surrounded on three sides by water.

"So what's that to know?" sniffs Billie.

"So what," counters Brock, "is this Sam Paine to know?"

He is disgusted to learn that Tom Paine, not Sam Paine, is dead, and demands of Paul what the hell he is learning her about dead people. "I just want her to know how to act with live people."

"Education is a difficult thing to control or to channel, Harry," soothes Paul. "One thing leads to another. It's a matter of awakening curiosity—stimulating imagination—developing a sense of independence."

Brock—Work on her, not me.

Paul—No extra charge.

BROCK—I don't need nothing you can tell me.

PAUL—Oh, I'm sure we could tell each other lots of interesting things, Harry.

BROCK (*warningly*)—What the hell does that mean?

PAUL—Just trying to be friendly.

BROCK—Who asked you? You know every time I see you I don't like you as much. For a chump who's got no place, you're pretty fresh. You better watch out—I got an eye on you.

PAUL—All right. Let's both watch out.

BROCK—You know, I could knock your block off, if I wanted.

PAUL—Yes, I know.

BROCK—All right, then—just go ahead and do what you're supposed to—and that's all.

PAUL—It's all right—we'll stop for now.

BROCK—No, go ahead. I want to see how you do it.

PAUL—Not just now if you don't mind—I've got to go lie down. You don't realize how hard I work.

BILLIE—Ha ha! Some joke.

BROCK (*petulant*)—Two hundred bucks a week and I can't even watch!

Paul departs. Billie turns her awakening mind upon Harry Brock. "What's this business we're in down here?"

"What do you mean—*we?*"

"Well, I figure I'm sort of a partner, in a way."

Brock informs her she is a silent partner and invites her to shut up, but she insists she has a right to know. She doesn't want to do anything if it's against the law. Billie has formed an opinion of her gentleman friend, but she has to go to the dictionary to find the words. He is, she announces, anti-social. "You're God damn right I am!" agrees Brock.

Devery, the lawyer, and Senator Hedges arrive and are bawled out by Brock for being late. To his demand to know what has happened they explain that there have been difficulties, and the deal is going to take more time and more money. The amendment will have to be redrafted, and the Senator is afraid that Brock will just have to wait.

Brock now turns his ill temper upon the Senator: "You better get moving or I'll butcher you—you'll wind up a God damn YMCA secretary again before you know it. . . . I'm gonna get it fixed so I can do business where I want and how I want and as big as I want. If you ain't with me, you're against me."

"I'm with you," agrees the pliant Senator.

"All right, then, you'll have to pull your weight in the God damn boat or I'll get somebody who can. You understand me?"

Brock slams out of the room, and the Senator makes a gentle comment upon his temper. "Don't mind him," says Devery. "He's always lived at the top of his voice."

This passage has been disturbing to Billie. "I don't think Harry should talk to you like that. After all, you're a senator," she says to Hedges. A senator, she muses, is a wonderful thing, and if a senator gets pushed around it's just like pushing a few million people around—the people who picked him. Hedges is more important than Harry Brock, for instance; nobody ever voted for *him.* Hedges is a little modest about his constituency—it's only 806,434. Billie, herself, has never voted for anybody.

The Senator, uncomfortable at Billie's serious turn of thought, eases himself out, and Lawyer Devery gets out some more papers for Billie to sign. This time she isn't signing blindly, even though Devery has his fountain pen all ready. She puts on her glasses and begins to read the first document—a maneuver which is amazing and disturbing to the lawyer. Billie wants to know what it is before she signs.

"A merger," explains Devery.

"What's that?"

"Several companies being formed into one. . . . A few of Harry's and some others. French, Italian and so on."

Dawn again breaks upon the developing Dawn mind. "A cartel!" she exclaims, remembering recent reading. Devery is dumbfounded, but smoothly tries to assure Billie that everything is all right and is eager for her signature. Billie will not be pushed. "Tomorrow," she says. "I want to look them over, so I'll know what I'm doing."

Devery tries to think of another approach when Billie ventures, "I know what you feel bad about. You don't like to be doing all his dirty work—because you know you're better than him." This shot strikes home. White and angry, Devery dashes up the stairs to get Brock, and Billie, picking up the documents, gets out a small dictionary and sits down to read.

Brock comes downstairs slowly—too slowly, and inquires if the reading is interesting. "Not very," replies Billie, without looking up. Brock wants to know what's the matter and Billie says something about not liking Ed Devery—not liking what he has done to himself. "He used to be Assistant Attorney General of the United States," she observes.

"So what's wrong with that?"

"Nothing's wrong. Just look at him now. . . . Did you know he once wrote a book? 'The Roots of Freedom.' That was the name of it. I read it. It was wonderful. . . . And look at him now. He hangs around and helps you promote and lets you walk all over him just because you pay for it."

Billie has now got a fair estimate of her friend Brock. He is selfish. All through history there have been bigger and better men—her $25-a-week father, for instance. Brock, puzzled, advises, "Listen, cutie, don't get nervous just because you read a book. You're as dumb as you ever were." Billie doubts this. "I'm still dumb," she admits, "but I know one thing I never knew before. There's a better kind of life than the one I got. Or you."

Brock's anger rises, and so does Billie's. She tells him his manners are lacking—he eats terrible, takes his shoes off all the time, picks his teeth.

"You're just not couth!" she accuses.

"I'm as couth as you are!" shouts Brock.

BILLIE—And that cheap perfume you put on yourself.

BROCK—I don't own nothin' cheap. Except you.

BILLIE (*very quietly*)—You don't own me. Nobody can own anybody. There's a law says.

BROCK—Don't tell me about the law. If I was scared of the law I wouldn't be where I am.

BILLIE—Where are you?

BROCK—All right, you've talked enough. If you don't like it here, beat it. You'll be back. (BILLIE *starts out.*) Wait a minute. (*He gets the documents.*) First this.

BILLIE—Not now.

BROCK—Right now.

BILLIE (*starting upstairs*)—No.

BROCK—Come here!

BILLIE—I'm not going to sign anything any more till I know what I'm signing. From now on.

BROCK—Do what I'm tellin' you! (*He raises his arm to strike her.*)

BILLIE—Harry, please! Don't! (*Her last word is cut by a stinging slap, then another.* BILLIE *sags and sobs, defeated, and* BROCK *shoves her to the desk. Still sobbing, she signs the documents one by one.*)

BROCK—All right, now get the hell out of here.

BILLIE—What?

BROCK—Don't be bawlin' around here, that's what. I don't like it. I been treatin' you too good, that's the trouble. You don't appreciate it. Nothin'. I ain't gonna have nobody around here who don't know their place. So get the hell out of here. Go sit on a park bench some place till you're ready to behave yourself. Go on! (*He points to the front door.*) This way out.

BILLIE (*in a small voice*)—I've got to put something on.

BROCK—Well, hurry up—I don't want you around here like this. You bother me.

BILLIE (*starting up the stairs and turning halfway up*)—Big Fascist!

Brock, alone, sees a pile of books and identifies them as the reason for his present despair. Violently he pushes them to the floor, kicks them, then picks one up and begins tearing out its pages with mingled fury, excitement and satisfaction. He is working on a second book when Devery comes down.

Devery wants, first, to know if the papers are signed—which they are—and, second, why Billie is crying. The book stuff, ventures Brock, has got her nervous—in reply to which Devery quotes, " 'A little learning is a dangerous thing.' " He opines that Brock's passion for educating her was a mistake.

Brock, miserable, confesses. "I love that broad. Ed, you think we could maybe find somebody to make her dumb again?"

Billie comes down the stair, dressed for the street, and moves toward the door. Without looking at her Brock advises, "And don't be late if you don't want a bloody nose."

Billie stops and moves a step into the room. Very, very gently she asks, "Would you do me a favor, Harry?"

"What?" snarls Brock.

"Drop dead?" Before Brock recovers Billie has left quickly.

The curtain falls.

ACT III

It is one-thirty that night. Devery, coatless and quite drunk, is working over a pile of documents, and Brock is worrying about Billie's not having come back. Eddie, who has been sent to find her, returns to report no luck. "The guy downstairs said he seen her go out and then he seen her come in."

Brock orders Eddie out on another hunt, but Eddie pleads that he has to change his shoes first. Devery again comes up with his favorite topic—marriage. The situation, he says, "seems to have gone beyond the reasons of appearance, Harry. If she's going to be truculent, I'm thinking of your legal safety. On paper, she owns—"

Brock is sour—on Billie, on books, on senators. Devery observes that not all senators are for sale—that the trouble with Washington is there are too many honest men in it. He goes into Brock's room and Brock, for want of anything else to do, picks up one of Billie's books—a very small one—and begins to read. This sight is quite astonishing to Eddie as he passes through to resume his hunt for the girl.

The book doesn't hold Brock long. He tears it in two, throws it away and goes up to his room.

Billie, letting herself in stealthily, goes quickly upstairs and listens at Brock's door. Returning to the hall door she whispers outside. Paul joins her, and the two begin a search of the papers on the desk. Billie hands them over and Paul makes a pile of documents, letters, checkbooks and papers, and Billie completes the raid by handing over the material left by Devery.

PAUL—This ought to do it fine.

BILLIE—I probably won't see you again, Paul—

PAUL—What?

BILLIE—Ssshh!

PAUL (*a whisper*)—What?

BILLIE—So I want to say good-by and thank you for everything.

PAUL—Where are you going?

BILLIE—Just away from here, that's all I know.

PAUL—Where? You can tell *me*.

BILLIE—I don't know. I thought I might go see my father for a while.

PAUL—And have a hot lunch every day?

BILLIE—Yeah.

PAUL—I've got a better idea.

BILLIE—What?

PAUL—Let's get married.

BILLIE—You must be daffy.

PAUL—I love you, Billie.

BILLIE—You don't love me. You just love my brain.

PAUL—That, too.

BILLIE—What would the boss of *The New Republic* say?

PAUL—I don't know. Probably—congratulations.

BILLIE—I'll think it over, but I can tell you now the answer is no. And I wish you'd hurry up out of here. (PAUL *kisses her.*) What are you doing?

PAUL—Well, if you don't know, I must be doing it wrong. (*He kisses her again.*)

BILLIE (*sitting on sofa*)—What's more important right now—crabbing Harry's act—or romancing?

PAUL—They're one and the same thing to me.

BILLIE—Honest, Paul, I wish you'd— (EDDIE *comes in, switches on the lights, stops, surprised.*)

EDDIE—What's this, night school? . . .

Eddie warns Paul he'd better leave. Billie, too, urges him to go. Paul leaves, and as Eddie goes upstairs into Brock's room Billie phones the hotel porter, gives the suite number, and asks that somebody be sent up for her bags right away.

Eddie reappears on the landing, rubbing his stomach. Brock has hit him.

"Why didn't you hit him back?" queries Billie. To Eddie the idea is astonishing.

Billie asks Eddie to pack her bags and he wants to know if she is sore at him, too. Billie confesses that, in a way, she is.

"It's a new thing with me, Eddie," she explains. "I'm going to be sore at anybody who just takes it. From now on."

Brock has come down the stairs. Billie greets him gaily. Brock morosely inquires what took her so long, then launches into a pronunciamento about where Billie stands. "Well—first thing, that Verrall stuff is through. It gets in my way—and I don't like you upset so much. It's bad for you. And the next thing—we're gonna get married."

"No."

Brock doesn't quite get the shock of the answer all at once. "Only," he continues, "you got to behave yourself. . . . No? What do you mean, no?"

"I don't want to, that's what I mean. No. In fact, I've never been so insulted."

The flabbergasted Brock whispers that this is the goddamnedest thing he has ever heard. He tries cajolery, essays apology. What if he did hit her a couple of times? It was for her own good. How about going upstairs and calming down? What about a trip to Florida? He even tries giving her a command again, but nothing avails. Billie's mind is made up.

Two bellhops appear to pick up her bags and Brock is further amazed—but not amazed enough to prevent him from chasing them out with the command of "Beat it!"

"Let's get organized around here! You can't just walk out, cutie. You're in too deep with me. I'm right in the middle of the biggest thing I ever done. Maybe I made a mistake hooking you in with it—but you're in."

Brock summons Devery from upstairs. He wants to wash up Billie's paper partnership. "What'd you do with that stuff you wanted her to—?" he asks Devery.

Devery points to the desk. "Right there."

But nothing is there, and the two men paw around feverishly while Billie inquires if what they are looking for had blue covers.

"Yeah."

"Three copies?"

"That's right," growls Brock.

"I gave 'em to Paul."

This information stuns Brock and Devery, and their horror increases as Billie nonchalantly informs them that she supposes Paul is going to put the documents in his paper because he says it is the worst swindle since "the Teapot."

Feverishly, Devery telephones Senator Hedges. Brock yells for Eddie and sends him for Paul. "Tell him Billie wants him," he suggests as bait. Brock is all set for a showdown, but Devery advocates conciliation. "If this stuff breaks," he predicts, "nobody'll play with us."

Eddie comes back with Paul, who immediately senses the trap. Brock, speaking with quiet menace, informs Paul, "I think you got something by mistake that belongs to me." Paul feigns ignorance. At a signal from Brock, Eddie pins his arms from behind while Brock frisks him.

At a command from Brock, Paul sits on the sofa—beside Billie, of whom he asks conversationally how she's been. Brock orders Devery to get "the stuff" out of Paul's room.

"Not there, Ed," says Paul, coolly.

"All right," snarls Brock, "if you want to play it rough. I know how to do that, too." He bolts the door of the service wing and Eddie, automatically, does the same to the front door. A kind of terror pervades the room as Brock speaks to the pair on the sofa:

"Now you listen, you two heels. I mean business. I got too much at stake around here. You got somethin' that belongs to me. And if you want to get out of here alive—you're gonna give it back. I'm no blowhard." To Billie he looks for confirmation. "Tell him."

"He's no blowhard," says Billie. "He's had people killed before. Like once, about six years ago, there was a strike at one of his—"

Brock shuts her up, and again Devery cuts in with some advice to lay off. Devery has been drinking, as usual, but his sense of moderation is now acute. Brock declares that Paul is the goddamnedest buttinsky he ever ran into, and Paul explains that this is his job—to find out what goes on and get it to the people.

"Never heard of the people," says Brock.

"You will, Harry, some day," advises Billie. "They're getting to be more well-known all the time."

Devery, the conciliator, wants to know what Paul would think if he were told the whole operation is strictly according to law, and Paul replies that in this case he thinks the law needs revision.

"Who are you?" demands Brock. "The Government?"

"Of course."

"Since when?"

"Since—uh—1779!"

This clincher is not from Paul, but from Billie, the bookreader. Another debate about democracy has begun when the buzzer rings again and this time Senator Hedges arrives, in response to the urgent telephone call. The Senator is genial because he does not know what is up—but Devery quickly puts him in touch. "Verrall, here, has—uh—stumbled on a whole pocketful of information."

Paul clarifies Devery's bulletin to the Senator by saying, "The connection between Harry's combine and the Senator's amendment is more than coincidence."

Hedges tries to bluster it out, but it doesn't work. When he righteously denies any implication of bribery, Billie chimes in with the right amount he was bribed for—$80,000.

Now, at last, it is Brock's turn to become a conciliator—because there is no other way out. He asks Paul what he will take.

"I'll take a drink, please, if I may."

Brock doesn't want fancy talk; he wants prices. He is talking about big numbers now.

"You and your big numbers," volunteers Billie. "If you don't watch out you'll be wearing one across your chest."

Brock, plunging on, dismisses Billie and concentrates on Paul. "Make up your mind. There's just two ways we can do business. One—you play ball—make it worth your while. Two—you better start watching your step. There'll be no place you can walk—no place you can live, if you monkey wrench me!"

Paul would like to think it over, and Brock gives him two minutes. Paul and Billie smile at each other, and they all look at one another. Quickly Paul rises. "Come on, Billie." They move toward the door, but Eddie maneuvers to intercept them and Brock steps in, menacingly.

There now are two conciliators—Devery, the lawyer, and Hedges, the senator. But Brock is not to be stopped. He clutches Paul's throat. Paul goes to his knees as Hedges, Devery and even Eddie try to haul Brock off. Billie rushes to the phone and screams for the operator.

At Devery's signal Eddie takes the phone from Billie's hand and sits her down. Devery and Hedges tear Brock loose from Paul and throw him to the sofa, where he sits, spent and subdued. Paul, groggy, sits on the stairs and Billie ministers to him.

"You goddamned fool! Where the hell do you think you are?" shouts Devery at Brock. "Can't you see all this muscle stuff is a thing of the past? You cut it out, or you'll be a thing of the past, too."

"I got mad!" explains Brock.

PAUL—Who are *you* to get mad? You big baboon! You ought to be grateful you're allowed to walk around free.

BROCK (*warning*)—You don't know me good enough for that kind of talk.

PAUL—I know you. I've seen your kind down here for years—with red hair and white hair and no hair—but you're always the same—you're usually right here in this room. What the hell do you guys want, any way? You've *got* all the oil and all the lumber and the steel and coal and aluminum—what do you want now—all the people? All the laws?

BROCK—Don't blow your top. I'm still ready to do business. How's a hundred grand?

PAUL—A hundred grand is beautiful—but I can't do it.

BROCK—Why not?

PAUL—My wife wouldn't like it.

BILLIE (*softly*)—She certainly wouldn't.

Brock wants to know what they are talking about and where is all this free enterprise. Devery, at the liquor table as usual, has poured himself a drink. He now toasts:

"To free enterprise."

BROCK—You're just sore because I made good and you ain't. Everybody had the same chance as me—all them kids I used to know—so where are they now?

Billie—No place. Because you beat them out, like you said. You always want to hold everybody down so you can get it all for yourself. That's why there's people like my father—and like me. He couldn't give me what he wanted—so I wind up with an empty head and with you.

Brock—I always did what I want and I'm always gonna.

Billie—Try it.

Brock—Who's gonna stop me?

Billie—Us two.

Brock—Youse two? Don't make me split a gut. Be some fine country where a hundred-and-a-quarter-a-week hick and a broad that ain't been off her end for ten years can stop *me*. (*In fury he crosses to* Devery.) What the hell are you standin' around like a deaf and dumby? What do I pay you for? Go on, say somethin'!

Devery—All right. I'll say something.

Brock—Well?

Devery—They're right.

Brock—You think they can stop me? Stop a senator? What the hell kind of world is it if your money's no good? How can they lick me? *I* got all the money.

Devery—The Republicans had all the money, too. Remember?

Paul—Maybe another time, Harry, not now. And if you're going to try again, do it fast. It gets harder all the time—people get wiser—they hear more—they read more—they talk more. When enough of them know enough—that'll be the end of you.

Brock—Don't worry about me.

Paul—I do, though. I worry like hell. I stay up nights. When you live in Washington, it's enough to break your heart. You see a perfect piece of machinery—the democratic structure—and somebody's always tampering with it and trying to make it hit the jackpot.

Devery (*toasting again*)—"To the jackpot."

Brock—I'm no gambler. I'm a business man.

Paul—You certainly are, but you're in the wrong business now.

Billie—When you steal from the Government, you're stealing from yourself, you dumb ox.

Paul—Sure, you near-sighted empire builders have managed to *buy* little pieces of it once in a while—but you can't have it all—if you do, it won't be this country any more.

Brock (*softly, to* Devery)—Of all the guys in this town—

why the hell did you have to pick *him* out? (*To* PAUL.) Do what you want. I'm goin' ahead.

BILLIE—Wait a minute! I'll tell you where you're going.

BROCK—You?

BILLIE—Sure. In this whole thing—I guess you forgot about me—about how I'm a partner? Ed once told me—a hundred and twenty-six different yards I own.

DEVERY—Control.

BILLIE—Same thing. So here's how it's going to be. I don't want them. I don't want anything of ours—or to do with you. So I'm going to sign them all back—only not all at once—just one at a time—*one a year!* (BROCK *is stunned.*) Only you've got to behave yourself—because if you don't, I'm going to let go on everything. For what you've done even since I've known you only—I bet you could be put in jail for about nine hundred years. You'd be a pretty old man when you got out.

BROCK (*to* DEVERY)—What's goin' on around here?

DEVERY—A revolution.

BROCK—You got me into this—*get me out!*

DEVERY—Somehow, I don't feel as clever as I used to.

BILLIE—Come on, Paul. (*To* BROCK.) I'll send for my things.

BROCK—You little crumb—you'll be sorry for this day—wait and see. Go on—go with him—you ain't got a chance. If I ever seen anybody outsmart themself, it's you.

BILLIE (*starting to go*)—Good-by, all.

BROCK (*to* PAUL)—And you!

PAUL—Me?

BROCK—Yeah—you're fired!

PAUL—I'm sorry, Harry. I've enjoyed working for you very much indeed.

BILLIE (*at the door*)—Eddie, open up!

EDDIE—All right, Harry?

BILLIE (*to* EDDIE, *in imitation of* BROCK)—Do what I'm telling you! (BILLIE *and* PAUL *go out, smiling.* DEVERY *pours himself a drink.*)

BROCK (*trying hard to laugh off this disaster*)—How do you like that? He coulda had a hundred grand—and she coulda had me. So they wind up with nothin'. . . . Dumb chump?

HEDGES—Yes.

BROCK—Crazy broad!

HEDGES—Quite right.

Devery (*toasting, his glass held high*)—"To all the dumb chumps and all the crazy broads, past, present and future—who thirst for knowledge—and search for truth—who fight for justice—and civilize each other—and make it so tough for sons-of-bitches like you—(*To* Hedges.)—and you (*To* Brock.)—and me."

THE CURTAIN FALLS

DREAM GIRL

A Comedy in Two Acts

By Elmer Rice

THE three Elmer Rice plays produced directly before his "Dream Girl" made its Broadway appearance December 14, 1945, were "Two on an Island," "Flight to the West," and "A New Life." In each of these Betty Field played a leading role. Then came "Dream Girl," with Miss Field as the star. Quite reasonably Mr. Rice has had a time convincing his public that he really and truly did not write "Dream Girl" for Betty (who became Mrs. Rice some seasons back). He had actually offered it to three other actresses (all of whom have made names for themselves in the movies), before it was decided that Mrs. Rice should play it.

Which goes to prove, if it proves anything important, that Betty Field is very active in Elmer Rice's bloodstream. There will be other actresses to play the heroine of "Dream Girl" as the seasons go on, but to the end of time it will always be Betty Field's play so far as Broadway is concerned.

There were other reasons why anyone familiar with his theatre life should believe that Mr. Rice had deliberately fashioned the role of Georgina Allerton for his wife. His thirty-one years on Broadway have produced twenty-five plays of which he has been author or co-author. A good majority of these have been plays dealing with subjects of that social significance of which drama critics write persistently and frequently, and often with admitted bias. Mr. Rice is a social and politically-minded liberal and proud of it. He says now that his first impressionistic drama, "The Adding Machine," is his own favorite Rice play, but he felt pretty serious about such dramas of protest as "We the People," "Judgment Day," "Between Two Worlds" and "American Landscape," not to mention such popular items as "Street Scene" and "Counsellor-at-Law." It did not seem likely that so serious-minded an author would devote a year's writing to a light and tricky comedy concerned with a young romantic who day-dreamed herself through

"Dream Girl," copyright 1945, 1946 *by Elmer Rice. Reprinted by permission of Coward-McCann, Inc., New York.*

obviously plausible but quite trivial adventures.

But that is what happened, and the result has proved satisfying to many thousands of playgoers, including the Elmer Rices. Betty Field, not too rugged physically, managed to play the season through in a role that contains something like 600 cues, and keeps her on the stage all but two minutes of the two-hour playing time that "Dream Girl" covers.

Approaching the story as it is told in the theatre, we discover that it quite definitely belongs to the "different" type of comedy. Our initial introduction is to a darkened stage, set with a series of tall, gray panels. From the immediate distance there comes the striking of a bell, followed by the insistent and irritating buzz of an alarm clock. As the lights go up slowly a canopied bed glides out from between the center panels toward the front of the stage. There is a night table by the side of the bed, and on this are the alarm clock and a small radio.

As the light increases we discover a girl in the bed; a girl turning, twisting, "struggling against the rude awakening." When she sits upright it is seen that she is "young, slender and pretty"; that "her hair is done up tightly in hairpins," and that she is about as mad at the alarm clock as a young, slender and pretty girl could well be. Her name is Georgina Allerton.

Georgina is a girl who frequently not only amuses herself, but also reveals many interestingly human sidelights of her character, by speaking her thoughts and even her more intimate cogitations. Just now she is rubbing her eyes, shaking her head, yawning and coming reluctantly to life. After she has angrily shut off the alarm clock, she leans over and raises an imaginary window-shade. The next second the bed is flooded with the morning sunlight and Georgina has finished a final stretch.

"Oh, dear! Another day! How awful!" she mutters. "Who was it that said: '*Must* we have another day?' Dorothy Parker, I suppose. I wonder if she really says all those things. . . . Well, time to get up, I guess."

From below stairs her mother's voice confirms that conclusion. "Goodness! You'd think sleep was some sort of a crime!" protests Georgina. But she goes dutifully about the business of getting out of bed and into her clothes.

The day—and it is a wonderful day of warm sunshine and cloudless skies—the day has barely started before Georgina begins to wonder. First she wonders how long a person can go on as she is going without developing a psychosis or something? For all she knows she may have a psychosis already! And what a terrifying thought that is! She does dream a lot, but she has never been able to make anything of her dreams— "That damned little psychic censor gets in your way," she mutters. "And, besides, I really don't know very much about dream-symbols. Just the obvious ones, like May-poles and church steeples, and I never seem to dream about them. . . . Oh, well, to hell with it!"

The radio has been devoting itself softly to music. Now the voice of an Announcer breaks through in the interest of Kellogg's Kidney Tablets and the suggestion that anyone who is mal-adjusted, or worried about some emotional problem, should certainly consult Dr. J. Gilmore Percival, the noted counselor on human relations, "whose wise and kindly counsel has helped hundreds."

"How ridiculous!" mutters Georgina, as she switches off the radio. "As though some little quack, sponsored by a patent-medicine company, could really solve people's emotional problems for them!"

Still—there is the thought . . .

"Maybe I should try psychiatry," Georgina is saying. "Only what's the use, when I know so well what is the matter with me? Except that the right psychiatrist might help me forget Jim. But, do I want to forget Jim? Oh, dear, I really am in a state!"

Try as she will, Georgina cannot dismiss from her mind the suggestion that she might get help from the right psychiatrist. But—wouldn't it cost a fortune? And, anyway, just what does she need a psychiatrist for?

"I'm a perfectly healthy, normal person," asserts Georgina, as she sits musing on the edge of the bed. "All that's the matter with me is that I'm in love with the wrong man! But that's plenty! Anyhow, how do I know I'm really normal? Is anybody? Everybody thinks they are—even murderers and nymphomaniacs, I suppose! Yes, it might be an interesting experience, having someone peel off layer after layer, until you get right down to your real naked self. And re-living everything that has happened to you—talking right out about things that you hardly even dare let yourself think about. Honestly, it's disgraceful that they allow charlatans like that Dr. Percival on the air!" A note of anger has crept into Georgina's voice. "Imagine standing up in front of a microphone and revealing the things that—"

The radio has lighted up again and the voice of the Announcer is heard: "And remember, folks, it is the kidneys that are the key to your health. And now, here is Dr. Percival." Georgina's first day-dream has begun.

From the radio comes Dr. Percival's voice. Georgina is listening intently, but without ever looking at the radio—

"Good evening, friends. Tonight we begin with the problem of Miss G. A. Now, Miss, just step right up to the microphone and tell me what is troubling you."

"Well, I'm—" Georgina's voice is very low.

"A little louder, please, so that we can all hear you. There's nothing to be nervous about."

"I'm not nervous. It's just—well, it's just that it is a little hard to discuss your personal problems with several million people listening in."

PERCIVAL'S VOICE—But that's what you've come here for, isn't it?

GEORGINA'S VOICE—Yes, it is—it was, but I—

PERCIVAL'S VOICE—I can't help you, unless you—

GEORGINA'S VOICE—I know. Well, you see, I'm in love with a man named Jim—

PERCIVAL'S VOICE—No names, please! No one's identity is ever revealed on this program. I treat your confidence as a sacred trust.

GEORGINA'S VOICE—Oh, I'm sorry! I—!

PERCIVAL'S VOICE—Go on, please. You are in love with a man named J. and he does not reciprocate your feeling for him, is that it?

GEORGINA'S VOICE—Oh, that's not the point! It's that he—he—

PERCIVAL'S VOICE—Well, what?

GEORGINA'S VOICE—Well, he happens to be my brother-in-law.

PERCIVAL'S VOICE—One moment, please! Do I understand you to say that you are in love with your brother-in-law?

GEORGINA'S VOICE—Yes. Yes, I am. I have been, for years and years.

PERCIVAL'S VOICE—This is really quite an extraordinary case. And, if I understand you correctly, he is not in love with you.

GEORGINA'S VOICE—No, unfortunately not! Oh, that sounds awful. I don't mean it that way. I—

PERCIVAL'S VOICE—Then what do you mean?

GEORGINA'S VOICE—Well, I used to think he was. And then suddenly he married Miriam and—

PERCIVAL'S VOICE—No names, please!

GEORGINA'S VOICE—Sorry! He married my sister, two years ago, and that was just about the end of everything for me.

Her brother-in-law is not aware of her feeling for him, Georgina admits; she would die before she would let him know. And she does have a feeling of guilt about it—

"Being in love with your own brother-in-law—well, it seems just a little—a little incestuous," Georgina admits.

"One moment, Miss A.," Dr. Percival promptly corrects! "That is not a word that is acceptable on the air . . . We must remember our youthful listeners, you know."

Georgina is pretty indignant at such an attitude, but she lets it pass. She also is prepared to accept the Doctor's advice that she put the brother-in-law business completely out of her mind, though she does not see exactly how she can do that—unless— Well, she's having lunch with a man this noon that she thought might help her to forget Jim. This would be a Mr. H. who keeps asking her out all the time. Yes, he's married, too. Isn't it awful that her involvements seem to concern married men exclusively? No, she doesn't feel guilty about Mr. H. So far she hasn't done anything to feel guilty about, but— After all, Mr. H. is very nice—good-looking and amusing and all that—

"Miss A., I think your situation is a very serious one, indeed. It is hard for me to believe that a young woman of refinement and education, as you evidently are, could deliberately contemplate—"

The light on the radio goes off, the Doctor's voice stops abruptly. Someone is knocking. Mrs. Allerton's voice can be heard in anxious inquiry:

"Georgina! Are you day-dreaming again in there? It's almost nine!"

"All right, Mother. I'm practically dressed."

As Georgina starts out the light fades on the bed and is focused on a large screen. The surface suggests the tiled wall of a bathroom. Only her head and shoulders are visible above the screen. Evidently she is removing her dressing gown and nightdress and putting on a cellophane cap for the shower. Throughout the bath there are few pauses in the flow of Georgina's conversation. Only the tooth brush gives her pause, and that but briefly. It is possible her mother is right—maybe she should cut out day-dreaming. It is just possible that she (Georgina) isn't an interesting psychological case at all. Maybe she is just a dull, ordinary, commonplace sort of girl. Yet, that's hard to believe. Compared with the average she really is intelligent and well-informed, and a good conversationalist. "And my looks are nothing to be ashamed of, either," mutters Georgina. "I have a neat little figure and my legs are really very nice. Of course my nose is sort of funny—but my face definitely has character—not just one of those magazine cover dead-pans." She is yawning again now. That may be one of the things that's wrong—she certainly doesn't get enough sleep!

It is while she is giving herself a brisk rub with a Turkish towel that Georgina decides this may be the day when things really will begin to happen to her. Maybe Wentworth & Jones will accept her novel. They have had it over a month, and all the other publishers to whom it had been submitted turned it down in less than two weeks. Besides, Jim had recommended it to W. & J. It would be pretty thrilling to be the author of a successful novel; to have the women in Schrafft's pointing her out and whispering: "Don't look now, but that girl over there—the one with the cute hair-do—that's Georgina Allerton, the novelist." Still, even that wouldn't make up for Jim!

Certainly something will have to happen pretty soon. "Here I am twenty-three years old—no, let's face it, twenty-four next month. And that's practically thirty. Thirty years old—and nothing to show for it. Supposing nothing ever does happen to me! That's a frightening thought! Just to go on and on, like this, on through middle-age, on to senility, never experiencing anything—what a prospect!"

Now Georgina is putting on her make-up—and still wondering. "Of course I suppose that up to a certain point there's nothing abnormal about virginity. But the question is, how can you ever be sure you haven't passed that point? Heavens, is that a gray hair? No, thank goodness! What a scare. Still there must be a lot of women who go right on being virgins until the very day they die. It can be done, I guess. Doesn't sound like much fun though. I *must* get a facial, Saturday. No, I can't! It's the last day of the Picasso show and I mustn't miss that. Well, our grandmothers didn't have all these problems. (*She giggles.*) Of course, they didn't, dope! If they'd been virgins, they wouldn't have been our grandmothers."

That brings her right smack up to George Hand. What is she going to do about George? Of course he is rushing her, but it doesn't necessarily follow that he has intentions. Yet, if he didn't have she probably would be a little miffed about that.

"So that puts it squarely up to me," sighs Georgina, getting into her slip. "What a problem! Am I more fastidious than other girls? Or could it be that I'm undersexed? How does one know about things like that? Well, anyhow, if I'm going to play with fire, I may as well look my best. So here goes!"

Georgina is struggling into her dress when Mrs. Allerton calls a warning that she is getting tired of keeping the coffee hot. "Coming! Coming!" Georgina calls back, as she steps into her shoes and hurries out from in back of the screen. . . .

The senior Allertons are at breakfast when Georgina joins them. Mr. Allerton has his morning's mail and Mrs. Allerton has a cold. She had come by the cold because she had slept near an open window the night before. "Your father, after consulting the calendar, decided that Spring is here, so of course up went the window all the way," Mother explains.

There is a letter from Wentworth & Jones. They have turned down Georgina's novel. Which naturally is discouraging—especially after Jim had recommended it for publication.

"Sounds to me like an excellent reason for turning it down," registers Mrs. Allerton, between sneezes.

"I don't think that's a bit funny."

"I wasn't—I wasn't trying—to be funny—" which is followed by another convincing sneeze.

"I don't see why you're always picking on poor Jim," protests Georgina.

"Well, I'm fed up with poor Jim," admits Mother. "I think a fellow of his age shouldn't just be sitting around reading manuscripts at thirty-five dollars a week."

"Oh, give the boy a chance, my dear," pleads Allerton. "He hasn't found himself yet."

"That's exactly it."

"Well," snaps Mrs. A., "I'm sick and tired of financing the search."

Mrs. Allerton feels that she is more or less afflicted with a family of idealists—Georgina, Jim and even Allerton, whom Georgina admires greatly for sticking unselfishly to his principles, "instead of just practicing law on a sordid commercial basis."

"There certainly is no taint of commercialism upon this family," agrees Mrs. A., "including the connections by marriage. And it's a fortunate coincidence that I am able to foot the bills on the income from Grandpa's sordid, commercial estate."

Georgina expects to pay her share, just as soon as her bookstore business improves. Last month they only lost a hundred and eighteen dollars. Claire Blakely, Georgina's partner, says it is the best month they have had. If it were not for the Summer months coming along they would shortly be breaking even. . . .

Miriam Lucas, Georgina's sister, young and attractive, is an early morning caller. She has, she says, come with news for the family, but is just as well pleased that she will have a chance to tell it to them one at a time. She has just been to the doctor's—

"Is there anything wrong?" inquires Georgina, anxiously.

MIRIAM—That's a matter of opinion. It seems that the old medico went into a huddle with some mouse or rabbit that he keeps around and they've decided that you're about to become an aunt.

GEORGINA—But, Miriam, how exciting! When's it going to be?

MIRIAM—Oh, not for a hell of a while—a good five or six months. All those boys at drafting boards knocking hours off the trans-continental flying time, but not one day do they save us mothers. We're right back in the old covered wagon days. Well, I guess I'll go break the news to Mother.

GEORGINA—I'll bet Jim is happy about it.

MIRIAM—He doesn't know it yet. I saw no point in getting him into an interesting condition until I was really sure myself. (*With sudden vehemence.*) And to come right out with it, I don't care a hoot in hell whether he's happy about it or not.

GEORGINA (*greatly embarrassed*)—Well, I know it's going to make all the difference in the world for you both. Gee, I certainly envy you!

MIRIAM—And may I say that I certainly envy *you?* Here am I, a seething mass of unpleasant symptoms and scared half to death, and there are you, fit as a fiddle and positively suffused with the soft glow of vicarious maternity.

GEORGINA—I just wish I could change places with you, that's all.

MIRIAM—It's a deal! I'll send my agent around after lunch. And I hope you have a boy.

GEORGINA—Maybe it'll be twins.

MIRIAM—Don't say things like that! You never know who's listening.

Miriam has gone. For a moment Georgina stands by the table gazing dreamily after her. Softly she begins to hum "Schlaf,

Kindchen, Schlaf." As the lights fade the humming is taken up by a chorus of female voices, merging in the darkness into a wailing of infants. Now the lights reveal a hospital bed completely surrounded by flowers, in which Georgina is propped up. "She wears a hospital nightgown and holds a large doll in each arm, one wrapped in a blue blanket, the other in pink. At one side of the bed stand an Obstetrician, who looks like Allerton; at the other side a Nurse, who looks like Mrs. Allerton."

OBSTETRICIAN—Well, my dear, you've come through wonderfully. In all my years, I've never known a harder confinement or a braver patient. Yes, you're a plucky little woman.

GEORGINA—A lucky one, you mean! (*Smiling down at the babies.*) Just look at my little darlings!

OBSTETRICIAN—I've never seen two finer ones.

NURSE—You're the envy of every mother in the hospital.

GEORGINA (*beaming*)—Well, what's a little suffering compared to that? Besides, pain is a part of life, and to live fully, we must taste every form of human experience.

NURSE—Oh, that's beautifully expressed!

OBSTETRICIAN (*nodding*)—I wish there were more women who had your imagination and courage.

GEORGINA—When I think that there are women who dread motherhood, women who shrink from it—well, it's just too much for me! And, Doctor, I definitely *don't* want them to go on the bottle. It's such a joy!

OBSTETRICIAN (*patting her head*)—Good girl!

The Obstetrician has left and Jim Lucas is calling. "He is an attractive young man with a face and manner that are almost too sensitive."

"Georgina, darling!" Jim's greeting is sincerely effusive.

"Oh, Jim!"

"Not too long, Mr. Lucas," cautions the nurse. "We mustn't tire her."

"No, no. I understand."

Together Jim and Georgina review the miracle that has meant everything to them; a double miracle that has meant birth for the twins, Gerald with Geraldine, and rebirth for their enraptured parents, as Georgina puts it.

But then Miriam arrives, and there is little sentiment in Miriam. She has come for her infants and she must hurry, because she is parked in front of a fire plug.

"No! You shan't have them!" declares Georgina, dramatically. "They're mine."

MIRIAM—Look, darling. I know you haven't been around much but you're really old enough to understand where babies come from. Jim, do you mind stepping outside, while I explain the facts of life to Georgina?

JIM—Facts! Facts! You're your mother's daughter, all over, Miriam. Dollars and cents. Nose to the grindstone. Man plus woman equals baby.

MIRIAM—Or two babies as the case may be. (*Angrily.*) Look, it wasn't my idea to have a baby! And I certainly did not invent the machinery of procreation. But having produced a couple of brats, in the customary antiquated manner, I don't think I'm unreasonable in contending that they're mine.

JIM—Only in the crudest physiological sense.

MIRIAM—Oh, forgive me! Is there some other sense?

GEORGINA—There is, indeed!

JIM—You wouldn't have to be told that, Miriam, if you had any feeling for the deeper values of life. There's no real marriage between you and me—no love, no understanding, no spiritual communion. The children of my body may be yours, but the children of my spirit will always be Georgina's.

Matter-of-factly Miriam calls the nurse, gathers in her babies and departs, leaving Jim to explain helplessly that though he knows things shouldn't be as they are, there is nothing he can do. Georgina, in tears, is still standing by the breakfast table when the lights are again shifted and Mrs. Allerton reappears with another warning that Georgina is sure to be late to the shop.

Why is Georgina weeping? Just because she is happy for Miriam our heroine explains, and a little wistful about becoming a maiden aunt. She's sorry for Jim, too, when her mother tells her that her brother-in-law is out of a job again. Poor Jim has had so much bad luck lately. Her sympathy is completely wasted on the cynical Mrs. Allerton, who hopes that Miriam now will have the good sense to get rid of Jim.

"She'd be a fool to hang on to him, now that he's accomplished what will probably be the only affirmative act of his life," declares Mrs. A. . . .

It was while Georgina was driving her sport-coupé to the bookshop that she began to wonder again about Jim Lucas. It was while she was stopped by a traffic light. Her car radio was play-

'hoto by Vandamm Studio.

"DREAM GIRL"

Hand—Georgina, if there is anything I can—
Georgina—To hell with that! I don't want your pity!

(*Betty Field, Edmon Ryan*)

ing softly and Georgina began to hum the tune. Then the light changed and she drove on. Presently she was day-dreaming again. She sees Jim sitting on a park bench, his face haggard, his clothes shabby. He stares despairingly into space, then suddenly reaches into his pocket, whips out a revolver and puts it to his temple. Before he can pull the trigger Georgina is by his side. Another minute and she would have been too late—

"It can't be as bad as all that," Georgina is saying, as Jim tries to explain. "What's happened to you? Why haven't I heard from you in all these months?"

"I was ashamed, Georgina. Ashamed to have you see what a complete failure I have become. . . . You were always the one to judge me sympathetically, Georgina. But I'm beyond sympathy now. There's nothing left to go on with. Cast off by my wife. Unable to find work. Homeless, friendless—a broken vagabond on a park bench!"

"Not friendless, Jim." She is holding his hand. "I still believe in you. I'll always believe in you."

"You're not just saying it?"

"No! There's never been anyone for me but you. Didn't you ever guess?"

"No! Never! Why, if I had dreamed that you—"

"I didn't want you to know. I would have died rather than come between you and Miriam. But now that you're out of her life—now that she's remarried, there's no longer any reason why you and I shouldn't— That is, if you want me."

"I thought I was dead and suddenly you open the door to life! But I can't, Georgina."

"Why?"

"Because I won't allow myself to be a burden to you—won't let my miserable failures be a drag on your splendid success. I knew that I was right about that novel!"

"Yes, you were the one who always believed in *me,* too. It's all been very exciting—money rolling in, receptions and interviews, Hollywood offers, my publishers clamoring for another book—"

"Don't let them make a hack of you, Georgina. Don't write until you're ready."

"Oh, indeed I won't. But, Jim, dear, it's all empty without somebody to share it with. I want love, companionship, children, your children, Jim! And, fortunately, I am able to provide for all of us now."

"If you really mean all that, then maybe there's still hope for me. Maybe, with your encouragement, your guidance, I can find a place for myself after all."

"All I want is a chance to prove it to you. That's all I ever wanted. Jim, darling, take me in your arms!"

But the embrace was not to be. The green light changes to red and out of the darkness a Rough Voice is shouting: "Hey, where do you think you're going? . . . What are you trying to do —kill somebody? Pull over there to the curb!"

"All right, I will," answers Georgina, but not too meekly. "You needn't be so rude about it!"

The jangle of police whistles, automobile horns, squeaking brakes and excited voices has died out. The lights have faded. When they come up again we are in a corner of the Mermaid Bookshop. There are walls of books and a flat-top desk, with a swivel-chair behind it, and another chair beside it. At the desk Claire Blakely, "a brisk young woman about Georgina's age," is seated.

A middle-aged woman customer comes in and goes to the shelves. She is looking for a copy of "Always Opal," but there is none. "We have a dozen copies, but they're all out," Claire explains. Perhaps the lady would like "My Heart Is Like a Trumpet"—a sort of idyllic love story about two horses? Or "The Dnieper Goes Rolling Along"—the new Soviet novel about the electrification of collective farms? No, the lady would not. What she wants is "Always Opal." All her friends are reading that one and she feels terribly out of it. If she can't get "Always Opal" she would like to buy a 3-cent stamp. And does. . . .

When Georgina arrives she explains about the red light and the traffic cop. She must have been day-dreaming to have been so dumb.

"You should watch that," Claire warns. "People sometimes get nasty bruises falling out of air-castles."

Has Claire had a busy morning, Georgina would know. "You betcha!" answers Claire, with enthusiasm. "I directed two people to Oppenheim Collins, one gal wanted to look at the phone book, another had to go to the john and I just made a cash sale of a 3-cent stamp."

"It's discouraging!" sighs Georgina.

"A little," admits Claire. "If we only had a hundred thousand copies of 'Always Opal' to slake the feminine thirst for fancy-dress pornography—"

Suddenly Claire remembers an offer they have had by phone from a Frank McClellan. Frank has been ordered to Arizona for his asthma and he wants to sell his bookshop. Says he has been clearing five or six hundred a month. He wants ten thousand dollars for the business. It's an opportunity—but does Georgina know where they can raise ten thousand? No, Georgina does not—

"Well, it's too bad," continues Claire, shaking her head dolefully. "We couldn't miss, right there in the middle of Radio City. Nobody ever walks down this Godforsaken street except folks on their way to the Morgue. Yes, it's really too bad!"

"Yes, it really is!" sadly agrees Georgina. "What's the good of opportunities if you can't take advantage of them?"

"I don't know the answer to that one, either. Georgie, I don't think you and I are cut out for business. I think the best thing for us to do is to board up this hole in the wall and call it a day."

Georgina is not quite that discouraged, but— What *are* they to do? She has used up practically all of her grandfather's estate and Claire's father has put his foot down—hard enough to rattle the chandeliers below. And neither of them is sure she could hold a job, even if she could find one.

"Of course," ventures Georgina, "we could go to secretarial school."

"Back to school at twenty-four," explodes Claire. "Listen, darling, beginning with play school at three, I went to school—let me see, now—(*Counting on her fingers.*)—sixteen, seventeen, eighteen, nineteen—! My God, nineteen consecutive years! Why, it's a lifetime. Do you realize that in the Renaissance they became cardinals at sixteen?"

"But not women, Claire."

"Don't make irrelevant remarks!" snaps Claire, irritably. "Nineteen years of intensive education—and what have we got to show for it? What are we good for? What can we do? Could either of us get a job as a telephone operator, a bookkeeper, a nurse, a chorus girl, a garage mechanic, a farmhand, a harpist, a laundress, or a short-order cook?"

"Even if we wanted to."

"Even if we wanted to! Now you've put your finger on it. Nineteen years, thousands of dollars and the efforts of hundreds of specially trained people have been spent just in making us not want to do all the useful things we don't know how to do."

Claire has gone to get out the month's bills. "Don't take any more reservations for 'Always Opal,' " she calls back, as she disappears behind the bookshelves. "Our lease will be up by the time we fill all we have now."

Georgina, with a sigh, has walked over to the bookshelves and taken down a book. She is standing, lost in thought, when the phone rings. She rushes back to the desk to answer it—

"Hello? Yes, this is she. What? Oh, no—I can't believe it! Yes! Yes! I'll be right there!"

As Georgina hurries out there is a brief darkness. When the lights come up they reveal a man in a surgeon's uniform with a stethoscope about his neck. The news he had given her over the phone is true. Georgina's mother is dead. The doctors had done everything they could, but—it was hopeless.

As the Doctor leaves, Georgina rushes into her father's arms. There are only the two of them now. Miriam and Jim will have the baby to look out for. With all her money, Georgina will be able to do whatever her heart desires, her father reminds her, but she quickly assures him that she will never leave him. The only use she might make of her money would be to go in with Claire—

The lights again reveal the Mermaid Bookshop. A young man, Clark Redfield, has come in staggering under a load of books. He dumps them on the desk and coughs tentatively. Darkness having blotted out Allerton, Georgina turns to meet the newcomer. Her greeting of Mr. Redfield is warm but formal.

"Good morning, Miss Allerton. You seem preoccupied. I hope I haven't derailed some train of cosmic thought."

"Of course not. I was just— Goodness! More review books?"

"You betcha! I've got—"

If Mr. Redfield doesn't mind, Georgina would like to call her mother. She hasn't been feeling well. It's only a cold, but—

As the phone rings the lights reveal Mrs. Allerton at home seated on the side of a sofa reading a book. When she answers the phone she is plainly irritated and still sneezing. Of course she's all right; if Georgina hasn't anything more important to do than to call up to find out about her mother's sneezing there must be precious little on her mind—

"I was appreciating Opal's hot affairs with Monseigneur de Montrouget and you interrupted me just as they were about to—to—" (*A generous sneeze.*) "So, if you have nothing more to say—"

Georgina has hung up the receiver and turned to Clark. "What have you there?" she asks, indicating the books.

CLARK—A fine mixed bag! Three who-dunits, a couple of epics of the soil, a survey of the natural resources of Bolivia and a volume called "Fun with a Chafing-Dish." And here is the prize of the lot. Professor Oglethorpe's two-volume "Life of

Napoleon," with the pages still uncut.

GEORGINA—You mean you haven't read it?

CLARK—Do I look like a boy who, six years out of college, would wade through eleven hundred pages on Napoleon?

GEORGINA—But I read your review of it in the *Globe*.

CLARK—I didn't say I didn't review it. I said I didn't read it.

GEORGINA—Well, I must say! How could you review it without reading it?

CLARK—Easy. I read the introduction, in which the author explains his approach. After quoting liberally from it, I attacked its validity. Then I intimated that this new work added little to what had already been written. Next I leafed quickly through and found three typographical errors, to which I called attention. Then, after praising the illustrations and complaining of the excessive number of footnotes, I said that the book would undoubtedly be of interest to all students of Bonaparte. Result, a scholarly column and all done in exactly fifty-seven minutes.

GEORGINA—That really is shocking!

CLARK—What's shocking about it? The author gets a column in a leading metropolitan newspaper and the publishers will discover several phrases which, torn from their context, will make excellent advertising copy.

GEORGINA—Is that your idea of literary criticism?

CLARK—I thought we were talking about book reviewing. I'm a working newspaper man and a member of the Newspaper Guild, whose contract guarantees me a minimum wage for a maximum working week. There's nothing that requires me to ruin my eyesight and addle my brain in the interest of the millionaire who owns the paper or the reading public that buys it in order to follow the adventures of Dick Tracy.

GEORGINA—Well, I've always heard that newspaper men are cynical, but I wouldn't have believed that a man who is entrusted with reviewing books could have so little sense of responsibility—! Why, I'll never be able to read a book review again, without wondering if the reviewer is really sincere.

CLARK—You make me feel like a great big brute. Yes, a woman's soul is a beautiful sanctuary and all we men can find to do is to profane it.

GEORGINA—I don't see anything funny about it. I think it's disgraceful.

CLARK—Don't twist the sword, Miss Allerton. Just give me the price of my shame and let me go in peace. (*Briskly.*) Well, what do you say? How much am I bid for the lot?

GEORGINA (*looking over the books*)—We're overstocked, as it is, and most of these aren't much use to us. How about five dollars?

CLARK—Like all idealists, you drive a hard bargain. But I'm not going to lug these damned things any further, so they're yours.

GEORGINA—Well, I don't want you to feel I'm taking advantage of you. I'll make it six dollars.

Clark's pride is slightly outraged, and he takes the five. There is one thing Georgina doesn't understand: If book reviewing is so distasteful to him, why does he do it? Well, for one thing, Clark explains, it is much easier on the legs than covering police courts; for another, he is hoping shortly to be given a chance on the sports page.

Georgina's amazement grows. Would Clark really rather be a sports writer than a literary critic? Yes, to be honest about it, Clark would. "You think that writing about books is on a higher level than writing about sports?" he queries.

"I just think there's no comparison," loftily insists Georgina.

"You're right; there isn't. Any young squirt, fresh out of college, can write book reviews. Just as any beginner in the theatre can play Polonius. In fact, the technique is much the same. You put on false whiskers and spout platitudes in a high, squeaky voice. But to go in there and play Hamlet and follow all the sinuous twists and turnings of that tortured soul; or, on the other hand, to analyze the strategy of an intricate football formation or judge a fast ten-round bout on points—that's something else again. To do that, you really have to know your stuff."

Furthermore Mr. Redfield would have the disillusioned Georgina know that to a really good sports' writer every door is open. "Look at Ring Lardner! Look at Heywood Broun! Look at John Kieran! Look even—if you can bear it—at Westbrook Pegler. In my day-dreams," Clark goes on, "I write a story about the deciding game of the World's Series that stampedes the Democratic convention and lands me in the White House. And on my tentative Cabinet slate, you're down for Secretary of Labor. Ta-ta, Madame Allerton. I'll see you in Washington!"

Before Clark can get away there is another matter Georgina would like to ask him about— Does he know Jim Lucas. Yes.

Clark knows Georgina's brother-in-law, though he is not boasting of the friendship. And does Georgina know the latest news about Jim? Yes, Georgina knows that Jim has parted company with Wentworth & Jones, if that is what Mr. Redfield means—

"Parted company, did you say?" asks Clark with amused surprise. "Really, Miss Allerton, you have a hyperbolic gift of understatement. The impact of Jim's violent explosion has rocked Publisher's Row to its foundations. If he is still sound of limb, it is only because there is some obscure and balmy saint who presides over congenital idiots. Would you mind telling an inquiring reporter, Miss Allerton, how it feels to be the sister-in-law of the man who sent back the manuscript of 'Always Opal,' without even turning in a report on it?"

"Is that really true? Did Jim do that?"

"Oh, so you haven't heard? An enterprising book-peddler like you should get around more, Miss Allerton. Mix with folks. Get acquainted with your own family. This Lucas is a celebrity, the greatest bonehead player since Fred Merkle forgot to touch second base, back in the year one thousand."

"Well, that book deserved to be turned down," declares Georgina, rallying to Jim's defense. "It's nothing but a lot of dressed-up smut, atrociously written and all in very bad taste, if you ask me."

Clark can't go along with that verdict. The fastest-selling book in forty years! Nearing the million mark in sales—!

But, getting back to Jim Lucas: "I got the impression that Jim thinks rather highly of that novel of yours that he asked me to read," says Clark.

"Oh, then he *did* give it to you?" Georgina is plainly eager for the Redfield verdict.

CLARK—Yes. Yes, he did. As a messenger boy, Jim has a great future, I think.

GEORGINA—And I suppose, following your usual practice, you haven't read it.

CLARK—No, you're wrong. I *have* read it. All of it—well, almost all.

GEORGINA (*after a pause*)—Well?

CLARK—You mean you want my opinion of it?

GEORGINA—Well, why do you suppose I let Jim give it to you?

CLARK—I wasn't sure. Well, to put the thing as delicately as possible, I think it stinks.

GEORGINA (*enraged*)—Oh, you do, do you?

CLARK—Yes, I do. (*Contemplatively.*) Yes, that really is an unsavory piece of tripe. In the first place—

GEORGINA (*almost in tears*)—Never mind, I'm not interested in what you have to say.

CLARK—Oh, then you really *didn't* want my opinion. That's what I thought.

GEORGINA—I don't call that an opinion. Just a nasty, insulting—

CLARK—I see! You only wanted a favorable opinion.

GEORGINA—Nobody wants criticism that's just destructive.

CLARK—That's the only kind of criticism that's worth a damn. A good truck-gardener doesn't waste his time nursing weeds. He yanks them up by the roots, so that the tomatoes and lima beans have a chance.

GEORGINA—What's that got to do with it? I say, if a critic can't be constructive—!

CLARK—You mean you want the critic to do the creative job that you failed to do? If that's his function, we might as well dispense with the writer in the first place. Now, if you'll let me give you another piece of friendly advice—

GEORGINA—I don't want your advice. If I had known how little your opinion is worth, I'd never have let Jim give you the manuscript. But I was under the mistaken impression that you were a literary man and not just a hockey fan.

CLARK—There's a good hockey match at the Garden, Saturday night. Want to go?

GEORGINA—No, I don't! And if you'll excuse me now, I have a lot of work to do.

CLARK—You haven't a damn thing to do. You just sit around this shop all day to give yourself the illusion that you're doing something.

GEORGINA—Will you please get out of here?

CLARK—Sore as a boil, aren't you?

GEORGINA—Not in the least. It just happens that I find you very unpleasant. I think you're not only lazy and dishonest, but sadistic and vulgar.

CLARK—Well, I'm glad you're not sore. And I think that novel of yours is just about the most terrific thing I've read since "War and Peace."

GEORGINA—And another thing, I wish you would not ever come here again.

CLARK—I'll try to remember that. 'By, now. And thanks for the five bucks.

GEORGINA (*with tears of anger*)—You great big ape!

It does not take Georgina long to dream up a perfectly lovely revenge for that insult. Trembling with rage and humiliation she paces the office, stopping at the desk long enough to shove Clark Redfield's books violently onto the floor. With sudden resolution she strides off into the darkness. As the lights fade on the bookshop they come up on Clark sitting before a typewriter in his shirtsleeves. He is twisting the tail of a cat, and the cat is meowing pitifully. With a fiendish laugh, and, after taking himself a stiff drink of whisky, Clark goes back to pecking at the typewriter.

There is a sharp knocking at the door, followed by the appearance of an angry Georgina, carrying a handbag.

"Oh, it's you, is it?" sneers Clark.

"Yes, it's me. I mean it's I!"

"I'm just having a little fun with the kitty."

"And I'm going to have a little fun with you!"

Thereupon Georgina opens the bag, takes out a revolver and fires two shots into Clark Redfield. An instant later two policemen have rushed into the room and seized Georgina roughly.

"All right, you needn't be rough about it," says Georgina, with quiet dignity. "I did it and I'm willing to take the consequences!"

As the policemen lead Georgina away the lights fade, to be turned up a moment later on a police court. There is a tumult of voices, followed by a threat from the Judge (who greatly resembles Georgina's father), to clear the courtroom if there are any more demonstrations. Georgina is sitting in the witness chair. She is being examined by the District Attorney. Jim Lucas is at the counsel table.

"Then you admit that you went there with the deliberate intention of killing Clark Redfield?" the District Attorney asks.

"Yes, I admit it. But I had every justification. He was a savage brute, a man without—"

"I object!" objects the District Attorney.

"Objection sustained," agrees the Judge, with a bang of his gavel.

"Your Honor, I protest," protests Jim Lucas. "This young woman is on trial for her life. Is she to be railroaded to the chair without even an opportunity to speak in her own defense?"

"The point is well taken. Proceed, Miss Allerton."

"Well, let me just ask you this. If he had attacked me wouldn't you all agree that I had a right—?"

"One moment! Are we to understand that Clark Redfield attempted to—?"

"No, he didn't. But compared to what he did to me, it would have been easy to submit to—to—well, not easy, but almost preferable. He struck at my dignity, humiliated me, trampled my pride in the dust. And if you men think that an injury to a woman's body is a greater provocation to murder than an injury to her spirit, then you know nothing about feminine nature. That's all. That's my case!"

"The prosecution rests. Your Honor, the people of the State of New York demand the death penalty!"

Jim has gone to Georgina and is patting her hand approvingly. "Counsel for the defense will now address the jury. Proceed, Mr. Lucas."

Jim rises to address an unseen jury. "Ladies and gentlemen of the jury. I speak to you not merely as counsel for Georgina Allerton, but as her brother. And by that I do not refer to my accidental marital relationship to her sister, but to the deep spiritual fraternal bond that has long existed between the defendant and myself. I can say, in all honesty, that no one understands her as I do; no other human being has plumbed so profoundly the depths of that tender, sensitive soul. And, in the light of my knowledge and understanding, I say to you that when she struck down Clark Redfield it was no act of murder, but a simple, human gesture of self-defense."

There is a murmur from the unseen jurors and Jim continues with mounting eloquence. What was this novel that Clark Redfield sought to annihilate with his sharp tongue and stabbing with—"It was her baby, ladies and gentlemen, the child of her spirit as real to her and as dear to her as though it had been indeed the flesh-and-blood creation of her body . . . the fruition of the gestative processes of her inner nature; the embodiment of her hopes, her aspirations, her dreams. And as it lay nestling in her bosom, so to speak, Clark Redfield struck at it with his lethal weapons. And with the noble, unerring instinct of outraged maternity she struck back, struck back at the would-be assassin of her baby. Could any mother—could any woman do less? I leave the answer to you."

He sits down, amid cheers and applause, and the jury is quick to return a verdict of not guilty. The defendant is dismissed by a sympathetic Judge, who ventures a paternal word of advice—let Georgina in future avoid the use of firearms. Incidentally the Judge is greatly enjoying Georgina's novel. "I think you have a splendid future as a writer," says he.

Georgina has turned to Jim. "Oh, Jim darling! I knew I could depend on you!" But just as Jim is about to take her in his arms the phone rings. The lights fade quickly. Georgina, back in the bookshop, is at the phone. "Mermaid Bookshop. No, madame, I'm sorry; we're all out of 'Always Opal.' You're welcome.". . .

Jim Lucas is worried. He has come to tell Georgina that he and Miriam are splitting up. Nor does the fact that Miriam had not told him she was going to have a baby change the picture to him. "When people have drifted as far apart as we have, nothing can bring them together," says Jim. Nor would it be fair, in his opinion, to expose an infant to the blight of parents who hate each other.

No, Jim would not have Georgina talk to Miriam. He really feels a new sense of freedom. Also he is convinced now that he and Georgina can be more to each other—as they used to be. But Georgina cannot subscribe to that. There is no going back to things, ever.

Jim has gone and Georgina remembers her luncheon date with George Hand. Claire would twit her a little about that.

"What a mind you have!" Georgina protests, with some spirit. "Just because Mr. Hand and I happened to discover that we have a few things in common—"

"Which he hopes will eventually include a bed," adds Claire.

Claire is also convinced that the Jim Lucas-Miriam Lucas split-up is all in Miriam's favor. She will be well rid of Jim.

"And that's another general opinion with which I disagree," announces Georgina, with conviction. "Oh, well, I may as well have lunch with George Hand and get it over with. I'll be back as soon as I can—"

"Don't hurry," Claire calls after her. "And don't say no until after the liqueurs!"

When the lights are up again the Mermaid Bookshop has been replaced by a semi-circular upholstered booth in a corner of the Canard Rouge, "a chi-chi midtown restaurant." Georgina and Hand are lingering over their coffee and brandy. "Hand is a brisk, good-looking man, getting on to forty." At the moment he is suggesting a third brandy to Georgina, but she is convinced that two cocktails and two brandies for lunch is not exactly her idea of being on the wagon.

Their conversation continues lightly. Mr. Hand is interested in Georgina's admission that the bookshop is not doing so well. He wonders that she should ever have chosen a business career. He is convinced she could have done much better in another line —love, for example. When he refuses to take her seriously, Hand suggests that if they both took her seriously that would certainly be overdoing it. Think of all the fun she misses by taking herself too seriously.

"Yes, maybe I do," confesses Georgina. "I've often wished that I could be just—well, just completely reckless and irresponsible, like—like—oh, I don't know who."

"Opal?"

"Well, yes, now that you mention it. Is that why everybody is so mad to read that silly book?"

"What are you being so snooty about? Why, that book is positively a boon to womankind! For two-fifty flat, or three cents a day, any Hausfrau in the land can identify herself with the most luscious yes-woman in all literature."

"Is that really what every woman wants?"

"All I can go by is the sales figures."

"So you think we're all harlots at heart?"

"Well, I wouldn't want to go on the air with that statement."

"Still even if you're right, there seems to be an awful lot of women who manage not to—"

"I know. That's what makes life so difficult for a man."

"Oh, poor Mr. Hand! Do we make things difficult for you?"

"Very. But I don't complain. No victory without labor, my Sunday school teacher used to say."

Their fencing match continues with honors easy until they finally arrive at the subject of marriage. Georgina isn't at all interested in marriage, she says. From what she has seen of it she has concluded that the odds are all stacked against you.

That, agrees George, makes everything simpler. At least it does not cramp Georgina's style; doesn't limit the range of her experiences.

"Why, that's true, isn't it?" sparkles Georgina. "You have a wonderful gift for clarifying things."

Hand—Don't be coy, Georgina. You'll never get me to believe that a sophisticated girl like you has never had any experiences.

Georgina—Well, it would be hard to believe that a sophisticated girl could get to be twenty-two without having had *some* experiences.

HAND—Then what the hell? Or does your aversion to marriage extend to men who are already married?

GEORGINA—I often wonder how I'd feel if I were the man's wife. Or is that very *un*sophisticated?

HAND—Not a bit. Does credit to your upbringing. Only Mollie isn't a bit like that. We get along fine together except when she has a drink too many and then we really go to town. Otherwise, I don't interfere with her and she doesn't interfere with me.

GEORGINA—That's what I mean about marriage.

HAND—I agreed with you, didn't I? But you'll admit I'm not one of the lads who comes crying for sympathy because he's so misunderstood.

GEORGINA—No, that's true. I knew there was *something* about you that was different.

HAND—No flattery, please! Tell me, have you ever been to Mexico?

GEORGINA—Thanks for changing the subject. No, I haven't been to Mexico. But I've always wanted to go.

HAND—Wonderful! But I haven't changed the subject. I have to go down next month and I've been thinking what fun it would be if we could sort of meet up there.

GEORGINA—Oh, have you? Well—

HAND—It's a great country. I've been there before and I know my way around. We'd take in jai-alai matches and bull-fights—

GEORGINA—I should say not!

HAND—All right, we'll stay away from bull-fights. Anyhow, we'd find some village fiestas, look at the Rivera frescoes and drift along on the flower boats at Xochimilco. And talk about food! Have you ever eaten mole?

GEORGINA—No, I don't think I have.

HAND—It's turkey with a sauce made of chocolate and about fifteen different kinds of pepper. Sounds revolting, doesn't it?

GEORGINA—It certainly does!

HAND—I'm telling you it's tops. Especially when washed down with a bottle of tequila. You've heard of Taxco, haven't you?

GEORGINA—Yes, of course.

HAND—Well, a friend of mine has a house there that he hardly ever uses. Up on a terraced hill, looking down onto the little village plaza. We'd have dinner in the patio and the local folks would come up and serenade us. Why, I can just see you, done up in a rebozo and—

GEORGINA—You *are* a salesman, aren't you?

Before Hand can reply, a man enters the room and passes their table. As it happens, he is the man who owns the house in Taxco. Hand is on his feet in a minute to follow his friend out. Nor does he heed Georgina's plea that he wait. "I won't be a minute," Hand calls back. Georgina, sitting back in her chair, continues to look after him dreamily. The lights begin to fade.

There is the sound of singing, growing nearer. The lights come up on the corner of an exotic patio, bathed in moonlight, where "a quartet of musical comedy Mexicans is strumming guitars and singing a sentimental Spanish love song. The leader of the quartet, a tall, good-looking young man, has the face of Clark Redfield."

After a moment Georgina and George Hand stroll in. Georgina is wearing a large, bright shawl. Hand has his arm around her as they stand listening to the music. As the song ends the serenaders cover their hearts with their sombreros and bow low.

"Oh, lovely, lovely!" cries Georgina, clapping her hands. "Buena! Buena! Muchos gracias!"

"That was great!" adds Hand, reaching into his pocket and dropping a fistful of coins into the leader's sombrero.

"Gracias, señor! Muchos gracias! Buenos noches, señor! Buenos noches, señorita!" He bends over to kiss Georgina's hand.

"Buenos noches! Hasta la vista!"

"Hasta la vista, señorita! Viva los Americanos!"

The serenaders back away into the darkness. The spell of the moon, the night, of memories of the last few weeks still hold Georgina in their grip—

"You're not sorry, are you, that you decided to come along?" Hand is saying, as he draws her closer to him.

"Not right now, I'm not. I only hope that—when it's all over—I won't feel a little cheap."

Now her companion has grown serious. There is something he would like to talk over with her. She will remember what she said at the luncheon when he first suggested this trip to Mexico—that she was not interested in marriage? Yes, she remembers. Well, George wasn't taken in by any of that. He knows that the reason she had decided finally to come with him was because she was trying to forget somebody it made her unhappy to think about.

Yes, admits Georgina, that's true. And has he helped her to forget? Yes, he has. That's why— But she decides not to go on.

"You've said all you need to say—all I wanted to know," Hand assures her, and hurries on: "Georgina, I thought I had nothing more to learn about women, but I was wrong. When we came down here together, I thought of it as just a gay adventure, just another romantic episode. But being here alone with you, getting to know you as I have, has opened my eyes to things I never dreamed of. It's made me want a kind of happiness I've never known. I don't want this to be the end of Georgina, but just the beginning."

"Why do you say such things, when you know that it is impossible?"

"No, it's not impossible. In fact it's all arranged. While you were at the market this afternoon I called up my wife. I told her I want a divorce, and—"

"No, I won't hear of it. I'm not one of those girls that breaks up marriages. That's one reason I've said no to every married man who—"

"Wait a minute! You're not breaking up any marriage. My wife jumped at the suggestion. It seems she's interested in someone, too, and she had just about made up her mind to ask *me* for a divorce."

"Are you telling me the truth?"

"I couldn't lie to you. I respect you too much and, anyhow, I know you're too smart for me to get away with it. Georgina, this is really from the gods! You can't say no!"

"I—don't know, George. You've got to give me time to think." The lights are beginning to fade. "I *must* have time to think!"

Georgina is still at table, dreamily gazing ahead of her, when Hand rushes back to tell her that everything has been arranged with his friend. They can have the cottage at Taxco! What does she say?

Georgina doesn't say much. She can't give him an answer just like that—

"Yes, you can!" enthuses Hand. "Never fight your impulses! Take it from me, the things we really regret in life are not those we do, but those we don't do!"

"Well, I'll—I'll think it over," agrees Georgina, hesitantly, as she glances at her watch. "Goodness, it's nearly three o'clock. I've got to get back to the shop. . . . Thanks for a lovely lunch."

He has taken her hand. "Remember what the voice of experience is saying to you: don't resist your impulses. Ta-ta! I won't leave you in peace for long!"

For a moment Georgina stands looking after him. When the waiter comes to clear the table she asks if she might have another brandy—

"So now you're taking to drink, are you?" Georgina is mumbling, as she resumes her seat at the table. "Just like all the other misfits who can't face their problems and try to make alcohol a substitute for character. Oh, Georgina, Georgina, my girl, you're really in a bad way!"

She shakes her head dolefully. The curtain falls.

ACT II

The lights are up on the corner of the bookshop. Claire is straightening books on the shelves when Georgina gets back from her luncheon with George Hand. It's about time, thinks Claire. She was just about to call the Juvenile Delinquents Court.

Well, they ate and ate, and drank and drank, and talked and talked, Georgina explains. Claire was quite right about Hand's intentions, Georgina admits. He wants Georgina to go to Mexico with him! He was nice and frank about the whole thing. He didn't try to pretend. And is Georgina thinking of going into it? Well, she has agreed to think it over. Even going that far is a bit of a surprise to Claire—

"It just doesn't sound like you," Claire insists. "Tell me, are you in love with him?"

"He's awfully attractive in many ways."

"That's what I mean, I guess. If you were swept off your feet by some great romantic impulse, that would be different. But this way it all sounds—well, just a little cold-blooded."

"But that's just it! If I were mad about him I wouldn't consider it for a minute. Because nothing could ever come of it, and I'd just end up being terribly unhappy."

"And as it is, you think you can eat your cake and have it, too. Is that it?"

"Well, that does sound cold-blooded. It isn't quite like that. He's a clever, successful, good-looking man. And I *am* attracted to him. He's not making any demand of me or pretending that he's in love with me. If it's all right for him, why isn't it for me?"

"You're desperately logical about it."

"Why do men have to have a monopoly on logic?"

"I don't know why. But, somehow, when a woman falls back on logic—"

"That's just a hangover from the days when women led sheltered lives; just another one of those superstitions that men have prompted to make women feel dependent and inferior. It's time we stopped being a lot of fluttery, scatterbrained little ninnies, who have to rely on something called intuition. Why can't we work out our problems, just as men do, by using our intelligence?"

"It really looks as though Mr. Hand *has* been using the right technique!"

Georgina is not being fooled by technique, she insists. She has thought everything out clearly. What if she should be hurt emotionally? It might be a good thing for her. Her life lately has been slipping into some pretty monotonous grooves.

"He thinks I'm puritanical. And I'm afraid he may be right," admits Georgina.

"Afraid?"

"Well, after all, what is a puritan? Just somebody with such strong desires that she doesn't dare let herself cut loose. Look at all the drunks and bachelor girls you meet who had the strictest kind of upbringing. And once they kick over the traces, there's no stopping them."

"Oh, so that's what you are afraid of. You think if you say yes to him it will be just your first step on the road to hell?"

"That would be pretty awful, wouldn't it?"

"It would, indeed! Well, darling, I think I'll pop out and do some shopping, while you wrestle with your little psychic censor. Think you can look after the trade by yourself?"

"Oh, damn it! I wish you'd be a little helpful."

"No, my pet! This is between you and your guardian angel. And I can't wait to see who wins."

"Neither can I."

Georgina sits for a moment, deep in thought. Then a lurid red light comes on, revealing a lamppost. A moment later Georgina, wearing a shabby scarlet coat, swaggers on, carrying a red handbag. She leans against the post, looking about with "a bold, alert glance."

Presently George Hand saunters in with a smartly-dressed girl on his arm; a girl who looks a lot like Georgina's sister Miriam. George is telling his friend about the food they serve at Antoine's in New Orleans. Out of the corner of his eye he sees Georgina. Before she can turn and run he has excused himself from his companion and caught Georgina by the arm.

"Hands off, you!" growls Georgina, in her best streetwalker manner.

"Why, I was right! It's Georgina Allerton!"

"Well, what's it *to* you?"

"What are you doing here, hanging around a street corner?"

"Looking after my trade, that's what."

"But—a girl like you! What's brought you to this?"

"It would give you a kick, wouldn't it, to hear all about it? You're all like that."

"But in Mexico you were such a gay, proud girl, full of the joy of living and dreaming of all the things you were going to do."

"I didn't know how easy it would be to say yes the next time someone asked me. And the next time after that it was easier still. Then they stopped asking me—and I began asking them. Now you know all about it. So, go ahead and scram!"

"Georgina, is there anything I can—"

"To hell with that! I don't want your pity."

"Well, let me at least—"

Hand has taken a bill from his pocket, which he presses on Georgina. She takes it, tears it in pieces and throws the pieces in his face. "Go on now! Beat it! Your girl friend is waiting for you!"

"For Heaven's sake, what was all that about?" demands his companion, as Hand rejoins her.

"It's tragic," sighs Hand. "I used to know that girl, years ago. And, believe it or not, she was a sweet, modest little—" They have disappeared.

For a moment Georgina is reduced to sobs, but the sound of someone approaching, whistling merrily, sets her up again.

"Got a date for tonight, dearie?" she asks the newcomer, who turns out to be Clark Redfield.

"Sorry, baby, but I've got a little wife waiting for me—" And then he recognizes Georgina as "the girl who used to run that crummy little bookshop on East—"

"Well, I'll be damned!" snorts Clark, and with raucous laughter he continues to sneer at this "highly cultivated young college grad" until she slaps him soundly in the face.

"Shut up, you great big ape!" she screams.

That is more than Clark can take. He starts away in a rage in search of an officer. No sooner has he disappeared than Georgina whips a small bottle from her pocket and drains it. From the near distance she can hear Jim Lucas calling to her to stop. The next minute she is in Jim's arms explaining between dying gasps that she could not have come to him for help—because—

". . . You have Miriam and those three lovely children," Georgina reminds him. "Once I brought you two together again there was no place for me in your life. There's no place for me anywhere." She totters and he catches her. "Hold me, Jim! Hold me! Don't say anything, Jim. Just hold me. I wanted to live in your arms but it wasn't to be. So let me die in them. Good-by, Jim! . . . It is a far, far better thing that I do than I have ever done! It is a far, far better rest I go to than I have ever known."

"Georgina, Georgina! My darling!"

Clark is back with an officer. Startled to discover what has happened, he is terribly, terribly sorry.

"Oh, why did I do it? If only I'd been a little human to her!" He turns to the policeman: "Officer, arrest me! Take me away!"

"What for?"

"I'm a murderer! I killed that girl as surely as though I had stabbed her to the heart."

"Then come along!" The law snaps a pair of handcuffs on Clark Redfield's wrists.

As the lights fade the clanging patrol-wagon bell is heard. It shortly merges with the ringing of a telephone. The lights are up on the bookshop and Georgina is answering the phone. A second light discloses Clark Redfield in a phone booth. It takes him a minute to recognize Georgina's voice. She sounds scared to death.

Georgina is soon in command of herself, however, and she is not at all inclined to talk with Clark. Certainly she does not want to hear any apologies. Nor is she at all interested in his suggestion that she go with him that evening to a show—

"You really have got the hide of an elephant!" says Georgina. "What makes you think I'd even consider—"

"Well, it's the opening of 'The Merchant of Venice' with James Zerney as Shylock. And I thought it might appeal to a lover of the classics."

That gives Georgina pause. Hilda Vincent is going to play Portia. Georgina had gone to college with Hilda. But Georgina is firm. No, it is not a date! No, she—

The operator has cut them off. Clark fishes for another nickel. He hasn't any. Nor can the operator change the five-dollar bill he is waving at the phone. He barely has time to shout that the number is Circle 5-7933 and ask Georgina to call him back. Then he is cut off.

Slowly Georgina copies the phone number on a pad. She has

just about decided to call back when the phone rings. In another spot of light George Hand is telephoning from his office.

Hand is excited because a dinner date has blown up on him and he wants Georgina to fill in. They could take their time over a good dinner and then go dancing—or to a show.

No, Georgina couldn't do that. She has just promised someone else to go to the theatre. No, she wouldn't consider cocktails and dinner before the show—she thinks that's all included. If anything should happen she will call George back.

"Well, I'll keep my fingers crossed," says Hand, resignedly. "Because I've got you very much on my mind. And if I do lose tonight, I'll owe you lunch tomorrow—yes?"

Yes, Georgina will consider that. A moment later she has begun slowly to dial Clark's number. Clark, meantime, has waited as long as his patience will hold and left the booth. But he comes rushing back just in time to get the call.

"The only reason I called back," Georgina is saying, "is that I don't want you to have the false impression that I'm sufficiently interested in anything you may have said, this morning or at any other time, to make me feel the slightest bit of resentment."

"Phew! (*Whistling.*) I was afraid you were never going to get to the end of that one! Now, to get back to the 'Merchant of Venice.' "

"Yes, exactly. In the first place, I have no interest whatever in being taken to the theatre by you. But I would like to see Hilda Vincent play Portia, so—"

"Right! So you'll—"

"Will you please let me finish?"

"If you think you can by eight-forty."

"What I started to say is that I'll consider it only on a strictly business basis."

"I have a feeling that neither of us knows what you're talking about."

"What I mean is, if you have an extra ticket on your hands, I'll be glad to buy it from you."

"Can't be done. These are press seats."

"Oh, are you going to review the play?"

"I am not. I got them from our movie critic. His mother is getting married tonight and he has to give her away."

"Do the movie critics get tickets for plays, too?"

"Look, Georgina, this is one of those booths where you have to stand up. How about meeting me at—"

"Are you dressing?"

"Certainly not! Nobody dresses for Shakespeare, unless Bea Lillie happens to be in it."

"Then I'll meet you in the lobby at eight-thirty."

But there is the question of dinner still to be settled. Georgina would escape that, too, unless they can "go Dutch." But Clark finally talks her into meeting him at Emilio's, "a spaghetti and red ink joint on Forty-seventh Street just west of Eighth Avenue."

Then another problem looms. Jim Lucas is in also to beg a dinner date. He is off for Reno next day and he wants to have a talk with Georgina before he goes. He has had another talk with Miriam. She doesn't want to leave her obstetrician, so Jim has agreed to make the Reno trip.

What Jim really wants to talk to Georgina about is the future—their future—after the divorce—

"Georgina, I came here this morning—confused, wounded, driven by some impulse I didn't even attempt to analyze," Jim relates. "And then, all at once, the moment I left you, I understood why I had come. . . . It was because instinctively, unconsciously, I knew it was you I always wanted."

Georgina would stop Jim from going on, if she could. She evades his demand for a direct answer to her feeling for him. After all Jim is still married to her sister. He is hurt, troubled, and she thinks he is imagining a good many things—"Just because I have tried to be a little sympathetic and understanding you've suddenly jumped to the conclusion—"

"No, that's not true! I may be a failure in a material sense, a mendicant in the market place, but emotionally I've come into my own, at last. I know what I want. It's a life with you, Georgina."

Georgina is not unmoved, but she is troubled. She had never dreamed of things happening this way. She had rather wait six weeks, until he is free and after they have had plenty of time to think things over. Then, after he gets back, and is free—

Jim isn't coming back. He is determined to get back to nature "where I can stretch my arms and legs, where I can see the stars and smell the earth. I know now that it's what I have always wanted."

"I've dreamed of that, sometimes, too," Georgina admits. "Just running off somewhere, anywhere."

With that encouragement Jim would have Georgina come with him now, this night. But that would hardly be decent, protests Georgina. Even if it weren't for Miriam, she couldn't do a thing like that. Of course people do day-dream about all sorts of things—but when they are faced with reality they have to stop and think. The best Jim can get from her is a hurried promise to see him off at the airport at midnight. . . .

Mrs. Allerton calls to warn Georgina of the situation in the Lucas family and to plead with her, should Jim come crying to her, to be very careful not to say anything that might discourage him from leaving at once for Reno. Of course she (Mrs. A.) is footing the bills, but she is sure this is one expenditure poor old Grandpa would approve of.

Georgina will not be home until late, she warns her mother. She is having dinner out and going to the opening of "The Merchant of Venice" and somewhere afterward. Not, as Mrs. Allerton hopes, with a promising male, but with no one but "just a boorish, conceited newspaper man in whom nobody could have the slightest interest."

"Sounds like a charming evening," Mrs. Allerton, stifling a sneeze, suggests.

"Well, I haven't been to a first night in years," explains Georgina. "Besides, Hilda Vincent is playing Portia and I want to see her."

"What is there in it for the young man?"

"I don't know. I haven't any idea why he asked me, except that he is sadistic and is planning to spend the evening making me feel uncomfortable."

"It certainly looks as though Mr. Right had come along at last," says Mrs. Allerton.

"Well, well—have fun."

The lights fade quickly on Mrs. Allerton and come up again on a table at Emilio's, "a modest but gay little Italian restaurant." Clark Redfield, impatiently reading a newspaper, is shortly joined by Georgina. Georgina is a little late, but by mutual consent they agree not to start fighting until later.

Calling Luigi, the waiter, Clark takes over the ordering. Georgina thinks she would like a Martini, but Clark decides not. With Italian food it would be better if she had a mixed vermouth, frappéed. She would skip the minestrone, but Clark thinks she should have at least a little. Then spaghetti Bolognese, scallopini à la Marsala, and eggplant Parmigiana. That will be much too much for her, Georgina protests, but Clark thinks otherwise. They will have what he has ordered, he tells Luigi, with a mixed green salad added. Finally they will top off the meal with a couple portions of Zuppe Inglese, a kind of rum cake. As for wine, Clark prefers the Falerno to the Lacrime Christi—

By which time Georgina has quit protesting.

Through dinner they talk of many things. Georgina is a little excited about seeing Hilda Vincent. Besides, Georgina had once played Portia in a High School production. She knows "The Merchant of Venice" by heart. At school she had very much wanted to become an actress. But her father wanted her to be a lawyer, so she tried one semester at law school. Now, of course, it is too late—

"So you turned to literature?" Clark is smiling.

"Let's keep off that subject, if you don't mind."

"Which reminds me that I have brought back your script." Clark produces a large envelope from underneath the table.

"That's very thoughtful of you, I'm sure," tartly admits Georgina. "But it might have been a little more practical to have brought it back tomorrow, instead of lugging it all through dinner and theatre."

"Aren't you forgetting that you told me never to enter your shop again?"

"You could have mailed it."

Clark is in a mood to celebrate. Oliver Quinn, one of his paper's best sports writers, is leaving to take the chair of Icelandic literature in the University of Michigan. That will mean promotions and a chance for Clark to break into sports. They drink to that. Still, Georgina is puzzled—

"I can't understand it. People getting all excited about which team scores the most runs or who knocks out who."

"Nothing hard about that. Every time the champ comes up with a haymaker, forty thousand customers are taking a swing at the boss or the traffic cop. And when the King of Swat whams it into the bleachers, a million flat-chested runs are right in there, whizzing around bases."

"That's nothing but escapism."

"That's right. Like the girls out of college who slam the door with Nora, take a nose dive into the brook with Ophelia, or tumble into a lot of Louis Quatorze beds with Opal."

"We'll just pass over the personal implications and confine ourselves to the abstract question whether an interest in sports and an interest in literature—"

"There is no such thing as an abstract discussion between a man and a woman."

"Well, that certainly reveals a narrow and conventional mind."

"Who's getting personal now? You see, every road we take

leads right back to that novel of yours."

"Will you stop harping on that?" Georgina demands, angrily. "What in hell has my novel got to do—! I certainly was an idiot ever to show it to you!"

"But you did! And the reason you did was that you thought you had produced something creative and wanted to show it off!"

"Nothing of the kind. I mistook you for a literary critic and I wanted—"

"Baloney! You were just a fond mama, showing off her baby, and blindly oblivious to the fact that it was just an old rag doll with straw stuffing coming through. Talk about escapism! Why, there wasn't a genuine moment in it—just a re-hash of all the English lady writers from Jane Austen to Katherine Mansfield and Virginia Woolf."

"All right, I've heard enough about it!"

An aroused Georgina is more interesting to Clark than a passive one. Despite her protests he continues to twit her about her novel; about her heroine who spends a lot of time "moony day-dreaming"; about her hero, "a balmy Jim Lucas," who might very well have sat for that portrait—

". . . For God's sake, hasn't anything ever happened to you? Have you never been drunk? Or socked a guy for making a pass at you? Or lost your panties on Fifth Avenue?"

"You think you're going to make me lose my temper, don't you?" snaps Georgina.

"Well, I'm sorry to disappoint you, but you're not. However, I do find you even more offensive than I had expected, so, if you'll excuse me, I think I'll just leave you to your splendid repast, while I—"

Georgina has started to rise, but with a curt "You'll certainly do nothing of the kind," Clark pushes her back in her seat and goes on with his analysis of character. Does she think that he is going to have Luigi's feelings lacerated? The preparation and serving of food is a serious business to Luigi and his helpers!

As they are eating their minestrone the lights fade out on the table. A few seconds later, and to the sound of a string quartet playing Elizabethan music, they come up dimly on a section of a theatre consisting of eight or ten seats arranged in rows and facing an unseen stage. Presently an usher appears, followed by Georgina and Clark, he with the script of Georgina's novel under his arm—

"Well, I'm glad we're not late," Georgina is saying. "I hate to come in after the curtain is up."

"I know a girl who was dropped from the Social Register for admitting that she had seen the first act of a play," reports Clark. "She finally put an end to herself by taking an overdose of caviar."

Clark and Georgina continue to shoot stinging, verbal arrows at each other until the music comes to an end and the lights are lowered for the rise of the curtain. A moment later the first lines of "The Merchant" come floating in from the darkness— Antonio is addressing Salarino and Salanio—

" 'In sooth, I know not why I am so sad;
It wearies me; you say it worries you,
But how I caught it, found it, or came by it,
I am to learn!" . . .

Salarino has barely started his reply ("Your mind is tossing on the ocean"), before Georgina's attention begins to wander. The voices of the actors grow fainter and fainter. Georgina is staring into space. "After a moment the Theatre Manager, wearing a dinner jacket and looking for all the world like Mr. Allerton," appears in the aisle and makes straight for Georgina, leaning across Clark to speak to her.

The Manager has come to tell Georgina, in a tense voice, that Hilda Vincent has collapsed in her dressing room and there is no understudy. Won't she (Georgina) please help them out? Miss Vincent has remembered that Miss Allerton is familiar with the role of Portia. It will save the refunding of thousands of dollars and the dismissal of the audience if she only will. "Miss Vincent told me to beg you in the name of your alma mater to—"

"All right! I will! I'll try!"

"You'll make a fool of yourself!" whispers Clark, as she pushes by him into the aisle.

"I'd rather be a fool than a coward!"

"That's the spirit, Miss Allerton!" agrees the manager. "I know you'll come through. This way, please."

A minute later the voice of the Manager can be heard making the announcement of Miss Vincent's illness, followed by his discovery of Miss Georgina Allerton in the audience—

"I am sure you will show Miss Allerton every indulgence, in view of the fact that she is going on at a moment's notice and without even a rehearsal. Thank you!"

Now the lights have come up on a small elevated stage. Georgina, in the dress of a Venetian Doctor of Laws, is facing the audience. A spotlight reveals Clark's face. He is grinning sardonically as Georgina begins to speak—

"'The quality of mercy is not strained,
It droppeth as the gentle rain from heaven
Upon the place beneath—'"

Gradually, as Georgina continues, the expression on Clark's face begins to soften. At the end of the speech he is almost in tears. There is an outburst of applause, cheers and cries of "Bravo!" Clark sniffles. Four ushers come down the aisle laden with flowers. Georgina, with her arms filled with flowers, is bowing to the right and to the left.

As Georgina comes back to her seat, Clark meets her in the aisle. "Georgina! You were magnificent!"

"Don't try to flatter me! I know you don't mean it!"

"But I do! I swear to you I do! You were superb; sincere, moving, eloquent, forceful, charming."

"That's a lot, isn't it, for a girl who doesn't know anything, a girl who can't do anything?"

"I take it all back, Georgina—every word of it. I've done you an injustice, completely misunderstood you—"

But the dream-Georgina is not to be mollified. She is through with Clark—

From the stage comes the voice of Portia—"'A gentle riddance. Draw the curtains, go. Let all of his complexion choose me so.'"

As the lights come up Georgina, startled, joins the applauders.

"Shall we have a smoke?" Clark is saying. The audience is beginning to file out.

"Yes, all right. It's good, isn't it?"

"Why, I don't believe you heard a word of it."

"Why, I heard every syllable." Georgina is quite indignant. "What do you mean—?"

"Go on! You were off in some cloud cuckoo-land."

A moment later Clark is trying quite seriously to elucidate his meaning. "The point is that you are a day-dreamer," he charges. "You live in a world of fantasy, instead of in a world of reality."

"What is this reality you keep talking about?" demands Georgina.

"I was hoping you wouldn't ask me that, because I'm not sure that I know the answer. But I'm pretty sure that it means living your life out and not dreaming it away."

"If a dream is real to you, why isn't it as real as something you do?"

"Because dreaming is easy and life is hard. Because when you dream, you make your own rules, but when you try to do something, the rules are made for you by the limitations of your own nature and the shape of the world you live in. Because no matter how much you win in your dreams, your gains are illusory, and you always come away empty-handed. But in life, whether you win or lose, you've always got something to show for it—even if it's only a scar or a painful memory."

"Scars are ugly and pain hurts."

"Without ugliness there would be no beauty. And if we never knew pain we'd never know the value of pleasure." . . .

They are still enjoying their first really sympathetic, understanding talk when Georgina, realizing the time, decides to call the airport. The waiter brings the phone to the table, and that is how Clark discovers that the midnight date is with Jim Lucas. He is not surprised, but he is plainly disgusted. So Lucas is going to Reno? Is Georgina going with him? No, but she may join him later. Then she and Jim will probably get married and get themselves a ranch—

This is too much for Clark. He is laughing immoderately. "A ranch! You and Jim Lucas! Why, it's right straight out of that novel of yours. 'Love Among the Heifers': a pastoral in nine cantos, with costumes by Abercrombie and Fitch."

A moment later Georgina feels like dancing and Clark is receptive. Soon they are exchanging compliments—bantering, satirical, self-conscious compliments. When the music stops they go back to the table and order another drink. And another sandwich—white fish on rye toast—without any onion.

Now Clark has borrowed three or four nickels from Georgina and gone to telephone. As Georgina gazes dreamily after him the lights fade out. A moment later they are up again on a bare stage. Following a persistent knocking a man in slippers and an old-fashioned flannel nightshirt appears. He looks a good deal like Mr. Allerton and he is very cross. Who's there and what do they want? Of course he's Justice of the Peace Billings or he wouldn't be there. So they want to get married? They do—

"Well, jimminy crickets, can't you wait until morning?" growls the Justice.

"No, we can't. It's an emergency," Clark's voice is heard to answer.

"Some folks ain't got the sense they were born with!" declares the Justice. And, as a clock is heard to cuckoo twice he adds: "Well, I'll be danged! Two o'clock! Time you young folks was in bed, 'stead of gallivantin' around."

"We know it. But we thought we ought to get married first," explains Clark.

On with the ceremony. But just as Justice Billings is about to pronounce them man and wife, Georgina suddenly calls out: "No! No! Stop it, Georgina! You mustn't go on like this! You mustn't!"

Now she is back at the table, twisting her hands in agony and mumbling to herself: "I'm at it again—drugging myself with dreams. And when I come to, all I'll get from him is a slap in the face. I don't really mean anything to him. He doesn't care a damn for me. He's just having fun with me—just giving me the run-around, that's all. He's calling up to find out if he won his bet on Wilinski—that means more to him than I do. And he'll come back and grin at me—make me feel like the ninny that I am. (*Springing to her feet.*) No! I can't! I can't take it! I can't face the pain of it! I'll go before he gets back. I'll never see him again. I'll—I'll never see him again. I'll—I'll—Oh, I don't know! Anything—anything not to hear the bitter truth from his lips."

She has started out when Jim Lucas appears. Thank God he's there! She had been bewildered, but now she sees things clearly. She wants him to take her with him. Let him forget what she said. Let him forget everything. Just take her away before it is too late—

Jim is confused and flustered. He will telephone the airport and see if there is space. Before he can do that Clark comes bursting back. Everything is lovely with Clark. He had won his bet on Wilinski. Then he sees Jim—and Georgina—

"You look as though you were going some place," he says to Georgina.

"I'm going away with Jim," she announces. "Good-by, and congratulate Wilinski for me."

CLARK—We'll send a joint wire from Grand Central. Better snap it up, Jim, or you'll miss your plane.

JIM—Yes. Come along, Georgina.

CLARK—She's not going with you.

GEORGINA—Who says I'm not?

CLARK—I do.

JIM—Who gave you the right to—?

CLARK—Nobody. I took it. (*To* GEORGINA.) We've got just twenty minutes to catch a train to Greenwich. I know it's a kind of a picayune trip for a girl who thinks in terms of Mexico and the high Sierras, but it's the best I could whip up on short notice.

GEORGINA (*chokingly*)—Clark—Clark, I'm a serious girl— I really am. It's my whole life. I wouldn't know how to take a joke.

CLARK—Neither would that fellow up there who issues marriage licenses. He was sore as a pup when I woke him. (GEORGINA *turns away.*)

JIM (*going to her*)—Georgina, think of what you're doing! You're just throwing yourself away on the impulse of a moment.

GEORGINA—It's the moment I've been waiting for, all my life. Please forgive me, Jim, if I've been cruel and inconsiderate. But, believe me, this is the way it has to be.

TAXI-DRIVER (*entering and approaching* JIM)—Say, Doc, if you wanna make that plane—

JIM (*despairingly*)—Georgina—

GEORGINA—Good-by, Jim. Good luck! (*He looks at her for a moment and then exits quickly. Her eyes fill with tears.*) Poor Jim!

CLARK—That form of contempt we call pity.

GEORGINA (*shocked*)—What a thing to say! You *are* a tough guy, aren't you? You scare me to death.

CLARK—Good! Well, come on! What are you waiting for?

GEORGINA—Are you sure you don't think we should sleep over it?

CLARK (*taking her arm*)—We will, eventually. Look, if we don't leave this minute, we'll miss that train. Oh, didn't you order that sandwich?

GEORGINA—Oh, I'm sorry! I forgot all about it.

CLARK—Day-dreaming again?

GEORGINA—Afraid so. About you and me.

CLARK—That was no day-dream. That was my wife. Come along!

Faint strains of the Lohengrin Wedding March are heard. The lights are out on the restaurant and a few seconds later are up to reveal a bedroom "through the frame of a double French window. In the room is a double bed with a baggage rack at the foot of it, and a bed table with telephone, beside it."

An elderly bellboy shows Georgina and Clark in and makes them comfortable in the usual elderly bellboy fashion.

"Well, Mrs. Redfield—!" Clark is holding out his arms.

Georgina evades him. "I *must* call up my parents," she says, sitting on the bed and picking up the telephone.

"Are you aware that all through our engagement and married life we have not exchanged as much as one kiss?" protests her groom.

"Well, when have we had time, for Heaven's sake?" demands Georgina.

"There was the taxi to the station."

"You were busy swearing at the driver for not getting us there faster."

"There was the train from New York."

"Filled with commuters! Besides we were sitting on opposite sides of the aisle."

"We could have leaned across!"

"I'd rather not start married life with a crick in the neck."

Georgina has got the operator and given the Allerton New York number. "They're going to think this is a little sudden," she predicts.

"Well, I suppose it is. Tell me something: when did you first know you really loved me?"

"When you canceled the onion with the sandwich."

A second light reveals a bedroom in the Allerton apartment. The senior Allertons are in twin beds. Mrs. A. answers the phone. Mr. A. groans and turns over. Mrs. A. is a little irritable. She is still sneezing, but manages to grope for some cleansing tissue under her pillow before she answers the phone. Georgina's message is a startler— She is at the Nickelby Head Hotel in Greenwich and married? Married, to whom? To a man she knows. His name is Clark Redfield. He had taken her to dinner and the theatre—and then—

"Good grief!" ejaculates Mrs. Allerton. "Don't tell me it's that boorish, conceited newspaper man!"

"Yes, that's the one!" answers Georgina, happily.

"Is he anything like Jim?"

"Nothing whatever."

"Well, thank God for that, anyhow." . . .

Georgina has hung up. "They seemed awfully pleased about it," she reports.

CLARK—Yes, and without even meeting me. (*Looking at his watch.*) It's two-thirty. I'm not used to being up so late. (*He tries again to take her in his arms.*)

GEORGINA—Wait! There's just one thing I'd like to know.

CLARK—Well, make it snappy.

GEORGINA—Do I have to give up dreaming altogether? Couldn't I just sort of taper off?

CLARK—Well, I'll be reasonable about it, as long as you run your dreams, instead of letting them run you.

GEORGINA—I know! "If you can dream and not make dreams your master—" Do you think Kipling will live?

CLARK—Look, I didn't come all the way up here to discuss literature. Oh, damn it!

GEORGINA—What?

CLARK—I left that script of yours at the night-club. Oh, well, I guess we won't need it tonight. (*He comes down to the window-frame and pulls a cord at the right, drawing a heavy drapery across the windows.*)

GEORGINA (*behind the drapery, ecstatically*)—Oh, darling, I feel as though this were all some wonderful dream!

THE CURTAIN FALLS

THE RUGGED PATH

A Drama in Two Acts

By Robert E. Sherwood

SOMETIMES it happens that a professional drama critic, aiming at a dramatist, also manages to hit a nail on the head. It happened so in the case of "The Rugged Path," the Robert E. Sherwood drama having to do with that esteemed liberal's first-hand observation of World War II.

"Because of its two separate parts 'The Rugged Path' often seems to be two separate plays," wrote Lewis Nichols in the New York *Times* the Sunday following the play's New York production on November 10, 1945. "The approach to the first is intellectual; the second is more active."

"The Rugged Path" was, in very fact, two separate plays originally. At least it came to life in the Sherwood mind as two plays. One was to be directly concerned with the editorial actions and reactions of influential journalists toward their government at a time of national and international crises. The other was to consider and report the adventure of a GI of better than average intelligence in his search for understanding as to what the whole blooming mess was about, and why he was mixed up in it.

The first play, naturally, would be focused on some segment of the American scene. The other, it was Mr. Sherwood's conviction, could be developed most reasonably in one of the occupied countries. The two ideas became fused after the dramatist, having finished his work for the government, and having just returned from a mission in the Pacific, decided that the Philippines presented the most reasonable locale. Thus the two plays became one play, with one hero representing both the journalistic crusader and the investigating GI.

The first months following the birth of "The Rugged Path" were rugged indeed. Spencer Tracy, one-time sturdy favorite of the Broadway drama, later an even sturdier favorite of the Hollywood drama, was announced for the leading role. Mr. Tracy, at first greatly enthused, later began to wonder if "The Rugged

"The Rugged Path," copyright 1946 *by Robert E. Sherwood. Published by Charles Scribner's Sons, New York.*

ɪto by *Graphic House.*

"THE RUGGED PATH"

)octor—You wanted to get to sea— You wanted combat duty—
Iorey—Well, sir, I guess my feelings are summed up by that quotation from Book of Job—"Yea, his soul draweth nearer unto the grave, and his life he destroyers."

(*Spencer Tracy, Howard Ferguson*)

Path" was really the best drama he could find for a temporary return to the legitimate theatre. One day he was sure. The next day he wondered. The third day he consulted with friends. And finally he decided: He would take on the Sherwood drama for a sort of test flight, but with mental reservations.

The first performance was in Providence, R. I., with Washington and Boston following. The critical reviews were varied, but never too enthusiastic. In Boston Mr. Tracy quit. His personal success was tremendous, his personal notices were highly flattering, and business at the box office was booming, but he dreaded facing the New York critics. Finally he was again won over, and the New York engagement was begun. Again the reception of the play was both satisfying and discouraging—satisfying as to business and audience response, discouraging as to the personal reactions of several critics—and Mr. Tracy.

Conferences went on for weeks—for ten weeks, in fact. Then the Playwrights' Company withdrew the play and Mr. Tracy returned to Hollywood, sadder, wiser and doubtless determined, so help him, never, never to leave his complicated but comparatively peaceful studio life again.

Despite its unhappy adventures, it seems to this editor that "The Rugged Path" is an interesting, frequently eloquent and always honest report on several vitally important aspects of a democracy at war. Hence its inclusion in this year book.

It is December, 1940. The scene is a small reception room in the White House, just outside the office of the President of the United States. The routine of an average day is being carried out. Christmas approaching, Jamieson, "an elderly, dignified Negro butler," is hanging a wreath on the door at the left side of the room. It isn't going to be a very merry Christmas, Jamieson fears, but—"We all try to keep the old spirit alive," he explains. "Peace on earth—good will to men. People like to know that the old spirit is alive, here in this house."

It is getting late. General MacGlorn, the President's Military Aide, is glad to report that there is but one more appointment—that of Morey Vinion, the newspaper correspondent. The President will probably want to talk to Morey, who is just back from Europe, a long time, but MacGlorn is reasonably sure that it will be safe to telephone Mrs. MacGlorn that her husband will be home for dinner by seven-thirty.

A moment later Morey Vinion arrives. He is a solid citizen in his early forties, calm, resourceful, well-poised. He is taking a cigarette from a somewhat battered metal case when General MacGlorn comes to greet him.

Morey, it appears, has been recalled from his correspondence job abroad, following the death of the owner of the paper on which he works. No, he has not been made boss of the paper, as MacGlorn has heard. The boss is George Bowsmith, Jr., son of the late publisher. Morey is only the editor.

MacGlorn understands that. "But, you can do a lot. You can steer the paper toward being a little more friendly to *my* boss in there," he suggests.

"Don't ask for the impossible, General," cautions Morey, with a grin.

The correspondent's report of his recent experiences on the other side are not too cheerful. He had not enjoyed writing the reports he had written about the way the English were taking the blitz.

"It took the bombs on London to convince them finally that there's a war on," he says. "Maybe we'll have to wait for the blitz to come to us here."

"If we do wait for that to happen," predicts MacGlorn, "it could mean nothing less than the end of this republic. You were at Dunkirk, weren't you, Morey?"

"Last Spring I came out of Dunkirk on a little old paddle wheel excursion boat called the *Belle of Brighton.* The Messerschmitts were after us and the U-boats and the E-boats and everything else they could throw in. But we got through and landed at Margate and I hitch-hiked a ride on a truck and we drove through the lovely English countryside. I tell you, General, it was unbelievable. You'd think that the people there would have been out frantically stringing barbed-wire or digging trenches to stop the German invasion. But they weren't—they were playing cricket. It was a week-end! Germans or no Germans, the English were playing cricket in their immaculate white pants."

"I imagine they're not playing much cricket now."

"They know how to take it, all right. And our people would know how to take it. But—this morning, after I landed in New York on the Clipper—I drove through the streets and saw the crowds out Christmas shopping. They seemed to have plenty of money and not a care in the world. I couldn't help thinking, General, that *we're* off for the week-end, too, an endless week-end. I couldn't help wondering whether we'll ever wake up and realize that it's Monday."

A moment later the buzzer buzzes and MacGlorn takes Morey in to see the President. The lights fade.

The curtain falls.

In June of the year following we are in the living room of the Morey Vinions' home "in one of the most fashionable suburbs of a medium-sized American city." A pleasant room, but everything in it seems to be there for purposes of ornament rather than for comfort or utility.

Called to the telephone, Harriet Vinion tries to explain to her friend Nora that she (Harriet) will do all she can to get George (her brother) to do what he can with the people he knows in the War Department in Washington to help keep her son, Johnny, from being drafted. The very idea! Johnny drafted? *That's terrible!*

Harriet's chance to speak to her brother about Johnny is practically immediate. George Bowsmith, a modestly aggressive, rather worried young man, on his way to Larry McLeod's camp in the Adirondacks to get some week-end fishing, stops in for a talk with Morey. Of course he will do what he can to get Johnny out of his mess.

But it is Morey about whom George is most concerned. There is something about Morey these days that George senses as a sort of vague dissatisfaction—

"You're crazy," Harriet is quick to inform her brother. "He's happier than he's ever been. He's got his own home, at last—the one thing that he wanted, after all the years of banging around Europe, when we hardly ever got to see each other. He *loves* this house. He has his own library in there—and that damned short-wave radio—and when he gets home at all hours of the night he can go out in the kitchen and cook scrambled eggs. What gives you the idea that he isn't happy?"

Then the story comes out. There is a young man named Gil Hartnick on the paper. "He's a young Jewish boy—very bright, like so many of them. Got his Phi Beta Kappa key at Cornell, and then he was a Rhodes Scholar, and now he's out to reform the world."

"You mean you think he's a Communist?"

"Nooo—maybe a little pinkish—but that's all," qualifies George, tolerantly. "Morey's very fond of him."

"Well—there's nothing new in that—Morey's fond of a lot of odd people."

Morey wants to send Hartnick to London to cover the war.

Leggatt Burt, the business manager of the Bowsmith paper, doesn't approve. And Morey has insisted that if he can't send Hartnick, he will have to go himself.

"Maybe that's why he's been listening to Berlin—and London —and all those places," suggests Harriet. "You mustn't pay any attention to what Leggatt Burt says about this. Let him worry about the advertising. Morey is the editor—and if he wants to send Hartnick to London, you ought to back him up."

George isn't sure about that. And another thing. Without wanting to get personal, George would like to know if Harriet and Morey have been getting along all right. In spite of everything, he doesn't believe that Morey *is* happy.

"There's nothing new in that," answers Harriet. "He's never been really happy—well—not since—not for a long time. When he got down to work in Europe, he began to take everything to heart as though he were personally involved, instead of being just an American reporter. He seemed to identify himself more and more with all the dreary business in Austria and Spain and the League of Nations and—and he's still doing it! This Spring, when the Germans went into Greece—whenever they bomb London—you'd think they were invading him."

In addition to this attitude, it was very plain to Harriet that Morey did not want her to stay with him in Europe and that he does not want to stay at home with her now.

"He hasn't got himself adjusted yet," says George, in an effort to ease Harriet's very evident unhappiness. "But—he'll settle down, and rediscover his own country, and he'll begin to realize that we have a few problems here at home that are a lot more important to us than all the wars and all the politics in Europe. Morey is a smart guy. He'll snap out of it."

Now Morey is home and can talk for himself. He greets George amiably, offers him a drink, listens to his plans for his fishing trip, and although he admits that in the newspaper business week-ends are traditionally dangerous, he thinks it will be fairly safe for George to take this holiday.

"I'll be back about a week from Monday," promises George, "and then I think we ought to get together for some staff conferences. Leggatt has some ideas for a campaign we ought to run this Summer—he thinks we ought to try to get people's minds off the war in Europe so that we can stimulate summer resort business. Some of the advertisers are hollering for it. Anyway, it's worth discussing, and I'd like to hear your views."

"You'll hear them."

"Fine! I'd like to see you and Leggatt get into a knock-down drag-out fight. I tell you, Morey—I can't tell you how wonderful it is to have you here. The paper's coming back to life, the way it was before the old man cracked up. Stick to it, kid. We're all with you. Good-by, Sis. 'By, Morey."

Morey, back from seeing George to the door, is of a mind to join Harriet in a drink. Also he would very much like to know what George had come for. Harriet is evasive.

"Oh, well—if it's family matters, Harriet—I apologetically withdraw the question."

"So you've got ants in your pants again!" says Harriet, looking at him over her drink.

MOREY (*surprised, but amiable*)—Now—really, Harriet—what leads you to that vulgar conclusion?

HARRIET—Why can't you be reasonably honest with me?

MOREY—I'll make every possible attempt to be honest with you as soon as I know just what it is you're talking about.

HARRIET—You want to go back to Europe, don't you?

MOREY—Europe? What do you mean, Europe? There isn't any such place, any more. There's only a continent named Hitler, and I pride myself that I wouldn't be admitted anywhere there.

HARRIET—Well, then—England. You want to leave here and go to London and watch the bombs come down, and even have the supreme satisfaction of getting yourself killed?

MOREY—What did George say to you?

HARRIET—He said that you'd had an argument about somebody—I've forgotten his name—some Jewish reporter.

MOREY—Oh—I'm sorry he bothered you about that. It wasn't a very pleasant episode.

HARRIET—Do you want to get out of here, Morey?

MOREY—No, I don't, I want to stay put for a change. I want to have my own home in my own country. I told you I wanted my own home—and I meant it. And now I've got it. It's a beautiful home. It might possibly be said that this isn't the most appropriate setting for me. But that's in its favor—and I love it—particularly the kitchen, with that automatic range, and the oven, and the ice-box that flashes a light when the cubes are congealed. Why should I want to leave this and go back to that tortured continent?

HARRIET—Only because you're incurably restless by nature. . . .

MOREY—I know, Harriet. That's a nice way of saying I'm a

natural-born tramp. But I suspect that even tramps get tired. I went to Europe in the first place because your father sent me there. He wanted me to learn my trade—that's what he told me at the time. He said to me, "It's tough luck, kid—but Europe's going to be the place where the main news will come from in the next ten years." I learned my trade, all right. And now—the ten years are up—and your father's dead, and George is publisher of the paper, and I'm the editor. And there are roses in the garden and Scotch in the cellarette, and the Germans are on the English Channel and the Isles of Greece. I repeat the question! Why in God's name should I want to go back to that mess over there?

HARRIET—But George said that—

MOREY—What difference does it make what George said? George is all right. He's doing his level best to be a worthy successor to the old man. . . . But—which do you want to be—your father's daughter—or George's sister?

HARRIET (*bitterly*)—I want most to be your wife—God help me.

MOREY (*melting*)—Now that's a very sweet thing to say. . . . (*He takes her hand.*) It hasn't been easy for any of us since your father died. He and I could fight with each other on matters of principle. The old man was a tough adversary—but a fair one. With George, it's different—he hasn't been through the mill—he listens to me and then he listens to the voice of the business department—the clanging, cash register voice of Leggatt Burt. . . . But it will work out, all right. We'll bring George around, eventually.

Harriet has let go Morey's hand. When he would know why, she explains that she felt he was only holding it because he felt sorry for her. Much has happened since he was in love with her, ventures Harriet. Much has happened since they were in love with each other, suggests Morey.

"I am sorry, Harriet. Your father had the situation sized up. When we first got engaged he said: 'You're a damned good newspaper man, Morey, which means that you'll be a damned poor husband.' And that's the way it has worked out. . . ."

But they've got along, Morey insists. They have, agrees Harriet—because they both have good manners. The only thing they really have had in common is their love of her father, and their gratitude to him. Yes, she is willing to admit that when they were married in 1929 it was a different world. Perhaps Morey is right—they haven't had a fair chance to catch up with all that has happened—together.

"I know—you've been in the thick of it—war and revolution—and you've changed, Morey," says Harriet. "But I haven't. I love the same things that I've always known and loved. I don't want to change. I want to live in my own house, with my own family, and friends—and if the rest of the world wants to go to hell, let it go. Is that criminal? Is that shockingly selfish?"

"No, Harriet—but—do you think you could keep the fires of that hell from licking in through those windows?"

"Yes! I do. And that's the real trouble between us. You can't live in peace. There are demons in you. . . . All right—if that's what you want, go on back to London, and have a fine time watching it burn."

For a long moment Morey is silent. "Why did George want to worry you about Gil Hartnick's assignment?" he ponders.

"George has always come to me with his troubles."

"Leggatt Burt must have put him up to this. I can just hear Leggatt saying, 'You go on out to the house and get Harriet to work on Morey. Explain to her that Hartnick is a Jew—not a member of the Country Club. . . .' Well—I'll tell you, dear, much as I admire Leggatt Burt for his sterling qualities as a business man, in this case he's wrong. Gil Hartnick is a good, decent, home-loving American citizen, he's a gentleman and a scholar and he's also one of the best damned writers I've ever seen."

The phone is ringing. Morey answers. The call is from the office. The news is apparently disturbing—

"City desk says there are 'disquieting reports' from Poland. Big German forces massing there—as if for an attack on Russia. That's what *they* say. But I'm late anyway."

"Morey, you're not going back there, are you?"

"No, Harriet, I'm not going back to Europe. Not now. . . . Good-by, dear. I won't be too late tonight. The Sunday edition goes to bed early."

He gives her a kiss and a pat on the back. Harriet sits silent for a moment and then picks up her drink. The lights fade.

The curtain falls.

The next day Morey and Leggatt Burt are sitting in Kenneally's Downtown Bar and Grill. It is a friendly establishment, but only a small part of it is shown—a booth built around a table at which Morey and Burt are sitting, and a part of the bar in the rear.

Morey is drinking orange juice. He is plainly weary and needs a shave. Burt, the business manager, "well-built, well-groomed, masterful but nervous," is finishing a cup of coffee. His nervousness stems partly from his conviction that George Bowsmith is still in the woods fishing when he should be in the office acting on the news.

"The New York *Times* plays it big," says Burt, picking up a paper from the litter on the table. " 'Hitler Begins War on Russia with Armies on March from the Arctic to the Black Sea.' Eight columns!"

"Those guys on the *Times* must have a nose for news," laconically suggests Morey.

Morey, who hasn't been home, is finishing his third breakfast. Yes, he'd knocked off a couple of hours of sleep, on top of his desk. "That pile of unanswered letters makes a good pillow," he tells Burt.

Burt had finally got in touch with Mrs. Bowsmith, but she didn't know when she would see George. That doesn't worry Morey. He can't see what George could do about it anyway. The German Army has invaded the Soviet Union. Could George do anything to stop Hitler—or to help him?

As for the story, Morey will play that for all it is worth, and as he believes the old man would have played it had he lived. Burt, feeling that there is nothing more he can do to boost his end of it, which would be paper sales, thinks he may as well go out to the Country Club for a round of golf, and dinner—

"You probably think that the future of the paper will depend on the stand we take today," Burt ventures. "But—you know as well as I do that the great bulk of our readers don't give a damn what happens in Russia. They're a lot more concerned with the fate of Little Orphan Annie. You'll play it right. You're a good man, Morey. I don't like you—but I've got to admit, you're good."

"On that point, at least, Leggatt, you and I seem to see eye to eye," agrees Morey. . . .

Gil Hartnick has come from the office with a handful of news-ticker sheets. "He is twenty-eight years old. He is good-looking and extremely alert, both physically and intellectually."

Gil's news sheets cover the full text of Winston Churchill's speech and, according to Gil, it's a hell of a good story. He hands the sheets to Morey, who skims them, and agrees. Certainly Churchill hasn't lost any time putting himself on record. And that, to Gil's way of thinking, is what the Bowsmith paper should do—

"What did you say, Gil?" Morey asks.

"I said—we've got to come out with an editorial supporting lend-lease aid for Russia—just like aid for Britain. We take the line that whatever we may have felt in the past about the Soviet Union, they're now fighting the Germans. . . ."

MOREY—Have we been supporting aid for Britain?

GIL—Oh, I know—we've been this way and that way about it. . . .

MOREY—The policy of pernicious anemia.

GIL—But we haven't actually opposed it. We've expressed polite sympathy for the British in their hour of agony. But now the big chips are really down. We could point out that if Hitler conquers Russia, his empire extends to the Pacific—to the Aleutian Islands. We can use those old weasel words about "enlightened self-interest," if you insist.

MOREY (*looking at* GIL)—So you feel that we should send our American goods to the Bolsheviks—give them the products of our American toil and sweat? Take the butter out of the ice-boxes of American housewives and give it to the enemies of religion? That's a fine, popular platform for us to stand on. That's a fine way to make friends with the National Association of Manufacturers.

GIL—Sure, Morey—that's why we've got to speak out before they do. You know what the isolationists will be saying. They'll be screaming for the President to send lend-lease to Hitler to stop the Red Menace. It won't only be America First. It will be all the Silver Shirts and the Christian mobilizers—all of our native Fascists. If we come out now—and show some guts in forcing the real issues—then we'll be performing the real mission of a newspaper. Whereas—if we wait to hear the views of the opposition—well—you know as well as I do what will happen. We'll be hesitating and shilly-shallying—and we'll be underwriting another tragedy of too little and too late.

MOREY—That's a mighty fine speech, my boy. You should have a microphone. But—have you thought this thing through?

GIL—I've tried to.

MOREY—Aid for Russia or for Britain doesn't only mean producing the stuff and paying for it. It means getting the stuff over there where it can be used. And that means convoys—the United States Navy. It means that American sailors—our boys—

may have to sacrifice their lives in order to deliver the goods. What about that?

GIL (*quietly*)—If that's a fact then we'd better face it now.

However, Gil understands Morey's position. As the editor of an eminent, dignified newspaper (or what used to be a newspaper, but is now a "property"), and as a realist, Morey knows when he's licked.

"And I suppose if you look at this realistically you can only come to the conclusion that people like Churchill and Roosevelt are as fatuous as King Canute—trying to command the Wave of the Future," adds Gil.

The jukebox is playing the tune called "Smiles" that was a big hit in the First World War. "I'm sentimental about that song," Morey is saying. "I learned it at my mother's knee. She was a waitress in the Coffee Shop at the Mohican House. She died in a flu epidemic. Went just like that. My father was in the Fire Department. He met a hero's death in a tenement fire in the colored district over on Fillmore Street. So I was orphaned at the age of fourteen. It's a pathetic story, isn't it? It's an authentic tear-jerker. Except for the fact that, from then on, I had it easy. Because a fund was raised for my upbringing and education, and that fund was raised by none other than the old man, George H. Bowsmith, Senior. He called it the Timothy Vinion Memorial Fund. A Testimonial to my heroic father. You'll find the whole story in the files of the paper. Mr. Bowsmith helped me through school and college and he gave me a job and he gave me all the best of the breaks on that job. He even gave me his daughter's hand in marriage. So I'm a success, and I wouldn't wonder if I ended up in the United States Senate."

"I understand, Morey. You've got your obligations of loyalty. But I've got one or two of my own—and I guess the best thing is for me to look elsewhere for a job."

"All right, Gil. You take a nice, fat job with the *New Republic*. But not until we've finished this night's work." (*He is speaking as if to himself, or to persons unseen.*) "A decision must be made, just as if the Old Man were here. He was a Black Republican. He was a product of the Robber Baron era. He believed in the doctrine of every man for himself. But he was an American—and a fighter. There were giants in the land in those days. 'Never compromise with your own convictions, son.' That's what he used to say to me. He called me 'son' because he felt that he had created me—not biologically, but spiritually. He felt he created me just as he created the paper, and the Bowsmith foundation, and all the other monuments to his greatness. He wanted a son-in-law and an editor of his paper and he thought that I provided the raw material for both. All right, Mr. Bowsmith. In your absence, I'll make the decision, attempting not to compromise with my own convictions. . . . I'll tell you what to do, Gil. You go back to the office and bat out an editorial along the lines you suggested. Bring it up to me and I'll see how it reads."

"All right, Morey. I'll take a whack at it."

His check paid, Morey gathers up the news-ticker sheets and starts back to the office.

"Will we be seeing you later, Morey?" asks Pete, the proprietor.

"Oh, sure. I'll probably be spending the night here. . . ."

"I'll keep the joint open, Morey."

"You damned well better. History is being made. Don't miss it."

The curtain falls.

George Bowsmith is back in his office the evening of the following day. "It is an old-fashioned office with old-fashioned furniture and a great many books and files in untidy arrangement."

At the moment George is in conference with Leggatt Burt, the business manager. Burt brought him the original manuscript of the editorial Gil Hartnick had written and Morey Vinion had okayed. The manuscript carries Hartnick's name at the top of each sheet, but there are also penciled revisions here and there in Morey's handwriting, and two inserts—

"He (Morey) enlarges on the idea that if the Germans conquer Russia, they will extend across Asia and link up by land with their Axis partners, the Japanese. That, of course, is intended to scare people into fearing that *we* might be endangered in the Pacific. Hal Fleury has phoned from Washington to say he's talked to some of his contacts in the State Department about that particular point, and they're very much upset about it; they say it's liable to do a powerful lot of damage, just when we're trying to keep our relations with Japan on an even keel."

"What else did Morey write?"

"Only that piece of dynamite at the finish, saying that aid for Russia means convoys, and that means risking the U. S. Navy."

"Did Hal say there's been any comment out of the White House?"

"Oh, I imagine the *White House* thinks the whole editorial is perfectly splendid," says Burt scornfully. "Morey has always been a prime favorite in that quarter."

Of course the advertisers have been driving Leggatt practically mad— He has had "One call after another—all saying the same thing, 'Why didn't you send out a circular letter saying the paper was going to go Communist?' " Only a scattered few had called to congratulate the paper on its courageous stand.

It is Burt's considered opinion that there is only one thing for George to do: "You've got to fire those responsible for that editorial!"

"I'm not so sure we ought to make a public issue of this. All the editorial says in effect is that we ought to support the position taken by Winston Churchill as regards Russia. We can't label Churchill as a Red."

"Churchill is fighting for England. He'll accept any ally. But we're not fighting. We may sympathize with the British—we may hope they'll pull through—but, if they don't—if the Germans win—okay, we do business with them. The main thing is, we've got to establish the fact once and for all that this paper stands four square against Communism, and the only way to do it is for you to repudiate that filthy, unauthorized editorial. . . ."

"My dad was very fond of Morey Vinion."

"If your dad were here today the first thing he'd do is kick Morey Vinion out of this shop and that Jew boy, Hartnick, with him."

George's state of indecision is pitiful. Perhaps the advertisers would be satisfied if he fired Hartnick and kept Morey? Maybe Morey would accept full responsibility and say the editorial slipped through without his knowing it? Then there's the family angle—and Harriet! As a member of the family Morey ought to see things right.

Of course Burt is awfully, awfully sorry for George. He'd do anything, anything he could. But—

"Actually, what has happened to us here on this paper in the last twenty-four hours has happened to the whole country in the last few years," says Burt. "While people like you and me were out fishing or playing golf—as we've got every right in the world to do—while we were looking the other way, some starry-eyed radicals got into positions of authority and jeopardized everything that we've worked for and fought for all our lives. You've got to realize that, George—there's more at stake in this than just that one editorial. It's the whole question of who is going to run this property—the man who owns it—or the men who are hired to operate it. You've got to make up your mind about that."

When Morey comes, Burt would move on, but George wants him to stay. Seeing Burt, Morey is quick to absolve him from all responsibility. He (Morey) could have consulted Burt about the editorial if he thought that necessary, but he didn't. Neither did Morey want Burt to drag George back from his vacation. There was no need of that. And now that the editorial, which is essentially right, has been published, and the yells from Burt's Chamber of Commerce friends have been heard, George might as well go back to the lake.

No. George must make his stand. Why did Morey do it? Was he drunk? Why didn't he consult with Leggatt?

Morey wasn't drunk. He didn't consult Leggatt because Leggatt wasn't responsible for the editorial policy of the paper. There was no divided control in the elder Bowsmith's day, and there shouldn't be any now. Whereupon George sends for Gil Hartnick.

Being questioned, Gil informs George that he has been on the paper since January; that he is married and has a son seven months old, and, yes, that he knew he was jeopardizing his job when he wrote the editorial. Then, why did he write it?—

GIL—Because I was convinced it was the best thing for the paper to say at this time.

GEORGE—I haven't any question of doubt that you're absolutely sincere in your convictions.

GIL—Now, please, Mr. Bowsmith—if you're going to fire me, fire me. But please don't fling that word "sincerity" in my face. Hitler is sincere in his desire to enslave the human race. I have no doubt that Judas Iscariot was sincere in feeling he had a right to collect those thirty pieces of silver.

GEORGE—I'm afraid I don't quite follow you on that. But no matter. What made you think that it was good policy for us to come out editorially in favor of aid for Russia?

GIL—When I read the text of Mr. Churchill's speech, it seemed obvious that we must either support that policy, or condemn it. . . .

BURT (*unable longer to keep out*)—But is Churchill deciding the policy for the United States—or for this paper? Isn't it within the bounds of possibility that Churchill may have been wrong in supporting the Reds?

GIL—It might be within the bounds of possibility, Mr. Burt. That point will have to be decided by history.

BURT—We're running a daily paper, Hartnick. We can't wait for history.

GEORGE—I'd like to know, Leggatt, just what position do you think we should have taken on this?

BURT—If we had had an editorial conference, I should have said that our line should be this: the primary enemy in the world today is Communism—and Germany has attacked the Communists. We have no sympathy with Nazism—we reject all dictatorial forms of government. But—in this war between Germany and Russia, we must remain completely neutral, giving no aid or comfort to either side.

GEORGE—How do you feel about it, Morey?

MOREY—I'm afraid I have nothing to contribute to this discussion.

BURT (*to* GIL)—Don't think I don't appreciate what a tough spot you're in, Hartnick. I fully realize that you have a particular emotional involvement in the war in Europe.

GEORGE—Of course, that's only natural, under the tragic circumstances.

GIL—What circumstances, Mr. Bowsmith?

GEORGE—It's a terribly difficult, delicate thing to talk about, whenever there's a racial issue involved. God knows, I don't blame you for hating the Nazis, for wanting vengeance—but—

GIL (*Face white. Speaks with painful quietness*)—You don't need to elaborate, Mr. Bowsmith. I get the idea. My employment is herewith terminated. I'll clean my desk out immediately.

Hartnick and Burt have left. Morey has remained at George's request. George can't understand what is the matter with Morey. Morey knows that George didn't want to "assert his inheritance," as Burt had put it; he had much rather have worked in a bank. But when his dad had died he had to take the job and he took it. He has tried to keep it the way his dad had wanted it. Even to this dreary old office. And how would Morey have handled this situation if he had been in George's place?

"Well, George—if I had been in your place," answers Morey, with complete frankness, "I should have given Gil Hartnick a raise in recognition of his fine services to the paper. And I should have fired Leggatt Burt."

"My father said before he died that Leggatt Burt is the best Business Manager we've ever had. He made Leggatt the executor of his estate."

"I know, George. Leggatt is part of your inheritance. And so am I. I suppose you can't fire me, either."

"For God's sake, Morey—I don't want to fire you. Oh—I know you want to walk out on me, and take a great virtuous position of martyrdom. But you can't do it. You've got to stick on the job out of respect for the Old Man's memory. In a way, you're more his son than I am. You understand what he was driving at. I don't—and I never will. This has been a hell of an unfortunate incident. But it is only an incident. The future of the paper is more important than Hartnick's feelings—or yours, or mine. If you go, Morey, the real spirit that my father put into this paper will go with you."

"I'll have to think about it, George, and decide what's best for me to do. But—I want you to know—I realize what you're up against. The dead hand is heavy. . . . I'll see you later."

Morey goes out. The lights fade.

The curtain falls.

A few days later Morey Vinion was in Pete's Bar and Grill, talking baseball with Pete, when Gil Hartnick came in with another bit of news. Gil had joined the Marine Corps—

". . . I talked it all over with Ruth, and she agreed with me that I ought to do it. So yesterday I just walked into the recruiting station and enlisted, and I passed the physical with flying colors and—well—I'm in."

Ruth and the baby will stay with Ruth's family in Pittsburgh. Ruth will get a job, and everything will work out fine.

"I'd like to be going with you, Gil," says Morey, with considerable feeling.

"I know that, Morey. But you can't. It's easy for me to get out. I'm new on this paper. I have no real roots here. But you have—you've got your devotion to the old man, and to tradition, and all that. All I've got to worry about is my self-respect."

"Self-respect? And is that part of the equipment they supply you with in the Marine Corps?"

"That's what I've heard. They give you a gun and a bayonet and a bolo knife and a little container marked "8 ounces Self-Respect—Government Issue."

They all stand up, Morey and Gil and Pete, and drink to the

Marines. They are considering having another drink as the lights fade.

The curtain falls.

We are back in the Vinions' living room. George Bowsmith, his wife, Edith, Leggatt Burt, and the Vinions are there. Morey is pouring champagne at the bar. (He had thought of making cocktails, but this champagne is too good for that.)

The occasion of this family gathering is to celebrate Morey's resignation from the paper—from the Bowsmith Enterprises, Inc. Edith is the first to wish him luck, which she does with marked indifference. But not George—

"I don't wish you the best of luck," says George, bitterly. "You owe everything you've got—your education, your job, your reputation, Harriet, this house—you owe everything to my father, and now that he's dead, you are walking out on us, in a crisis, and you're doing it in a manner to discredit us and to hurt the paper that my father created."

As for Burt, he is a bit worried. Has Morey been offered another job? Yes, in a way. Morey has joined the Navy. Making this announcement Morey adds:

"I consider your looks of amazement and incredulity distinctly insulting."

What he is going to do in the Navy, Morey doesn't know. Whatever they find for him to do, after he finishes his boot training. He might even qualify as a ship's cook. Yes, his was a straight enlistment, quite casual and quite simple. He had walked down State Street looking for employment. Coming to a Marine Recruiting Station he momentarily considered becoming a Marine, but lacked the nerve. Then he came upon a Navy Station and went in, pretending he was looking for a story on recruiting—

"The Chief Petty Officer on duty told me that even old men of forty could get sea duty," Morey tells them, "since there are a few jobs on a ship that don't demand the same amount of youth and vigor required for service in fox-holes. So—when I'd got all the facts—I put away my press card and offered my body. After considerable argument, they took it."

George thinks that Morey might at least have let his friends help him get a commission, but Morey is convinced he has done the right thing—

"This will be the final laying of the scandal about the pro-Russian editorial. Look at what happened to the two culprits involved—Hartnick and Vinion. Both of them are off the paper —both of them cast into outer darkness—one in the Marine Corps, the other in the Navy. And you'll be able to give the advertisers solemn assurance that there'll be no more Bolshevism on the editorial page."

George, Morey admits, has done his best to "achieve a compromise between Leggatt Burt and me," but that was impossible. So he is relieving George of all responsibility. Now he will open another bottle of champagne, and they will all drink to the Chamber of Commerce.

To that suggestion there is practically no response. A few minutes later the company has left.

"When will we get to see you in that sailor suit?" Edith asks Morey on the way to the hall.

"Well—first—I've got to get myself tattooed," cracks Morey.

Coming back into the room Morey is prepared to open more champagne, though Harriet gives him no encouragement. She wants to talk; wants to know whatever impelled him to do what he has done—

"I don't know that I can ever explain it to you, or to myself," Morey confesses. "But—I've seen some faint glimmering of light. Maybe it's deceptive, but it's there—and what it's showing me is this: I've failed—I'm not the thing your father tried to create—I'm not the right editor for his paper. I can't achieve the old winning combination of superficial liberalism with fundamental reaction. I can't fight on equal terms with Leggatt Burt. And—in addition to all that—I'm not the right son-in-law that your father tried to imagine me. I'm not the right husband for you."

HARRIET—Then joining the Navy is your means of leaving me.

MOREY—You'll be making a cruel mistake if you believe that.

HARRIET—What can I believe, Morey?

MOREY—That there's a chance that after this experience, whatever it may be, you and I will have found a way to live at peace with each other.

HARRIET—Suppose you're killed.

MOREY—Oh. . . . Even when we do get into the war, it's unlikely that anyone of my advanced age should ever get near to combat—unless I suddenly become an Admiral.

HARRIET (*standing up and looking about the room*)—I've made another mistake—just one more addition to a long list. I thought this house would be the answer. I thought you would love it and again love me.

MOREY—You're blaming yourself because this house is beautiful?

HARRIET—Yes—beautiful and utterly wrong.

MOREY (*coming close to her*)—For God's sake, Harriet—this isn't a matter of who's to blame—you or me—or distribution of the guilt between us. We both share in our own unhappiness. . . . The trouble is that we're both, in a way, casualties of this war.

HARRIET—The trouble is, Morey—I love you—I've never stopped loving you since the first moment long ago when I knew that I was going to compel you to ask me to marry you.

MOREY (*taking her in his arms*)—You see, Harriet—the thing is that history has brought us all to a Great Divide, and every one of us has got to make his own decision—whether to try to stay put, or to turn back, or to push on over the ridge into the unknown. Maybe going into the Navy is the craziest, silliest thing I could have done. But I'm tired of being merely someone who stands by and watches. I want to be part of something. You said I have demons in me—and maybe you're right. They're demons of doubt. I want to dispel them. I want to find out whether there really is anything in this world worth fighting for and dying for.

HARRIET—You said you're leaving tonight?

MOREY—Yes. I've got to take the 8:20 train for Chicago. That's where I'm to report. I suppose I go to the Great Lakes station.

HARRIET—You probably won't be taking much luggage.

MOREY—No—just enough for overnight—a toothbrush and that stuff.

HARRIET—I'll go up and get it together.

Morey stands still for a moment. He considers pouring himself another drink and decides against it. He goes to the window, and is staring into the garden, as—

The curtain falls.

ACT II

Nearly three years later—in June, 1944—we are in a corner of the men's mess compartment of the Destroyer *Townsend*. There is a ladder leading up to the main deck, a door leading to the galley and a mess table flanked with benches.

Two or three of the crew are busying themselves in the mess—writing letters, drinking coffee, the idle ones heckling those who are trying to complete off-duty tasks.

Coming from the galley, Morey Vinion brings a pot of coffee. One of the men has heard from the radio room that Allied forces have landed in Northern France. But what the hell does that mean to them—they being on a destroyer in the Pacific? Is it significant, or isn't it? Morey, the cook, ought to know. Morey doesn't know, but he has an idea—

"If that had happened it wouldn't be any rumor," he tells them; "every radio transmitter in the world would be broadcasting the official communiqué. Probably the skipper would announce it to us."

"There ain't no invasion of Europe," ventures Kavanagh, bosun's mate and a Navy veteran. "That war there is going on for years. How can they land an Army in Europe unless they've got enough Navy to do it. And they ain't got enough Navy—unless they move *us* out of the Pacific."

"You mean this tin-can could lick the Germans?"

"That's what I said."

"If they put us into Europe, who'd take care of the Japs?"

"Nobody. Does that answer your question?"

"Well, all I want to know is, where are we going now? Why are we all alone? Where's the rest of the fleet?"

"There ain't no 'rest of the fleet.' We're a one-ship task force."

"Then why don't we go back to base and unload those guys who got wounded?"

"Get back to your writing and stop asking questions!"

The loudspeaker has started to blare a message through the shrill whistle of a bosun's pipe—

"Now hear this! Now hear this! Set condition one Easy. Set condition one Easy. We're cruising pretty deep into enemy water on a rescue mission to search for two fliers from the Sara. They went down this morning when attacking that enemy task force that we met up with last night. We may meet up with some of them again, so there won't be much sleeping done on board for the time being. That's all."

"By God—that skipper is all right. He explains things," declares Kavanagh.

"What did he mean, Kavanagh? What did he mean we're on a 'rescue mission'?"

"Just what he said—we're going out to look for a couple of fliers from a CV."

"So we risk our lives to save a couple of *aviators?*"

"Maybe some day you'll be floating around yourself in the

sea, with nothing but a Mae West to keep you alive. You'll be damned glad to see a couple of aviators looking for *you*."

Morey has brought in a plate of sliced bread for peanut butter sandwiches. The bosun's whistle is shrieking again,—

"'Damage control parties report to their stations!'"

The men go up the ladder. The platter of sandwiches goes up with Kavanagh. The Ship's Doctor, a Lt. J.G., "young but weary," is in for a cup of Java.

"Pretty tough day for you, sir," ventures Morey. "Any more men die?"

DOCTOR—No. Conway and Vogel are in pretty bad shape, but the others will pull through—that is, if the ship does. This is a nice mission we're on—and we're all alone. We're naked. But that's the sterling old Navy tradition. They'll risk a good ship and three hundred men to save two who may or may not be floating around in rubber rafts out there someplace.

MOREY—Well—that's the beautiful part of my job on this ship. I never know where we are or why. If I knew more about the situation I'd only be more scared.

DOCTOR—Were you scared when we were in that scrap last night?

MOREY—Yes, sir—I was.

DOCTOR—Why? You must have been under fire plenty of times in Europe.

MOREY—That was strictly another matter. Then I was a correspondent—an Olympian observer—stationed far above the sordid tides of battle. But last night, I was just another Joe, passing the ammunition. When those Jap planes came in low, I didn't think of it in terms of phrases. And I saw another Jap plane coming in low and I thought our gun might be the target, and it was. But I wasn't standing up to the gun. I was flat on my face. So I'm able to stand up now—instead of having to be slid silent over the fan-tail like Harry Husman and Jack MacLaggen were this morning. And now—we're heading west—deep into enemy waters. And if you want to know how I feel now, Doctor—I'm again scared.

DOCTOR—I don't want to pry, Vinion—but, since you joined this ship, I couldn't help wondering about you. You've been quite a subject for speculation in the Ward Room.

MOREY—I'm honored, sir.

DOCTOR—Now and then, I censor your mail, and it makes very interesting reading—especially those long letters you write to some friend of yours in the Marines.

MOREY—That was Gil Hartnick. He used to be on the paper with me.

DOCTOR—Why did you get into service like this—as a ship's cook second-class on a destroyer? A man of your experience—

MOREY—I know, Doctor, a man of my experience ought to be doing dignified work in the Public Relations outfit. And that's where they put me at first. But—if I was going to spend the war pounding a typewriter, I might as well have stayed home. I heard there was a call for cooks, and I got admitted to a course. I learned to make coffee the Navy way, so that when you put a spoon in it, it won't sink.

DOCTOR—You wanted to get to sea. You wanted combat duty.

MOREY (*smiles*)—Well, sir, I guess my feelings are summed up by that quotation from the Book of Job you've got in the Ward Room: "Yea, his soul draweth near unto the grave, and his life to the Destroyers." And last night I thought—"Here's where they take it!"

For the next few minutes the Doctor and Morey are busy looking after Costanzo, a twenty-year-old curly head who appears suddenly, wearing no more than his pajama pants. His left arm and shoulder are heavily bandaged, his arm taped to his chest. Guffey had told him, he reports to the Doctor, that he could go on deck to get some air. He's feeling fine. To prove it he breaks into a wild bit of jitterbugging. Next minute he is leaning weakly on Morey and looking a little silly. Now Guffey has come for him.

"You spoke of the letters I wrote to my friend in the Marines," Morey is saying to the Doctor. "I don't think he got any of those letters. I heard from his wife last week—the last mail we got on board. He was killed in action on one of the islands out here. Why do they do it, Doctor?"

"Why do who do what?"

"All these kids—this generation. Who do they fight? That kid Costanzo, for instance. He saw service in the North Atlantic against U-boats, and he's been out here in the Pacific for over a year. He and all the rest of them have no reason to believe that they'll ever get back alive. What's in their minds? What do they think they're accomplishing?"

The Doctor wouldn't know. He's a surgeon, not a psychiatrist. "The Medical Department isn't supposed to fathom their innermost secrets," says he.

"Maybe if I'm in the Navy long enough," Morey says, "I'll be able to find out why they think they've got a country that's worth fighting for and dying for."

Now, amid an increasing confusion on deck, General Quarters is sounded. The lights go out, except for one red lamp. As Morey and the Doctor run out, the General Alarm is heard. There are the sounds of men running to their battle stations—"pounding up the ladders; water-tight doors and hatches being slammed shut and dogged down." And over all the sound of the Loudspeaker—

"All hands man your battle stations! Man your battle stations" . . . "Bandit bears 283, distance ten miles, closing.". . . "Stand by to repel air attack" . . . "All guns report when manned and ready . . ."

"Gun one manned and ready . . . Never mind the gab—lay out some more ammunition! This ain't no drill . . ."

"Bandit closing fast! All guns—action port! Action port! Match pointers—shift to automatic . . ."

"Gun three in automatic!"

"Target bears 270! Position angle six . . ."

"Commence firing! Commence firing!"—

And now the first reports of damage suffered begin to come in: "One bomb hit, aft, sir! Skin and bulkheads ruptured! Making water fast, sir!"

"Engine room! Maintain all possible speed!"

"Give 'em hell!" . . . "Coming in! Coming in! Get the bastard!"

And now the beginning of the end. There are several explosions as shells from Jap ships hit the *Townsend* aft. Again the bad news spreads—

"Heavy hit aft, sir! Steering aft flooded, sir!" . . . "Lost power on both shafts, sir!" . . . "Losing speed, rapidly, sir!" . . . "Settling heavily astern, sir!" . . . "Breaking up aft, sir!" . . . "Forward spaces are flooding, sir!" . . .

There is a pause, and then—"Prepare to abandon ship!"

"'All hands stand by to abandon ship! Stand by to abandon ship!'"

"'Get all wounded into life rafts! Don't bunch up on any one raft!'" Another pause. Then, over the P.A. system: "'Men, the *Townsend's* on her way down! She's a fighting ship! She paid her way! Leave her proud! Keep together—and good luck!'"

" 'All hands abandon ship! All hands abandon ship! All hands aband—' "

There is a heavy explosion—with the sound of aircraft fading into the distance.

The curtain falls.

The little flags stuck in the large wall map of Europe and Asia hung in George Bowsmith's office indicate that the date is June 20, 1944. In the office we find in addition to George, his sister, Harriet Vinion; Leggatt Burt, and Hal Fleury. Fleury, the paper's Washington correspondent, has just come from Washington to report, very confidentially, what he has been able to learn from his contacts in the Navy Department of the fate of the destroyer *Townsend*. So secret is Mr. Fleury's information that he has not been permitted to write it, or telephone, but must deliver it in person. Not a word of what he reports must be repeated outside this room.

The story of the *Townsend*, so far as the Navy knows, is that she was lost while cruising deep in enemy waters in the Southwest Pacific.

"She radioed that she was being attacked by the enemy—Then, total silence," reports Hal. No survivors have been found, but search is being kept up by long-range bombers.

"Morey's presence on the *Townsend* on this date is confirmed," Fleury is saying. "Therefore he is listed as 'missing.' But so is the entire crew of this destroyer and the Navy Department is not yet notifying the next of kin, since such notification might reveal to the enemy the possible loss of the ship.

It is possible that they will know nothing more for weeks, or years, or even until after the war. It is possible that *Townsend* survivors have been picked up, and that Morey may be among them.

"It's going to be a tough job, Sis—tough for all of us," sympathizes George. "We've got to take this standing up. Whatever has happened to Morey, we can't allow it to get us down."

"You don't need to worry about me. I'm prepared for it—whatever it is. Morey is 'missing.' But I've become accustomed to that. He was missing when he was here. I didn't know where he was, even when I could see him."

George would have his sister avoid the dangerously morbid state of mind that she is getting herself into. He would have her get away from her home. But Harriet has no intention of doing that—

"The only luxury I have these days," she says, "is remembering—and regretting—and wondering whether he has found what he was looking for. He went to war to find peace . . . Perhaps, now, I shall never know. But I'm not going to stop wondering."

Harriet has left. Leggatt Burt is in with a page proof of a large layout of photographs of Morey. He has had the Art Department get it up against the day the news of Morey's heroic sacrifice is released. There will be a big feature story to go with it—

"And we'd better tell in that story that Morey left us because we objected to an editorial favoring Lend-Lease for Russia," says George, with a touch of sarcasm. "And we could make it even more dramatic by bringing in Gil Hartnick, whom we fired for that same editorial, and who now is buried in the Marine Corps cemetery on Guadalcanal."

"I can't see that we are responsible for the developments of this war."

"You're damned right we aren't. If we had been, maybe the Russians today wouldn't be pushing the Germans back. Maybe there wouldn't be any Russian armies left." He points to the big map on the wall. "Maybe those German flags wouldn't be here on the map. Maybe they'd be down here in Asia—linked up with the Japs."

"Maybe—maybe—maybe," protests Burt. "You can't run a newspaper or a world on maybes. I know you feel sentimental —and regretful—about Morey. But I still insist that the action we took on that editorial three years ago was right. Certainly it proved our good faith to the business community of which we're an essential part. But—even granting that we were wrong—we'd do no good now by indulging in cringing apologies."

George thinks he will go out and get a drink. No. Not at the Club. He thinks he will go over to Kenneally's Bar and Grill.

Leggatt Burt is at the phone talking to Ralph Jessup. He would have Jessup redesign the big service flag the paper has displayed at the corner of Seventh and State. "The idea is to get the blue stars grouped around the margin, leaving white space in the middle for a big gold star . . ." he is saying.

The curtain falls.

That same day, on one of the smaller Philippine islands, Col. Rainsford is seated at a table inside the Nipa hut that is serving as his headquarters. Outside from time to time, Filipino boy passes and repasses the entrance, a rifle slung over his shoulder.

Rainsford, seated in a wicker chair holding a cane, is very

haggard. "His khaki shirt and trousers are old and have been repaired in many places—he wears very battered shoes and no socks—but the silver eagle and the crossed sabers on his shirt-collar gleam defiantly, and he presents a clean, soldierly appearance."

Morey is seated near by, drinking. Gregorio, a native, had found him crawling up the hill from Banana Beach. Morey had thought Gregorio a Jap.

Outside a group of natives has gathered to stare through the door at Morey. "Look at this!" Gregorio is saying to them; "a U.S. Navy sailor! Do you know what this means? It means the U.S. Navy has come back to us. He was on a battle-ship. And that means—more battle-ships are near to us—the whole U.S. Navy. That means we are not forgotten."

Col. Rainsford thinks it would be well for Gregorio to return to his post. They will all have a chance to meet the American sailor later. Dr. Querin, "a middle-aged Filipino, quiet, scholarly, observant," brings a report that such facts as they have been able to gain from Morey's identity card have been duly transmitted. The Doctor is also convinced that he has recognized Morey as a writer—

"I was in the States for two years before the war," Doctor Querin explains. "I was on leave from the University of Manila. I was particularly interested in all that you wrote about the Munich Conference. What a tragic business that was . . . But—It's a pleasure to have you here, Mr. Vinion."

"He's read my stuff," a surprised Morey exclaims to Col. Rainsford. "What kind of a Doctor is he—M.D.?"

"No. He was a Professor of Philosophy. Now he runs our radio transmitter. There are many people like Dr. Querin who have had to learn new trades these past few years."

So far Morey has refused to tell his captors the name of his ship. Nor will he now tell Col. Rainsford. How can he be sure of Rainsford's identity? There is no way, the Colonel admits. All his papers were taken from him at the time of the surrender on Bataan, April 9, 1942. For a year he was a prisoner. He was hit in the leg while escaping.

"I was in the class of 1912 at West Point," Col. Rainsford says. "I was Corps G-2 under General MacArthur in USAFFE. . . ."

"May I ask, Colonel—why do you keep it up? What is it that keeps you going?"

"You wouldn't ask that if you had been in a Jap prison camp. And pathetic as this guerrilla operation may seem, it isn't an irresponsible rabble, a Robin Hood outlaw band. All of us out here are organized under General MacArthur. We are units in an orderly chain of command. This is a containing campaign. As long as we keep the flag flying here—as long as these brave people know there's a living proof here of the United States Army—then the whole population remains confident and active in resistance."

"Did they teach you all this at West Point, Colonel—how to behave in a situation like this?"

"I was educated at my country's expense. I learned that it was my duty to repay that debt with my life. 'Duty, Honor, Country'—that's our motto at West Point. I don't know what they teach at Annapolis—but it's probably along somewhat similar lines."

"My God, Colonel—it's funny—"

"What's funny?"

"Forgive me, sir. But do you mind if I say something, not as an Able Seaman, but as an old newspaper man?"

"No—I don't mind. Tonight you're my guest—you haven't gone on duty yet. And besides—I gather you're a little bit drunk."

"Yes, sir. You see, sir—for years, as a civilian, I had dealings with high-ranking officers—'brass hats.' And I heard them talking in that sententious, pompous manner about that old sense of duty—that old West Point or Annapolis code of Honor. And I laughed at it—and sneered at it. I sneered at it in print. And now the time has come when all of us—the whole nation—the whole miserable world—depend on officers like you, and your 'sense of duty,' and your old code and your old red tape. We depend on you for the mere fact of survival. It's a strange commentary on the march of events."

Morey is ready to tell them the story of the *Townsend* now. Doctor Querin is back to hear it. He makes notes as Morey relates the adventure of the rescue mission; the attack of the Japs; of the battle that ended with the *Townsend's* salvo of torpedoes, two of which had found the Jap carrier, and sent it down.

The *Townsend* was badly hit. When she sank Morey found himself on a raft. He had pulled two wounded men on with him. They were badly hurt. When they died, Morey had buried them at sea. He had managed to rig a sail of sorts. How long he kept going on the raft he doesn't know—

"I've been part of a ship, and that ship went down—she went down fighting," Morey concludes. "Those kids are dead—those kids who were griping to me about the quality of the chow—who were writing letters home while they were waiting for the next attack to come in."

"Take it easy, sailor. Lots of good men are dead. You'll accomplish nothing by getting emotional about it."

"Colonel, I'm probably the most incompetent, most reluctant fighting man you ever saw." (MOREY *has risen to his feet.*) "But—I may be the only living survivor of the crew of the *Townsend*—and that means I'm the unworthy bearer of a good tradition. I want assignment to duty here, sir—whatever it is, whatever I can do."

"You'll have plenty to do around here, Vinion. You'll get your assignment to duty."

"When, sir?"

"Soon enough. But—you'll be no damned good to anybody until you've had some rest."

Catalino, "a lean, sad-faced Filipino in a clean white suit and large straw hat and no shoes," has appeared with a harmonica. He blows mess call. Catalino, explains the Colonel, is the camp bugler. And it's a good thing he hasn't a bugle. If he had, the enemy would hear him.

Groups of natives are passing the hut, all of them stopping to bow, or to salute the Colonel with one gesture or another. Gregorio reappears. He fixes a place for the brave American sailor that God has sent them. Let Morey rest. "There is all the time in the world for you to sleep," Gregorio assures him.

Morey has begun to sing: " 'There are smiles that make us happy—there are smiles that make us blue—there are smiles that steal away the tear drops—' "

Col. Rainsford is at the desk jotting down notes. Gregorio is gazing at the sleeping Morey. "The United States Navy!" mutters Gregorio reverently.

The curtain falls.

A week later in Col. Rainsford's hut there is considerable activity. The Colonel is at the table, plotting positions on a map. Doctor Querin is near by making grenades—"using old beer bottles and small pottery jugs on which inscriptions have been made. He pours into each vessel some black powder and some of the generator fuel, then seals it with a fiber cork."

When the Colonel has the positions worked out he explains them to the men. Gregorio's detachment is to be deployed on Cabul Point. The command post will be at the scene of the unloading. Doctor Querin, with the radio transmitter, will superintend the dispersal of supplies.

There is still the detachment on Banana Beach to be looked after. Who will take care of that? The Colonel thinks Lareza is the best man available, but Doctor Querin reports Lareza is still suffering from his wounds. There's young Golez, but he's a little too young. Why not try Morey Vinion? The suggestion is Doctor Querin's.

Col. Rainsford is not impressed. It's just their luck, he reminds the Doctor, a little bitterly, that the sole survivor of the *Townsend* is, unhappily, not an officer, but a cook. ". . . I can understand why the men are fond of him. He's an agreeable sort of chap—a bit on the radical side, perhaps—but intelligent and courageous . . ."

"I don't like to dispute superior authority, Colonel," persists the Doctor, "but I think you're wrong."

A moment later Morey has joined them. He is feeling fit, he announces. And when is he going to be assigned to duty?

That, replies the Colonel, will be for the Navy to decide. The next day they are expecting a submarine to come into the channel south of Cabul Point. It will be bringing them twenty tons of arms and equipment—the first since 1942.

That's great news to Morey. But what about the Japs? If there is likely to be a fight, Morey wants in, wherever they can use him. He will be helpful with the unloading, the Colonel agrees. And then, when the submarine gets away, Morey will go with it. At this decision, Morey is plainly distressed.

"It was the suggestion of headquarters," the Colonel explains, "that you be put on that submarine. Evidently the Navy wants you back. We've enjoyed your stay here, Vinion. We're sorry to see you go."

The Colonel has left them. Morey is still puzzled. He tries to get the Doctor to explain matters to him. What is likely to happen tomorrow?

"The submarine will flash a blinker signal from offshore just before dawn," Querin explains. "Some Jap patrols will surely see it—they will report a strange ship coming in. Then there will be an attack."

"From which direction?"

"Probably from the north—from San Isidro."

"That's the road that runs along Banana Beach?"

"Yes—that's it."

"The Japs would have to be held there to cover the landing."

"Naturally."

"Do you think they can be held?"

"That remains to be seen."

"Then how can the Colonel spare a single man who might be useful—even me?"

"There's no reason for you to feel unhappy about it. The submarine will take you back to some base, and from there you may be sent back home. You wouldn't object to that."

"Home?—When I think of home, Doctor, I think of a little tin-can that now lies broken to pieces on the bottom of the Pacific. And all my folks, all my own people, are down there, dead."

Morey volunteers to help with the making of the hand grenades. As he works he continues his effort to find out just what is happening to him, and why. Why, when he wants so very much to be a part of this war for freedom, is he going to be sent home?

It is probably because they think he can be of great use at home, suggests the Doctor. There is a very important story to be told there—the story of the Filipinos' need of friendship and leadership. ". . . And what is true of us Filipinos is true of all peoples who have known defeat and oppression—in Europe, in Asia, everywhere. Oh—you will have a lot to write about."

Morey—I understand, Doctor. But I am no longer impressed by the power of the pen. For years I wrote about what was coming. I tried to tell what I had seen and heard and felt. I wrote my heart out. But it did no good.

Doctor—You have a low opinion of your own profession. I'm afraid you have known too much, you have seen too much of the evil that is abroad in the world.

Morey—I'm a newspaperman. We're trained to be contemptuous. We're trained to doubt, to suspect and ultimately to despise. Oh—there are some of our papers that are honorable—and some that are degraded—and a lot that are neither one thing nor the other nor anything else. But the practice of journalism in general does not tend to promote faith, or hope, or charity. And that, Doctor, is the basic reason why I joined the Navy.

Querin—Perhaps your press is not so unrepresentative as you think. I want to tell you that I am afraid of you Americans—not that you will be imperialistic in the old sense. I am afraid that you will not have the courage and the wisdom to be great in times of peace as you have been in times of war.

Morey—You think we're too short-sighted, mean-spirited, greedy?

QUERIN—I did not say that.

MOREY—I heard what you said, Doctor—and I know what you mean. I used to feel somewhat the same way myself. I used to wonder—where are all the real Americans? I kept trying to find whatever became of those rugged, crazy idealists who made this country—the men and women of the *Mayflower,* and the Alamo, and the covered wagons. I thought they were gone and forgotten.

QUERIN—And have you found them?

MOREY—Yes—I've found them here—in the Colonel, and you, and Gregorio, and all your people. I found them in those guys I was with on the *Townsend,* DD-346. I've known them, I've seen them, living and fighting. And what this has meant to me is beyond measurement, beyond expression. It's a revival of the spirit—a restoration of faith—the discovery of life. You don't get these things free, Doctor. And I don't want to go back until I'm sure I've paid for them.

QUERIN—But—after the war—do you think you will find this militant still surviving in your own countrymen?

MOREY—I don't know, Doctor. I've resigned from the role of prophet. But it's hard for me to believe that we can forget—that we can ever slip back into the old complacency, the old suicidal selfishness. But—God forgive me if I'm turning into an optimist.

Two natives have appeared with orders from Gregorio to take the grenades to Post Eleven. As Morey and the Doctor quit their job, the Doctor suggests, casually, that maybe Morey will not have to go back if he chooses not to.

"I think I know what Col. Rainsford has in his mind," says Querin. "It's not doubt of your courage. It is the same doubt that I have felt about your country—fear that you will not take responsibility for leadership, for the lives of other men."

When Col. Rainsford returns Morey again brings up the subject—

"Colonel—I greatly appreciate your desire to restore me to the Navy and to my proper work of cooking Spam. But, by your leave, sir, I must say that I prefer to remain here. . . . I like this outfit of yours, sir. I'd be honored to serve with it in any capacity."

"Do you realize, Vinion, that by choosing to stay here, you are probably condemning yourself to death?"

"We are all condemned to death, sir. We were born that way."

For a moment the Colonel pauses to consider. Then he summons Gregorio. Let him fall in the guard. There is going to be a ceremony.

"I'd make you a Second Lieutenant, Vinion—but this is the only insignia we have available at the moment," the Colonel explains, reaching in his pocket. "I borrowed this from one of our Captains who was wounded. So you will have to be a Captain —a temporary one. Are you ready to accept this honor and the duties and responsibilities it entails?"

"Yes, sir. I'm as nearly ready as I'll ever be, sir."

"In that case, Vinion, I'm happy to have the privilege of commissioning you. You will not be a very conventional sort of officer. But this is not a conventional sort of war."

So, with the Guerrilla Detachment standing at attention just outside the hut, its home-made flag with three magenta stripes replacing the last three red stripes for which there was no more material, Morey Vinion is solemnly sworn into the Army of the United States of America. He raises his right hand and firmly repeats after the Colonel, phrase by phrase, the oath of allegiance —from "I, Morey Vinion," through to "SO HELP ME GOD!"

The Guerrillas come to the "Present." Col. Rainsford salutes. Morey, looking a bit confused, but unquestionably deeply moved, returns the salute.

The curtain falls.

Very early next morning we are at a jungle outpost. Col. Rainsford and Capt. Vinion are standing at the crest of the hill, looking off toward the beaches. Morey has the Captain's bars attached to his collar and a revolver holster on his belt—

"Perhaps it will help you to think that Banana Beach is the Pass at Thermopylae and you are Leonidas," the Colonel is saying. "But you will not have three hundred Spartans. You will have thirty-five guerrillas, armed mostly with home-made shotguns."

"Yes, sir. I'll try to remember Thermopylae. But I'll try to do this job with the minimum number of casualties, including myself."

"And another thing—if you don't hold down there—if the Japs break through to Cabul Point—not only will the unloading be frustrated, the submarine itself will be trapped until the next high tide. She will probably be destroyed and her entire crew killed or captured. Therefore—even though you are temporarily in the Army, this morning you will be covering an operation of the United States Navy."

As to how long it will be, the Colonel is convinced the first hour will be decisive; after that they should have new arms and ammunition from the submarine, and they will be strong. It might well be, the Colonel muses, that with the supplies they can hold out on the island for months, and keep on transmitting intelligence until the glorious day of victory comes, and they can all go home.

Task Force Zero (that is what the Colonel has said Morey can call his detachment if he likes) is moving nervously about. This, suggests the Colonel, would be a good time for Morey to address his soldiers, if he has anything he wants to say. A kind of pep talk, as Morey sees it.

"Well, I take it you all know that this is apt to be quite an interesting operation," says Morey, turning to the men. "It's not on exactly the same scale as the landings in Normandy—and perhaps nobody will ever hear about it—but it's the only operation we've got at the moment, so I'm sure that we shall all make the most of it."

"We do better than they did in Normandy," speaks up Gregorio, proudly. "*They* didn't kill any Japs."

"That's the right attitude, Gregorio. But—we mustn't feel too superior toward those boys who are fighting in France. After all, they're our Allies. And they are playing a part in the overall grand strategy, just as we are."

Yes. Morey agrees, it is really more tough here than it is in Europe. The beaches over there are much wider; they can use tanks. Here they will have to hold their tanks strictly in reserve. But, if they hold their strip of beach, and litter it with a lot of dead Japs, the Colonel will be much pleased. Task Force Zero will be mentioned in the dispatches. And what's more, right now, in Washington there is a map—a map of that little island. On it there will be a row of pins along Banana Beach—"and the President and the Chiefs of Staff will be watching that row of pins to see if we hold."

Gregorio would like to hear more about the White House. Did Morey ever go there? Oh, sure, Morey went there for press conferences whenever he got back from his travels—

"You saw the President of the United States?"

MOREY—Yes. Sometimes he would ask me to stay after the conference and he asked me questions about what I had seen in Europe. The last time I was there was December, 1940. I had just come home from London. They were bombing London night after night, and it seemed that nothing could ever stop them. I felt despairing then. I thought that the Germans and the Japs were going to knock off one opponent after another, one at a time, until they had all of creation divided between them—and then they would tangle up in a final, gruesome World Series. Well—when I got to Washington, they had Christmas decorations in the White House, and I saw the President. He was cheerful and confident, but I couldn't figure out why. I guess that was just his nature.

GREGORIO—He was right! He knew those Germans and Japs would never beat *us!*

MOREY—Yes, Gregorio. He was right and so are you. But I couldn't see it that way in December, 1940. That night I was walking through Lafayette Square—that's a little park out in front of the White House. It was a bitter cold night. I saw the big lamp that hangs over the main entrance of the White House, and I stood there, looking at it, and I thought, "There is the last light that is left shining anywhere on earth." I guess I was unduly emotional. But I had the thought that the fuel that kept that light burning was the living spirit of a hundred and thirty million people who were strong and weak, rich and poor, wise and ignorant, black and white, Christian and Jew. And I thought—if only that living spirit could be projected all over the world, it would restore the light to guide the tortured people out of the darkness. I said to myself, "That is a beautiful poetic thought. I must write it down at once and have it printed and broadcast across the nation." But I walked on through Lafayette Square and went around the corner to the Press Club and forgot all about it. But—the funny part of it is—it has come true. That living spirit has gone out, all over the world, and the light shines more strongly every day. Some of it is coming here, to us, right now. If we can hold that strip of beach long enough, the submarine will land thirty tons of equipment made especially for us by the people at home, seven thousand miles away from here. One submarine may not seem like so much. I guess that in Normandy, by this time, hundreds of ships have landed millions of tons. But thirty tons here will look much bigger to us.

RAINSFORD—It's 0603. The submarine is late.

GREGORIO—Maybe it will not come, after all.

MOREY—Gregorio! Would you dare to question the reliability of the United States Navy? Obviously, the Colonel's watch is fast.

Gregorio—But maybe the Japs sink that submarine like that destroyer you were on.

Morey—When you say "maybe" you're indulging in speculation, and that is not permitted among junior officers . . . There's one piece of equipment we've got for this fight—and it wasn't manufactured yesterday and it won't be destroyed tomorrow—and that one piece of equipment is faith. It's the faith of the people—the devotion of the people to the God who created man in His own image. That faith is our weapon and our hope. You people here on this island—you have proved the power of that weapon and that hope. You may not seem to have much to fight with, but you know what you've got to fight for, and that gives you dignity. It makes you unconquerable.

Col. Rainsford is still looking off toward Cabul Point. Morey moves over to stand a moment by his side. There is still no signal. As Morey turns back he sees that Gregorio and the others have removed their caps and are on their knees in silent prayer. He stands with bared and bowed head until the soldiers bless themselves with the sign of the cross.

"Let nobody here doubt that your prayers will be answered," he says to them. "We'll carry this one off, not because we're great fighting men but because we've got to do it. There's been a very narrow margin between victory and defeat in this war—it was no wider than the English Channel, no wider than one street in Stalingrad—it may be no wider than Banana Beach. But God has decreed that it must be wide enough—and we shall be obedient to that decree."

A moment later Col. Rainsford speaks, excitedly. "There it is! We've got the signal! Give me that lantern! Get going, Captain!"

"Okay, Colonel! Task Force Zero—March!"

They start over the ridge. Morey and the Colonel shake hands. The curtain falls.

We are back in the same room in the White House where we met Morey Vinion in 1940. Jamieson, the faithful servitor, is still there. This time he is bringing in a bowl of lilacs to put on the console table below the portrait of Washington.

There are a lot of people with the President, Jamieson reports. And a lot of camera men, too. The President is awarding a medal to the family of Morey Vinion.

Presently the Vinion party is ushered out by Gen. MacGlorn,

the President's Military Aide. They are Edith and George Bowsmith, Gregorio and Col. Rainsford, Harriet Vinion and Dr. Querin. Harriet is carrying the leather case with the medal.

George would thank Col. Rainsford and the others who have come on for the ceremony.

"We were all devoted to Morey," says the Colonel. "I wish you could have seen the funeral service that we held up at our headquarters."

GREGORIO—People came there from all over the mountains and villages.

RAINSFORD—The Priest read them those beautiful words of St. Paul's: "For the trumpet shall sound, and the dead shall be raised incorruptible, and we shall be changed . . . then shall it be brought to pass the saying that is written, Death is swallowed up in Victory."

HARRIET—"We shall be changed." Do you think that is true?

QUERIN—It must be true, Mrs. Vinion. We cannot believe otherwise.

HARRIET (*to* GEORGE)—Are you changed, George, because of what Morey did? Am I changed? Has his death had any effect on all the things he fought against and hated in his life?

GEORGE—You know we'll never forget him—never cease to honor his memory.

HARRIET—Colonel Rainsford, I never heard from Morey after he reached the Philippines.

RAINSFORD—We lacked means of communication out there, Mrs. Vinion.

HARRIET—Of course, I realize that. But—while he was there —did he ever speak to you about his home?

RAINSFORD—He said very little to us about himself. But I can tell you, Mrs. Vinion, I have had a lifetime of experience in the profession of arms, and I have observed that men who are as faithful, as devoted, as your husband was, have a very deep attachment for their homes.

QUERIN—The day before Morey died, Mrs. Vinion, he told me that he had been looking for the Americans—the real, old-fashioned, fighting Americans. He said he had found them, in the Colonel here, and all of us—and in his friends on that destroyer. But—I think the important thing is—he found them in himself. He believed that we *have* changed.

HARRIET—You said you're going back to the Philippines, Dr. Querin?

QUERIN—Yes, Mrs. Vinion.

HARRIET—There must be some museum or university or something out there that would like to have Morey's Medal of Honor. I'd be grateful if you would take it to them.

GEORGE—Harriet! The President conferred it on you, Morey's wife.

HARRIET—The President will not object to having it go back where it was earned. Here—take it.

A moment later good-bys are being exchanged. Dr. Querin is looking again at the medal. Col. Rainsford voices a common regret that Morey could not have been there during the excitement of the presentation. "How he would have enjoyed it! How he would have laughed!"

"I think he was there, Colonel," says Gregorio, soberly.

MacGlorn has brought in the home-made flag with the magenta stripes. It is to be flown over the White House, at the President's request. And the President has asked the Philippine delegation to stay to supper, if they have nothing else to do. The President would like to hear all about their radio station.

Now, at MacGlorn's suggestion, they have started on a tour of the White House. "It's an interesting old place," MacGlorn assures them. "It's full of memories."

"And hope," adds Col. Rainsford.

A shaft of light has struck the flag of Task Force Zero, which MacGlorn has laid on his desk. The light is fading.

THE CURTAIN FALLS

LUTE SONG

Oriental Drama with Music in Two Acts

BY WILL IRWIN AND SIDNEY HOWARD

(Adapted from the Oriental "Pi-Pa-Ki" by Kao-Tong-Kia, 1940)

IT was in early February that Michael Meyerberg, who had stepped in when other prospective Broadway producers had stepped out, brought "Lute Song" to Broadway. The play had had a series of strange and interesting experiences, starting with Will Irwin's ambition as a young enthusiast of the Chinese theatre in San Francisco in the 1890s to adapt it to the Occidental stage. It had been written and rewritten many times before Sidney Howard and Mr. Irwin agreed in the late 1920s to collaborate in a new version. Their play, then without musical interpolations, was tried in the summer theatre at Stockbridge, Massachusetts, in August, 1930. Many playgoers were enthusiastic about it, but no Broadway producer was willing to chance a production. "The Yellow Jacket," emphasizing the appeal of a comedy property man, was their idea of how a Chinese play should be written and played for English-speaking audiences.

Following that first hearing, "Lute Song" was played at a number of universities, and notably at the University of Hawaii, where the actors were young American citizens of Chinese parentage. It was not until 1944 that Producer Meyerberg, at the suggestion of John Byram of Paramount, decided the play would do admirably as a starring vehicle for Mary Martin, if a somewhat sketchy musical score could be added to it. This started a new chain of research, following which everybody was delighted to discover that in the original Fourteenth Century production songs were also interspersed with the text.

As to the original play, naturally not too much is known. "Although scholars, both Oriental and Occidental, are in agreement as to the identity of the author," Mr. Irwin has written, "they disagree as to his name. A majority favors Kao-Tong-Kia, but others call him Tse-Tching.

"It is certain that he had been a schoolmaster in an interior province and came to the capital of the Flowery Kingdom to make

"Lute Song," copyright, 1945, *under title of "Pi-Pa-Ki," by Will Irwin and Sidney Howard. Revised and published version, copyright,* 1946, *under title of "Lute Song," by Will Irwin and Leopoldine Howard.*

his fortune with his pen. Editors of the play have drawn from internal evidence the inference that he had taken the literary examinations, which were for more than a thousand years the gateway to service under the Imperial Government (and which form such an important motive in this play), and had failed to pass them. Even the date of the play in its original and lost form is disputed. In the Nineteenth Century, Chinese and American editors favored the last decade of the Fourteenth Century, although Anton Pierre Louis Bazin, greatest French sinologist of his time, called attention to the fact that certain features suggested the Yuan period, which ended when the Mongol Emperors fell in 1368. Recent research by Chinese scholars points to the probability that it was in existence as early as the 1350s of our era."

After its Summer production in Stockbridge in 1930, "Lute Song" had many contacts with the professional play-producing world of Broadway. It was read at one time or another by dozens of prospective producers. But it was not until 1944, when Mr. Meyerberg, a little proud of his success with another unusual play script that had been generously refused production, the same being Thornton Wilder's "The Skin of Our Teeth," decided that he wanted to do it for Miss Martin. Raymond Scott was engaged to write an incidental musical score and "Lute Song" had its first Broadway hearing the night of February 6, 1946.

Audience introduction to "Lute Song" is by way of a short explanatory prologue spoken by the Manager. The overture has been played; the lights are lowered; the theatre curtain rises to reveal a second and much more beautiful series of dropped panels done in the Oriental manner, and with close approximation to the better Chinese art. Then the Manager, a robust gentleman of quiet authority, swathed in a beautiful Mandarin coat, appears to address us.

"Honorable gentlemen and ladies, whose radiant presence will inspire our actors to their highest art, we have engaged to perform for you tonight, 'The Lute Song.'" He pauses to survey the audience impassively and then continues: "It is a venerable tale of the time when the gods walked upon earth and wrought their magic in the sight of men. Since that time, cycles have swept over China. The Scarlet Gate has fallen; the Emerald Throne is dust. Through our skies today men dart more swiftly than the swallow; they speak to far lands with voices that outrun the sunbeam. They kill with pitiless machines and subtle essences. But still through the ages the voice of an ancient lute sings on —sings of life's cruelty, but also of its beauty; sings of ambition which consumes itself, but also of affection and fidelity; sings of harshness, but of pity also; sings of love, which is stronger than the Voice of Jade from the Imperial Throne. And now, with your permission, our play begins. We shall leave nothing out; we hope to be finished before morning."

Other curtains are raised, including the Blue Curtain of the House of Tsai in the village of Tchin-lieou. Tsai-Yong, whom we are to know as Husband the rest of the evening, is sitting at a table reading a book. There are other books around him.

"Six thousand volumes have I read," announces Husband, "all with the utmost concentration, yet have I never been tempted to turn my knowledge to the base uses of personal advancement."

At this point the Manager, who has been standing modestly by, resumes his part in the play—"that of the Honorable Tchang, an old friend of the family." The First Property Man appears with a change of hats for the Honorable Tchang, and takes away his robe. Tchang, to be known frequently hereafter simply as Friend, steps confidently into the action to explain that all his good neighbors depend upon him for counsel and protection; in the last three days he has advised no fewer than nine families, and now he is called to consider the affair of the obstinate young man, Tsai-Yong, the Husband.

The Emperor of the Middle Kingdom, Friend reports, has summoned all the young men of learning to the Capital that they may prove by examination their right to be exalted in the Imperial service. Before Husband can answer, his mother and father appear. Father, too, would like to know why his son continues to linger in the village, when he might well be on his way. Mother, however, is of a mind to keep him, Tsai being the only son she has.

Husband's excuse is reasonable enough: He doesn't want to go because his parents are old, his father blind. Who will provide for and cherish them if he should desert them now?

Father is not fooled. He knows well that it is his love for his young and beautiful wife, Tchao-ou-niang, that holds his son in the village. "His ship clings to the shore," says Father. "He dare not steer his course for the wide horizon." A moment later, after the beautiful young Wife has joined the circle, Father has turned to his son and asked—

"What do the sages teach you of the nature of filial piety?"

"A son's duty is to know, in Winter as in Summer, that his parents lack no single necessity of life," recites Tsai-Yong, as though he were in class. "He shall himself each evening make their bed. Each morning at cockcrow he shall himself enquire, in the most affectionate and respectful tone, concerning the state of their health. Many and many times each day he shall enquire whether they be hot or cold and upon what thing great or small their desire of the moment is inclined. He shall love the very dogs and horses his father loves. Such is the perfect filial piety of the ancients."

"My son, you neglect the loftier aspects. To attain greatness in the world and so to make glorious the name of the father and mother who conceived and bore you—that is the son's noblest expression of filial piety."

"I, who am a venerable Chinese," speaks up Friend, "remember what was said by a great scholar of the past. 'Youth sees too far today to see how near it is to seeing farther.' "

"Enough, enough, Honorable Tchang!" protests Mother. "You both certainly do not lack magnificent words to urge my son to leave! For three years now, we've poured our money like water into books and teachers for him. Books, books, until the house smells of ink! Our money is gone and you want to send him away."

But though Mother pleads eloquently, and there are many meaningful exchanges of glances between Wife and Husband, it is decreed that Tsai-Yong shall go. As for his obligations to his parents, his thoughtful and devoted wife will look after them—

"Heaven that made my parents virtuous, make my wife generous," prays Husband. "I confide my parents to my wife's care, trusting that when the time comes for my return to the land of my birth, robed in the splendors of a Mandarin, my parents will not have forgotten me, my wife will recognize and welcome my unworthy person."

"The day on which the Emperor creates my husband Mandarin, I will serve his parents from morning until nightfall upon tables of carved teakwood inlaid with pearls in the symbols of the Emperor. I will serve his parents upon dishes of fine porcelain. When my husband returns robed in the garments of a Mandarin, his glory will be my pride."

Husband and Wife have now knelt before Father, Mother and Friend. A "going-away" curtain is lowered behind them. Husband places a pin in the shape of a Golden Phoenix in Wife's hair. A second Property Man places a staff and wallet on Husband's shoulder, and gives a lute to Wife, who promptly passes it on to Husband.

The curtain that is lowered now is of the North Road that leads from Tchin-lieou to the Capital. We see Husband starting on his journey, Wife following him and singing softly the "Mountain High, Valley Low" song—

> " 'If you need me I will be near by—
> Mountain high,
> Valley low.
> My love follows you until the last,
> Lightning fast,
> Turtle slow.
> Journey to the North Star.
> South winds blow my thoughts to you.
> If you need me I will be near by,
> Mountain high,
> Valley low.' "

To which Husband answers—

> " 'I'll be with you 'tho our fortunes sway.
> Lantern gay,
> Willow sad.
> Spring will stroll our meadows ev'ry day,
> Winter gray,
> Summer glad.
> When your hair turns snow white,
> You will find me by your side.
> I'll be with you 'tho our fortunes sway,
> Lantern gay,
> Willow sad.' "

Now Wife has turned back to her home and Husband has continued on his journey. A ballet moves in to depict briefly adventures of the journey; the meeting and passing of a number of typical Chinese travelers—"Beggars and Merchants, a Rich Man and His Servant, a Woman, a Small Boy and Others."

Again the scene changes. Now we are in the Palace of Prince Nieou. The Prince is a large, important person, gorgeously arrayed. He is surveying condescendingly a formal tea ceremony.

Princess Nieou-Chi, his daughter, stands back of him with her Waiting Women and two Hand Maidens, who hold the tea service.

As soon as the others depart at the end of the ceremony, Prince Nieou makes an announcement: "I am Prince Nieou of the eminent House of Han, Preceptor of Morals to the Imperial Household," says he. "The effulgent goodness of the Son of Heaven arises from me, with some slight assistance from the Gods. My palace is as sumptuous as my virtues are exalted. No one speaks to me except to praise my zeal and my integrity. I govern my establishment with wise benevolence. It is my constant desire to promote tranquillity and happiness among those about me. At the merest suggestion of an argument, I simply sever their unworthy necks. No one has more authority than I except, of course, the Emperor."

This matter being settled, the Prince gives audience to a Marriage Broker who is eager and authorized to serve him. To the Marriage Broker he repeats a recent experience at court. The Son of Heaven had deigned to address him and to enquire whether or not his daughter, the Princess Nieou-Chi, had married yet. Learning that she had not, the Voice of Jade had said—

"Since that is so, it is my divine wish that she shall be given in marriage to the new Chief Magistrate of the Middle Kingdom, a young man of eminent merit and agreeable exterior. I shall myself preside at the marriage ceremony."

The Marriage Broker is greatly impressed by this Imperial Mandate, and hopeful that so auspicious a union shall last a thousand years.

"I honor this young man by my proposal and my daughter has certain undeniable merits of her own. Go to him, propose this marriage, return here with your answer. Your recompense will be in accordance with your success."

A short time later Prince Nieou seeks the Princess in her rooms to apprise her of the good fortune that has come to her. "My daughter," he says, after he has dismissed the Waiting Women, "you will be gratified to learn that I am now engaged in making arrangements for your marriage. At the Imperial command, I have at this moment sent a proposal to the latest recipient of the favor of the Son of Heaven, who is also the chief young scholar of the Middle Kingdom. Instruct your women to make due preparations and hold yourself in appreciative readiness."

"My father's will is my wish," answers the Princess, dutifully.

"I think I may safely conclude that my daughter is not unworthy of such a father."

The news has spread. The Steward brings in gossip of a spectacularly magnificent celebration in the Capital. "Not for a generation has the Imperial City witnessed such a display of pomp!"

"What was magnificent? What was superb?" demands a listener.

"The ceremony! The procession! For the new Chief Magistrate of the Middle Kingdom! Such a horse he rode. None of the horses of antiquity could have equaled it! They called him Flying Demon, Red Stag, Son of the Mountain, Lion Flower and Dragon's Spawn! And the doors of his stable are the twin arches of triumph."

"Never mind the horse! What about the man?"

"The Man? Oh, some young fellow who came when the moon was new from a far province and passed from the examinations through the Scarlet Gate into the very enclosure of the Son of Heaven under a triple parasol!"

And now the procession itself, or one very like it, moves excitingly across the scene. "First is a Sweeper of Heaven and Earth. Then a Major Domo. These are followed by two imperial guards carrying insignia with long streamers. Next comes a Drum Player wildly beating a large tom-tom which is carried by two guards. Directly back of these is a small boy playing a flute. Following are two imperial attendants with banners and then two imperial attendants with triple parasols. Next are two secretaries, then the Husband in his Magistrate's robe. He is followed by two imperial attendants carrying a very large single parasol. Bringing up the rear are two more guards with banners, a Fan-bearer and another Sweeper of Heaven and Earth. As the procession passes from view the curtain falls.

We are back in the village of Tchin-lieou, before the House of Tsai. Father, his robe more somber than before, has been telling the four children who troop after him one of the older stories—the one that ends: "'. . . and that was the end of the dragon, and they lived happily ever after.'"

It is time for the children to go home, but they continue to beg for another story until the wife of the absent Tsai-Yong agrees to substitute for Father. She will sing for them the song, "Who's the Monkey?" and play with them the game that goes with it. And she does.

But this is not at all to the liking of Mother, who breaks in upon their laughter. This is no time for games, says Mother. This is a time for them all, especially Father, to be about gathering food for the family. Where now is the brave son who had promised to serve them from morning to evening with rare meats? And who was it sent him away?

"Food is scarce, our money is gone! In the weeks to come if our son does not return what will become of us?"

"I will keep the promises I made to my husband," says Wife. "I will serve his parents the savory food suitable to their age and station. I shall manage, my mother."

"But how?"

"I will sell my long tunics of silk, and my jackets of stiff embroidery, the pearls and precious gems that I wore on my wedding day—even this—(*She takes from her hair the pin the* HUSBAND *put there.*)—this Golden Phoenix he pinned in my hair the day he went away."

"It was the last gift he gave you."

"And the last he will ever give to her," predicts Mother.

"My parents, listen to me," pleads the wife of Tsai-Yong. "The sun looks down upon the roofs of the Capital and through the windows and doors of the Emperor's palace. The wind spreads itself over the land and across the thresholds of the Emperor. The sun and the wind know the greatness of my husband. In our time we too shall know."

"My daughter!"

"My mother, let us have faith in one another. Your son will return with honor, with riches, and with greatness. All else is hidden but that I know."

The curtain falls.

Now we stand before the Gates of the Palace of the Voice of Jade, where Prince Nieou has come to meet the Marriage Broker and learn, he assumes, of the happy consummation of their joint interests. But there is no good news for the Prince. Do what she could the Marriage Broker could not gain the permission of the so fortunate young man to marry the Princess Nieou-Chi. He is even now preparing his petition to be returned to his native town.

Now Husband comes to answer for himself. He cannot marry the Princess, first, for reasons of filial piety; second, because he is already married—

"Hear me, my Lord," pleads Tsai-Yong. "The ancients sometimes counseled the gods. Suffer your abased servant to advise your Lordship. (*The* PRINCE *nods.*) The Princess is noble. My wife, whom I love, is of common birth. It was that I meant. If I marry your daughter, the sacred rites lower my wife to the station of concubine. This I will not allow."

"You cannot—" The Prince is suddenly infuriated.

"It is written that the chrysanthemum is not the only flower in the field," calmly answers Tsai-Yong. "Find another son-in-law, my Lord."

"I am not proud, but I cannot submit to humiliation," firmly answers the Prince. "Should you balk my will in this, fortified as it is by the Imperial Decree, what then would become of my authority and of the consideration which now surrounds me? (*In a burst of rage.*) Tsai-Yong, I insist upon this marriage!"

"It cannot be, my Lord!"

"This very hour I shall prostrate myself before the Voice of Jade," declares Prince Nieou, calmly but menacingly. "We shall see how far this young upstart can defy my rank!" With this he storms out in the direction of the Imperial Palace.

"Oh, the gods give eloquence to my tongue, for it is my only hope," mutters Tsai-Yong, as he follows after. "Surely the Son of Heaven will understand."

The curtain falls.

The air is filled with ritual music. Before a great gold screen stands the Imperial Chamberlain in all his robes, attended by four Imperial Guards. "The Emperor of the Heavens is at its zenith!" announces the Chamberlain. "The Emperor of Earth holds court!"

And now, with great ceremony and to an elaborate musical accompaniment, the Imperial Chamberlain proceeds "to raise the jeweled curtain in the crimson apartment of Divine Wisdom!" Now he reveals "the Hall of Undying Autumn," and "the Hall of perpetual Sincerity," and finally "the Palaces of the Golden Bells." After this and more he is prepared to listen to the "Lord Chief Magistrate newly created of the Middle Kingdom."

"Now, speak your purpose," says he, facing Tsai-Yong.

HUSBAND—Shadow of our Imperial Lord—(*Bows.*)—I have sought honors, but not all those that have been showered upon me.

CHAMBERLAIN—Is any honor unwelcome to the Chief Magistrate?

HUSBAND—If I beg the Son of Heaven to withdraw one of his favors, it is because I cannot in conscience accept it.

CHAMBERLAIN—Has the Chief Magistrate a conscience independent of his Emperor's?

HUSBAND—I have written all here upon this ivory tablet, according to the prescribed rites. My desire is to return forthwith to the land of my birth.

CHAMBERLAIN (*turning*)—Chief Magistrate of the Middle Kingdom, why?

HUSBAND—I have duties to fulfill in the land of my birth. Duties toward my father and mother who are growing old; other duties no less exacting. My country is a far province that lies beyond high mountains and wide southern rivers. I am uneasy for my parents.

CHAMBERLAIN—Your uneasiness is natural enough, Chief Magistrate. Tell me, what favor of the Emperor's do you desire to have withdrawn?

HUSBAND—I am ordered to contract a marriage here with a Princess of high rank.

CHAMBERLAIN—In which you are envied of all men, Chief Magistrate.

HUSBAND—How dare I contract a marriage without my father's consent?

CHAMBERLAIN—The Son of Heaven is your Celestial father.

HUSBAND—I have a wife already, a young wife whom I love.

CHAMBERLAIN (*starting to leave*)—The antechamber of the Hall of Audiences, my Lord Chief Magistrate, is no place for tears.

HUSBAND—Will not the Son of Heaven free me from this command? Will not his mercy and justice release me from this marriage?

CHAMBERLAIN—That is unlikely. The Imperial Preceptor waits even at this moment upon the Emperor. I am afraid your petition will not greatly avail you.

HUSBAND—What of my own wife? What of her?

CHAMBERLAIN—This is a question of obedience to the Emperor's will.

HUSBAND—This is a question of right and wrong and of justice and injustice.

CHAMBERLAIN—Of the Emperor's will and a young man's folly. Give me the tablet.

HUSBAND—Present my petition! Say to the Emperor that

rather than make this marriage, the Chief Magistrate craves leave to resign his office and his honors!

Prince Nieou has seen the Emperor, and has won the decision. What is past for Tsai-Yong is past forever and must be forgotten. "You must pay the price of your greatness in a certain amount of personal discomfort. The Emperor is your father now. Your life began anew with your elevation to his favor. Be advised, accept all he may deign to bestow upon you, and do not look back."

With an anguished cry of "My wife! My wife!" Tsai-Yong would make a break for liberty. Whichever way he turns there are Imperial Guards to stop him. Soon he is surrounded by guards and spears.

And now the Imperial Chamberlain has come from the Emperor to announce to Tsai-Yong that, because of the great generosity of Prince Nieou, the wedding is to take place at once. All is in readiness.

Still Tsai-Yong protests. In the face of all that the Emperor might decree to his hurt he still rebels. But to no avail.

To further bursts of music, attendants enter bearing the young man's golden wedding robe and hat and drape them upon him.

Now the great doors of the Palace are opened and there stands the Princess, gorgeous in a red and gold wedding dress. The Prince is at her side and the Imperial Chamberlain is near by.

Tsai-Yong starts toward the steps and stops. At a threatening gesture from the guards he continues on. Now he stands dutifully beside the Princess. Bride and groom are bowing to the assembled dignitaries as—

The curtain falls.

Now we have further news from Tchang, our Friend. It is his report on conditions in the village of Tchin-lieou. "Rain, rain, day after day," reports Tchang. "Rivers breaking their boundaries and flooding the land. Today the last of our rice fields slipped away beneath the water. There is no food, only what has been hoarded by the rich and what was stored in the Provincial Granary against the time of famine. Now, that too is almost gone."

A rising curtain reveals the Provincial Granary in the village. The Food Commissioner and Two Clerks are doling out rice. There are many Beggars in the crowd, and among them the wife of Tsai-Yong.

One by one the beggars advance and get what rations the Commissioner will allow. The Clerks have some trouble keeping them in line. One, who is paralyzed, is given three rations. One, with a family of six, since his wife died, interests the Commissioner—

"I'm sorry to hear about your wife. Did she die of starvation in the present famine?"

"My wife died of catching cold as the result of selling her wearing apparel, and both my daughters-in-law are threatened with the same fate."

"This family will become a menace to public decency," comments the Commissioner. "Six rations. Next!"

Wife, discovered as the only woman among the Beggars, interests the Commissioner. What would be her story?

"My name is Tchao-ou-niang; I am the wife of Tsai-Yong, only son of the one-time magistrate, Tsai. I ask the food of charity."

"Times are strange when a woman of good family and respectable environment comes unescorted to a public office."

"The times are strange indeed, my Lord. My husband is some months gone from home on an expedition to the Capital for the Imperial Examinations. My husband's father and mother are old and broken."

"And who is there to support your husband's parents during his absence?"

"Only myself, your Excellency. They have no worthier staff to lean upon."

"A frail staff. I wonder your husband was willing to trust much to it."

"It is not for me to wonder."

"Let us hope your husband's success in life will compensate his family for his neglect. Three rations. Next!"

Suddenly it is discovered that there is no more rice in the Provincial Granary. The Commissioner and the Clerks must announce this fact and withdraw. As the bewildered crowd moves away, some of the Beggars set upon Wife, take her rations from her and throw her to the ground. A blind Beggar stumbles over her as he follows the crowd.

"So low have we fallen—the poor robbing the starving," mutters Wife, bitterly, as she gets to her feet and starts away. "Every day brings death in a thousand and ten different guises, but the end of life, which is the true death, comes only once. . . ."

It is better, she decides, to throw herself into an abandoned

Photo by George Karger, Pix, Inc.

"LUTE SONG"

Now Tchao-ou-niang approaches, her raven hair hanging about her shoulders. Softly she sings—

"And now it's harvest time,
My hair is in its prime;
Who'll buy my bitter harvest,
Who'll buy my hair?"

(*Walter Stane, Mary Martin, Ronald Fletcher*)

well she had noted on her way to the Granary. ". . . I shall have gathered my thousand daily deaths into one complete oblivion."

But Friend Tchang is there to save Wife from this decision. Tchang will share with her his provisions. He will walk with her and see her safely home. And he would cheer her with a prophecy—

"I say to you that your present misfortune is the compensation the gods exact for your happiness to come when your husband says to you: 'I am the work of your hands, Tchao-ou-niang, my wife, and my glory is the fruit of your devotion. But for you, my honors will be dross.'"

As they walk the lights fade. The curtain falls.

It is night. The Garden of Prince Nieou's Palace is bathed in soft lights. Tsai-Yong is there, sitting on the steps of the Palace, trying to compose his mind with music. It is his wedding night, but he is not happy. He can neither play nor sing. The times and the lute are out of tune.

Suddenly Tsai-Yong recognizes an old friend in the Steward who has come to do him service. This would be Youen-Kong and he would be the one man in the Palace whom Tsai-Yong can trust. Tsai-Yong would have the steward find a trustworthy servant and send him at once to the village of Tchin-lieou with gold coins and pearls for the daughter of the retired magistrate, Tsai. They are for the wife of Tsai's son—

"And on no account is he to give any report of me," instructs Tsai-Yong. "He is to be as discreet there as you must be secret here. Give him money for his journey. When he returns, he shall have a bar of gold."

"Your Lordship's generosity is boundless."

The Princess has come from the Palace. She had heard the lute and would hear more—

"This is our wedding night. Play to me, my good Lord. I, too, have misgivings. I, too, have need of calm."

"What shall I play?" asks Tsai, as an attendant hands him the lute. "'The Snow on the Pines?'"

"No, that is the song of Widowhood. Are we not together here, my Lord? Sing some old song of longing and of love fulfilled."

But it is no use. Though he tries a few bars of "Mountain High, Valley Low" Tsai cannot go on. Soon he has reluctantly drunk a toast to his bride—and left her. . . .

The Steward has found the servant he would select for the journey to the village. He has given him the purses and Tsai's letter for Wife. But before the servant can leave, Prince Nieou appears suddenly and relieves him of both jewels and letter, which he reads aloud—

"'I am doing well. I am in the government service. I cannot, owing to circumstances, reveal' . . . h'm . . . 'You will hear from me further in time!' . . . h'm . . . 'I hope someday . . .' He says little enough. I might without harm let it go after all. (*He starts to return the letter to* YOUEN-KONG.) Ah, if it were not for the other woman. No, I must protect my daughter from her and from himself. I am sorry for the old people, but the past must be past and the crown of wisdom goes to him who knows how to forget. Pu-Kiong has said that when a member of a household stoops to folly, the head of the house must be wise for him. Put those pearls into the household treasury. He shall have them back."

"When, my Lord?"

"When? When he has learned to forget."

"My Lord, what of the old people?"

"They'll manage. They always do!"

From near-by Tsai-Yong has been a witness to what has happened. He would follow after Prince Nieou, but armed guards step quickly from the darkness and bar his way. The lights fade. The curtain falls.

We are back in the village of Tchin-lieou, at the House of Tsai—a battered and run-down house by now. Father and Mother, stricken by the famine, are seated at a broken table hoping for food. The wife of Tsai, trying to serve them, has fetched a tray with three bowls. But, being stricken with hunger pains, the unsalted rice, which is all Wife has, does not satisfy them. Mother is particularly bitter.

"In famine time one eats only to preserve life," Father chides. "Set down the rice, my daughter. I give thanks for it. Sometimes I think that Heaven sent this calamity to prove to us the goodness of our son's wife."

"Only a month ago our larders were stored with salt fish . . ." wails Mother, "and there were fine turnips and sweet preserved fruits. Now this . . . Take it away." She sweeps the bowl from the table.

"Anger will only weaken you, my mother. Perhaps I still can find a few grains of salt."

Wife has gone back to her own bowl before the stove. This, to Mother, is a suspicious act. Can it be Wife has plenty for herself, but is denying her husband's parents? But when she investigates,

Mother finds that Wife has even less than they—no more than a bowl of roots and rice husks—pig's food!

"I am ashamed of my suspicions," now wails Mother. "May the gods forgive me the injustice that I thought." And as she starts back to the table she falls. When they go to her, Mother is dead.

Father does not linger long in his grief. He, too, knows that he is dying and would, in his misery, call down punishment on his absent son's head. To this the loyal Wife objects—

"Your son, when he returns robed in honors as you would have him come," she promises, "will stand at my side to honor his parents. Together we will marvel at the strange ways of the gods, for whom the gardens of life grow only in the dust of suffering."

Father is not impressed. He calls upon his old friend, Tchang, to write down a will. In the will Father decrees that his son's wife shall go from his house, forget his son and take unto herself a new home and a new husband. To Tchang he bequeaths his staff, that Tchang may use it to beat Tsai's son when he shall come home, and drivc him from the village in disgrace everlasting.

Even though it is written, Wife will not respect this will. She would break the staff of her husband's father if she could—

"Strike me with it if you will, but lift this curse," she cries out. "Lift this curse! My faith is stronger than doubt or anger. You are going beyond the Nine Rivers. Think what you do last in this life. Think, before you leave me here alone with the memory of bitterness and curses. . . . Father! Father!"

Father is dead. "A sage of ancient times has said: 'The root which is cloven in twain shall perish in both parts,'" quotes Tchang. "It is over, Tchao-ou-niang."

Together they pass in front of the curtain of the House of Tsai. "I promised my parents a funeral worthy of their station and their life," Wife is saying. "Parents of my dear love, I shall find boards for your coffins and fine linen cloth for your shrouds. I shall find white raiment for my mourning and a dry place in the yellow earth for your tombs. Rest in peace, my parents, rest in peace." She has raised her hands in supplication. "High Gods, do not abandon me now! Help me to find a way!"

The curtain falls.

We are in the Street of the Hair Buyers. There is a milling crowd: Coolies, Rich Merchants, Hawkers, Children and Two Hair Buyers.

From time to time women approach the Buyers, prepared to part with their hair. There is bargaining and buying. It is nearing night. As the shadows fall the crowd thins out.

Now Tchao-ou-niang approaches, her raven hair hanging about her shoulders. The street is deserted. Softly she sings—

> " 'And now it's harvest time,
> My hair is in its prime.
> Who'll buy my bitter harvest
> Rich and ripe? . . .
>
> " 'My lover's gaze is there
> Should you appraise my hair
> You could never pay
> A price too high,
> Money couldn't buy
> What's in my harvest!
> Who'll buy my hair?' "

Two Hair Buyers chip off Wife's tresses and go back into their shop.

Friend Tchang is witness to the proceeding and is startled. What is this that Wife has done?

"I have sold my hair for the burial rites of my dead. When my parents are suitably laid in their tombs, I shall go to a nunnery and ask shelter until my husband returns."

"In you, Tchao ou niang, I salute a being more faithful than any I have ever known. I promise you, your parents will have a funeral worthy of a magistrate and of a magistrate's wife.

They start to leave. The curtain falls.

In a Burial Place in the village of Tchin-lieou a funeral procession appears, headed by Two Priests, Two Willow Bearers and a Flute Player. The procession assembles for prayer around two small headstones.

"Oh, ye gods of the Upper Kingdom who preside over the living and the dead, hear our petitions and accept our sacrifices . . ." intones the First Priest.

"Give them a happy sleep, O ye Gods of the Sky," adds the Second Priest. "Wake them this day only to hear their descendants raise their petitions in prayer to the just and administering gods."

Friend and Wife have come to bring Wife's offering and to

kneel at the graves. Now the others have withdrawn and Wife is alone—

"Mother and Father of my love and duty," she prays, "your daughter stays alone here in this place of eternal rest. Mother and Father of my love and duty, it is a time of famine and this is little enough food that I have given you for your Heavenly journey. . . . Mother and Father of my love and duty, forgive me that I have borne no man-child to complete the three-fold circuit of your graves. Forgive me that I have been too poor to have raised above you the shrine which is your due. I have stayed alone to raise some semblance of a mound with my hands."

As Wife is scooping earth from the ground to place on the graves there is a blinding flash of light and a great burst of music. Now a rising curtain reveals a high pyramid of Buddhisatvas and Lesser Gods, surmounted by a Genie—

"Touched by the virtue and devotion of Tchao-ou-niang, the Sovereign of the Heavens decrees divine assistance to her final act of perfect piety," proclaims the Genie. "Hosts of the Shadowy Empire! Ape of the Mountain! White Tiger of the South! Comc to my work here and raise this mound!"

A ballet of Lesser Gods moves in and at the height of their ritualistic dancing "a cloud of smoke rises from the earth and out of it comes a gleaming white and gold shrine."

And now from the Genie Tchao-ou-niang receives further instructions. She is to proceed to the convent of O-mi-to Buddha, tell her story to the Holy Abbess and obtain the raiment of a novice. Then, as a Beggar and Holy Pilgrim, she is to proceed to the Capital of the Middle Kingdom, earning her bread through song. Finding her husband she is to tell him of his parents' passing, that he may perform the appointed rites that will bring their souls rest. The end of her journey will be reward.

At the top of the pyramid the Genie holds aloft the lute of Tsai-Yong. It is passed down the pyramid and into Wife's hands. "Go now, in the name of Him who is everlasting and Glorious and Serene!" directs the Genie.

Wife has taken the lute to hold it lovingly in her arms. As the light fades on the pyramid she starts on her journey—

"Singing over the roads to the Scarlet Gates of the Emperor's Palace; to the Capital of the Son of Heaven, in my arms my lover's lute . . . my lover's lute . . ."

There is a final burst of music. Wife is holding the lute before her.

The curtain falls.

ACT II

Our friend, the Manager, has returned. He stands for a moment or two before a figured curtain, satisfying himself that the audience is seated before he speaks.

"Eminent gentlemen! Ladies whose virtue is incense in the temple of domestic tranquillity! After this brief interval for contemplation and reflection, our play continues. . . .

"Our story is indeed sad; our men—Tsai, the Venerable Magistrate, the Young Scholar, the Exalted Prince—all these have found that the ropes by which they hoped to climb were cords to bind and strangle them. Their way is hard. But our women! Ah! Woman is sister to the white blossoming willow. She is cheering to the eye, downy to the touch, and pliant in the hand—more or less."

"But when the gods wish to dam a mighty river—yes, even the giant Yangtze Kiang—they pass by the sturdy sycamore and choose the slender willow. Why? I do not know. Perhaps the gods themselves do not understand willows and women. But it is so, as you shall see." . . .

Now we are back in the garden of Prince Nieou's Palace. It is night. Tsai-Yong, surrounded by attendants, is idly watching two dancers who are doing their best to entertain him. Soon he sends them away and dismisses his attendants.

Nor is he cheered by the appearance of the Princess, who has come to discover, if possible, what it is that has for five months kept the veils of sorrow drawn around her lord's heart—

"My husband," gently protests the Princess, "in this house you are served with the rarest meats. You have tunics of lilac silk and girdles of yellow gold, and fillets of pale jade. When you ride into the city, maidens strew flowers beneath your horse's hoofs, and youths shade your head with triple parasols. Do not reproach me, my Lord, if I remind you how, only five short months ago, you were a poor student."

HUSBAND—Five months . . .

PRINCESS (*moving down to step*)—Do not reproach me if I remind you that today you live in a palace of the House of Han, surrounded by all abundance of honor and of substance, and fulfill the most lofty functions of the Middle Kingdom. It is strange to me that such an ascent leaves you dissatisfied.

HUSBAND—You are right. I lack nothing—neither rare meats nor girdles of gold and jade, nor the tunics of lilac silk. I have shoes, too, that are black and polished to be worthy of the floors of the Son of Heaven. But my tunics and girdles only burden me, and I stumble in my shoes.

PRINCESS—Have I, then, succeeded only in shackling my husband?

HUSBAND—Not you. Sorrow is a thing either of memory or of fear.

PRINCESS—Is it that the Son of Heaven exacts too much of you?

HUSBAND—No . . .

PRINCESS—Your servant, then, does not govern her household to please you?

HUSBAND—It is not that . . .

PRINCESS—If I do not understand, how can I hope to set things right? Perhaps, in some other palace, in the pavilion of some other garden, you have found a sweeter love than mine!

HUSBAND—No. Those whom I love—dwell far beyond the horizon of the South.

PRINCESS—Trust me, my husband. Tell me . . .

It is then Husband does tell his Princess of the aging Father and Mother he had been forced to desert, and of his great desire to return to them. The Princess suggests that it might be better if he were to bring his parents to the Capital, to live in the Palace with him.

Then Tsai-Yong tells of his loyal Wife. That is his real secret, his real sorrow. Stunned for a moment, the Princess would hear more of this wife—

"She is the daughter of the people," explains Tsai-Yong, "and her beauty is like the light and her virtues are manifold. She lives in my father's house and she is safe there. But my heart is torn for her . . . and my spirit restless and uneasy over the wrong I have done her—even though I intended no wrong."

It is then the Princess learns for the first time that she has been twice deceived—by her husband and by her father. And these wrongs must be corrected—

"My father is Preceptor of the Imperial Family," she says, with determination. "His household must set an example of honorable living. I shall go to him now with what I propose."

"What is that?"

"To make with you a penitential pilgrimage to your village, to your parents and to your neglected wife."

"Your father will never permit it."

"Reason and justice and right are on my side."

"What right?"

"The right of womanhood. One of us, your first wife or I, must be the wife and one—the concubine."

A moment later they have started on their way to have audience with the Prince.

The curtain falls.

We are back now on the North Road. The Honorable Tchang has come a way with Tchao-ou-niang on her way to the Capital. It is strange to Tchang that one should travel so far at the bidding of a dream. But Tsai-Yong's wife would correct him. If he had seen the rich shrine that was raised over her dead he would know it was not a dream. Could a dream transport so material a thing as a lute over mountains and rivers to the place of the dead?

"The gods said to me: 'Take this lute. It is the lute of your husband, Tsai-Yong. Find him and tell him what has befallen.' "

There is one thing about which Tchang would warn Tchao-ou-niang. "When your husband left you," says he, "beauty flowered in your face and your body was supple as a willow branch in springtime, but when he sees you now. . . ."

"I understand."

"What will become of you?"

"It does not matter. These things are as the gods ordained. Were I as withered as an old leaf, yet I would go."

When Tchang has turned back, Wife sits by the road a little and sings again the words of the song she and Tsai-Yong knew—" 'If you need me I will be near-by, Mountain High, Valley Low . . .' "

Wife is still singing as the curtain falls.

In a room in the Palace, Prince Nieou is awaiting the Princess and her husband. He is prepared to submit a new plan to them in answer to their request to be permitted to visit the remote village of Tchin-lieou. "In the ancient book of etiquette," ruminates the Prince, "it is written that he who would rule a kingdom must first govern his own household."

When the Princess and Husband are seated before him the Prince first tells them of his objections to the proposed journey. Tchin-lieou is far-distant; the district in which it lies has been swept by floods and is devastated by famine; the way is over mountains and through swollen rivers; the Princess would never survive the journey.

"As to you, my son-in-law, we have already discussed this matter and I am much too cognizant of your inclinations to run the risk of permitting you to indulge them," the Prince continues, turning to Tsai-Yong. "The character of man is the noblest work of the gods—so long as it is preserved from any temptation whatsoever. The merest approach of temptation is, unfortunately, sufficient to degrade it. This is a fact which we are bound to recognize in order to get the best results from the higher sex. Women—women, I have observed, are singularly immune to temptation. This is due to women's general spiritual, imaginative and intellectual inferiority. (*To* HUSBAND.) If I allowed you to make this journey, you would probably never return. You would probably abandon both my daughter and your position here at court and thus not only ruin your own career but also cause myself unnecessary embarrassment."

It is the Prince's conclusion that a caravan properly outfitted for the journey should proceed at once to the village of Tchin-lieou and, hunting out the wife and parents of the Chief Magistrate, bring them forthwith to the Palace.

With one instruction added, the Princess approves the plan: "Let him not tell—her—of my Lord's marriage to me," she pleads.

"And if he does mention that great honor?" queries Prince Nieou.

"My father, it will do no good to bring her here with hatred in her heart."

"That is a wise suggestion, my daughter. If she has any visionary expectations, let her enjoy them while she may. Life, I have observed, is a sovereign remedy for the disease of optimism."

The Princess and Husband are kneeling before Prince Nieou as the curtain falls.

We stand now in the gorgeous Temple of O-Mi-To-Fo. A Priest is kneeling before the altar. A Bonze is beating a prayer drum. There is a great din. A group of beggars kneels on the floor of the Temple. After the curtain has risen, the Priest gets to his feet and addresses the people—

"Oh, all ye who sorrow for the shades of parents departed, this day we celebrate in this Temple the Festival of Souls. . . ."

It is to this celebration that Tchoa-ou-niang has come, still carrying the lute of her husband. The Priest sees her, and following his exhortation to the crowd he approaches her—

"Holy Sister!"

"Is this the Temple of O-Mi-To-Buddha?"

"It is. Can I help you?"

"I need charity, Reverend Father, money to buy incense and prayers for my dead."

"Incense costs money, Sister, but the poorest can pray. Come into the shrine, Sister. May the gods give heed to you."

Wife has moved up to kneel before the altar. The Priest has turned to greet the Steward Youen-song who comes to announce the approach of the Chief Magistrate.

"Joyfully the shrine of Fo welcomes your master's advent," declares the Priest. "An offering will be prepared." And summoning the beggars he advises them: "Listen to me, all ye who ask charity! You will not ask in vain of this one!"

The Bonze has gone to the altar to motion Tchoa-ou-niang to one side, that there shall be more room for the Chief Magistrate and his party. And now the procession of Guards and Parasol Bearers enters the temple with a great fanfare of music and beating of cymbals.

Tsai-Yong has come in search of the Shrine of Ancestors. He is a little surprised to find it harboring so many beggars, but, seeing this is the Day of Souls, he orders his Steward to give them alms.

From her place near the altar Tchao-ou-niang has seen and recognized her husband. She cowers timidly on the steps before him. He, recognizing her for a holy woman, would give her a silver coin—

"Pray for me, Sister," he says. At this Wife bursts into tears and Tsai-Yong is greatly puzzled. He would say more, but the Priests are calling him. His ancestor offering has been prepared. The Priest has begun:

"Address with profound heart the prayers of the eternal life! Bow you down before the Lotus Flower. Open your soul to the Lotus Flower! Jewel of the Lotus Flower, I pray you that the relatives of this worshiper enjoy rest, happiness and health everlasting!"

The great gong has been struck. The prayers continue. Wife, edging timidly toward the Steward, touches his arm. She would know his master's rank.

"Chief Magistrate of the Middle Kingdom, trusted and honored of the Son of Heaven," answers the Steward, proudly. He is surprised at Wife's tears.

"Will you give him this?" she asks, handing him the lute.

"It is a strange gift."

"I think your master will understand; if he does not, no matter."

"But what shall I tell him?"

"Tell him they wait no longer," she says, and is gone.

The prayers are finished. Tsai-Yong has come back, looking for the holy woman. The Steward hands him the lute, with the message.

"Curious! In the South where I come from I used to play upon such an instrument."

"There's a word painted on it there . . . She bade me . . ."

" 'Tsai-Yong!' My lute! My old lute! What did she say?"

" 'They wait no more.' "

"That beggar—that holy woman was my wife! Where did she go?"

"She went into the crowd, Master."

"Find her! Find her!"

The guards have rushed off. Husband is kneeling in shame.

The curtain falls.

It is late in the day. A storm has come up. The street is teeming with beggars and others. The guards are searching frantically for Tchao-ou-niang, who, seeing them, runs on again.

The Steward is there to report that every nunnery in and near the city has been searched. Runners have been sent to every nunnery within fifty leagues of the city.

Let them continue the search, commands Tsai-Yong.

The curtain falls.

In a room in the Palace the Princess stands distraught. The Steward has been summoned, but still has no news of the one for whom they search. If they do not find her this day, the Princess fears it will be too late.

Tsai-Yong has gone back to his books. In the garden he is listening to a secretary read, but this does not divert him for long. Nor can the Princess do aught to comfort him—

"I have been thinking that, had I never learned to read and write," Husband is saying, "I would have been a better son and a better man. Learning is too strong a wine for such weak souls as mine."

"Why do you reproach yourself, my husband? We are what we are. At the most we can affect the world only a little. You should have better courage."

"That I have not is only another sign of the malady that destroys me—weakness and pretense. Forgive me. I shall do well enough by myself."

Prince Nieou has come at the request of his daughter. She is afraid. She would know from him if there is any danger that her husband may commit suicide? The Prince is reassuring—

"No gentleman kills himself except upon the order of the Emperor or to take revenge upon an enemy," he says. "Were any other than himself to blame for your husband's predicament, he might then be justified in taking his life upon that other's doorstep, thus discrediting that other in the sight of the world. Since he has no one but himself to blame, he will scarcely commit suicide to discredit himself."

Li Wang, the servant who had headed the caravan to Tchin-lieou in search of the parents and wife of Tsai-Yong, has returned.

"The old people died of starvation in the famine . . . The house is in ruins . . . The Wife has fled, no one knows where," he reports.

And now the Steward has come to tell the Princess that she whom they seek is at the gates of the Palace. But she does not yet know whose palace this is. A moment later Tchoa-ou-niang stands before the Princess—

PRINCESS—Rest yourself. You must be weary. Have you traveled far, Sister?

WIFE—I have come a long way, my Lady.

PRINCESS—And how have you fared?

WIFE—I have gone from place to place, begging charity.

PRINCESS—Your speech is of a far province, Holy Sister.

WIFE—My only home is the home of my birth and my birth was beyond the southern mountains.

PRINCESS—In what province? What town?

WIFE—In a small village beside the great river. It is called Tchin-lieou. (*The* PRINCESS *tightens a bit.*) A village so humble, the great Lady has doubtless never heard its name.

PRINCESS—Sister, how long is it since you took your vows?

WIFE—I have not yet passed through the Jeweled Gate to Peace, my Lady. I am still only a novice. Before that . . . before that, I was married.

PRINCESS—You must find it hard to beg in the streets. Have you no other means of livelihood?

WIFE—In my childhood I was taught the golden accomplishments of woman. I can read and paint and embroider and I can sing and play the lute. On my way to the Capital, that was the way I earned my bread. My Lady, it was not just to beg that I came to the Capital.

PRINCESS—Why then?

WIFE—To find my husband.

PRINCESS—Have you found him?

WIFE—I have found him. He has risen to greatness, leaving his parents to starve. He saw me . . . he did not know me.

PRINCESS—And then, Sister?

WIFE—And then—I ran away. . . .

Wife has fallen to the floor. There is an excited rush of attendants to revive her. A waiting woman has brought a cup which the Princess puts to Wife's lips. "Drink this. It will bring back your strength."

When Wife has recovered, it is the Princess' suggestion that she should stay on in the Palace in the Princess' service. There is a great need of a waiting woman with the golden accomplishments. At first Tchao-ou-niang refuses, but soon she is won over.

The Princess sends attendants for a robe of gold and a headdress of precious stones. "In this house you cannot wear that nun's robe. My hus . . . my father would not permit it."

"I dare not change it. It is my sign of mourning."

"I honor your piety, Sister, but you must change that dress. Come! Come! We'll have need of all your beauty."

In the process of dressing Tchoa-ou-niang, the Princess notices that her hair has been cut. When she hears that it was to pay for the burial rites of her dead, the Princess orders that it shall be her finest headdress that Wife shall wear—a headdress in the form of a Phoenix.

"If I wear it, will I not be overwhelmed with shame?" demands Wife; "I whose husband forsook her."

"You shall wear it with pride, because you have been faithful," answers the Princess. . . .

Presently the whole story is told. Tchao-ou-niang knows in whose house she is, and why she has been dressed thus extravagantly. "I wanted him to see you as he remembered you . . . his very life depends on that," explains the Princess.

"His life!" repeats Tchoa-ou-niang, bitterly. "My nun's cloak! Tell them to find my nun's cloak!"

PRINCESS—Not yet, Tchao-ou-niang! Listen to me! He married me at the command of the Emperor. What could he do? He sent a letter and money to his parents and gifts to you, but . . .

WIFE—In that letter, did he tell us . . . about you?

PRINCESS—He is a man and men are frail. He was not strong enough to break out of the trap, nor I alone, to help him . . .

WIFE—Help him—to what?

PRINCESS—To some end worthy of your hopes and mine and his father's dreams for him. We can be very strong together, Tchao-ou-niang. We can make his life the harvest of our united faith and joint mercy.

WIFE—Mercy! Had he mercy for his father and mother when he left them to starve? Princess, what are you trying to make me do?

PRINCESS—Not to make you but to persuade you to stay in this house with me—and with him. Stay and love him and tend him and bear him the man-child who will make the three-fold circuit of his tomb when he is gone.

WIFE—I was his wife, Princess. While he got his learning, night and day I cherished him. When he came to the Capital to find greatness, I cared for his father and his mother. Freely I gave them my love—all my love. Through hunger and humiliation and injustice and blows and madness, I cared for them. I saw them die, Princess. I buried them in the yellow earth. And now you in the pride of your high station, you ask me . . .

PRINCESS—I ask you to stand with me at his side to help him and guard him.

WIFE—You as his wife—and I as his concubine? Is that what he wants? (*The* PRINCESS *cannot answer.*) If that is what my husband desires, his wish shall be my will. Only, Princess, I must hear it from him.

Tsai-Yong is called. As he faces the Princess he follows her gaze to where Tchao-ou-niang is standing. With a glad cry he bounds down the steps and kneels at his wife's feet, crying "Tchao-ou-niang, my wife! My wife!"

"You as the wife, Tchao-ou-niang," murmurs the Princess, leaving the two together.

"Can you forgive me?" pleads Tsai-Yong.

"My husband!"

"Help me to be worthy. I shall not fail in my penitence."

They have moved up the steps. Now Husband is sitting on a stool and Wife kneels at his feet. It is thus that Prince Nieou finds them and turns to the audience:

"That is indeed extremely touching, my children, though I find the sentiment somewhat overwrought. As for this unfortunate marriage of my daughter, it is written in the maxims that what the Voice of Jade has ordained, the Voice of Jade may revoke. I shall prostrate myself before his radiance and relate this unique tale of filial piety. I am not sure I may not, myself, compose an historical monograph to perpetuate this episode. For though women may be our slaves and are certainly our inferiors, we cannot overlook their virtues. As generous men, we cannot possibly do that."

Husband and Wife are singing the final bars of "The Lute Song."

THE CURTAIN FALLS

THE PLAYS AND THEIR AUTHORS

"State of the Union," a comedy in three acts by Howard Lindsay and Russel Crouse. Copyright, 1944, by the authors. Copyright and published, 1946, by Random House, Inc., New York.

This is the second appearance of the collaborating team of Lindsay and Crouse in this theatre record. They made their debut as Best Play authors in the issue of 1939-40 with their long-running comedy, "Life with Father," which, at this writing, is still playing and is well within reach of the record-holding "Tobacco Road," which achieved a total of 3,182 performances over a span of seven years.

Mr. Lindsay, born in Waterford, New York, 1889, devoted his early years as a writer of plays to comedy collaborations with Bertrand Robinson. A solo effort that was hugely successful was a dramatization of Edward Hope's "She Loves Me Not" in 1934.

Mr. Crouse, born in Findlay, Ohio, in 1893, devoted his first years as a writer to newspaper work, serving the Cincinnati *Commercial-Tribune,* the Kansas City *Star,* and three New York dailies, the *Globe, Mail* and *Post,* as reporter and columnist. He was the author of several books, notably "Mr. Currier and Mr. Ives" (1930), before he teamed with Corey Ford on "Hold Your Horses," for Joe Cook, and with Mr. Lindsay for the production of a highly successful musical comedy, "Anything Goes," introducing the happy trio of William Gaxton, Victor Moore and Ethel Merman.

Since they joined forces Mr. Lindsay and Mr. Crouse have written "Red, Hot and Blue" and "Hooray for What?", musical comedies; "Life with Father," "Strip for Action," and "State of the Union," comedies. As producers they have presented "Arsenic and Old Lace," "Strip for Action," "The Hasty Heart" and "State of the Union"—four hits out of five tries.

"Home of the Brave," a drama in three acts by Arthur Laurents. Copyright, 1945, by the author. Copyright and published, 1946, by Random House, Inc., New York.

Arthur Laurents was born in New York City, July 14, 1918, and in 1937 got a Bachelor of Arts degree from Cornell University. He began his professional career as a writer of radio scripts, and when he joined the Army in August, 1941, he continued in this field. He wrote or helped write a great number of Army broadcast programs, including such series as "Assignment Home" and "The Man Behind the Gun." "Home of the Brave" is his first play, and a second one has been completed for possible production in the 1946-47 season. On the strength of the drama-writing ability shown in "Home of the Brave," he was given a grant of $1,000 by the American Academy of Arts and Letters.

"Deep Are the Roots," drama in three acts by Arnaud d'Usseau and James Gow. Copyright, 1945, by the authors. Copyright and published by Charles Scribner's Sons, New York.

A year after their success with "Tomorrow the World" (Best Plays, 1942-43), Arnaud d'Usseau and James Gow decided to leave scenario writing to the Hollywood field and transferred their activities to Broadway and the living theatre. They had not been in New York long, however, before they were inducted into the Army and assigned to the Signal Corps. In the Army it took them a year and a half to write "Deep Are the Roots." This study of a Negro war hero returned to his home in the Deep South proved as quick a success as a post-war problem drama as "Tomorrow the World" had proved as a World War I study of a Nazi-trained youth's reactions in the democratic world of the U.S.A.

Both d'Usseau and Gow are Western-born—d'Usseau a native son of California (Los Angeles, April, 1916) and Gow a cornhusker from Creston, Iowa (August 23, 1907). D'Usseau had his schooling in California; Gow in both Iowa and Colorado. Both had newspaper experience, Gow on the old New York *World*, d'Usseau as a United Press correspondent in Arizona. After they had turned to scenario writing in Hollywood they met on the RKO lot. One thing led to another until they decided to collaborate on a play. Two or three minor failures taught them a lot about what not to do. Elliott Nugent, who staged "Tomorrow the World," taught them more in six weeks than they had learned before in six years, they are happy to confess. They are completely in agreement as to politics and religion, which saves them time in argument and adds a lot to their joy of living.

"The Magnificent Yankee," a comedy in three acts by Emmet Lavery. Copyright, 1945, by the author. Copyright and published, 1946, by Samuel French, Inc., New York.

The year he wrote his first produced play, "The First Legion," which was in 1935 or thereabouts, Emmet Lavery spoke of himself as "a newspaperman and occasional lawyer who lives happily in Poughkeepsie with his wife and two children." Because there has been no drastic change in this domestic situation in twelve years, it is fair to assume that Mr. Lavery is practically the same man today, though now he is living in Beverly Hills, California, and devoted himself recently to running for Congress. He has had quite a bit of experience in show business since then, however. He served as one of the executives who helped Hallie Flanagan with the conduct of the nearest thing to a national theatre America has ever boasted—that being the Federal Theatre, which grew out of the great depression of the middle nineteen thirties. "The First Legion" traveled practically around the world, being produced in several different languages. A short play, "Monsignor's Hour," also had several productions by amateur dramatic societies, and a Vassar piece called "The Daisy Chain" had a tryout at the Pasadena Playhouse. But it was not until he wrote "The Magnificent Yankee" that Mr. Lavery bounced back to Broadway attention. He was born in Poughkeepsie in 1902, got an LL.B. from Fordham University in 1924, and was admitted to the bar in New York in 1925. He has gone in actively for picture assignments since settling in California. He is now president of the Screen Writers' Guild and vice president of the Motion Picture Academy of Arts and Sciences.

"Antigone," a tragedy in one act by Jean Anouilh. English adaptation by Lewis Galantiere. Copyright, 1945, by Lewis Galantiere. Copyright and published, 1946, by Random House, Inc., New York.

Jean Anouilh has been an active and successful playwright in the Paris theatre since 1932, when his first play, "L'Hermine," was produced at the Théâtre de l'Œuvre. He was twenty-two then, and the Paris newspaper critics were well pleased with his work. To bear out this critical faith Anouilh came back in 1933 with a comedy called "Mandarine," which was also a success. That the playwright has variety is indicated by the fact that the first of these two successful plays was fairly heavy drama, concerning a youth disgusted with the society rich who expressed his disgust by committing murder, and the second the story of a gigolo "who scoffed at the bourgeois honesties." Anouilh continued to write plays up to the German occupation, his "Laocadia" having been staged in 1941 and his "Eurydice" in 1942. "Antigone and the Tyrant" was, of course, a sly slap at Fascist dictators. That it got by the German censors during the occupation was a surprise to many people. M. Anouilh was born in Bordeaux and was working for an advertising agency in Paris when he wrote his first play.

Lewis Galantiere, who made the English adaptation of "Antigone," although a native of Chicago (1893), has spent much of his life, the last thirty years, in and around Paris. From 1920 to 1927 he was associated with the International Chamber of Commerce in Paris; from 1928 to 1939 he was chief of the foreign division of the Federal Reserve Bank of New York, and from 1942 on he was director of French overseas operations in the Office of War Information. He is the author of a book attractively entitled "France Is Full of Frenchmen," and has translated and written introductions for the works of many French men of letters, including the translating and editing of "The Goncourt Journals, 1851-1870." In 1932 he had a fling at the stage, writing a play called "And Be My Love," and, with John Houseman, another entitled "Three and One."

"O Mistress Mine," a comedy in three acts by Terence Rattigan. Copyright, 1945, by the author. Revised and published version, copyright, 1946, by Terence Rattigan.

The best-known of Terence Rattigan's comedies previous to the arrival of Alfred Lunt and Lynn Fontanne with "O Mistress Mine" was one called "French Without Tears," which ran for 111 performances at the Henry Miller Theatre, New York, starting in September, 1937. A war play concerned with the Royal Air Force, which was Mr. Rattigan's assignment during the war, did not fare so well. It was called "Flare Path," was produced in December, 1942, and was withdrawn after 14 performances. "O Mistress Mine" was called "Love in Idleness" in London, where it enjoyed a long tour of the English provinces before being taken by the Lunts to the continent to help celebrate V-Day with the GI's.

Mr. Rattigan was born in London in 1912. He attended Harrow and Oxford and was headed for the diplomatic service when he wrote a play called "First Episode," afterward renamed "College Sinners." This first effort served the purpose, the author agrees, of teaching him a lot about what not to do in playwriting. Taught him so much, in fact, that the following year he wrote the successful "French Without Tears." His biggest success in London to date is a piece called "While the Sun Shines." Over there it long since passed its 1,000-performance mark. Over here it was discovered to be too British for our taste, getting only 39 performances in September, 1944.

"Born Yesterday," a comedy in three acts by Garson Kanin. Copyright, 1946, by Garson Kanin and Ruth Gordon. Copyright and published, 1946, by Viking Press, Inc., New York.

Garson Kanin is a graduate of what might be called Abbott Academy—but not the New England school of that name. He is one of the young men and women who have been trained in showmanship by George Abbott.

Kanin was born November 24, 1912, in Rochester, New York. He studied at the American Academy of Dramatic Arts and subsequently appeared in a number of Broadway plays, including "Spring Song" and "Little Ol' Boy." Then he became a production assistant to Abbott on a series of successful comedies including "Three Men on a Horse," "Brother Rat" and "Room Service." He directed two plays, "Hitch Your Wagon" and "Too Many Heroes."

In 1937 Kanin joined Samuel Goldwyn's film production staff, and a year later joined RKO as a producer-director. His first notable screen-directing job was on "A Man to Remember," a so-called B picture which was highly praised.

In 1942 he became a film producer for the U. S. Offices of Emergency Management. Subsequently he joined the Signal Corps, next transferred to the O.S.S., and finally became a member of General Dwight D. Eisenhower's staff. In this latter post he produced "The True Glory," which the New York Film Critics' Circle voted one of the two best documentary films of the war. It was a history of the European campaign from D-Day on. Kanin left the army with the rank of captain.

"Born Yesterday" is Kanin's first play. He is married to Ruth Gordon, the actress, and when Miss Gordon wrote a comedy for herself titled "Over 21" it was stated inaccurately that Kanin had helped write it. Mr. and Mrs. Kanin insist that Mrs. Kanin's plays are her own—and his is his own.

"Dream Girl," a comedy in two acts, by Elmer Rice. Copyright, 1945, 1946, by the author. Copyright and published, 1946, by Coward-McCann, Inc., New York.

Elmer Rice insists, so help him, that he had no idea that his wife, the attractive Betty Field, who has been the star of most of his dramas the last several years, would also star in "Dream Girl." He is, after all, a commercial dramatist. He knew that practically every female motion picture star is hoping desperately that she can find a play with which she could return to Broadway. When he came upon an idea that would fit such an ambition he just naturally wrote the comedy suggested and tried to sell it in Hollywood. But the screen stars he had in mind could not see it, and those who could see it he didn't particularly fancy. So-o-o—Betty had to play it after all. Mr. Rice has been in these theatre yearbooks several times before—with "Street Scene" in 1928-29, which was his first appearance, down to "Flight to the West," with which he temporarily bowed out in 1940-41. He was headed for the law when he quit college, but quickly switched to the drama when his first play, "On Trial," proved an overnight hit. He has written twenty-five plays since then, and his average of successes is higher than most.

"The Rugged Path," a drama in three acts by Robert E. Sherwood. Copyright, 1945, by the author. Copyright and published, 1946, by Charles Scribner's Sons, New York.

Robert Emmet Sherwood gave up playwriting at the outbreak of World War II. When it became our war as well as that of the Allies, he became associated with various departments of the government's war effort, notably the O.W.I. with which he served in Europe for many months, his official title being that of Director of Overseas Operations Branch, Office of War Information. In World War I he served with the Black Watch, joining up in Canada.

Mr. Sherwood's first appearance as a Best Plays author was the season of 1926-27, when his first produced play, "The Road to Rome," was a great success, starring Jane Cowl, supported by the late Philip Merivale. Sherwood successes that followed included "Reunion in Vienna," "Idiot's Delight," "The Petrified Forest," "Abe Lincoln in Illinois," and what many consider the best of all the war plays, "There Shall Be No Night." Mr. Sherwood was born in New Rochelle, New York, in 1896, got his A.B. at Harvard in 1918. He served his time as drama editor of *Vanity Fair,* and as editor of *Life* magazine when it was a humorous weekly.

"Lute Song," an Oriental drama in two acts, adapted by Will Irwin and Sidney Howard from the Chinese classic, "Pi-Pa-Ki." Copyright, 1945, under title of "Pi-Pa-Ki," by Will Irwin and Sidney Howard. Revised and published version, copyright, 1946, under title of "Lute Song," by Will Irwin and Leopoldine Howard.

In his autobiography, Will Irwin confessed that his curse was a yearning for experience. Beginning with his childhood and youth in the pioneer West, carrying through war and politics and militant journalism, he seems to have got what he wanted. The by-product was hundreds of short stories and magazine articles and thirty books or so. Perhaps he is best known for the correspondence for the London *Times* and *The Saturday Evening Post* during the First World War—Lord Northcliffe of the *Times* once called him "the ace of correspondents"—and for his analytical writing on the subject of journalism itself. His early experiences included a term as a barn-storming actor; he collaborated with Bayard Veiller in *The Thirteenth Chair* and he has taken other whirls at the drama both professional and amateur. Now, his roving done, he lives with his novelist wife, Inez Haynes Irwin, in a state of relative tranquillity in an old house in Greenwich Village, nursing a bad leg which he got playing center at Stanford, and wired for sound because of a head-wound he took at the Battle of Caporetto. The first Irwin-Howard version of "Lute Song" was tried at the Stockbridge, Massachusetts, Summer theatre in 1930. Broadway scouts who saw it could see no commercial value in it.

The late Sidney Howard (he died in August, 1939) made his first appearance as a Best Plays author with "They Knew What They Wanted" in 1924-25, and his last appearance with "Dodsworth" in 1933-34. He enjoyed a fine success as a dramatist for many years. He was a Californian, born in Oakland in 1891, a graduate of the University of California, and the commander of a combat air squadron in the First World War.

PLAYS PRODUCED IN NEW YORK

June 17, 1945—June 1, 1946

(Plays marked "continued" were still playing June 1, 1946)

OH, BROTHER!

(23 performances)

A comedy in three acts by Jacques Deval. Produced by Maximilian Becker and Peter Warren at the Royale Theatre, New York, June 19, 1945.

Cast of characters—

Allen Kilmer....Don Gibson
Sue Atkins....Susana Garnett
Charles Craddock....Hugh Herbert
Ethel Shores....Eva Condon
Rose....Sally Archdeacon
Larry....Kendall Bryson
Marion Cosgrove....Arleen Whelan
Amelia Broadwell....Catherine Doucet
Steve Foley....Lyle Bettger
Julian Trumbull....Forrest Orr
Connie Rowland....Jutta Wolfe
Joan Massuber....Gloria Stroock

Acts I, II and III.—Study at the Cosgrove Home, Daytona Beach, Florida.

Staged by Bretaigne Windust; setting by Samuel Leve.

Charles Craddock is an expert at chess. He needs $1,000 to enter a tournament. A little on the crook side, Craddock hopes to get the money by inducing a young friend of his named Kilmer to impersonate a long missing heir to a fortune. Kilmer helps build complications by falling in love with his supposed sister, Marion Cosgrove, who is also a bathing suit model of generously exposed attractions.

(Closed July 7, 1945)

THE WIND IS NINETY

(108 performances)

A play in three acts by Ralph Nelson. Produced by the Messrs. Shubert in association with Albert de Courville at the Booth Theatre, New York, June 21, 1945.

Cast of characters—

Nana..Blanche Yurka
Joan..Joyce Van Patten
Tommy..Roy Sterling
Jimmy..Kevin Mathews
Chris..Donald Devlin
Bert..Teddy Rose
Doc Ritchie..Bert Lytell
Mr. Wheeler..Scott Moore
Jean..Frances Reid
Ernie Sheffield..Dickie Van Patten
Dan..Wendell Corey
Soldier..Kirk Douglas
Boy..Marty Miller
Youth..James Dobson
Young Man..Henry Barnard
2nd Lieutenant..Gordon McDonald

Acts I, II and III.—The Front Lawn of a Home.
Staged by Albert de Courville; setting by Frederick Fox.

Don Ritchie, a lieutenant in the Air Force, is shot down over Germany. Hoping to save his family from the shock of his passing when the official news reaches them, Don comes home in spirit form, accompanied by the spirit of the Unknown Soldier. Don, unable to get through to his wife, his parents and his two small children, discovers that each of them remembers him differently—his father as a college freshman, his mother as a small boy with a black eye, his wife as the youth who awkwardly proposed to her. He finally manages to give them the idea that whenever the wind is 90, which would be from the east, he will always be with them in spirit.

(Closed September 22, 1945)

MARINKA

(165 performances)

A romantic musical in two acts by George Marion, Jr., and Karl Farkas; music by Emmerick Kalman; orchestrations by Hans Spialek. Produced by Jules J. Leventhal and Harry Howard at the Winter Garden, New York, July 18, 1945.

Cast of characters—

Nadine..Ruth Webb
Countess Von Diefendorfer..Elline Walther
Bratfisch..Romo Vincent
Crown Prince Rudolph..Harry Stockwell
Count Lobkowitz..Taylor Holmes
Naval Lieutenant..Noel Gordon
Count Hoyos..Paul Campbell
Francis..Leonard Elliott
Tilly..Ronnie Cunningham
Marinka..Joan Roberts
Madame Sacher..Ethel Levey
Countess Landovska..Luba Malina

Waiter..Jack Leslie
Lieutenant Baltatzy....................................Bob Douglas
Emperor Franz Josef............................Reinhold Schunzel
Countess Huebner...................................Adrienne Gray
Sergeant Negulegul...............................Michael Barrett
Lieutenant Palafy......................................Jack Gansert

Act I.—Scene 1—Open Air Movie Theatre, Connecticut, 1945. 2 and 7—Gardens of the Imperial Palace of Schoenbrunn, 1888. 3—Bratfisch's Cab. 4—Living Room of Lodge at Mayerling. 5—Street in Vienna. 6—Red Room of Sacher Restaurant. Act II.—Scenes 1 and 3—The Austro-Hungarian Border. 2—Corner of Parade Ground, Budapest. 4—Mayerling. 5—Open Air Movie Theatre, Connecticut, 1945.

Staged by Hassard Short; book directed by the authors; choreography by Albertina Rasch; music directed by Ray Kavanaugh; sets by Howard Bay; costumes by Mary Grant.

A retelling of the story of the Mayerling tragedy that took Crown Prince Rudolph of Austria and the last of his mistresses, Marie Vetsera (Marinka), mysteriously from our midst, and from the hunting lodge in Mayerling as well. In this version the audience is permitted to complete the story as it wishes. The Crown Prince and his love just disappear.

(Closed December 8, 1945)

MR. STRAUSS GOES TO BOSTON

(12 performances)

A comedy with music in two acts by Leonard L. Levenson based on an original story by Alfred Gruenwald and Geza Herczeg; music by Robert Stolz; lyrics by Robert Sour. Produced by Felix Brentano at the Century Theatre, New York, September 6, 1945.

Cast of characters—

Dapper Dan Pepper......................................Ralph Dumke
Policeman McGillicudy...............................Brian O'Mara
Inspector Gogarty...Don Fiser
1st Reporter...Dennis Dengate
2nd Reporter...Larry Gilbert
3rd Reporter...Joseph Monte
Pepi...Florence Sundstrom
Bellhop...Frank Finn
Johann Strauss..George Rigaud
Elmo Tilt...Edward J. Lambert
Hotel Manager...Lee Edwards
Brook Whitney...Virginia MacWatters
A Waiter...Paul Mario
Mrs. Dexter..Laiyle Tenen
Mrs. Blakely...Rose Perfect
Mr. Whitney...Sydney Grant
Mrs. Taylor..Arlene Dahl
Mrs. Hastings...Selma Felton
Mrs. Iverson..Mario Barova
Mrs. Byrd...Cecile Sherman
Butler..John Oliver
Tom Avery...Jay Martin
A Photographer..John Harrold

Earl...Brian O'Mara
Hetty Strauss.......................................Ruth Matteson
Aide to President....................................Lee Edwards
President Grant....................................Norman Roland
Mr. Pottinger...Don Fiser
Man in Overalls......................................Paul Mario
Solo Dancers..............Harold Lang, Babs Heath, Margit Dekova

Ladies and Gentlemen of Singing Ensemble: Nancy Baskerville, Jeanne Beauvais, Arlene Carmen, Doris Elliott, Alma Fernandez, Lucy Hillary, Olga Pavlova, Mia Stenn, Mary Lou Wallace, Dennis Dengate, Lee Edwards, Frank Finn, Larry Gilbert, John Harrold, Philip Harrison, Paul Mario, Joseph Monte, John Oliver, Brian O'Mara.

Corps de Ballet: Mary Burr, Jacqueline Cezanne, Sylvia de Penso, Andrea Downing, Helen Gallagher, Arlene Garver, Mary Grey, Fiala Mraz, Virginia Poe, Stephen Billings, Paul Olson, William Sarazen, Tilden Shanks, Terry Townes.

Act I.—Scene 1—Lobby of Grand Palace Hotel, New York, June 16, 1872. 2—Corridor in Hotel. 3—Sitting Room of Strauss Suite. 4—Off to Boston. 5—Whitney Drawing Room, Boston. 6—Reception in Honor of Johann Strauss. Act II.—Scene 1—Strauss Bedroom at Governor Winthrop House. 2—Balcony of the Governor Winthrop House. 3—Along the Charles River.

Staged by Felix Brentano; choreography by George Balanchine; settings by Stewart Chaney; costumes by Walter Florell.

Johann Strauss, Jr., the waltz king, visits Boston during the Jubilee in 1872, and is made much of by the women—by Miss Brook Whitney in particular. But Mrs. Strauss has followed her husband, and, with the aid of Ulysses S. Grant, leads him back into the marital path.

(Closed September 15, 1945)

A BOY WHO LIVED TWICE

(15 performances)

A drama in two parts by Leslie Floyd Egbert and Gertrude Ogden Tubby. Produced by Hall Shelton at the Biltmore Theatre, New York, September 11, 1945.

Cast of characters—

Braxton..Stapleton Kent
Ellen Blake...Cecil Elliott
Jeane Hastings....................................Anne Sargent
Randall Hastings................................Grandon Rhodes
Martha Hastings...................................Claire Windsor
Dr. Cecil Blake (Dockaby).......................W. O. McWatters
Philip Hastings.......................................John Heath
Anne Cunningham...................................Strelsa Leeds
Dr. Broulette....................................Vaughan Glaser
Mother..Nellie Burt

Parts I and II.—Living Room of the Hastings Home, Long Island, New York.

Staged by Paul Foley; setting by John Root.

On horsy Long Island Philip Hastings falls off a horse and is pronounced dead by a doctor—only to come to life apparently unhurt. Philip does, however, think he is somebody else—a lad who was killed in an airplane accident. His family try to cure him by employing a hypnotist, but Philip still persists in his belief. This is embarrassing, because he and his "sister" have fallen in love, she with his new soul and he with all of her. The solution deals with a transference of souls, in which the two boys, twins, made a trade. Philip was one of the twins. His supposed father confesses that he kidnaped a baby which was not his, which cleans up the love affair.

(Closed September 22, 1945)

DEVILS GALORE

(5 performances)

A comedy in three acts by Eugene Vale. Produced by William Cahn at the Royale Theatre, New York, September 12, 1945.

Cast of characters—

Effie Thurston....................Tony Eden
Bernie Grant....................Michael King
Cecil Brock....................George Baxter
Miss Pierce....................Betty Kelley
Mrs. Isabel Goodwyn....................Jean Cleveland
Dr. Aguirra....................Harry Sothern
A Devil....................Ernest Cossart
Larry....................Paul Byron
Bobbie....................John (Red) Kullers
Inspector Brandon....................Malcolm Lee Beggs
Atamar....................Rex O'Malley
Packey "The Flash" Gurney....................Solen Burry

Acts I, II and III.—Cecil Brock's Office on the 34th Floor of a Fifth Avenue Skyscraper, New York.

Staged by Robert Perry; setting by Howard Bay; costumes by Peggy Clark.

When Cecil Brock, an amorous literary agent, is more or less accidentally killed by a virtuous young lady novelist, a sub-devil is dispatched from hell to claim his soul. The agent talks the devil into letting him have two more weeks of life, during which time he guarantees to overcome the young woman's reserve and thus provide the devil with a second fallen soul. The spirit from hell assumes human identity in order to watch events—and finds that New Yorkers are so far ahead of the nether regions in devilment that he accepts a bid from St. Peter to try heaven for a while.

(Closed September 15, 1945)

MAKE YOURSELF AT HOME

(4 performances)

A comedy in two acts by Vera Mathews. Produced by Albert Chapereau and Johnnie Walker at the Barrymore Theatre, New York, September 13, 1945.

Cast of characters—

Luther Quinn....................................Donald McClelland
Honeybelle Collins....................................Bonnie Nolan
Vic Arnold....................................Philip Huston
Ray Gilbert....................................Donald White
Porter....................................Charles Carol
Dwight Waring....................................Wm. Valentine
Mona Gilbert....................................Bernadene Hayes
(Mama) Gilbert....................................Suzanne Jackson
Ivy....................................Elizabeth Brew
Ferris Delmar....................................Robert Carleton
Barney....................................Grey Stafford
Bob....................................Robert Noe
Sammy....................................Loy Nilson

Acts I and II.—Living Room of Mona Gilbert's New York Apartment.
Staged by Johnnie Walker; setting by William Noel Saulter; costumes by Janice Walker.

Mona Gilbert, a fading movie star, returns to New York to try a comeback in a play. She moves back into her own apartment, in spite of the fact that it is leased to and occupied by Honeybelle Collins, a Southern cutie, and her protector. The action deals farcically with the housing shortage.

(Closed September 15, 1945)

THE RYAN GIRL

(48 performances)

A comedy in three acts by Edmund Goulding. Produced by Messrs. Shubert in association with Albert De Courville at the Plymouth Theatre, New York, September 24, 1945.

Cast of characters—

Weavy Hicks....................................Una O'Connor
Miley Gaylon....................................Edmund Lowe
Venetia Ryan....................................June Havoc
Harold Tyler....................................Curtis Cooksey
Lt. George Clark....................................John Compton
2nd Lt. Victor Sellers....................................Richard Gibbs
Jane Clark....................................Doris Dalton
Edwin Rourke....................................Calvin Thomas

Radio Broadcast by Lowell Thomas

Acts I, II and III.—Venetia Ryan's Apartment, New York City.
Staged by Edmund Goulding; setting by Raymond Sovey.

Miley Gaylon, a hoodlum, returns from seven years in Venezuela to visit his wife, Venetia Ryan, a former "Follies" girl. New York detectives still want him on a murder charge. Gaylon has read that his and Venetia's son, known now as Lt. George Clark, has been awarded the Congressional Medal. Shortly after his birth the boy, unwanted by both parents, had been adopted by a second "Follies" girl, who married a millionaire and brought the lad up as a gentleman. It is Gaylon's plan to reveal the hero's true parentage—and thus, he thinks, escape the electric chair. "They" wouldn't dare execute the father of a national hero! Venetia saves "them" trouble by shooting Gaylon and preserving her son's good, though adopted, name.

(Closed November 3, 1945)

YOU TOUCHED ME!

(109 performances)

A romantic comedy in three acts by Tennessee Williams and Donald Windham, suggested by a short story by D. H. Lawrence. Produced by Guthrie McClintic in association with Lee Shubert at the Booth Theatre, New York, September 25, 1945.

Cast of characters—

Matilda Rockley....................................Marianne Stewart
Emmie Rockley....................................Catherine Willard
Phoebe....................................Norah Howard
Hadrian....................................Montgomery Clift
Cornelius Rockley....................................Edmund Gwenn
The Reverend Guildford Melton....................Neil Fitzgerald
A Policeman....................................Freeman Hammond

Acts I, II and III.—A House in Rural England, Spring of 1943.
Staged by Guthrie McClintic; setting by Motley.

Cornelius Rockley, retired from the sea, and living with his acidulous and hopelessly frustrated sister, Emmie, is distressed to discover that Emmie's influence over Matilda, his daughter, is far from helpful. Cornelius, an amiable rumpot, would bring Matilda out of the narrow depression she is settling into and back to life by furthering her interest in Hadrian, his adopted son. Hadrian, a flyer from Canada, is not averse to the assignment, and the life force wins.

(Closed January 5, 1946)

DEEP ARE THE ROOTS

(289 performances)

(Continued)

A play in three acts by Arnaud d'Usseau and James Gow. Produced by Kermit Bloomgarden and George Heller at the Fulton Theatre, New York, September 26, 1945.

Cast of characters—

Honey Turner....................................Helen Martin
Bella Charles....................................Evelyn Ellis
Senator Ellsworth Langdon........................Charles Waldron
Genevra Langdon..................................Barbara Bel Geddes
Alice Langdon....................................Carol Goodner
Roy Maxwell......................................Harold Vermilyea
Howard Merrick...................................Lloyd Gough
Brett Charles....................................Gordon Heath
Sheriff Serkin...................................Andrew Leigh
Chuck Warren.....................................George Dice
Bob Izay...Douglas Rutherford

Acts I, II and III.—Living Room of Langdon Home on the Outskirts of a Small Town in the Deep South, Spring of 1945.

Staged by Elia Kazan; setting by Howard Bay; costumes by Emeline Roche.

See page 94.

CARIB SONG

(36 performances)

A musical play in two acts by William Archibald; music by Baldwin Bergersen; orchestrations by Ted Royal. Produced by George Stanton at the Adelphi Theatre, New York, September 27, 1945.

Cast of characters—

The Singer.......................................Harriet Jackson
The Fat Woman....................................Mable Sanford Lewis
The Tall Woman...................................Mercedes Gilbert
The Husband......................................William Franklin
The Fisherman....................................Avon Long
The Woman..Katherine Dunham
The Fishwoman....................................Elsie Benjamin
The Shango Priest................................La Rosa Estrada
The Boy Possessed by a Snake.....................Tommy Gomez
The Leader of the Shango Dancers.................Vanoye Aikens

The Village Friends: Lucille Ellis, Lauwanne Ingram, Eartha Kitt, Ora Leak, Mary Lewis, Gloria Mitchell, Eulabel Riley, Priscilla Stephens, James Alexander, Byron Cutler, John Diggs, Jesse Hawkins, Lenwood Morris, William C. Smith, Charles Welch, Norman Coker, Richardena Jackson, Eddy Clay, Roxie Foster, Eugene Lee Robinson, Enid Williams, Julio Mendez.

Act I.—Scene 1—The Wake. 2—Early Morning by the River. 3—The New House. 4—The Corn Sorting. 5—The Market. 6—The Lie. 7—The Road to the Shango. 8—The Shango. Act II.—Scene 1—Dry Season. 2—"Today I Is So Happy." 3—The Market. 4—The

Quarrel. 5—The Forest at Night. 6—"Go to Church, Sunday." 7—"Wash Clothes, Monday." 8—The Rain Comes. Action takes place in Small West Indian Village.

Staged by Katherine Dunham and Mary Hunter; settings and lighting by Jo Mielziner; costumes by Motley; music directed by Pembroke Davenport; choreography by Katherine Dunham.

Woman, being pursued by Fisherman, gives Husband the run-around, suffering the familiar penalty in the end.

(Closed October 27, 1945)

NEW YORK CITY CENTER OF MUSIC AND DRAMA

The Ballet Russe de Monte Carlo opened the 1945-46 season at the City Center, New York, September 9, 1945. (See Dance Drama.)

The New York City Opera Company under the direction of Laszlo Halasz opened its 1945-46 season at the City Center, New York, September 27, 1945.

TOSCA

An opera in three acts by V. Sardou, L. Mica and G. Giacosa; music by G. Puccini. Presented at City Center, New York, September 27, October 7, 20, 28 and November 4, 1945.

Cast of characters—

Floria Tosca....................Doris Doree, Dorothy Sarnoff
Mario Cavaradossi....................Eugene Conley
Baron Scarpia....................George Doubrovsky
Cesare Angelotti....................Grant Garnell
Spoletta....................Hubert Norville
A Sacristan....................George Lipton
Sciarrone....................Arthur Newman
Gaoler....................Allen Winston
A Shepherd....................Elsa Rozner

Act I.—Interior of Church in Rome. Act II.—Scarpia's Study in Farnese Palace. Act III.—Citadel of San Angelo. June, 1800.

Staged by Leopold Sachse; music directed by Laszlo Halasz.

CAVALLERIA RUSTICANA

A melodrama in one act by G. Targioni-Jozzetti and G. Menasci; music by P. Mascagni. Presented at City Center, New York, September 28 and October 4, 14 and 21, 1945.

Cast of characters—

Santuzza....................Doris Doree
Turiddu....................Giulio Gari, Ian Cosman
Alfio....................Grant Garnell
Lola....................Gladys Zieher, Louise Bernhardt
Mamma Lucia....................Carroll Taussig, Mary Kreste

A Sicilian Village.

Staged by Eugene Bryden; music directed by Julius Rudel and Laszlo Halasz.

Followed by—

PAGLIACCI

An opera in two acts by Ruggiero Leoncavallo.

Cast of characters—

Canio.............................Rafael La Gares, John Dudley
Nedda..Helen George
Tonio..Todd Duncan
Beppo.....................................Nathaniel Sprinzena
Silvio.......................................Gordon Dilworth

Acts I and II.—A Calabrian Village.

Staged by Eugene Bryden; music directed by Laszlo Halasz and Julius Rudel; setting by Richard Rychtarik.

LA BOHEME

An opera in four acts by G. Giacosa and L. Illica after the novel by Henry Murger; music by G. Puccini. Presented at City Center, New York, September 29, October 7, 17 and 27, November 2, 1945, May 10 and 26, 1946.

Cast of characters—

Mimi.................Lucille Manners, Irma Gonzalez, Alice Ribeiro
Musetta..Natalie Bodanya, Nadine Ray, Lillian Fawcett, Helen George
Rudolpho............................Eugene Conley, Giulio Gari
Marcello.............Enzo Mascherini, Daniel Duno, John de Surra
Schaunard.....................................Arthur Newman
Colline.................James Pease, Gean Greenwell, Carlton Gauld
Benoit.............................Emil Renan, George Lipton
Alcindoro.....................................Hubert Norville
Parpignol.................................Nathaniel Sprinzena

Acts I and IV.—Attic Studio on Montmartre. Act II.—Café Momus. Act III.—At the Gate of Paris.

Staged by Sally Stanfield and Leopold Sachse; music directed by Thomas P. Martin. Settings by H. A. Condell.

LA TRAVIATA

An opera in four acts by Francesco M. Piave after the novel by A. Dumas; music by Giuseppe Verdi. Presented at City Center, New York, September 30, October 13, 25 and November 8, 19, 25 and 29, 1945.

Cast of characters—

Violetta Valery.............................Rosemarie Brancato
Alfred Germont.......Rafael La Gares, John Dudley, Eugene Conley
George Germont.......................Daniel Duno, Gordon Dilworth
Flora Bervoix...................................Susan Griska
Annina...........................Elsa Rosner, Blanche Archambault
Gaston de Letorieres...........John Harrold, Nathaniel Sprinzena
Baron Douphol...................................Grant Garnell
Marquis D'Orgibny...............Morton Davenport, Gil Gallagher
Doctor Grenville...............................Arthur Newman

Act I.—Terrace of Violetta's Mansion, Paris. About 1850. Act II.—Villa Near Paris. Act III.—Ballroom in Flora's Mansion. Act IV.—Violetta's Bedroom.

Staged by Sally Stanfield; music directed by Thomas Martin and Jean Morel; choreography by Carl Randall and Igor Schwezoff; settings by Richard Rychtarik.

CARMEN

An opera in four acts by Meilhac and Halevy; music by Georges Bizet. Presented at City Center, New York, September 30, October 6, 11, 19, 24, November 1, 4, 9, 1945, and May 12, 18, 25, June 1, 1946.

Cast of characters—

Carmen...Winifred Heidt
Don Jose.................................John Dudley, Ramon Vinay
Escamillo............George Doubrovsky, James Pease, Todd Duncan
Micaela....................Alice Ribeiro, Nadine Ray, Helen George
Frances Anderson, Lucille Manners
Zuniga................Grant Garnell, George Lipton, Gean Greenwell
Frasquita...Lenore Parker
Mercedes..Susan Griska
Remendado......................................Nathaniel Sprinzena
Dancairo..Hubert Norville
Morales..Arthur Newman
Solo Dancers.........Jane Kiser, Zoya Leporska, Anthony Werbitsky

Act I.—Public Square in Seville. Act II.—Tavern. Act III.—Ravine in Mountains. Act IV.—Entrance to Arena.

Staged by Leopold Sachse; music directed by Jean Morel; choreography by Carl Randall and Igor Schwezoff; settings by Richard Rychtarik and H. A. Condell.

THE BARTERED BRIDE

A folk opera in three acts with English version by Joan Cross and Eric Crozier after the translation by Rosa Newmarch; music by Bedrich Smetana. Presented at City Center, New York, October 3, 14, 20, 26, November 3, 11, 1945, and May 11, 24, 1946.

Cast of characters—

Marenka............Brenda Lewis, Lucille Manners, Polyna Stoska
Jenik.................................John Dudley, Morton Bowe
Kecal.................James Pease, Gean Greenwell, Carlton Gauld
Krushina...Grant Garnell
Ludmilla...Enid Szantho
Vashek..........................John Harrold, Hubert Norville
Tobias Micha......................................Arthur Newman
Hata...Mary Kreste
Principal............................Emil Renan, Gil Gallagher
Esmeralda..Lillian Fawcett
An Indian..Alan Winston

Acts I, II and III.—Village Square in Bohemia.

Staged by Eugene S. Bryden; music directed by Laszlo Halasz, Julius Rudel and Thomas P. Martin; setting by Richard Rychtarik; choreography by Carl Randall and Igor Schwezoff.

"The Bartered Bride" was also presented for three weeks in December beginning the week of December 6, playing from Thursdays through Sundays.

FAUST

An opera in four acts by L. Barbier and M. Carre after Goethe's drama; music by Charles Gounod. Presented at City Center, New York, October 5, 13, 21, and November 11, 1945.

Cast of characters—

Marguerite.........Brenda Lewis, Dorothy Sarnoff, Lucille Manners
Faust..................................Giulio Gari, Eugene Conley
Mephistopheles...................George Doubrovsky, Carlton Gauld
Valentin..............................Grant Garnell, Daniel Duno
Siebel...........................Lenore Parker, Louise Bernhardt
Martha..................................Mary Kreste, Enid Szantho
Wagner..........................Nathan Newman, Arthur Newman

Prologue.—Faust's Study. Act I.—Courtyard of Tavern. Act II.—Marguerite's Garden. Act III.—Street in Front of Marguerite's Home. Act IV.—Scene 1—The Church. 2—The Prison.

Staged by Sally Stanfield; music directed by Jean Morel; settings by H. A. Condell; choreography by Carl Randall.

THE GYPSY BARON

An opera in three acts adapted into English by George Mead; music by Johann Strauss. Presented at City Center, New York, October 6, 12 and 28, and November 10, 1945.

Cast of characters—

Barinkay..Gordon Dilworth
Czipra...Enid Szantho
Saffi...Brenda Lewis
Zsupan..George Lipton
Arsena...Helen George
Ottokar.........................John Harrold, Nathaniel Sprinzena
Carnero...Hubert Norville
Count Homonnay...................................Grant Garnell

Act I.—Remote Region in Transylvania Countryside. Act II.—Gypsy Encampment around Ruins of Barinkay's Castle. Act III.—Public Square in Vienna.

Staged by Leopold Sachse; music directed by Julius Rudel; settings by H. A. Condell; choreography by Carl Randall.

FLYING DUTCHMAN

An opera in three acts by Richard Wagner. Presented at City Center, New York, October 10, 18 and 27, 1945.

Cast of characters—

Daland..........................Sidor Belarsky, Gean Greenwell
The Dutchman.....................................Frederick Destal
The Steersman.........................Irwin Dillon, John Dillon
Erik...Giulio Gari
Senta...............................Doris Doree, Polyna Stoska
Mary..Enid Szantho

Act I.—A Landing Place. Act II.—Daland's Home. Act III.—Two Ships Anchored Side by Side Not Far from Daland's Home.

Staged by Sally Stanfield; music directed by Laszlo Halasz; setting by Richard Rychtarik.

RIGOLETTO

An opera in three acts by Francesco Maria Piave; music by Giuseppe Verdi. Presented at City Center, New York, May 9, 17, and 26, 1946.

Cast of characters—

The Duke of Mantua....................Giulio Gari, Eugene Conley
Rigoletto....................................Ivan Petroff
Sparafucile..........................Gean Greenwell, James Pease
Count Monterone...............................Grant Garnell
Count Ceprano...................................Emile Renan
Marullo.......................................Arthur Newman
Borsa......................................Nathaniel Sprinzena
Gilda....................Virginia MacWatters, Rosemarie Brancato
Maddalena......................Margery Mayer, Rosalind Nadelle
Giovanna......................................Mary Kreste
Countess Ceprano...............................Susan Griska
A Page..............................Irene Freyhan, Lenore Parker

Act I.—Scene 1—Palace of the Duke of Mantua. 2—A Square with Home of Rigoletto and Palace of Ceprano. Act II.—Palace of Duke of Mantua. Act III.—Sparafucile's Inn.

Staged by Leopold Sachse; music directed by Laszlo Halasz; choreography by Igor Schwezoff; settings by Richard Rychtarik.

THE PIRATES OF PENZANCE

An opera in two acts by W. S. Gilbert; music by Arthur Sullivan. Presented at City Center, New York, May 12, 16, 22 and 31, 1946.

Cast of characters—

The Pirate King.......................Gean Greenwell, James Pease
Samuel, His Lieutenant...........................Hubert Norville
Frederic, Pirate Apprentice...........................John Hamill
Ruth, Pirate Maid-of-all-work....................Catherine Judah
Major-General Stanley..................................John Dudley
Major-General Stanley's Daughters:
Mabel..................Virginia MacWatters
Edith..........................Susan Griska
Kate..........................Lenore Parker
Isabel.......................Mary Polynack
Sergeant of Police.......................................Emile Renan

Act I.—Rocky Shore on Coast of Cornwall. Act II.—Ruined Chapel on General Stanley's Estate.

Staged by Eugene Bryden; music directed by Julius Rudel; choreography by Igoe Schwezoff; settings by H. A. Condell.

MADAMA BUTTERFLY

An opera in two acts founded upon the book by John L. Long and the drama by David Belasco; music by Giacomo Puccini. Presented at City Center, New York, May 15, 19, 23 and 30, 1946.

Cast of characters—

Madama Butterfly................Enya Gonzalez, Camilla Williams
Suzuki...........................Rosalind Nadell, Margery Mayer

Benjamin F. Pinkerton..................Giulio Gari, Eugene Conley
Sharpless, U. S. Consul..............................Ivan Petroff
Goro...Hubert Norville
Yamadori...Emile Renan
The Bonze.........................Grant Garnell, Gean Greenwell
Imperial Commissioner...................................Arthur Newman
Kate Pinkerton.....................................Irene Freyhan

Act I.—Japanese House, Terrace and Garden Overlooking Nagasaki Harbor. Act II.—Interior of House.

Staged by Eugene Bryden; music directed by Laszlo Halasz; settings by H. A. Condell.

THE NEW YORK CITY SYMPHONY

The New York City Symphony opened the season at City Center, New York, October 8, 1945, under the direction of Leonard Bernstein. Guest conductors during the series of concerts were Erich Leinsdorf, Walter Hendl, Lukas Foss and Robert Shaw. The premiere of Marc Blitzstein's "Airborne," with Orson Welles as narrator and the Collegiate Chorale conducted by Robert Shaw participating, was presented April 1, 1946. The season closed April 2, 1946, after 24 performances.

THE TEMPEST

(24 performances)

A comedy in prologue and two acts by William Shakespeare; interpreted by Margaret Webster, based on a production idea by Eva Le Gallienne; music by David Diamond. Presented by Cheryl Crawford at City Center, November 12, 1945.

Cast of characters—

Ship-Master.................................Beaumont Bruestle
Boatswain......................................Angus Cairns
Alonso, King of Naples.............................Bram Nossen
Gonzalo.......................................Robert Harrison
Antonio, brother to Prospero.......................Joseph Hardy
Sebastian, brother to Alonzo...................Eugene Stuckmann
Prospero..Arnold Moss
Miranda, his daughter.............................Diana Sinclair
Ariel..Vera Zorina
Caliban..Canada Lee
Ferdinand, Prince of Naples.................Albert Hachmeister
Adrian, a Lord.....................................Jack Bostick
Trinculo, a Jester...............................Wallace Acton
Stephano, a butler.................................Benny Baker
Master of Ceremonies } Spirits.........................{ Bernard Miller
Dancer } { Peggy Allardice

Mariners, Shapes and Spirits: Peggy Allardice, Beaumont Bruestle, Angus Cairns, Cebert LaVine, Bernard Miller, Thomas Vize.

Prologue.—On a Ship at Sea. Acts I and II.—On an Island.

Staged by Margaret Webster; music directed by David Diamond; settings and costumes by Motley; lighting by Moe Hack; music directed by Drago Jovanovich.

The original presentation of this production opened at the Alvin Theatre, New York, January 25, 1945, and ran for 100 performances.

(Closed December 1, 1945)

LITTLE WOMEN

(16 performances)

A play in four acts adapted by Marian De Forest from Louisa M. Alcott's book. Revived by Frank McCoy at City Center, New York, December 23, 1945.

Cast of characters—

Jo..Margaret Hayes
Meg..Gloria Stroock
Amy..Billie Lou Watt
Beth..Dortha Duckworth
Mrs. March..Velma Royton
Hannah..Georgia Harvey
Brooke..Clark Williams
Laurie..Richard Camp
Aunt March..Grace Mills
Mr. March..David Lewis
Mr. Laurence..Harrison Dowd
Professor Bhaer..Jack Lorenz

Acts I, II, III and IV.—Sitting Room of March Home in Small Town of New England. 1863 and 1864.
Staged by Frank McCoy.

Larry Adler, harmonica player, and Paul Draper, tap dancer, began their fourth season at City Center, New York, December 25, 1945, alternating with "Little Women" until January 1, 1946, giving 9 performances.

(Closed January 5, 1946)

THE DESERT SONG

(45 performances)

An operetta in two acts by Otto Harbach, Oscar Hammerstein 2nd and Frank Mandel; music by Sigmund Romberg. Revived by Russell Lewis and Howard Young at City Center, New York, January 8, 1946.

Cast of characters—

Mindar..Edward Wellman
Sid El Kar..Richard Charles
Ahmed..Keith Gingles
Omar..Jack Saunders
Hassi..Thayer Roberts
Pierre Birabeau..Walter Cassel
Benjamin Kidd..Jack Goode

Sentinel....................................William Bower
Captain Paul Fontaine....................................Wilton Clary
Sergeant Le Verne....................................Joseph Claudio
Sergeant De Boussac....................................Antonio Rovano
Azuri....................................Clarissa
Edith....................................Tamara Page
Susan....................................Sherry O'Neil
Mardi....................................Barbara Bailey
Florette....................................Betina Orth
Yvette....................................Florette Hillier
Yvonne....................................Maria Taweel
Margot Bonvalet....................................Dorothy Sandlin
General Birabeau....................................Lester Matthews
Clementina....................................Jean Bartel
Harem Guard....................................Richard Hughes
Ali Ben Ali....................................George Burnson
Nogi....................................Louis DeMagnus
Riff Runner....................................Paul Ruth

Act I.—Scene 1—Hiding Place of Red Shadow, Riff Mountains. 2—Garden Outside General Birabeau's Villa. 3—Inside the Villa. Act II.—Scene 1—Desert Retreat of Ali Ben Ali. 2—Corridor to the Bath. 3—Room of the Silken Couch. 4—Edge of Desert. 5—General Birabeau's Villa.

Staged by Sterling Halloway; choreography by Aida Broadbent; music directed by Waldemar Guterson; settings by Boris Aronson.

"The Desert Song" was originally produced by Laurence Schwab and Frank Mandel at the Casino Theatre, New York, November 30, 1926, and ran for 471 performances. The theatrically exciting story has to do with the adventure of Pierre Birabeau, son of a Colonel in the French Army, when he takes on the cause of a band of Riffian rebels. With the rebels he is known as the Red Shadow, and looks it. With the Army he is a little dumbly in love with a lovely Margot Bonvalet. He sings equally well in either part, and finally wins military favors for the Riffs and the love of Margot for himself.

(Closed February 16, 1946)

CARMEN JONES

(32 performances)

A musical play in two acts by Oscar Hammerstein 2d, based on Meilhac and Halevy's adaptation of Prosper Merimee's "Carmen"; music by Georges Bizet; orchestral arrangements by Robert Russell Bennett. Presented by Billy Rose at City Center, April 7, 1946.

Cast of characters—

Corporal Morrell....................................Robert Clarke
Foreman....................................George Willis
Cindy Lou....................Elton J. Warren, Coreania Hayman
Sergeant Brown....................................Jack Carr
Joe....................Napoleon Reed, Le Vern Hutcherson
Carmen....................Muriel Smith, Urylee Leonardos
Sally....................................Sibol Cain

T-Bone....................Edward Roche
Tough Kid....................James May
Drummer....................Oliver Coleman
Bartender....................Andrew J. Taylor
Waiter....................Edward Christopher
Myrt....................Ruth Crumpton
Frankie....................Theresa Merritte
Rum....................John Bubbles
Dink....................Ford Buck
Boy....................Bill O'Neil
Girl....................Erona Harris
Husky Miller....................Glenn Bryant
Soldiers....................{Robert Clarke, Randall Steplight, George Willis, Elijah Hodges}
Mr. Higgins....................Jack Carr
Miss Higgins....................Fredye Marshall
Photographer....................Harold Taylor
Card Players....................{Fredye Marshall, Doris Brown, Sibol Cain}
Waiter.................... Richard de Vaultier
Dancing Girl....................Audrey Vanterpool
Poncho....................Frank Palmer
Dancing Boxers....................{Sheldon B. Hoskins, Randolph Sawyer}
Bullet Head....................George Willis

Act I.—Scene 1—Outside Parachute Factory near Southern Town. 2—Near-by Roadside. 3—Billy Pastor's Café. Act II.—Scene 1—Terrace, Meadowland Country Club, Southside of Chicago. 2—Outside Sport Stadium.

Staged by Hassard Short; libretto directed by Charles Friedman; choreography by Eugene Loring; choral direction by Robert Shaw; music directed by David Mordecai; settings by Howard Bay; costumes by Raoul Pene duBois.

"Carmen Jones" played on Broadway from December 2, 1943, to February 10, 1945 (503 performances), prior to this engagement.

(Closed May 4, 1946)

LIVE LIFE AGAIN

(2 performances)

A play in three acts by Dan Totheroh. Produced by S. S. Krellberg at the Belasco Theatre, New York, September 29, 1945.

Cast of characters—

Preacher Hill....................Edward Bushman
Mrs. Jones....................Kay MacDonald
Mrs. Smith....................Isabel Bishop
Mrs. Brown....................Ruth Saville
Mrs. White....................Phoebe Mackay
Mrs. Black....................Mathilde Baring
Mrs. Green....................Florence Beresford
Mr. Smith....................Lester Lonergan, Jr.
Mr. Jones....................Bruce Halsey
Mr. Brown....................Pat Smith
Mr. White....................Robert Gardet
Mr. Black....................Kenneth Bowles
Mr. Green....................James Coyle

Spiers.......................................Parker Fennelly
Nathan Spiers.................................Zachary A. Charles
Judith Spiers.......................................Mary Rolfe
Greer, the Gravedigger..........................John O. Hewitt
Mark Orme...Donald Buka
Saul Orme......................................Thomas Chalmers
Hilda Paulson...............................Beatrice de Neergaard
Doctor Bush.....................................Harold McGee
Rose...Mary Boylan
Mrs. Hansen..Grace Mills

Act I.—Scene 1—The Graveyard, Near Prairie Village of Bison Run, Nebraska. 2—Saul Orme's House. Act II.—Scene 1—Pleasant Grove. 2—Saul's House. 3—Julia Spier's Bedroom. Act III.—Scene 1—The Orme House. 2—A Cornfield. 3—Saul Orme's Bedroom.

Staged by Sawyer Falk; settings by Albert Johnson; costumes by Grace Houston.

Mark Orme, a Nebraska Hamlet, suspects his mother's death can be traced to his father. When father decides to marry the maid, Hilda Paulson, Mark is convinced his suspicions are correct. He shoots father dead and then realizes his mistake. Everybody is pretty unhappy about the whole thing.

(Closed October 1, 1945)

POLONAISE

(113 performances)

A musical in two acts by Gottfried Reinhardt and Anthony Veiller; lyrics by John Latouche; music by Frederic Chopin; adaptations by Bronislaw Kaper; orchestrations by Don Walker. Produced by W. Horace Schmidlapp in association with Harry Bloomfield at the Alvin Theatre, New York, October 6, 1945.

Cast of characters—

Captain Adams...............................John V. Schmidt
General Washington..........................Walter Munroe
Colonel Hale...................................Martin Lewis
General Thaddeus Kosciusko....................Jan Kiepura
Sergeant Zapolski...................................Curt Bois
Private Tompkins...........................Sidney Lawson
Private Skinner..............................Arthur Lincoln
Private Motherwell..........................Martin Cooke
Marisha.......................................Marta Eggerth
Vladek...Rem Olmsted
Tecla......................................Tania Riabouchinska
General Boris Volkoff........................Harry Bannister
Count Casimir Zaleski........................Graham Velsey
Countess Ludwika Zaleski......................Rose Inghram
Peniatowski..................................Lewis Appleton
Kollontaj...................................Andrew Thurston
Potocki..Gary Green
Old Nobleman.................................Victor Savidge
Blacksmith...................................George Spelvin
Butcher..Larry Beck
Priest..Larry O'Dell
King Stanislaus Augustus......................James MacColl
Count Gronski.................................Walter Appler

Courtier..Jay Dowd
Princess Margarita..............................Candy Jones
Princess Lydia.....................................Leta Mauree
Princess Lania..............................Sherry Shadburne
Princess Anna..............................Martha E. Watson
Peasant Girl..Alicia Krug

"THE MARQUIS' SNUFF BOX"

The Princess......................................Ruth Riekman
The Prince......................................Shawn O'Brien
The Highwayman..............................Sergei Ismaeloff
The Page..Amalia Valez

The Ballerinas: Jean Harris, Virginia Barnes, Adele Bodroghy, Joan Collenette.

Act I.—Scene 1—The Ramparts—West Point—1783. 2—The Waterfront, New York. 3 and 7—A Hayfield Near Cracow, Poland. 4—The Road to Manor House. 5—The Manor House. 6—The Road to the Hayfield. Act II.—Scenes 1 and 3—The Royal Palace, Warsaw. 2—A Balcony of the Palace. 4—The Battle of Maciejowice. 5—Cell—St. Petersburg. 6—The Waterfront—Philadelphia.

Staged by Stella Adler; music directed by Irving Landau; choreography by David Lichine; settings by Howard Bay; costumes by Mary Grant.

After Thaddeus Kosciuszko had helped out the American revolutionists in 1776 he returned to Poland and ran into a home revolution. He also ran into Marisha, a pretty peasant girl. The result was a good deal of singing and dancing, and some little romance.

(Closed January 12, 1946)

THERESE

(96 performances)

A drama in two acts by Thomas Job, based on Emile Zola's "Therese Raquin." Produced by Victor Payne-Jennings and Bernard Klawans at the Biltmore Theatre, New York, October 9, 1945.

Cast of characters—

Camille..Berry Kroeger
Madame Raquin..............................Dame May Whitty
Therese......................................Eva Le Gallienne
Laurent..Victor Jory
Madame Louise....................................Doris Patston
Mr. Grivet......................................John F. Hamilton
Inspector Michaud..............................Averell Harris
Suzanne..Annette Sorell

Acts I and II.—Living Room Above a Milliner's Shop in the Pont Neuf District in Paris. 1875-1876.

Staged by Margaret Webster; setting and costumes by Raymond Sovey.

Therese Raquin, unhappily married to Camille, conspires with her lover, Laurent, to dump Camille in the river, from whence they know he will not be able to save himself. Thereafter they are so persistently haunted by a memory of their deed that they can no longer enjoy their love, even though married. When Mme. Raquin, Camille's mother, overhears their confession of the murder she suffers a stroke that puts her in a wheelchair for the rest of her life. She cannot move a muscle save those of her flashing eyes, but her dirty looks are terrific. One day she manages to spell out what she knows of the guilt of Therese and Laurent and they are promptly taken over by the authorities.

(Closed December 31, 1945)

THE RED MILL

(265 performances)
(Continued)

An operetta in two acts by Henry Blossom; music by Victor Herbert; additional lyrics by Forman Brown. Revived by Paula Stone and Hunt Stromberg, Jr., at the Ziegfeld Theatre, New York, October 16, 1945.

Cast of characters—

Town Crier....................P. J. Kelly
Willem....................Hal Price
Franz....................George Meador
Tina....................Dorothy Stone
Bill-Poster....................Gordon Boelzner
Flora....................Hope O'Brady
Lena....................Lois Potter
Dora....................Betty Galavan
The Burgomaster....................Frank Jaquet
Juliana....................Lorna Byron
Con Kidder....................Michael O'Shea
Kid Conner....................Eddie Foy, Jr.
Gretchen....................Ann Andre
Capt. Hendrik Van Damn....................Robert Hughes
Gaston....................Charles Collins
Pennyfeather....................Billy Griffith
Madame La Fleur....................Odette Myrtil
Georgette....................Jean Walburn
Suzette....................Nony Franklin
Fleurette....................Kathleen Ellis
Nanette....................Jacqueline Ellis
Lucette....................Patricia Gardner
Yvette....................Joan Johnston
The Governor....................Edward Dew

Act I.—The Inn at the Red Mill. Act II.—Scene 1—Neighborhood Street. 2—Hall in the Burgomaster's House. 3—Ballroom in the Burgomaster's House.

Staged by Billy Gilbert; technical supervision by Adrian Awan; choreography by Aida Broadbent; music directed by Edward Ward; chorus by William Tryoler; vocal numbers directed by George Cunningham; settings by Arthur Lonergan; costumes by Walter Israel and Emile Santiago.

The adventures of Kid Conner and Con Kidder, the time they were stranded in Holland, was told originally by David Montgomery and Fred Stone in Victor Herbert and Henry Blossom's

"The Red Mill," produced in 1906 at the Knickerbocker Theatre in New York. Montgomery and Stone played "The Red Mill" for three seasons. The above is the first New York revival in a revised version.

THE ASSASSIN

(13 performances)

A drama in three acts by Irwin Shaw. Produced by Carly Wharton and Martin Gabel in association with Alfred Bloomingdale, at the National Theatre, New York, October 17, 1945.

Cast of characters—

Monsieur Popinot....William Hansen
Gustav Boubard....Alfred White
Lucien Gerard....Guy Sorel
Christine Theodore....Frances Chaney
Charles Ganneracs....Ralph Stantley
Helene Mariotte....Lesley Woods
Sophie Vauquin....Elena Karam
Robert de Mauny....Frank Sundstrom
Victor Mallasis....Harold Huber
David Stein....Henry Sharp
Ida Stein....Carmen Mathews
Andre Vauquin....Karl Malden
Steingel....Peter Gregg
General Roucheau....Richard Keith
General Mousset....Clay Clement
General Kley....Robert Ober
Colonel Von Kohl....William Malten
Admiral Marcel Vespery....Roger De Koven
Haynes....Harrison Dowd
A Captain....Alan Dreeben
Lieutenant Crane....Stuart Nedd
Sergeant....Frank DeLangton
A Lieutenant....Bill Weyse
Monsieur Jacques....Booth Colman
A Woman....Florence Robinson
Guard....Alan Dreeben
Priest....William Marceau

Soldiers: Booth Colman, Ralph Smiley, Bill Weyse, William Marceau.

Act I.—Scenes 1 and 3—A Café in Algiers, November, 1942. 2—Room in French Army Headquarters. Act II.—Scene 1—Room at Headquarters. 2—Small Villa Outside Algiers. 3—Café. Christmas Eve. Act III.—Scene 1—The Café. 2—A Cell in Military Jail. Just Before Dawn.

Staged by Martin Gabel; settings by Boris Aronson.

Royalist Robert de Mauny, working with the underground in Algiers for the defeat of the Germans and the rededication of France, assassinates Admiral Marcel Vespery (Darlan) while he is making a speech over the radio Christmas Eve, 1942. Taken to jail Robert is double-crossed by those patriots who had agreed to effect his release the day set for his execution. He goes bravely to his death, to the great distress of Helene Mariotte, his quondam sweetheart.

(Closed October 27, 1945)

THE BLACKFRIARS' GUILD

The Blackfriars' Guild opened its fifth season October 25, 1945, with "Seven Mirrors" (an experiment in social drama), written by the classes in play production of the Immaculate Heart College. The production was staged by Dennis Gurney; dances directed by Patricia Newman and verse choir by Frances Mohan. There were 22 performances, closing November 18, 1945. Other Blackfriars' productions follow.

A YOUNG AMERICAN

(26 performances)

A play in three acts by Edwin Bronner. Presented at Blackfriars' Theatre, New York, January 17, 1946.

Cast of characters—

Mrs. Hastings....................Joan Field
Jacob Geismar....................Howard Swaine
Alexander Cortell....................Alex Wilson
Lynn Cortell....................Martha Jean
Steven Willoughby....................Murray C. Stewart
William Farrell....................Louis Peterson, Jr.
Sophie Baines....................Marion L. Douglas
Professor Arnold Harmon....................Harry Gerard

Act I, II and III.—Duplex Apartment of Alexander Cortell, New York.

Staged by Dennis Gurney; setting by Blackfriars' Guild Studio.

(Closed February 10, 1946)

MARY OF MAGDALA

(25 performances)

A play in three acts by Ernest Milton. Presented at Blackfriars' Theatre, March 25, 1946.

Cast of characters—

Zillah....................Gladys Edgecomb
Bodmin....................Douglas Gordon
Quintus Superbus....................Ray Colcord
Elkan....................Joseph Nash
Pappus....................Jay Welles
Pamphylia....................Jean Lovelace
Ibn-el-Hadjaz....................Hugh Thomas, Jr.
Zimora....................Margaret Roberts
Cleonice....................Barbara Stanton
Orontes....................Ralph Curtis
Rachel....................Florence Interrante
Zebulun....................Oskar Soroko
Tammuzadad....................Joseph F. Gilbert
Mary....................Helen Horton
Othmar....................Robert Carroll

Amil, An Itinerant Merchant........................Frank Schofield
Zepta, His Daughter................................Anne Osterhout
Aletta, His Assistant..............................Jean Spelvin

Acts I, II and III.—Atrium of Quintus' House in Jerusalem.

Staged by Dennis Gurney; setting by Avril Gentles; costumes by Valerie and Virginia Todahl.

(Closed April 16, 1946)

COME MARCHING HOME

(19 performances)

(Continued)

A play in three acts by Robert Anderson. Presented at Blackfriars' Theatre, New York, May 18, 1946.

Cast of characters—

Robert Hughes......................................Robert Fierman
Sarah Bliven.......................................Jean Lovelace
Professor Cunningham...............................Edwin C. Hugh
Mrs. Comstock......................................Florence Brown
Antoinette Bosworth................................Inge Adams
John Bosworth......................................Clark Howat
Joe Zaccanino......................................Thomas G. Monahan
Mrs. Bosworth, Sr..................................Florence Pendleton
Chester Powell.....................................James Rafferty
Dr. Belmont..Frank Ford

Acts I, II and III.—Living Room of the Bosworths' Cottage Outside small Eastern City.

Staged by Dennis Gurney; setting by Avril Gentles; costumes by Valerie; lighting by Ray Colcord.

BEGGARS ARE COMING TO TOWN

(25 performances)

A play in three acts by Theodore Reeves. Produced by Oscar Serlin at the Coronet Theatre, New York, October 27, 1945.

Cast of characters—

Maurice..Herbert Berghof
Felix..Alfred Linder
Emile..Julius Bing
Dave...E. G. Marshall
Pasqual..Joseph Rosso
Noll Turner..Luther Adler
Lou..Harry Kadison
Frankie Madison....................................Paul Kelly
Florrie Dushaye....................................Dorothy Comingore
Jonathan Webley....................................Harold Young
Mrs. Bennett Richardson............................Adrienne Ames
Bennett Richardson.................................Austin Fairman
Ziggie...Louis Gilbert
Wilson's Wastrels..................................Cedric Wallace Trio
Nick Palestro......................................George Mathews
Heinz..Tom Pedi
Skinner..Arthur Hunnicutt
Goldie...Harry M. Cooke

Acts I, II and III.—Office of the Avignon, New York Supper Club.
Staged by Harold Clurman; setting by Jo Mielziner; costumes by Ralph Alswang.

Noll Turner and Frankie Madison were fellow gangsters in Prohibition days. During a hijacking job in which murder was done, Turner got away and Madison took the rap. After fourteen years in Sing Sing, Madison comes back expecting to be again taken into partnership by Turner, now become a big-shot night club proprietor. Turner, however, would pay Frankie off and let him go. Frankie, after failing to stage a comeback with the old mob, finally does go, taking with him Florrie Dushaye, the handsome cigarette girl of Noll Turner's night club.

(Closed November 10, 1945)

THE NEXT HALF HOUR

(8 performances)

A drama in three acts by Mary Chase. Produced by Max Gordon at the Empire Theatre, New York, October 29, 1945.

Cast of characters—

Barney Brennan....................................Conrad Janis
Margaret Brennan....................................Fay Bainter
Pat Brennan....................................Jack Ruth
Frances Brennan....................................Pamela Rivers
Peter O'Neill....................................Francis Compton
James O'Neill....................................Art Smith
Rosie Higgins....................................Esther Owen
Jessie Shoemaker....................................Thelma Schnee
Bridget O'Neill....................................Jean Adair
McCracken....................................Larry Oliver

Acts I, II and III.—Living-Room of Home of Margaret Brennan in Early April, 1931, in an American City.
Staged by George S. Kaufman; setting by Edward Gilbert; costumes by Mary Percy Schenck.

Margaret Brennan brought with her from her native Ireland a reverence for and a belief in the pagan superstitions of Irish folk. She can note the work of the little people in many a fantastic happening of nature, and hear the wail of the banshee that heralds the approach of death. Hearing the banshee on one occasion, Margaret feared it heralded the death of her oldest son, who had been carrying on with a married trollop. She sends her younger son to warn the older, and the younger boy is killed. This, Margaret is told, was due to her interference with fate. "The next half hour always belongs to God."

(Closed November 3, 1945)

THE SECRET ROOM

(21 performances)

A drama in three acts by Robert Turney. Produced by Joseph M. Hyman and Bernard Hart in association with Haila Stoddard at the Royale Theatre, New York, November 7, 1945.

Cast of characters—

Noonie Beverly....................Jane Earle
Susan Beverly....................Frances Dee
Sister....................Fuzzy McQuade
Dr. John Beverly....................Reed Brown, Jr.
Mrs. Smitkin....................Juanita Hall
Margaret Beverly (Meg)....................Grace Coppin
Dr. Jackson....................Ivan Simpson
Leda Ferroni....................Eleonora Mendelssohn
Colonel Hammond....................Albert Bergh
Samuels, an Interne....................Charles S. Dubin

Act I, II and III.—Living-Room of the Beverly House in the Country.

Staged by Moss Hart; setting by Carolyn Hancock; lighting by Frederick Fox.

Leda Ferroni, suffering capture and defilement by the Nazis, bears one of her captors a child in the concentration camp of Dachau. The experience unsettles her mind. Out of prison Dr. Jackson, believing he has effected a cure, asks Dr. John Beverly, an American psychiatrist, to let the convalescent Leda live in his home until her return to normal is complete. Knowing Dr. Jackson is leaving a report of her case history with the Beverlys, Leda smothers the good Doctor. The smothering is overseen by two young Beverly children from a secret room they have discovered accidentally. Leda proceeds to win the children's affection and to turn them against their mother. She also tries to smother Mother, but is caught at it just before the final curtain.

(Closed November 24, 1945)

THE GIRL FROM NANTUCKET

(12 performances)

A musical comedy in two acts by Paul Stamford and Harold M. Sherman, based on a story by Fred Thompson and Berne Giler; lyrics by Kay Twomey; dialogue by Hi Cooper. Produced by Henry Adrian at the Adelphi Theatre, New York, November 8, 1945.

Cast of characters—

Michael Nicolson.......................................Bob Kennedy
Betty Ellis.............................Evenings, Adelaide Bishop
Matinees, Pat McClarney
Tom Andrews.......................................George L. Headley
Ann Ellis...Marion Niles
Dodey Ellis...Jane Kean
Keziah Getchel.....................................Helen Raymond
Judge Peleg...John Robb
Captain Matthew Ellis...............................Billy Lynn
Dick Oliver..Jack Durant
Enrico Nicoletti...................................Richard Clemens
Cornelius B. Van Winkler.........................Norman Roland
Roy, Caleb and Several Other Fellows..............Johnny Eager
Mary...Connie Sheldon
Dance Specialists.........................Kim and Kathy Gaynes
Solo Dancer...Tom Ladd

The Four Buccaneers: Paul Shiers, John Panter, Don Cortez, Joseph Cunneff.

Act I.—Prologue—An Apartment House in New York City. Scene 1—Office of Nantucket Steamship Company. 2 and 4—Nantucket Pier. 3—Mike and Dick's Apartment, New York City. 5—Whaler's Bar. 6—Outside Nantucket Museum. 7—Keziah's Beach Home. Act II.—Scene 1—Nantucket Pier. 2—Mike and Dick's Bungalow in Nantucket. 3—Outside the Museum. 4—Old Nantucket. 5—Inside the Museum. 6—Nantucket Square.

Staged by Edward Clarke Lilley; ballets directed by Val Raset; dances directed by Van Grona; music directed by Harry Levant; settings and lighting by Albert Johnson; costumes by Lou Eisele.

A costly mistake having to do with the complications created when a house painter is hired to do a series of murals in the Nantucket Museum.

(Closed November 17, 1945)

THE RICH FULL LIFE

(27 performances)

A comedy in three acts by Vina Delmar. Produced by Gilbert Miller at the Golden Theatre, New York, November 9, 1945.

Cast of characters—

Lou Fenwick...Judith Evelyn
Mother Fenwick......................................Jessie Busley
Carrie...Edith Meiser
Cynthia...Virginia Weidler
Fredonia..Sandra Holman
Lawrence..Frederic Tozere
Fred..Frank M. Thomas
Ricky Latham......................................Jonathan Braman
Miss McQuillen....................................Ann Shoemaker

Acts I, II and III.—Living Room of Fenwick Home.

Staged by Gilbert Miller; setting by Raymond Sovey.

Lou Fenwick, having experienced a drab life with a dull husband, is determined that her daughter, Cynthia, shall live something at least resembling a rich, full life. Cynthia is a frail child. When Mother lets her go to the senior hop with Ricky Latham, the captain of the swimming team, she catches cold and nearly dies of pneumonia. Only the emotional satisfaction inspired by a visit from Ricky pulls Cynthia through.

(Closed December 1, 1945)

ARE YOU WITH IT?

(235 performances)
(Continued)

A musical comedy in two acts by Sam Perrin and George Balzer, adapted from "Slightly Imperfect," a novel by George Malcolm-Smith; lyrics by Arnold B. Horwitt; music by Harry Revel. Produced by Richard Kollmar and James W. Gardiner at the Century Theatre, New York, November 10, 1945.

Cast of characters—

Marge Keller..........Jane Dulo
Mr. Bixby..........Sydney Boyd
Mr. Mapleton..........Johnny Stearns
Wilbur Haskins..........Johnny Downs
Vivian Reilly..........Joan Roberts
Policeman..........Duke McHale
"Goldie"..........Lew Parker
Bartender..........Lou Wills, Jr.
Carter..........Lew Eckels
Snake Charmer's Daughter..........Jane Deering
Cicero..........Bunny Briggs
Cleo..........June Richmond
A Barker..........Johnny Stearns
Balloon Seller..........Mildred Jocelyn
Bunny La Fleur..........Dolores Gray
Sally Swivelhips..........Diane Adrian
Georgetta..........Buster Shaver
Olive.......... Olive
George.......... George
Richard.......... Richard
Strong Man..........William Lundy
Aerialist..........Jane Deering
Office Boy..........Hal Hunter
1st Musician..........Lou Hurst
2nd Musician..........David Lambert
3rd Musician..........Jerry Duane
4th Musician..........Jerry Packer
Loren..........Loren Welch

Act I.—Scene 1—Boarding House in Hartford, Conn. 2 and 4—Bushnell Park. 3—Office of Nutmeg Insurance Co. 5—Joe's Barroom. 6, 8 and 10—Behind Tent of the "Plantation Minstrels." 7 and 11—The Midway. 9—Two Train Compartments. Act II.—Scene 1—Office of Nutmeg Insurance Co. 2 and 4—The Tent. 3—"Acres of Fun" in Worcester. 5—The Train. 6—Carter's Office on the Train. 7—Inside the Midway Frolics Tent. 8—The Midway.

Staged by Edward Reveaux; musical numbers directed by Jack Donohue; vocalization supervised by H. Clay Warnick; music directed by Will Irwin; settings and lighting by George Jenkins; costumes by Raoul Pene Du Bois.

"Goldie," a carnival barker, induces Wilbur Haskins, an insurance solicitor who has been fired for having misplaced a decimal point, to join the show. Wilbur thereafter devotes his attention to adding up feminine figures, concentrating, for obvious reasons, on Vivian Reilly.

THE RUGGED PATH

(81 performances)

A drama in two acts by Robert E. Sherwood. Produced by The Playwrights' Company at the Plymouth Theatre, New York, November 10, 1945.

Cast of characters—

Morey Vinion....Spencer Tracy
Harriet Vinion....Martha Sleeper
George Bowsmith....Clinton Sundberg
Leggatt Burt....Lawrence Fletcher
Charlie....Henry Lascoe
Pete Kenneally....Ralph Cullinan
Fred....Nick Dennis
Gil Hartnick....Rex Williams
Edith Bowsmith....Jan Sterling
Firth....Theodore Leavitt
Albok....Paul Alberts
Dix....Sandy Campbell
Stapler....Lynn Shubert
Kavanagh....Sam Sweet
Doctor....Howard Ferguson
Costanzo....William Sands
Guffey....David Stone
Hal Fleury....Gordon Nelson
Colonel Rainsford....Clay Clement
Gregorio Felizardo....Vito Christi
Catalino....Robin Taylor
Hazel....Kay Loring
Jamieson....Emory Richardson
Major General MacGlorn....Ernest Woodward

Filipino Soldiers and Civilians

Act I.—Scenes 1 and 5—The Vinions' Home. 2 and 4—Kenneally's Downtown Bar & Grill. 3—George Bowsmith's Office. Act II.—Scene 1—Mess Compartment on the Destroyer *Townsend*. June, 1944. 2—George Bowsmith's Office. 3 and 4—Colonel Rainsford's Headquarters. 5—A Jungle Outpost. 6—A Room in the White House. Spring, 1945.

Staged by Captain Garson Kanin; settings and lighting by Jo Mielziner; gowns by Valentina.

See page 308.

(Closed January 19, 1946)

SKYDRIFT

(7 performances)

A drama in three acts by Harry Kleiner. Produced by Rita Hassan at the Belasco Theatre, New York, November 13, 1945.

Cast of characters—

Private Paul Rennard....Paul Crabtree
Corporal Kenneth Brody....Elliott Sullivan

Private Fitzroy Donovan..........................Arthur Keegan
Private Mario Bucelli..........................Zachary A. Charles
Private Edward Freling..........................William Chambers
Co-Pilot..........................Sid Martoff
Private Nickie Bucelli..........................Carl Specht
Crew Chief..........................Eli Wallach
Sergeant Robert A. Kane..........................Alfred Ryder
Donovan, Sr...........................Roger Quinlan
Francey..........................Olive Deering
Danny..........................Marty Miller
Mrs. Bucelli..........................Lili Valenty
Mr. Bucelli..........................Wolfe Barzell
Angelina..........................Rosita Cosio
Audra..........................Elsbeth Hofmann
Waiter..........................David Stewart

Acts I, II and III.—The Past and Present.
Staged by Roy Hargrave; settings and costumes by Motley.

Seven paratroopers flying a mission in the Pacific theatre are shot out of the air. Finding themselves dead in their shattered plane, they decide to bail out and seek out their kin for a last earthly visit. They are pleasantly received at home and try to make their kin believe that they (the dead) will be happy if they are just left to make their spiritual way alone.

(Closed November 17, 1945)

STATE OF THE UNION

(231 performances)
(Continued)

A comedy in three acts by Howard Lindsay and Russel Crouse. Produced by Leland Hayward at the Hudson Theatre, New York, November 14, 1945.

Cast of characters—

James Conover..........................Minor Watson
Spike McManus..........................Myron McCormick
Kay Thorndyke..........................Kay Johnson
Grant Matthews..........................Ralph Bellamy
Norah..........................Helen Ray
Mary Matthews..........................Ruth Hussey
Stevens..........................John Rowe
Bellboy..........................Howard Graham
Waiter..........................Robert Toms
Sam Parrish..........................Herbert Heyes
Swenson..........................Fred Ayres Cotton
Judge Jefferson Davis Alexander..........................G. Albert Smith
Mrs. Alexander..........................Maidel Turner
Jennie..........................Madeline King
Mrs. Draper..........................Aline McDermott
William Hardy..........................Victor Sutherland
Senator Lauterback..........................George Lessey

Act I.—Scene 1—Study in James Conover's Home in Washington, D. C. 2—Bedroom in Conover's Home. Act II.—Living Room of a Suite in Book-Cadillac Hotel in Detroit. Act III.—Living Room of the Matthews' Apartment in New York City.
Staged by Bretaigne Windust; settings by Raymond Sovey.

See page 29.

A SOUND OF HUNTING

(23 performances)

A drama in three acts by Harry Brown. Produced by Irving L. Jacobs at the Lyceum Theatre, New York, November 20, 1945.

Cast of characters—

Pfc. Charles Coke....................Frank Lovejoy
Pfc. John Hunter....................James McGrew
Pvt. Dino Collucci....................Sam Levene
T/5 Frank Daggert....................William Beal
Lt. Allan Crane....................Charles J. Flynn
Sgt. Joseph Mooney....................Burton Lancaster
Pfc. Saul Shapiro....................George Tyne
Pfc. Karl Muller....................Kenneth Brauer
Sgt. Thomas Carter....................Carl Frank
Pfc. Morris Ferguson....................Ralph Brooke
Capt. John Telawny....................Stacy Harris
Frederick Finley....................Bruce Evans

Acts I, II and III.—War-Ruined House in Town of Cassino, Italy.
Staged by Anthony Brown; setting by Samuel Leve.

A squad of American GIs has been on patrol in the battered city of Cassino in Italy. One of their number has been trapped by German machine gunners between the lines. The squad is about to be relieved for a rest period. They refuse to go back without the trapped comrade, even though they do not like him much. Against orders they try to rescue their comrade. Pvt. Dino Collucci silences the machine gun and gets to the trapped man only to find him dead. The squad goes back.

(Closed December 28, 1945)

MARRIAGE IS FOR SINGLE PEOPLE

(6 performances)

A comedy in three acts by Stanley Richards. Produced by Ruth Holden and Virginia Kronberg at the Cort Theatre, New York, November 21, 1945.

Cast of characters—

Mrs. Sibyl Hecuba....................Nana Bryant
Lily Packer....................Florence Sundstrom
Reena Rowe....................Anne Francine
Cynthia Murdock....................Marguerite Lewis
Dudley Packer....................Frank Otto
Kenneth Hecuba....................Joel Marston
Una....................Nancie Hobbes
Lottie Disenhower....................Gertrude Beach
Spencer Shilling....................Robert Sully
An Expressman....................Sherman Lazarus
Reginald Hecuba....................Nicholas Saunders
A Young Lady....................Vivian Mallah

Acts I, II and III.—Reginald Hecuba's Penthouse Apartment in New York City.
Staged by Stanley Logan; setting by Frederick Fox.

A little stinker relating the adventure of a simple California girl, Lottie Disenhower, who is sent by her fiancé, a comic playwright, to visit his folks in New York. The girl wins a night club glamor contest and marries the playwright's younger brother.

(Closed November 24, 1945)

THE DAY BEFORE SPRING

(165 performances)

A musical in two acts by Alan Jay Lerner; music by Frederick Loewe; orchestrations by Harold Byrns. Produced by John C. Wilson at the National Theatre, New York, November 22, 1945.

Cast of characters—

Katherine Townsend....Irene Manning
Peter Townsend....John Archer
Bill Tompkins....Bert Freed
May Tompkins....Lucille Benson
Alex Maitland....Bill Johnson
Marie....Karol Loraine
Lucille....Bette Anderson
Leonore....Lucille Floetman
Marjorie....Estelle Loring
Susan....Arlounine Goodjohn
Anne....Betty Jean Smythe
Girls (1)....Eleanore Treiber
Girls (2)....Eva Soltesz
Girls (3)....June Morris
Gerald Barker....Tom Helmore
Joe McDonald....Don Mayo
Harry Scott....Robert Field
Eddie Warren....Dwight Marfield
Christopher Randolph....Patricia Marshall
Voltaire....Paul Best
Plato....Ralph Glover
Freud....Hermann Leopoldi

Scenes in New York City and at Harrison University.
Staged by John C. Wilson; book directed by Edward Padula; ballets by Antony Tudor; music directed by Maurice Abravanel; settings by Robert Davison; costumes by Miles White.

The Peter Townsends go back to Harrison University for the celebration of the tenth reunion of their class. There they meet Alex Maitland with whom Katherine Townsend would have eloped in her senior year if the car had not broken down. Now they think perhaps they will try it again. Again the car breaks down. This time Katherine's husband catches up with them. Results pleasant.

(Closed April 14, 1946)

THE MERMAIDS SINGING

(53 performances)

A comedy in three acts by John Van Druten. Produced by Alfred de Liagre, Jr., at the Empire Theatre, New York, November 28, 1945.

Cast of characters—

Clement Waterlow....................Walter Abel
George....................Arthur Griffin
Bertha Corrigan....................Lois Wilson
Thad Greelis....................Walter Starkey
Dee Matthews....................Beatrice Pearson
Mrs. James....................Jane Hoffman
Mrs. Matthews....................Frieda Inescort
Professor James....................Harry Irvine
Luther Cudworth....................Jack Manning
An Elderly Gentleman....................Wallace Widdecombe
A Waiter....................Leon Forbes
A Drunk....................Frank Lyon
A Girl....................Dina Merrill
A Man....................David Van Winkle

Act I.—Living Room of a Suite in the Best Hotel in any Large American City Other Than New York. Act II.—Scenes 1 and 3—Corner of Hotel Bar. 2—Mrs. Matthews' House. Act III.—Scene 1—The Park. 2—Living Room of Hotel Suite.

Staged by John Van Druten; settings by Raymond Sovey.

Clement Waterlow, playwright, is directing the first production of a comedy concerning adultery in a sizable city near New York. Dee Matthews, 22 and impressionable, falls in love with Waterlow. She would go back to New York with him, even though he confesses that he is happily married and the father of two children. Honor and reason triumph and Dee is eased back into the grooves of her normal life.

(Closed January 12, 1946)

STRANGE FRUIT

(60 performances)

A drama in two acts and twelve scenes dramatized by Lillian and Esther Smith from a novel of the same name by Lillian Smith. Produced by Jose Ferrer at the Royale Theatre, New York, November 29, 1945.

Cast of characters—

A Mill Hand....................Murray Hamilton
Another Mill Hand....................Robert Daggett
Ed Anderson....................George B. Oliver
Little Miss Nobody....................Doris Block
Preacher Dunwoodie....................Stephen Chase
Tom Harris....................Ralph Theadore

Dee Cassidy..Ted Yaryan
Gabe..Alonzo Bosan
Doug..Jay Norris
Harriet Harris..Eugenia Rawls
Charlie Harris..Francis Letton
Tracy Deen..Melchor Ferrer
Crazy Carl..Robinson Stone
Alma Deen..Vera Allen
Sam Perry..Juano Hernandez
Laura Deen..Charlotte Keane
Tut Deen..Frank Tweddell
Corporal..Herbert Junior
Nonnie Anderson..Jane White
Bess Anderson..Dorothy Carter
Jackie (Bess' Child)..Juan Jose Hernandez
Henry McIntosh..Earl Jones
Salamander..Hanson W. Elkins
Chuck..Ralph Meeker
Miss Sadie..Mary Fletcher
Miss Belle..Esther Smith
Mamie McIntosh..Edna Thomas
Tracy Deen (As a Child)..Peter Griffith
Henry McIntosh (As a Child)..Richard W. Williams
A Little Girl..Phyllis De Bus
Laura Deen (As a Child)..Betty Lou Keim
Ten McIntosh..Ken Renard
A Colored Man..Ellsworth Wright
A Maid..Doris Block

Act I.—Scenes 1 and 5—Deen's Drug Store, Maxwell, Georgia. 2—Anderson's Home. 3—Deen's Sun Porch. 4—The Ridge. Act II.—Scenes 1 and 2—Deen's Yard. 3—Salamander's Café. 4 and 6—Anderson's Gate. 5—Deen's Sun Porch. 7—Tom Harris' Mill Office.

Staged by Jose Ferrer; supervised by Arthur S. Friend; settings by George Jenkins; costumes by Patricia Montgomery.

Tracy Deen and Nonnie Anderson have been lovers from childhood. Denied marriage because he represents the white, she the black race, their romance approaches its tragic end before the birth of her child. Tracy bribes his houseboy to marry Nonnie to give her child a name. Nonnie's brother shoots Tracy. A village mob, demanding a Negro victim, lynches the houseboy.

(Closed January 19, 1946)

THE FRENCH TOUCH

(33 performances)

A comedy in two acts by Joseph Fields and Jerome Chodorov. Produced by Herbert H. Harris at the Cort Theatre, New York, December 8, 1945.

Cast of characters—

Patard..John Regan
Roublard..Brian Aherne
Giselle Roublard..Jacqueline Dalya
Schwartz..William Malten
Felix von Brenner..John Wengraf
Jacqueline Carlier..Arlene Francis
Boucot..Ralph Simone
Henri..Jerome Thor
Georgette..Louise Kelley

Nanette....................................Mary Cooper
Toto....................................Richard Bengali
Marcel....................................John Graham
Robert....................................Stewart Stern
Madeleine....................................Sara Strengell
Odette Renoux....................................Madeleine Le Beau
Reiner....................................Dave Hyatt

Acts I and II.—The Theatre Roublard in Paris, Spring of 1943.
Staged by Rene Clair; setting and lighting by George Jenkins.

The Roublards, he a popular Parisian actor, she his third wife, are living in the Roublard Theatre the last year of the German occupation. The invaders have demanded that Roublard shall write a propaganda play favorable to the Germans. Forced to agree, Roublard plans to trick the enemy by writing two last acts. He will rehearse the German act openly, but be ready to play the patriotic French act when the day of production comes. The Roublard company is reassembled. All three Roublard wives are present, causing temperamental comedy outbreaks. The enterprise is abandoned when the German agent is shot and killed accidentally.

(Closed January 5, 1946)

BRIGHTEN THE CORNER

(29 performances)

A comedy in three acts by John Cecil Holm. Produced by Jean Dalrymple at the Lyceum Theatre, New York, December 12, 1945.

Cast of characters—

Opal Harris....................................Dulcie Cooper
Jeri Carson....................................Phyllis Avery
Neil Carson....................................George Petrie
Dell Marshall....................................Lenore Lonergan
Jeffrey Q. Talbot....................................Charles Butterworth
Townsend Marshall, Lt., U.S.N....................................Gene Blakely
Delivery Boy....................................Paul Stanley
Officer Robertson....................................Robert Simon

Acts I, II and III.—Living Room and Outer Hall of the Carsons' Upper East Side Apartment in New York City.
Staged by Arthur O'Connell; setting by Willis Knighton.

Jeffrey Q. Talbot, slightly eccentric man of means, has decided to give his recently married nephew, Neil Carson, a check for $10,000 before he (Uncle) returns to Australia, and a $25,000 bond on the appearance of a Carson heir. Coming unexpectedly into the Carson apartment in the first act, Uncle Jeff mistakes Dell Marshall for Neil's bride. He is increasingly mystified by the Carson-Marshall goings-on right up to the end of the last act.

(Closed January 5, 1946)

HAMLET

(131 performances)

A streamlined, GI version in two acts of William Shakespeare's play, by Maurice Evans; music by Roger Adams. Produced by Michael Todd at Columbus Circle Theatre, New York, December 13, 1945.

Cast of characters—

Bernardo....................William Weber
Franciscus....................John Bryant
Marcellus....................Alexander Lockwood
Horatio....................Walter Coy
Ghost of Hamlet's Father....................Victor Thorley
Claudius, King of Denmark....................Thomas Gomez
Hamlet, Prince of Denmark....................Maurice Evans
Gertrude, Queen of Denmark....................Lili Darvas
Polonius....................Thomas Chalmers
Laertes....................Emmett Rogers
Ophelia....................Frances Reid
Reynaldo....................Franz Bendtsen
Rosencrantz....................Howard Morris
Guildenstern....................Booth Colaman
Player King....................Nelson Leigh
Player Queen....................Blanche Collins
Player Villain....................Alan Dreeben
Player Prologue....................Alan Masters
Fortinbras, Prince of Norway....................Leon Shaw
Norwegian Captain....................Nelson Leigh
Osric....................Morton Da Costa

Act I.—Scenes 1 and 4—Battlements at Castle at Elsinore, Denmark. 2 and 6—Main Hall of Castle. 3 and 5—Apartment of Polonius. 7—Chapel in the Castle. Act II.—Scenes 1 and 8—Open Court in Castle. 2—Chapel in the Castle. 3—The Queen's Apartment. 4—Cellar Room in Castle. 5—Hall in Castle. 6—Street Leading to Port. 7—Main Hall in the Castle.

Staged by George Schaefer; music directed by William Brooks; settings by Frederick Stover; costumes by Irene Sharaff.

Maurice Evans' first American revival of Shakespeare's "Hamlet" was made in 1938 and revived in 1939, with Margaret Webster serving as director. This was the first uncut version of the tragedy to be seen in New York. It ran for 96 performances in 1938, 40 in 1939. The shortened, or GI version, taking numerous liberties with the text, runs the speech to the players into a rehearsal of "The Mousetrap," and eliminates the scenes of Ophelia's death and burial, thus cutting out the gravediggers' scene. It was this version that Maj. Evans played frequently in the South Pacific during World War II.

(Closed April 6, 1946)

DREAM GIRL

(195 performances)
(Continued)

A comedy in two acts by Elmer Rice. Produced by The Playwrights' Company (Maxwell Anderson, Robert Sherwood, S. N. Behrman, Elmer Rice, John F. Wharton) at the Coronet Theatre, New York, December 14, 1945.

Cast of characters—

Georgina Allerton.......Betty Field
Lucy Allerton.......Evelyn Varden
Radio Announcer.......Keene Crockett
Dr. J. Gilmore Percival.......William A. Lee
George Allerton.......William A. Lee
Miriam Allerton Lucas.......Sonya Stokowski
The Obstetrician.......William A. Lee
The Nurse.......Evelyn Varden
Jim Lucas.......Kevin O'Shea
Claire Blakeley.......Helen Marcy
A Stout Woman.......Philippa Bevans
The Doctor.......Don Stevens
Clark Redfield.......Wendell Corey
A Policeman.......James Gregory
The Judge.......William A. Lee
The District Attorney.......Keene Crockett
George Hand.......Edmon Ryan
Bert.......Don Stevens
A Mexican.......Wendell Corey
Two Other Mexicans.......David Pressman, James Gregory
A Waiter.......Stuart Nedd
Arabella.......Sonya Stokowski
Luigi.......David Pressman
An Usher.......Gaynelle Nixon
Miss Delehanty.......Helen Bennett
Antonio.......Don Stevens
Salarino.......Robert Fletcher
A Theatre Manager.......William A. Lee
A Head-Waiter.......Keene Crockett
A Waiter.......Robert Fletcher
Justice of the Peace Billings.......William A. Lee
A Chauffeur.......Stuart Nedd

Acts I and II.—Scenes in Georgina's Home, in a Bookstore, a Night Club and a Street Corner.

Staged by Elmer Rice; settings by Jo Mielziner; costumes by Mainbocher.

See page 267.

THE AMERICAN NEGRO THEATRE

HOME IS THE HUNTER

A drama in two acts by Samuel M. Kootz. Presented at the A.N.T. Playhouse, New York, December 20, 1945.

Cast of characters—

Dawson Drake, Sr.......Evelio Grillo
Rusty Saunders.......Maxwell Glanville

Ann Drake....................................Clarice Taylor
Dawson Drake, Jr..................................Elwood Smith
Acts I and II.—Living Room of Drake Residence in Industrial Town in U.S.A.
Staged by Abram Hill; setting by Irene Bresadola.

ON STRIVERS ROW

(27 performances)

A comedy in three acts by Abram Hill. Presented at the A.N.T. Playhouse, New York, February 28, 1946.

Cast of characters—

Dolly Van Striven..................................Dorothy Carter
Sophie..Isabell Sanford
Professor Hennypest..............................Draynard Clinton
Tillie Petunia......................................Letitia Toole
Chuck..Oliver Pitcher
Cobina Van Striven................................Javotte Sutton
Mrs. Pace......................................Hattie King-Reavis
Oscar Van Striven..................................Stanley Greene
Lily Livingston...................................Verneda La Selle
Louise Davis.......................................Hilda Haynes
Dr. Leon Davis................................Charles Henderson
Rowena...Courtenaye Olden
Acts I, II and III.—Van Striven Residence on Harlem's Strivers Row, New York City.
Staged by Abram Hill; setting by Charles Seebree.

(Closed April 15, 1946)

BILLION DOLLAR BABY

(188 performances)
(Continued)

A musical revue in two acts by Betty Comden and Adolph Green; music by Morton Gould. Produced by Paul Feigay and Oliver Smith at the Alvin Theatre, New York, December 21, 1945.

Cast of characters—

Ma Jones..Emily Ross
Pa Jones...William David
Esme..Shirley Van
Neighbors........Maria Harriton, Edward Hodge, Howard Lenters, Douglas Deane, Helen Gallagher, Beverly Hosier
Champ Watson.......................................Danny Daniels
Photographer.......................................Anthony Reed
Reporter...Alan Gilbert
Maribelle Jones...................................Joan McCracken
Newsboys...........................Douglas Jones, Richard Thomas
Master of Ceremonies..............................Richard Sanford
Miss Texas..Althea Elder
Georgia Motley.......................................Mitzi Green
Violin Player..Tony Cardell
Jerry Bonanza..Don De Leo
Dapper Welch..David Burns
Rocky Barton.....................................William Tabbert

Cigarette Girl....................................Jeri Archer
Waiter....................................David Thomas
M. M. Montague....................................Robert Chisholm
Marathon M. C....................................Allan Gilbert
Chorines..Joan Mann, Lorraine Todd, Virginia Gorski, Virginia Poe, Helen Gallagher, Maria Harriton
Comic....................................Douglas Deane
Danny....................................Tony Gardell
J. C. Creasy....................................Horace Cooper
Art Leffenbush....................................Eddie Hodge
Rodney Gender....................................Richard Sanford
Watchman....................................Robert Edwin
Rocky (Who Dances)....................................James Mitchell
Policeman....................................Howard Lenters

Dancers: Jacqueline Dodge, Helen Gallagher, Virginia Gorski, Maria Harriton, Ann Hutchinson, Cecille Mann, Joan Mann, Virginia Poe, Lorraine Todd, Lucas Aco, Allan Waine, Douglas Deane, Fred Hearne, Joe Landis, Arthur Partington, Bill Summer.

Singers: Peggy Anne Ellis, Jeri Archer, Future Fulton, Lyn Gammon, Doris Hollingsworth, Beverly Hosier, Sydney Wylie, Betty Saunders, Thelma Stevens, Beth Shea, Tony Caffaro, Tony Gardell, Robert Morrissey, Franklin Powell, Anthony Reed, David Thomas, Philip La Torre.

Act I.—Scenes 1, 3 and 8—Staten Island Living Room. 2—Atlantic City Boardwalk. 4—Staten Island Ferry. 5—Front of Speakeasy. 6—Chez Georgia. 7—Georgia's Dressing Room. 9—Street. 10 and 12—Dapper's Apartment. 11—The Marathon. 13—Backstage of Jollities. 14—On Stage of Jollities. Act II.—Scene 1—A Funeral. 2—Porch of Plaza Hotel, Palm Beach. 3 and 5—Entrance of Marathon. 4—The Marathon. 6—Maribelle's Bedroom. 7—Church Vestry. 8—Wedding. 1928-29.

Staged by George Abbott; choreography and musical numbers staged by Jerome Robbins; music directed by Max Goberman; settings by Oliver Smith; costumes by Irene Sharaff.

Maribelle Jones, tired of Staten Island humdrum, vows to make her dreams come true and dashes into the "Terrific Twenties" with that thought uppermost in her mind. Thereafter she dances and romances with a variety of monied adventurers of the prohibition era and barely escapes the 1929 crash.

DUNNIGAN'S DAUGHTER

(38 performances)

A drama in three acts by S. N. Behrman. Produced by The Theatre Guild at the Golden Theatre, New York, December 26, 1945.

Cast of characters—

Jim Baird....................................Richard Widmark
Robert....................................Hale Norcross
Zelda Rainier....................................Jan Sterling
Miguel Riachi....................................Luther Adler
Ferne Rainier....................................June Havoc
Clay Rainier....................................Dennis King
Jesus y Blasco Hernandez....................................Arthur Gondra

Acts I, II and III.—Clay Rainier's Mexican Residence Outside a Small Mining Town.

Staged by Elia Kazan; production supervised by Theresa Helburn and Lawrence Langner; settings by Stewart Chaney.

Clay Rainier, ruthless American industrialist, is in Mexico with his third wife, the beautiful daughter of a political henchman named Dunnigan. Rainier is riding rough-shod over the rights of the natives. Occasionally he takes time out to mistreat his wife. Ferne Rainier, resenting her husband's treatment, turns for sympathy to a Mexican artist of standing, one Hernandez, and also to a sweetheart of her youth, Jim Baird. Baird, representing the U. S. State Department, is in Mexico checking up on Rainier. During the checking he succeeds in reawakening Mrs. Rainier's interest in himself. He also proves to her that her father's suicide in a Chicago jail was directly traceable to her husband's influence. Dunnigan's daughter thereupon ditches Rainier and returns to the United States with Baird.

(Closed January 26, 1946)

PYGMALION

(179 performances)

A comedy in prologue and three acts by George Bernard Shaw. Revived by Theatre Incorporated (Richard Aldrich, managing director) at the Barrymore Theatre, New York, December 26, 1945.

Cast of characters—

Clara Eynsford-Hill....................Wendy Atkin
Mrs. Eynsford-Hill....................Myrtle Tannehill
Bystander....................J. P. Watson
Freddy Eynsford-Hill....................John Cromwell
Eliza Doolittle....................Gertrude Lawrence
Colonel Pickering....................Cecil Humphreys
Henry Higgins....................Raymond Massey
Sarcastic Bystander....................Jay Black
Taxicab Driver....................Rudolph Watson
Mrs. Pearce....................Anita Bolster
Alfred Doolittle....................Melville Cooper
Mrs. Higgins....................Katherine Emmet
Parlourmaid....................Hazel Jones
Pedestrians and Bystanders....................Lucy Storm, Barbara Pond, Walter Kapp, John Parks, Frieda Smith

Prologue.—Portico of Saint Paul's Church, Covent Garden, London, England. 1908. Act I.—Henry Higgins' Laboratory, Wimpole Street. Act II.—Mrs. Higgins' Drawing Room, Chelsea Embankment. Act III.—Scene 1—Henry Higgins' Laboratory. 2—Mrs. Higgins' Drawing Room.

Staged by Cedric Hardwicke; settings by Donald Oenslager; costumes by Motley.

Sir Herbert Beerbohm Tree produced "Pygmalion" originally at the Lyceum Theatre, London, April 4, 1914. Sir Herbert played Henry Higgins, Mrs. Patrick Campbell was the Eliza Doolittle and Philip Merivale the Pickering. The play was revived in England in 1920, 1927 and 1939. George C. Tyler brought "Pygmalion" to America in November, 1914, starring Mrs. Campbell as Eliza. Philip Merivale was the Higgins. In November, 1926, the Theatre Guild revived the play with Lynn Fontanne as Eliza and Reginald Mason as Higgins. The story is of the phonetics professor who wagers he can so correct the speech and manners of a flower girl that she can be passed off as a lady at a Buckingham Palace garden party within six months' time. He wins.

(Closed June 1, 1946)

HOME OF THE BRAVE

(69 performances)

A drama in three acts by Arthur Laurents. Produced by Lee Sabinson in association with William R. Katzell at the Belasco Theatre, New York, December 27, 1945.

Cast of characters—

Capt. Harold Bitterger....................Eduard Franz
Major Dennis Robinson, Jr....................Kendall Clark
T. J....................Russell Hardie
Coney....................Joseph Pevney
Finch....................Henry Barnard
Mingo....................Alan Baxter

Act I.—Scene 1—Hospital Room. Pacific Base. 2—The Office.
Act II.—Scene 1—Another Clearing. The Island. 2—Hospital Room.
Act III.—Scenes 1 and 2—The Hospital Room. 3—The Office.
Staged by Michael Gordon; settings and lighting by Ralph Alswang.

See page 75.

(Closed February 23, 1946)

SHOW BOAT

(170 performances)
(Continued)

A musical comedy in two acts by Oscar Hammerstein 2nd; based on the novel by Edna Ferber; music by Jerome Kern, orchestration by Robert Russell Bennett. Revived by Oscar Hammerstein 2nd at the Ziegfeld Theatre, New York, January 5, 1946.

Cast of characters—

Windy....................Scott Moore
Steve....................Robert Allen
Pete....................Seldon Bennett
Queenie....................Helen Dowdy
Parthy Ann Hawks....................Ethel Owen
Captain Andy....................Ralph Dumke
Ellie....................Colette Lyons
Frank....................Buddy Ebsen
Rubber Face....................Francis Mahoney

Julie....................Carol Bruce
Gaylord Ravenal....................Charles Fredericks
Vallon....................Ralph Chambers
Magnolia....................Jan Clayton
Joe....................Kenneth Spencer
Backwoodsman....................Howard Frank
Jeb....................Duncan Scott
Sal....................Pearl Primus
Sam....................Laverne French
Fatima....................Jean Reeves
Old Sport....................Willie Torpey
Strong Woman....................Paula Kaye
Spanish....................Andrea Downing
Italian....................Vivian Cherry
French....................Janice Bodenhoff
Scotch....................Elana Keller
Greek....................Audrey Keane
English....................Marta Becket
Russian....................Olga Lunick
Indian....................Eleanor Boleyn
Dahomey Queen....................Pearl Primus
Ata....................Alma Sutton
Mala....................Claude Marchant
Bora....................Talley Beatty
Landlady....................Sara Floyd
Ethel....................Assota Marshall
Sister....................Sheila Hogan
Mother Superior....................Iris Manley
Kim (Child)....................Alyce Mace
Jake....................Max Showalter
Jim....................Jack Daley
Man with Guitar....................Thomas Bowman
Doorman at Trocadero....................William C. Smith
Lottie....................Nancy Kenyon
Dolly....................Lydia Fredericks
Sally....................Bettina Thayer
Kim (In Her Twenties)....................Jan Clayton
Old Lady on Levee....................Frederica Slemons
Jimmy Craig....................Charles Tate

Act I.—Scene 1—Levee at Natchez on the Mississippi. 2—Kitchen Pantry of the "Cotton Blossom." 3 and 5—Auditorium and Stage. 4—Box-Office on Foredeck. 6—The Top Deck. 7—Levee at Greenville. Act II.—Scene 1—Midway Plaisance, World's Fair at Chicago, 1893. 2—Room on Ontario Street, 1904. 3 and 5—Rehearsal Room, Trocadero Music Hall. 4—St. Agatha's Convent. 6—Stern of Show Boat, 1927. 7—Top Deck of "Cotton Blossom." 8—Levee at Greenville.

Staged by Hassard Short; book directed by Oscar Hammerstein 2nd; music directed by Edwin McArthur; chorus by Bill Vodery; choreography by Helen Tamiris; settings by Howard Bay; costumes by Lucinda Ballard.

"Show Boat" was originally produced by Florenz Ziegfeld at the Ziegfeld Theatre, New York, December 27, 1927, and ran for 572 performances. It was revived by Ziegfeld at the Casino with practically the same cast May 19, 1932, and ran for 180 performances.

A JOY FOREVER

(16 performances)

A comedy in three acts by Vincent McConnor. Produced by Blevins Davis and Archie Thomson at the Biltmore Theatre, New York, January 7, 1946.

Cast of characters—

Tina....Dorothy Sands
Frith....Charles Laffin
Benjamin Vinnicum....Guy Kibbee
Young Dan....William Nunn
Old Dan....Seth Arnold
Constance Sherman....Ottilie Kruger
Harrison Eames....Loring Smith
Archer Barrington....Nicholas Joy
Wallace....Joe Johnson
Mrs. Tillery....Frieda Altman
Guard....Rollin Bauer
Allora Eames....Natalie Schafer
Model....Charles Boaz, Jr.
Delivery Man....Fred Knight
Assistant Delivery Man....Lucian Self
Mrs. Danforth....Lois Bolton

Acts I, II and III.—Studio of Benjamin Vinnicum, Overlooking Fort Tryon Park, New York City.

Staged by Reginald Denham; setting by Stewart Chaney.

Benjamin Vinnicum, artist, embittered with life, retires from the world and is soon forgotten. Living as an eccentric recluse in a studio barn, with a favorite ex-model to cook for him and minister unto his needs, Benjamin goes on painting so furiously that when he is rediscovered years later by Archer Barrington, art critic, his piled-high canvases are appraised at a million dollars. The rush to buy them is so disturbing that Vinnicum decides to give them away, first come, first served, and go back to his ex-model and their simple life.

(Closed January 19, 1946)

THE WOULD-BE GENTLEMAN

(77 performances)

A musical comedy in two acts adapted by Bobby Clark from Molière's classic, "Le Bourgeois Gentilhomme"; music adapted by Jerome Morass from the original by Lully. Revived by Michael Todd at the Booth Theatre, New York, January 9, 1946.

Cast of characters—

Music Master....Donald Burr
Dancing Master....Alex Fisher
Criquet....Fred Werner
Nicole....Ann Thomas
Marcel....Rand Elliot
Baptiste....Albert Henderson
Monsieur Jourdain....Bobby Clark
Mademoiselle Valere....Ruth Harrison
Singers....Constance Brigham, Mary Godwin, Lewis Pierce
Madame Jourdain....Edith King
Fencing Master....Earl MacVeigh
Philosopher....Frederic Persson
Count Dorante....Gene Barry
Lucille Jourdain....Eleanore Whitney

Covielle....................................Leonard Elliott
Cleonte....................................John Heath
Tailor....................................LeRoi Operti
Raymond....................................Lester Towne
Marquise Dorimene....................................June Knight

Acts I and II.—Drawing Room of Monsieur Jourdain's House in Paris—Circa 1670.

Staged by John Kennedy; setting by Howard Bay; costumes by Irene Sharaff.

Eva Le Gallienne included Molière's "Would-Be Gentleman," in the F. Anstey version, in her Civic Repertory Theatre revivals, opening with it in October, 1928, and reviving it in September, 1929. Egon Brecher was the Jourdain and Beatrice Neergaard the Nicole. With this version Bobby Clark took many liberties, adding extracts from other Molière comedies.

(Closed March 16, 1946)

THE WINTER'S TALE

(39 performances)

A comedy by William Shakespeare adapted to prologue and two acts; incidental music by Anthony Bernard and Leo Russotto. Revived by The Theatre Guild Shakespearean Repertory Company at the Cort Theatre, New York, January 15, 1946.

Cast of characters—

Prologue....................................Romney Brent
Archidamus, a Lord of Bohemia....................................Michael Bey
Camillo, a Lord of Sicilia....................................Colin Keith-Johnston
Polixenes, King of Bohemia....................................David Powell
Leontes, King of Sicilia....................................Henry Daniell
Hermione, Queen to Leontes....................................Jessie Royce Landis
Mamillius, Young Prince of Sicilia....................................Maurice Cavell
1st Lady....................................Denise Flynn
2nd Lady....................................Lucille Patton
3rd Lady....................................Jennifer Howard
1st Lord....................................Baldwin McGaw
Antigonus, a Lord of Sicilia....................................Charles Francis
2nd Lord....................................Lionel Ince
3rd Lord....................................Frank Leslie
Paulina....................................Florence Reed
Keeper of the Jail....................................Michael Bey
Emilia....................................Genevieve Frizzell
Cleomenes, a Lord of Sicilia....................................Charles Atkin
Dion, a Lord of Sicilia....................................Philip Huston
Old Shepherd....................................Whitford Kane
Clown....................................Kurt Richards
Time....................................Philip Huston
Autolycus....................................Romney Brent
Florizel, Prince of Bohemia....................................Robert Duke
Perdita....................................Geraldine Stroock
Dorcas....................................Jo Van Fleet
Mopsa....................................Helen Wagner
Servant....................................Victor Beecroft
Dancing Ram....................................James Starbuck
Dancing Ewe....................................Lili Mann
Dancing Horsemen....................................Francis "Buster" Burnell, Jules Racine

Act I.—Scene 1—King Leontes' Palace. Sicilia. 2—Corridor in Palace. 3 and 5—Room in Palace. 4—Prison Corridor. 6—Road in Bohemia. 7—Cave in Bohemia. 8—Near Leontes' Palace. 9—Court of Justice. Act II.—Scenes 1 and 3—Road in Bohemia. 2—Outside a Shepherd's Cottage. 4—Room in Leontes' Palace. 5—Corridor in Palace. 6—Chapel in Paulina's House.

Staged by B. Iden Payne and Romney Brent; supervised by Lawrence Langner and Theresa Helburn; choreography by William Bales; settings by Stewart Chaney.

With a first New York performance at the John Street Theatre, June 1, 1795, under the title of "Florizel and Perdita," Shakespeare's "The Winter's Tale" has been played variously through the years. There was a major revival by Edwin Booth at Booth's Theatre in April, 1871, with Lawrence Barrett as Leontes, Ada Clifton as Hermione and Bella Pateman as Perdita. This ran for six weeks and was much talked about. Later revivals were sponsored by Madame Janauschek, Rose Eytinge, Kathryn Kidder (who doubled Hermione and Perdita), and Viola Allen, who also doubled the roles in 1905. Edith Wynne Matthison played Hermione to the Leontes of Henry Kolker with the New Theatre Company, New York, in March, 1910.

(Closed February 16, 1946)

NELLIE BLY

(16 performances)

A musical comedy in two acts by Joseph Quillan based on story by Jack Emmanuel; lyrics by Johnny Burke; music by James Van Heusen; orchestration by Ted Royal and Elliott Jacoby. Produced by Nat Karson and Eddie Cantor at the Adelphi Theatre, New York, January 21, 1946.

Cast of characters—

Pulitzer....Walter Armin
Bennett....Edward H. Robins
Newsboy....William O'Shay
Frank Jordan....William Gaxton
Ferry Captain....Fred Peters
Deckhand....Harold Murray
Phineas T. Fogarty....Victor Moore
First Reporter....Robert Strauss
Murphy....Artells Dickson
Wardheeler....Jack Voeth
Second Reporter....Larry Stuart
Third Reporter....Eddy Di Genova
Nellie Bly....Joy Hodges
Battle Annie....Benay Venuta
Steward....Larry Stuart
Honeymoon Couple....Doris Sward, Jack Voeth
French Girl....Drucilla Strain
Grisette....Lubov Roudenko
French Dandy....Jack Whitney
French Mayor....Walter Armin

Santos Dumont....................................Fred Peters
Reporters....................................The Debonairs
Czar....................................Walter Armin
Russian Captain....................................Fred Peters
First Sheik....................................Robert Strauss
Second Sheik....................................Edward H. Robins
Third Sheik....................................Larry Stuart
Official....................................Harold Murray
Copygirl....................................Suzie Baker

Act I.—Scene 1—Barclay Street Ferry Slip, New York. 2—Front of Ferry House. 3—Battle Annie's Saloon. 4—City Hall Square. 5—Steamship Pier in Hoboken. 6—The After Deck. 7—Stateroom, "S.S. Augusta Victoria." 8—Gates of Paris Exposition. 9—Paris Exposition. Act II.—Scene 1—City Room of New York *Herald.* 2—Stratosphere. 3—Public Square, Moscow. 4 and 6—Street in Aden. 5—The Pass. 7—Somewhere in Texas. 8—In Transit. 9—Barclay Street Ferry Slip.

Staged by Edgar McGregor; choreography by Lee Sherman; musical supervision by Joseph Lilley; music directed by Charles Drury; settings and lighting by Nar Karson.

Frank Jordan, managing editor of the New York *Herald,* is excited by the threat of a promotional beat staged by the New York *World*. The *World* assigns a reporter, Nellie Bly, to circle the globe in an attempt to beat the eighty-day record of Jules Verne. Jordan of the *Herald* engages Phineas T. Fogarty, who has been working as a "stable boy for the Hoboken Ferry," to race Nellie. To be sure Phineas doesn't loaf on the job, Jordan goes along and manages to fall in love with Miss Bly before the evening is well started.

(Closed February 2, 1946)

THE MAGNIFICENT YANKEE

(152 performances)
(Continued)

A comedy in three acts by Emmet Lavery. Produced by Arthur Hopkins at the Royale Theatre, New York, January 22, 1946.

Cast of characters—

Dixon....................................Mason Curry
Mr. Justice Holmes....................................Louis Calhern
Fanny Dixwell Holmes....................................Dorothy Gish
Henry Adams....................................Fleming Ward
Copeland....................................Christopher Marvin
Mason....................................Nicholas Saunders
Mary....................................Eleanor Swayne
Mr. Palmer, of "The Transcript"....................................William Roerick
Owen Wister....................................Sherling Oliver
Northrop....................................Philip Truex
Hamilton....................................Robert Healy
Mr. Justice Brandeis....................................Edgar Barrier
Mapes....................................Grey Stafford
Rogers....................................Edward Hudson

Jackson....................................Edwin Whitner
Halloran....................................Bruce Bradford

Acts I, II and III.—Library of Mr. Justice Holmes. December, 1902, to March 4, 1933.

Staged by Arthur Hopkins; setting and costumes by Woodman Thompson.

See page 141.

O MISTRESS MINE

(150 performances)

(Continued)

A comedy in three acts by Terence Rattigan. Produced by The Theatre Guild and John C. Wilson at the Empire Theatre, New York, January 23, 1946.

Cast of characters—

Olivia Brown....................................Lynn Fontanne
Polton....................................Margery Maude
Miss Dell....................................Esther Mitchell
Sir John Fletcher....................................Alfred Lunt
Michael Brown....................................Dick Van Patten
Diana Fletcher....................................Ann Lee
Miss Wentworth....................................Marie Paxton

Acts I and II.—House in Westminster, London, 1944. Act II.—A Flat in Baron's Court.

Staged by Alfred Lunt; settings by Robert Davison.

See page 201.

JANUARY THAW

(48 performances)

A comedy in three acts by William Roos, from a novel by Bellamy Partridge. Produced by Michael Todd at the Golden Theatre, New York, February 4, 1946.

Cast of characters—

Sarah Gage....................................Lorna Lynn
Frieda....................................Norma Lehn
Paul Gage....................................Charles Nevil
Herbert Gage....................................Robert Keith
Marge Gage....................................Lulu Mae Hubbard
Barbara Gage....................................Natalie Thompson
George Husted....................................John Hudson
Jonathan Rockwood....................................Charles Middleton
Mathilda Rockwood....................................Helen Carew
Mr. Loomis....................................John McGovern
Uncle Walter....................................Charles Burrows
Matt Rockwood....................................Irving Morrow
Carson....................................Henry Jones
Melvin Gorley....................................Paul Weiss

Acts I, II and III.—Living Room of an Old House in Connecticut. The Gage Family, after restoring it to its Colonial State, have Just Moved In.

Staged by Ezra Stone; setting by Watson Barratt.

After Herbert Gage rents a place in Connecticut he discovers that the owner's heirs have a legal right to live in the house as long as they care to. After the Gages move in the Jonathan Rockwoods appear from nowhere and announce an intention of taking advantage of their relative's will. There are complications and contests of wit between the city slickers and the country folk until curtain time.

(Closed March 16, 1946)

BORN YESTERDAY

(138 performances)
(Continued)

A comedy in three acts by Garson Kanin. Produced by Max Gordon at the Lyceum Theatre, New York, February 4, 1946.

Cast of characters—

Helen....................Ellen Hall
Paul Verrall....................Gary Merrill
Eddie Brock....................Frank Otto
Bellhop....................William Harmon
Bellhop....................Rex King
Harry Brock....................Paul Douglas
The Assistant Manager....................Carroll Ashburn
Billie Dawn....................Judy Holliday
Ed Devery....................Otto Hulett
Barber....................Ted Mayer
Manicurist....................Mary Laslo
Bootblack....................Paris Morgan
Senator Norval Hedges....................Larry Oliver
Mrs. Hedges....................Mona Bruns
Waiter....................C. L. Burke

Acts I, II and III.—Washington, D. C., September, 1945.
Staged by Garson Kanin; setting by Donald Oenslager; costumes by Ruth Kanin Aronson.

See page 235.

APPLE OF HIS EYE

(118 performances)

A comedy in two acts by Kenyon Nicholson and Charles Robinson. Produced by Jed Harris in association with Walter Huston at the Biltmore Theatre, New York, February 5, 1946.

Cast of characters—

Stella Springer....................Doro Merande
Foss Springer....................Arthur Hunnicutt
Lily Tobin....................Mary James
Tude Bowers....................Roy Fant
Sam Stover....................Walter Huston
Carol Ann Stover....................Jimsey Somers

Ott Tobin....................................Joseph Sweeney
Nettie Bowers....................................Claire Woodbury
Glen Stover....................................Tom Ewell

Acts I and II.—Sam Stover's Maple Lawn Farm, Highland Township, Montgomery County, Indiana.

Staged by Jed Harris; setting by Raymond Sovey.

Sam Stover, Indiana farmer, eleven years a widower, falls precipitately in love with Lily Tobin, twenty years his junior. Lily has come to his farm to look after him while his regular housekeeper is hospitalized. Sam takes Lily to a carnival and attempts to demonstrate his youth in a wrestling match that puts him on his back. After that he would let Lily go and forget his love, but Lily has a different idea.

(Closed May 18, 1946)

LUTE SONG

(134 performances)

(Continued)

A love story with music in three acts by Sidney Howard and Will Irwin, from the Chinese Classic, "Pi-Pa-Ki"; music by Raymond Scott; lyrics by Bernard Hanighen. Produced by Michael Myerberg at Plymouth Theatre, New York, February 6, 1946.

Cast of characters—

The Manager } The Honorable Tschang }....................................Clarence Derwent
Tsai-Yong, the Husband....................................Yul Brynner
First Property Man....................................Albert Vecchio
Second Property Man....................................Leslie Rheinfeld
Tsai, the Father....................................Augustin Duncan
Madame Tsai, the Mother....................................Mildred Dunnock
Tchao-Ou-Niang, the Wife....................................Mary Martin
Prince Nieou, the Imperial Perceptor....................................McKay Morris
Princess Nieou-Chi, His Daughter....................................Helen Craig
Si-Tchun, a Lady in Waiting....................................Nancy Davis
Waiting Women....................................Pamela Wilde, Sydelle Sylovna
Hand Maidens....................................Blanche Zohar, Mary Ann Reeve
Youen-Kong, the Steward....................................Rex O'Malley
A Marriage Broker....................................Diane De Brett
A Messenger....................................Jack Amoroso
The Imperial Chamberlain....................................Ralph Clanton
The Food Commissioner....................................Gene Galvin
First Clerk....................................Max Leavitt
Second Clerk....................................Bob Turner
First Applicant....................................Tom Emelyn Williams
Second Applicant....................................Michael Blair
Imperial Guards....................................John Robert Lloyd, John High
Imperial Attendants....................................Gordon Showalter, Ronald Fletcher
The Genie....................................Ralph Clanton
The White Tiger....................................Lisa Maslova
The Ape....................................Lisan Kay
Phoenix Birds....................................Lisa Maslova, Lisan Kay
Li-Wang....................................Max Leavitt
Priest of Amida Buddha....................................Tom Emelyn Williams
A Bonze....................................Gene Galvin

Two Lesser Bonzes................Joseph Camiolo, Leslie Rheinfeld
A Rich Man..Bob Turner
A Merchant..John High
A Little Boy...Donald Rose
The Lion..........................Walter Stane, Alberto Vecchio
Children..............Mary Ann Reeve, Blanche Zohar, Teddy Rose
A Secretary...Michael Blair

Travelers on the North Road, Beggars, Guards, Attendants, Gods, and Others: Mary Burr, Arlene Gaver, Sydelle Sylovna, Pamela Wilde, Alan Banks, Victor Burset, Jack Amoroso, Joseph Camiolo, Jack Cooper, Ronald Fletcher, John High, John Robert Lloyd, Lang Page, Bernard Pisarski, Leslie Rheinfeld, Gordon Showalter, Walter Stane, Alberto Vecchio.

Act I.—Scenes 1 and 4—House of Tsai in the Village of Tchin-lieou. 2—North Road. 3—Gardens of the Palace of Prince Nieou. 5—Gate to Palace of Voice of Jade. Act II.—Scenes 1 and 3—Gardens of Palace. 2—Public Granary in Village of Tchin-lieou. 4—House of Tsai. 5—Market Place. 6—Burial Place. Act III.—Scene 1—Gardens of Palace. 2—North Road. 3—In the Palace. 4—Temple of Amidha. 5—Street in the Capital. 6—Blue Pavilion in the Palace of Prince Nieou.

Staged by John Houseman; music directed by Eugene Kusmiak; choreography by Yeichi Nimura; settings, lighting and costumes by Robert Edmond Jones.

See page 345.

THE DUCHESS MISBEHAVES

(5 performances)

A musical comedy in two acts by Gladys Shelly; additional dialogue by Joe Bigelow; music by Frank Black; orchestrations by Don Walker; vocal arrangements by Clay Warnick. Produced by A. P. Waxman at the Adelphi Theatre, February 13, 1946.

Cast of characters—

(In Carlton's Department Store)

Woman...Grace Hayle
Franchot..Buddy Ferraro
1st Sister..Elena Boyd
2nd Sister..Mildred Boyd
3rd Sister..Edith Boyd
Butterfly...Penny Edwards
Paul..Larry Douglas
Fitzgerald..James MacColl
Woonsocket..Joey Faye
1st Girl..Gail Adams
2nd Girl..Ethel Madson
Miss Kiester.....................................Paula Laurence
Crystal Shalimar................................Audrey Christie
Reporter..Al Downing
Neville Goldglitter................................Philip Tonge

(In Spain)

Pablo...Larry Douglas
Amber...Grace Hayle
Goya..Joey Faye
Model...Joanne Jaap
Roberto...James MacColl
Duchess of Alba.................................Audrey Christie
Mariposa...Penny Edwards
Barber...Paul Marten
Manicurist...Joanne Jaap

Tailor..Ken Martin
Ass't Tailor..Bernie Williams
Messenger..Buddy Ferraro
1st Student..Victor Clark

Act I.—Scene 1—Carlton's Department Store. 2—Goya's Studio in Spain. 3—Street in Madrid. 4—Outside Fiesta Grounds. Act II.—Scene 1—Public Square, Madrid. 2—Side Street. 3—Goya's Studio. 4—Carlton's Department Store.

Staged by Martin Manulis; dances directed by George Tapps; music directed by Charles Sanford; settings by A. A. Ostrander; costumes by Willa Kim; lighting by Carlton Winckler.

Woonsocket, suffering a swoon-sock, dreams that he is the artist, Francisco Goya, engaged in painting the Duchess of Alba in the nude. Much sly comment, mostly dirty.

(Closed February 16, 1946)

ANTIGONE

(64 performances)

The Sophocles tragedy adapted by Lewis Galantiere from a play by Jean Anouilh. Produced by Katharine Cornell in association with Gilbert Miller at the Cort Theatre, New York, February 18, 1946.

Cast of characters—

Chorus..Horace Braham
Antigone..Katharine Cornell
Nurse..Bertha Belmore
Ismene..Ruth Matteson
Haemon..Wesley Addy
Creon..Cedric Hardwicke
First Guard..George Mathews
Second Guard..David J. Stewart
Third Guard..Michael Higgins
Messenger..Oliver Cliff
Page..Albert Biondo
Eurydice..Merle Maddern

A Room in a Palace draped in Gray Silk.

Staged by Guthrie McClintic; setting by Raymond Sovey; costumes by Valentina.

See page 176.

(Closed May 4, 1946)

JEB

(9 performances)

A drama in two acts by Robert Ardrey. Produced by Herman Shumlin at the Martin Beck Theatre, New York, February 21, 1946.

Cast of characters—

Solly....................................Morris McKenney
Don....................................Charles Holland
Cynthie....................................Carolyn Hill Stewart
Hazy Johnson....................................Wardell Saunders
Jeb Turner....................................Ossie Davis
Bush....................................P. Jay Sidney
Flabber....................................Percy Verwayen
Simpson....................................G. Harry Bolden
Mr. Touhy....................................W. J. Hackett
Amanda Turner....................................Laura Bowman
Rachel....................................Reri Grist
Libby George....................................Ruby Dee
Libe....................................Rudolph Whitaker
Jefferson....................................Christopher Bennett
Julian....................................Maurice Ellis
Paul Devoure....................................Santos Ortega
Mrs. Devoure....................................Grace McTarnahan
Charles Bard....................................Frank M. Thomas
Dr. Hazelton....................................Edwin Cushman
Mr. Gibney....................................Grover Burgess
Joseph....................................Milton Shirah
Mr. Dowd....................................Edward Forbes
White Man....................................Owen Hewitt

Act I.—Scene 1—Elite Café in Negro Section of Northern City. 2—Amanda Turner's Kitchen, Small Louisiana Town. 3—The Devoure Back Parlor. Act II.—Scene 1—Timekeeper's Shed at Sugar Mill. 2—Amanda's Kitchen. 3—Behind Dr. Hazelton's Church. 4—Elite Café.

Staged by Herman Shumlin; settings and lighting by Jo Mielziner; costumes by Patricia Montgomery; production associate, David Merrick.

Jeb Turner, a colored Silver Star and Purple Heart hero who lost a leg in the war, comes home to Louisiana expecting to find a job and be taken back into the community. In the Army he has learned to operate an adding machine. There is need of such an operator in the mills, and the sympathetic proprietor is eager to give it to Jeb, but is overruled by the town's "best" citizens, who refuse to see a Negro in a white man's job. When Jeb tries to fight this prejudice, he is accused of having been seen with a white girl and is forced to leave town. In New York Jeb is robbed by crooks of his own race in a Harlem café. Still undaunted, he decides to go back to Louisiana and continue his fight for justice.

(Closed February 28, 1946)

TRUCKLINE CAFE

(13 performances)

A comedy in three acts by Maxwell Anderson. Produced by Harold Clurman and Elia Kazan in association with The Playwrights' Company at the Belasco Theatre, New York, February 27, 1946.

Cast of characters—

Toby.....Frank Overton
Kip.....Ralph Theadore
Stew.....John Sweet
Maurice.....Kevin McCarthy
Min.....June Walker
Wing Commander Hern.....David Manners
Anne.....Virginia Gilmore
Stag.....Karl Malden
Angie.....Irene Dailey
Celeste.....Joanne Tree
Patrolman Gray.....Robert Simon
Evvie Garrett.....Joann Dolan
Hutch.....Kenneth Tobey
Matt.....Louis A. Florence
June.....Jutta Wolf
Sissie.....Leila Ernst
Tory McRae.....Ann Shepherd
Sage McRae.....Marlon Brando
Man With a Pail.....Lou Gilbert
The Breadman.....Peter Hobbs
Janet.....Peggy Meredith
Mildred.....June March
Bimi.....Richard Paul
Tuffy Garrett.....Eugene Steiner
First Man.....Solen Hayes
First Woman.....Lorraine Kirby
Mort.....Richard Waring
Second Man.....Joseph Adams
Second Woman.....Rose Steiner
First Girl.....Ann Morgan
Second Girl.....Gloria Stroock

Acts I, II and III.—Interior of Diner Café on Ocean Highway between Los Angeles and San Francisco.

Staged by Harold Clurman; settings by Boris Aronson; costumes by Millia Davenport.

Anne, a girl of gentle rearing in the East, believing that her war-time husband, Mort, has been killed in Europe, gives herself up to drink and other men. When she hears Mort is alive, she submits to an abortion and tries to hide herself as a waitress in a Truckline Café in California. Mort finds her. He, too, has violated his marital obligations and is the father of a French child whose mother had died giving birth. After a variety of emotional crises, Mort is able to convince Anne that they should both forget the sins of the past and start a new life.

(Closed March 9, 1946)

LITTLE BROWN JUG

(5 performances)

A drama in three acts by Marie Baumer. Produced by Courtney Burr at the Martin Beck Theatre, New York, March 6, 1946.

Cast of characters—

Irene Haskell.....Katharine Alexander
Henry Barlow.....Ronald Alexander

Carol Barlow................................Marjorie Lord
Ira................................Percy Kilbride
Lydia................................Frieda Altman
Michael Andrews................................Arthur Kranz
Norman Barlow................................Arthur Margetson

Act I.—Scene 1—Henry Barlow's Combined Lodge and Boat House in Maine, 1945. 2—Irene Haskell's House in Connecticut. Acts II and III.—Irene Haskell's House.

Staged by Gerald Savory; settings and lighting by Frederick Fox.

Irene Haskell, taking her daughter's side in a quarrel with the daughter's drunken husband, Henry Barlow, slaps his face. Henry, losing balance, falls out a window and is killed. A witness to the accident turns up in the person of a shifty handyman, Ira, who blackmails the two women into taking him into their home. Unless they do his bidding he will swear Barlow's death was not accidental, but a deliberate murder. Norman Barlow, the dead man's brother, sees through Ira and his schemes, and forces the handyman's confession.

(Closed March 9, 1946)

THREE TO MAKE READY

(100 performances)
(Continued)

A revue in two acts by Nancy Hamilton; music by Morgan Lewis; orchestrations by Russell Bennett, Charles L. Cooke, Elliott Jacoby, Ted Royal and Hans Spialek. Produced by Stanley Gilky and Barbara Payne at the Adelphi Theatre, New York, March 7, 1946.

Principals engaged—

Brenda Forbes	Ray Bolger
Rose Inghram	Gordon MacRae
Bibi Osterwald	Harold Lang
Jane Deering	Garry Davis
Althea Elder	Joe Jonson
Meg Mundy	Carleton Carpenter
Mary Alice Bingham	Martin Kraft
Mary McDonnell	Jack Purcell
Edythia Turnell	Irwin Charles
Candace Montgomery	Jimmy Venable
Iris Linde	Jim Elsegood

Arthur Godrey

Staged by John Murray Anderson; sketches directed by Margaret Webster; dances and musical numbers directed by Robert Sidney; music directed by Ray M. Kavanaugh; settings by Donald Oenslager; costumes by Audre.

FLAMINGO ROAD

(7 performances)

A comedy in three acts by Robert and Sally Wilder. Produced by Rowland Stebbins at the Belasco Theatre, New York, March 19, 1946.

Cast of characters—

Boatright....................Olvester Polk
Titus Semple....................Francis J. Felton
Fielding Carlisle....................Lauren Gilbert
Henry Veech....................Frank McNellis
"Doc" Watterson....................Will Geer
Dan Curtis....................Philip Bourneuf
Ulee Jackson....................Paul Ford
Tate Hadley....................Bernard Randall
Lute-Mae Saunders....................Doris Rich
Goldie....................Martha Jensen
Another Girl....................Sally Carthage
Lane Ballou....................Judith Parrish
Burrell Lassen....................Tom Morrison
"Red"....................Marcella Markham
Matron....................Hazele Burgess
Virgie....................Evelyn Davis
Grocery Boy....................Mahlon Naill

Act I.—Front Porch of the Palmer House, Florida. Act II.—Scene 1—Yard of Women's Prison Farm. 2—Room at Lute-Mae Saunders'. Act III.—Scene 1—Living Room at 32 Flamingo Road. 2—Front Porch of Palmer House.

Staged by Jose Ruben; settings by Watson Barratt; lighting by Leo Kerz; costumes by Emeline Roche.

Titus Semple, small-town Florida sheriff and political overlord of his territory, railroads a carnival girl, Lane Ballou, when she threatens to interfere with his plans by attracting the attention of Fielding Carlisle. Lane comes out of a house of correction bent on revenge. As an inmate of the town's chief bordello, she wins her freedom by going to live with Dan Curtis, a Semple rival. When Semple breaks up this romance, Lane shoots three or four bullets into his expansive viscera.

(Closed March 23, 1946)

HE WHO GETS SLAPPED

(46 performances)

A drama by Leonid Andreyev; English version in two acts by Judith Guthrie. Revived by The Theatre Guild at the Booth Theatre, New York, March 20, 1946.

Cast of characters—

Tilly....................Bobby Barry
Polly....................John M. O'Connor

Count Mancini.......................................John Abbott
Papa Briquet.......................................Wolfe Barzell
Zinaida.......................................Stella Adler
Funny.......................................Dennis King
Jim Jackson.......................................Russell Collins
Consuela.......................................Susan Douglas
Alfred Bezano.......................................Jerome Thor
A Gentleman.......................................Tom Rutherford
Baron Regnard.......................................Reinhold Schunzel

Other Characters

Housekeeper.......................................Edith Shayne
Ringmaster.......................................Arthur Foran
1st Jockey.......................................George Cory
2nd Jockey.......................................Tony Albert
3rd Jockey.......................................Ellis Eringer
Thomas, Head Usher.......................................Ernest Sarracino
Equestrienne.......................................Cynthia Blake
Tap Dancing Trio.........Phil Sheridan, Jack Orton, Leatta Miller
Strong Man.......................................Paul Alberts
Jugglers.......................................Frank de Silva, Robin Taylor
Waiter.......................................Frank de Silva

Dancers: Cynthia Carlin, Letitia Fay, Sydna Scott, Jackie Jones, Elsbeth Fuller.

Clowns: Michael Wyler, Joseph Singer, Carl Specht, Douglas Hudelson.

Acts I and II.—Backstage of Circus in City in France, 1919.

Staged by Tyrone Guthrie; production under supervision of Theresa Helburn and Lawrence Langner; settings and costumes by Motley.

The original production of "He Who Gets Slapped" was staged by the Theatre Guild at the Garrick Theatre, New York, January 9, 1922. It continued for 308 performances. Richard Bennett and Margalo Gillmore played the leads. The adaptation was by Gregory Zilboorg.

The 1946 version was written by Judith Guthrie, who renamed the hero "Funny" in place of "He," leaving the story practically intact. "Funny," a citizen of social prominence, deceived by his wife and his best friend, joins a small circus and becomes the clown who submits to the slaps of his colleagues in the cause of comedy. Falling in love with Consuela, a youthful bareback rider who is being sold by a dissolute father to a more dissolute Baron, "Funny" poisons the girl and himself to save them both from a fate he decides would be several times worse than death.

(Closed April 27, 1946)

I LIKE IT HERE

(52 performances)

A comedy in three acts by A. B. Shiffrin. Produced by William Cahn at the Golden Theatre, New York, March 22, 1946.

Cast of characters—

Mr. Smedley.......................................Seth Arnold
Captain Leroux.......................................John Effrat

Laura Merriweather....................................Mardi Bryant
Matilda Merriweather....................................Beverly Bayne
Sebastian Merriweather....................................Bert Lytell
Brad Monroe....................................William Terry
Willie Kringle....................................Oscar Karlweis
David Bellow....................................Donald Randolph
Saphronia Lawrence....................................Ellis Baker

Acts I, II and III.—New England Home of the Merriweathers.
Staged by Charles K. Freeman; setting by Ralph Alswang.

Willie Kringle, answering an ad announcing the need of a handyman at the home of Prof. Sebastian Merriweather, of the New England Merriweathers, talks himself into the job and practically talks the Merriweathers out of the freedom of their home. A superior type of Austrian refugee, Willie helps daughter Laura land her true love, Brad Monroe, the village taxi driver, by inducing Brad to run for Congress against the village politician, phony David Bellow. Brad wins.

(Closed May 4, 1946)

THE SONG OF BERNADETTE

(3 performances)

A drama in three acts dramatized by Jean and Walter Kerr from Franz Werfel's novel of the same name. Produced by Victor Payne-Jennings and Frank McCoy at the Belasco Theatre, New York, March 26, 1946.

Cast of characters—

Sister Marie....................................Jean Mann
Jeanne Abadie....................................Christina Soulias
Bernadette Soubirous....................................Elizabeth Ross
Marie Soubirous....................................Pamela Rivers
Dean Peyramale....................................Keinert Wolff
Louise Soubirous....................................Marjorie Hurtubise
Soubirous....................................Whit Vernon
Croisine Bouhouhorts....................................Mimi Norton
Louis Bouriette....................................Anthony Messuri
Bernarde Casterot....................................Gertrude Kinnell
Madame Sajou....................................Cavada Humphrey
Antoine Nicolau....................................Bruce Hall
Mayor Lacade....................................Michael Vallon
Jacomet....................................Richard Karlan
Dr. Dozous....................................Francis Compton
Celeste....................................Octavia Kenmore
Madame Pernet....................................Ray Macdonald
Mother Josephine....................................Ruth Gregory
Schoolgirl....................................Jane Thomas

Act I.—Scene 1—Schoolroom in Lourdes, 1858. 2—Grotto of Massabielle. 3 and 4—The Cachot, Home of the Soubirouses. Act II.—Scene 1—Office of Mayor Lacade. 2—Dean Peyramale's Garden. 3 and 4—The Grotto. Act III.—Scene 1—The Cachot. 2—Convent at Nevers.

Staged by Walter Kerr; settings by Willis Knighton; production equipment designed by Ralph Brown.

Bernadette Soubirous, daughter of a poor miller and his wife, sees herself in a vision speaking with the Virgin in the Grotto of Massabielle. Thereafter she holds steadfastly to her faith in her vision, against the persistent opposition of her family, and most of the village folk, including the local dean. In the end she becomes one with the sisters of the convent of Nevers.

(Closed March 27, 1946)

WALK HARD

(7 performances)

A drama in three acts adapted by Abram Hill from Len Zinberg's novel, "Walk Hard—Talk Aloud." Produced by Gustav Blum at the Chanin Auditorium, New York, March 27, 1946.

Cast of characters—

Bobby	Richard Kraft
Mack Jeffris	Leonard Yorr
Andy Whitman	Maxwell Glanville
Mr. Berry	Fred C. Carter
Lou Foster	Joseph Kamm
Happy	Howard Augusta
Mickey	Stephen Elliott
Larry Batcheller	Mickey Walker
Becky	Jacqueline Andre
Charlie	Maurice Lisby
Susie	Lulu Mae Ward
Ruth Lawson	Dorothy Carter
Bartender	John O. Hewitt
Sadie	Jean Normandy
Dorothy	Miriam Pullen
George, the Bellhop	Leslie Jones
Hotel Clerk	Richard Kraft
Lady Friend	Fiona O'Shiel
Reporter	Edward Kreisler
Announcer	Richard Kraft

Act I.—Scene 1—Street Corner at Dusk, New York. 2—Lou Foster's Office. 3—Whitman Home. Act II.—Scene 1—Jersey Tavern. 2—Hotel Lobby. 3—Ringside. Act III.—Scene 1—Hotel Room. 2—Whitman Home.

Staged by Gustav Blum and Gilbert Weiss; settings by John Wenger.

Andy Whitman, a Negro prizefighter, becomes convinced that he should fight the prejudice involving his race outside as well as inside the ring. The decision embroils him in a good deal of trouble with family and friends. In the end he is still fighting. The Mickey Walker of the above cast marks the stage debut of the former welterweight and middleweight champion.

(Closed March 31, 1946)

ST. LOUIS WOMAN

(73 performances)

(Continued)

A musical play in three acts by Arna Bontemps and Countee Cullen based on a novel, "God Sends Sunday," by Bontemps; lyrics by Johnny Mercer; music by Harold Arlen. Produced by Edward Gross at the Martin Beck Theatre, New York, March 30, 1946.

Cast of characters—

Barfoot....Robert Pope
Little Augie....Harold Nicholas
Barney....Fayard Nicholas
Lila....June Hawkins
Slim....Louis Sharp
Butterfly....Pearl Bailey
Della Green....Ruby Hill
Biglow Brown....Rex Ingram
Ragsdale....Elwood Smith
Pembroke....Merritt Smith
Jasper....Charles Welch
The Hostess....Maude Russell
Drum Major....J. Mardo Brown
Mississippi....Milton J. Williams
Dandy Dave....Frank Green
Leah....Juanita Hall
Jackie....Joseph Eady
Celestine....Yvonne Coleman
Piggie....Herbert Coleman
Joshua....Lorenzo Fuller
Mr. Hopkins....Milton Wood
Preacher....Creighton Thompson
Waiter....Carrington Lewis

Act I.—Scene 1—A Stable, St. Louis, 1898. 2—Biglow's Bar. 3—Outside Barney's Room. 4—Ballroom. Act II.—Scene 1—Augie's and Della's Home. 2—The Alley. 3—Funeral Parlor. Act III.—Scene 1—Augie's and Della's Home. 2—The Alley. 3—The Bar. 4—The Stable. 5—Street Corner Close to Race Track.

Staged by Rouben Mamoulian; dances directed by Charles Walters; music by Leon Leonardi; settings and costumes by Lemuel Ayers.

Della Green, a reigning queen of fast colored society in St. Louis in 1898, is Biglow Brown's woman until Little Augie comes along. Augie is a winning jockey and the sporting favorite of the hour. Della switches to Augie; Biglow gives her a beating; Augie sets out to get Biglow. He'd have done it, too, if one of Biglow's castoffs had not beaten him to the shooting. Biglow's dying curse changes Augie's winning streak and Della leaves him until just before curtain time.

CANDIDA

(24 performances)

A comedy in three acts by Bernard Shaw. Revived by Katharine Cornell in association with Gilbert Miller at the Cort Theatre, New York, April 3, 1946.

Cast of characters—

Miss Proserpine Garnett.......................... Mildred Natwick
James Mavor Morell.............................. Wesley Addy
Alexander Mill.................................. Oliver Cliff
Mr. Burgess..................................... Cedric Hardwicke
Candida... Katharine Cornell
Eugene Marchbanks............................... Marlon Brando
Acts I, II and III.—Sitting Room in St. Dominic's Parsonage in Northeast Suburb of London.
Staged by Guthrie McClintic.

"Candida" was first played in New York by Katharine Cornell on December 12, 1924, with Pedro de Cordoba as Morell and Richard Bird as Marchbanks. The play ran for 143 performances. Miss Cornell's last New York appearance in the play was April 27, 1942, when the American Theatre Wing War Service, Inc. revived it for the benefit of the Army Emergency Fund and the Navy Relief Society for four matinees and one evening performance. Raymond Massey played Morell; Dudley Digges, Mr. Burgess; Burgess Meredith, Marchbanks; Mildred Natwick, Proserpine Garnett; and Stanley Bell, Alexander Mill. This revival proved sensationally successful and was continued for twenty-seven performances following the benefit dates.

(Closed May 4, 1946)

WOMAN BITES DOG

(5 performances)

A comedy in three acts by Bella and Samuel Spewack. Produced by Kermit Bloomgarden at the Belasco Theatre, New York, April 17, 1946.

Cast of characters—

Amanda Merkle.................................. Eda Heinemann
Tony Flynn...................................... Frank Lovejoy
Betsy Louis Eric................................ Himself
Commander Southworth............................ Taylor Holmes
Sims.. E. G. Marshall
Wilson.. Harold Grau
Betty Lord...................................... Mercedes McCambridge
Major Southworth................................ Royal Beal
Lizzie Southworth............................... Ann Shoemaker
Hopkins... Kirk Douglas

1st Attorney....Richard Clark
2nd Attorney....Arthur Russell
Slim....Dudley Sadler
Waiter....Sam Bonnell
Valet....Russell Morrison
Breckenridge....Robert Le Sueuer
Maurice Crash....Maury Tuckerman
Sokonovski....Boris Kogan
Lee....John Shellie
Mayor Stevens....Ed Nannery
Dean West....Roger Quinlan

Acts I and III.—Office of the Publisher of the *Herald*. Act II.—Living Room of Commander Southworth's Suite at the Royal Hotel.

Staged by Coby Ruskin; settings by Howard Bay; costumes by Mary Grant.

Once upon a time there were two brothers, Commander and Major Southworth, and a cousin, Lizzie Southworth. The Commander owned a newspaper in Chicago and exploited a practically uncontrolled ego. The Major owned a sensationally popular newspaper in New York and had developed an acute cynicism as self-protection against his gentler humanitarian impulses. Cousin Lizzie owned a newspaper in Washington, D. C., which ran its more personal and socially destructive columns on its first page. All three hated communism like poison. Comes a young air hero home from the wars bent on exposing the Southworths to themselves. He frames the Commander with a story revealing the Joseph Stalin influence in Danville, Ill. The Commander falls for it and would have been terribly embarrassed if it had not been for his ego.

(Closed April 20, 1946)

CALL ME MISTER

(52 performances)
(Continued)

A musical revue in two acts; music and lyrics by Harold Rome; sketches by Arnold Auerbach and Arnold B. Horwitt; musical arrangements by Ben Ludlow assisted by Charles Huffine and Julian Work. Produced by Melvyn Douglas and Herman Levin at the National Theatre, New York, April 18, 1946.

Principals engaged—

Jules Munshin	Betty Garrett
David Nillo	Maria Karnilova
Bill Callahan	Paula Bane
Lawrence Winters	Betty Lou Holland
George Hall	Ruth Feist
Harry Clark	Kate Friedlich
Alan Manson	Virginia Davis
Danny Scholl	Evelyn Shaw
Chandler Cowles	Betty Gilpatrick
George Irving	Joan Bartels
Glenn Turnbull	Marjorie Oldroyd

Assisting GI's, Wacs, Waves, etc.: Steve Allison, Robert Baird, Joe Calvan, Fred Danieli, Francis Dometrovich, Alex Dunaeff, Peter Fara, Shellie Filkins, Ward Garner, Tommy Knox, Henry Lawrence, Sid Lawson, Betty Lorraine, Howard Malone, William Mende, Patricia Penso, Ray Ross, Edward Silkman, Eugene Tobin, Alvis A. Tinnin, Doris Parker, Paula Purnell, Bruce Howard, Kevin Smith, Rae MacGregor, Darcy Gardner and Betty Durrence.

Act I.—Sketch 1—"Going Home Train." 2—"Welcome Home." 3—"Love Story." 4—"The Army Way." 5—"Surplus Blues." 6—"Off We Go." 7—"The Red Ball Express." 8—"Military Life." 9—"Call Me Mister." Act II.—Sketch 1—"Yuletide, Park Avenue." 2—"Love Story." 3—"Once Over Lightly." 4—"The Face on the Dime." 5—"A Home of Our Own." 6—"South America, Take It Away." 7—"South Wind." 8—"The Senators' Song."

Staged by Robert H. Gordon; dances directed by John Wray; music by Lehman Engel; settings by Lester Polokov; costumes by Grace Houston.

THIS, TOO, SHALL PASS

(39 performances)
(Continued)

A drama in three acts by Don Appell. Produced by Richard Krakeur and David Shay at the Belasco Theatre, New York, April 30, 1946.

Cast of characters—

Janet Alexander....................Jan Sterling
Martha Alexander....................Kathryn Givney
Dr. Steven Alexander....................Ralph Morgan
Mac Sorrell....................Sam Wanamaker
Buddy Alexander....................Walter Starkey

Acts I, II and III.—Home of Dr. Steven Alexander in Small Midwestern Town.

Staged by Don Appell; setting by Raymond Sovey.

Mac Sorrell was the soldier who saved Buddy Alexander's life in World War II. That's how he came to correspond with Buddy's sister Janet, which resulted in their becoming engaged. Everybody was very happy about everything when the boys came home from the war—until Mrs. Alexander discovered that Mac was a Jew and that the old, unreasoning, intolerant, anti-Semitic prejudice still gripped her. That led to the split-up of the Alexanders as a family unit. Later the accidental death of Buddy Alexander under the wheels of Mac's car, and the final marriage of Mac and Janet in defiance of all prejudice and in final justification of their love, helped to bring the family together.

SAN CARLO OPERA COMPANY

The San Carlo Opera season for 1945-46 opened at the Rockefeller Center Theatre, New York, May 1, 1946, and ended the season May 12, having presented 12 operas in 16 performances.

AIDA

An opera in four acts by Giuseppe Verdi. Produced by Fortune Gallo at the Center Theatre, New York, May 1, 1946.

Cast of characters—

Aida, an Ethiopian slave............................Willa Stewart
Amneris..Coe Glade
Rhadames...Rafael Lagares
Amonasro...Mostyn Thomas
Ramfis...John Gurney
The King of Egypt..................................William Wilderman
Messenger..Adrien La Chance
Priestess..Emily Kalter

Dance Spectacles by the San Carlo Ballet, Lydia Arlova, Premiere Danseuse; Lucien Prideaux, Premier Danseur.

Moorish Slave Dancers: Mlles. Mueller, Ammon and Davidova.

Triumphal Dance: Lucien Prideaux, Lydia Arlova and Corps de Ballet.

Act I.—Scene 1—Hall in King's Palace at Memphis. 2—Temple of Isis. Act II.—Scene 1—Hall in Amneris' Apartment. 2—Gate of Thebes. Act III.—Shores of Nile, Near Temple of Isis. Act IV.—Scene 1—Outside Judgment Hall. 2—In the Temple of Vulcan. 3—Vault Beneath Temple.

Staged by Mario Valle; music directed by Victor Trucco and Isaac Van Grove.

"Aida" was repeated May 10 with the same cast except for Marie Powers, Rocco Pandiscio and Lloyd Harris who replaced Coe Glade, Mostyn Thomas and John Gurney.

Other operas presented during the San Carlo season were:

MADAMA BUTTERFLY—May 2 and 11. Cast—Hizi Koyke, Olympia diNapoli, Joan Bishop, Sydney Rayner, Mario Valle, William Wilderman, Adrien La Chance, Fausto Bozza and Mario Palermo.

LA TRAVIATA—May 3. Cast—Stella Andreva, Virginia Blair, Loraine Calcagno, Mario Palermo, Carlo Morelli and Adrian La Chance. Ballet.

CARMEN—May 4 and 11. Cast—Coe Glade, Mina Cravi, Virginia Blair, Emily Kalter, Sydney Rayner, Mostyn Thomas, William Wilderman, Lloyd Harris, Adrien La Chance, Ernice Lawrence and Stephan Ballerini.

IL TROVATORE—May 4 and 12. Cast—Willa Stewart, Marie Powers, Lorraine Calcagno, Rafael Lagares, Stephan Ballarini, William Wilderman, Adrien La Chance and Mostyn Thomas. Ballet.

RIGOLETTO—May 5. Cast—Doris Marinelli, Emily Kalter, Joan Bishop, Loraine Calcagno, Ernice Lawrence, Carlo Morelli, John Gurney, William Wilderman and Adrien La Chance. Ballet.

LA BOHEME—May 5 and 12. Cast—Mina Cravi, Biruta Ramoska, Bernice Fontayne, Mario Palermo, Mario Valle, Stephan Ballarini, John Gurney, Lloyd Harris, Adrien La Chance and Sydney Rayner.

LA TOSCA—May 6. Cast—Rachelle Carlay, Lorraine Calcagno, Sydney Rayner, Carlo Morelli, William Wilderman, Oscar Lassner and Adrien La Chance.

THE BARBER OF SEVILLE—May 7. Cast—Doris Marinelli, Emily Kalter, Mario Palermo, Carlo Morelli, Mario Valle, Valfrido Patacchi, Fausto Bozza and Adrien La Chance.

CAVALLERIA RUSTICANA—May 8. Cast—Gertrude Ribla, Dorothy Hartigan, Lorraine Calcagno, Ernice Lawrence, and Stephan Ballarini.

PAGLIACCI—May 8. Cast—Mina Cravi, Sydney Rayner, Mostyn Thomas, Stephan Ballarini and Adrien La Chance.

FAUST—May 9. Cast—Virginia Blair, Emily Kalter, Lorraine Calcagno, Mario Palermo, Stephan Ballarini, John Gurney, Henry Whiting, and Fausto Bozza. Ballet.

(Closed May 12, 1946)

OLD VIC REPERTORY COMPANY

(33 performances)
(Continued)

HENRY IV, PART I

(14 performances)

A drama in three parts by William Shakespeare. Presented by Theatre Incorporated (Richard Aldrich, Managing Director) for the Old Vic Theatre Company of London, England, at the Century Theatre, New York, May 6, 1946.

Cast of characters—

King Henry IV.....Nicholas Hannen
Henry, Prince of Wales.....Michael Warre
John of Lancaster.....Robin Lloyd
Earl of Westmoreland.....Peter Copley
Earl of Warwick.....Kenneth Edwards
Sir Walter Blunt.....Cecil Winter
Earl of Worcester.....George Relph
Earl of Northumberland.....Miles Malleson
Henry Percy (Hotspur).....Laurence Olivier
Lord Mortimer, Earl of March.....David Kentish
Owen Glendower.....Harry Andrews
Archibald, Earl of Douglas.....William Monk
Sir Richard Vernon.....Frank Duncan

Sir John Falstaff.............................Ralph Richardson
Bardolph.............................Michael Raghan
Poins.............................Sidney Tafler
Peto.............................George Rose
Mistress Quickly.............................Ena Burrill
Lady Percy.............................Margaret Leighton
Lady Mortimer.............................Diana Maddox
Servant to Hotspur.............................Joseph James
A Traveler.............................Frank Duncan
Another Traveler.............................William Squire
Francis.............................John Garley
Vintner of the Boar's Head.............................Kenneth Edwards
Sheriff.............................William Monk

Lords, Attendants and Soldiers: Lawrence Carr, George Cooper, Frank Duncan, John Garley, Carl James, Joseph James, John Reilly, Sandy Roe.

Scene—England.

Staged by John Burrell; music directed by Herbert Menges; fights arranged by Peter Copley; settings by Gower Parks; costumes by Roger Furse; lighting by John Sullivan.

"Henry IV, Part I" has had several revivals in both England and America, starting in London in 1667 at the Theatre Royal, and in New York at the new Beekman St. Theatre in 1761, with David Douglass as Falstaff. The Fat Knight was a favorite role with James H. Hackett through the 1860s. The Players staged a notable all-star revival in 1926, with Philip Merivale the Hotspur and Otis Skinner the Falstaff. Maurice Evans played Falstaff in his revival in 1939.

HENRY IV, PART II

(6 performances)

Presented May 7, 1946.

Cast of characters—

Rumour, The Presenter.............................Nicolette Bernard
King Henry IV.............................Nicholas Hannen
Henry, Prince of Wales (Afterwards King Henry V).............................Michael Warre
Prince John of Lancaster.............................Robin Lloyd
Thomas, Duke of Clarence.............................George Rose
Prince Humphrey of Gloucester.............................John Garley
Earl of Warwick.............................Kenneth Edwards
Earl of Westmoreland.............................Peter Copley
The Lord Chief Justice.............................Cecil Winter
His Servant.............................Max Brent
Fang.............................Frank Duncan
Snare.............................Joseph James
Gower.............................Kenneth Edwards
Earl of Northumberland.............................Miles Malleson
Lady Northumberland.............................Bryony Chapman
Lady Percy, Widow of Henry Hotspur.............................Margaret Leighton
Travers.............................Robin Lloyd
Morton.............................Peter Copley
Scroop, Archbishop of York.............................Harry Andrews
Lord Mowbray.............................William Squire
Lord Hastings.............................David Kentish
Lord Bardolph.............................George Rose
Sir John Coleville.............................Sidney Tafler
Sir John Falstaff.............................Ralph Richardson

His Page....................Brian Parker
Mistress Quickly, Hostess of the Boar's Head..........Ena Burrill
Bardolph....................Michael Raghan
Poins....................Sidney Tafler
Peto....................George Rose
Doll Tearsheet....................Joyce Redman
Pistol....................George Relph
Francis, a Winedrawer....................John Garley
Another Winedrawer....................Robin Lloyd
Justice Shallow....................Laurence Olivier
Justice Silence....................Miles Malleson
Davy, Servant to Shallow....................William Monk
Mouldy....................George Rose
Wart....................John Garley
Shadow....................Frank Duncan
Feeble....................David Kentish
Bullcalf....................Joseph James

Lords, Attendants, Soldiers, Citizens: Eleanora Barrie, Bryony Chapman, Julie Harris, Dee Sparks, Jane Wenham, Lawrence Carr, Rudolph Cavell, George Cooper, Will Davis, Frank Duncan, Carl James, Elmer Lehr, Bernard Pollack, John Reilly, Paul Riley, Sandy Roe, William Squire, Al Studer, Alvin Sullum, Richard Wendley.

"Henry IV, Part II" has been seldom played here. The last previously recorded performance in America was in 1867.

UNCLE VANYA

(5 performances)

A drama in three acts translated from the Russian of Anton Chekhov by Constance Garnett. Revived by Theatre, Inc., presenting the Old Vic Theatre Company at the Century Theatre, New York, May 13, 1946.

Cast of characters—

Marina....................Ena Burrill
Astrov....................Laurence Olivier
Voynitsky ("Uncle Vanya")....................Ralph Richardson
The Professor....................Nicholas Hannen
Yelena....................Margaret Leighton
Sonya....................Joyce Redman
Telyegin ("Waffles")....................George Relph
Marya Voynitsky....................Byrony Chapman
Yefim....................William Monk

Act I.—Outside the Professor's House on Southern Russian Estate at end of Nineteenth Century. Act II.—Room in the House. Act III.—Uncle Vanya's Room.

Staged by John Burrell; settings and costumes by Tanya Moiseiwitsch; lighting by John Sullivan.

New York has seen two previous revivals of "Uncle Vanya"—one the season of 1928-29, with Morris Carnovsky in the title role, and a cast including Franchot Tone and Hubert Druce, which gave two performances. The season following, in April, 1930, Jed Harris staged a revival with Walter Connolly as Uncle Vanya, and a cast including Osgood Perkins, Lillian Gish and Joanna Roos. This showing achieved a run of seventy-one performances.

ŒDIPUS

(8 performances)

A tragedy by Sophocles; English version by W. B. Yeats; music by Anthony Hopkins. Revived by Theatre, Inc., presenting the Old Vic Theatre Company at the Century Theatre, New York, May 20, 1946.

Cast of characters—

Œdipus....Laurence Olivier
A Priest....Cecil Winter
Creon....Harry Andrews
Tiresias....Ralph Richardson
Boy....Brian Parker
Jocasta....Ena Burrill
Attendants to Jocasta....Joyce Redman, Margaret Leighton, Nicolette Bernard
First Messenger....Miles Malleson
Herdsman....George Relph
Second Messenger....Michael Warre
Antigone....Jane Wenham
Ismene....Dee Sparks
Chorus Leader....Nicholas Hannen

Chorus of Theban Elders: Max Brent, George Cooper, Peter Copley, Frank Duncan, Kenneth Edwards, John Garley, Joseph James, David Kentish, Robin Lloyd, William Monk, Michael Raghan, George Rose, William Squire, Sydney Tafler.

Attendants, Guards, Priests, Servants, Crowd: Eleanora Barrie, Byrony Chapman, Julie Harris, Diana Maddox, Jane Wenham, Lawence Carr, Will Davis, Carl James, Elmer Lehr, Rudolph Cavell, Bernard Pollack, John Reilly, Paul Riley, Sandy Roe, Al Studer, Alvin Sullum, Richard Wendley.

Scene.—In Front of the Palace of King Œdipus in Thebes.

Staged by Michel Saint-Denis; music directed by Norman Feasey; setting by John Piper; lighting by John Sullivan; costumes by Marie-Helene Daste.

The Greek tragedy, under the title of "Œdipus Tyrannus," was produced for two weeks starting January 30, 1882, by Daniel Frohman at Booth's Theatre, New York. George Riddle played the leading character in Greek and Georgia Cayvan as Jocasta, Lewis Morrison as Creon and other members of the cast spoke English. Signori Paradossi and Consigli presented Ernesti Novelli as Œdipus in the Franco Liberata adaptation at the Lyric Theatre, March, 1907. The most recent revival was a single performance in the William Butler Yeats adaptation by the Abbey Theatre Irish Players in association with The Theatre Guild, January 15, 1932.

Followed by—

THE CRITIC

A comedy in two scenes by Richard Brinsley Sheridan.

Cast of characters—

Mr. Dangle....George Relph
Mrs. Dangle....Margaret Leighton
Servant....Robin Lloyd
Mr. Sneer....Peter Copley
Sir Fretful Plagiary....Miles Malleson
Mr. Puff....Laurence Olivier
First Scene Shifter....William Squire
Under Prompter....John Garley
First Sentinel....Frank Duncan
Second Sentinel....George Cooper
Sir Christopher Hatton....George Rose
Sir Walter Raleigh....Michael Warre
Earl of Leicester....Michael Raghan
Governor of Tilbury....Nicholas Hannen
Master of the Horse....Kenneth Edwards
Tilburina....Nicolette Bernard
Confidant....Joyce Redman
Whiskerandos....Sydney Tafler
Second Scene Shifter....Max Brent
Beefeater....William Monk
Lord Burleigh....Ralph Richardson
First Niece....Diana Maddox
Second Niece....Jane Wenham
Thames....Kenneth Edwards
First Bank....Robin Lloyd
Second Bank....Joseph James
Neptune....George Cooper

Scene 1—Mr. Dangle's House, 1779. 2—Drury Lane Theatre.

Staged by Miles Malleson; music directed by Herbert Menges; lighting by John Sullivan; fight arranged by Peter Copley; settings and costumes by Tanya Moiseiwitsch.

"The Critic" was first produced in New York at the John Street Theatre, July 10, 1786. A Daly revival at the Fifth Ave. Theatre, September 13, 1874, had Louis James as Sir Christopher, Fanny Davenport as Tilburina and James Lewis as Puff. Whitford Kane played in a production revived at the Princess Theatre, January 25, 1915. The most recent revival was at the Neighborhood Playhouse, May 8, 1925, when the cast included Whitford Kane, Dorothy Sands, Charles Warburton and Ian Maclaren.

ON WHITMAN AVENUE

(30 performances)
(Continued)

A drama in two acts by Maxine Wood. Produced by Canada Lee and Mark Marvin in association with George McLain at the Cort Theatre, New York, May 8, 1946.

Cast of characters—

Johnnie Tilden....Martin Miller
Kate Tilden....Ernestine Barrier
Ed Tilden....Will Geer
Owen Bennett....Richard Williams
Gramp Bennett....Augustus Smith
Wini Bennett....Vivienne Baber

Bernie Lund.....Kenneth Terry
Aurie Anderson.....Hilda Vaughn
Cora Bennett.....Abbie Mitchell
Toni Tilden.....Perry Wilson
David Bennett.....Canada Lee
Jeff Hall.....Philip Clarke
Belle Hall.....Betty Greene Little
Walter Lund.....Robert Simon
Ellen Lund.....Jean Cleveland
Wilbur Reed.....Stephen Roberts
Edna Reed.....Joanna Albus

Acts I and II.—The Tildens' Home in Lawndale, a Suburban Development in the Mid-West.

Staged by Margo Jones; setting and lighting by Donald Oenslager.

Toni Tilden, who has achieved liberalism in college, takes advantage of her parents' absence to rent the upper apartment in their home in a high-class Western city suburb to David Bennett, a Negro veteran of World War II, and his wife. On the Tildens' return a neighborhood mess is stirred up, expanding into a community protest, and the final forced eviction of the Bennetts. Toni's father sticks by her, but her mother is active in the social ranks of the opposition.

SWAN SONG

(22 performances)
(Continued)

A drama in three acts by Ben Hecht and Charles MacArthur, based on a story by Ramon Romero and Harriett Hinsdale. Produced by John Clein at the Booth Theatre, New York, May 15, 1946.

Cast of characters—

Louise Kubin.....Marianne Stewart
Titogh.....Ivan Simpson
Eric Moore.....Scott McKay
Stella Hemingway.....Mary Servoss
Victor Remezoff.....Michael Dalmatoff
Stanislaus Kubin.....Theo Goetz
Vera Novak.....Jacqueline Horner
Leo Pollard.....David Ellin
Katya.....Kasia Orzazewski
Sister Agatha.....Leni Stengel
Max Vonzell.....Harry Sothern
Gustav Wexler.....Louis Sorin
Oscar Mutzenbauer.....Rand Elliot
Ruth Trefon.....Barbara Perry
Dr. Corbett.....Owen Coll
Captain Bartow.....Arthur L. Sachs
Nurse.....Mary Jones

Acts I, II and III.—Long Island Living Room of Stanislaus Kubin.

Staged by Joseph Pevney; setting and lighting by Ralph Alswang.

Leo Pollard, whose career as a concert pianist has suffered frustration, becomes a victim of his own ambitions. The death of a sister who stood in his way as a boy is followed by his visit to a sanitarium. Out of the sanitarium he would resume his career and again finds his progress threatened by the genius of a youthful fellow student, Vera Novak. His plotting of this young girl's killing is providentially thwarted.

ANNIE GET YOUR GUN

(20 performances)
(Continued)

A musical comedy by Herbert and Dorothy Fields; music and lyrics by Irving Berlin. Produced by Richard Rodgers and Oscar Hammerstein 2nd, at the Imperial Theatre, New York, May 16, 1946.

Cast of characters—

Little Boy....Clifford Sales
Little Girl....Mary Ellen Glass
Charlie Davenport....Marty May
Iron Tail....Daniel Nagrin
Yellow Foot....Walter John
Mac....Cliff Dunstan
Cowboys....Rob Taylor, Bernard Griffin, Jack Pierce
Cowgirls....Mary Grey, Franca Baldwin
Foster Wilson....Art Barnett
Coolie....Beau Tilden
Dolly Tate....Lea Penman
Winnie Tate....Betty Anne Nyman
Tommy Keeler....Kenny Bowers
Frank Butler....Ray Middleton
Girl With Bouquet....Katrina Van Oss
Annie Oakley....Ethel Merman
Minnie....Nancy Jean Raab
Jessie....Camilla De Witt
Nellie....Marlene Cameron
Little Jake....Bobby Hookey
Harry....Don Liberto
Mary....Ellen Hanley
Col. Wm. F. Cody (Buffalo Bill)....William O'Neal
Mrs. Little Horse....Alma Ross
Mrs. Black Tooth....Elizabeth Malone
Mrs. Yellow Foot....Nellie Ranson
Trainman....John Garth III
Waiter....Leon Bibb
Porter....Clyde Turner
Riding Mistress....Lubov Roudenko
Major Gordon Lillie (Pawnee Bill)....George Lipton
Chief Sitting Bull....Harry Bellaver
Mabel....Mary Woodley
Louise....Ostrid Lind
Nancy....Dorothy Richards
Andy Turner....Earl Sauvain
Clyde Smith....Victor Clarke
John....Rob Taylor
Freddie....Robert Dixon
Wild Horse....Daniel Nagrin
Pawnee's Messenger....Walter John
Major Domo....John Garth III
1st Waiter....Clyde Turner
2nd Waiter....Leon Bibb

Mr. Schuyler Adams....................................Don Liberto
Mrs. Schuyler Adams..............................Dorothy Richards
Dr. Percy Ferguson....................................Bernard Griffin
Mrs. Percy Ferguson....................................Marietta Vore
Debutante...Ruth Vrana
Mr. Ernest Henderson....................................Art Barnett
Mrs. Ernest Henderson................................Truly Barbara
Sylvia Potter-Porter..............................Marjorie Crossland
Mr. Clay...Rob Taylor
Mr. Lockwood...Fred Rivett
Girl in Pink..Christina Lind
Girl in White...Mary Grey

Act I.—Scene 1—The Wilson House, Summer Hotel, Outskirts of Cincinnati, Ohio. 2—Pullman Parlor in Overland Steam Train. 3—Fair Grounds at Minneapolis and Arena of Big Tent. 4—Dressing Room Tent. Act II.—Scene 1—Deck of Cattle Boat. 2—Ballroom of Hotel Brevoort. 3—Aboard the Ferry. 4—Governor's Island.

Staged by Joshua Logan; music directed by Jay S. Blackton; dances by Helen Tamiris; settings and lighting by Jo Mielziner; costumes by Lucinda Ballard.

Little Annie Oakley joins the Buffalo Bill Wild West Show and falls in love with Frank Butler, its sure-shot champion, whom she dethrones. To hold Frank's love Annie finally has to let him win a match.

AROUND THE WORLD

(1 performance)
(Continued)

A musical extravaganza in two acts adapted by Orson Welles from Jules Verne's novel "Around the World in Eighty Days"; music and lyrics by Cole Porter. Produced by Mercury Productions at the Adelphi Theatre, New York, May 31, 1946.

Cast of characters—

Dick Fix..Orson Welles
A Lady...Genevieve Sauris
Mr. Phileas Fogg......................................Arthur Margetson
Avery Jevity...Stefan Schnabel
Molly Muggins...Julie Warren
Passepartout...Larry Laurence
Mr. Benjamin Cruett-Spew.........................Brainerd Duffield
Mr. Ralph Runcible..Guy Spaull
Sir Charles Mandiboy...................................Bernard Savage
Lord Upditch..Billy Howell
Meerahlah..Dorothy Bird
Lee Toy..Jackie Cezanne
Mr. Oka Saka..Brainerd Duffield
Mrs. Aouda..Mary Healy
Lola...Victoria Cordova

Other principals engaged: Nathan Baker, Jack Pitchon, Myron Speth, Gordon West, Lucas Aco, Spencer James, Eddy Di Genova, Allan Lowell, Victoria Cordova, Bruce Cartwright, Victor Savidge, Stanley Turner, Arthur Cohen and Phil King.

Act I.—Scenes 1, 3 and 17—Movies. 2—Jevity's Bank, London, England. 4—Hyde Park. 5 and 7—London Street. 6 and 9—Fogg's Flat. 8—Card Room in Whist Club. 10—Charing Cross Railroad Station. 11—Suez, Egypt. 12—End of Railway Tracks, British India. 13—Great Indian Forest. 14—Pagoda of Pilagi. 15—Jungle Encampment in Himalayas. 16—Aboard S.S. *Tankadere* on China Sea. 18—Street of Evil Repute, Hong Kong. 19—

Opium Den. 20—Oka Saka Circus, Yokohama, Japan. Act II.—Scenes 1 and 4—Movies. 2—Lola's, low place in California. 3—Railroad Station, San Francisco. 5—Passenger Car, Central Pacific Railway—Rocky Mountains. 6—Pass at Medicine Bow. 7—Water Stop, Banks of Republican River. 8—Bald Mountain. 9—Harbor, Liverpool. 10—Gaol, Liverpool. 11—Cell, Liverpool. 12—Street in London. 13—Outside London Whist Club. 14—Grand Tableau.

Staged by Orson Welles; music directed by Harry Levant; choreography by Nelson Barclift; circus arranged by Barbette; settings by Robert Davison; costumes by Alvin Colt.

EQUITY-LIBRARY THEATRE

By George Freedley

The Equity-Library Theatre maintained its top standard of quality from the previous season, and during 1945-46 frequently topped it with a series of really outstanding productions, forty-eight in all. Its system of operation remained the same. Actors filed applications and were cast from the ELT headquarters at Actors' Equity Association, 45 West 47th Street, where directors held readings. Producers, all Equity, sponsored the choice of casts which *can* include 80% Equity and 20% non-Equity members. Thus a limited number of available theatre people from the armed services, universities and community theatres may be absorbed into the training ground and viewing stand for the professional New York stage.

The season opened with Oscar Wilde's "The Importance of Being Earnest," a fiftieth anniversary showing, on November 7, 1945. During that month came "Rain," "The Enchanted Cottage," "Jason," "Golden Boy" and "Hay Fever." December brought "The Good Hope," "A New Way to Pay Old Debts" (not seen on Manhattan Island for sixty years), "The Drunkard" and "Blithe Spirit." The new year began with "The Green Bay Tree," "Springtime for Henry," "Night Must Fall," "The Letter," "Dangerous Corner," "Tonight at 8:30" (which was composed of "Red Peppers," "Hands Across the Sea" and "Still Life") and Goethe's "Faust," which was extraordinarily well directed by John Reich.

"Outward Bound" (with a black and white cast) began February and was followed by "The Vortex," "Those Endearing Young Charms," "Ghosts" and "A Doll's House." In March came "Candlelight," "Live Life Again" together with "This Property Condemned," "The Silver Cord," "Thunder Rock," "High Tor," "A Chekhov Carnival" and "Theatre." Not seen since the visit of Max Reinhardt's touring troupe nearly twenty years ago, "The Servant of Two Masters" was seen again in April. Then came "Coquette," "Waiting for Lefty," "Mandragola" (first professional production in America); "The Last Mile," "The Lawyer,"

"Blind Alley," "The Hasty Heart," "Othello" and "Family Portrait."

May brought "Anna Christie," "The Cherry Orchard," "The Animal Kingdom," "The Infernal Machine," "One-Man Show," "All for Love" (last seen in New York in 1797), "The World We Make" and "The Physician in Spite of Himself" (first professional performance in English in New York) and, finally, Mady Christians' production of "The Affairs of Anatol."

Four branches of The New York Public Library were utilized for performances (Hudson Park, George Bruce, Fort Washington and Hamilton Grange), though several others have been utilized for rehearsal purposes. Anne Gerlette acted as permanent Executive Secretary while John Golden, through the John Golden Theatre Fund, financed the small budgets allowed for each ELT production and paid the salary of an executive secretary. Sam Jaffe, for Equity, and George Freedley, for the Library, remained as co-chairmen.

DANCE DRAMA

"Ballet Russe Highlights," organized by Leonide Massine, started the 1945-46 dance season in New York at the Lewisohn Stadium, June 30. In the company were Irina Baranova, André Eglevsky, Yurek Lazowski, Anna Istomena, Kathryn Lee and Leonide Massine. Music was directed by Franz Allers. The program included "Pas de deux" from Tchaikovsky's "Nutcracker" suite; "Bohemian Dance" with music by Brahms; "Vision" to music by Bach; "Contradances," music by Beethoven; "The Warrior," music by Rachmaninoff; "Premiere Polka" and "Polish Festival," music by Glinka; "Spectre de la Rose," music by Weber; "The Barman," music by Nabokoff; "Bumble Bee," music by Rimsky-Korsakoff; "Russian Dance" by Gliere; "The Bluebird," music by Tchaikovsky; "At the Dentist" to music by Shostakovich and choreography by Massine; and "Cappriccio Espagnol," with music by Rimsky-Korsakoff. The July program included Fokine's "Les Syphides," "Dragon Fly," "Beau Danube," by Massine. "Dancing Poodles" from "Boutigue Fantasque," Ravel's "Pavane," "Leningrad Symphony," "Black Swan," "Gypsy Dance," "Farucca" from "Three-Cornered Hat," and "Gopak" choreographed by Yrek Lazowski.

A second dance event at the Lewisohn Stadium in New York took place in July, when Alicia Markova and Anton Dolin gave a program of pas de deux, suites and divertissements. Supporting them were Anne Simpson, Albia Kavan, Bettina Rosay and John Kriza. The conductor was Maurice Abravanel. The program included "Suite de Danse" (Chopin); "Taglioni and the Scotsman," (Mendelssohn); "Pas Espagnol" (Favina), choreographed by Anne Simpson; "The Polka" (Strauss), choreographed by Vincenzo Celli; "Vestris Solo" (Mozart's "Les Petite Riens") choreographed by Celli; "Pas de Quatre" (Pagni); "Blue Bird" from Tchaikovsky's "Princess Aurora"; "Serenade" (Malats), choreographed by Anne Simpson and pas de deux from Tchaikovsky's "Nutcracker."

Also in July La Meri and her Natya Dancers presented a program of Latin-American dances at Ethnologic Theatre, New York, featuring South American, Philippine and Caribbean impressions.

In August this dancer added Arabic dances from North Africa, Western Asia and Southern Europe, India, Java, Spain and Panama.

At the City Center

The Ballet Russe de Monte Carlo, directed by Sergei Denham (music directed by Emanuel Balaban and Ivan Boutnikoff), opened its season at the New York City Center, September 9, with "Danses Concertantes" by Igor Stravinsky. Choreography was by George Balanchine, costumes and scenery by Eugene Berman. The dance dramas which followed were: "Concerto Barocco," arranged to D Minor concerto of Bach and choreographed by George Balanchine; "Afternoon of a Faun," music by Claude Debussy, choreography by Vaslav Nijinsky, scenery and costumes by Leon Bakst; "The Beautiful Danube," music by Johann Strauss, arranged and orchestrated by Roger Desormieres, choreography by Leonid Massine, scenery and costumes after Constantin Guys, by Count Etienne de Beaumont; "Mozartiana," music by Peter Ilytch Tchaikovsky, choreography by George Balanchine, scenery and costumes by Christian Berard; "Pas De Deaux Classique," music by Tchaikovsky; "Rodeo," music by Aaron Copland, ballet by Agnes de Mille, scenery by Oliver Smith, costumes by Kermit Love; "Le Bourgeois Gentilhomme," music by Richard Strauss, choreography by George Balanchine; "Scheherazade," music by Nicolai Rimsky-Korsakoff, choreography by Michel Fokine, scenery and costumes by Leon Bakst; "The Nutcracker," a fairy-tale ballet in two acts by Tchaikovsky, choreography by Ivanov, revised by Mme. A. Fedorova, scenery and costumes by Alexander Benois. "Ballet Imperial," music by Tchaikovsky, choreography by George Balanchine, scenery and costumes by M. Doboujinsky; "The Red Poppy," a ballet in a prologue and three scenes by Igor Schwezoff, music by Reinhold Gliere, arranged by Arthur Cohn, scenery and costumes by Boris Aronson; "Les Sylphides," a romantic reverie by Michel Fokine, music by Frederic Chopin, scenery by Adrian Awan; "Grand Adagio," music by Tchaikovsky, choreography by George Balanchine; "Coppelia," a drama in three acts, music by Delibes, scenery and costumes by Pierre Roy, choreography by Petipa and Cecchetti, reconstructed by N. Sergeieff; "Comedia Balletica" (premiere), music from "Pulcinella" by Stravinsky-Pergolesi, choreography by Todd Bolender, scenery and costumes by Robert Davison; "Chopin Concerto," choreography by Bronislava Nijinska, settings by Alexander Ignatieff.

Winter Ballet

The Ballet Russe ended its Fall season at City Center, September 23, and began a six weeks' winter season February 17, with a program which included the revival of George Balanchine's "Baiser de la Fee," devised to the scenario and music of Stravinsky. Other dance dramas not presented in the earlier season included "Gaite Parisienne," music by Jacques Offenbach, choreography by Leonide Massine; "Frankie and Johnny," an American melodrama with music by Jerome Moross, choreography by Ruth Page and Bentley Stone, scenery by Clive Ricksbaugh, costumes by Paul DuPont; "The Swan Lake," a choreographic poem in one act by Tchaikovsky; "The Snow Maiden," ballet in one act based on a Russian folk legend, music by Alexander Glazounov, choreography by Bronislava Nijinska, scenery and costumes by Boris Aronson; "The Night Shadow" (premiere), ballet in one act by Vittorio Rieti on themes from Vincenzo Bellini; scenery and costumes by Dorothea Tanning; "Raymonda" (premiere), a ballet in three acts by Lydia Pashkova and Marius Petipa, choreography by Alexandra Danilova and George Balanchine, music by Alexander Glazounov, scenery and costumes by Alexandre Benois.

The principals engaged were Alexandra Danilova, Frederic Franklin, Nathalie Krassovska, Leon Danielian, Ruthanna Boris, Nicolas Magallanes, Maria Tallchief, Dorothy Etheridge, Nikita, Michel Katcharoff, Gertrude Tyven, Marie-Jeanne, Claire Pasch, Herbert Bliss, Nikita Talin, Yvonne Chouteau, Pauline Goddard, Nora White, Beatrice Tompkins, Julia Horvath and Robert Lindgren.

At the Metropolitan

The Ballet Theatre launched its 1945-46 season at the Metropolitan Opera House, October 7. The new ballets presented were "On Stage" by Michael Kidd, music by Norman Dello Joio, scenery and costumes by Oliver Smith; "Graziana," music by Mozart, choreography by John Taras; "The Gift of the Magi," adapted from the O. Henry story by Simon Semenoff with music by Lukas Foss, setting and costumes by Raoul Pene DuBois; "Interplay," by Jerome Robbins, scenery by Oliver Smith, costumes by Irene Sharaff; "Firebird," music by Stravinsky, new version by Adolph Bolm, scenery and costumes by Marc Chagall.

The company closed its Fall season November 6, and reopened

in the Spring, presenting dance dramas from April 7 to 13 and from April 21 to May 5. Included in the repertoire for both Fall and Spring seasons were "Pas de Deux" from "Pavillon d'Armide," by Anatole Oboukhoff to music of Tcherepnin; "Judgment of Paris," by Anthony Tudor; "Gala Performance," "Fancy Free," "Helen of Troy," "Giselle," "Swan Lake," "Bluebeard," "Romeo and Juliet," "Pillar of Fire," "Princess Aurora," "Graduation Ball," "Aleko," "Fair at Sorochinsk," "Firebird," "Les Sylphides," "Lilac Garden," "Pas de Quatre," "Peter and the Wolf," "Petrouchka," "Spectre de la Rose," "Tally-ho," "Undertow," "Waltz Academy," "Black Swan," "Apollo," "Pas de Deux" from "The Nutcracker."

The principals engaged were Alicia Markova, Anton Dolin, Maria Karnilova, Andre Egglevsky, John Kriza, Dimitri Romanoff, Harold Lang, Janet Reed, Muriel Bentley, Shirley Eckl, Marjorie Tallchief, Nora Kaye, John Taras, Lucia Chase, Alicia Alonzo, Stanley Herbertt, Michael Kidd, Hugh Laing, Alpheous Koon, Nicholas Orloff, Diana Adams, Margaret Banks, Fernando Alonzo, Barbara Fallis, Roszika Sabo, Mildred Herman, Tommy Rall and Mary Heater.

Ballets in Musical Comedy

During the season in New York many ballets were presented in musical comedies, including "Lute Song," "Show Boat," "Carib Song," "Three to Make Ready," "The Girl from Nantucket," "The Duchess Misbehaves," "Call Me Mister," "Marinka," "Polonaise," "The Red Mill," "St. Louis Woman," "Annie Get Your Gun," "Carmen Jones," "The Desert Song," "Nellie Bly," "Mr. Strauss Goes to Boston," "The Day Before Spring," "Are You with It?" and others. Names of choreographers and principal dancers may be found in the "Plays Produced in New York" section of this volume. Musical comedies which had continued into this season having ballets were "Carousel," "Oklahoma!" "Bloomer Girl," "On the Town," "Up in Central Park" and "Song of Norway."

Le Meri and her Natya Dancers presented programs featuring Hindu Dance Drama. In October her company danced "Krishna and Radha," with setting by George Duberg. In February with a company of 15 she presented Rimsky-Korsakov's "Scheherazade" in Hindu idiom.

Regina Devi presented a Katha-Kali dance drama, "Sita Harana" at the Barbizon-Plaza Theatre, December 4, 1945. Carmencita Maracci, assisted by Marie Groscup, Margaret Kilroy, Shirley Lopez, Julia Randall and Ron gave two performances at Carnegie Hall, December 30 and 31, 1945. New dance dramas on her programs included "Nightingale and the Maiden" and "Portrait in Raw Espana."

Martha Graham and her company began a two-week engagement at the Plymouth Theatre, January 21. "Dark Meadow" with score by Carlos Chavez had its world premiere January 23. Among other dance dramas on her program were "Appalachian Spring," to music by Aaron Copland; "Herodiade," music by Paul Hindesmith; "Letter to the World," "Salem Shore," "Deaths and Entrances," music by Hunter Johnson; "Punch and Judy," "John Brown," and "Every Soul Is a Circus," music by Paul Nordoff. The company included Erick Hawkins, Merce Cunningham, May O'Donnel, Nina Fonaroff, Pearl Lang, David Zellner, Douglas Watson, Marjorie Mazia, Ethel Winter and Yuriko. Guest artists were Jane Dudley and Jean Erdman. Costumes were by Edythe Gifond, decor by Isamu Noguchi and Philip Stapp and music was directed by Louis Horst.

Rosario and Antonio, assisted by Sinda Iberia, Pastora Ruiz and Carmen Lopez, presented a program at Carnegie Hall, March 3, consisting of selections from "El Amor Brujo," "Jota," "Cordoba," "El Mansiero," "The Three Cornered Hat" and other dance dramas.

The African Academy of Arts and Sciences presented "A Tale of Old Africa" in two performances at Carnegie Hall, April 25 and 26. Asadata Defora wrote this dramatic ballet with Etukio C. Okala-Abuta and staged it with Herbert Gellendre. A company of fifty were headed by Asadata Defora, Clementine Blount, Abdul Essen, Princess Orelia, Julie Adams, Berenice Samuels and Randolph Scott.

OFF BROADWAY

A modernized version by Beverly Bush and John Burgess of the Shakespearean comedy, "As You Like It," was presented by the authors for seven performances at the President Theatre, New York, July 3, after a tour through California. It was originally given at the University of Washington. Miss Bush directed the play, the settings were by Charles Elson and the lighting by Stanley Jennings. The cast included Margarette Ramsey, Marian Hall, Nancy Hoadley, John Burgess, Norman Budd, Beverly Bush and others.

At the Provincetown Playhouse, under the direction of John F. Grahame, "The Playboy of the Western World" was given July 22. "Claudia," staged by David Alexander, was presented August 1 to 6 with John McQuade, Eda Reiss Merin and Robert Harris in the cast and from August 8 through August 13, "Gold in the Hills" was played by the same cast. Also in August, Rodney Ackman's "Strange Orchestra" was played by Ellen Demming, Les Mahoney, John Leighton and Paz Davilla. "Night Must Fall" was revived by Modern Play Productions February 21, 1946.

Grace Moore sang Mimi and Jan Peerce Rudolfo in a presentation of "La Boheme" at the Lewisohn Stadium, August 2. Others in the cast were Martial Singher (Marcello), Lorenzo (Collins), George Cehanobsky (Schaunard) and Mimi Benzel as Musetta. The opera was staged by Herbert Graf; music directed by Alexander Smallens.

At the Cherry Lane Theatre in Greenwich Village Paul McCullough presented "Murder Without Crime," September 4, and "Art and Mrs. Bottle" with Paula Houston playing Judy, October 19. Paul and Virginia Gillmore opened their season at the same theatre with "This Thing Called Love" December 5.

The Light Opera Theatre, under the direction of John F. Grahame and Alexander Maissel, opened its tenth season at the Provincetown Playhouse November 9, with "The Pirates of Penzance." Josephine Lombardo, Robert Feyti and Fred Barry were in the cast. The second production was "The Gondoliers," with John Francis, Cecile Carol, Robert Feyti and Josephine Lombardi in the cast. The Gilbert and Sullivan repertory, which continued through the season, included "The Sorcerer," "The Mikado," "Pirates of Penzance," an altered version of "Princess Ida," "Trial by Jury" and "H.M.S. Pinafore," "Yeoman of the Guard" and "Iolanthe." In February a puppet performance of "Trial by Jury" was given two performances, members of the Light Opera Company singing the various roles. Eighteen-inch marionettes for this performance were created and directed by Sally Nusbaum.

Ice Shows and Others

The Ice Follies of 1946, produced by Eddie and Roy Shipstad and Oscar Johnson at the Madison Square Garden, opened November 20 and continued through December 2, with a cast of 165 headed by Evelyn Chandler. Other principals were Heine Brock, Hazel Franklin, Bobbie Blake, Harris and Phyllis Legg, Frick, Mae Ross, Dick Rasmussen, Bill Cameron and Ross Tucky.

The Lighthouse Players, from the New York Association for the Blind, produced "The Damask Cheek" in December.

"The First Wife," by Pearl Buck, was presented in English by the Chinese Theatre at the Barbizon-Plaza Theatre, in December. Also seen at the Barbizon-Plaza Theatre were "Alice My Wife," written and staged by Rhyissa Van Ross and presented by Eddie Shanley; Virginia Sale in a monodramo, "Americana," "Tidbits of '46," a variety entertainment presented by Youth Theatre Alumni in April, and "The Ruptured Duck" by Walter Armitage, presented by The Veterans Association.

Readers Theatre, Inc., presented a series of plays without scenery, and with the roles read from scripts, at the Majestic Theatre. James Light, Joel Schenker and Henry G. Alsberg produced the plays. They started in December with Sophocles' "Œdipus Rex," in a version by William Butler Yeats. The narrator was Eugene O'Neill, Jr., and Frederic Tozere read the part of Œdipus. Others engaged were Blanche Yurka (Jocasta), Williams Adams (Creon), Henry Irvine (Tiresias), Martin Wolfson, Robert Harris, Frederic Downs, Art Smith, Bram Nossen and William Hughes. The play was staged by James Light. "The Mayor of Zolamea," by Pedro Calderon, translated from the Spanish by Edward Fitzgerald, was presented January 27, with James Light directing and Eugene O'Neill, Jr., serving as narrator. The cast included Philip and Amelia Robinson, Will Davis, Jack Manning, Marriott Wilson, Robert Gardet, Leonard Cimino, Ellen Andrews, Herbert Berghof, Philip Gordon, Gregory Morton and Frederic Downs.

College Shows

At the McMillen Academic Theatre, April 25, Joseph H. O'Reilly presented the Columbia University Players in "Step Right Up," a musical comedy in two acts by Robert Lovett; music by Louis A. Garisto. The production was staged by Ferdinand N. Monjo, choreography by Tracy Morrison and settings by Joseph O'Reilly.

The Columbia Theatre Associates, in co-operation with the University's Department of Music, presented the premiere of Gion-Carlo Menotti's two-act chamber opera, "The Medium," at Brander Matthews Hall, May 8. The cast included Evelyn Keller, Leo Coleman, Claramae Turner, Beverly Dame, Jacques La Rochelle and Virginia Beeler.

The Playhouse des Artistes presented a stock company under the management of T. C. Upham, with productions directed by Philip Earle. Starting in January with "Little Eyolf" by Henrik Ibsen, and a cast including Romolo Robb, Jean Aubuchon, Frank Scholfield, Richard Marlowe, Geraldine Page and Lee Malbourne, the company added "Her Husband's Wife" by A. E. Thomas in February, with Bill Remick, Bob Fierman, Lee Malbourne, Romola Robb, Audrey Swanson and Geraldine Page. Later they offered "Lady Windermere's Fan" by Oscar Wilde, "Footsteps" (new) by Dr. Robert Bachmann, and "Craig's Wife" by George Kelly.

The Dramatic Workshop of the New School of Social Research, directed by Erwin Piscator, gave a series of plays under the heading of "March of Drama Repertory," illustrating the history of drama. These continued from January until June at the President Theatre.

Foreign Language Plays

The Downtown National Theatre opened the New York Yiddish season August 31, with a vaudeville show headed by Irving Grossman, Diana Goldberg, Irving Jacobson and Mae Shoenfeld. Included in the program was an intimate revue, "Our Victory," with Esther Field, Chaim Tauber and Shirley Gross in the cast; "Open the Gates," played by Diana Goldberg, Jack Rechtzeit, Ola Shliftko, Betty Simonov, Max and Rose Bozik, and "Laugh, Clown, Laugh," a miniature Yiddish musical with Herman Yablokoff as the star.

Mollie Picon was starred in "It's a Great Life," in condensed version, at the Downtown National Theatre in November. "Mazol Tov Mama," a musical comedy, was presented in November. In January, Herman Yablokoff was starred in "Don't Worry," in a condensed version of his own musical production, "Semele's Bar Mitzval," in a musical comedy, "The Dishwasher," and "Bessarabia," a revue by Isidore Lilian.

The Yiddish Theatre Ensemble gave two performances of "Downfall of Haman," November 10 and 18, and "Tragic Jest," by Sholem Aleichem, November 24, at the Barbizon-Plaza Theatre, New York.

The twenty-sixth season of the Yiddish Art Theatre began October 1, with "Three Gifts," a play in two parts adapted by Melach Ravitch and Maurice Schwartz. This was from the works of I. L. Peretz, with music by Joseph Rumshinsky, dances directed by Lillian Shapero, settings and costumes by H. A. Condell. The cast was headed by Maurice Schwartz and included Sam Levine, Muriel Gruber, Celia Lipzin, Luba Kadison, Victor Bergman and Yudel Dubinsky. "Three Gifts" closed in November, after 50 performances, and was followed by "Doctor Herzl," by H. R. Lenz and G. Nilioff, which ran from December 28 to February 17.

"Wish Me Luck," a musical comedy in two acts by Isidor Friedman and Israel Rosenberg, with lyrics by Jacob Jacobs and Isidor Lillian, music by Abe Ellstein, was presented at the Second Ave. Theatre, October 11. Dances were directed by Valentina Belova, settings by Edward Sundquist and costumes by Gropper. Leading the cast were Menasha Skulnik, Miriam Kressyn, Muni Serebrov and Yetta Zwerling. In January, Skulnik produced "My Wedding Night," which ran until March 3.

Ibsen's "Ghosts," in German, was produced at the Barbizon-Plaza April 2 through April 8, by Albert and Elsa Basserman and Ernst Deitsch.

Les Comedians Associes, a professional French troupe, played "Frenesie" by Peret Chapuis at the Barbizon-Plaza Theatre, April 29.

STATISTICAL SUMMARY

(Last Season Plays Which Ended Runs After June 17, 1945)

Plays	*Number Performances*	
A Bell for Adano	304	(Closed October 27, 1945)
Bloomer Girl	654	(Closed April 27, 1946)
Common Ground	69	(Closed June 23, 1945)
Concert Varieties	36	(Closed June 28, 1945)
Dark of the Moon	320	(Closed December 15, 1945)
Follow the Girls	882	(Closed May 18, 1946)
Foxhole in the Parlor	45	(Closed June 30, 1945)
Hats Off to Ice	889	(Closed April 27, 1946)
Hollywood Pinafore	53	(Closed July 14, 1945)
Kiss and Tell	956	(Closed June 23, 1945)
Kiss Them for Me	111	(Closed June 23, 1945)
Laffing Room Only	233	(Closed July 14, 1945)
Memphis Bound	36	(Closed June 23, 1945)
On the Town	463	(Closed February 2, 1946)
School for Brides	375	(Closed June 23, 1945)
Ten Little Indians	426	(Closed June 30, 1945)
The Hasty Heart	207	(Closed June 30, 1945)
The Late George Apley	385	(Closed November 17, 1945)
The Overtons	175	(Closed July 7, 1945)
Up in Central Park	504	(Closed April 13, 1946)

LONG RUNS ON BROADWAY

To June 1, 1946

(Plays marked with asterisk were still playing June 1, 1946)

Plays	*Number Performances*
Tobacco Road	3,182
*Life with Father	2,755
Abie's Irish Rose	2,327
Arsenic and Old Lace	1,444
Hellzapoppin	1,404
*Oklahoma!	1,372
Angel Street	1,295
Lightnin'	1,291
Pins and Needles	1,108
Kiss and Tell	956
*The Voice of the Turtle	891
Hats Off to Ice	889
Follow the Girls	882
The Bat	867
My Sister Eileen	865
White Cargo	864
You Can't Take It with You	837
Three Men on a Horse	835
Stars on Ice	830
The Ladder	789
The First Year	760
*Song of Norway	748
*Anna Lucasta	747
Sons o' Fun	742
The Man Who Came to Dinner	739
Claudia	722
Junior Miss	710
Seventh Heaven	704
Peg o' My Heart	692
The Children's Hour	691
Dead End	687
*I Remember Mama	682
East Is West	680
*Harvey	677
Chauve Souris	673
The Doughgirls	671
Irene	670
Boy Meets Girl	669
Blithe Spirit	657
The Women	657
A Trip to Chinatown	657
Bloomer Girl	654
Rain	648
Janie	642
The Green Pastures	640
*Dear Ruth	619
Is Zat So	618
Separate Rooms	613
Star and Garter	609
Student Prince	608
Broadway	603
Adonis	603
Street Scene	601
Kiki	600
Blossom Time	592
The Two Mrs. Carrolls	585
Brother Rat	577
Show Boat	572
The Show-Off	571
Sally	570
One Touch of Venus	567
Rose Marie	557

Plays	Number Performances	Plays	Number Performances
Strictly Dishonorable .	557	The Vagabond King . .	511
Ziegfeld Follies	553	The New Moon	509
Good News	551	Shuffle Along	504
Let's Face It	547	Up in Central Park . .	504
Within the Law	541	Carmen Jones	503
The Music Master . . .	540	Personal Appearance .	501
What a Life	538	Panama Hattie	501
The Boomerang	522	Bird in Hand	500
Rosalinda	521	Sailor, Beware!	500
Blackbirds	518	Room Service	500
Sunny	517	Tomorrow the World .	500
Victoria Regina	517		

NEW YORK DRAMA CRITICS' CIRCLE AWARD

The New York drama critics found themselves stymied when they met to select the best play of American authorship to represent the theatre season of 1945-46. Four of its leading members decided there just hadn't been any one play that they felt was entitled to their votes. As there were nineteen critics voting, ten votes were needed for a simple majority. On the final and decisive ballot Howard Lindsay and Russel Crouse's "State of the Union" got seven votes, Garson Kanin's "Born Yesterday" five, Elmer Rice's "Dream Girl" one and Harry Brown's "A Sound of Hunting" one. The first, or test ballot, gave "State of the Union" four, "Home of the Brave," "Carousel" and "A Sound of Hunting" three each, "Born Yesterday" two, "Dream Girl" and the d'Usseau-Gow "Deep Are the Roots" one each. One critic voted no award. "State of the Union" picked up three votes, but needed six, and the four "no award" votes sabotaged the selection.

Eleven critics voted "no award" when an effort was made to select the best play of the season of foreign authorship. But there were five votes for the Jean Anouilh-Lewis Galantiere "Antigone," which Katharine Cornell brought home with her, and one for Terence Rattigan's "O Mistress Mine," which the Lunts also brought home with them from their soldier camp tour of the continent. A special citation was awarded the Richard Rodgers-Oscar Hammerstein "Carousel" as an outstanding contribution.

This is the fourth time since it was organized in 1935 that the Critics' Circle has refused to select a best American play of the season. Its record stands:

1935-36—Winterset, by Maxwell Anderson
1936-37—High Tor, by Maxwell Anderson
1937-38—Of Mice and Men, by John Steinbeck
1938-39—No award.
1939-40—The Time of Your Life, by William Saroyan
1940-41—Watch on the Rhine, by Lillian Hellman
1941-42—No award.
1942-43—The Patriots, by Sidney Kingsley
1943-44—No award.
1944-45—The Glass Menagerie, by Tennessee Williams
1945-46—No award.

PULITZER PRIZE WINNERS

"For the original American play performed in New York which shall best represent the educational value and power of the stage in raising the standard of good morals, good taste and good manners."—The Will of Joseph Pulitzer, dated April 16, 1904.

In 1929 the advisory board, which, according to the terms of the will, "shall have the power in its discretion to suspend or to change any subject or subjects . . . if in the judgment of the board such suspension, changes or substitutions shall be conducive to the public good," decided to eliminate from the above paragraph relating to the prize-winning play the words "in raising the standard of good morals, good taste and good manners."

The present terms of the Pulitzer award are "for an original American play performed in New York, which shall represent in marked fashion the educational value and power of the stage, preferably dealing with American life."

The Columbia University committee delegated to select the best play of American authorship presented during the year 1945-46 for the Pulitzer award did not fumble its opportunity this season, as did the Drama Critics' Circle. It plumped promptly for the Howard Lindsay-Russel Crouse "State of the Union," which could not command a majority vote at the Circle's election because four members refused to vote at all. The Pulitzer prize of $500 therefore went to the Messrs. Lindsay and Crouse.

Previous Pulitzer prize play awards have been—

1917-18—Why Marry? by Jesse Lynch Williams
1918-19—No award.
1919-20—Beyond the Horizon, by Eugene O'Neill
1920-21—Miss Lulu Bett, by Zona Gale
1921-22—Anna Christie, by Eugene O'Neill
1922-23—Icebound, by Owen Davis
1923-24—Hell-bent fer Heaven, by Hatcher Hughes
1924-25—They Knew What They Wanted, by Sidney Howard
1925-26—Craig's Wife, by George Kelly
1926-27—In Abraham's Bosom, by Paul Green
1927-28—Strange Interlude, by Eugene O'Neill
1928-29—Street Scene, by Elmer Rice
1929-30—The Green Pastures, by Marc Connelly

1930-31—Alison's House, by Susan Glaspell
1931-32—Of Thee I Sing, by George S. Kaufman, Morrie Ryskind, Ira and George Gershwin
1932-33—Both Your Houses, by Maxwell Anderson
1933-34—Men in White, by Sidney Kingsley
1934-35—The Old Maid, by Zoe Akins
1935-36—Idiot's Delight, by Robert E. Sherwood
1936-37—You Can't Take It with You, by Moss Hart and George S. Kaufman
1937-38—Our Town, by Thornton Wilder
1938-39—Abe Lincoln in Illinois, by Robert E. Sherwood
1939-40—The Time of Your Life, by William Saroyan
1940-41—There Shall Be No Night, by Robert E. Sherwood
1941-42—No award.
1942-43—The Skin of Our Teeth, by Thornton Wilder
1943-44—No award.
1944-45—Harvey, by Mary Coyle Chase
1945-46—State of the Union, by Howard Lindsay and Russel Crouse

PREVIOUS VOLUMES OF BEST PLAYS

Plays chosen to represent the theatre seasons from 1899 to 1945 are as follows:

1899-1909

"Barbara Frietchie," by Clyde Fitch. Published by Life Publishing Company, New York.

"The Climbers," by Clyde Fitch. Published by the Macmillan Co., New York.

"If I Were King," by Justin Huntly McCarthy. Published by Samuel French, New York and London.

"The Darling of the Gods," by David Belasco. Published by Little, Brown & Co., Boston, Mass.

"The County Chairman," by George Ade. Published by Samuel French, New York and London.

"Leah Kleschna," by C. M. S. McLellan. Published by Samuel French, New York.

"The Squaw Man," by Edwin Milton Royle.

"The Great Divide," by William Vaughn Moody. Published by Samuel French, New York, London and Canada.

"The Witching Hour," by Augustus Thomas. Published by Samuel French, New York and London.

"The Man from Home," by Booth Tarkington and Harry Leon Wilson. Published by Samuel French, New York, London and Canada.

1909-1919

"The Easiest Way," by Eugene Walter. Published by G. W. Dillingham, New York; Houghton Mifflin Co., Boston.

"Mrs. Bumpstead-Leigh," by Harry James Smith. Published by Samuel French, New York.

"Disraeli," by Louis N. Parker. Published by Dodd, Mead and Co., New York.

"Romance," by Edward Sheldon. Published by the Macmillan Co., New York.

"Seven Keys to Baldpate," by George M. Cohan. Published by Bobbs-Merrill Co., Indianapolis, as a novel by Earl Derr Biggers; as a play by Samuel French, New York.

"On Trial," by Elmer Reizenstein. Published by Samuel French, New York.

"The Unchastened Woman," by Louis Kaufman Anspacher. Published by Harcourt, Brace and Howe, Inc., New York.

"Good Gracious Annabelle," by Clare Kummer. Published by Samuel French, New York.

"Why Marry?" by Jesse Lynch Williams. Published by Charles Scribner's Sons, New York.

"John Ferguson," by St. John Ervine. Published by the Macmillan Co., New York.

1919-1920

"Abraham Lincoln," by John Drinkwater. Published by Houghton Mifflin Co., Boston.

"Clarence," by Booth Tarkington. Published by Samuel French, New York.

"Beyond the Horizon," by Eugene G. O'Neill. Published by Boni & Liveright, Inc., New York.

"Déclassée," by Zoe Akins. Published by Liveright, Inc., New York.

"The Famous Mrs. Fair," by James Forbes. Published by Samuel French, New York.

"The Jest," by Sem Benelli. (American adaptation by Edward Sheldon.)

"Jane Clegg," by St. John Ervine. Published by Henry Holt & Co., New York.

"Mamma's Affair," by Rachel Barton Butler. Published by Samuel French, New York.

"Wedding Bells," by Salisbury Field. Published by Samuel French, New York.

"Adam and Eva," by George Middleton and Guy Bolton. Published by Samuel French, New York.

1920-1921

"Deburau," adapted from the French of Sacha Guitry by H. Granville Barker. Published by G. P. Putnam's Sons, New York.

"The First Year," by Frank Craven. Published by Samuel French, New York.

"Enter Madame," by Gilda Varesi and Dolly Byrne. Published by G. P. Putnam's Sons, New York.

"The Green Goddess," by William Archer. Published by Alfred A. Knopf, New York.

"Liliom," by Ferenc Molnar. Published by Boni & Liveright, New York.

"Mary Rose," by James M. Barrie. Published by Charles Scribner's Sons, New York.

"Nice People," by Rachel Crothers. Published by Charles Scribner's Sons, New York.

"The Bad Man," by Porter Emerson Browne. Published by G. P. Putnam's Sons, New York.

"The Emperor Jones," by Eugene G. O'Neill. Published by Boni & Liveright, New York.

"The Skin Game," by John Galsworthy. Published by Charles Scribner's Sons, New York.

1921-1922

"Anna Christie," by Eugene G. O'Neill. Published by Boni & Liveright, New York.

"A Bill of Divorcement," by Clemence Dane. Published by the Macmillan Company, New York.

"Dulcy," by George S. Kaufman and Marc Connelly. Published by G. P. Putnam's Sons, New York.

"He Who Gets Slapped," adapted from the Russian of Leonid Andreyev by Gregory Zilboorg. Published by Brentano's, New York.

"Six Cylinder Love," by William Anthony McGuire.

"The Hero," by Gilbert Emery.

"The Dover Road," by Alan Alexander Milne. Published by Samuel French, New York.

"Ambush," by Arthur Richman.

"The Circle," by William Somerset Maugham.

"The Nest," by Paul Geraldy and Grace George.

1922-1923

"Rain," by John Colton and Clemence Randolph. Published by Liveright, Inc., New York.

"Loyalties," by John Galsworthy. Published by Charles Scribner's Sons, New York.

"Icebound," by Owen Davis. Published by Little, Brown & Company, Boston.

"You and I," by Philip Barry. Published by Brentano's, New York.

"The Fool," by Channing Pollock. Published by Brentano's, New York.

"Merton of the Movies," by George Kaufman and Marc Connelly, based on the novel of the same name by Harry Leon Wilson.

"Why Not?" by Jesse Lynch Williams. Published by Walter H. Baker Co., Boston.

"The Old Soak," by Don Marquis. Published by Doubleday, Page & Company, New York.

"R.U.R.," by Karel Capek. Translated by Paul Selver. Published by Doubleday, Page & Company.

"Mary the 3d," by Rachel Crothers. Published by Brentano's, New York.

1923-1924

"The Swan," translated from the Hungarian of Ferenc Molnar by Melville Baker. Published by Boni & Liveright, New York.

"Outward Bound," by Sutton Vane. Published by Boni & Liveright, New York.

"The Show-Off," by George Kelly. Published by Little, Brown & Company, Boston.

"The Changelings," by Lee Wilson Dodd. Published by E. P. Dutton & Company, New York.

"Chicken Feed," by Guy Bolton. Published by Samuel French, New York and London.

"Sun-Up," by Lula Vollmer. Published by Brentano's, New York.

"Beggar on Horseback," by George Kaufman and Marc Connelly. Published by Boni & Liveright, New York.

"Tarnish," by Gilbert Emery. Published by Brentano's, New York.

"The Goose Hangs High," by Lewis Beach. Published by Little, Brown & Company, Boston.

"Hell-bent fer Heaven," by Hatcher Hughes. Published by Harper Bros., New York.

1924-1925

"What Price Glory?" by Laurence Stallings and Maxwell Anderson. Published by Harcourt, Brace & Co., New York.

"They Knew What They Wanted," by Sidney Howard. Published by Doubleday, Page & Company, New York.

"Desire Under the Elms," by Eugene G. O'Neill. Published by Boni & Liveright, New York.

"The Firebrand," by Edwin Justus Mayer. Published by Boni & Liveright, New York.

"Dancing Mothers," by Edgar Selwyn and Edmund Goulding.

"Mrs. Partridge Presents," by Mary Kennedy and Ruth Warren. Published by Samuel French, New York.

"The Fall Guy," by James Gleason and George Abbott. Published by Samuel French, New York.

"The Youngest," by Philip Barry. Published by Samuel French, New York.

"Minick," by Edna Ferber and George S. Kaufman. Published by Doubleday, Page & Company, New York.

"Wild Birds," by Dan Totheroh. Published by Doubleday, Page & Company, New York.

1925-1926

"Craig's Wife," by George Kelly. Published by Little, Brown & Company, Boston.

"The Great God Brown," by Eugene G. O'Neill. Published by Boni & Liveright, New York.

"The Green Hat," by Michael Arlen.

"The Dybbuk," by S. Ansky, Henry G. Alsberg-Winifred Katzin translation. Published by Boni & Liveright, New York.

"The Enemy," by Channing Pollock. Published by Brentano's, New York.

"The Last of Mrs. Cheyney," by Frederick Lonsdale. Published by Samuel French, New York.

"Bride of the Lamb," by William Hurlbut. Published by Boni & Liveright, New York.

"The Wisdom Tooth," by Marc Connelly. Published by George H. Doran & Company, New York.

"The Butter and Egg Man," by George Kaufman. Published by Boni & Liveright, New York.

"Young Woodley," by John Van Druten. Published by Simon and Schuster, New York.

1926-1927

"Broadway," by Philip Dunning and George Abbott. Published by George H. Doran Company, New York.

"Saturday's Children," by Maxwell Anderson. Published by Longmans, Green & Company, New York.

"Chicago," by Maurine Watkins. Published by Alfred A. Knopf, Inc., New York.

"The Constant Wife," by William Somerset Maugham. Published by George H. Doran Company, New York.

"The Play's the Thing," by Ferenc Molnar and P. G. Wodehouse. Published by Brentano's, New York.

"The Road to Rome," by Robert Emmet Sherwood. Published by Charles Scribner's Sons, New York.

"The Silver Cord," by Sidney Howard. Published by Charles Scribner's Sons, New York.

"The Cradle Song," translated from the Spanish of G. Martinez Sierra by John Garrett Underhill. Published by E. P. Dutton & Company, New York.

"Daisy Mayme," by George Kelly. Published by Little, Brown & Company, Boston.

"In Abraham's Bosom," by Paul Green. Published by Robert M. McBride & Company, New York.

1927-1928

"Strange Interlude," by Eugene G. O'Neill. Published by Boni & Liveright, New York.

"The Royal Family," by Edna Ferber and George Kaufman. Published by Doubleday, Doran & Company, New York.

"Burlesque," by George Manker Watters. Published by Doubleday, Doran & Company, New York.

"Coquette," by George Abbott and Ann Bridgers. Published by Longmans, Green & Company, New York, London, Toronto.

"Behold the Bridegroom," by George Kelly. Published by Little, Brown & Company, Boston.

"Porgy," by DuBose Heyward. Published by Doubleday, Doran & Company, New York.

"Paris Bound," by Philip Barry. Published by Samuel French, New York.

"Escape," by John Galsworthy. Published by Charles Scribner's Sons, New York.

"The Racket," by Bartlett Cormack. Published by Samuel French, New York.

"The Plough and the Stars," by Sean O'Casey. Published by the Macmillan Company, New York.

1928-1929

"Street Scene," by Elmer Rice. Published by Samuel French, New York.

"Journey's End," by R. C. Sherriff. Published by Brentano's, New York.

"Wings Over Europe," by Robert Nichols and Maurice Browne. Published by Covici-Friede, New York.

"Holiday," by Philip Barry. Published by Samuel French, New York.

"The Front Page," by Ben Hecht and Charles MacArthur. Published by Covici-Friede, New York.

"Let Us Be Gay," by Rachel Crothers. Published by Samuel French, New York.

"Machinal," by Sophie Treadwell.

"Little Accident," by Floyd Dell and Thomas Mitchell.

"Gypsy," by Maxwell Anderson.

"The Kingdom of God," by G. Martinez Sierra; English version by Helen and Harley Granville-Barker. Published by E. P. Dutton & Company, New York.

1929-1930

"The Green Pastures," by Marc Connelly (adapted from "Ol' Man Adam and His Chillun," by Roark Bradford). Published by Farrar & Rinehart, Inc., New York.

"The Criminal Code," by Martin Flavin. Published by Horace Liveright, New York.

"Berkeley Square," by John Balderston. Published by the Macmillan Company, New York.

"Strictly Dishonorable," by Preston Sturges. Published by Horace Liveright, New York.

"The First Mrs. Fraser," by St. John Ervine. Published by the Macmillan Company, New York.

"The Last Mile," by John Wexley. Published by Samuel French, New York.

"June Moon," by Ring W. Lardner and George S. Kaufman. Published by Charles Scribner's Sons, New York.

"Michael and Mary," by A. A. Milne. Published by Chatto & Windus, London.

"Death Takes a Holiday," by Walter Ferris (adapted from the Italian of Alberto Casella). Published by Samuel French, New York.

"Rebound," by Donald Ogden Stewart. Published by Samuel French, New York.

1930-1931

"Elizabeth the Queen," by Maxwell Anderson. Published by Longmans, Green & Co., New York.

"Tomorrow and Tomorrow," by Philip Barry. Published by Samuel French, New York.

"Once in a Lifetime," by George S. Kaufman and Moss Hart. Published by Farrar and Rinehart, New York.

"Green Grow the Lilacs," by Lynn Riggs. Published by Samuel French, New York and London.

"As Husbands Go," by Rachel Crothers. Published by Samuel French, New York.

"Alison's House," by Susan Glaspell. Published by Samuel French, New York.

"Five-Star Final," by Louis Weitzenkorn. Published by Samuel French, New York.

"Overture," by William Bolitho. Published by Simon & Schuster, New York.

"The Barretts of Wimpole Street," by Rudolf Besier. Published by Little, Brown & Company, Boston.

"Grand Hotel," adapted from the German of Vicki Baum by W. A. Drake.

1931-1932

"Of Thee I Sing," by George S. Kaufman and Morrie Ryskind; music and lyrics by George and Ira Gershwin. Published by Alfred Knopf, New York.

"Mourning Becomes Electra," by Eugene G. O'Neill. Published by Horace Liveright, Inc., New York.

"Reunion in Vienna," by Robert Emmet Sherwood. Published by Charles Scribner's Sons, New York.

"The House of Connelly," by Paul Green. Published by Samuel French, New York.

"The Animal Kingdom," by Philip Barry. Published by Samuel French, New York.

"The Left Bank," by Elmer Rice. Published by Samuel French, New York.

"Another Language," by Rose Franken. Published by Samuel French, New York.

"Brief Moment," by S. N. Behrman. Published by Farrar & Rinehart, New York.

"The Devil Passes," by Benn W. Levy. Published by Martin Secker, London.

"Cynara," by H. M. Harwood and R. F. Gore-Browne. Published by Samuel French, New York.

1932-1933

"Both Your Houses," by Maxwell Anderson. Published by Samuel French, New York.

"Dinner at Eight," by George S. Kaufman and Edna Ferber. Published by Doubleday, Doran & Co., Inc., Garden City, New York.

"When Ladies Meet," by Rachel Crothers. Published by Samuel French, New York.

"Design for Living," by Noel Coward. Published by Doubleday, Doran & Co., Inc., Garden City, New York.

"Biography," by S. N. Behrman. Published by Farrar & Rinehart, Inc., New York.

"Alien Corn," by Sidney Howard. Published by Charles Scribner's Sons, New York.

"The Late Christopher Bean," adapted from the French of René Fauchois by Sidney Howard. Published by Samuel French, New York.

"We, the People," by Elmer Rice. Published by Coward-McCann, Inc., New York.

"Pigeons and People," by George M. Cohan.

"One Sunday Afternoon," by James Hagan. Published by Samuel French, New York.

1933-1934

"Mary of Scotland," by Maxwell Anderson. Published by Doubleday, Doran & Co., Inc., Garden City, N. Y.

"Men in White," by Sidney Kingsley. Published by Covici, Friede, Inc., New York.

"Dodsworth," by Sinclair Lewis and Sidney Howard. Published by Harcourt, Brace & Co., New York.

"Ah, Wilderness," by Eugene O'Neill. Published by Random House, New York.

"They Shall Not Die," by John Wexley. Published by Alfred A. Knopf, New York.

"Her Master's Voice," by Clare Kummer. Published by Samuel French, New York.

"No More Ladies," by A. E. Thomas.

"Wednesday's Child," by Leopold Atlas. Published by Samuel French, New York.

"The Shining Hour," by Keith Winter. Published by Doubleday, Doran & Co., Inc., Garden City, New York.

"The Green Bay Tree," by Mordaunt Shairp. Published by Baker International Play Bureau, Boston, Mass.

1934-1935

"The Children's Hour," by Lillian Hellman. Published by Alfred Knopf, New York.

"Valley Forge," by Maxwell Anderson. Published by Anderson House, Washington, D. C. Distributed by Dodd, Mead & Co., New York.

"The Petrified Forest," by Robert Sherwood. Published by Charles Scribner's Sons, New York.

"The Old Maid," by Zoe Akins. Published by D. Appleton-Century Co., New York.

"Accent on Youth," by Samson Raphaelson. Published by Samuel French, New York.

"Merrily We Roll Along," by George S. Kaufman and Moss Hart. Published by Random House, New York.

"Awake and Sing," by Clifford Odets. Published by Random House, New York.

"The Farmer Takes a Wife," by Frank B. Elser and Marc Connelly.

"Lost Horizons," by John Hayden.

"The Distaff Side," by John Van Druten. Published by Alfred Knopf, New York.

1935-1936

"Winterset," by Maxwell Anderson. Published by Anderson House, Washington, D. C.

"Idiot's Delight," by Robert Emmet Sherwood. Published by Charles Scribner's Sons, New York.

"End of Summer," by S. N. Behrman. Published by Random House, New York.

"First Lady," by Katharine Dayton and George S. Kaufman. Published by Random House, New York.

"Victoria Regina," by Laurence Housman. Published by Samuel French, Inc., New York and London.

"Boy Meets Girl," by Bella and Samuel Spewack. Published by Random House, New York.

"Dead End," by Sidney Kingsley. Published by Random House, New York.

"Call It a Day," by Dodie Smith. Published by Samuel French, Inc., New York and London.

"Ethan Frome," by Owen Davis and Donald Davis. Published by Charles Scribner's Sons, New York.

"Pride and Prejudice," by Helen Jerome. Published by Doubleday, Doran & Co., Garden City, New York.

1936-1937

"High Tor," by Maxwell Anderson. Published by Anderson House, Washington, D. C.

"You Can't Take It with You," by Moss Hart and George S. Kaufman. Published by Farrar & Rinehart, Inc., New York.

"Johnny Johnson," by Paul Green. Published by Samuel French, Inc., New York.

"Daughters of Atreus," by Robert Turney. Published by Alfred A. Knopf, New York.

"Stage Door," by Edna Ferber and George S. Kaufman. Published by Doubleday, Doran & Co., Garden City, New York.

"The Women," by Clare Boothe. Published by Random House, Inc., New York.

"St. Helena," by R. C. Sherriff and Jeanne de Casalis. Published by Samuel French, Inc., New York and London.

"Yes, My Darling Daughter," by Mark Reed. Published by Samuel French, Inc., New York.

"Excursion," by Victor Wolfson. Published by Random House, New York.

"Tovarich," by Jacques Deval and Robert E. Sherwood. Published by Random House, New York.

1937-1938

"Of Mice and Men," by John Steinbeck. Published by Covici-Friede, New York.

"Our Town," by Thornton Wilder. Published by Coward-McCann, Inc., New York.

"Shadow and Substance," by Paul Vincent Carroll. Published by Random House, Inc., New York.

"On Borrowed Time," by Paul Osborn. Published by Alfred A. Knopf, New York.

"The Star-Wagon," by Maxwell Anderson. Published by Anderson House, Washington, D. C. Distributed by Dodd, Mead & Co., New York.

"Susan and God," by Rachel Crothers. Published by Random House, Inc., New York.

"Prologue to Glory," by E. P. Conkle. Published by Random House, Inc., New York.

"Amphitryon 38," by S. N. Behrman. Published by Random House, Inc., New York.

"Golden Boy," by Clifford Odets. Published by Random House, Inc., New York.

"What a Life," by Clifford Goldsmith. Published by Dramatists' Play Service, Inc., New York.

1938-1939

"Abe Lincoln in Illinois," by Robert E. Sherwood. Published by Charles Scribner's Sons, New York and Charles Scribner's Sons, Ltd., London.

"The Little Foxes," by Lillian Hellman. Published by Random House, Inc., New York.

"Rocket to the Moon," by Clifford Odets. Published by Random House, Inc., New York.

"The American Way," by George S. Kaufman and Moss Hart. Published by Random House, Inc., New York.

"No Time for Comedy," by S. N. Behrman. Published by Random House, Inc., New York.

"The Philadelphia Story," by Philip Barry. Published by Coward-McCann, Inc., New York.

"The White Steed," by Paul Vincent Carroll. Published by Random House, Inc., New York.

"Here Come the Clowns," by Philip Barry. Published by Coward-McCann, Inc., New York.

"Family Portrait," by Lenore Coffee and William Joyce Cowen. Published by Random House, Inc., New York.

"Kiss the Boys Good-bye," by Clare Boothe. Published by Random House, Inc., New York.

1939-1940

"There Shall Be No Night," by Robert E. Sherwood. Published by Charles Scribner's Sons, New York.

"Key Largo," by Maxwell Anderson. Published by Anderson House, Washington, D. C.

"The World We Make," by Sidney Kingsley.

"Life with Father," by Howard Lindsay and Russel Crouse. Published by Alfred A. Knopf, New York.

"The Man Who Came to Dinner," by George S. Kaufman and Moss Hart. Published by Random House, Inc., New York.

"The Male Animal," by James Thurber and Elliott Nugent. Published by Random House, Inc., New York, and MacMillan Co., Canada.

"The Time of Your Life," by William Saroyan. Published by Harcourt, Brace and Company, Inc., New York.

"Skylark," by Samson Raphaelson. Published by Random House, Inc., New York.

"Margin for Error," by Clare Boothe. Published by Random House, Inc., New York.

"Morning's at Seven," by Paul Osborn. Published by Samuel French, New York.

1940-1941

"Native Son," by Paul Green and Richard Wright. Published by Harper & Bros., New York.

"Watch on the Rhine," by Lillian Hellman. Published by Random House, Inc., New York.

"The Corn Is Green," by Emlyn Williams. Published by Random House, Inc., New York.

"Lady in the Dark," by Moss Hart. Published by Random House, Inc., New York.

"Arsenic and Old Lace," by Joseph Kesselring. Published by Random House, Inc., New York.

"My Sister Eileen," by Joseph Fields and Jerome Chodorov. Published by Random House, Inc., New York.

"Flight to the West," by Elmer Rice. Published by Coward, McCann, Inc., New York.

"Claudia," by Rose Franken Meloney. Published by Farrar & Rinehart, Inc., New York and Toronto.

"Mr. and Mrs. North," by Owen Davis. Published by Samuel French, New York.

"George Washington Slept Here," by George S. Kaufman and Moss Hart. Published by Random House, Inc., New York.

1941-1942

"In Time to Come," by Howard Koch. Published by Dramatists' Play Service, Inc., New York.

"The Moon Is Down," by John Steinbeck. Published by The Viking Press, New York.

"Blithe Spirit," by Noel Coward. Published by Doubleday, Doran & Co., Garden City, New York.

"Junior Miss," by Jerome Chodorov and Joseph Fields. Published by Random House, Inc., New York.

"Candle in the Wind," by Maxwell Anderson. Published by Anderson House, Washington, D. C.

"Letters to Lucerne," by Fritz Rotter and Allen Vincent. Published by Samuel French, Inc., New York.

"Jason," by Samson Raphaelson. Published by Random House, Inc., New York.

"Angel Street," by Patrick Hamilton. Published by Constable & Co., Ltd., London, under the title "Gaslight."

"Uncle Harry," by Thomas Job. Published by Samuel French, Inc., New York.

"Hope for a Harvest," by Sophie Treadwell. Published by Samuel French, Inc., New York.

1942-1943.

"The Patriots," by Sidney Kingsley. Published by Random House, Inc., New York.

"The Eve of St. Mark," by Maxwell Anderson. Published by Anderson House, Washington, D. C.

"The Skin of Our Teeth," by Thornton Wilder. Published by Harper & Brothers, New York and London.

"Winter Soldiers," by Dan James.

"Tomorrow the World," by James Gow and Arnaud d'Usseau. Published by Charles Scribner's Sons, New York.

"Harriet," by Florence Ryerson and Colin Clements. Published by Charles Scribner's Sons, New York.

"The Doughgirls," by Joseph Fields. Published by Random House, Inc., New York.

"The Damask Cheek," by John Van Druten and Lloyd Morris. Published by Random House, Inc., New York.

"Kiss and Tell," by F. Hugh Herbert. Published by Coward-McCann, Inc., New York.

"Oklahoma!", by Oscar Hammerstein 2nd and Richard Rodgers. Published by Random House, Inc., New York.

1943-1944

"Winged Victory," by Moss Hart. Published by Random House, Inc., New York.

"The Searching Wind," by Lillian Hellman. Published by Viking Press, Inc., New York.

"The Voice of the Turtle," by John Van Druten. Published by Random House, Inc., New York.

"Decision," by Edward Chodorov.

"Over 21," by Ruth Gordon. Published by Random House, Inc., New York.

"Outrageous Fortune," by Rose Franken. Published by Samuel French, New York.

"Jacobowsky and the Colonel," by S. N. Behrman. Published by Random House, Inc., New York.

"Storm Operation," by Maxwell Anderson. Published by Anderson House, Washington, D. C.

"Pick-up Girl," by Elsa Shelley.

"The Innocent Voyage," by Paul Osborn.

1944-1945

"A Bell for Adano," by Paul Osborn. Published by Alfred A. Knopf, New York.

"I Remember Mama," by John Van Druten. Published by Harcourt, Brace and Co., Inc., New York.

"The Hasty Heart," by John Patrick. Published by Random House, Inc., New York.

"The Glass Menagerie," by Tennessee Williams. Published by Random House, Inc., New York.

"Harvey," by Mary Chase.

"The Late George Apley," by John P. Marquand and George S. Kaufman.

"Soldier's Wife," by Rose Franken. Published by Samuel French.

"Anna Lucasta," by Philip Yordan. Published by Random House, Inc., New York.

"Foolish Notion," by Philip Barry.

"Dear Ruth," by Norma Krasna. Published by Random House, Inc., New York.

WHERE AND WHEN THEY WERE BORN

(Compiled from the most authentic records available.)

Abbott, George	Hamburg, N. Y.	1895
Abel, Walter	St. Paul, Minn.	1898
Adams, Maude	Salt Lake City, Utah	1872
Addy, Wesley	Omaha, Neb.	1912
Adler, Luther	New York City	1903
Adler, Stella	New York City	1904
Aherne, Brian	King's Norton, England	1902
Anders, Glenn	Los Angeles, Cal.	1890
Anderson, Judith	Australia	1898
Anderson, Maxwell	Atlantic City, Pa.	1888
Andrews, A. G.	Buffalo, N. Y.	1861
Andrews, Ann	Los Angeles, Cal.	1895
Arden, Eve	San Francisco, Cal.	1912
Arling, Joyce	Memphis, Tenn.	1911
Arliss, George	London, England	1868
Astaire, Fred	Omaha, Neb.	1899
Bainter, Fay	Los Angeles, Cal.	1892
Bankhead, Tallulah	Huntsville, Ala.	1902
Barbee, Richard	Lafayette, Ind.	1887
Barry, Philip	Rochester, N. Y.	1896
Barrymore, Diana	New York City	1921
Barrymore, Ethel	Philadelphia, Pa.	1879
Barrymore, John	Philadelphia, Pa.	1882
Barrymore, Lionel	Philadelphia, Pa.	1878
Barton, James	Gloucester, N. J.	1890
Beecher, Janet	Jefferson City, Mo.	1887
Behrman, S. N.	Worcester, Mass.	1893
Bell, James	Suffolk, Va.	1891
Bellamy, Ralph	Chicago, Ill.	1905
Berghof, Herbert	Vienna, Austria	1909
Bergner, Elisabeth	Vienna	1901
Berlin, Irving	Russia	1888
Blackmer, Sydney	Salisbury, N. C.	1898
Bolger, Ray	Dorchester, Mass.	1906
Bondi, Beulah	Chicago, Ill.	1892

Bordoni, Irene	Paris, France	1895
Bourneuf, Philip	Boston, Mass.	1912
Bowman, Patricia	Washington, D. C.	1912
Brady, William A.	San Francisco, Cal.	1863
Braham, Horace	London, England	1896
Brent, Romney	Saltillo, Mex.	1902
Brice, Fannie	Brooklyn, N. Y.	1891
Broderick, Helen	New York	1891
Brotherson, Eric	Chicago, Ill.	1911
Bruce, Carol	Great Neck, L. I.	1919
Bruce, Nigel	San Diego, Cal.	1895
Burke, Billie	Washington, D. C.	1885
Burr, Ann	Boston, Mass.	1920
Butterworth, Charles	South Bend, Ind.	1896
Byington, Spring	Colorado Springs, Colo.	1898
Cagney, James	New York	1904
Cagney, Jeanne	New York	1920
Cahill, Lily	Texas	1891
Calhern, Louis	New York	1895
Cannon, Maureen	Chicago, Ill.	1927
Cantor, Eddie	New York	1894
Carlisle, Kitty	New Orleans, La.	1912
Carnovsky, Morris	St. Louis, Mo.	1898
Carroll, Leo G.	Weedon, England	1892
Carroll, Nancy	New York City	1906
Catlett, Walter	San Francisco, Cal.	1889
Caulfield, Joan	New York City	1924
Chandler, Helen	Charleston, N. C.	1906
Chatterton, Ruth	New York	1893
Christians, Mady	Vienna, Austria	1907
Claire, Helen	Union Springs, Ala.	1908
Claire, Ina	Washington, D. C.	1892
Clark, Bobby	Springfield, Ohio	1888
Clayton, Jan	Alamogordo, N. M.	1921
Clift, Montgomery	Omaha, Neb.	1921
Clive, Colin	St. Malo, France	1900
Coburn, Charles	Macon, Ga.	1877
Cohan, George M.	Providence, R. I.	1878
Colbert, Claudette	Paris	1905
Collins, Russell	New Orleans, La.	1901
Colt, Ethel Barrymore	Mamaroneck, N. Y.	1911
Colt, John Drew	New York	1914

Conroy, Frank	London, England	1885
Cook, Donald	Portland, Ore.	1902
Cooper, Gladys	Lewisham, England	1888
Cooper, Melville	Birmingham, England	1896
Cooper, Violet Kemble	London, England	1890
Corbett, Leonora	London, England	1908
Corey, Wendell	Dracut, Mass.	1907
Cornell, Katharine	Berlin, Germany	1898
Cossart, Ernest	Cheltenham, England	1876
Coulouris, George	Manchester, England	1906
Coward, Noel	Teddington, England	1899
Cowl, Jane	Boston, Mass.	1887
Crothers, Rachel	Bloomington, Ill.	1878
Cummings, Constance	Seattle, Wash.	1911
Dale, Margaret	Philadelphia, Pa.	1880
Davis, Owen	Portland, Me.	1874
Davis, Owen, Jr.	New York	1910
Digges, Dudley	Dublin, Ireland	1880
Douglas, Susan	Prague, Czechoslovakia	1925
Dowling, Eddie	Woonsocket, R. I.	1895
Drake, Alfred	New York City	1914
Dressler, Eric	Brooklyn, N. Y.	1900
Duncan, Augustin	San Francisco	1873
Dunning, Philip	Meriden, Conn.	1890
Edney, Florence	London, England	1879
Eggerth, Marta	Budapest, Hungary	1915
Eldridge, Florence	Brooklyn, N. Y.	1901
Evans, Edith	London, England	1888
Evans, Maurice	Dorchester, England	1901
Evans, Wilbur	Philadelphia, Pa.	1908
Fabray, Nanette	New Orleans, La.	1921
Fay, Frank	San Francisco	1897
Ferber, Edna	Kalamazoo, Mich.	1887
Ferrer, Jose	Puerto Rico	1912
Field, Sylvia	Allston, Mass.	1902
Fields, W. C.	Philadelphia, Pa.	1883
Fitzgerald, Barry	Dublin, Ireland	1888
Fitzgerald, Geraldine	Dublin, Ireland	1914
Fletcher, Bramwell	Bradford, Yorkshire, Eng.	1904
Fontanne, Lynn	London, England	1887
Forbes, Brenda	London, England	1909

Forbes, Ralph	London, England	1905
Foy, Eddie, Jr.	New Rochelle, N. Y.	1907
Francis, Arlene	Boston, Mass.	1908
Fraser, Elizabeth	Brooklyn, N. Y.	1920
Garrett, Betty	St. Louis, Mo.	1919
Gaxton, William	San Francisco, Cal.	1893
Geddes, Barbara Bel	Cleveland, Ohio	1912
Geddes, Norman Bel	Adrian, Mich.	1893
Gershwin, Ira	New York	1896
Gielgud, John	London, England	1904
Gillmore, Margalo	England	1901
Gilmore, Virginia	El Monte, Cal.	1919
Gish, Dorothy	Dayton, Ohio	1898
Gish, Lillian	Springfield, Ohio	1896
Gleason, James	New York	1885
Golden, John	New York	1874
Goodner, Carol	New York City	1904
Gordon, Ruth	Wollaston, Mass.	1896
Gough, Lloyd	New York City	1906
Grant, Sydney	Boston, Mass.	1873
Greaza, Walter	St. Paul, Minn.	1900
Green, Mitzi	New York City	1920
Greenstreet, Sydney	England	1880
Groody, Louise	Waco, Texas	1897
Gwenn, Edmund	Glamorgan, Wales	1875
Hampden, Walter	Brooklyn, N. Y.	1879
Hannen, Nicholas	London, England	1881
Hardie, Russell	Griffin Mills, N. Y.	1906
Hardwicke, Sir Cedric	Lye, Stourbridge, England	1893
Hart, Richard	Providence, R. I.	1915
Havoc, June	Seattle, Wash.	1916
Haydon, Julie	Oak Park, Ill.	1910
Hayes, Helen	Washington, D. C.	1900
Heflin, Frances	Oklahoma City, Okla.	1924
Heflin, Van	Walters, Okla.	1909
Heineman, Eda	Japan	1891
Heming, Violet	Leeds, England	1893
Henie, Sonja	Oslo, Norway	1912
Hepburn, Katharine	Hartford, Conn.	1907
Henreid, Paul	Trieste, Italy	1905
Hobbes, Halliwell	Stratford, England	1877

Hoey, Dennis	London, England	1893
Holliday, Judy	New York City	1924
Hopkins, Arthur	Cleveland, Ohio	1878
Hopkins, Miriam	Bainbridge, Ga.	1904
Holmes, Taylor	Newark, N. J.	1872
Hull, Henry	Louisville, Ky.	1888
Humphreys, Cecil	Cheltenham, England	1880
Hussey, Ruth	Providence, R. I.	1917
Huston, Walter	Toronto	1884
Inescort, Frieda	Hitchin, Scotland	1905
Ingram, Rex	Dublin, Ireland	1892
Ives, Burl	Hunt Township, Ill.	1909
Jagger, Dean	Columbus Grove, Ohio	1904
Jameson, House	Austin, Texas	1902
Jolson, Al	Washington, D. C.	1883
Johnson, Harold J. (Chic)	Chicago, Ill.	1891
Joy, Nicholas	Paris, France	1892
Kane, Whitford	Larne, Ireland	1882
Karloff, Boris	Dulwich, England	1887
Kaufman, George S.	Pittsburgh, Pa.	1889
Kaye, Danny	New York City	1914
Keith, Robert	Scotland	1899
Kelly, Gene	Pittsburgh, Pa.	1912
Kerrigan, J. M.	Dublin, Ireland	1885
Kiepura, Jan	Warsaw, Poland	1902
Kilbride, Percy	San Francisco, Cal.	1880
King, Dennis	Coventry, England	1897
Kingsford, Walter	England	1876
Lackland, Ben	Waco, Texas	1901
Landi, Elissa	Venice, Italy	1904
Landis, Jessie Royce	Chicago, Ill.	1904
Laughton, Charles	Scarborough, England	1899
Lawrence, Gertrude	London	1898
Lee, Canada	New York City	1907
Le Gallienne, Eva	London, England	1899
Leighton, Margaret	Barnt Green, England	1922
Lillie, Beatrice	Toronto, Canada	1898
Loeb, Philip	Philadelphia, Pa.	1892

Lonergan, Lenore	Toledo, Ohio	1928
Lord, Pauline	Hanford, Cal.	1890
Lukas, Paul	Budapest, Hungary	1895
Lund, John	Rochester, N. Y.	1916
Lunt, Alfred	Milwaukee, Wis.	1893
Lytell, Bert	New York City	1885
MacMahon, Aline	McKeesport, Pa.	1899
March, Fredric	Racine, Wis.	1897
Margetson, Arthur	London, England	1897
Margo	Mexico	1918
Marshall, Everett	Worcester, Mass.	1902
Marshall, Herbert	London, England	1890
Massey, Raymond	Toronto, Canada	1896
Matteson, Ruth	San Jose, Cal.	1905
McClintic, Guthrie	Seattle, Wash.	1893
McCormick, Myron	Albany, Ind.	1907
McCracken, Joan	Philadelphia, Pa.	1923
McGrath, Paul	Chicago, Ill.	1900
McGuire, Dorothy	Omaha, Neb.	1918
Meredith, Burgess	Cleveland, Ohio	1908
Merivale, Philip	Rehutia, India	1886
Merman, Ethel	Astoria, R. I.	1909
Middleton, Ray	Chicago, Ill.	1907
Miller, Gilbert	New York	1884
Miranda, Carmen	Portugal	1912
Mitchell, Grant	Columbus, Ohio	1874
Mitchell, Thomas	Elizabeth, N. J.	1892
Moore, Grace	Del Rio, Tenn.	1901
Moore, Victor	Hammondton, N. J.	1876
Morgan, Claudia	New York	1912
Morgan, Ralph	New York City	1889
Morris, Mary	Boston	1894
Morris, McKay	San Antonio, Texas	1890
Moss, Arnold	Brooklyn, N. Y.	1910
Muni, Paul	Lemberg, Austria	1895
Myrtil, Odette	Paris, France	1898
Nagel, Conrad	Keokuk, Iowa	1897
Natwick, Mildred	Baltimore, Md.	1908
Nolan, Lloyd	San Francisco, Cal.	1903
Nugent, Elliott	Dover, Ohio	1900

O'Brien-Moore, Erin	Los Angeles, Cal.	1908
Odets, Clifford	Philadelphia	1906
Olivier, Laurence	Dorking, Surrey, England	1907
Olsen, John Siguard (Ole)	Peru, Ind.	1892
O'Malley, Rex	London, England	1906
O'Neal, Frederick	Brookville, Miss.	1905
O'Neill, Eugene Gladstone	New York	1888
Ouspenskaya, Maria	Tula, Russia	1876
Patterson, Elizabeth	Savannah, Tenn.	1898
Pemberton, Brock	Leavenworth, Kansas	1885
Petina, Irra	Leningrad, Russia	1900
Pickford, Mary	Toronto	1893
Picon, Molly	New York City	1898
Pollock, Channing	Washington, D. C.	1880
Price, Vincent	St. Louis, Mo.	1914
Rains, Claude	London, England	1889
Raitt, John	Santa Ana, Cal.	1917
Rathbone, Basil	Johannesburg	1892
Raye, Martha	Butte, Mont.	1916
Redman, Joyce	Newcastle, Ireland	1918
Reed, Florence	Philadelphia, Pa.	1883
Rennie, James	Toronto, Canada	1890
Richardson, Ralph	Cheltenham, England	1902
Roberts, Joan	New York City	1918
Robinson, Bill	Richmond, Va.	1878
Robinson, Edward G.	Bucharest, Roumania	1893
Ross, Anthony	New York	1906
Royle, Selena	New York	1905
Ruben, José	Belgium	1886
Sands, Dorothy	Cambridge, Mass.	1900
Sarnoff, Dorothy	Brooklyn, N. Y.	1919
Scheff, Fritzi	Vienna, Austria	1879
Scott, Martha	Jamesport, Mo.	1914
Segal, Vivienne	Philadelphia, Pa.	1897
Shannon, Effie	Cambridge, Mass.	1867
Sherwood, Robert Emmet	New Rochelle, N. Y.	1896
Sidney, Sylvia	New York	1910
Simms, Hilda	Minneapolis, Minn.	1920
Skinner, Cornelia Otis	Chicago	1902
Smith, Kent	Smithfield, Me.	1910

Stickney, Dorothy	Dickinson, N. D.	1903
Stoddard, Haila	Great Falls, Mont.	1914
Stone, Carol	New York	1917
Stone, Dorothy	New York	1905
Stone, Ezra	New Bedford, Mass.	1918
Stone, Fred	Denver, Colo.	1873
Sullavan, Margaret	Norfolk, Va.	1910
Taliaferro, Mabel	New York	1887
Taylor, Laurette	New York	1884
Tetzel, Joan	New York	1923
Thomas, John Charles	Baltimore, Md.	1887
Tone, Franchot	Niagara Falls, N. Y.	1907
Tozere, Frederick	Brookline, Mass.	1901
Tracy, Spencer	Milwaukee, Wis.	1900
Travers, Henry	Berwick, England	1874
Truex, Ernest	Red Hill, Mo.	1890
Van Patten, Dickie	New York	1929
Van Patten, Joyce	New York City	1934
Varden, Evelyn	Venita, Okla.	1893
Venuta, Benay	San Francisco, Cal.	1912
Walker, Nancy	Philadelphia, Pa.	1922
Walker, June	New York	1904
Warfield, David	San Francisco, Cal.	1866
Waring, Richard	Buckinghamshire, England	1912
Waters, Ethel	Chester, Pa.	1900
Watson, Lucile	Quebec, Canada	1879
Watson, Minor	Marianna, Ark.	1889
Webb, Clifton	Indiana	1891
Webster, Margaret	New York City	1905
Welles, Orson	Kenosha, Wis.	1915
West, Mae	Brooklyn, N. Y.	1892
Weston, Ruth	Boston, Mass.	1911
Whiting, Jack	Philadelphia, Pa.	1901
Whorf, Richard	Winthrop, Mass.	1908
Widmark, Richard	Sunrise, Minn.	1914
Willard, Catherine	Dayton, Ohio	1895
Williams, Rhys	Wales	1903
Wiman, Dwight Deere	Moline, Ill.	1895
Winwood, Estelle	England	1883

Wood, Peggy	Brooklyn, N. Y.	1894
Wyatt, Jane	Campgaw, N. J.	1912
Wynn, Ed.	Philadelphia, Pa.	1886
Wynn, Keenan	New York City	1917
Yurka, Blanche	Bohemia	1893

NECROLOGY

June 19, 1945—June 1, 1946

Ainley, Henry, actor, producer and director, 66. English actor; London debut (1900) in "Henry V"; played in New York opposite Maude Adams in "The Pretty Sister of José." Born Leeds, England; died London, England, October 31, 1945.

Amber, Mabel, actress, 79. First stage appearance with Augustin Daly Company in "The Magistrate" (1889); toured in "The Nominee," "A Gay Divorcée," "In Missouri," "Rupert of Hentzau," etc.; last engagement in "Just Out of College" (1905). Born Elmira, New York; died Englewood, New Jersey, October 7, 1945.

Atwill, Lionel, actor and producer, 61. Forty-year career began in London; came to America with Lillie Langtry (1915) and toured in "Mrs. Thompson"; appeared in many Ibsen plays in London and New York; films included "The Age of Innocence," "The Firebird," "The Great Profile," etc. Born Croyden, England; died Pacific Palisades, Calif., April 22, 1946.

Arliss, George (Augustus George Andrews), actor and author, 77. 60 years on stage; first appearance in London, 1887; first in America touring with Mrs. Patrick Campbell (1901); first in New York with David Belasco company as Zakkuri in "The Daughter of the Gods" with Blanche Bates (1902); with Mrs. Fiske in "Leah Kleschna," etc.; starred in "Disraeli," "Voltaire," "The Merchant of Venice," "Old English," "Green Goddess," etc.; appeared in many screen plays, winning Photoplay Gold Medal (1929) for performance in "Disraeli"; president Episcopal Actors Guild for fifteen years. Born London, England; died London, England, February 5, 1946.

Barbier, George, actor, 80. 54 years on stage and screen; appeared in New York in "The Hunchback of Notre Dame," "The Man Who Came Back," "That's Gratitude," "The Beggar on Horseback," etc.; played more than forty screen roles since 1930. Born Philadelphia, Pa.; died Hollywood, Calif., July 19, 1945.

Benchley, Robert C., humorist, dramatic critic, film and radio actor, 56. Dramatic editor of *Life* magazine and *New Yorker* (1920-29); wrote "The Treasurer's Report," at request of Irving Berlin read it in "Music Box Revue of 1923-24"; received Motion Picture Academy award for "How to Sleep." Born Worcester, Mass.; died New York City, November 21, 1945.

Craven, Frank, actor, author and director, 70. Member of theatrical family; first appeared as child actor in "The Silver King"; first New York appearance in "Artie" (1907); first New York hit in "Bought and Paid For"; wrote "New Brooms," "Spite Corner," "The First Year," "Too Many Cooks," "That's Gratitude," "The 19th Hole," etc.; last appearance on Broadway with Billie Burke in "Mrs. January and Mr. X" (1944). Born Boston, Mass.; died Beverly Hills, Calif., September 1, 1945.

Dixon, Thomas, author, 82. Author of "The Clansman," adapted to stage from "The Leopard's Spots," presented on Broadway (1906); rewritten for the movies by David Wark Griffith; produced as "The Birth of a Nation" (1915). Born Shelby, N. C.; died Raleigh, N. C., April 3, 1946.

Edwards, Gus (Simon), song writer, actor, movie director, 66. Best known as song writer and talent scout for vaudeville; pioneer of the revue in vaudeville; wrote "By the Light of the Silvery Moon," "Schooldays," "In My Merry Oldsmobile," "I Can't Tell Why I Love You," "I Just Can't Make My Eyes Behave" (for Anna Held), etc.; helped discover and develop many stars including Elsie Janis, Groucho Marx, Georgie Jessel, Eddie Cantor, Walter Winchell, Mae Murray and many others; wrote for and appeared in motion pictures. Born Hohensalza, Germany; died Hollywood, Calif., November 7, 1945.

Fielding, Edward, actor, 71. Veteran stage and screen actor; stage debut in "The Great Ruby" in England (1899); with Sir Herbert Beerbohm Tree, Olga Nethersole, Charles Hawtrey and others in London; debut in New York with Grace George in "A Woman's Way"; with Otis Skinner in "Your Humble Servant"; with Laurette Taylor in "Peg O' My Heart." Born Brooklyn, New York; died Hollywood, Calif., January 10, 1946.

Giffen, Robert Lawrence, producer, director, author's agent, 73. Stock company manager in Richmond and Norfolk, Va., Denver and St. Louis; press representative for Minnie Maddern Fiske, Lawrence D'Orsay, Nazimova, etc.; once partner of Alice Kauser, play broker. Born Tecumseh, Neb.; died Brooklyn, New York, March 16, 1946.

Harned, Virginia, actress, 78. Leading American actress in the nineties; New York debut at 14th St. Theatre in "A Long Lane, or Pine Meadows" (1890); with Wilton Lackaye in "Trilby"; played Ophelia to her husband's, E. H. Sothern's, Hamlet; remembered in "The Dancing Girl," "Captain Letterblair," "The Love Letter," "An Enemy to the King," etc.; second marriage was to William Courtnay; retired from stage in 1918. Born Boston, Mass.; died New York City, April 29, 1946.

Hatton, Frederic H., drama critic, author, 66. Shared drama critic job on Chicago *Post* with his wife, Fanny Hatton; wrote (with her) "Years of Discretion," "The Great Lover" (with Leo Ditrichstein), "Lombardi, Ltd.," etc. Born Peru, Ill.; died Rutland, Ill., April 13, 1946.

Holmes, Ralph, actor, 30. Son of Taylor Holmes and husband of Libby Holman; appeared in "Where Do We Go from Here," "Thanks for Tomorrow" and many screen plays. Born New York; died New York City, November 15, 1945.

Hughes, Hatcher, playwright, 64. Won Pulitzer Prize in 1924 with "Hell-Bent for Heaven"; other plays "Wake Up Jonathan" (with Elmer Rice), "Ruint," and "The Lord Blesses the Bishop"; taught English and organized play-writing course at Columbia University. Born Polkville, N. C.; died New York City, October 18, 1945.

Hunter, Glenn, actor, 49. Started with Washington Square Players (1916); on Orpheum Circuit in vaudeville; appeared on Broadway in "Pollyanna," "Seventeen," "Merton of the Movies," "Young Woodley," etc. Born Highland Mills, New York; died New York City, December 30, 1945.

Jefferson, William Winter, actor, 70. Started stage career in company of his father, Joseph Jefferson; with his brother Thomas, revived "Rip Van Winkle" and other plays which had brought fame to his father; retired in 1925. Born London, England; died Honolulu, 1945.

Jessup, Stanley, actor, 67. Began stage career with Richard Mansfield in "Cyrano de Bergerac"; remembered in "The Merry Widow," "Potash and Perlmutter," "Shore Leave," "Nina Rosa," "I'd Rather Be Right," "Candle in the Wind," etc. Born Chester, New York; died New York City, October 26, 1945.

Kappeler, Alfred, actor, 69. On stage 48 years, starting with "Bride Elect," an operetta by Sousa (1897); with Denman Thompson in "The Old Homestead," sang Ernest in "Parsifal" (1905); remembered in "Seventh Heaven," "The Great Lover," "Dodsworth," etc., last Broadway appearance in "The Mermaids Singing." Born Zurich, Switzerland; died New York City, October 30, 1945.

Kauser, Alice, author's agent and play broker, 73. For half a century represented many great American and foreign playwrights, including Anatole France, Sardou, Hauptmann, Ibsen, Edward Sheldon, Rupert Hughes, Channing Pollock, etc.; daughter of Berta Gerster, famous operatic star and god-daughter of Franz Liszt. Born Budapest, Hungary; died New York City, September 10, 1945.

Keane, Doris, actress, 63. First appearance in New York in "Whitewashing Julia" (1903); best remembered in "Romance" (1913) which she played in England and America for 7 years; other plays "Gypsy," "The Other Girl," "De Lancey," "The Hypocrites," "The Czarina," etc. Born Michigan; died New York City, November 25, 1945.

Kern, Jerome David, composer, 60. Credited with music for 104 stage and screen shows; wrote scores for "Showboat," "Music in the Air," "Roberta," "Sally," "Very Warm for May," "The Cat and the Fiddle," etc.; remembered songs are "Ol' Man River," "I Told Every Little Star," "Smoke Gets in Your Eyes," etc.; working with Oscar Hammerstein 2d on revival of "Showboat" at time of his death. Born New York City; died New York City, November 11, 1945.

Knoblock, Edward, actor, author, 71. Internationally known playwright; first play "The Club Baby" (with Lawrence Sterner), 1895; next forty years wrote fifty plays, including "Kismet," "Milestones" (with Arnold Bennett), "Tiger, Tiger!", "Sister Beatrice," etc.; dramatized "Grand Hotel" (by Vicki Baum); screen plays included "Thief of Bagdad" and "Moonlight Sonata"; last play "Bird of Passage" (1943). Born New York City; died London, England, July 19, 1945.

Lambart, Ernest, actor, 71. Prominent comedian for more than 30 years; first appearance in "The Girl from Kays" (1903); was with Weber and Fields at the Music Hall; played in "The Squaw Man" with William Faversham and was with Anna Held's company for two years; last engagement in "The Great Waltz" (1934). Born Ireland; died New York, June 27, 1945.

Lewis, Frederick G., actor, 73. First stage appearance in "Camille" in Savannah (1891); toured with Lyceum Stock Company; supported John Barrymore in "Hamlet," Henry Miller in "Pasteur," Mary Shaw in "Ghosts," Henrietta Crosman in "As You Like It"; was with Sothern-Marlowe Company in Shakespearean repertoire for many years; last appearance on Broadway in "Come of Age" (1934). Born Oswego, New York; died Amityville, Long Island, March 19, 1946.

McCormack, John, singer, 61. World famous tenor; noted ballad singer; first success in "Cavalleria Rusticana" at London's Covent Garden Opera House (1907); American debut in "La Traviata" (1909); remembered for Irish song repertory, "Mother Machree," "I Hear You Calling Me," etc.; last public appearance on Red Cross Concert tour in England (1945). Born Athlone, Ireland; died Booterstown, Ireland, September 16, 1945.

Merivale, Philip, actor, 59. Professional debut with Sir Frank Benson in "Orestes" (1905); three years with Sir Herbert Beerbohm Tree; came to America as Mrs. Patrick Campbell's leading man in "Pygmalion" (1914); toured with George Arliss in "The Mollusc"; other plays "Cynara," "The Road to Rome," "Death Takes a Holiday" and "Mary of Scotland"; played and produced "Othello" and "Macbeth" with his wife, Gladys Cooper. Born Rehutia, India; died Los Angeles, Calif., March 13, 1946.

Mitchell, Earl, actor, 64. In acting career of 40 years supported Leo Ditrichstein 16 years; debut in Dallas, Texas (1901); played in "Way Down East," "Strongheart," "Under Cover," "The Dove," etc.; last Broadway appearance with Eva Le Gallienne in "Madam Capet" (1938). Born La Plata, Mo.; died New York City, February 17, 1946.

Morosco, Oliver (Mitchell), producer and author, 70. Started as acrobat in his father's troupe; became owner of many theatres in California and one in New York; was co-author of "The Judge and Jury," "So Long Letty," "Merely Mary Ann," etc.; produced "Bird of Paradise," "Beyond the Horizon," "Peg O' My Heart," "The Unchastened Woman" and "The Bat"; last New York production "The Morning After the Night Before" (1927). Born Logan, Utah; died Hollywood, Calif., August 25, 1945.

Nazimova, Alla, actress, 66. Russian actress well known in London and New York; first stage appearance in Poland in "L'Aiglon" (1901); with Paul Orlenoff produced "The

Chosen People" in Berlin; made first appearance in London and New York as Lia in that play (1905); remembered in Ibsen's and Chekhov's plays; also in "Good Earth," "Mourning Becomes Electra," "Bella Donna," etc. Born Yalta, Crimea, Russia; died Los Angeles, Calif., July 13, 1945.

O'Hara, Fiske, singer, 67. Lyric tenor who became famous singing Irish ballads; veteran of concert and vaudeville stage, screen and radio; sang in "Robin Hood," "Down Limerick Way," "Springtime in Mayo," "Jerry for Short," etc. Born Ireland; died Hollywood, Calif., August 2, 1945.

Pollock, Anna (Marble), author, theatrical press agent, 65. Descendant of William Warren of the first English company of actors to come to America; daughter of Edward Marble, actor and playwright, and wife of Channing Pollock, playwright; wrote one-act plays; press representative for "Floradora," Elsie de Wolfe and Nazimova. Born Chicago, Ill.; died New York City, March 31, 1946.

Pollock, John, theatrical representative and manager, 64. General manager for John Golden; publicity agent for Orpheum and Keith's circuits; prominent as booker of stage attractions; agented "The Great Waltz," "Claudia," "Susan and God," etc.; served on USO Advisory Committee. Born Salt Lake City, Utah; died New York City, July 29, 1945.

Shaw, Arthur W., actor, 65. Forty years on Broadway, starting with "Brown of Harvard" (1906); other plays "The Yellow Jacket," "The Torchbearers," "Craig's Wife," "The Traveling Salesman," etc.; son of Mary Shaw, actress. Born New York; died Washington, D. C., March 22, 1946.

Scott, Cyril, actor, 79. Began 53-year stage career in "The Girl I Love" (1883); was with Minnie Maddern Fiske, Richard Mansfield, Lotta, E. H. Sothern and Empire Theatre Stock Co.; remembered in "Prince Chap" and "Seven Keys to Baldpate"; last appearance in "Holmeses of Baker Street" (1936). Born Banbridge, Ireland; died Flushing, New York, August 16, 1945.

Sheldon, Edward Brewster, playwright, 60. Started career with "Salvation Nell" (1908) starring Minnie Maddern Fiske; wrote "Romance" (1913) starring Doris Keane; adapted "The Jest" (1919) for John and Lionel Barrymore; other plays included "The Nigger," "The High Road," "Lulu Belle" (with Charles MacArthur); last play "Dishonored Lady" (1930) written with Margaret Ayer Barnes, played by Katharine Cornell. Born Chicago, Ill.; died New York City, April 1, 1946.

Tarkington, Newton Booth, author and dramatist, 76. Dean of American novelists; wrote 40 novels and 20 plays; first play "The Man from Home" (1907) in collaboration with Harry Leon Wilson; others, "The Gentleman from Indiana," "Mister Antonio" for Otis Skinner, "Beaucaire," "Cameo Kirby," "Clarence," "The Man on Horseback," etc.; last play "Aaron Burr" (1938); two of his novels, "The Magnificent Ambersons" and "Alice Adams," won Pulitzer Prizes and were made into movies; latest work a novel, "Image of Josephine" (1945). Born Indianapolis, Ind.; died Indianapolis, Ind., May 19, 1946.

Tracy, Virginia, actress and author, 72. Stage debut in early 90s in stock companies in Milwaukee, Denver and Hartford, Conn.; appeared with Maurice Barrymore in "Aristocracy," Robert Mantell in Shakespearean repertory and Mrs. Leslie Carter in "The Heart of Maryland"; last appearance in "Sweet Mystery of Life" (1935); wrote "Merely Players" and several novels with theatrical background. Born New York City; died New York City, March 4, 1946.

Tyler, George Crouse, producer and manager, 78. For 30 years outstandingly successful producer of American plays and importer of leading foreign stars; entered show business in 1894 as manager for James O'Neill and "The Count of Monte Cristo"; organized Liebler & Co. in 1897; starred Viola Allen in "The Christian," William Faversham in "The Squaw Man," William Hodge in "The Man from Home" and George Arliss in "Disraeli"; imported Mrs. Patrick Campbell, Eleanora Duse, Olga Nethersole, Mme. Rejane, Mme. Simone and The Irish Players; leased Century (New) Theatre for production of "Garden of Allah," "Joseph and His Brethren," etc.; toured Laurette Taylor and "Out There" with all-star cast and collected $700,000 for Red Cross in World War I. Born Chillicothe, Ohio; died Yonkers, New York, March 13, 1946.

Waldorf, Wilella, drama critic, 46. Play reviewer for New York *Evening Post* since 1941; champion of repertory theatre and supporter of experimental and trial theatre groups; last play review "Show Boat," Jan. 7, 1946; treasurer N. Y. Drama Critics' Circle. Born South Bend, Ind.; died New York City, March 12, 1946.

Waldron, Charles D., actor, 71. Stage and screen actor for 48 years in more than 400 roles; started at Murray Hill Theatre, New York, in stock (1898); continued in stock for 9 years; first appearance on Broadway in "The Warrens of Virginia" (1907); toured Australia and New Zealand starring in "The Squaw Man" and "The Virginian"; first Broadway success in "The Fourth Estate" (1909); remembered in "Daddy Long Legs," "A Bill of Divorcement," "Alien Corn," "Coquette," "Winterset," "Barretts of Wimpole Street" and "Saint Joan"; last appearance in "Deep Are the Roots." Born Waterford, New York; died Hollywood, Calif., March 4, 1946.

Werfel, Franz, author, composer and poet, 54. First Broadway play "The Goat Song" presented by The Theatre Guild, followed same year by "Juarez and Maximilian" (1926); "The Eternal Road," a pageant, was presented in 1937; other plays included "Jacobowsky and the Colonel," adapted by S. N. Behrman; "Embezzled Heaven" with Ethel Barrymore, and "The Song of Bernadette." Born Prague, Czechoslovakia; died Beverly Hills, Calif., Aug. 26, 1945.

Yost, Herbert A., actor, 65. Favorite character actor 48 years beginning with "Over Night" (1898); other plays "Post Road," "Mr. Pim Passes By," "Paris Bound," "Masque of Kings" and "Mornings at Seven"; last appearance in "Jacobowsky and the Colonel" (1944). Born Harrison, Ohio; died New York City, October 25, 1945.

Youmans, Vincent, composer, 47. Wrote full scores and popular interpolations for many musical successes; composed music for "Two Little Girls in Blue" (1921), "No, No, Nanette," "Hit the Deck," "Wildfire," "Mary Jane McKane," "Great Day," etc.; remembered for song hits "Tea for Two," "Bambolina," "I Want to be Happy," "Oh me! Oh my! Oh You!", etc. Born New York City, died Denver, Colo., April 5, 1946.

THE DECADES' TOLL

(Persons of Outstanding Prominence in the Theatre Who Have Died in Recent Years)

	Born	*Died*
Baker, George Pierce	1866	1935
Barrymore, John	1882	1942
Belasco, David	1856	1931
Bernhardt, Sarah	1845	1923
Campbell, Mrs. Patrick	1865	1940
Cohan, George Michael	1878	1942
De Koven, Reginald	1861	1920
De Reszke, Jean	1850	1925
Drew, John	1853	1927
Drinkwater, John	1883	1937
Du Maurier, Sir Gerald	1873	1934
Duse, Eleanora	1859	1924
Fiske, Minnie Maddern	1865	1932
Frohman, Daniel	1851	1940
Galsworthy, John	1867	1933
Gorky, Maxim	1868	1936
Greet, Sir Philip (Ben)	1858	1936
Herbert, Victor	1859	1924
Patti, Adelina	1843	1919
Pinero, Sir Arthur Wing	1855	1934
Russell, Annie	1864	1936
Schumann-Heink, Ernestine	1861	1936
Skinner, Otis	1858	1942
Sothern, Edwin Hugh	1859	1933
Tarkington, Booth	1862	1946
Terry, Ellen	1848	1928
Thomas, Augustus	1857	1934
Tyler, George C.	1867	1946
Yeats, William Butler	1865	1939

INDEX OF AUTHORS

INDEX OF PLAYS AND CASTS

INDEX OF PRODUCERS, DIRECTORS AND DESIGNERS